Cloud Computing

A Hands-On Approach

Arshdeep Bahga, Vijay Madisetti

Cloud Computing - A Hands-On Approach

Published by Arshdeep Bahga & Vijay Madisetti

ISBN-13: 978-1494435141
ISBN-10: 1494435144

Book Website: www.cloudcomputingbook.info

Contents

Preface

About This Book

Cloud computing is a transformative paradigm that enables scalable, convenient, on-demand access to a shared pool of configurable computing and networking resources, for efficiently delivering applications and services over the Internet. This book is written as a textbook on cloud computing for educational programs at colleges and universities, and also for cloud service providers who may be interested in offering a broader perspective of cloud computing to accompany their own customer and developer training programs. The typical reader is expected to have completed a couple of courses in programming using traditional high-level languages at the college-level, and is either a senior or a beginning graduate student in one of the science, technology, engineering or mathematics (STEM) fields.

We have tried to write a comprehensive book that transfers knowledge through an immersive "hands on" approach, where the reader is provided the necessary guidance and knowledge to develop working code for real-world cloud applications. Concurrent development of practical applications that accompanies traditional instructional material within the book further enhances the learning process, in our opinion.

Organizationally, the book is organized into 3 main parts, comprising of a total of 13 chapters. Part I covers basic technologies that form the foundations of cloud computing. These include topics such as virtualization, load balancing, scalability & elasticity, deployment, replication. Real-world examples of cloud-based services and their characteristics are described.

Part II introduces the reader to the programming aspects of cloud computing with a view towards rapid prototyping complex applications. We chose Python as the primary programming language for this book, and an introduction to Python is also included within the text to bring readers to a common level of expertise. We also describe packages and frameworks for Python that allows rapid prototyping of practical cloud applications. Reference architectures for different classes of cloud applications, including e-Commerce, Business-to-Business,

Banking, Retail and Social Networking in the context of commonly used design methodologies are examined in detail. Other languages, besides Python, may also be easily used within the methodology outlined in this book.

Part III introduces the reader to specialized aspects of cloud computing including cloud application benchmarking, multimedia cloud applications, cloud security and big data analytics. Case studies on the applications of the cloud in industry, healthcare, transportation systems, smart grids, and education are provided.

Through generous use of hundreds of figures and tested code samples, we have attempted to provide a rigorous "no hype" guide to cloud computing. It is expected that diligent readers of this book can use these exercises to develop their own applications on cloud platforms, such as those from Amazon Web Services, Google Cloud, and Microsoft's Windows Azure. Review questions and exercises are provided at the end of each chapter so that the readers (students or instructors) can improve their understanding of the technologies conveyed. We adopted an informal approach to describing well-known concepts primarily because these topics are covered well in existing textbooks, and our focus instead is on getting the reader firmly on track to developing robust cloud applications as opposed to more theory.

While we frequently refer to offerings from commercial vendors, such as Amazon, Google or Microsoft, this book is not an endorsement of their products or services, nor is any portion of our work supported financially (or otherwise) by these vendors. All trademarks and products belong to their respective owners and the underlying principles and approaches, we believe, are applicable to other cloud vendors as well. The opinions in this book are those of the authors alone.

Chapter-1: Introduction to Cloud Computing

Provides an overview of cloud computing, including cloud deployment models, cloud service models, and development of cloud-based applications.

Chapter-2: Cloud Concepts & Technologies

Provides an introduction to underlying technologies, including virtualization, load balancing, scalability & elasticity, deployment, replication, monitoring, identity and access management, service level agreements (SLAs) and billing.

Chapter-3: Cloud Services & Platforms

Describes a classification of common cloud services including computing, storage, database, application, analytics, network and deployment services.

Chapter-4: Hadoop & MapReduce - Concepts

Provides an overview of Hadoop ecosystem, including MapReduce architecture, MapReduce job execution flow and MapReduce schedulers, with examples.

Chapter-5: Cloud Application Design

Provides the principles and methodologies of rapid cloud application design including common cloud application reference architectures.

Chapter-6: Python Basics

Provides an introduction to Python, installing Python, Python data types & data structures, control flow, functions, modules, packages, file input/output, data/time operations and classes.

Chapter-7: Python for Cloud

Provides an introduction to the use of Python for cloud development. Practical examples rely on Amazon Web Services, Python for Google Cloud Platform, Python for Windows Azure, Python for MapReduce, Python web application framework (i.e., Django) and development with Django.

Chapter-8: Cloud Application Development in Python

Provides instruction on the design of several case studies including Image Processing App, MapReduce App, Document Storage App and Social Media Analytics App.

Chapter-9: Big Data Analytics

Provides an introduction to big data analytics approaches, including clustering and classification of big data

Chapter-10: Multimedia Cloud

Provides a description of reference architectures for multimedia cloud for real-time applications and live streaming.

Chapter-11: Cloud Application Benchmarking & Tuning

Provides a description of cloud application workload characteristics, performance metrics for cloud applications, cloud application testing, and performance testing tools.

Chapter-12: Cloud Security

Provides an introduction to cloud security, including approaches for authorization authentication, identify & access management, data security, data integrity encryption & key management.

Chapter-13: Cloud for Industry, Healthcare & Education

Provides an introduction to applications of cloud computing in healthcare, energy, smart grids, manufacturing industry, transportation systems and education.

Book Website

For more information on the book, copyrighted source code of all examples in the book, lab exercises, and instructor material, visit the book website: www.cloudcomputingbook.info

Acknowledgments

From Arshdeep Bahga
I would like to thank my father, Sarbjit Bahga, for inspiring me to write a book and sharing his valuable insights and experiences on authoring books. This book could not have been completed without the support of my mother Gurdeep Kaur, wife Navsangeet Kaur, and brother Supreet Bahga, who have always motivated me and encouraged me to explore my interests.

From Vijay Madisetti
I thank my family, especially Anitha and Jerry (Raj) for their support.

About the Authors

Arshdeep Bahga

Arshdeep Bahga is a Research Scientist with Georgia Institute of Technology. His research interests include cloud computing and big data analytics. Arshdeep has authored several scientific publications in peer-reviewed journals in the areas of cloud computing and big data.

Vijay Madisetti

Vijay Madisetti is a Professor of Electrical and Computer Engineering at Georgia Institute of Technology. Vijay is a Fellow of the IEEE, and received the 2006 Terman Medal from the American Society of Engineering Education and HP Corporation.

Part I

INTRODUCTION & CONCEPTS

1 — Introduction to Cloud Computing

This Chapter Covers

- Definition of cloud computing
- Characteristics of cloud
- Cloud deployment models
- Cloud service models
- Driving factors and challenges of cloud
- Overview of applications of Cloud
- Generic case studies

1.1 Introduction

Cloud computing is a transformative computing paradigm that involves delivering applications and services over the internet. Many of the underlying technologies that are the foundation of cloud computing have existed for quite some time. Cloud computing involves provisioning of computing, networking and storage resources on demand and providing these resources as metered services to the users, in a "pay as you go" model. In this chapter you will learn about the various deployment models, service models, characteristics, driving factors and challenges of cloud computing.

1.1.1 Definition of Cloud Computing

The U.S. National Institute of Standards and Technology (NIST) defines cloud computing as [1]:

> **Definition:** Cloud computing is a model for enabling ubiquitous, convenient, on-demand network access to a shared pool of configurable computing resources (e.g., networks, servers, storage, applications, and services) that can be rapidly provisioned and released with minimal management effort or service provider interaction.

1.2 Characteristics of Cloud Computing

NIST further identifies five essential characteristics of cloud computing:

On-demand self service

Cloud computing resources can be provisioned on-demand by the users, without requiring interactions with the cloud service provider. The process of provisioning resources is automated.

Broad network access

Cloud computing resources can be accessed over the network using standard access mechanisms that provide platform-independent access through the use of heterogeneous client platforms such as workstations, laptops, tablets and smartphones.

Resource pooling

The computing and storage resources provided by cloud service providers are pooled to serve multiple users using multi-tenancy. Multi-tenant aspects of the cloud allow multiple users to be served by the same physical hardware. Users are assigned virtual resources that run on top of the physical resources. Various forms of virtualization approaches such as full virtualization, para-virtualization and hardware virtualization are described in Chapter 2.

Rapid elasticity

Cloud computing resources can be provisioned rapidly and elastically. Cloud resources can be rapidly scaled up or down based on demand. Two types of scaling options exist:

- **Horizontal Scaling (scaling out):** Horizontal scaling or scaling-out involves launching and provisioning additional server resources.

- **Vertical Scaling (scaling up):** Vertical scaling or scaling-up involves changing the computing capacity assigned to the server resources while keeping the number of server resources constant.

Measured service

Cloud computing resources are provided to users on a pay-per-use model. The usage of the cloud resources is measured and the user is charged based on some specific metric. Metrics such as amount of CPU cycles used, amount of storage space used, number of network I/O requests, etc. are used to calculate the usage charges for the cloud resources.

In addition to these five essential characteristics of cloud computing, other characteristics that again highlight savings in cost include:

Performance

Cloud computing provides improved performance for applications since the resources available to the applications can be scaled up or down based on the dynamic application workloads.

Reduced costs

Cloud computing provides cost benefits for applications as only as much computing and storage resources as required can be provisioned dynamically, and upfront investment in purchase of computing assets to cover worst case requirements is avoid. This saves significant cost for organizations and individuals. Applications can experience large variations in the workloads which can be due to seasonal or other factors. For example, e-Commerce applications typically experience higher workloads in holiday seasons. To ensure market readiness of such applications, adequate resources need to be provisioned so that the applications can meet the demands of specified workload levels and at the same time ensure that service level agreements are met.

Outsourced Management

Cloud computing allows the users (individuals, large organizations, small and medium enterprises and governments) to outsource the IT infrastructure requirements to external cloud providers. Thus, the consumers can save large upfront capital expenditures in setting up the IT infrastructure and pay only for the operational expenses for the cloud resources used. The outsourced nature of the cloud services provides a reduction in the IT infrastructure management costs.

Reliability

Applications deployed in cloud computing environments generally have a higher reliability since the underlying IT infrastructure is professionally managed by the cloud service. Cloud service providers specify and guarantee the reliability and availability levels for their cloud resources in the form of service level agreements (SLAs). Most cloud providers promise 99.99% uptime guarantee for the cloud resources, which may often be expensive to achieve with in-house IT infrastructure.

Multi-tenancy

The multi-tenanted approach of the cloud allows multiple users to make use of the same shared resources. Modern applications such as e-Commerce, Business-to-Business, Banking and

Financial, Retail and Social Networking applications that are deployed in cloud computing environments are multi-tenanted applications. Multi-tenancy can be of different forms:

- **Virtual multi-tenancy:** In virtual multi-tenancy, computing and storage resources are shared among multiple users. Multiple tenants are served from virtual machines (VMs) that execute concurrently on top of the same computing and storage resources.
- **Organic multi-tenancy:** In organic multi-tenancy every component in the system architecture is shared among multiple tenants, including hardware, OS, database servers, application servers, load balancers, etc. Organic multi-tenancy exists when explicit multi-tenant design patterns are coded into the application.

1.3 Cloud Models

1.3.1 Service Models

Cloud computing services are offered to users in different forms. NIST defines at least three cloud service models as follows:

Infrastructure-as-a-Service (IaaS)

IaaS provides the users the capability to provision computing and storage resources. These resources are provided to the users as virtual machine instances and virtual storage. Users can start, stop, configure and manage the virtual machine instances and virtual storage. Users can deploy operating systems and applications of their choice on the virtual resources provisioned in the cloud. The cloud service provider manages the underlying infrastructure. Virtual resources provisioned by the users are billed based on a pay-per-use paradigm. Common metering metrics used are the number of virtual machine hours used and/or the amount of storage space provisioned.

Platform-as-a-Service (PaaS)

PaaS provides the users the capability to develop and deploy application in the cloud using the development tools, application programming interfaces (APIs), software libraries and services provided by the cloud service provider. The cloud service provider manages the underlying cloud infrastructure including servers, network, operating systems and storage. The users, themselves, are responsible for developing, deploying, configuring and managing applications on the cloud infrastructure.

Software-as-a-Service (SaaS)

SaaS provides the users a complete software application or the user interface to the the application itself. The cloud service provider manages the underlying cloud infrastructure including servers, network, operating systems, storage and application software, and the user is unaware of the underlying architecture of the cloud. Applications are provided to the user through a thin client interface (e.g., a browser). SaaS applications are platform independent and can be accessed from various client devices such as workstations, laptop, tablets and smartphones, running different operating systems. Since the cloud service provider manages both the application and data, the users are able to access the applications from anywhere.

Figure 1.1 shows the cloud computing service models and Figure 1.2 lists the benefits, characteristics and adoption of IaaS, PaaS and SaaS.

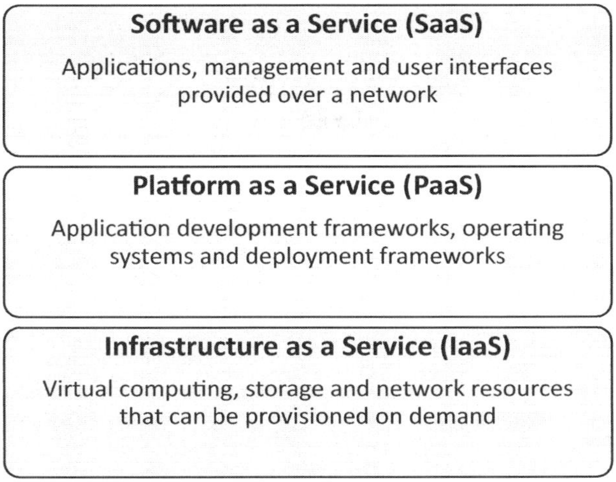

Software as a Service (SaaS)
Applications, management and user interfaces provided over a network

Platform as a Service (PaaS)
Application development frameworks, operating systems and deployment frameworks

Infrastructure as a Service (IaaS)
Virtual computing, storage and network resources that can be provisioned on demand

Figure 1.1: Cloud computing service models

1.3.2 Deployment Models

NIST also defines four cloud deployment models as follows:

Public cloud

In the public cloud deployment model, cloud services are available to the general public or a large group of companies. The cloud resources are shared among different users (individuals, large organizations, small and medium enterprises and governments). The cloud services are provided by a third-party cloud provider. Public clouds are best suited for users who want to use cloud infrastructure for development and testing of applications and host applications in the cloud to serve large workloads, without upfront investments in IT infrastructure.

Private cloud

In the private cloud deployment model, cloud infrastructure is operated for exclusive use of a single organization. Private cloud services are dedicated for a single organization. Cloud infrastructure can be setup on premise or off-premise and may be managed internally or by a third-party. Private clouds are best suited for applications where security is very important and organizations that want to have very tight control over their data.

Hybrid cloud

The hybrid cloud deployment model combines the services of multiple clouds (private or public). The individual clouds retain their unique identities but are bound by standardized or proprietary technology that enables data and application portability. Hybrid clouds are best suited for organizations that want to take advantage of secured application and data hosting on a private cloud, and at the same time benefit from cost savings by hosting shared applications and data in public clouds.

Community cloud

In the community cloud deployment model, the cloud services are shared by several organizations that have the same policy and compliance considerations. Community clouds are

IaaS
Benefits
- Shift focus from IT management to core activities
- No IT infrastructure management costs
- Pay-per-use/pay-per-go pricing
- Guaranteed performance
- Dynamic scaling
- Secure access
- Enterprise grade infrastructure
- Green IT adoption
Characteristics
- Multi-tenancy
- Virtualized hardware
- Management & monitoring tools
- Disaster recovery
Adoption
- Individual users: Low
- Small & medium enterprises: Medium
- Large organizations: High
- Government: High
Examples
- Amazon Elastic Compute Cloud (EC2)
- RackSpace
- GoGrid
- Eucalyptus
- Joyent
- Terremark
- OpSource
- Savvis
- Nimbula
- Enamoly
PaaS
Benefits
- Lower upfront & operations costs
- No IT infrastructure management costs
- Improved scalability
- Higher performance
- Secured access
- Quick & easy development
- Seamless integration
Characteristics
- Multi-tenancy
- Open integration protocols
- App development tools & SDKs
- Analytics
Adoption
- Individual users: Low
- Small & medium enterprises: Medium
- Large organizations: High
- Government: Medium
Examples
- Google App Engine
- Windows Azure Platform
- Force.com
- RightScale
- Heroku
- Github
- Gigaspaces
- AppScale
- OpenStack
- LongJump
SaaS
Benefits
- Lower costs
- No infrastructure required
- Seamless upgrades
- Guaranteed performance
- Automated backups
- Easy data recovery
- Secure
- High adoption
- On-the move access
Characteristics
- Multi-tenancy
- On-demand software
- Open integration protocols
- Social network integration
Adoption
- Individual users: High
- Small & medium enterprises: High
- Large organizations: High
- Government: Medium
Examples
- Google Apps
- Salesforce.com
- Facebook
- Zoho
- Dropbox
- Taleo
- Microsoft Office 365
- Linkedin
- Slideshare
- CareCloud

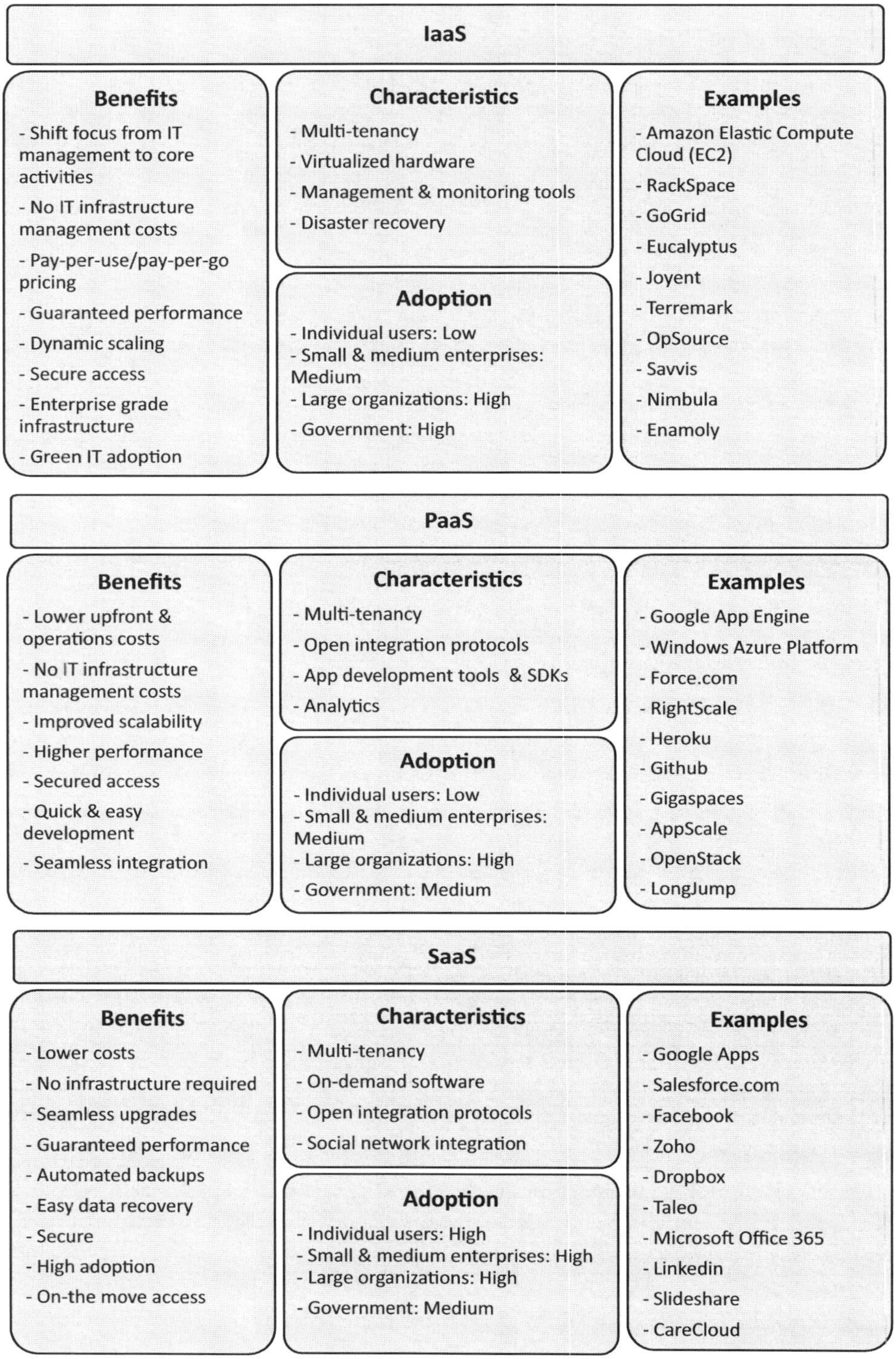

Figure 1.2: Benefits, characteristics and adoption of IaaS, PaaS and SaaS

best suited for organizations that want access to the same applications and data, and want the cloud costs to be shared with the larger group.

Figures 1.3 and 1.4 show the cloud deployment models.

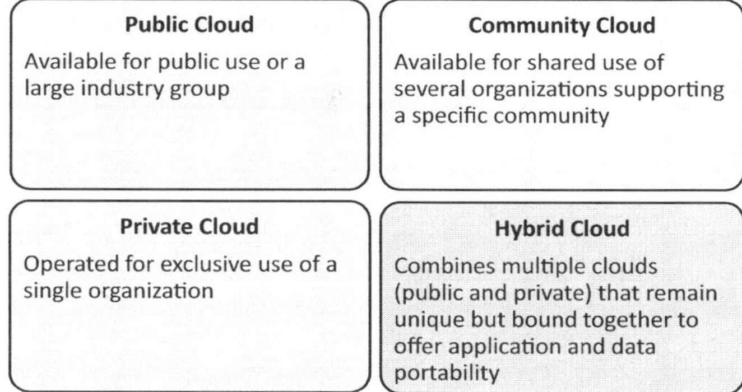

Figure 1.3: Cloud deployment models

1.4 Cloud Services Examples

1.4.1 IaaS: Amazon EC2, Google Compute Engine, Azure VMs

Amazon Elastic Compute Cloud (EC2) [3] is an Infrastructure as a Service (IaaS)n offering from Amazon.com. EC2 (TM) is a web service that provides computing capacity in the form of virtual machines that are launched in Amazon's cloud computing environment. Amazon EC2 allows users to launch instances on demand using a simple web-based interface. Amazon provides pre-configured Amazon Machine Images (AMIs) which are templates of cloud instances. Users can also create their own AMIs with custom applications, libraries and data. Instances can be launched with a variety of operating systems. Users can load their applications on running instances and rapidly and easily increase or decrease capacity to meet the dynamic application performance requirements. With EC2, users can even provision hundreds or thousands of server instances simultaneously, manage network access permissions, and monitor usage resources through a web interface. Amazon EC2 provides instances of various computing capacities ranging from small instances (e.g., 1 virtual core with 1EC2 compute unit, 1.7GB memory and 160GB instance storage) to extra large instances (e.g., 4 virtual cores with 2 EC2 compute units each, 15GB memory and 1690 GB instance storage). Amazon C2 also provides instances with high memory, high CPU resources, cluster compute instances, cluster graphical processor unit (GPU) instances and high Input/Output (I/O) instances. The pricing model for EC2 instances is based on a pay-per-use model. Users are billed based on the number on instance hours used for on-demand instances. EC2 provides the option of reserving instances by one-time payment for each instance that the user wants to reserve. In addition to these on-demand and reserved instances, EC2 also provides spot instances that allow users to bid on unused Amazon EC2 capacity and run those instances for as long as their bid exceeds the current spot price. Amazon EC2 provides a number of powerful

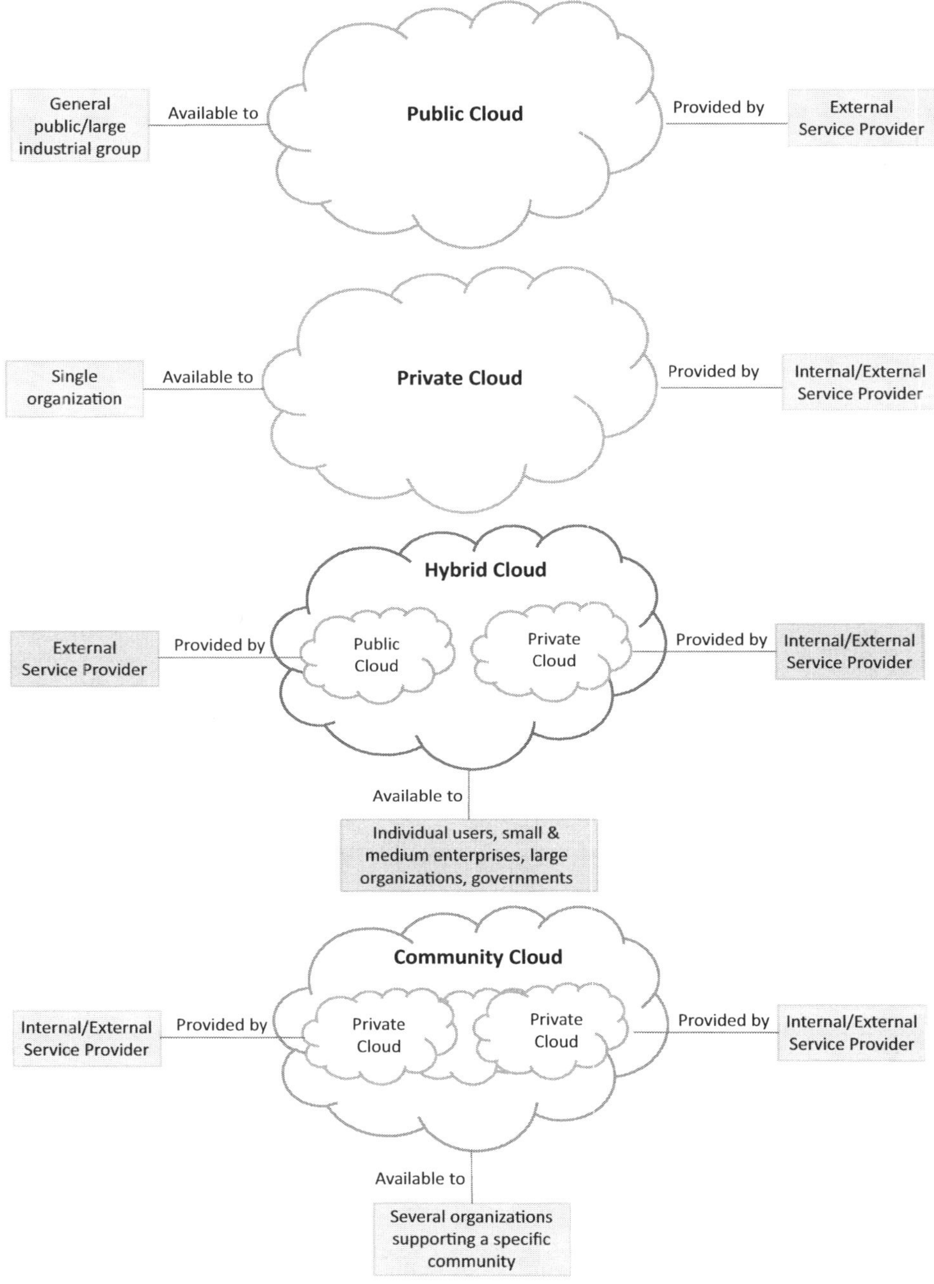

Figure 1.4: Cloud deployment models

features for building scalable and reliable applications such as auto scaling and elastic load balancing. Figure 1.5 shows a screenshot of Amazon EC2 dashboard.

Google Compute Engine (GCE) [4] is an IaaS offering from Google. GCE provides virtual machines of various computing capacities ranging from small instances (e.g., 1 virtual core with 1.38 GCE unit and 1.7GB memory) to high memory machine types (e.g., 8 virtual cores with 22 GCE units and 52GB memory). Figure 1.6 shows a screenshot of Google Compute Engine dashboard.

Windows Azure Virtual Machines [83] is an IaaS offering from Microsoft. Azure VMs provides virtual machines of various computing capacities ranging from small instances (1 virtual core with 1.75GB memory) to memory intensive machine types (8 virtual cores with 56GB memory). Figure 1.7 shows a screenshot of Windows Azure Virtual Machines dashboard.

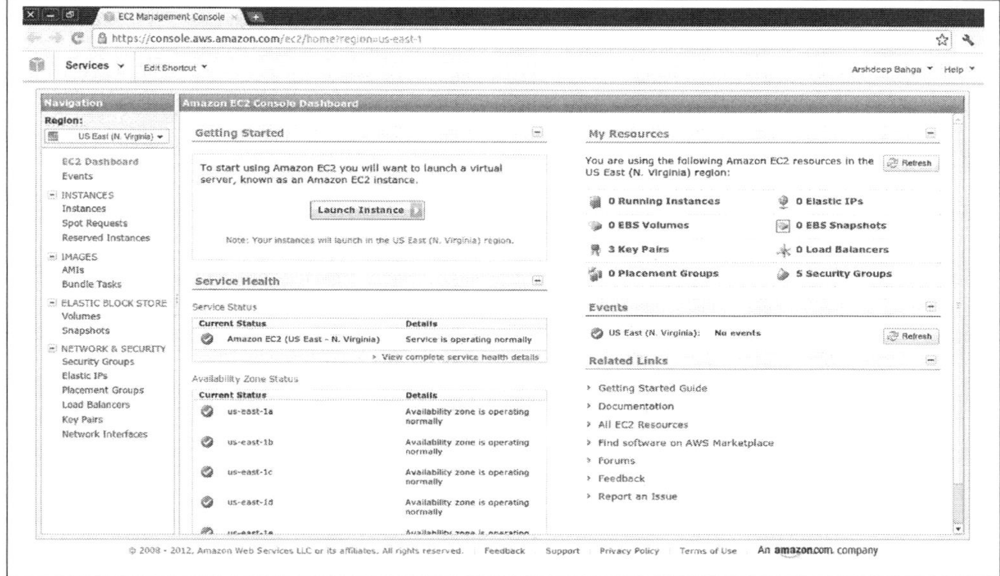

Figure 1.5: Amazon EC2 dashboard

1.4.2 PaaS: Google App Engine

Google App Engine (GAE) [105] is a Platform-as-a-Service (PaaS) offering from Google. GAE(TM) is a cloud-based web service for hosting web applications and storing data. GAE allows users to build scalable and reliable applications that run on the same systems that power Google's own applications. GAE provides a software development kit (SDK) for developing web applications software that can be deployed on GAE. Developers can develop and test their applications with GAE SDK on a local machine and then upload it to GAE with a simple click of a button. Applications hosted in GAE are easy to build, maintain and scale. Users don't need to worry about launching additional computing instances when the application load increases. GAE provides seamless scalability by launching additional instances when application load increases. GAE provides dynamic web serving based on common web technologies. Applications hosted in GAE can use dynamic technologies. GAE provides automatic scaling and load balancing capability.

GAE supports applications written in several programming languages. With GAE's

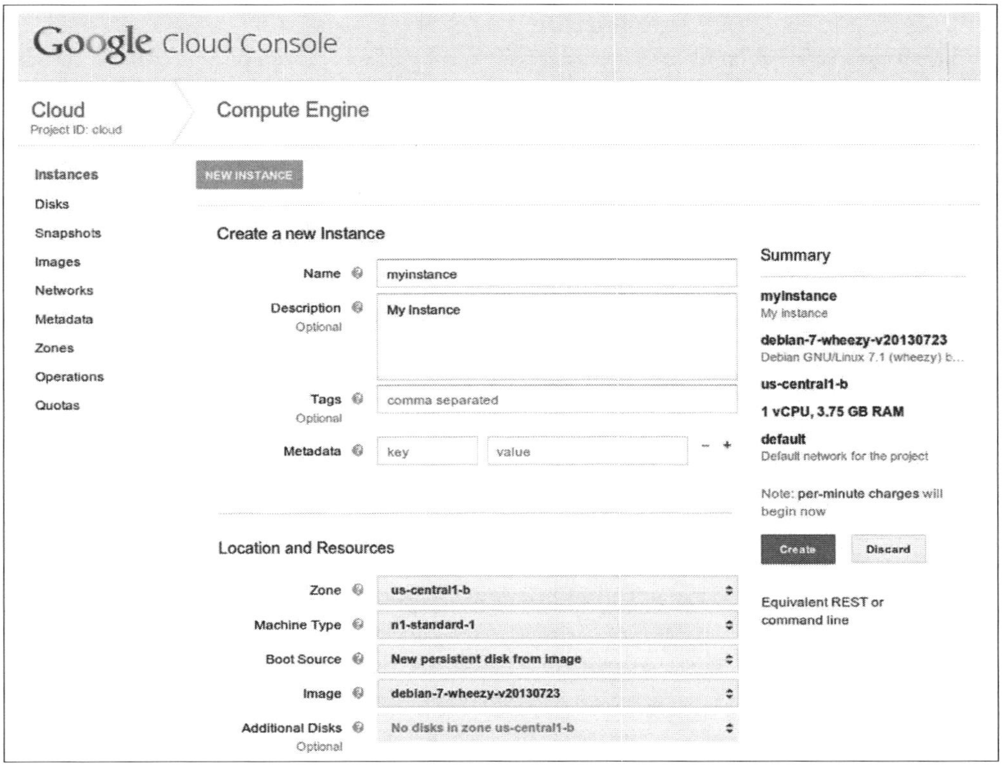

Figure 1.6: Google Compute Engine dashboard

Java runtime environment developers can build applications using Java programming language and standard Java technologies such as Java Servlets. GAE also provides runtime environments for Python and Go programming languages. Applications hosted in GAE run in secure sandbox with limited access to the underlying operating system and hardware. The benefit of hosting applications in separate sandboxes is that GAE can distribute web requests for applications across multiple servers thus providing scalability and security.

The pricing model for GAE is based on the amount of computing resources used. GAE provides free computing resources for applications up to a certain limit. Beyond that limit, users are billed based on the amount of computing resources used, such as amount bandwidth consumed, number of resources instance hours for front-end and back-end instances, amount of stored data, channels, and recipients emailed. Figure 1.8 shows a screenshot of GAE dashboard.

1.4.3 SaaS: Salesforce

Salesforce [7] Sales Cloud(TM) is a cloud-based customer relationship management (CRM) Software-as-a-Service (SaaS) offering. Users can access CRM application from anywhere through internet-enabled devices such as workstations, laptops, tablets and

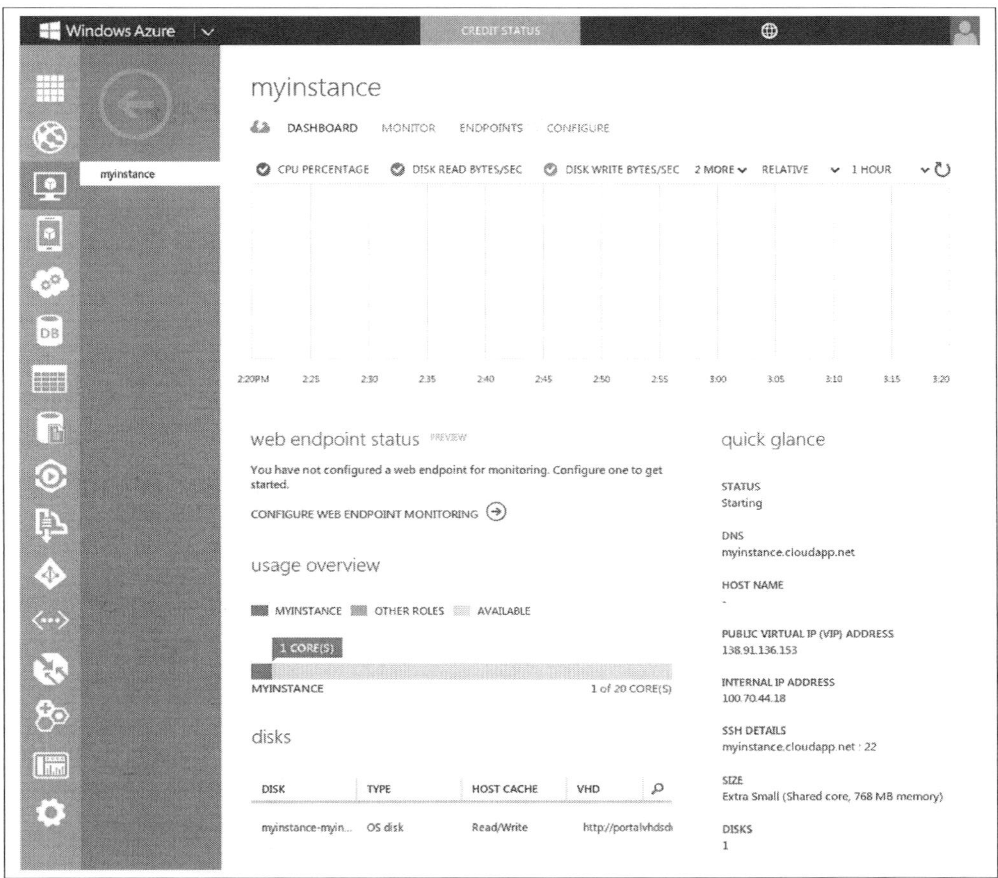

Figure 1.7: Windows Azure Virtual Machines dashboard

smartphones. Sales Cloud allows sales representatives to manage customer profiles, track opportunities, optimize campaigns from lead to close and monitor the impact of campaigns.

Salesforce Service Cloud (TM) is a cloud based customer service management SaaS. Service Cloud provides companies a call-center like view and allows creating, tracking, routing and escalating cases. Service Cloud can be fully integrated with a company's call-center telephony and back office apps. Service Cloud also provides self service capabilities to customers. Service Cloud includes a social networking plug-in that enables social customer service where comments from social media channels can be used to answer customer questions.

Salesforce Marketing Cloud (TM) is cloud based social marketing SaaS. Marketing cloud allows companies to identify sales leads from social media, discover advocates, identify the most trending information on any topic. Marketing Cloud allows companies to pro-actively engage with customers, manage social listening, create and deploy social content, manage and execute optimized social advertisement campaigns and track the performance of social campaigns. Figure 1.9 shows a screenshot of Salesforce dashboard.

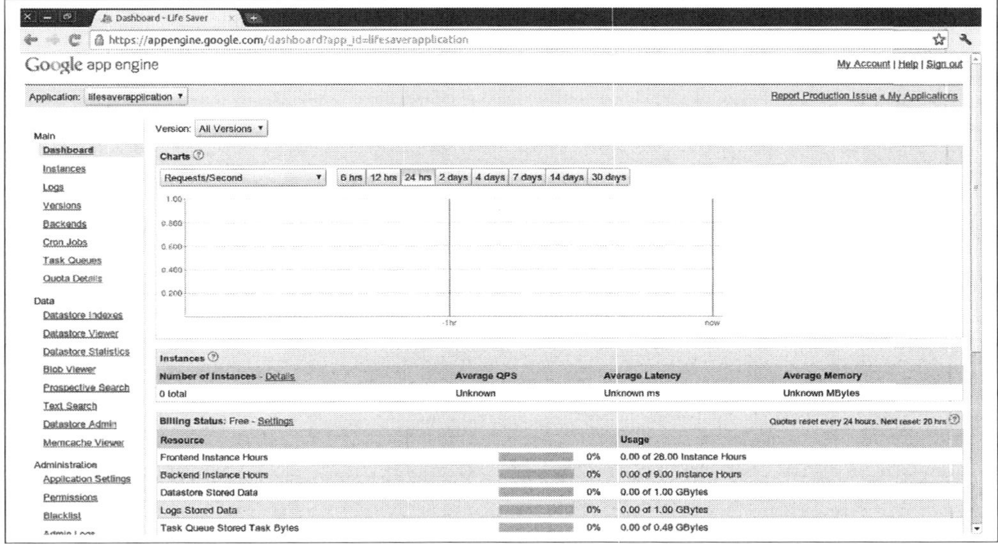

Figure 1.8: Google App Engine dashboard

Some of the tools included in the Salesforce Sales, Service and Marketing Clouds include:

- Accounts and contacts
- Leads
- Opportunities
- Campaigns
- Chatter
- Analytics and Forecasts

1.5 Cloud-based Services & Applications

Having discussed the characteristics, service and deployment models of cloud computing, let us now consider a few examples of the cloud-based services and applications.

1.5.1 Cloud Computing for Healthcare

Figure 1.10 shows the application of cloud computing environments to the healthcare ecosystem [10]. Hospitals and their affiliated providers can securely access patient data stored in the cloud and share the data with other hospitals and physicians. Patients can access their own health information from all of their care providers and store it in a personal health record (PHR) providing them with an integrated record that may even be a family health record. The PHR can be a vehicle for e-prescribing, a technique known to reduce medication dispensing errors and to facilitate medication reconciliation. History and information stored in the cloud (using SaaS applications) can streamline the admissions, care and discharge processes by eliminating redundant data collection and entry. Health payers can increase the effectiveness and lower the cost of their care management programs by providing value added services and giving access to health information to members.

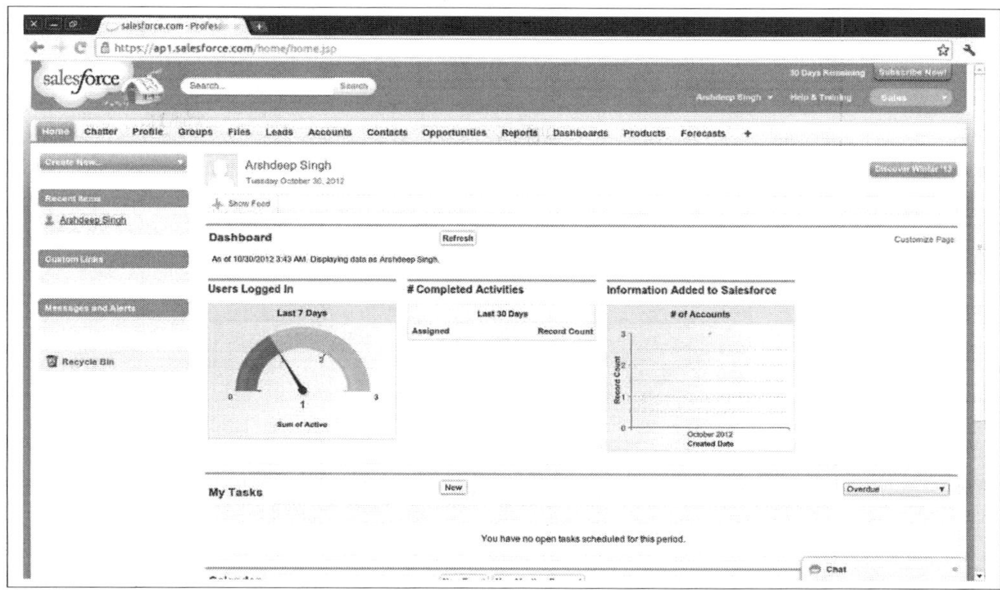

Figure 1.9: Salesforce dashboard

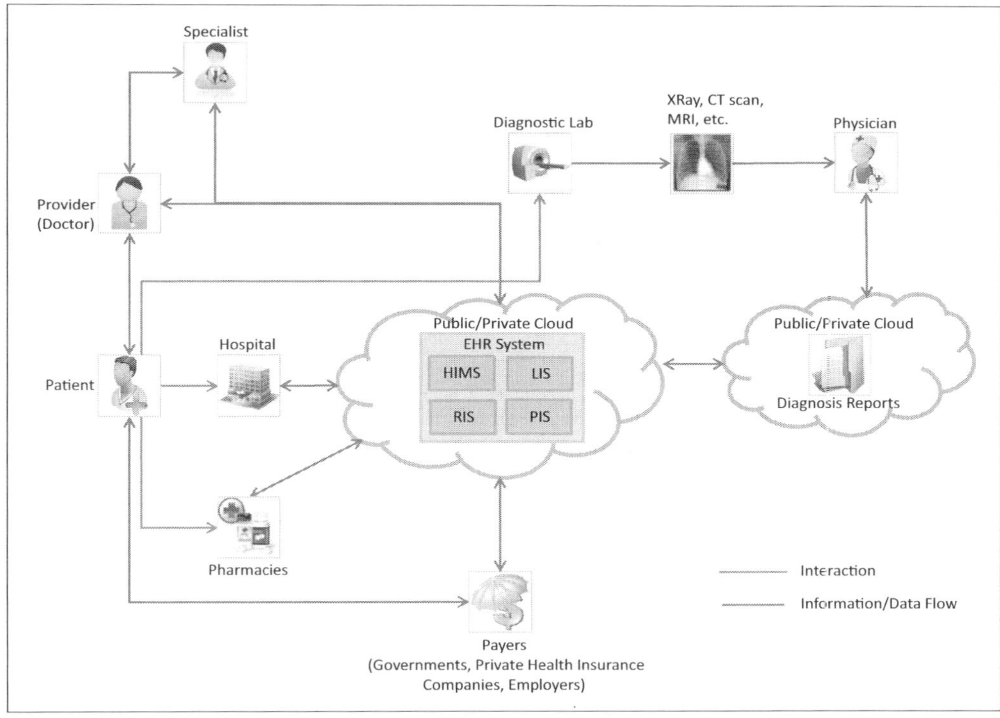

Figure 1.10: Cloud computing for healthcare

1.5.2 Cloud Computing for Energy Systems

Energy systems (such as smart grids, power plants, wind turbine farms, etc.) have thousands of sensors that gather real-time maintenance data continuously for condition monitoring and failure prediction purposes. These energy systems have a large number of critical components that must function correctly so that the systems can perform their operations correctly. For example, a wind turbine has a number of critical components, e.g., bearings, turning gears, etc. that must be monitored carefully as wear and tear in such critical components or sudden change in operating conditions of the machines can result in failures. In systems such as power grids, real-time information is collected using specialized electrical sensors called Phasor Measurement Units (PMU) at the substations. The information received from PMUs must be monitored in real-time for estimating the state of the system and for predicting failures. Maintenance and repair of such complex systems is not only expensive but also time consuming, therefore failures can cause huge losses for the operators, and supply outage for consumers. In [8], the Bahga & Madisetti have proposed a generic framework, CloudView, for storage, processing and analysis of massive machine maintenance data, collected from a large number of sensors embedded in industrial machines, in a cloud computing environment. The approach proposed in [8], in addition to being the first reported use of the cloud architecture for maintenance data storage, processing and analysis, also evaluated several possible cloud-based architectures that leverage the advantages of the parallel computing capabilities of the cloud to make local decisions with global information efficiently, while avoiding potential data bottlenecks that can occur in getting the maintenance data in and out of the cloud. Figure 1.11 shows a generic use case of cloud for energy systems.

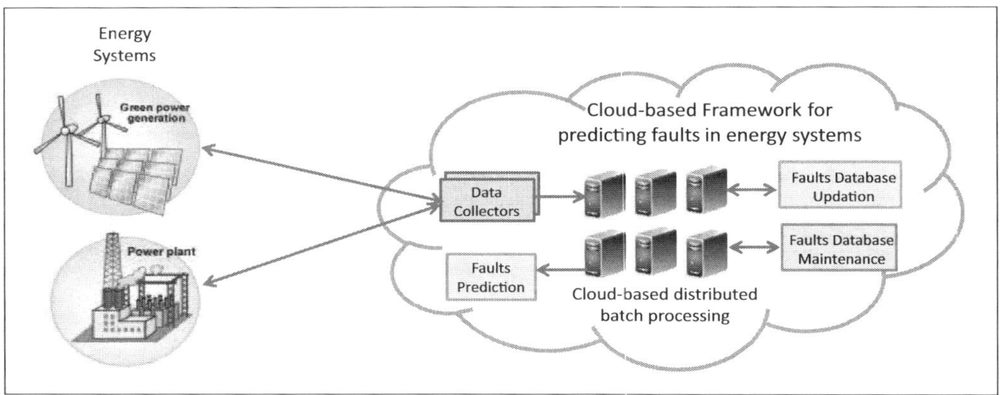

Figure 1.11: Cloud computing for energy systems

1.5.3 Cloud Computing for Transportation Systems

Intelligent transportation systems (ITS) have evolved significantly in recent years. Modern ITS are driven by data collected from multiple sources which is processed to provide new services to their users. By collecting large amount of data from various sources and processing the data into useful information, data-driven ITS can provide new services such as advanced route guidance, dynamic vehicle routing, anticipating customer demands for pickup and delivery problem, etc. Collection and organization of data from multiple sources in real-time and using the massive amounts data for providing intelligent decisions for operations and supply chains, is a major challenge, primarily because the size of the databases involved is very large, and real-time analysis tools have not been available. As a result large organizations are faced with a seemingly unsurmountable problem of analyzing terabytes of unorganized data stored on isolated and distinct geographical locations. However, recent advances in massive scale data processing systems, utilized for driving business operations of corporations provide a promising approach to massive ITS data storage and analysis.

In recent work, we have proposed a cloud-based framework that can be leveraged for real-time fresh food supply tracking and monitoring [9]. Fresh food can be damaged during transit due to unrefrigerated conditions and changes in environmental conditions such as temperature and humidity, which can lead to microbial infections and biochemical reactions or mechanical damage due to rough handling. Spoilage of fruits and vegetables during transport and distribution not only results in losses to the distributors but also presents a hazard to the food safety. Therefore tracking and monitoring of fresh food supply is an important problem that needs to be addressed. Typically medium and large container trucks are used for fresh food supply.

Since fresh foods have short durability, tracking the supply of fresh foods and monitoring the transit conditions can help identification of potential food safety hazards. The analysis and interpretation of data on the environmental conditions in the container and food truck positioning can enable more effective routing decisions in real time. Therefore, it is possible to take remedial measures such as, (1) the food that has a limited time budget before it gets rotten can be re-routed to a closer destinations, (2) alerts can be raised to the driver and the distributor about the transit conditions, such as container temperature exceeding the allowed limit, humidity levels going out of the allowed limit, etc., and corrective actions can be taken before the food gets damaged. Figure 1.12 shows a generic use case of cloud for transportation systems.

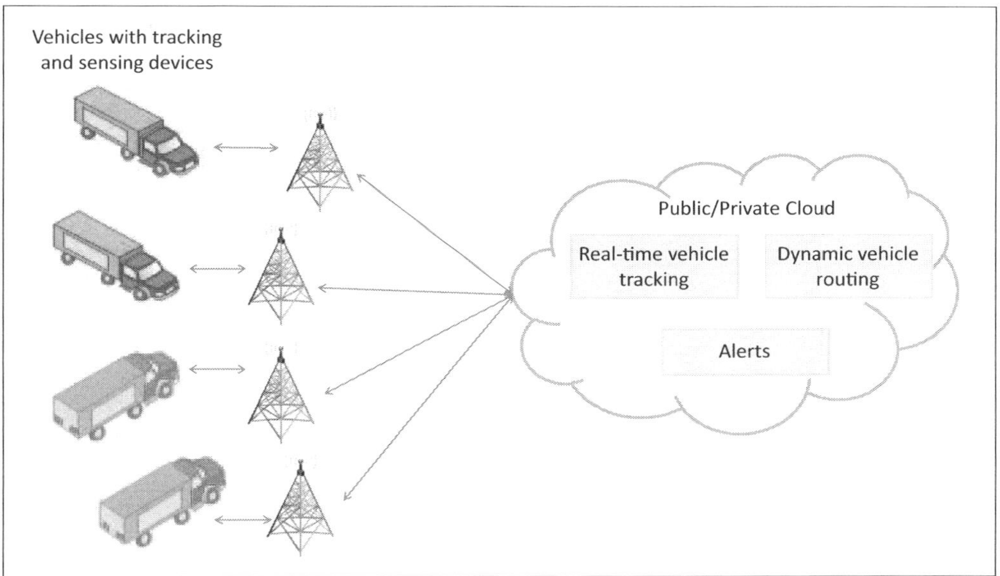

Figure 1.12: Cloud computing for transportation systems

1.5.4 Cloud Computing for Manufacturing Industry

Industrial Control Systems (ICS), such as supervisory control and data acquisition (SCADA) systems, distributed control systems (DCS), and other control system configurations such as Programmable Logic Controllers (PLC) continuously generate monitoring and control data. Real-time collection, management and analysis of data on production operations generated by ICS, in the cloud, can help in estimating the state of the systems, improve plant and personnel safety and thus take appropriate action in real-time to prevent catastrophic failures. Figure 1.13 shows a generic use case of cloud for manufacturing industry.

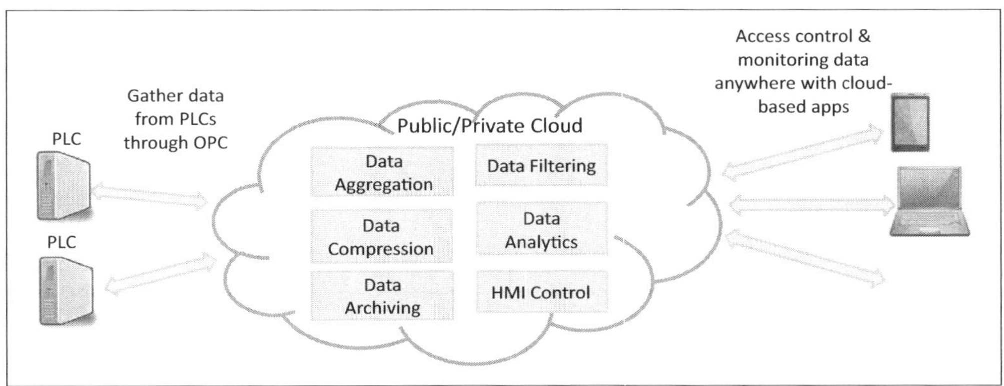

Figure 1.13: Cloud computing for manufacturing industry

1.5.5 Cloud Computing for Government

Cloud computing can play significant role for improving the efficiency and transparency of government operations. Cloud-based e-Governance systems can improve delivery of services to citizens, business, government employees and agencies, etc. and also improve the participation of all responsible parties in various government schemes and policy formation processes. Public services such as public transport reservations, vehicle registrations, issuing of driving licenses, income tax filing, electricity and water bill payments, birth or marriage registration, etc. can be facilitated through cloud-based applications. The benefit of using cloud for such public service applications is that the applications can be scaled up to serve a very large number of citizens. Cloud-based applications can share common data related to citizens. Data on utilization of government schemes can be collected from the citizens and used in the policy formation process and improvement of schemes. Figure 1.14 shows a generic use case of cloud for government.

1.5.6 Cloud Computing for Education

Cloud computing can help in improving the reach of quality online education to students. Cloud-based collaboration applications such as online forums, can help student discuss common problems and seek guidance from experts. Universities, colleges and schools can use cloud-based information management systems to admissions, improve administrative efficiency, offer online and distance education programs, online exams, track progress of students, collect feedback from students, for instance. Cloud-based online learning systems

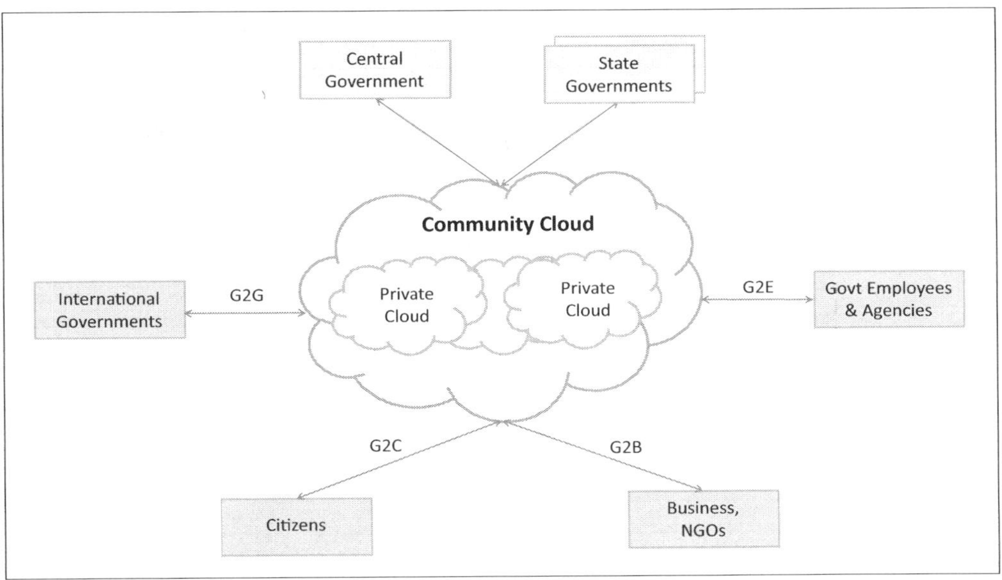

Figure 1.14: Cloud computing for government

can provide access to high quality educational material to students. Figure 1.15 shows a generic use case of cloud for education. Cloud-based systems can help universities, colleges and schools in cutting down the IT infrastructure costs and yet provide access to educational services to a large number of students.

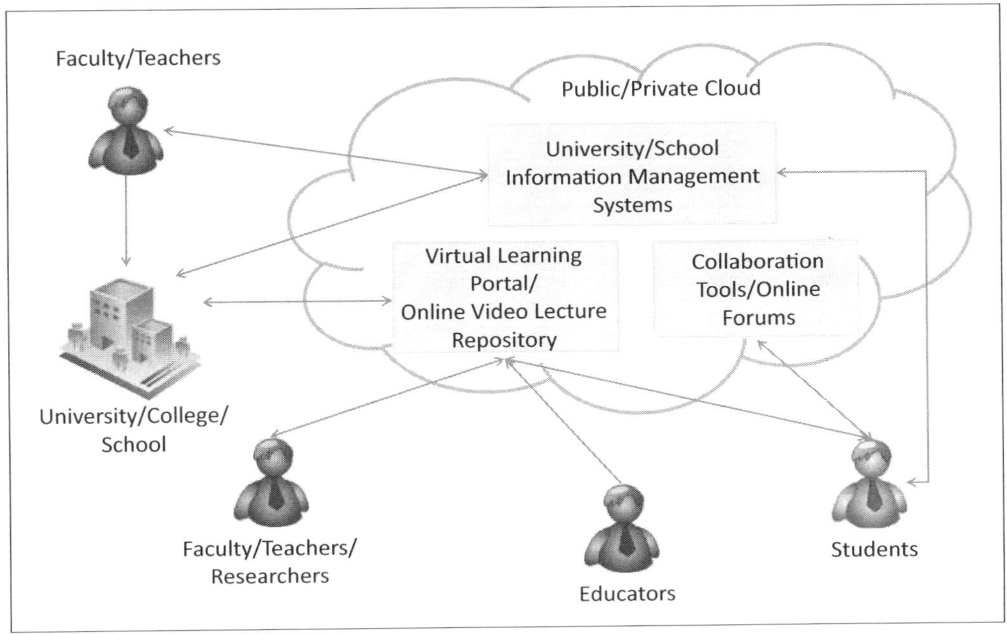

Figure 1.15: Cloud computing for education

1.5.7 Cloud Computing for Mobile Communication

Mobile communication infrastructure involves heterogeneous network devices for the radio access network (RAN) and the core network (CN). A variety of proprietary hardware components and systems are used for these network devices adding to their cost and inflexibility. Expansion and upgradation of the mobile network requires significant capital investments to meet the hardware and space requirements. Due to the increasing speed of innovation, the lifecycles of the network devices are becoming shorter. Network Function Virtualization (NFV) is being seen as a key enabling technology for the fifth generation of mobile communication networks (5G) in the next decade. NFV will leverage cloud computing to consolidate the heterogeneous network devices into the cloud. The NFV architecture, as being standardized by the European Telecommunications Standards Institute (ETSI) comprises of NFV infrastructure, virtual network functions and NFV management and orchestration layers [11]. NFV comprises of network functions implemented in software that run on virtualized resources in the cloud. NFV enables a separation the network functions which are implemented in software from those of the underlying hardware. Thus, network functions can be easily tested and upgraded by installing new software while the hardware remains the same. This flexibility will speed up innovation and reduce the time-to-market. By leveraging the cloud for mobile communication network functions significant savings in capital and operational expenditure can be achieved.

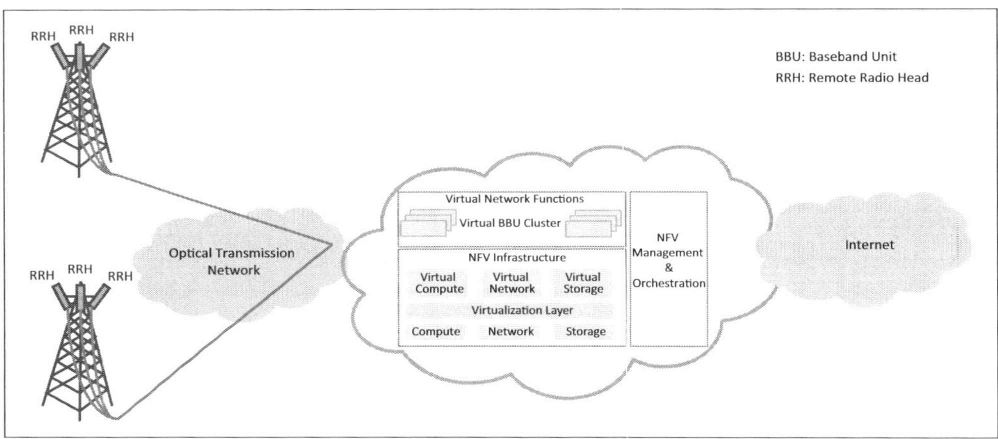

Figure 1.16: Cloud computing for virtualizing radio access network

Figure 1.16 shows a use case of cloud-based NFV architecture for cloud-based radio access networks (C- RANs) with virtualized mobile base stations (baseband units). The baseband units (BBUs), such as eNodeB in 4G, in current mobile communication networks are co-located with the cell towers on-site and run on proprietary hardware. The BBUs are typically designed for worst-case peak loads. However, typical workload levels are much lower than the peak loads, therefore, the excess capacity goes unused. With NFV and cloud the BBUs can be virtualized and only as many resources as required to meet the workload levels can be provisioned on-demand. This will result in significant power savings. Centralized cloud-based virtual BBU clusters can replace on-site installations of BBUs in distributed geographical locations. This will result in reduction of management and

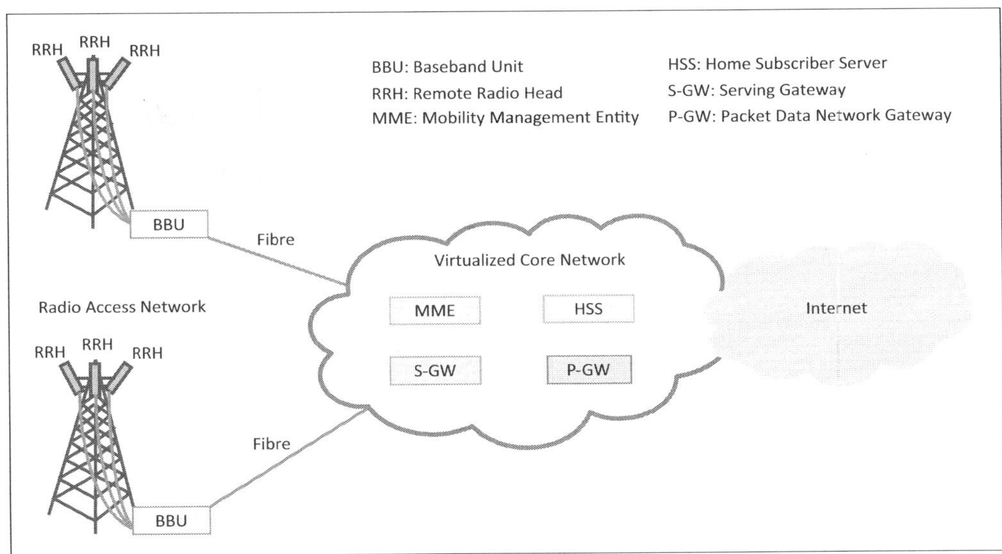

Figure 1.17: Cloud computing for virtualizing mobile core network

operational expenses.

Figure 1.17 shows a use case of cloud-based NFV architecture for mobile core network. With NFV, the core network devices such as Mobility Management Entity (MME), Home Subscriber Server (HSS), Serving Gateway (S-GW) and Packet Data Network Gateway (P-GW) in 4G can be implemented in software and deployed on virtualized resources in the cloud. This will reduce the total cost of ownership due to consolidation of network component that run on industry standard networking hardware. Other benefits of using cloud-based NFV architecture for mobile core network include improved resource utilization efficiency, improved network resilience, improved flexibility in scaling up capacity.

Summary

In this chapter you learned the definition and characteristics of cloud computing. Cloud computing offers Internet-based access to low cost computing and applications that are provided using virtualized resources. On-demand service, remote accessibility through a variety of networks, resource pooling, rapid elasticity and measured service are the key characteristics of cloud computing. Cloud computing resources can be provisioned on-demand by the users. Cloud computing resources can be accessed over the network with standard access mechanisms. Cloud resources are pooled to serve multiple users using multi-tenancy.

Cloud computing has three service models - IaaS, PaaS and SaaS. IaaS provides the users the capability to provision computing and storage resources. PaaS provides the users the capability to develop and deploy their own applications in the cloud. SaaS provides applications hosted in the cloud through thin client interfaces.

Cloud computing is being increasingly adopted by individual users, small and large enterprises, large organizations and governments. Cloud computing is being applied in various fields such as healthcare, education, governance, energy systems, manufacturing industry, transportation systems, etc.

Review Questions

1. Define cloud computing
2. List the pros and cons of cloud computing.
3. Distinguish between IaaS, PaaS and SaaS.
4. Define multi-tenancy. What is the difference between virtual and organic multi-tenancy?
5. What is the difference between horizontal scaling and vertical scaling? Describe scenarios in which you will use each type of scaling.
6. Define virtualization. What is the difference between full, para- and hardware-assisted virtualization?
7. Assume your company wants to launch an e-commerce website. Which cloud services and deployment models will you consider for the website?

2 — Cloud Concepts & Technologies

This Chapter Covers
Concepts and enabling technologies of cloud computing including:

- Virtualization
- Load balancing
- Scalability & Elasticity
- Deployment
- Replication
- Monitoring
- MapReduce
- Identity and Access Management
- Service Level Agreements
- Billing

In this chapter you will learn the key concepts and enabling technologies of cloud computing. We will introduce and build upon technologies such as virtualization, load balancing,and on-demand provisioning. A popular programming model, called MapReduce, will also be covered.

2.1 Virtualization

Virtualization refers to the partitioning the resources of a physical system (such as computing, storage, network and memory) into multiple virtual resources. Virtualization is the key enabling technology of cloud computing and allows pooling of resources. In cloud computing, resources are pooled to serve multiple users using multi-tenancy. Multi-tenant aspects of the cloud allow multiple users to be served by the same physical hardware. Users are assigned virtual resources that run on top of the physical resources. Figure 2.1 shows the architecture of a virtualization technology in cloud computing. The physical resources such as computing, storage memory and network resources are virtualized. The virtualization layer partitions the physical resources into multiple virtual machines. The virtualization layer allows multiple operating system instances to run currently as virtual machines on the same underlying physical resources.

Hypervisor

The virtualization layer consists of a hypervisor or a virtual machine monitor (VMM). The hypervisor presents a virtual operating platform to a guest operating system (OS). There are two types of hypervisors as shown in Figures 2.2 and 2.3 . Type-1 hypervisors or the native hypervisors run directly on the host hardware and control the hardware and monitor the guest operating systems. Type 2 hypervisors or hosted hypervisors run on top of a conventional (main/host) operating system and monitor the guest operating systems.

Guest OS

A guest OS is an operating system that is installed in a virtual machine in addition to the host or main OS. In virtualization, the guest OS can be different from the host OS.

Various forms of virtualization approaches exist:

Full Virtualization

In full virtualization, the virtualization layer completely decouples the guest OS from the underlying hardware. The guest OS requires no modification and is not aware that it is being virtualized. Full virtualization is enabled by direct execution of user requests and binary translation of OS requests. Figure 2.4 shows the full virtualization approach.

Para-Virtualization

In para-virtualization, the guest OS is modified to enable communication with the hypervisor to improve performance and efficiency. The guest OS kernel is modified to replace non-virtualizable instructions with hypercalls that communicate directly with the virtualization layer hypervisor. Figure 2.5 shows the para-virtualization approach.

Hardware Virtualization

Hardware assisted virtualization is enabled by hardware features such as Intel's Virtualization Technology (VT-x) and AMD's AMD-V. In hardware assisted virtualization, privileged and sensitive calls are set to automatically trap to the hypervisor. Thus, there is no need for either binary translation or para-virtualization.

Table 2.1 lists some examples of popular hypervisors.

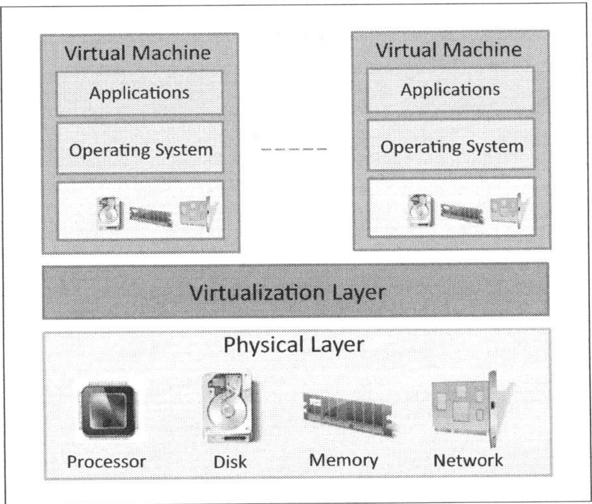

Figure 2.1: Virtualization architecture

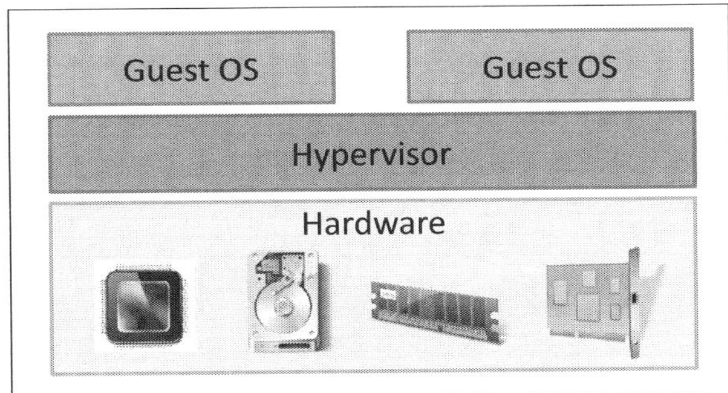

Figure 2.2: Hypervisor design: Type-1

2.2 Load Balancing

One of the important features of cloud computing is scalability. Cloud computing resources can be scaled up on demand to meet the performance requirements of applications. Load balancing distributes workloads across multiple servers to meet the application workloads. The goals of load balancing techniques are to achieve maximum utilization of resources, minimizing the response times, maximizing throughput. Load balancing distributes the incoming user requests across multiple resources. With load balancing, cloud-based applications can achieve high availability and reliability. Since multiple resources under a load balancer are used to serve the user requests, in the event of failure of one or more of the resources, the load balancer can automatically reroute the user traffic to the healthy resources. To the end user accessing a cloud-based application, a load balancer makes the pool of servers under the

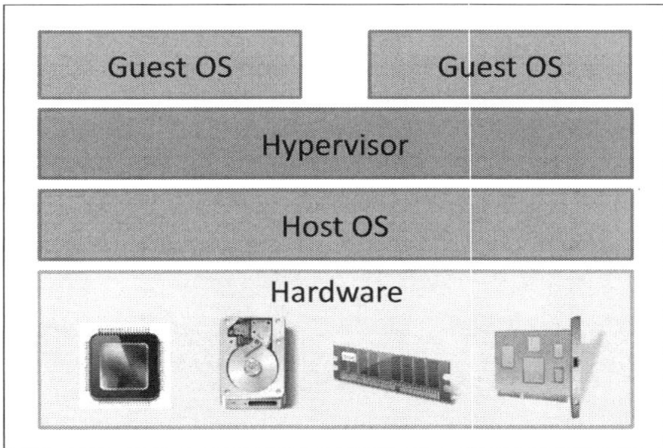

Figure 2.3: Hypervisor design: Type-2

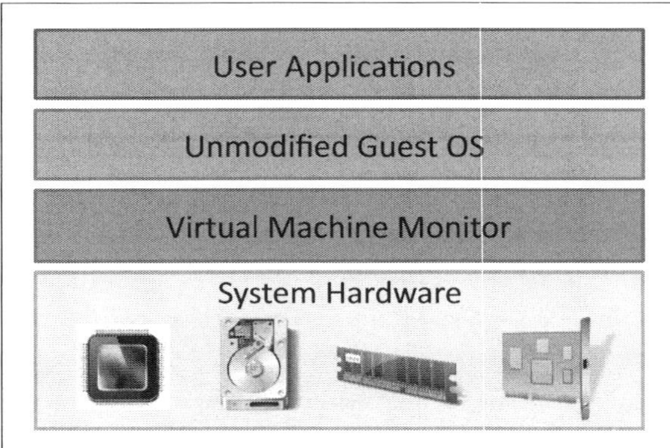

Figure 2.4: Full virtualization

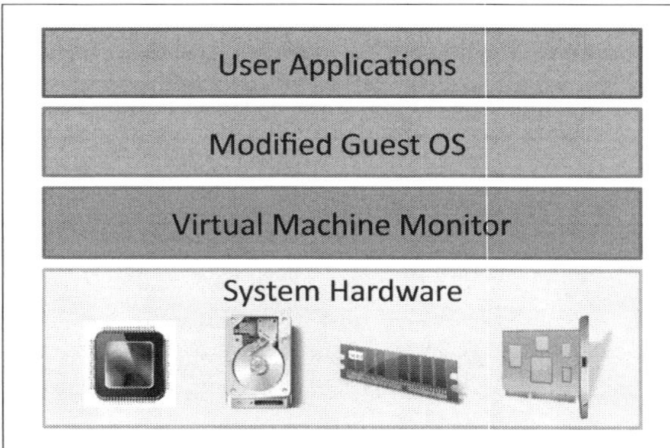

Figure 2.5: Para-virtualization

load balancer appear as a single server with high computing capacity. The routing of user requests is determined based on a load balancing algorithm. Commonly used load balancing algorithms include:

Hypervisor	Type
Citrix XenServer	Type-1
Oracle VM Server	Type-1
KVM	Type-1
VMWare ESX/ESXi	Type-1
Microsoft Hyper-V	Type-1
Xen Hypervisor	Type-1
VMWare Workstation	Type-2
VirtualBox	Type-2

Table 2.1: Examples of popular hypervisors

Round Robin

In round robin load balancing, the servers are selected one by one to serve the incoming requests in a non-hierarchical circular fashion with no priority assigned to a specific server.

Weighted Round Robin

In weighted round robin load balancing, severs are assigned some weights. The incoming requests are proportionally routed using a static or dynamic ratio of respective weights.

Low Latency

In low latency load balancing the load balancer monitors the latency of each server. Each incoming request is routed to the server which has the lowest latency.

Least Connections

In least connections load balancing, the incoming requests are routed to the server with the least number of connections.

Priority

In priority load balancing, each server is assigned a priority. The incoming traffic is routed to the highest priority server as long as the server is available. When the highest priority server fails, the incoming traffic is routed to a server with a lower priority.

Overflow

Overflow load balancing is similar to priority load balancing. When the incoming requests to highest priority server overflow, the requests are routed to a lower priority server.

Figure 2.6 depicts these various load balancing approaches. For session based applications, an important issue to handle during load balancing is the persistence of multiple requests from a particular user session. Since load balancing can route successive requests from a user session to different servers, maintaining the state or the information of the session is important. Three commonly used persistence approaches are described below:

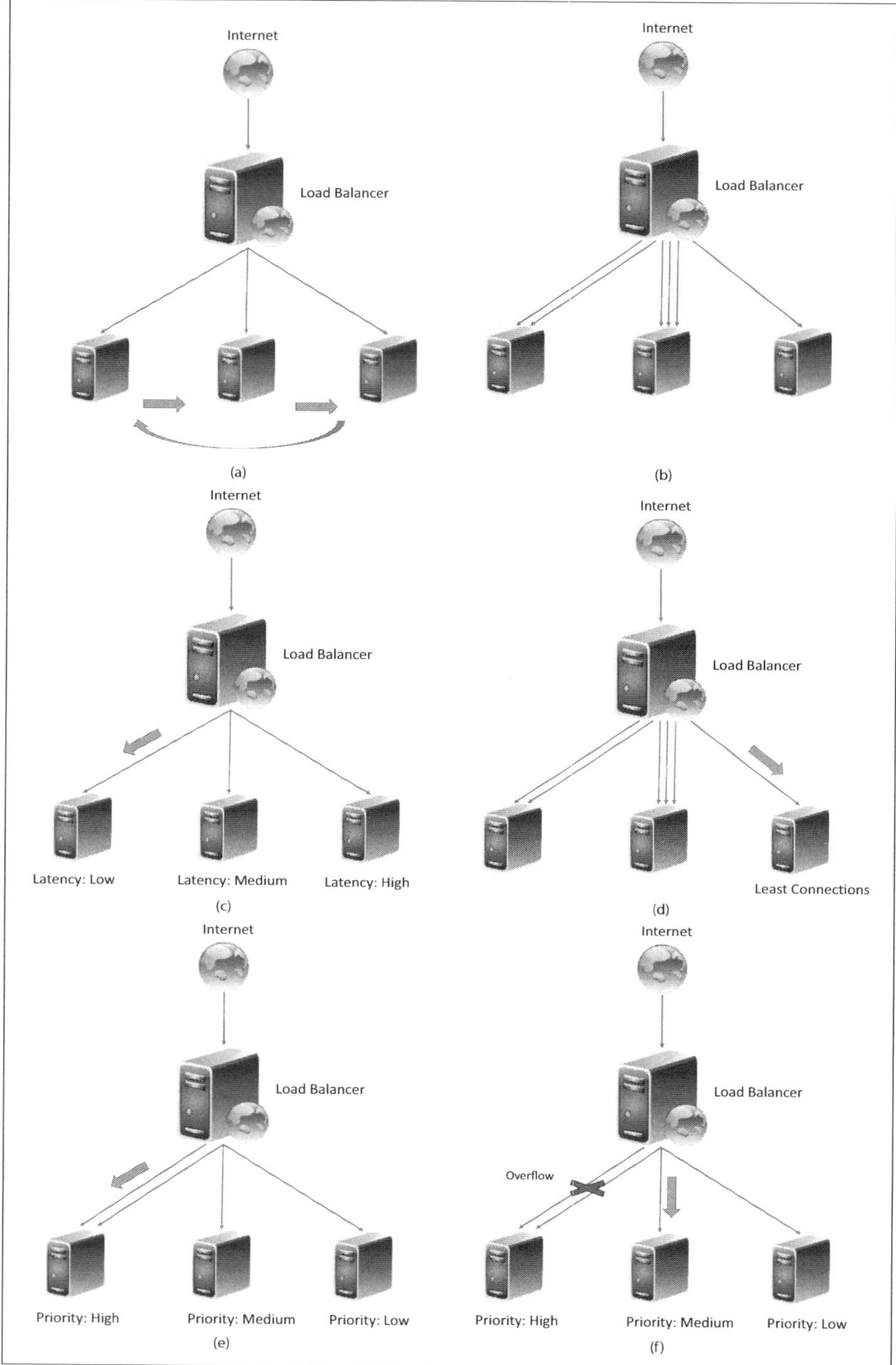

Figure 2.6: (a) Round robin load balancing, (b) Weighted round robin load balancing, (c) Low latency load balancing, (d) Least connections load balancing, (e) Priority load balancing, (f) Overload load balancing

Sticky sessions

In this approach all the requests belonging to a user session are routed to the same server. These sessions are called sticky sessions. The benefit of this approach is that it makes session management simple. However, a drawback of this approach is that if a server fails all the sessions belonging to that server are lost, since there is no automatic failover possible.

Session Database

In this approach, all the session information is stored externally in a separate session database, which is often replicated to avoid a single point of failure. Though, this approach involves additional overhead of storing the session information, however, unlike the sticky session approach, this approach allows automatic failover.

Browser cookies

In this approach, the session information is stored on the client side in the form of browser cookies. The benefit of this approach is that it makes the session management easy and has the least amount of overhead for the load balancer.

URL re-writing

In this approach, a URL re-write engine stores the session information by modifying the URLs on the client side. Though this approach avoids overhead on the load balancer, a drawback is that the amount of session information that can be stored is limited. For applications that require larger amounts of session information, this approach does not work.

Load balancing can be implemented in software or hardware. Software-based load balancers run on standard operating systems, and like other cloud resources, load balancers are also virtualized. Hardware-based load balancers implement load balancing algorithms in Application Specific Integrated Circuits (ASICs). In a hardware load balancer, the incoming user requests are routed to the underlying servers based on some pre-configured load balancing strategy and the response from the severs are sent back either directly to the user (at layer-4) or back to the load balancer (at layer-7) where it is manipulated before being sent back to the user. Table 2.2 lists some examples of load balancers.

2.3 Scalability & Elasticity

Multi-tier applications such as e-Commerce, social networking, business-to-business, etc. can experience rapid changes in their traffic. Each website has a different traffic pattern which is determined by a number of factors that are generally hard to predict beforehand. Modern web applications have multiple tiers of deployment with varying number of servers in each tier. Capacity planning is an important task for such applications. Capacity planning involves determining the right sizing of each tier of the deployment of an application in terms of the number of resources and the capacity of each resource. Capacity planning may be for computing, storage, memory or network resources. Figure 2.7 shows the cost versus capacity curves for traditional and cloud approaches.

Traditional approaches for capacity planning are based on predicted demands for applications and account for worst case peak loads of applications. When the workloads of applications increase, the traditional approaches have been either to scale up or scale

Load Balancer	Type
Nginx	Software
HAProxy	Software
Pound	Software
Varish	Software
Cisco Systems Catalyst 6500	Hardware
Coyote Point Equalizer	Hardware
F5 Networks BIG-IP LTM	Hardware
Barracuda Load Balancer	Hardware

Table 2.2: Examples of popular load balancers

out. Scaling up involves upgrading the hardware resources (adding additional computing, memory, storage or network resources). Scaling out involves addition of more resources of the same type. Traditional scaling up and scaling out approaches are based on demand forecasts at regular intervals of time. When variations in workloads are rapid, traditional approaches are unable to keep track with the demand and lead to either over-provisioning or under-provisioning of resources. Over-provisioning of resources leads to higher capital expenditures than required. On the other hand, under-provisioning of resources leads to traffic overloads, slow response times, low throughputs and hence loss of opportunity to serve the customers. Analyzing the real traffic history plots for top websites shown in Figure 2.7 we observe that the off peak workloads are significantly lower than peak workloads. Traditional capacity planning approaches which are designed to meet the peak loads result in excess capacity and under utilization of resources. Moreover, the infrastructure resources for traditional applications are fixed, rigid and provisioned in advance. This involves up-front capital expenditures for setting up the infrastructure.

2.4 Deployment

Figure 2.8 shows the cloud application deployment lifecycle. Deployment prototyping can help in making deployment architecture design choices. By comparing performance of alternative deployment architectures, deployment prototyping can help in choosing the best and most cost effective deployment architecture that can meet the application performance requirements. Table 2.3 lists some popular cloud deployment management tools. Deployment design is an iterative process that involves the following steps:

Deployment Design

In this step the application deployment is created with various tiers as specified in the deployment configuration. The variables in this step include the number of servers in each tier, computing, memory and storage capacities of severs, server interconnection, load balancing and replication strategies. Deployment is created by provisioning the cloud

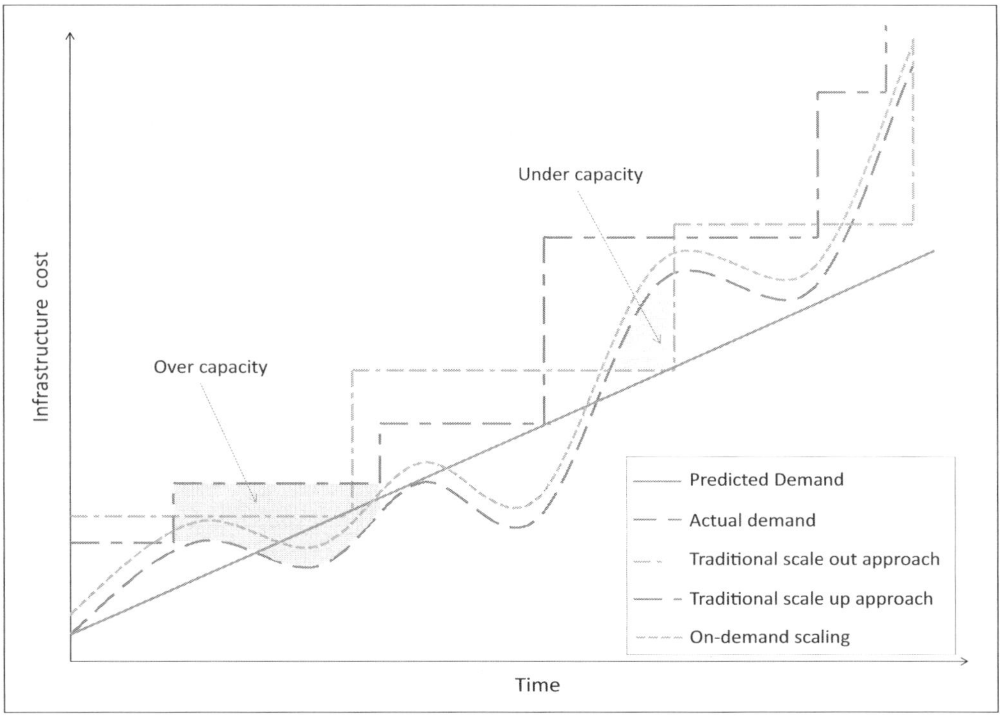

Figure 2.7: Cost versus capacity curves

resources as specified in the deployment configuration. The process of resource provisioning and deployment creation is often automated and involves a number of steps such as launching of server instances, configuration of servers, and deployment of various tiers of the application on the servers.

Performance Evaluation

Once the application is deployed in the cloud, the next step in the deployment lifecycle is to verify whether the application meets the performance requirements with the deployment. This step involves monitoring the workload on the application and measuring various workload parameters such as response time and throughput. In addition to this, the utilization of servers (CPU, memory, disk, I/O, etc.) in each tier is also monitored.

Deployment Refinement

After evaluating the performance of the application, deployments are refined so that the application can meet the performance requirements. Various alternatives can exist in this step such as vertical scaling (or scaling up), horizontal scaling (or scaling out), alternative server interconnections, alternative load balancing and replication strategies, for instance.

2.5 Replication

Replication is used to create and maintain multiple copies of the data in the cloud. Replication of data is important for practical reasons such as business continuity and disaster recovery.

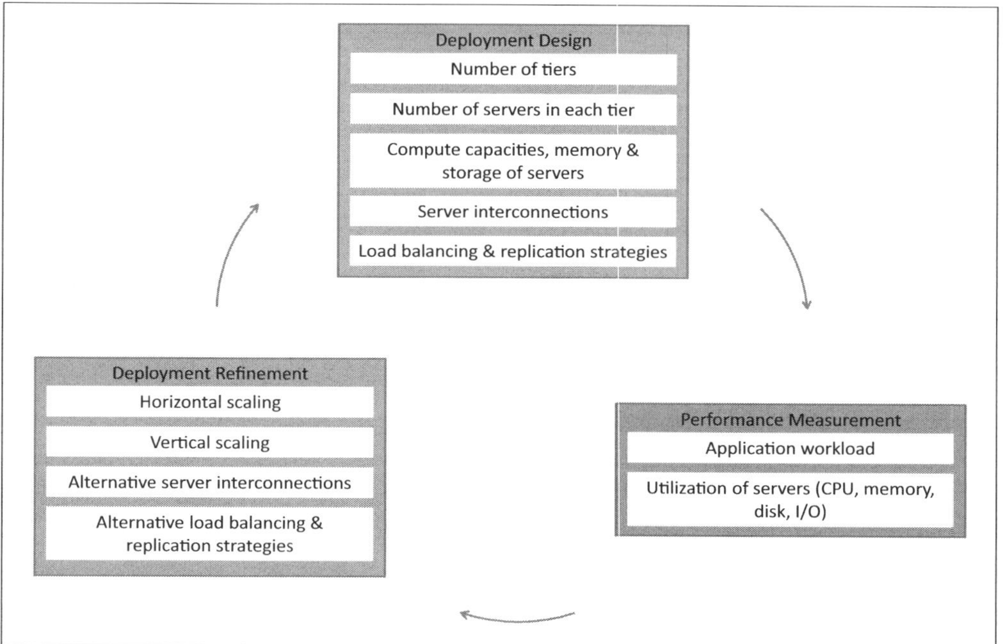

Figure 2.8: Cloud application deployment lifecycle

In the event of data loss at the primary location, organizations can continue to operate their applications from secondary data sources. With real-time replication of data, organizations can achieve faster recovery from failures. Traditional business continuity and disaster recovery approaches don't provide efficient, cost effective and automated recovery of data. Cloud based data replication approaches provide replication of data in multiple locations, automated recovery, low recovery point objective (RPO) and low recovery time objective (RTO). Cloud enables rapid implementation of replication solutions for disaster recovery for small and medium enterprises and large organizations. With cloud-based data replication organizations can plan for disaster recovery without making any capital expenditures on purchasing, configuring and managing secondary site locations. Cloud provides affordable replication solutions with pay-per-use/pay-as-you-go pricing models. There are three types of replication approaches as shown in Figure 2.9 and described as follows:

Array-based Replication

Array-based replication uses compatible storage arrays to automatically copy data from a local storage array to a remote storage array. Arrays replicate data at the disk sub-system level, therefore the type of hosts accessing the data and the type of data is not important. Thus array-based replication can work in heterogeneous environments with different operating systems. Array-based replication uses Network Attached Storage (NAS) or Storage Area Network (SAN), to replicate. A drawback of this array-based replication is that it requires similar arrays at local and remote locations. Thus the costs for setting up array-based replication are higher than the other approaches.

Cloud Deployment Management Tool	Features
RightScale	Design, deploy and manage cloud deployments across multiple public or private clouds.
Scalr	Provides tools to automate the management of servers, monitors servers, replaces servers that fail, provides auto scaling and backups.
Kaavo	Allows deploying applications easily across multiple clouds, managing distributed applications and automating high availability.
CloudStack	Allows simple and cost effective deployment management and configuration of cloud computing environments.

Table 2.3: Examples of popular cloud deployment management tools

Network-based Replication

Network-based replication uses an appliance that sits on the network and intercepts packets that are sent from hosts and storage arrays. The intercepted packets are replicated to a secondary location. The benefits of this approach is that it supports heterogeneous environments and requires a single point of management. However, this approach involves higher initial costs due to replication hardware and software.

Host-based Replication

Host-based replication runs on standard servers and uses software to transfer data from a local to remote location. The host acts the replication control mechanism. An agent is installed on the hosts that communicates with the agents on the other hosts. Host-based replication can either be block-based or file-based. Block-based replication typically require dedicated volumes of the same size on both the local and remote servers. File-based replication requires less storage as compared to block-based storage. File-based replication gives additional allows the administrators to choose the files or folders to be replicated. Host-based replication with cloud-infrastructure provides affordable replication solutions. With host-based replication, entire virtual machines can be replicated in real-time.

2.6 Monitoring

Cloud resources can be monitored by monitoring services provided by the cloud service providers. Monitoring services allow cloud users to collect and analyze the data on various monitoring metrics. Figure 2.10 shows a generic architecture for a cloud monitoring service. A monitoring service collects data on various system and application metrics from the cloud computing instances. Monitoring services provide various pre-defined metrics. Users can also define their custom metrics for monitoring the cloud resources. Users can define various actions based on the monitoring data, for example, auto-scaling a cloud deployment when the CPU usage of monitored resources becomes high. Monitoring services also provide various statistics based on the monitoring data collected. Table 2.4 lists the commonly

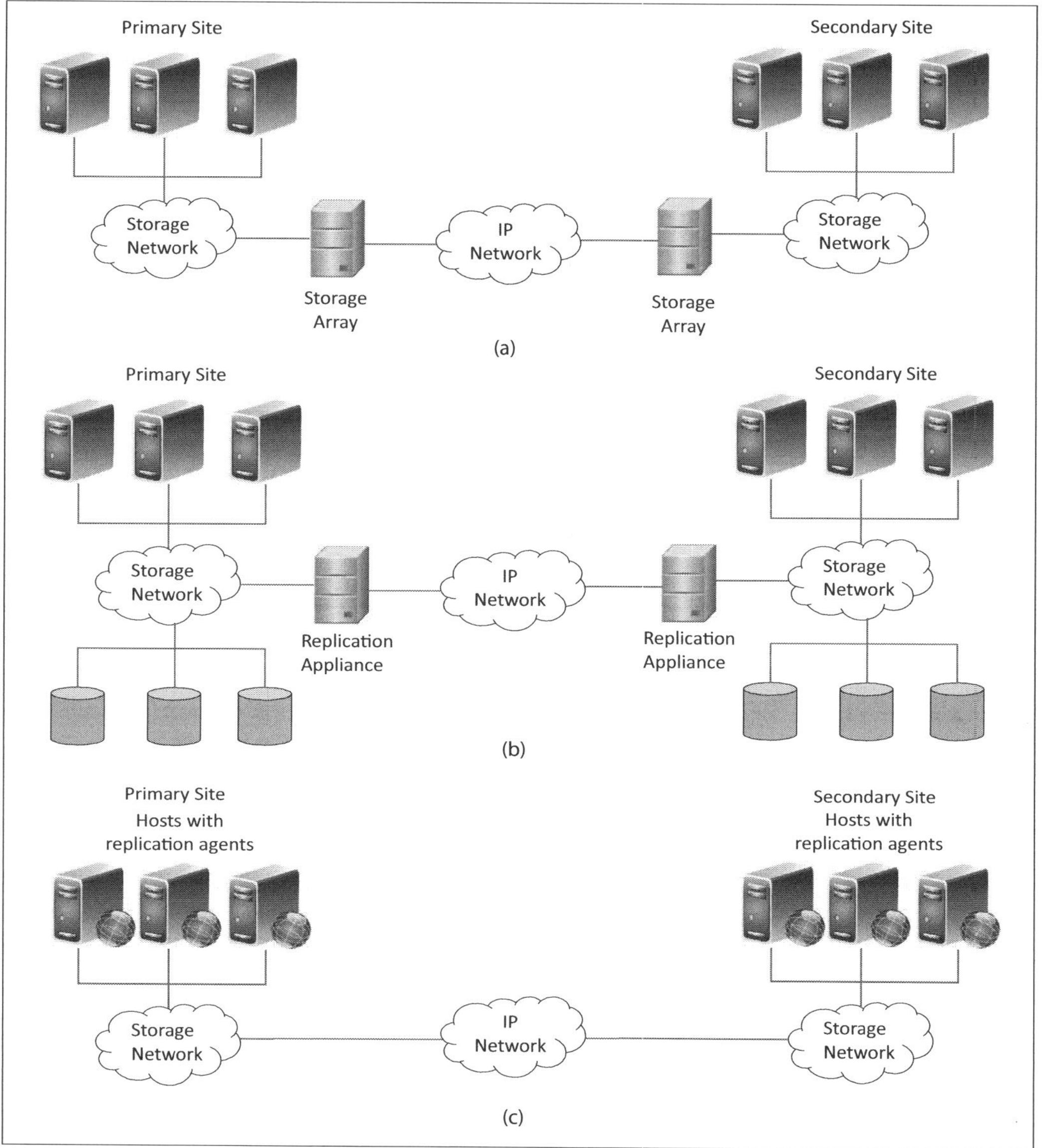

Figure 2.9: Replication approaches: (a) Array-based replication, (b) Network-based replication, (c) Host-based replication

used monitoring metrics for cloud computing resources. Monitoring of cloud resources is important because it allows the users to keep track of the health of applications and services deployed in the cloud. For example, an organization which has its website hosted in the cloud can monitor the performance of the websit and also the website traffic. With the monitoring data available at run-time users can make operational decisions such as scaling up or scaling down cloud resources.

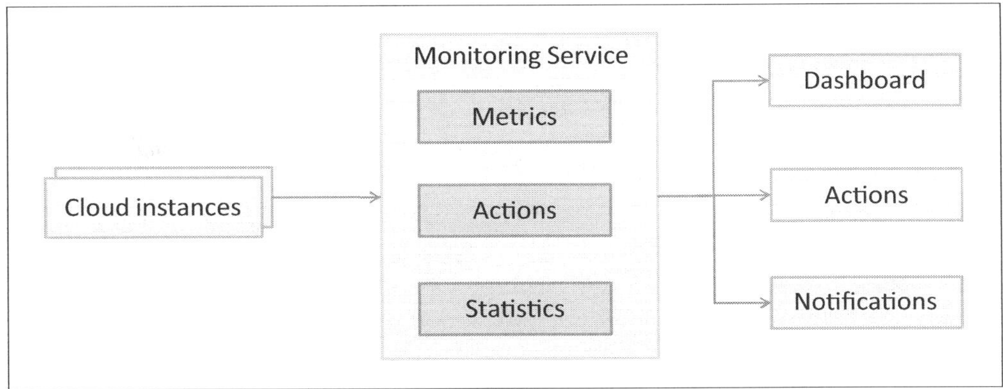

Figure 2.10: Typical cloud monitoring service architecture

Type	Metrics
CPU	CPU-Usage, CPU-Idle
Disk	Disk-Usage, Bytes/sec (read/write), Operations/sec
Memory	Memory-Used, Memory-Free, Page-Cache
Interface	Packets/sec (incoming/outgoing), Octets/sec(incoming/outgoing)

Table 2.4: Typical monitoring metrics

2.7 Software Defined Networking

Software-Defined Networking (SDN) is a networking architecture that separates the control plane from the data plane and centralizes the network controller. Figure 2.11 shows the conventional network architecture built with specialized hardware (switches, routers, etc.). Network devices in conventional network architectures are getting exceedingly complex with the increasing number of distributed protocols being implemented and the use of proprietary hardware and interfaces. In the conventional network architecture the control plane and data plane are coupled. Control plane is the part of the network that carries the signaling and routing message traffic while the data plane is the part of the network that carries the payload data traffic.

The limitations of the conventional network architectures are as follows:

- **Complex Network Devices**: Conventional networks are getting increasingly complex with more and more protocols being implemented to improve link speeds and reliability. Interoperability is limited due to the lack of standard and open interfaces. Network devices use proprietary hardware and software and have slow product lifecycles limiting innovation. The conventional networks were well suited for static traffic patterns and had a large number of protocols designed for specific applications. With the emergence of cloud computing and proliferation of internet access devices, the traffic patterns are becoming more and more dynamic. Due to the complexity of conventional network devices, making changes in the networks to meet the dynamic traffic patterns has

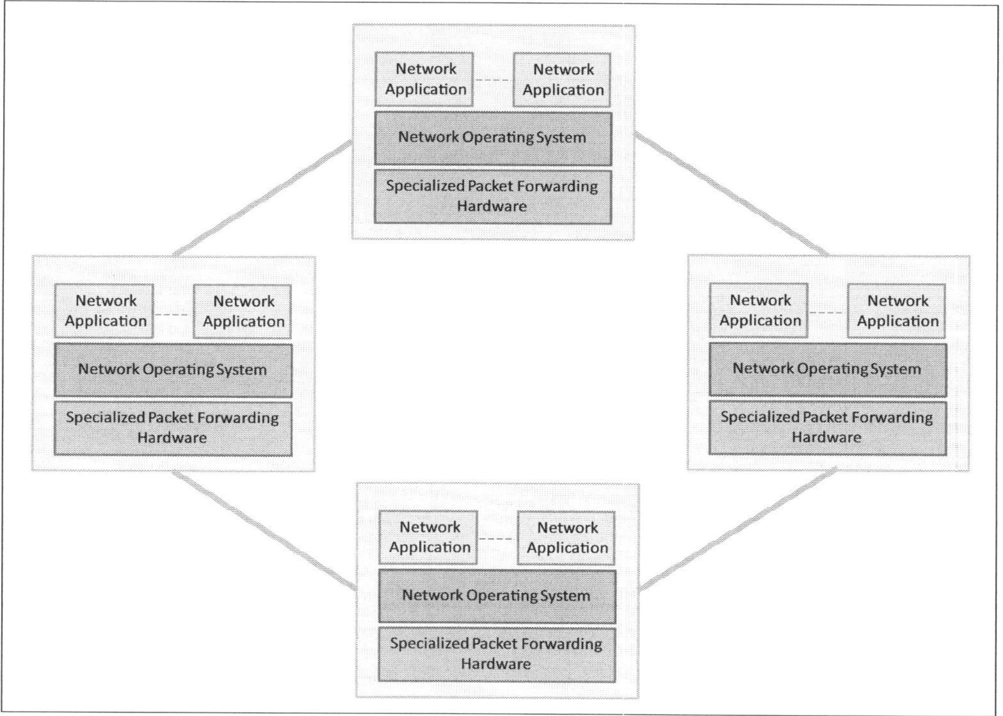

Figure 2.11: Conventional network architecture

become increasingly difficult.

- **Management Overhead**: Conventional networks involve significant management overhead. Network managers find it increasingly difficult to manage multiple network devices and interfaces from multiple vendors. Upgradation of network requires configuration changes in multiple devices (switches, routers, firewalls, etc.)
- **Limited Scalability**: The virtualization technologies used in cloud computing environments has increased the number of virtual hosts requiring network access. Multi-tenanted applications hosted in the cloud are distributed across multiple virtual machines that require exchange of traffic. Big data applications run distributed algorithms on a large number of virtual machines that require huge amounts of data exchange between virtual machines. Such computing environments require highly scalable and easy to manage network architectures with minimal manual configurations, which is becoming increasingly difficult with conventional networks.

SDN attempts to create network architectures that are simpler, inexpensive, scalable, agile and easy to manage. Figures 2.12 and 2.13 show the SDN architecture and the SDN layers in which the control and data planes are decoupled and the network controller is centralized. Software-based SDN controllers maintain a unified view of the network and make configuration, management and provisioning simpler. The underlying infrastructure in SDN uses simple packet forwarding hardware as opposed to specialized hardware in conventional networks. The underlying network infrastructure is abstracted from the applications. Network devices become simple with SDN as they do not require implementations of a large number of

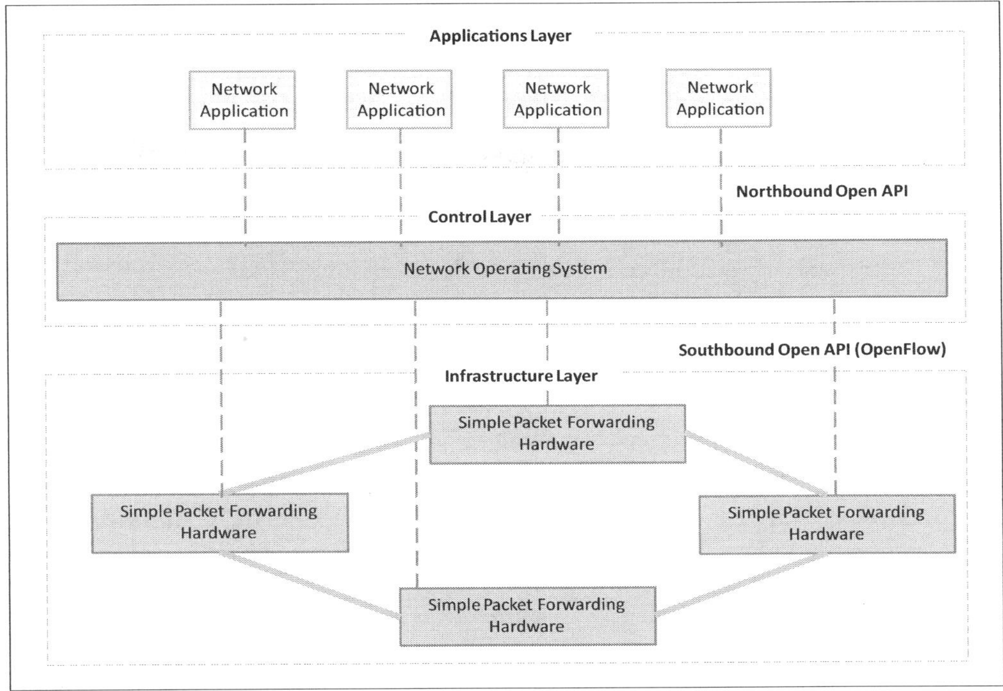

Figure 2.12: SDN architecture

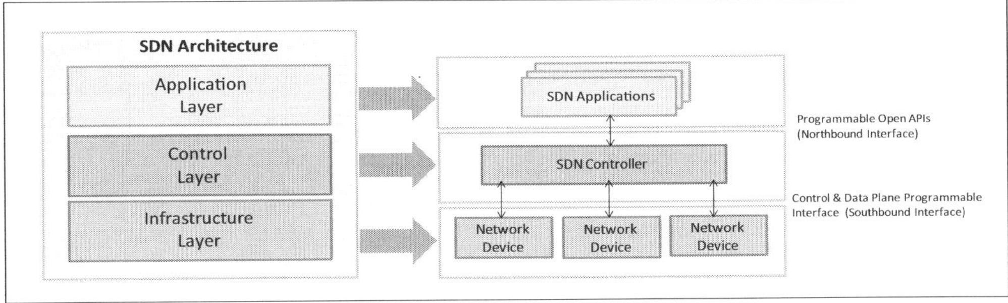

Figure 2.13: SDN layers

protocols. Network devices receive instructions from the SDN controller on how to forward the packets. These devices can be simpler and cost less as they can be built from standard hardware and software components.

Key elements of SDN are as follows:

- **Centralized Network Controller**: With decoupled the control and data planes and centralized network controller, the network administrators can rapidly configure the network. SDN applications can be deployed through programmable open APIs. This speeds up innovation as the network administrators no longer need to wait for the device vendors to embed new features in their proprietary hardware.
- **Programmable Open APIs**: SDN architecture supports programmable open APIs for interface between the SDN application and control layers (Northbound interface).

These open APIs that allow implementing various network services such as routing, quality of service (QoS), access control, etc.

- **Standard Communication Interface (OpenFlow)**: SDN architecture uses a standard communication interface between the control and infrastructure layers (Southbound interface). OpenFlow, which is defined by the Open Networking Foundation (ONF) is the broadly accepted SDN protocol for the Southbound interface. With OpenFlow, the forwarding plane of the network devices can be directly accessed and manipulated. OpenFlow uses the concept of flows to identify network traffic based on pre-defined match rules. Flows can be programmed statically or dynamically by the SDN control software. Figure 2.14 shows the components of an OpenFlow switch comprising of one or more flow tables and a group table, which perform packet lookups and forwarding, and OpenFlow channel to an external controller. OpenFlow protocol is implemented on both sides of the interface between the controller and the network devices. The controller manages the switch via the OpenFlow switch protocol. The controller can add, update, and delete flow entries in flow tables. Figure 2.15 shows an example of an OpenFlow flow table. Each flow table contains a set of flow entries. Each flow entry consists of match fields, counters, and a set of instructions to apply to matching packets. Matching starts at the first flow table and may continue to additional flow tables of the pipeline [12].

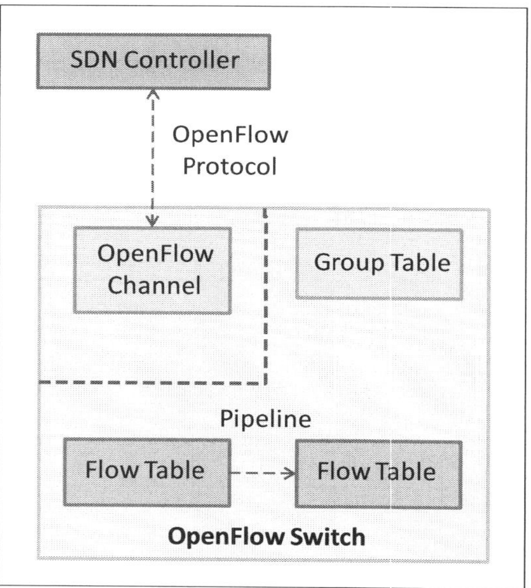

Figure 2.14: OpenFlow switch

2.8 Network Function Virtualization

Network Function Virtualization (NFV) is a technology that leverages virtualization to consolidate the heterogeneous network devices onto industry standard high volume servers, switches and storage. NFV is complementary to SDN as NFV can provide the infrastructure on which SDN can run. NFV and SDN are mutually beneficial to each other but not dependent.

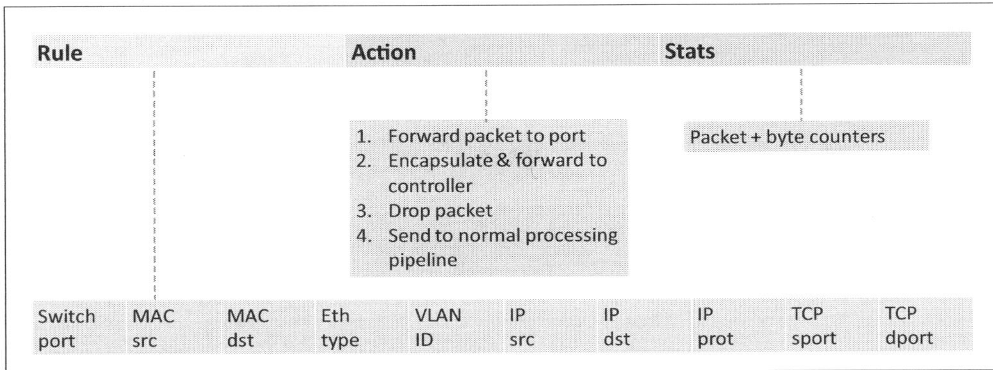

Figure 2.15: OpenFlow flow table

Network functions can be virtualized without SDN, similarly, SDN can run without NFV.

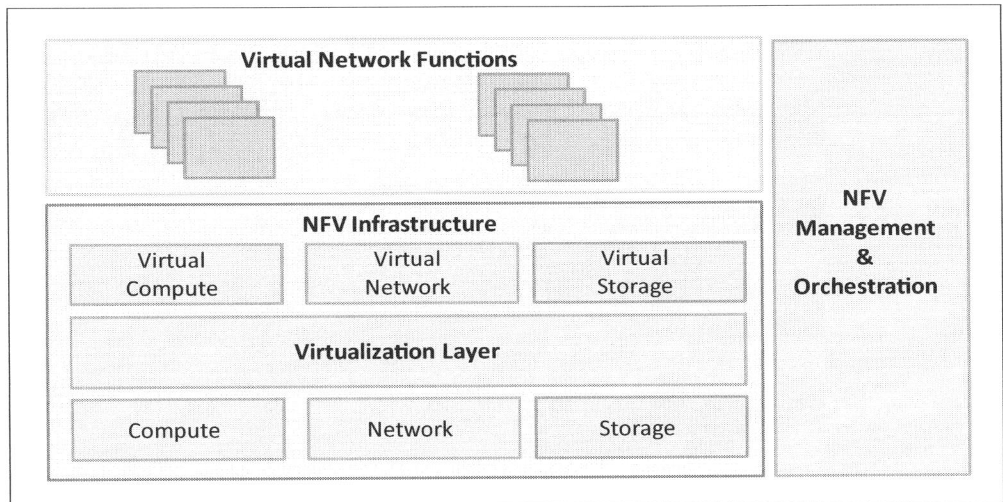

Figure 2.16: NFV architecture

Figure 2.16 shows the NFV architecture, as being standardized by the European Telecommunications Standards Institute (ETSI) [11]. Key elements of the NFV architecture are as follows:

- **Virtualized Network Function (VNF)**: VNF is a software implementation of a network function which is capable of running over the NFV Infrastructure (NFVI).
- **NFV Infrastructure (NFVI)**: NFVI includes compute, network and storage resources that are virtualized.
- **NFV Management and Orchestration**: NFV Management and Orchestration focuses on all virtualization-specific management tasks and covers the orchestration and lifecycle management of physical and/or software resources that support the infrastructure virtualization, and the lifecycle management of VNFs.

NFV comprises of network functions implemented in software that run on virtualized resources in the cloud. NFV enables a separation the network functions which are implemented

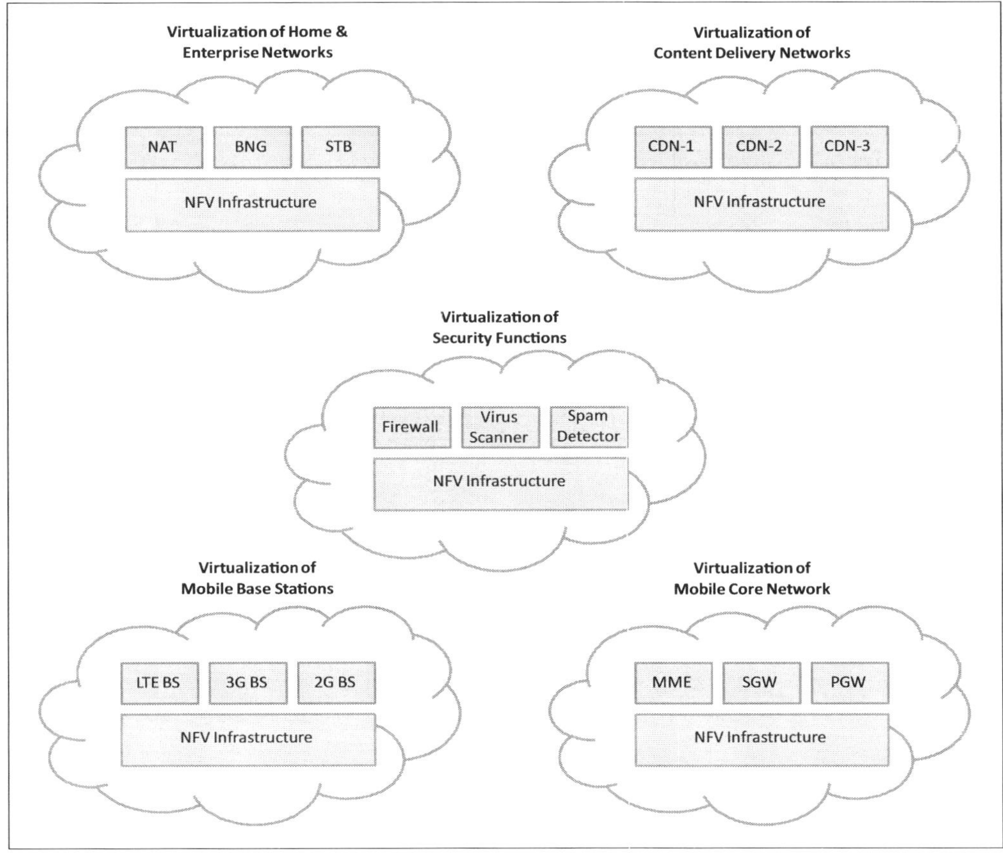

Figure 2.17: NFV use cases

in software from the underlying hardware. Thus network functions can be easily tested and upgraded by installing new software while the hardware remains the same. Virtualizing network functions reduces the equipment costs and also reduces power consumption. The multi-tenanted nature of the cloud allows virtualized network functions to be shared for multiple network services. NFV is applicable only to data plane and control plane functions in fixed and mobile networks. Figure 2.17 shows use cases of NFV for home and enterprise networks, content delivery networks, mobile base stations, mobile core network and security functions.

2.9 MapReduce

MapReduce is a parallel data processing model for processing and analysis of massive scale data [14]. MapReduce model has two phases: Map and Reduce. MapReduce programs are written in a functional programming style to create Map and Reduce functions. The input data to the map and reduce phases is in the form of key-value pairs. Run-time systems for MapReduce are typically large clusters built of commodity hardware. The MapReduce run-time systems take care of tasks such partitioning the data, scheduling of jobs and communication between nodes in the cluster. This makes it easier for programmers to analyze massive scale data without worrying about tasks such as data partitioning and scheduling. Figure 2.18 shows the workflow of MapReduce. In the Map phase, data is read from a distributed file system, partitioned among a set of computing nodes in the cluster, and sent to the nodes as a set of key-value pairs. The Map tasks process the input records independently of each other and produce intermediate results as key-value pairs. The intermediate results are stored on the local disk of the node running the Map task. When all the Map tasks are completed, the Reduce phase begins in which the intermediate data with the same key is aggregated. An optional Combine task can be used to perform data aggregation on the intermediate data of the same key for the output of the mapper before transferring the output to the Reduce task. Figure 2.19 shows the flow of data for a MapReduce job. MapReduce programs take a set of input key-value pairs and produce a set of output key-value pairs. MapReduce programs take advantage of locality of data and the data processing takes place on the nodes where the data resides. In traditional approaches for data analysis, data is moved to the compute nodes which results in significant of data transmission between the nodes in a cluster. MapReduce programming model moves the computation to where the data resides thus decreasing the transmission of data and improving efficiency. MapReduce programming model is well suited for parallel processing of massive scale data in which the data analysis tasks can be accomplished by independent map and reduce operations.

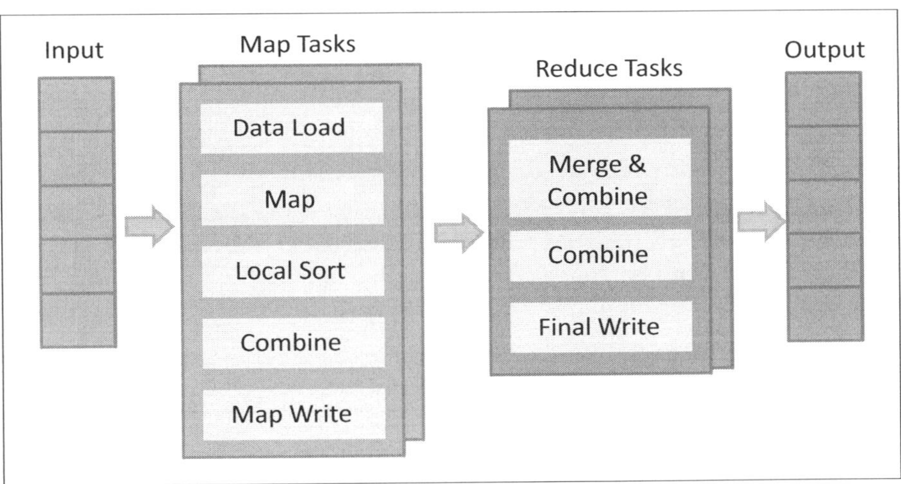

Figure 2.18: MapReduce workflow

2.10 Identity and Access Management

Identity and Access Management (IDAM) for cloud describes the authentication and authorization of users to provide secure access to cloud resources. Organizations with multiple users can use IDAM services provided by the cloud service provider for management of user identifiers and user permissions. IDAM services allow organizations to centrally manage users, access permissions, security credentials and access keys. Organizations can enable role-based access control to cloud resources and applications using the IDAM services. IDAM services allow creation of user groups where all the users in a group have the same

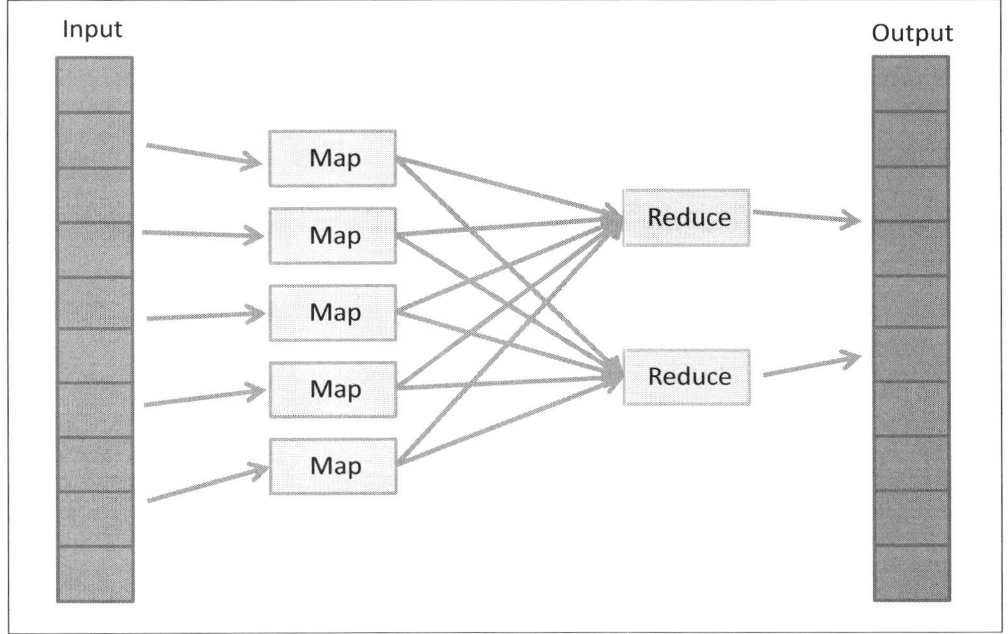

Figure 2.19: Data flow in MapReduce

access permissions. Identity and Access Management is enabled by a number of technologies such as OpenAuth, Role-based Access Control (RBAC), Digital Identities, Security Tokens, Identity Providers, etc. Figure 2.20 shows the examples of OAuth and RBAC. OAuth is an open standard for authorization that allows resource owners to share their private resources stored on one site with an- other site without handing out the credentials. In the OAuth model, an application (which is not the resource owner) requests access to resources controlled by the resource owner (but hosted by the server). The resource owner grants permission to access the resources in the form of a token and matching shared-secret. Tokens make it unnecessary for the resource owner to share its credentials with the application. Tokens can be issued with a restricted scope and limited lifetime, and revoked independently. RBAC is an approach for restricting access to authorized users. Figure 2.21 shows an example of a typical RBAC framework. A user who wants to access cloud resources is required to send his/her data to the system administrator who assigns permissions and access control policies which are stored in the User Roles and Data Access Policies databases respectively.

2.11 Service Level Agreements

A Service Level Agreement (SLA) for cloud specifies the level of service that is formally defined as a part of the service contract with the cloud service provider. SLAs provide a level of service for each service which is specified in the form of minimum level of service guaranteed and a target level. SLAs contain a number of performance metrics and the corresponding service level objectives. Table 2.5 lists the common criteria cloud SLAs.

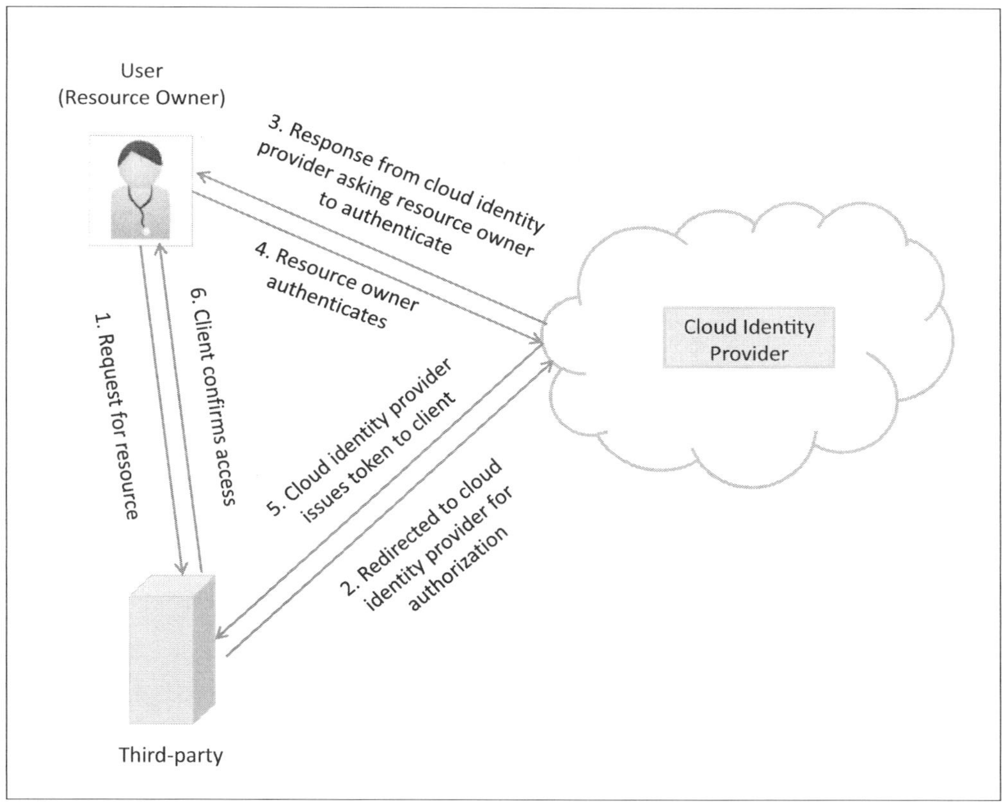

Figure 2.20: OAuth example

2.12 Billing

Cloud service providers offer a number of billing models described as follows:

Elastic Pricing

In elastic pricing or pay-as-you-use pricing model, the customers are charged based on the usage of cloud resources. Cloud computing provides the benefit of provision resources on-demand. On-demand provisioning and elastic pricing models bring cost savings for customers. Elastic pricing model is suited for customers who consume cloud resources for short durations and who cannot predict the usage beforehand.

Fixed Pricing

In fixed pricing models, customers are charged a fixed amount per month for the cloud resources. For example, fixed amount can be charged per month for running a virtual machine instance, irrespective of the actual usage. Fixed pricing model is suited for customers who want to use cloud resources for longer durations and want more control over the cloud expenses.

Spot Pricing

Spot pricing models offer variable pricing for cloud resources which is driven by market demand. When the demand for cloud resources is high, the prices increase and when the

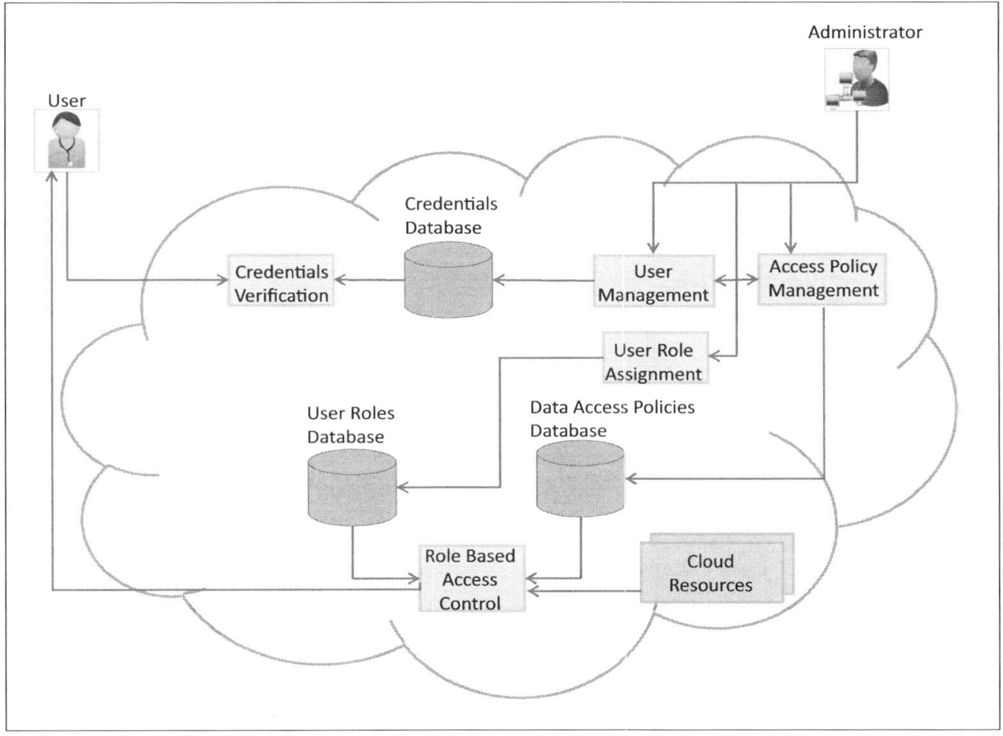

Figure 2.21: Role-based Access Control example

demand is lower, the prices decrease.

Table 2.6 lists the billable resources for cloud including virtual machines, network, storage, data services, security services, support, application services, deployment and management services.

Summary

In this chapter you learned cloud computing concepts and enabling technologies such as virtualization, load balancing, scalability & elasticity, deployment, replication, MapReduce, identity & access management, service level agreements and billing. Virtualization partitions the resources of a physical system (such as computing, storage, network and memory) into multiple virtual resources and enables resource pooling and multi-tenancy.

Review Questions

1. What are the various layers in a virtualization architecture?
2. What is the difference between full and para-virtualization?
3. What are the benefits of load balancing?
4. What are sticky sessions?
5. What are the differences between traditional and on-demand scaling approaches?
6. What are the various stages in the deployment lifecycle?
7. What is the difference between array-based and host-based replication?

Criteria	Details
Availability	Percentage of time the service is guaranteed to be available
Performance	Response time, Throughput
Disaster Recovery	Mean time to recover
Problem resolution	Process to identify problems, support options, resolution expectations
Security and privacy of data	Mechanisms for security of data in storage and transmission

Table 2.5: List of criteria for cloud SLAs

Resource	Details
Virtual machines	CPU, memory, storage, disk I/O, network I/O
Network	Network I/O, load balancers, DNS, firewall, VPN
Storage	Cloud storage, storage volumes, storage gateway
Data services	Data import/export services, data encryption, data compression, data backup, data redundancy, content delivery
Security services	Identity and access management, isolation, compliance
Support	Level of support, SLA, fault tolerance
Application services	Queuing service, notification service, workflow service, payment service
Deployment and management services	Monitoring service, deployment service

Table 2.6: List of billable resources for cloud

8. In MapReduce, what are the functions of map, reduce and combine tasks?
9. Describe three applications that can benefit from the MapReduce programming model?
10. What are the various criteria for service level agreements?

3 — Cloud Services & Platforms

This Chapter covers

- Compute Services
- Storage Services
- Database Services
- Application Services
- Content Delivery Services
- Analytics Services
- Deployment & Management Services
- Identity & Access Management Services

In this chapter you will learn about various types of cloud computing services including compute, storage, database, application, content delivery, analytics, deployment & management and identity & access management. For each category of cloud services, examples of services provided by various cloud service providers including Amazon, Google and Microsoft are described.

Figure 3.1 (a) shows the cloud computing reference model along with the various cloud service models (IaaS, PaaS and SaaS). Infrastructure-as-a-Service (IaaS) provides virtualized dynamically scalable resources using a virtualized infrastructure. Platform-as-a-Service (PaaS) simplifies application development by providing development tools, application programming interfaces (APIs), software libraries that can be used for wide range of applications. Software-as-a-Service (SaaS) provides multi-tenant applications hosted in the cloud.

The bottommost layer in the cloud reference model is the infrastructure and facilities layer that includes the physical infrastructure such as datacenter facilities, electrical and mechanical equipment, etc. On top of the infrastructure layer is the hardware layer that includes physical compute, network and storage hardware. On top of the hardware layer the virtualization layer partitions the physical hardware resources into multiple virtual resources that enabling pooling of resources. Chapter 2 described various types of virtualization approaches such as full virtualization, para-virtualization and hardware virtualization. The computing services are delivered in the form of Virtual Machines (VMs) along with the storage and network resources.

The platform and middleware layer builds upon the IaaS layers below and provides standardized stacks of services such as database service, queuing service, application frameworks and run-time environments, messaging services, monitoring services, analytics services, etc. The service management layer provides APIs for requesting, managing and monitoring cloud resources. The topmost layer is the applications layer that includes SaaS applications such as Email, cloud storage application, productivity applications, management portals, customer self-service portals, etc.

Figure 3.1 (b) shows various types of cloud services and the associated layers in the cloud reference model.

3.1 Compute Services

Compute services provide dynamically scalable compute capacity in the cloud. Compute resources can be provisioned on-demand in the form of virtual machines. Virtual machines can be created from standard images provided by the cloud service provider (e.g. Ubuntu image, Windows server image, etc.) or custom images created by the users. A machine image is a template that contains a software configuration (operating system, application server, and applications). Compute services can be accessed from the web consoles of these services that provide graphical user interfaces for provisioning, managing and monitoring these services. Cloud service providers also provide APIs for various programming languages (such as Java, Python, etc.) that allow developers to access and manage these services programmatically.

Features

- **Scalable**: Compute services allow rapidly provisioning as many virtual machine instances as required. The provisioned capacity can be scaled-up or down based on the

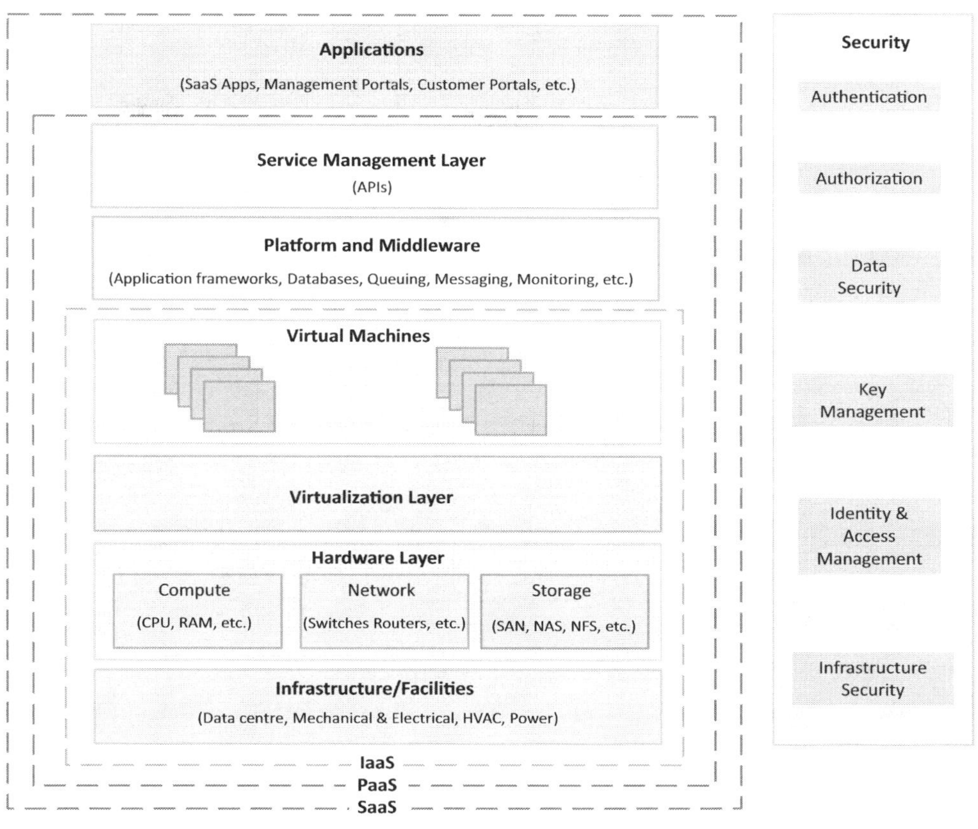

(a) Cloud reference model

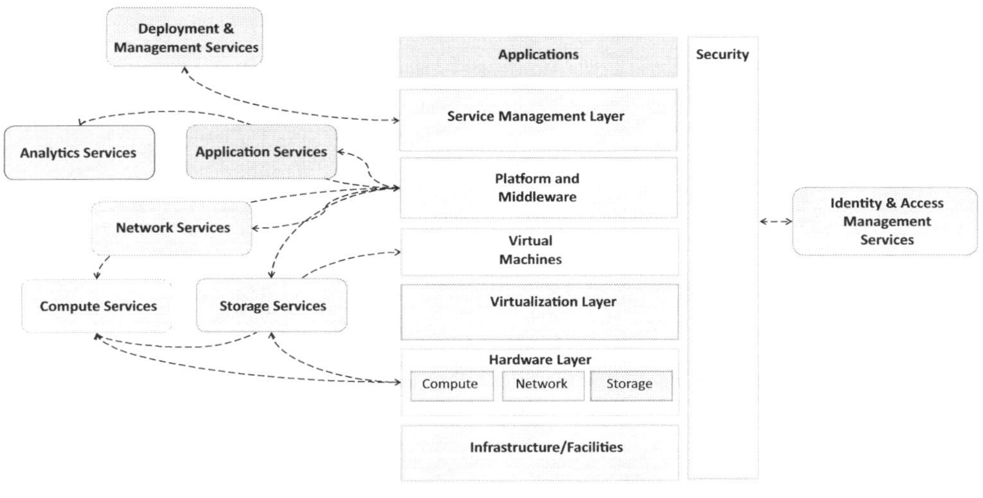

(b) Cloud services

Figure 3.1: Cloud Computing reference model & services

workload levels. Auto-scaling policies can be defined for compute services that are triggered when the monitored metrics (such as CPU usage, memory usage, etc.) go above pre-defined thresholds.

- **Flexible**: Compute services give a wide range of options for virtual machines with multiple instance types, operating systems, zones/regions, etc.
- **Secure**: Compute services provide various security features that control the access to the virtual machine instances such as security groups, access control lists, network firewalls, etc. Users can securely connect to the instances with SSH using authentication mechanisms such as OAuth or security certificates and keypairs.
- **Cost effective**: Cloud service providers offer various billing options such as on-demand instances which are billed per-hour, reserved instances which are reserved after one-time initial payment, spot instances for which users can place bids, etc.

3.1.1 Amazon Elastic Compute Cloud

Amazon Elastic Compute Cloud (EC2) is a compute service provided by Amazon. Figure 3.2 shows a screenshot of the Amazon EC2 console. To launch a new instance click on the launch instance button. This will open a wizard where you can select the Amazon machine image (AMI) with which you want to launch the instance. You can also create their own AMIs with custom applications, libraries and data. Instances can be launched with a variety of operating systems. When you launch an instance you specify the instance type (micro, small, medium, large, extra-large, etc.), the number of instances to launch based on the selected AMI and availability zones for the instances. The instance launch wizard also allows you to specify the meta-data tags for the instance that simplify the administration of EC2 instances. When launching a new instance, the user selects a key-pair from existing keypairs or creates a new keypair for the instance. Keypairs are used to securely connect to an instance after it launches. The security groups to be associated with the instance can be selected from the instance launch wizard. Security groups are used to open or block a specific network port for the launched instances.

When the instance is launched its status can be viewed in the EC2 console. Upon launching a new instance, its state is pending. It takes a couple of minutes for the instance to come into the running state. When the instance comes into the running state, it is assigned a public DNS, private DNS, public IP and private IP. The public DNS can be used to securely connect to the instance using SSH.

3.1.2 Google Compute Engine

Google Compute Engine is a compute service provided by Google. Figure 3.3 shows a screenshot of the Google Compute Engine (GCE) console. GCE console allows users to create and manage compute instances. To create a new instance, the user selects an instance machine type, a zone in which the instance will be launched, a machine image for the instance and provides an instance name, instance tags and meta-data. Every instance is launched with a disk resource. Depending on the instance type, the disk resource can be a scratch disk space or persistent disk space. The scratch disk space is deleted when the instance terminates. Whereas, persistent disks live beyond the life of an instance. Network option allows you to control the traffic to and from the instances. By default, traffic between instances in the same network, over any port and any protocol and incoming SSH connections from anywhere are

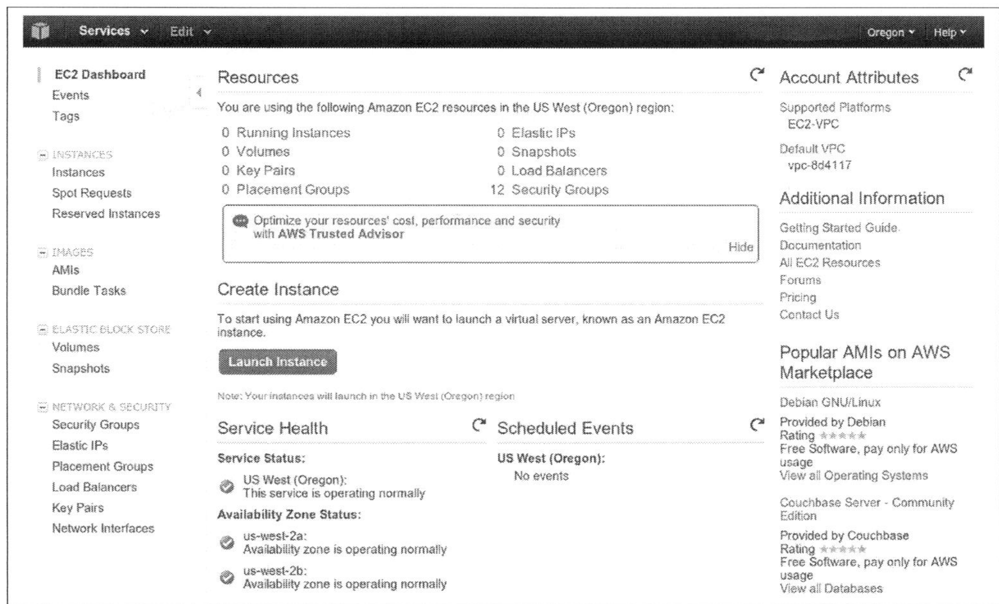

Figure 3.2: Screenshot of Amazon EC2 console

enabled. To enable other connections, additional firewall rules can be added.

3.1.3 Windows Azure Virtual Machines

Windows Azure Virtual Machines is the compute service from Microsoft. Figure 3.4 shows a screenshot of Windows Azure Virtual Machines console. To create a new instance, you select the instance type and the machine image. You can either provide a user name and password or upload a certificate file for securely connecting to the instance. Any changes made to the VM are persistently stored and new VMs can be created from the previously stored machine images.

3.2 Storage Services

Cloud storage services allow storage and retrieval of any amount of data, at any time from anywhere on the web. Most cloud storage services organize data into buckets or containers. Buckets or containers store objects which are individual pieces of data.

Features

- **Scalability**: Cloud storage services provide high capacity and scalability. Objects upto several tera-bytes in size can be uploaded and multiple buckets/containers can be created on cloud storages.
- **Replication**: When an object is uploaded it is replicated at multiple facilities and/or on multiple devices within each facility.
- **Access Policies**: Cloud storage services provide several security features such as Access Control Lists (ACLs), bucket/container level policies, etc. ACLs can be used to selectively grant access permissions on individual objects. Bucket/container level

Figure 3.3: Screenshot of Google Compute Engine console

policies can also be defined to allow or deny permissions across some or all of the objects within a single bucket/container.

- **Encryption**: Cloud storage services provide Server Side Encryption (SSE) options to encrypt all data stored in the cloud storage.
- **Consistency**: Strong data consistency is provided for all upload and delete operations. Therefore, any object that is uploaded can be immediately downloaded after the upload is complete.

3.2.1 Amazon Simple Storage Service

Amazon Simple Storage Service(S3) is an online cloud-based data storage infrastructure for storing and retrieving any amount of data. S3 provides highly reliable, scalable, fast, fully redundant and affordable storage infrastructure. Figure 3.5 shows a screenshot of the Amazon S3 console. Data stored on S3 is organized in the form of buckets. You must create a bucket before you can store data on S3. S3 console provides simple wizards for creating a new bucket and uploading files. You can upload any kind of file to S3. While uploading a

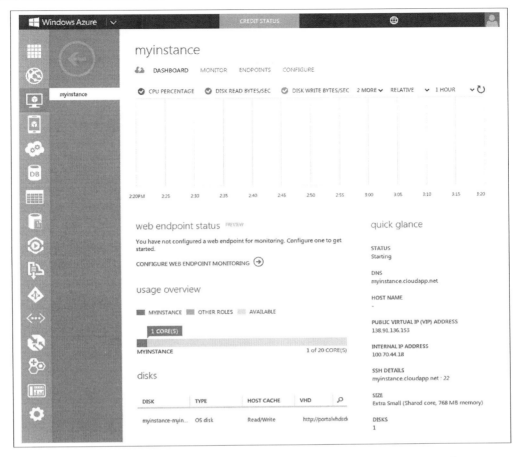

Figure 3.4: Screenshot of Windows Azure Virtual Machines console

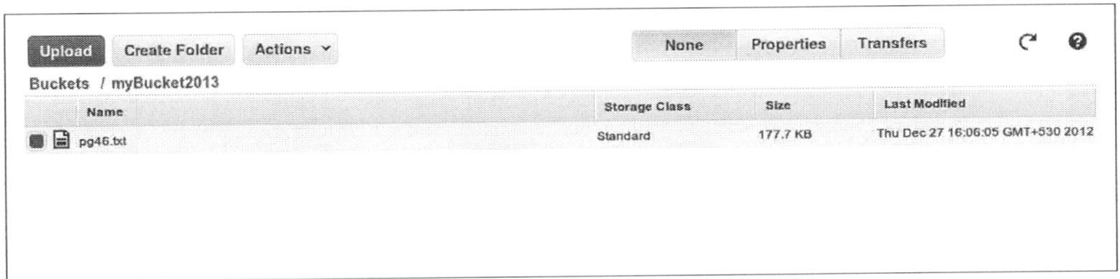

Figure 3.5: Screenshot of Amazon S3 console

file, you can specify the redundancy and encryption options and access permissions.

3.2.2 Google Cloud Storage

Figure 3.6 shows a screenshot of the Google Cloud Storage (GCS) console. Objects in GCS are organized into buckets. ACLs are used to control access to objects and buckets. ACLs can be configured to share objects and buckets with the entire world, a Google group, a Google-hosted domain, or specific Google account holders.

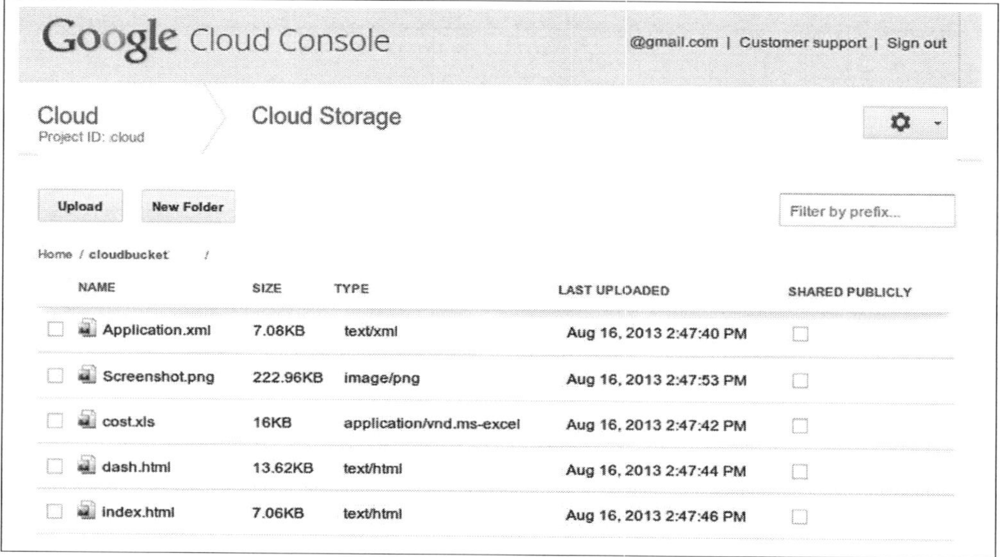

Figure 3.6: Screenshot of Google Cloud Storage console

3.2.3 Windows Azure Storage

Windows Azure Storage is the cloud storage service from Microsoft. Figure 3.7 shows a screenshot of the Windows Azure Storage console. Windows Azure Storage provides various storage services such as blob storage service, table service and queue service. The blob storage service allows storing unstructured binary data or binary large objects (blobs). Blobs are organized into containers. Two kinds of blobs can be stored - block blobs and page blobs. A block blob can be subdivided into some number of blocks. If a failure occurs while transferring a block blob, retransmission can resume with the most recent block rather than sending the entire blob again. Page blobs are divided into number of pages and are designed for random access. Applications can read and write individual pages at random in a page blob.

3.3 Database Services

Cloud database services allow you to set-up and operate relational or non-relational databases in the cloud. The benefit of using cloud database services is that it relieves the application developers from the time consuming database administration tasks. Popular relational databases provided by various cloud service providers include MySQL, Oracle, SQL Server, etc. The non-relational (No-SQL) databases provided by cloud service providers are mostly proprietary solutions. No-SQL databases are usually fully-managed and deliver seamless throughput and scalability. The characteristics of relational and non-relational databases are described in Chapter 5.

Features

- **Scalability**: Cloud database services allow provisioning as much compute and storage resources as required to meet the application workload levels. Provisioned capacity

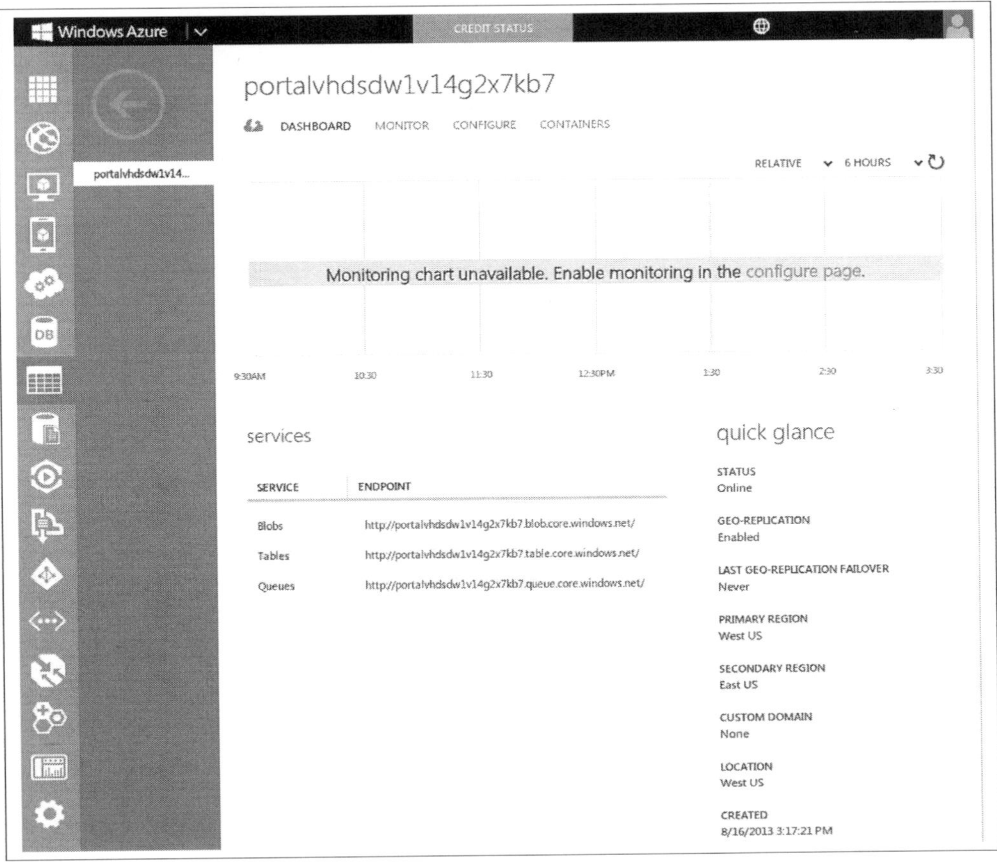

Figure 3.7: Screenshot of Windows Azure Storage console

can be scaled-up or down. For read-heavy workloads, read-replicas can be created.

- **Reliability**: Cloud database services are reliable and provide automated backup and snapshot options.
- **Performance**: Cloud database services provide guaranteed performance with options such as guaranteed input/output operations per second (IOPS) which can be provisioned upfront.
- **Security**: Cloud database services provide several security features to restrict the access to the database instances and stored data, such as network firewalls and authentication mechanisms.

3.3.1 Amazon Relational Data Store

Amazon Relational Database Service (RDS) is a web service that makes it easy to setup, operate and scale a relational database in the cloud. Figure 3.8 shows a screenshot of the Amazon RDS console. The console provides an instance launch wizard that allows you to select the type of database to create (MySQL, Oracle or SQL Server) database instance size, allocated storage, DB instance identifier, DB username and password. The status of the launched DB instances can be viewed from the console. It takes several minutes for the instance to become available. Once the instance is available, you can note the instance end point from the instance properties tab. This end point can then be used for securely connecting to the instance.

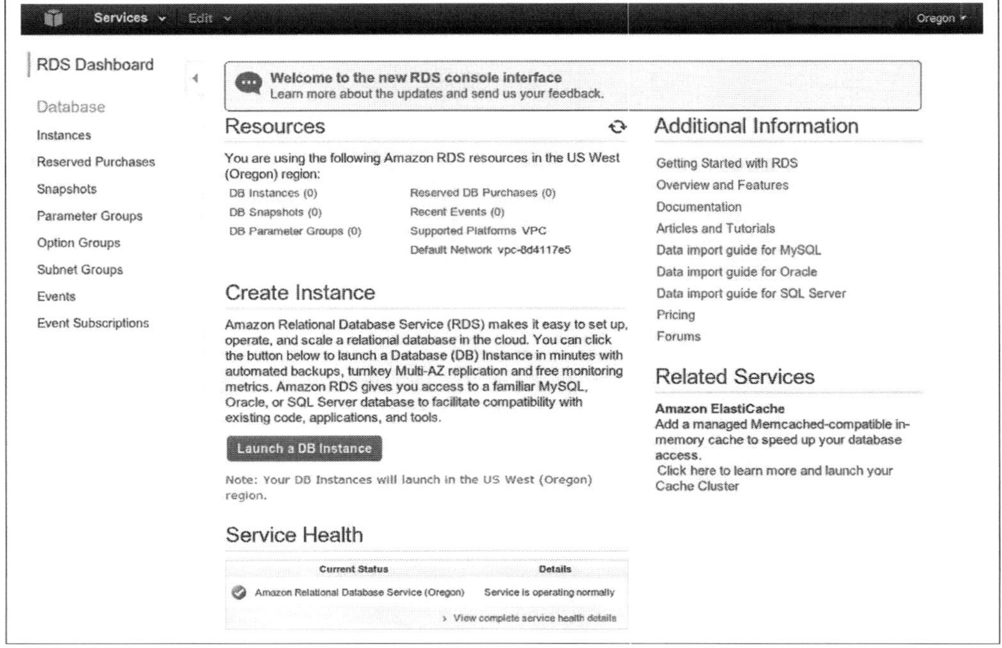

Figure 3.8: Screenshot of Amazon RDS console

3.3.2 Amazon DynamoDB

Amazon DynamoDB is the non-relational (No-SQL) database service from Amazon. Figure 3.9 shows a screenshot of the Amazon DynamoDB console. The DynamoDB data model includes include tables, items and attributes. A table is a collection of items and each item is a collection of attributes. To store data in DynamoDB you have to create a one or more tables and specify how much throughput capacity you want to provision and reserve for reads and writes. DynamoDB is a fully managed service that automatically spreads the data and traffic for the stored tables over a number of servers to meet the throughput requirements specified by the users. All stored data is automatically replicated across multiple availability zones to provide data durability.

3.3.3 Google Cloud SQL

Google SQL is the relational database service from Google. Google Cloud SQL service allows you to host MySQL databases in the Google's cloud. Cloud SQL provides both synchronous or asynchronous geographic replication and the ability to import/ export databases. Figure 3.10 shows a screenshot of the Google Cloud SQL console. You can create new database instances from the console and manage existing instances. To create a new instance you select a region, database tier, billing plan and replication mode. You can schedule daily backups for your Google Cloud SQL instances, and also restore backed-up databases.

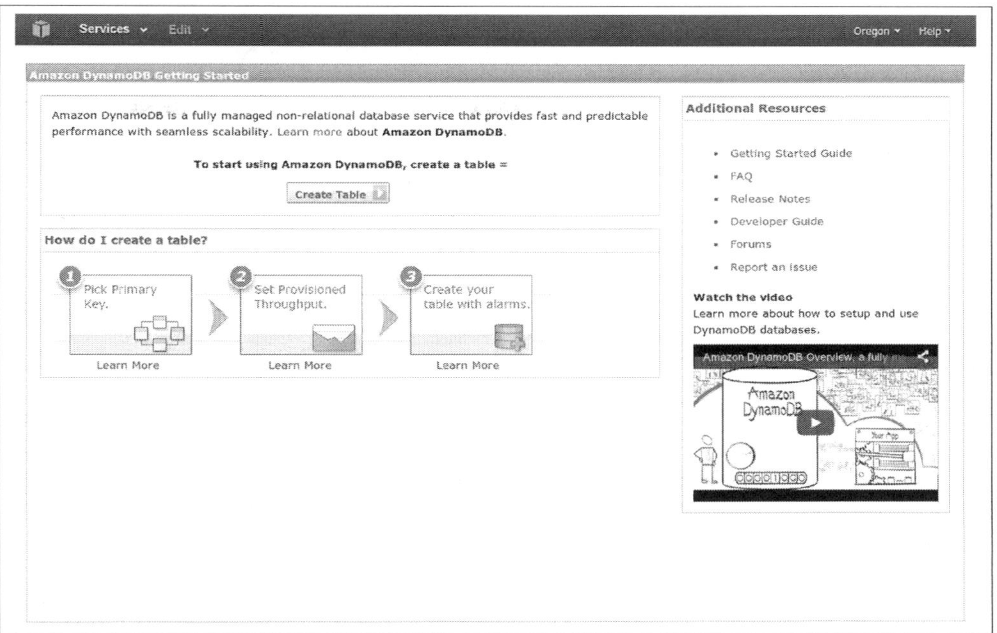

Figure 3.9: Screenshot of Amazon DynamoDB console

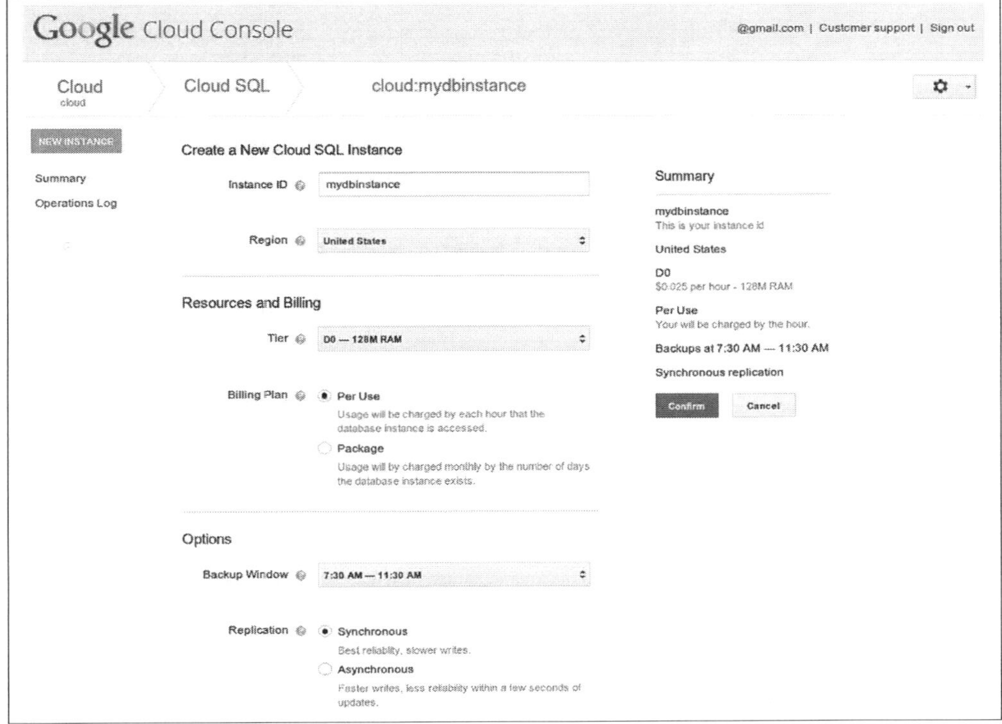

Figure 3.10: Screenshot of Google Cloud SQL console

3.3.4 Google Cloud Datastore

Google Cloud Datastore is a fully managed non-relational database from Google. Cloud Datastore offers ACID transactions and high availability of reads and writes. The Cloud Datastore data model consists of entities. Each entity has one or more properties (key-value pairs) which can be of one of several supported data types, such as strings and integers. Each entity has a kind and a key. The entity kind is used for categorizing the entity for the purpose of queries and the entity key uniquely identifies the entity. Figure 3.11 shows a screenshot of the Google Cloud Datastore console.

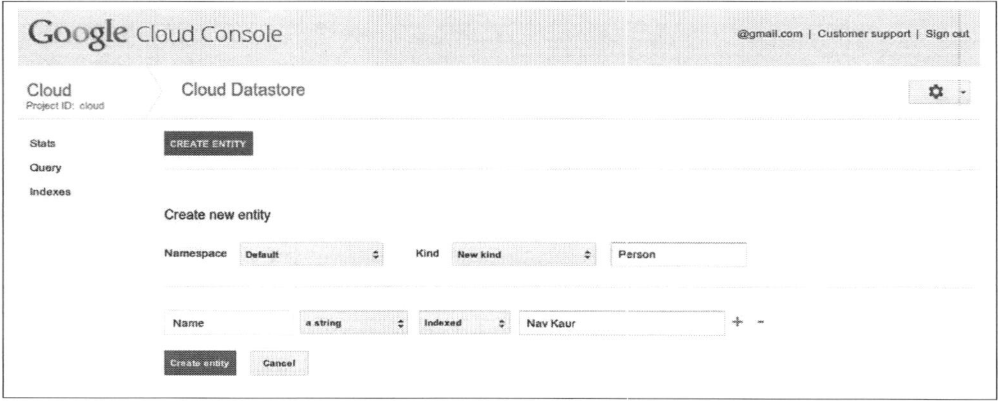

Figure 3.11: Screenshot of Google Cloud Datastore console

3.3.5 Windows Azure SQL Database

Windows Azure SQL Database is the relational database service from Microsoft. Azure SQL Database is based on the SQL server, but it does not give each customer a separate instance of SQL server. Instead the SQL Database is a multi-tenant service, with a logical SQL Database server for each customer. Figure 3.12 shows a screenshot of the Windows Azure SQL Database console.

3.3.6 Windows Azure Table Service

Windows Azure Table Service is a non-relational (No-SQL) database service from Microsoft. The Azure Table Service data model consists of tables having multiple entities. Tables are divided into some number of partitions, each of which can be stored on a separate machine. Each partition in a table holds a specified number of entities, each containing as many as 255 properties. Each property can be one of the several supported data types such as integers and strings. Tables do not have a fixed schema and different entities in a table can have different properties.

3.4 Application Services

In this section you will learn about various cloud application services such as application runtimes and frameworks, queuing services, email services, notification services and media services.

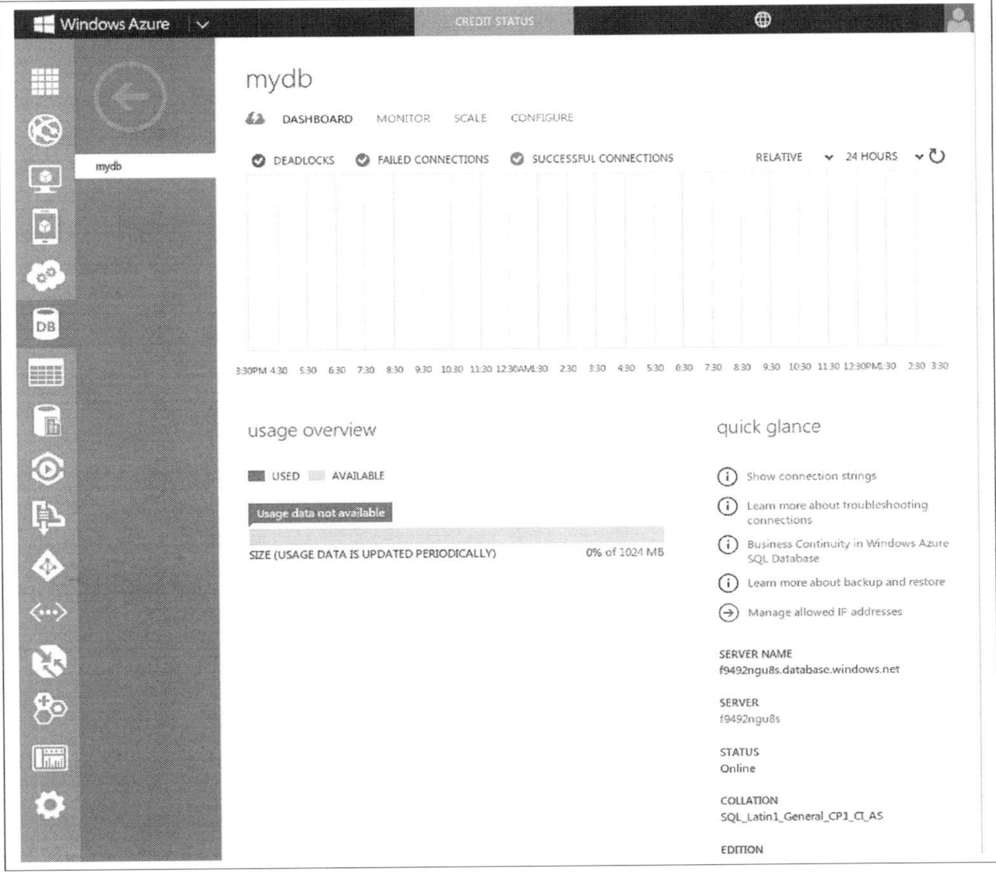

Figure 3.12: Screenshot of Windows Azure SQL Database console

3.4.1 Application Runtimes & Frameworks

Cloud-based application runtimes and frameworks allow developers to develop and host applications in the cloud. Application runtimes provide support for programming languages (e.g., Java, Python, or Ruby). Application runtimes automatically allocate resources for applications and handle the application scaling, without the need to run and maintain servers.

Google App Engine

Google App Engine is the platform-as-a-service (PaaS) from Google, which includes both an application runtime and web frameworks. Figure 3.13 shows a screenshot of the Google App Engine console.

App Engine features include:

- **Runtimes**: App Engine supports applications developed in Java, Python, PHP and Go programming languages. App Engine provides runtime environments for Java, Python, PHP and Go programming language.
- **Sandbox**: Applications run in a secure sandbox environment isolated from other applications. The sandbox environment provides a limited access to the underlying operating system. App Engine can only execute application code called from HTTP

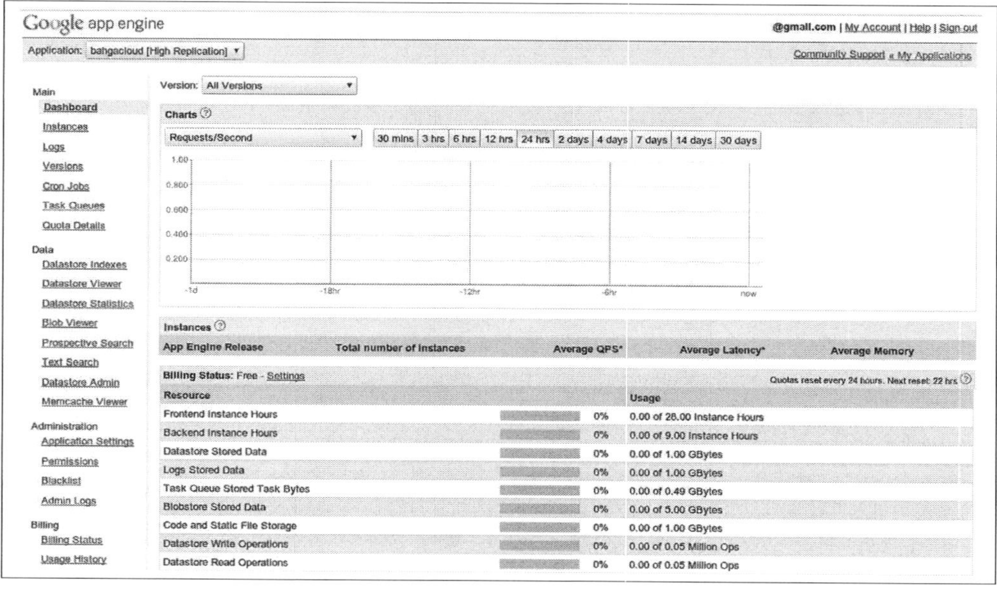

Figure 3.13: Screenshot of Google App Engine console

requests. The sandbox environment allows App Engine to distribute web requests for the application across multiple servers.

- **Web Frameworks**: App Engine provides a simple Python web application framework called webapp2. App Engine also supports any framework written in pure Python that speaks WSGI, including Django, CherryPy, Pylons, web.py, and web2py.
- **Datastore**: App Engine provides a no-SQL data storage service.
- **Authentication**: App Engine applications can be integrated with Google Accounts for user authentication.
- **URL Fetch service**: URL Fetch service allows applications to access resources on the Internet, such as web services or other data
- **Email service**: Email service allows applications to send email messages.
- **Image Manipulation service**: Image Manipulation service allows applications to resize, crop, rotate, flip and enhance images.
- **Memcache**: Memcache service is a high performance in-memory key-value cache service that applications can use for caching data items that do not need a persistent storage.
- **Task Queues**: Task queues allow applications to do work in the background by breaking up work into small, discrete units, called tasks which are enqueued in task queues.
- **Scheduled Tasks service** : App Engine provides a Cron service for scheduled tasks that trigger events at specified times and regular intervals. This service allows applications to perform tasks at defined times or regular intervals.

Windows Azure Web Sites

Windows Azure Web Sites is a Platform-as-a-Service (PaaS) from Microsoft. Azure Web Sites allows you to host web applications in the Azure cloud. Azure Web Sites provides shared and standard options. In the shared option, Azure Web Sites run on a set of virtual machines that may contain multiple web sites created by multiple users. In the standard option, Azure Web Sites run on virtual machines (VMs) that belong to an individual user. Azure Web Sites supports applications created in ASP.NET, PHP, Node.js and Python programming languages. Multiple copies of an application can be run in different VMs, with Web Sites automatically load balancing requests across them.

3.4.2 Queuing Services

Cloud-based queuing services allow de-coupling application components. The de-coupled components communicate via messaging queues. Queues are useful for asynchronous processing. Another use of queues is to act as overflow buffers to handle temporary volume spikes or mismatches in message generation and consumption rates from application components. Queuing services from various cloud service providers allow short messages of a few kilo-bytes in size. Messages can be enqueued and read from the queues simultaneously. The enqueued messages are typically retained for a couple of days to a couple of weeks.

Amazon Simple Queue Service

Amazon Simple Queue Service (SQS) is a queuing service from Amazon. SQS is a distributed queue that supports messages of up to 256 KB in size. SQS supports multiple writers and readers and locks messages while they are being processed. To ensure high availability for delivering messages, SQS service trade-offs on the first in, first out capability and does not guarantee that messages will be delivered in FIFO order. Applications that require FIFO ordering of messages can place additional sequencing information in each message so that they can be re-ordered after retrieving from a queue. Figure 3.14 shows a screenshot of the Amazon Simple Queue Service console.

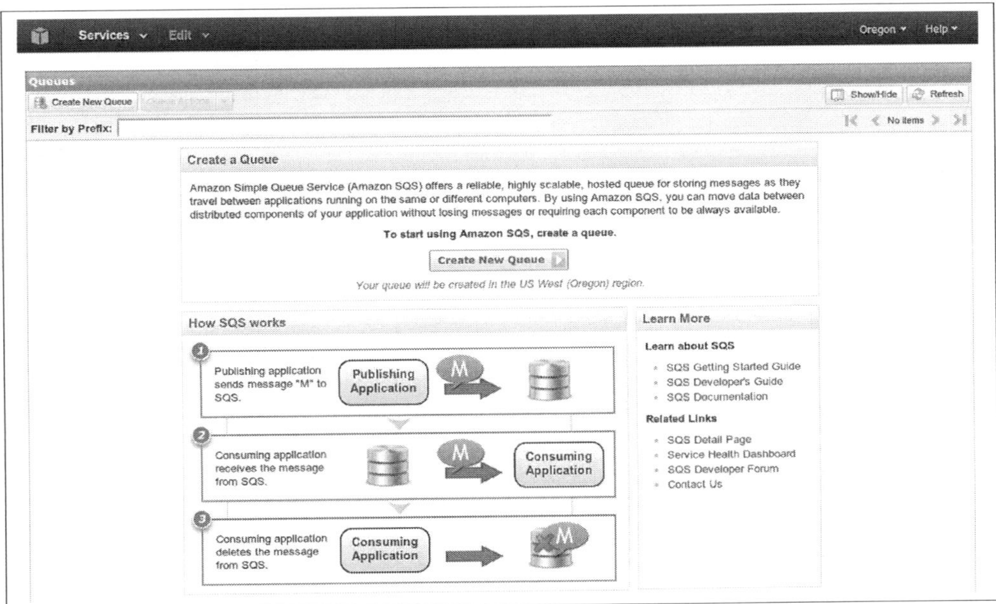

Figure 3.14: Screenshot of Amazon SQS console

Google Task Queue Service

Google Task Queues service is a queuing service from Google and is a part of the Google App Engine platform. Task queues allow applications to execute tasks in background. Task is a unit of work to be performed by an application. The task objects consist of application-specific URL with a request handler for the task, and an optional data payload that parameterizes the task. There are two different configurations for Task Queues - Push Queue and Pull Queue. Push Queue is the default queue that processes tasks based on the processing rate configured in the queue definition. Pull Queues allow task consumers to lease a specific number of tasks for a specific duration. The tasks are processed and deleted before the lease ends.

Windows Azure Queue Service

Windows Azure Queue service is a queuing service from Microsoft. Azure Queue service allows storing large numbers of messages that can be accessed from anywhere in the world via authenticated calls using HTTP or HTTPS. The size of a single message can be up to 64KB.

3.4.3 Email Services

Cloud-based email services allow applications hosted in the cloud to send emails.

Amazon Simple Email Service

Amazon Simple Email Service is bulk and transactional email-sending service from Amazon. SES is an outbound-only email-sending service that allows applications hosted in the Amazon cloud to send emails such as marketing emails, transactional emails and other types of correspondence. To ensure high email deliverability, SES uses content filtering technologies to scan the outgoing email messages to help ensure that they do not contain material that is typically flagged as questionable by ISPs. SES service can be accessed and used from the SES console, the Simple Mail Transfer Protocol (SMTP) interface, or the SES API.

Google Email Service

Google Email service is part of the Google App Engine platform that allows App Engine applications to send email messages on behalf of the app's administrators, and on behalf of users with Google Accounts. App Engine apps can also receive emails. Apps send messages using the Mail service and receive messages in the form of HTTP requests initiated by App Engine and posted to the app.

3.4.4 Notification Services

Cloud-based notification services or push messaging services allow applications to push messages to internet connected smart devices such as smartphones, tablets, etc. Push messaging services are based on publish-subscribe model in which consumers subscribe to various topics/channels provided by a publisher/producer. Whenever new content is available on one of those topics/channels, the notification service pushes that information out to the consumer. Push notifications are used for such smart devices as they help in displaying the latest information while remaining energy efficient. Consumer applications on such devices can increase their consumer engagement with the help of push notifications.

Amazon Simple Notification Service

Amazon Simple Notification Service is a push messaging service from Amazon. SNS has two types of clients - publishers and subscribers. Publishers communicate asynchronously with subscribers by producing and sending messages to topics. A topic is a logical access point and a communication channel. Subscribers are the consumers who subscribe to topics to receive notifications. SNS can deliver notifications as SMS, email, or to SQS queues, or any HTTP endpoint. Figure 3.15 shows a screenshot of the Amazon Simple Notification Service console. The SNS console has wizards for creating a new topic, publishing to a topic and subscribing to a topic.

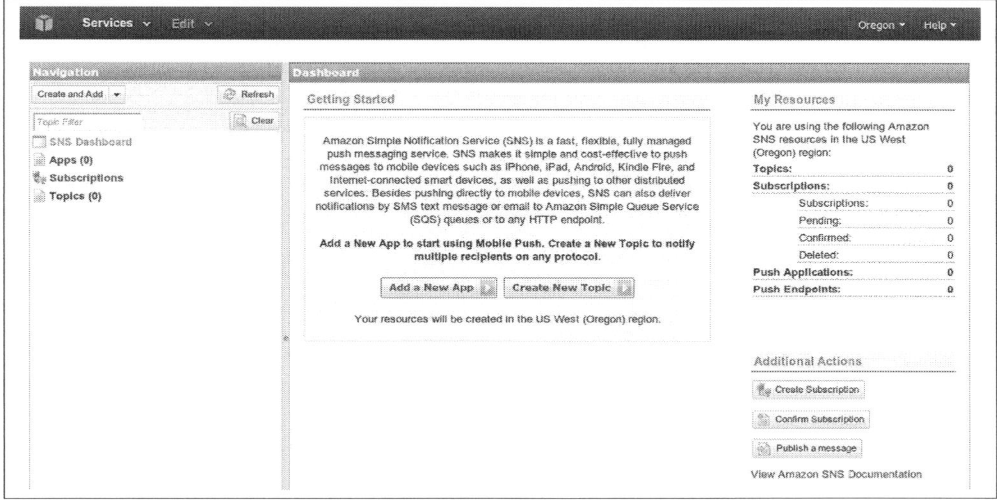

Figure 3.15: Screenshot of Amazon SNS console

Google Cloud Messaging

Google Cloud Messaging for Android provides push messaging for Android devices. GCM allows allows applications to send data from the application servers to their users' Android devices, and also to receive messages from devices on the same connection. GCM is useful for notifying applications on Android devices that there is new data to be fetched from the application servers. GCM supports messages with payload data upto 4 KB. GCM provides a 'send-to-sync' message capability that can be used to inform an application to sync data from the server.

Google Cloud Messaging for Chrome is another notification service from Google that allows messages to be delivered from the cloud to apps and extensions running in Chrome.

Windows Azure Notification Hubs

Windows Azure Notification Hubs is a push notification service from Microsoft that provides a common interface to send notifications to all major mobile platforms including Windows Store/Windows Phone 8, iOS, and Android. Platform specific infrastructures called Platform Notification Systems (PNS) are used to deliver notification messages. Devices register their PNS handles with the Notification Hub. Each notification hub contains credentials for each supported PNS. These credentials are used to connect to the PNSs and send push notifications to the applications.

3.4.5 Media Services

Cloud service providers provide various types of media services that can be used by applications for manipulating, transforming or transcoding media such as images, videos, etc.

Amazon Elastic Transcoder

Amazon Elastic Transcoder is a cloud-based video transcoding service from Amazon. Elastic Transcoder can be used to convert video files from their source format into various other formats that can be played on devices such as desktops, mobiles, tablets, etc. Elastic Transcoder provides a number of pre-defined transcoding presets. Transcoding pipelines are used to perform multiple transcodes in parallel. Elastic Transcoder works with the Amazon S3 storage where the input and output video files are stored. Users can create transcoding jobs by specifying the input and output locations (on S3), preset to use, and optional thumbnails and job specific parameters such as frame-rate.

Google Images Manipulation Service

Google Images Manipulation service is a part of the Google App Engine platform. Image Manipulation service provides the capability to resize, crop, rotate, flip and enhance images. The Images service can accept image data directly from the App Engine apps, or from Google Blobstore or Google Cloud Storage. Image Service accepts images in various formats including JPEG, PNG, WEBP, GIF, BMP, TIFF and ICO formats and can return transformed images in JPEG, WEBP and PNG formats.

Windows Azure Media Services

Windows Azure Media Services provides the various media services such as encoding & format conversion, content protection and on-demand and live streaming capabilities. Azure Media Services provides applications the capability to build media workflows for uploading, storing, encoding, format conversion, content protection, and media delivery. To use Azure Media Services, you can create jobs that process media content in several ways such as encoding, encrypting, doing format conversions, etc. Each Media Services job has one or more tasks. Each task has preset string, an input asset and an output asset. Media assets in the Azure Media Service can be delivered either by download or by streaming.

3.5 Content Delivery Services

Cloud-based content delivery service include Content Delivery Networks (CDNs). A CDN is a distributed system of servers located across multiple geographic locations to serve content to end-users with high availability and high performance. CDNs are useful for serving static content such as text, images, scripts, etc., and streaming media. CDNs have a number of edge locations deployed in multiple locations, often over multiple backbones. Requests for static or streaming media content that is served by a CDN are directed to the nearest edge location. CDNs cache the popular content on the edge servers which helps in reducing bandwidth costs and improving response times.

3.5.1 Amazon CloudFront

Amazon CloudFront is a content delivery service from Amazon. CloudFront can be used to deliver dynamic, static and streaming content using a global network of edge locations. The content in CloudFront is organized into distributions. Each distribution specifies the original location of the content to be delivered which can be an Amazon S3 bucket, an Amazon EC2 instance, or an Elastic Load Balancer, or your own origin server. Distributions can be accessed by their domain names. Figure 3.16 shows a screenshot of the Amazon CloudFront console. CloudFront helps in improving the performance of websites in several ways: (1) by caching the static content (such as JavaScript, CSS, images, etc.) at the edge location, (2) by proxying requests for dynamic or interactive content back to the origin (such as an Amazon EC2 instance) running in the AWS cloud.

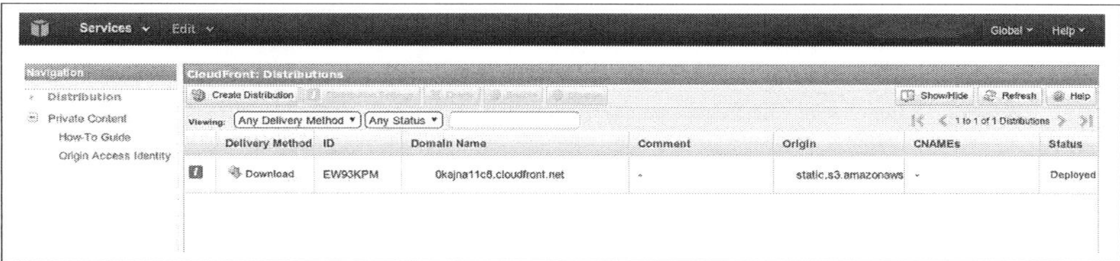

Figure 3.16: Screenshot of Amazon CloudFront console

3.5.2 Windows Azure Content Delivery Network

Windows Azure Content Delivery Network (CDN) is the content delivery service from Microsoft. Azure CDN caches Windows Azure blobs and static content at the edge locations to improve the performance of web sites. Azure CDN can be enabled on a Windows Azure storage account.

3.6 Analytics Services

Cloud-based analytics services allow analyzing massive data sets stored in the cloud either in cloud storages or in cloud databases using programming models such as MapReduce. Using cloud analytics services applications can perform data-intensive tasks such as such as data mining, log file analysis, machine learning, web indexing, etc.

3.6.1 Amazon Elastic MapReduce

Amazon Elastic MapReduce is the MapReduce service from Amazon based the Hadoop framework running on Amazon EC2 and Amazon S3. EMR supports various job types:

- Custom JAR: Custom JAR job flow runs a Java program that you have uploaded to Amazon S3.
- Hive program: Hive is a data warehouse system for Hadoop. You can use Hive to process data using the SQL-like language, called Hive-QL. You can create a Hive job flow with EMR which can either be an interactive Hive job or a Hive script.
- Streaming job: Streaming job flow runs a single Hadoop job consisting of map and reduce functions implemented in a script or binary that you have uploaded to Amazon

S3. You can write map and reduce scripts in Ruby, Perl, Python, PHP, R, Bash, or C++.

- Pig programs: Apache Pig is a platform for analyzing large data sets that consists of a high-level language (Pig Latin) for expressing data analysis programs, coupled with infrastructure for evaluating these programs. You can create a Pig job flow with EMR which can either be an interactive Pig job or a Pig script.
- HBase: HBase is a distributed, scalable, No-SQL database built on top of Hadoop. EMR allows you to launch an HBase cluster. HBase can be used for various purposes such as referencing data for Hadoop analytics, real-time log ingestion and batch log analytics, etc.

Figure 3.17 shows a screenshot of the Amazon EMR console. The EMR console provides a simple wizard for creating new MapReduce job flows. To create a MapReduce job you enter the job name, select the streaming option for the job flow, specify the locations of input, output and the mapper and reducer programs and specify the number of nodes to use in the Hadoop cluster and the instance sizes. The job flow takes several minutes to launch and configure. A Hadoop cluster is created as specified in the job flow and the MapReduce program specified in the input is executed. On completion of the MapReduce job, the results are copied to the output location specified and the Hadoop cluster is terminated.

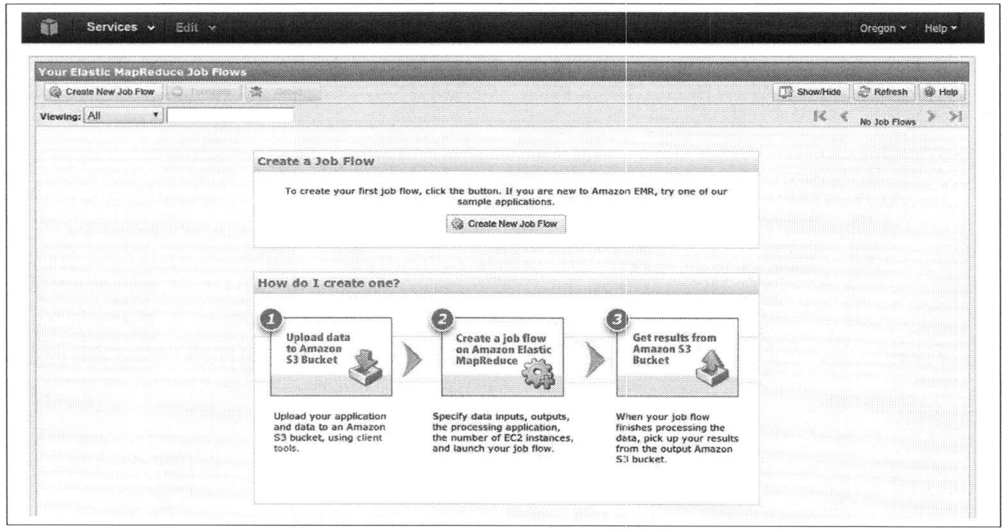

Figure 3.17: Screenshot of Amazon EMR console

3.6.2 Google MapReduce Service

Google MapReduce Service is a part of the App Engine platform. App Engine MapReduce is optimized for App Engine environment and provides capabilities such as automatic sharding for faster execution, standard data input readers for iterating over blob and datastore data, standard output writers, etc. The MapReduce service can be accessed using the Google MapReduce API. To execute a MapReduce job a MapReduce pipeline object is instantiated within the App Engine application. MapReduce pipeline specifies the mapper, reducer, data input reader, output writer.

3.6.3 Google BigQuery

Google BigQuery is a service for querying massive datasets. BigQuery allows querying datasets using SQL-like queries. The BigQuery queries are run against append-only tables and use the processing power of Google's infrastructure for speeding up queries. To query data, it is first loaded into BigQuery using the BigQuery console or BigQuery command line tool or BigQuery API. Data can be either in CSV or JSON format. The uploaded data can be queried using BigQuery's SQL dialect.

3.6.4 Windows Azure HDInsight

Windows Azure HDInsight is an analytics service from Microsoft. HDInsight deploys and provisions Hadoop clusters in the Azure cloud and makes Hadoop available as a service. HDInsight Service uses Windows Azure Blob Storage as the default file system. HDInsight provides interactive consoles for both JavaScript and Hive.

3.7 Deployment & Management Services

Cloud-based deployment & management services allow you to easily deploy and manage applications in the cloud. These services automatically handle deployment tasks such as capacity provisioning, load balancing, auto-scaling, and application health monitoring.

3.7.1 Amazon Elastic Beanstalk

Amazon provides a deployment service called Elastic Beanstalk that allows you to quickly deploy and manage applications in the AWS cloud. Elastic Beanstalk supports Java, PHP, .NET, Node.js, Python, and Ruby applications. With Elastic Beanstalk you just need to upload the application and specify configuration settings in a simple wizard and the service automatically handles instance provisioning, server configuration, load balancing and monitoring. Figure 3.18 shows a screenshot of the Amazon Elastic Beanstalk console. The launch wizard allows you to specify the environment details such as name, URL, application file, container type, instance type, etc. When the environment is launched Elastic Beanstalk automatically creates a new load balancer, launches and configures application and database servers as specified in the launch wizard, and deploys the application package on the application servers. The load balancer sits in front of the application servers which are a part of an Amazon Auto Scaling group. If the load on the application increases, Auto Scaling automatically launches new application servers to handle the increased load. If the load decreases, Auto Scaling stops additional instances and leaves at least one instance running.

3.7.2 Amazon CloudFormation

Amazon CloudFormation is a deployment management service from Amazon. With CloudFront you can create deployments from a collection of AWS resources such as Amazon Elastic Compute Cloud, Amazon Elastic Block Store, Amazon Simple Notification Service, Elastic Load Balancing and Auto Scaling. A collection of AWS resources that you want to manage together are organized into a stack. CloudFormation stacks are created from CloudFormation templates. You can create your own templates or use the predefined templates. The AWS infrastructure requirements for the stack are specified in the template. Figure 3.19 shows a screenshot of the Amazon CloudFormation console.

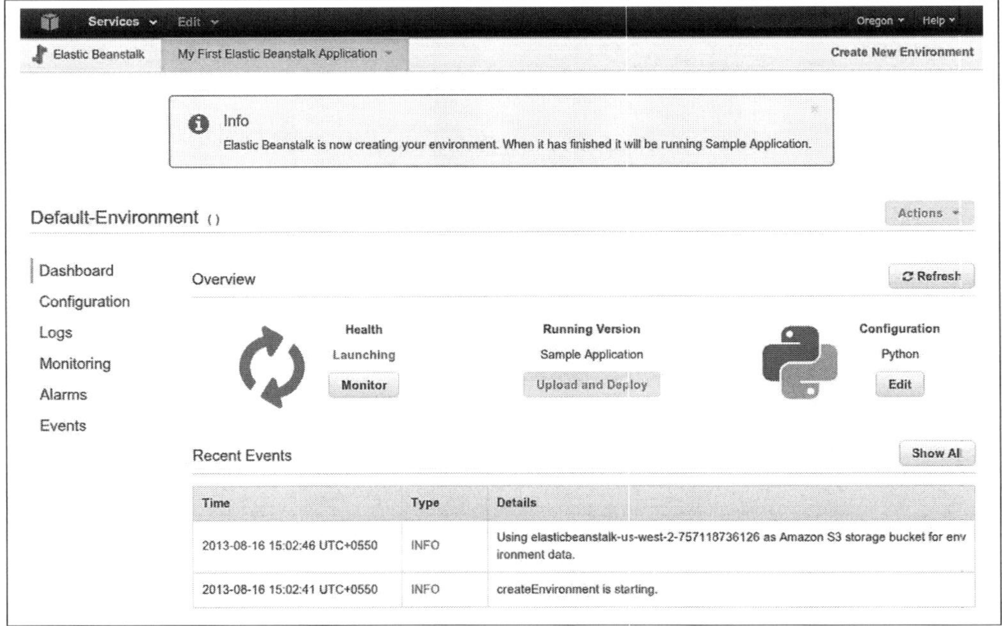

Figure 3.18: Screenshot of Amazon Elastic Beanstalk console

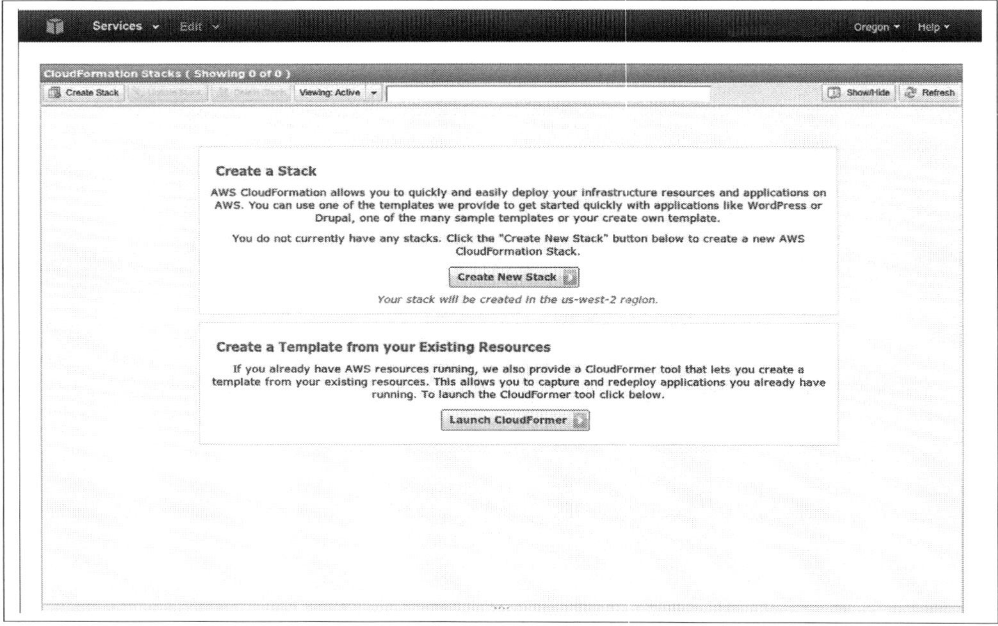

Figure 3.19: Screenshot of Amazon CloudFormation console

3.8 Identity & Access Management Services

Identity & Access Management (IDAM) services allow managing the authentication and authorization of users to provide secure access to cloud resources. IDAM services are useful for organizations which have multiple users who access the cloud resources. Using IDAM services you can manage user identifiers, user permissions, security credentials and access keys.

3.8.1 Amazon Identity & Access Management

AWS Identity and Access Management (IAM) allows you to manage users and user permissions for an AWS account. With IAM you can manage users, security credentials such as access keys, and permissions that control which AWS resources users can access. Using IAM you can control what data users can access and what resources users can create. IAM also allows you to control creation, rotation, and revocation security credentials of users. Figure 3.20 shows a screenshot of the Amazon Identity & Access Management console.

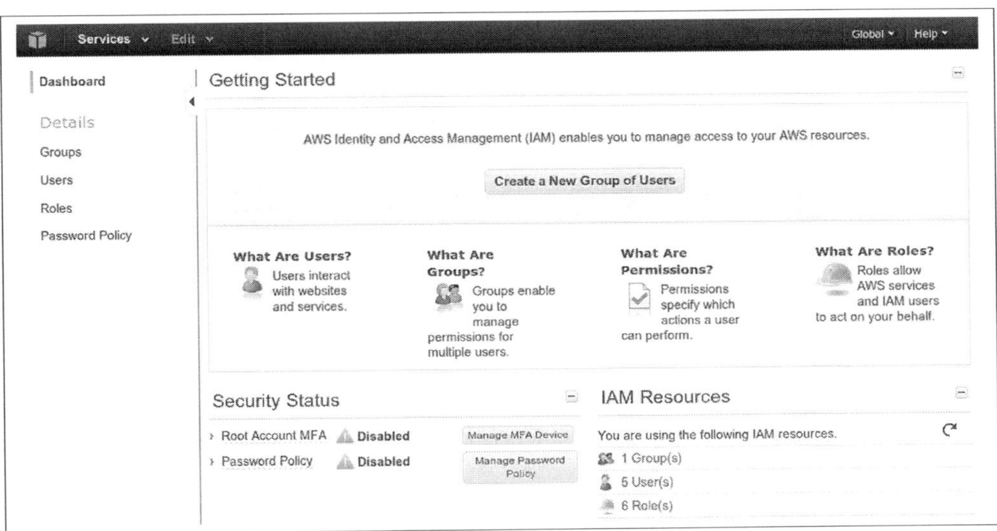

Figure 3.20: Screenshot of Amazon IAM console

3.8.2 Windows Azure Active Directory

Windows Azure Active Directory is an Identity & Access Management Service from Microsoft. Azure Active Directory provides a cloud-based identity provider that easily integrates with your on-premises active directory deployments and also provides support for third party identity providers. By integrating your on-premises active directory, you can authenticate users to Windows Azure with their existing corporate credentials. With Azure Active Directory you can control access to your applications in Windows Azure.

3.9 Open Source Private Cloud Software

In the previous sections you learned about popular public cloud platforms. This section covers open source cloud software that can be used to build private clouds.

3.9.1 CloudStack

Apache CloudStack is an open source cloud software that can be used for creating private cloud offerings [15]. CloudStack manages the network, storage, and compute nodes that make up a cloud infrastructure. A CloudStack installation consists of a Management Server and the cloud infrastructure that it manages. The cloud infrastructure can be as simple as one host running the hypervisor or a large cluster of hundreds of hosts. The Management Server allows you to configure and manage the cloud resources. Figure 3.21 shows the architecture of CloudStack which is basically the Management Server. The Management Server manages one or more zones where each zone is typically a single datacenter. Each zone has one or more pods. A pod is a rack of hardware comprising of a switch and one or more clusters. A cluster consists of one or more hosts and a primary storage. A host is a compute node that runs guest virtual machines. The primary storage of a cluster stores the disk volumes for all the virtual machines running on the hosts in that cluster. Each zone has a secondary storage that stores templates, ISO images, and disk volume snapshots.

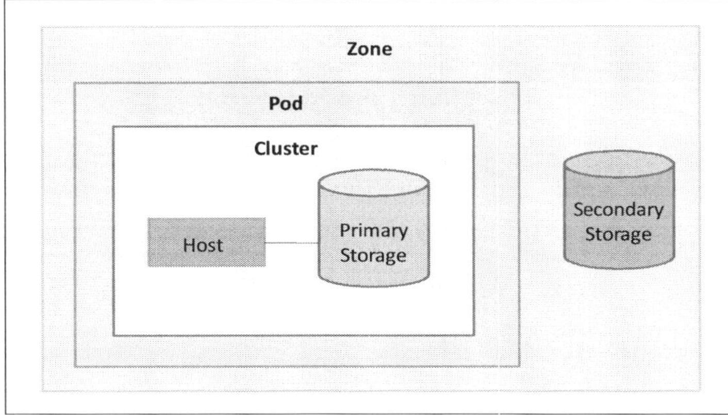

Figure 3.21: CloudStack architecture

3.9.2 Eucalyptus

Eucalyptus is an open source private cloud software for building private and hybrid clouds that are compatible with Amazon Web Services (AWS) APIs [16]. Figure 3.22 shows the architecture of Eucalyptus. The Node Controller (NC) hosts the virtual machine instances and manages the virtual network endpoints. The cluster-level (availability-zone) consists of three components - Cluster Controller (CC), Storage Controller (SC) and VMWare Broker. The CC manages the virtual machines and is the front-end for a cluster. The SC manages the Eucalyptus block volumes and snapshots to the instances within its specific cluster. SC is equivalent to AWS Elastic Block Store (EBS). The VMWare Broker is an optional component that provides an AWS-compatible interface for VMware environments. At the cloud-level there are two components - Cloud Controller (CLC) and Walrus. CLC provides an administrative interface for cloud management and performs high-level resource scheduling, system accounting, authentication and quota management.

Walrus is equivalent to Amazon S3 and serves as a persistent storage to all of the virtual machines in the Eucalyptus cloud. Walrus can be used as a simple Storage-as-a-Service solution.

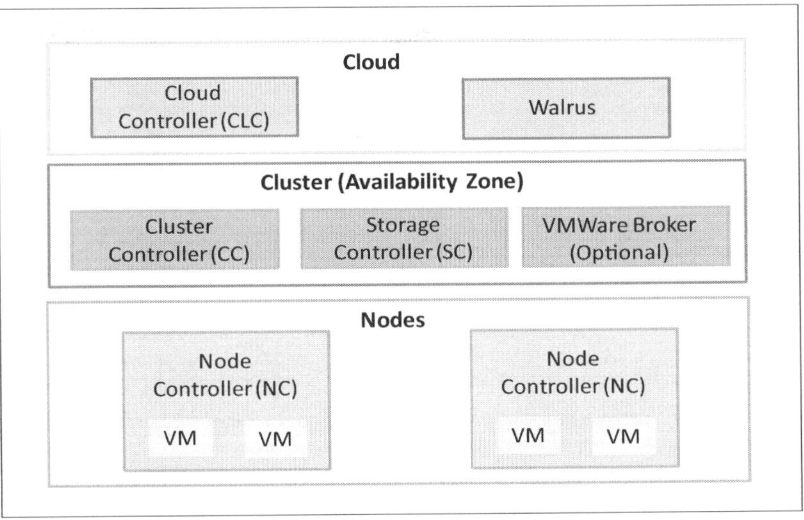

Figure 3.22: Eucalyptus architecture

3.9.3 OpenStack

OpenStack is a cloud operating system comprising of a collection of interacting services that control computing, storage, and networking resources [17]. Figure 3.23 shows the architecture of OpenStack. The OpenStack compute service (called nova-compute) manages networks of virtual machines running on nodes, providing virtual servers on demand. The network service (called nova-networking) provides connectivity between the interfaces of other OpenStack services. The volume service (Cinder) manages storage volumes for virtual machines. The object storage service (swift) allows users to store and retrieve files. The identity service (keystone) provides authentication and authorization for other services. The image registry (glance) acts as a catalog and repository for virtual machine images. The OpenStack scheduler (nova-scheduler) maps the nova-API calls to the appropriate OpenStack components. The scheduler takes the virtual machine requests from the queue and determines where they should run. The messaging service (rabbit-mq) acts as a central node for message passing between daemons. Orchestration activities such as running an instance are performed by the nova-api which accepts and responds to end user compute API calls. The OpenStack dashboard (called horizon) provides web-based interface for managing OpenStack services.

Summary

In this chapter you learned about the cloud reference model that includes the infrastructure/facilities layer, hardware layer, virtualization layer, virtual machines, platform & middleware, service management layer and applications layer and security layer. Cloud computing services can be of various types including compute service, storage services, database services application services, content delivery services, analytics services deployment & management services, identity & access management services, etc. Compute services provide dynami-

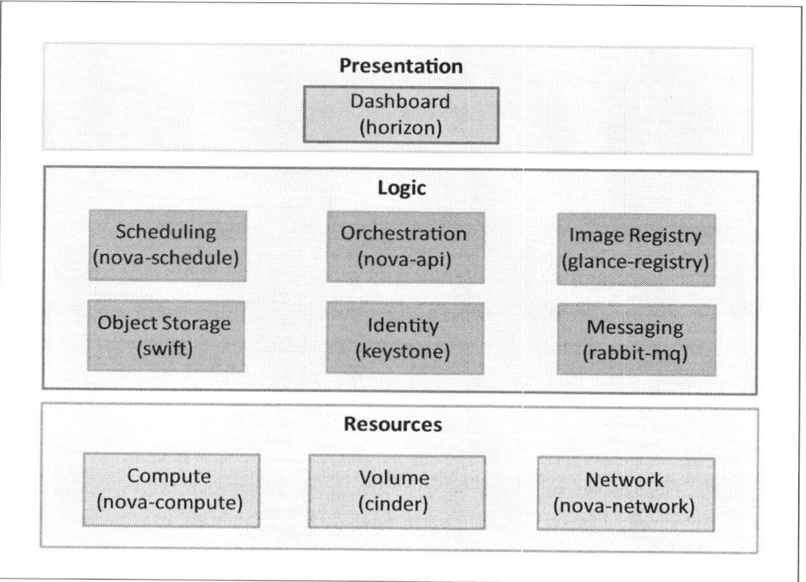

Figure 3.23: OpenStack architecture

cally scalable compute capacity in the cloud which can be provisioned on-demand in the form of virtual machines. Amazon Elastic Compute Cloud, Google Compute Engine and Windows Azure Virtual Machines are popular compute services. Cloud storage services allow storage and retrieval of any amount of data and at any time from anywhere on the web. Amazon Simple Storage Service, Google Cloud Storage and Windows Azure Storage are popular cloud storage services. Cloud database services allow you to set-up and operate relational or non-relational databases in the cloud. Amazon Relational Data Store, Google Cloud SQL and Windows Azure SQL Database are popular cloud-based relational database services. Amazon DynamoDB, Google Cloud Datastore and Windows Azure Table Service are popular cloud-based non-relational database services. Cloud-based application runtimes and frameworks allow developers to develop and host applications in the cloud. Google App Engine and Windows Azure Web Sites are popular PaaS services. Cloud-based queuing services allow asynchronous processing in applications. Amazon Simple Queue Service, Google Task Queue Service and Windows Azure Queue Service are popular queuing services. Cloud-based email services allow applications hosted in the cloud to send emails. Amazon Simple Email Service and Google Email Service are popular cloud-based email services.

Cloud-based notification services or push messaging services allow applications to push messages to internet connected smart devices such as smartphones, tablets, etc. Amazon Simple Notification Service, Google Cloud Messaging and Windows Azure Notification Hubs are popular notification services. Cloud-based media services that can be used by applications for manipulating, transforming or transcoding media such as images, videos, etc. Amazon Elastic Transcoder, Google Image Manipulation Service and Windows Azure Media Services are popular cloud-based media services. Content Delivery Network is a distributed system of servers located across multiple geographic locations to serve content to end-users with high availability and high performance. Amazon CloudFront and Windows

Azure CDN are popular CDNs. Cloud-based analytics services allow analyzing massive data sets stored in the cloud either in cloud storages or in cloud databases using programming models such as MapReduce. Amazon Elastic MapReduce, Google MapReduce Service, Google BigQuery, Windows Azure HDInsight are popular analytics services. Cloud-based deployment & management services allow you to easily deploy and manage applications in the cloud. Amazon Elastic Beanstalk and Amazon CloudFormation are popular deployment & management services. Identity & Access Management (IDAM) Services allow you to manage user identifiers, user permissions, security credentials and access keys. Amazon Identity & Access Management is a popular IDAM service.

Review Questions

1. What are the various layers in the cloud reference model?
2. Describe three applications of compute services.
3. Describe the various security mechanisms of cloud-storage services.
4. What are the differences between an SQL and No-SQL databases?
5. What is the benefit of using a sandbox environment for a PaaS?
6. Which cloud service is most important for developing loosely coupled applications?
7. What is a push messaging service? What are its uses?
8. What is a Content Delivery Network?
9. What are the various types of MapReduce jobs supported by Amazon EMR?
10. Describe a real-world application that can benefit from Google BigQuery.

Lab Exercises

1. In this exercise you will create an Amazon EC2 instance and setup a web-server on the instance and associate an Amazon Elastic IP address with the instance. Follow the steps below:
    - Create and Amazon Web Services account.
    - Log into the AWS account and open the Amazon EC2 console. Click on the launch instances button.
    - Select an 'Ubuntu Server' AMI. In the create instance wizard select *t1.micro* instance type. Proceed with the instance creation wizard with default settings. On the create key-pair page, create a new key-pair. On the security groups page, create a new security group. In the security group, create a custom TCP rule with port 80. Proceed with the wizard and launch the instance.
    - View the instance status in the console and wait till the status becomes running. When the status becomes running, note the public DNS of the instance from the console.
    - Connect to the instance using SSH. You will need the key-pair you specified while creating the instance. Use the following command for ssh:
      ssh -i /path/to/myKeyPair.pem ubuntu@publicDNS
    - After connecting to the EC2 instance, install Apache server using the following command:

sudo apt-get install apache2

- Create a web page as follows:
  cd /var/www/html
  sudo vim index.html

- Restart the Apache server as follows:
  sudo /etc/init.d/apache2 restart
- In a browser open the public DNS of the EC2 instance and see the web page you just created.
- Now to associate an Elastic IP address with the instance, go back to the EC2 console and click on the Elastic IPs link. Click on Allocate New Address button and allocate a new address. You can see the allocated Elastic IP address in the console. Right-click on it and choose Associate from the menu. Choose the EC2 instance you created previously and associate it with the Elastic IP address. Now enter the Elastic IP address in a browser and view the web page you created.

2. Repeat Exercise-1 using Google Compute Engine. Follow the steps below:
   - Create and Google Cloud Platform account and then create a new project.
   - Log into the Google Cloud Platform account and open the Google Compute Engine console.
   - Create a new instance with *f1.micro* machine type and a CentOS image.
   - Download and Install the gcutil command line tool.
   - Connect to your Google cloud project using the following command:
     gcutil getproject –project=<project-id> –cache_flag_values

   - When the instance status changes to running in the GCE console, SSH into the instance using the following command: gcutil ssh my-instance-name

   - Create a new firewall rule to allow incoming HTTP 80 as follows:
     gcutil addfirewall http2 –description="Incoming HTTP" –allowed="tcp:http"

   - Install Apache server and create a web page.
   - Open the IP address of the instance in a browser and view the web page you created.

3. Repeat Exercise-1 using Windows Azure Virtual Machine. Follow the steps below:
   - Create Windows Azure account.
   - From the Azure console, create a new instance with *ExtraSmall* machine type and a Ubuntu image.
   - Add an endpoint to allow incoming HTTP.
   - When the instance status changes to running in the Azure console, SSH into the instance.
   - Install Apache server and create a web page.
   - Open the IP address of the instance in a browser and view the web page you

created.

4. In this exercise you will create a cloud deployment with two web-servers under a load balancer using Amazon EC2 and Amazon ELB. Follow the steps below:
   - Follow the steps in Exercise-1 and launch two web servers.
   - In a browser open the public DNS of the EC2 instances and see if both the web servers are working.
   - Now from the Amazon EC2 console, create an Elastic Load Balancer (ELB).
   - In the ELB creation wizard, select the web server instances to add them to the ELB.
   - When the ELB is ready note the DNS name. Open the DNS in a browser and see the web page you created.

5. In this exercise you will create a database instance in the cloud using Amazon RDS. Follow the steps below:
   - From the Amazon RDS console, launch a new RDS instance with the following settings: DB Engine - MySQL, DB Instance Class - db.t1.micro, DB Port - 3306.
   - When the DB instance status changes to running, note the DB endpoint.
   - Edit the security group associated with the DB instance and add your local machine's IP address to the allowed hosts.
   - Now connect to the DB instance as follows:
     mysql -h dB-endpoint-name -P 3306 -u myuser -p
   - At the MySQL prompt, create a new database table, insert data into the table and query the table as follows:
     mysql>CREATE TABLE users (
     username VARCHAR(100) PRIMARY KEY,
     password VARCHAR(100) NOT NULL,
     firstname VARCHAR(100) NOT NULL,
     lastname VARCHAR(100) NOT NULL
     );
     mysql>INSERT INTO users VALUES ('testuser','password','test','user');
     mysql>SELECT * FROM users

6. Repeat Exercise-5 using Google Cloud SQL.

7. In this exercise you will learn how to host a static website from a cloud storage and create a CDN distribution to serve static files such as images. Follow the steps below:
   - Create an HTML web page with some static files embedded such as CSS, images, etc.
   - From the Amazon S3 console create a new bucket and upload the web page and dependent files to the bucket.
   - Now enable your bucket for static website hosting.
   - From a browser, access the web page via the Amazon S3 website endpoint for your bucket.
   - Now create another bucket and copy the static files in the web page (CSS, image

files, etc.) to the bucket.

- From the Amazon CloudFront console, create a new download distribution and specify the name of the bucket in which you copied the static files.
- When the distribution becomes available, note the distribution URL.
- Now edit the URLs of the static files in the web page and append the CloudFront distribution URL (e.g. files/img.jpg to mycloudfrontdist.com/files/img.jpg).
- Open the web page again in a browser and note if the response time improves.

4 — Hadoop & MapReduce

This Chapter Covers

- Overview of Hadoop ecosystem
- MapReduce architecture
- MapReduce job execution flow
- MapReduce schedulers

4.1 Apache Hadoop

Apache Hadoop [102] is an open source framework for distributed batch processing of big data. MapReduce has also been proposed as a parallel programming model [14]suitable for the cloud. The MapReduce algorithm allowed large scale computations to be parallelized across a large cluster of servers.

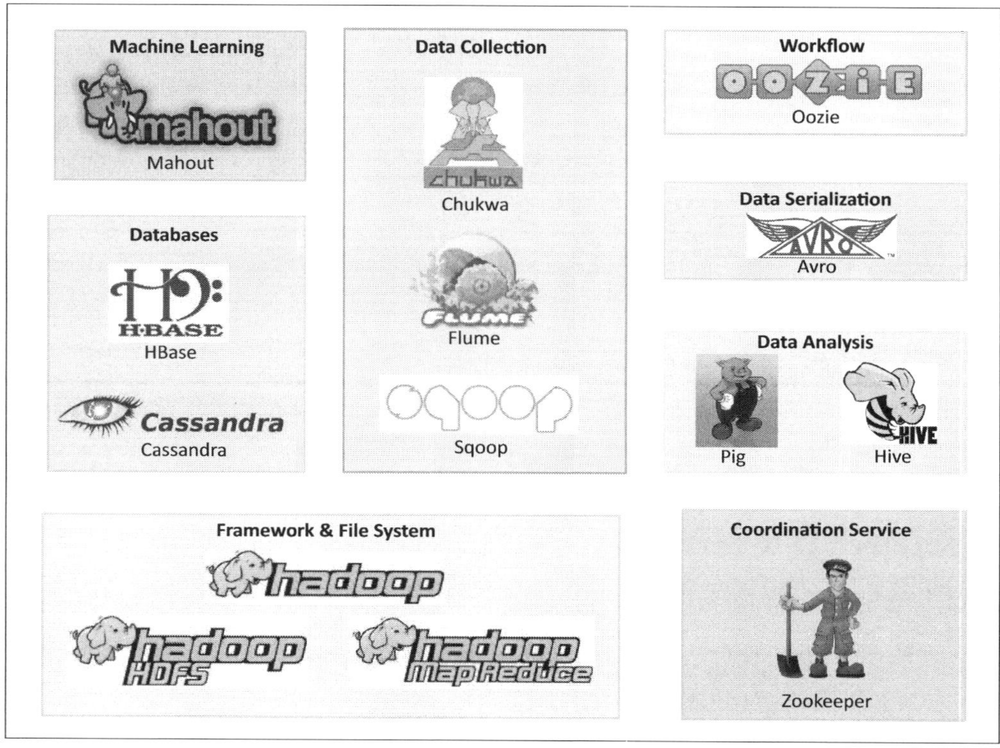

Figure 4.1: Hadoop ecosystem

The Hadoop ecosystem consist of a number of projects as shown in Figure 4.1. These projects are described briefly as follows:

- **Hadoop Common:** Hadoop Common consists of common utilities that support other Hadoop modules. Hadoop common has utilities and scripts for starting Hadoop, components and interfaces to access the file systems supported by Hadoop.
- **Hadoop Distributed File System (HDFS):** HDFS is a distributed file system (DFS) that runs on large clusters and provides high throughput access to data. HDFS was built to reliably store very large files across machines in a large cluster built of commodity hardware. HDFS stores each file as a sequence of blocks all of which are of the same size except the last block. The blocks of each file are replicated on multiple machines in a cluster with a default replication factor of 3 to provide fault tolerance.
- **Hadoop MapReduce:** MapReduce is a parallel programming model that allows distributing large scale computations in a sequence of operations on data sets of key-value pairs. The Hadoop MapReduce provides a data processing model and an execution environment for MapReduce jobs for large scale data processing.

- **Hadoop YARN:** A framework for job scheduling and cluster resource management.
- **HBase:** HBase is a scalable, non-relational, distributed, column-oriented database that provides structured data storage for large tables [19]. HBase data storage can scale linearly and automatically by addition of new nodes. As the tables grow, they are automatically split into regions and distributed across all available datanodes.
- **Zookeeper:** Zookeeper is a high performance distributed coordination service for maintaining configuration information, naming, providing distributed synchronization and group services [22].
- **Pig:** Pig is a data flow language and an execution environment for analyzing large datasets. Pig compiler produces a sequence of MapReduce jobs that analyze data in HDFS using the Hadoop MapReduce framework [29].
- **Hive:** Hive is a distributed data warehouse infrastructure for Hadoop. Hive provides an SQL-like language called HiveQL that allows easy data summarization, ad-hoc querying, and analysis of large datasets stored in HDFS [18].
- **Chukwa:** Chukwa is a data collection system for monitoring large distributed systems. Chukwa is built on top of HDFS and Hadoop MapReduce and allows collecting and analyzing data [20].
- **Mahout:** Mahout is a scalable machine learning library for Hadoop. Mahout provides a large collection of machine learning algorithms for clustering, classification and collaborative filtering which are implemented on top of Hadoop using the MapReduce parallel programming model [68].
- **Cassandra:** Cassandra is scalable multi-master database with no single points of failure. Cassandra is designed to handle massive scale data spread across many servers and provides a highly available service with no single point of failure. Cassandra is a No-SQL solution that provides a structured key-value store [27].
- **Avro:** Avro is a data serialization system that provides rich data structures, a compact and fast binary data format, a container file to store persistent data, cross-language RPC and simple integration with dynamic languages [23].
- **Oozie:** Oozie is a workflow scheduler system for managing Hadoop jobs. Oozie is integrated with the Hadoop stack and supports several types of Hadoop jobs such as MapReduce jobs, Pig, Hive, Sqoop, Distcp and system specific jobs [24].
- **Flume:** Flume is a distributed, reliable and available service for collecting, analyzing and moving large amounts of data from applications to HDFS [21].
- **Sqoop:** Sqoop is a tool that allows efficiently transferring bulk data between Hadoop and structured datastores such as relational databases [30].

4.2 Hadoop MapReduce Job Execution

In Chapter 2 you were introduced to the MapReduce parallel programming model. You may recall that a MapReduce job consists of two phases. In the Map phase, data is read from a distributed file system and partitioned among a set of computing nodes in the cluster. The data is sent to the nodes as a set of key-value pairs. The Map tasks process the input records independently of each other and produce intermediate results as key-value pairs. The intermediate results are stored on the local disk of the node running the Map task. When all the Map tasks are completed, the Reduce phase begins in which the intermediate data with the same key is aggregated. An optional Combine task can be used to perform data aggregation on the intermediate data of the same key for the output of the mapper before transferring the output to the Reduce task. In this section you will learn about the MapReduce job execution workflow and the steps involved in job submission, job initialization, task selection and task execution. Figure 4.2 shows the components of a Hadoop cluster. A Hadoop cluster comprises of a Master node, backup node and a number of slave nodes. The master node runs the NameNode and JobTracker processes and the slave nodes run the DataNode and TaskTracker components of Hadoop. The backup node runs the Secondary NameNode process. The functions of the key processes of Hadoop are described as follows:

4.2.1 NameNode

NameNode keeps the directory tree of all files in the file system, and tracks where across the cluster the file data is kept. It does not store the data of these files itself. Client applications talk to the NameNode whenever they wish to locate a file, or when they want to add/copy/move/delete a file. The NameNode responds to the successful requests by returning a list of relevant DataNode servers where the data lives. NameNode serves as both directory namespace manager and 'inode table' for the Hadoop DFS. There is a single NameNode running in any DFS deployment.

4.2.2 Secondary NameNode

HDFS is not currently a high availability system. The NameNode is a Single Point of Failure for the HDFS Cluster. When the NameNode goes down, the file system goes offline. An optional Secondary NameNode which is hosted on a separate machine creates checkpoints of the namespace.

4.2.3 JobTracker

The JobTracker is the service within Hadoop that distributes MapReduce tasks to specific nodes in the cluster, ideally the nodes that have the data, or at least are in the same rack.

4.2.4 TaskTracker

TaskTracker is a node in a Hadoop cluster that accepts Map, Reduce and Shuffle tasks from the JobTracker. Each TaskTracker has a defined number of slots which indicate the number of tasks that it can accept. When the JobTracker tries to find a TaskTracker to schedule a map or reduce task it first looks for an empty slot on the same node that hosts the DataNode containing the data. If an empty slot is not found on the same node, then the JobTracker it looks for an empty slot on a node in the same rack.

4.2.5 DataNode

A DataNode stores data in an HDFS file system. A functional HDFS filesystem has more than one DataNode, with data replicated across them. DataNodes connect to the NameNode on startup. DataNodes respond to requests from the NameNode for filesystem operations. Client applications can talk directly to a DataNode, once the NameNode has provided the location of the data. Similarly, MapReduce operations assigned to TaskTracker instances near a DataNode, talk directly to the DataNode to access the files. TaskTracker instances can be deployed on the same servers that host DataNode instances, so that MapReduce operations are performed close to the data.

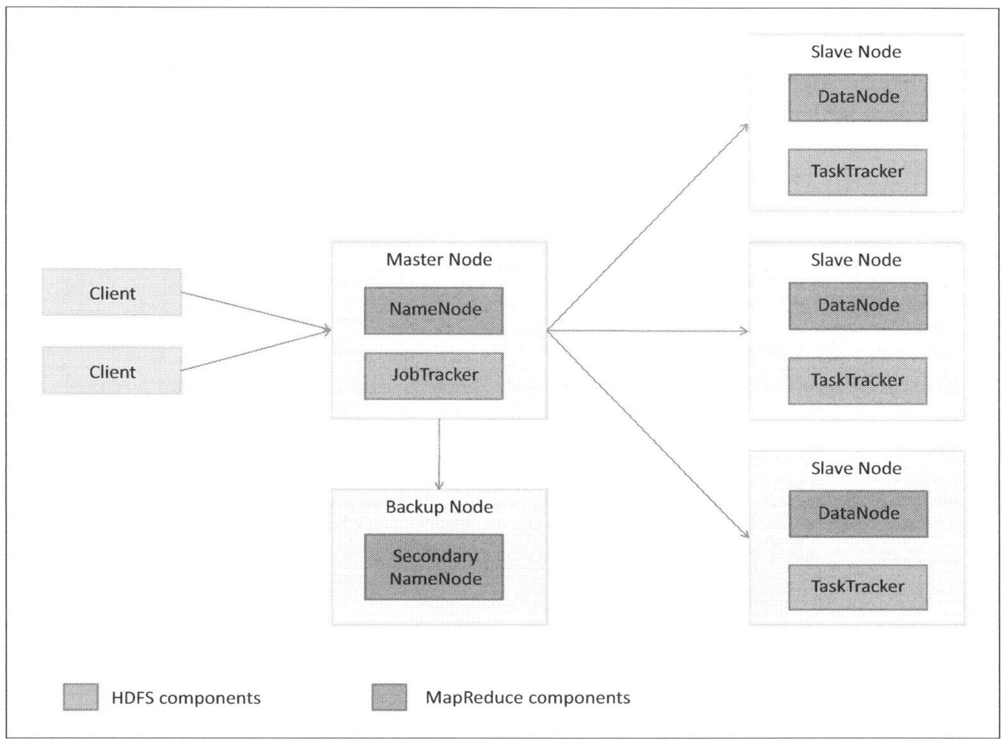

Figure 4.2: Components of a Hadoop cluster

4.2.6 MapReduce Job Execution Workflow

Figure 4.3 shows the MapReduce job execution workflow for first generation Hadoop MapReduce framework (MR1). The job execution starts when the client applications submit jobs to the Job tracker. The JobTracker returns a JobID to the client application. The JobTracker talks to the NameNode to determine the location of the data. The JobTracker locates TaskTracker nodes with available slots at/or near the data. The TaskTrackers send out heartbeat messages to the JobTracker, usually every few minutes, to reassure the JobTracker that they are still alive. These messages also inform the JobTracker of the number of available slots, so the JobTracker can stay up to date with where in the cluster, new work can be delegated. The JobTracker submits the work to the TaskTracker nodes when they poll for tasks. To choose a task for a TaskTracker, the JobTracker uses various scheduling algorithms. The default scheduling algorithm in Hadoop is FIFO (first-in, first-out). In FIFO scheduling a work queue is maintained and JobTracker pulls the oldest job first for scheduling. There is no notion of the job priority or size of the job in FIFO scheduling. Hadoop, however, implements the ability for pluggable schedulers. There are other advanced scheduling algorithms that come with Hadoop. These are explained later in this chapter.

The TaskTracker nodes are monitored using the heartbeat signals that are sent by the TaskTrackers to JobTracker. The TaskTracker spawns a separate JVM process for each task

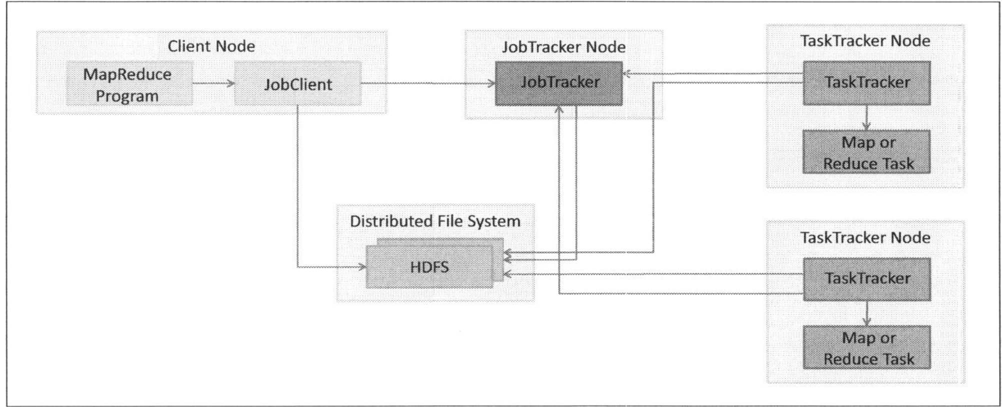

Figure 4.3: Hadoop MapReduce job execution

so that any task failure does not bring down the TaskTracker. The TaskTracker monitors these spawned processes while capturing the output and exit codes. When the process finishes, successfully or not, the TaskTracker notifies the JobTracker. When a task fails the TaskTracker notifies the JobTracker and the JobTracker decides whether to resubmit the job to some other TaskTracker or mark that specific record as something to avoid. The JobTracker can blacklist a TaskTracker as unreliable if there are repeated task failures. When the job is completed, the JobTracker updates its status. Client applications can poll the JobTracker for status of the jobs.

Recently, the next generation of Hadoop MapReduce has been introduced. The new MapReduce architecture is called YARN or MapReduce 2.0 (MR2). In Hadoop 2.0 the original processing engine of Hadoop (MapReduce) has been separated from the resource management (which is now part of YARN) as shown in Figure 4.4. This makes YARN effectively an operating system for Hadoop that supports different processing engines on a Hadoop cluster such as MapReduce for batch processing, Apache Tez [26] for interactive queries, Apache Storm [25] for stream processing, etc.

Figure 4.5 shows the MapReduce job execution workflow for next generation Hadoop MapReduce framework (MR2). The next generation MapReduce architecture divides the two major functions of the JobTracker - resource management and job life-cycle management - into separate components – ResourceManager and ApplicationMaster. The key components of YARN are described as follows:

- **Resource Manager (RM):** RM manages the global assignment of compute resources to applications. RM consists of two main services:
  - Scheduler: Scheduler is a pluggable service that manages and enforces the resource scheduling policy in the cluster.
  - Applications Manager (AsM): AsM manages the running Application Masters in the cluster. AsM is responsible for starting application masters and for monitoring and restarting them on different nodes in case of failures.
- **Application Master (AM):** A per-application AM manages the application's life cycle. AM is responsible for negotiating resources from the RM and working with the NMs to execute and monitor the tasks.

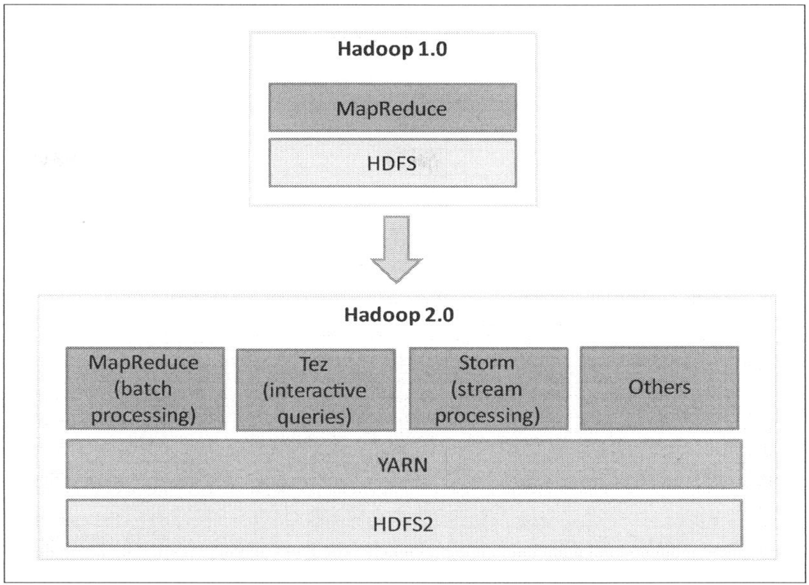

Figure 4.4: Comparison of Hadoop 1.0 and 2.0 architectures

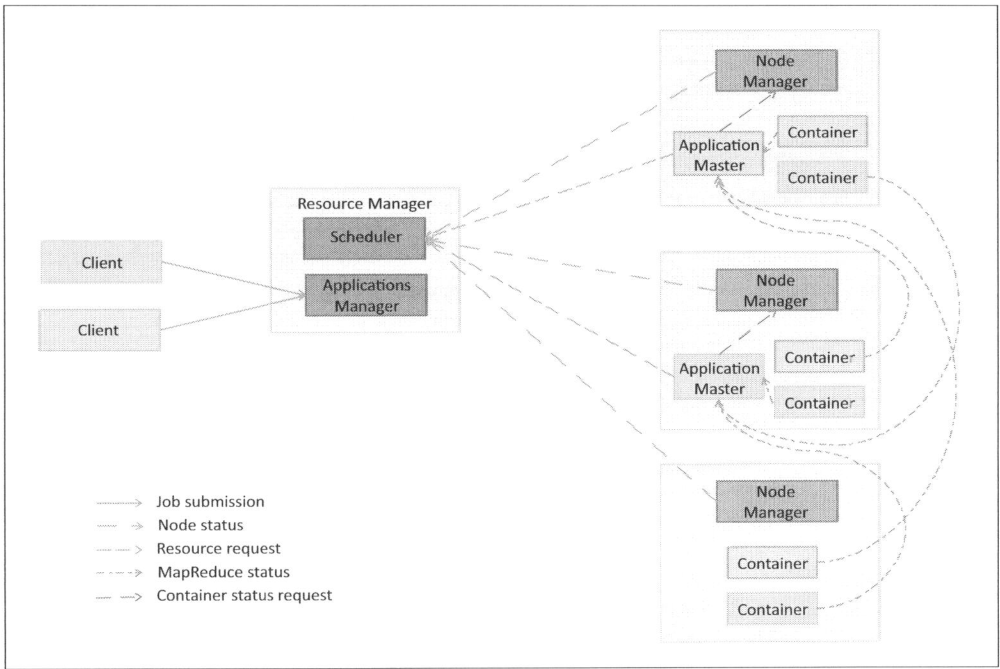

Figure 4.5: Hadoop MapReduce Next Generation (YARN) job execution

- **Node Manager (NM):** A per-machine NM manages the user processes on that machine.
- **Containers:** Container is a bundle of resources allocated by RM (memory, CPU, network, etc.). A container is a conceptual entity that grants an application the privilege

to use a certain amount of resources on a given machine to run a component task. Each node has an NM that spawns multiple containers based on the resource allocations made by the RM.

Figure 4.5 shows a YARN cluster with a Resource Manager node and three Node Manager nodes. There are as many Application Masters running as there are applications (jobs). Each application's AM manages the application tasks such as starting, monitoring and restarting tasks in case of failures. Each application has multiple tasks. Each task runs in a separate container. Containers in YARN architecture are similar to task slots in MR1. However, unlike MR1 which differentiates between map and reduce slots, each container in YARN can be used for both map and reduce tasks. The resource allocation model in MR1 consists of a predefined number of map slots and reduce slots. This static allocation of slots results in low cluster utilization. The resource allocation model of YARN is more flexible with introduction of resource containers which improve cluster utilization.

To better understand the YARN job execution workflow let us analyze the interactions between the main components on YARN. Figure 4.6 shows the interactions between a Client and Resource Manager. Job execution begins with the submission of a new application request by the client to the RM. The RM then responds with a unique application ID and information about cluster resource capabilities that the client will need in requesting resources for running the application's AM. Using the information received from the RM, the client constructs and submits an Application Submission Context which contains information such as scheduler queue, priority and user information. The Application Submission Context also contains a Container Launch Context which contains the application's jar, job files, security tokens and any resource requirements. The client can query the RM for application reports. The client can also "force kill" an application by sending a request to the RM.

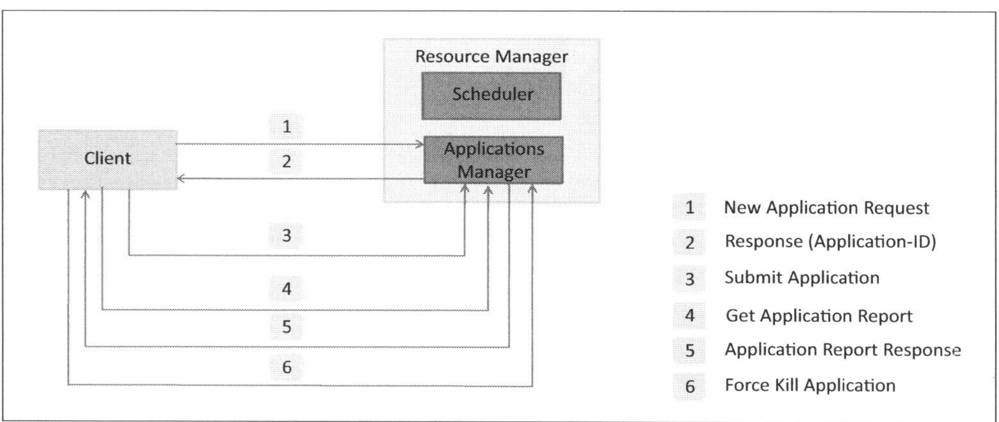

Figure 4.6: Client – Resource Manager interaction

Figure 4.7 shows the interactions between Resource Manager and Application Master. Upon receiving an application submission context from a client, the RM finds an available container meeting the resource requirements for running the AM for the application. On finding a suitable container, the RM contacts the NM for the container to start the AM process on its node. When the AM is launched it registers itself with the RM. The registration process consists of handshaking that conveys information such as the RPC port that the AM will be

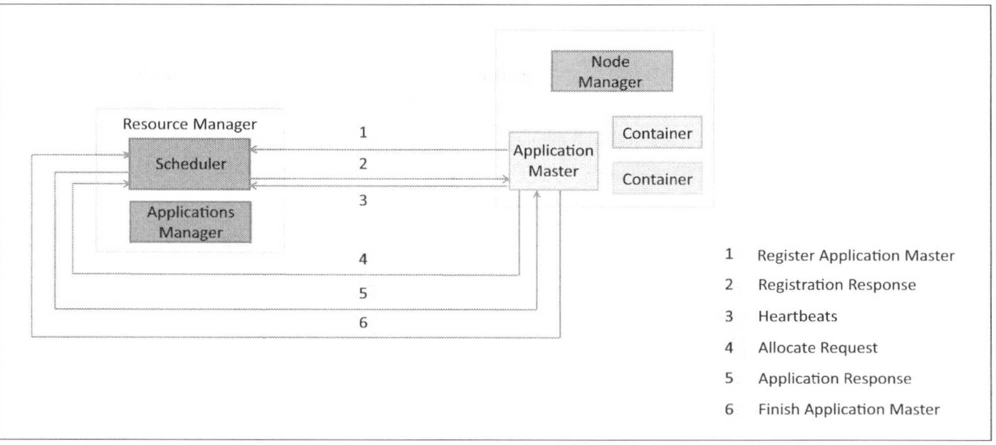

Figure 4.7: Resource Manager – Application Master interaction

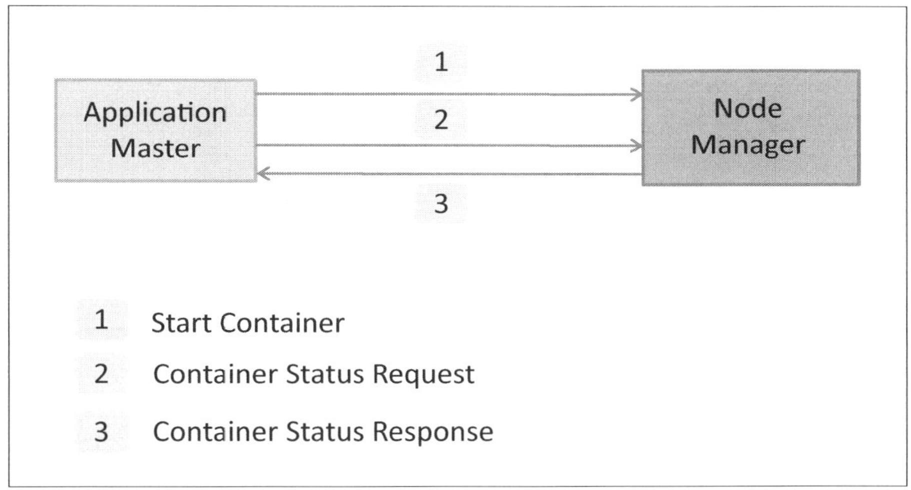

Figure 4.8: Application Master- Node Manager interaction

listening on, the tracking URL for monitoring the application's status and progress, etc. The registration response from the RM contains information for the AM that is used in calculating and requesting any resource requests for the application's individual tasks (such as minimum and maximum resource capabilities for the cluster). The AM relays heartbeat and progress information to the RM. The AM sends resource allocation requests to the RM that contains a list of requested containers, and may also contain a list of released containers by the AM. Upon receiving the allocation request, the scheduler component of the RM computes a list of containers that satisfy the request and sends back an allocation response. Upon receiving the resource list, the AM contacts the associated NMs for starting the containers. When the job finishes, the AM sends a Finish Application message to the RM.

Figure 4.8 shows the interactions between the an Application Master and Node Manager. Based on the resource list received from the RM, the AM requests the hosting NM for each container to start the container. The AM can request and receive a container status report from the Node Manager.

4.3 Hadoop Schedulers

Hadoop scheduler is a pluggable component that makes it open to support different scheduling algorithms. The default scheduler in Hadoop is FIFO (first in, first out). In addition to this, two advanced schedulers are also available - the Fair Scheduler, developed at Facebook, and the Capacity Scheduler, developed at Yahoo. The pluggable scheduler framework provides the flexibility to support a variety of workloads with varying priority and performance constraints. Efficient job scheduling makes Hadoop a multi-tasking system that can process multiple data sets for multiple jobs for multiple users simultaneously. The Hadoop scheduling algorithms are discussed in the sections that follow.

4.3.1 FIFO

FIFO is the default scheduler in Hadoop that maintains a work queue in which the jobs are queued. The scheduler pulls jobs in first in first out manner (oldest job first) for scheduling. There is no concept of priority or size of job in FIFO scheduler.

4.3.2 Fair Scheduler

The Fair Scheduler allocates resources evenly between multiple jobs and also provides capacity guarantees. Fair Scheduler assigns resources to jobs such that each job gets an equal share of the available resources on average over time. Unlike the FIFO scheduler, which forms a queue of jobs, the Fair Scheduler lets short jobs finish in reasonable time while not starving long jobs. Tasks slots that are free are assigned to the new jobs, so that each job gets roughly the same amount of CPU time. The Fair Scheduler maintains a set of pools into which jobs are placed. Each pool has a guaranteed capacity. A configuration file is used for specifying the pools and the guaranteed capacities. When there is a single job running, all the resources are assigned to that job. When there are multiple jobs in the pools, each pool gets at least as many task slots as guaranteed. Each pool receives at least the minimum share. When a pool does not require the guaranteed share the excess capacity is split between other jobs. This lets the scheduler guarantee capacity for pools while utilizing resources efficiently when these pools don't contain jobs.

All the pools have equal share by default. It is possible to provide more or less share to a pool by specifying the share in the configuration file. The Fair Scheduler keeps track of the compute time received by each job. The scheduler computes periodically the difference between the computing time received by each job and the time it should have received in ideal scheduling. The job which has the highest deficit of the compute time received is scheduled next. This ensures that over time, each job gets its fair share of compute time. When multiple users are submitting jobs, to ensure fairness, each user is assigned to a pool. It is possible to limit the number of running jobs per user or per pool by specifying the limits in the configuration file. This is useful when a user submits a large number of jobs and permits greater responsiveness of the Hadoop cluster. Table 4.1 lists the configurable properties of the Fair Scheduler.

Property Name	Details
mapred.fairscheduler. allocation.file	Absolute path to an XML file which contains the allocations for each pool, as well as the per-pool and per-user limits on number of running jobs. If this property is not provided, allocations are not used.
mapred.fairscheduler. assignmultiple	Allows the scheduler to assign a map task and a reduce task on each heartbeat, which improves cluster throughput when there are many small tasks to run.
mapred.fairscheduler. sizebasedweight	Take into account job sizes in calculating their weights for fair sharing. By default, weights are only based on job priorities. Setting this flag to true will make them based on the size of the job (number of tasks needed) as well.
mapred.fairscheduler. poolnameproperty	Specify which jobconf property is used to determine the pool that a job belongs in.
mapred.fairscheduler. weightadjuster	An extensibility point that lets you specify a class to adjust the weights of running jobs.
mapred.fairscheduler. loadmanager	An extensibility point that lets you specify a class that determines how many maps and reduces can run on a given TaskTracker.
mapred.fairscheduler. taskselector	An extensibility point that lets you specify a class that determines which task from within a job to launch on a given tracker.

Table 4.1: List of configurable properties of Fair Scheduler

4.3.3 Capacity Scheduler

The Capacity Scheduler has similar functionally as the Fair Scheduler but adopts a different scheduling philosophy. In Capacity Scheduler, you define a number of named queues each with a configurable number of map and reduce slots. Each queue is also assigned a guaranteed capacity. The Capacity Scheduler gives each queue its capacity when it contains jobs, and shares any unused capacity between the queues. Within each queue FIFO scheduling with priority is used. For fairness, it is possible to place a limit on the percentage of running tasks per user, so that users share a cluster equally. A wait time for each queue can be configured. When a queue is not scheduled for more than the wait time, it can preempt tasks of other queues to get its fair share.

Capacity Scheduler allows enforcing strict access control on queues. The access controls are defined on a per-queue basis and restrict the ability to submit jobs to queues and the ability to view and modify jobs in queues. Capacity Scheduler provides support for memory-intensive jobs, wherein a job can optionally specify higher memory-requirements than the default. Tasks of the high-memory jobs are run only on TaskTrackers that have enough memory to spare. When a TaskTracker has free slots, the Capacity Scheduler picks a queue for which the ratio of the number of running slots to capacity is the lowest. The scheduler then picks a job from the selected queue to run. Jobs are sorted based on when they're submitted and their priorities. Jobs are considered in order, and a job is selected if its user is within the user-quota for the queue, i.e., the user is not already using queue resources above the defined limit. In case special memory requirements are specified for a job, the scheduler makes sure there is enough free memory in the TaskTracker to run the job's task. Table 4.2 lists the configurable properties of the Capacity Scheduler. Capacity Scheduler is configured within multiple Hadoop configuration files. The queues are defined within hadoop-site.xml, the queue configurations are set in capacity-scheduler.xml and access control lists are configured within mapred-queue-acls.xml.

Property Name	Details
mapred.capacity-scheduler.queue.<queue-name>.guaranteed-capacity	Percentage of the number of slots in the cluster that are guaranteed to be available for jobs in this queue. The sum of guaranteed capacities for all queues should be less than or equal 100.
mapred.capacity-scheduler.queue.<queue-name>.reclaim-time-limit	The amount of time, in seconds, before which resources distributed to other queues will be reclaimed.
mapred.capacity-scheduler.queue.<queue-name>.supports-priority	If true, priorities of jobs will be taken into account in scheduling decisions.
mapred.capacity-scheduler.queue.<queue-name>.minimum-user-limit-percent	Each queue enforces a limit on the percentage of resources allocated to a user at any given time, if there is competition for them. This user limit can vary between a minimum and maximum value. The former depends on the number of users who have submitted jobs, and the latter is set to this property value.

Table 4.2: List of configurable properties of Capacity Scheduler

4.4 Hadoop Cluster Setup

In this section you will learn how to setup a Hadoop cluster. Hadoop framework is written in Java and has been designed to work with commodity hardware. The Hadoop's filesystem HDFS is highly fault-tolerant. In our opinion, the suitable operating system to host Hadoop is Linux, however, it can be set up on Windows operating systems with Cygwin environment.

Figure 4.9 shows the multi-node Hadoop cluster configuration that will be described in this section. This Hadoop cluster comprises of one master node that runs the NameNode and JobTracker and two slave nodes that run the TaskTracker and DataNode. The hardware used for the Hadoop cluster example described in this section comprised of three Amazon EC2 (m1.Large) instances running Ubuntu linux. In Chapter 3 we described how to launch Amazon EC2 instances and connect to them securely using SSH.

The steps involved in setting up a Hadoop cluster are described as follows:

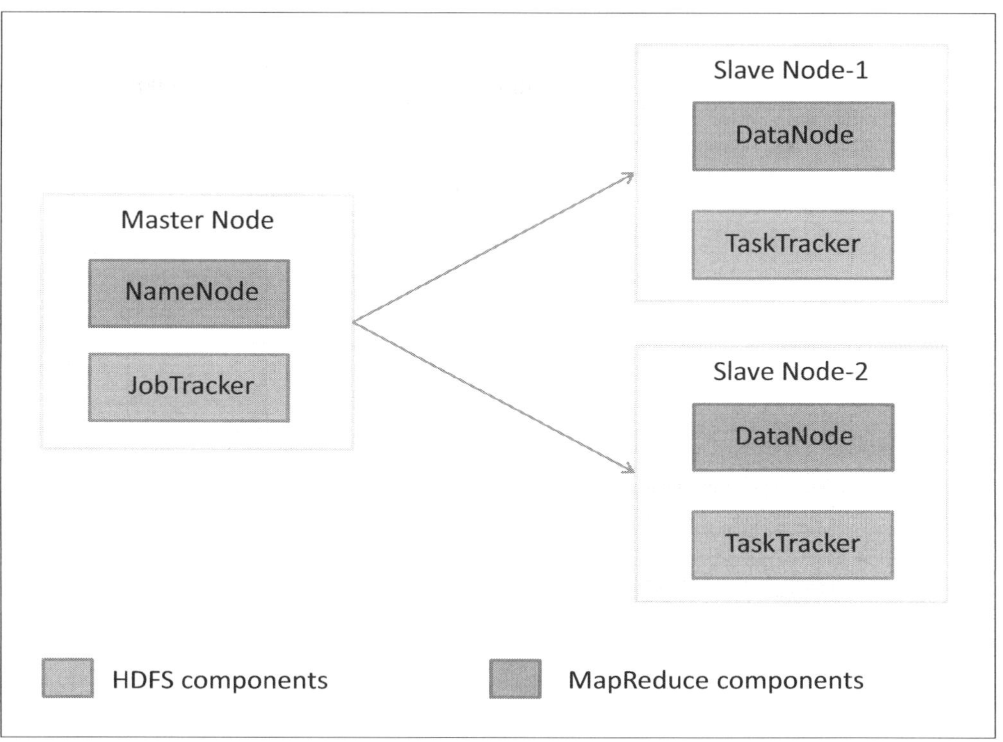

Figure 4.9: Hadoop cluster example

4.4.1 Install Java

Hadoop required Java 6 or later version. Box 4.1 lists the commands for installing Java 6.

4.4.2 Install Hadoop

To setup a Hadoop cluster, the Hadoop setup tarball is downloaded and unpacked on all the nodes. The Hadoop version used for the cluster example in this section is 1.0.4. Box 4.2 lists the commands for installing Hadoop.

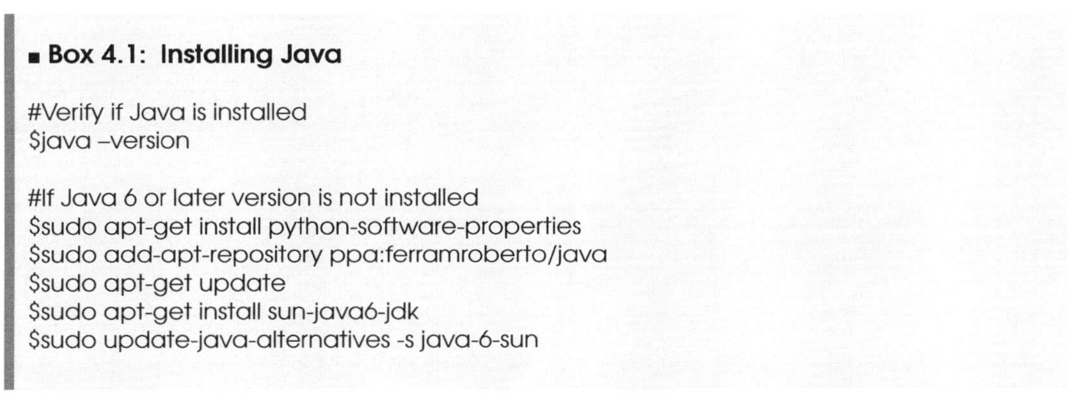

■ Box 4.1: Installing Java

```
#Verify if Java is installed
$java –version

#If Java 6 or later version is not installed
$sudo apt-get install python-software-properties
$sudo add-apt-repository ppa:ferramroberto/java
$sudo apt-get update
$sudo apt-get install sun-java6-jdk
$sudo update-java-alternatives -s java-6-sun
```

■ **Box 4.2: Install and configure Hadoop**

```
$wget http://apache.techartifact.com/mirror/hadoop/common/hadoop-1.0.4/
hadoop-1.0.4.tar.gz
$tar xzf hadoop-1.0.4.tar.gz
#Change hostname of node
#sudo hostname master
#sudo hostname slave1
#sudo hostname slave2

#Modify /etc/hosts file and add private IPs of Master and Slave nodes:
$sudo vim /etc/hosts
#<private_IP_master> master
#<private_IP_slave1> slave1
#<private_IP_slave2> slave2

$ssh-keygen -t rsa -f /.ssh/id_rsa
$sudo cat /.ssh/id_rsa.pub >> /.ssh/authorized_keys

#Open authorized keys file and copy authorized keys of each node
$sudo vim /.ssh/authorized_keys

#Save host key fingerprints by connecting to every node using SSH
#ssh master
#ssh slave1
#ssh slave2
```

File Name	Description
core-site.xml	Configuration parameters for Hadoop core which are common to MapReduce and HDFS
mapred-site.xml	Configuration parameters for MapReduce daemons – JobTracker and TaskTracker
hdfs-site.sml	Configuration parameters for HDFS daemons – NameNode and Secondary NameNode and DataNode
hadoop-env.sh	Environment variables for Hadoop daemons
masters	List of nodes that run a Secondary NameNode
slaves	List of nodes that run TaskTracker and DataNode
log4j.properties	Logging properties for the Hadoop daemons
mapred-queue-acls.xml	Access control lists

Table 4.3: Hadoop configuration files

4.4.3 Networking

After unpacking the Hadoop setup package on all the nodes of the cluster, the next step is to configure the network such that all the nodes can connect to each other over the network. To make the addressing of nodes simple, assign simple host names to nodes (such master, slave1 and slave2). The /etc/hosts file is edited on all nodes and IP addresses and host names of all the nodes are added.

Hadoop control scripts use SSH for cluster-wide operations such as starting and stopping NameNode, DataNode, JobTracker, TaskTracker and other daemons on the nodes in the cluster. For the control scripts to work, all the nodes in the cluster must be able to connect to each other via a password-less SSH login. To enable this, public/private RSA key pair is generated on each node. The private key is stored in the file /.ssh/id_rsa and public key is stored in the file /.ssh/id_rsa.pub. The public SSH key of each node is copied to the /.ssh/authorized_keys file of every other node. This can be done by manually editing the /.ssh/authorized_keys file on each node or using the ssh-copy-id command. The final step to setup the networking is to save host key fingerprints of each node to the known_hosts file of every other node. This is done by connecting from each node to every other node by SSH.

4.4.4 Configure Hadoop

With the Hadoop setup package unpacked on all nodes and networking of nodes setup, the next step is to configure the Hadoop cluster. Hadoop is configured using a number of configuration files listed in Table 4.3. Boxes 4.3, 4.4, 4.5 and 4.6 show the sample configuration settings for the Hadoop configuration files core-site.xml, mapred-site.xml, hdfs-site.xml, masters/slaves files respectively.

■ Box 4.3: Sample configuration – core-site.xml

```
<?xml version="1.0"?>
<configuration>
<property>
<name>fs.default.name</name>
<value>hdfs://master:54310</value>
</property>
</configuration>
```

■ Box 4.4: Sample configuration hdfs-site.xml

```
<?xml version="1.0"?>
<configuration>
<property>
<name>dfs.replication</name>
<value>2</value>
</property>
</configuration>
```

■ Box 4.5: Sample configuration mapred-site.xml

```
<?xml version="1.0"?>
```

```
<configuration>
<property>
<name>mapred.job.tracker</name>
<value>master:54311</value>
</property>
</configuration>
```

■ **Box 4.6: Sample configuration masters and slave files**

```
$cd hadoop/conf/

#Open the masters file and add hostname of master node
$vim masters
#master

#Open the masters file and add hostname of slave nodes
$vim slaves
#slave1
#slave2
```

■ **Box 4.7: Starting and stopping Hadoop cluster**

```
$cd hadoop-1.0.4
#Format NameNode
$bin/hadoop namenode –format

#Start HDFS daemons
$bin/start-dfs.sh

#Start MapReduce daemons
$bin/start-mapred.sh

#Check status of daemons
$jps

#Stopping Hadoop cluster
# bin/stop-mapred.sh
$bin/stop-dfs.sh
```

4.4.5 Starting and Stopping Hadoop Cluster

Having installed and configured Hadoop the next step is to start the Hadoop cluster. Box 4.7 lists the commands for starting and stopping the Hadoop cluster.

If the Hadoop cluster is correctly installed, configured and started, the status of the Hadoop daemons can be viewed using the administration web-pages for the daemons. Hadoop publishes the status of HDFS and MapReduce jobs to an internally running web server on the master node of the Hadoop cluster. The default addresses of the web UIs as follows:

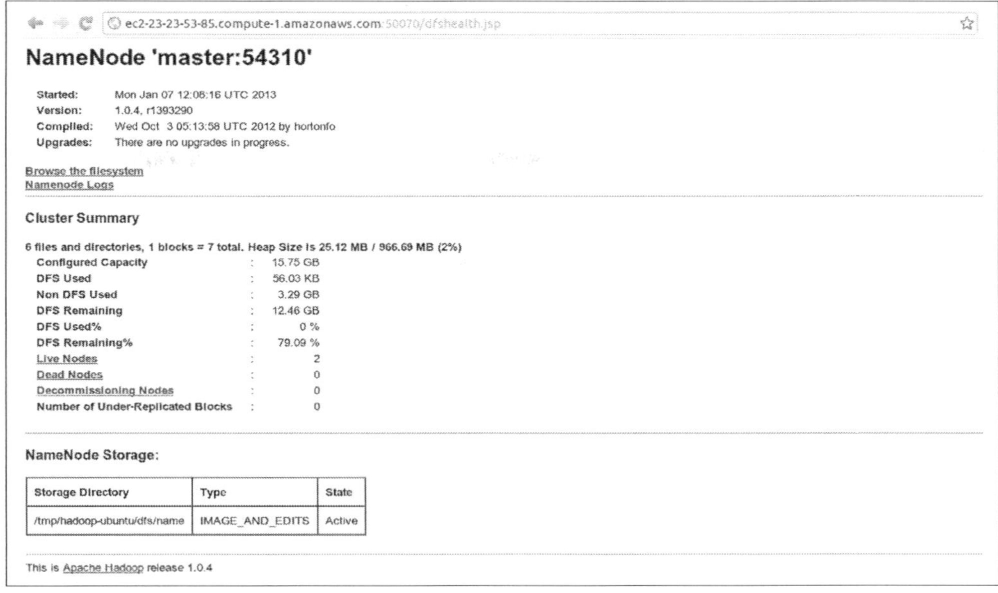

Figure 4.10: Hadoop NameNode status page

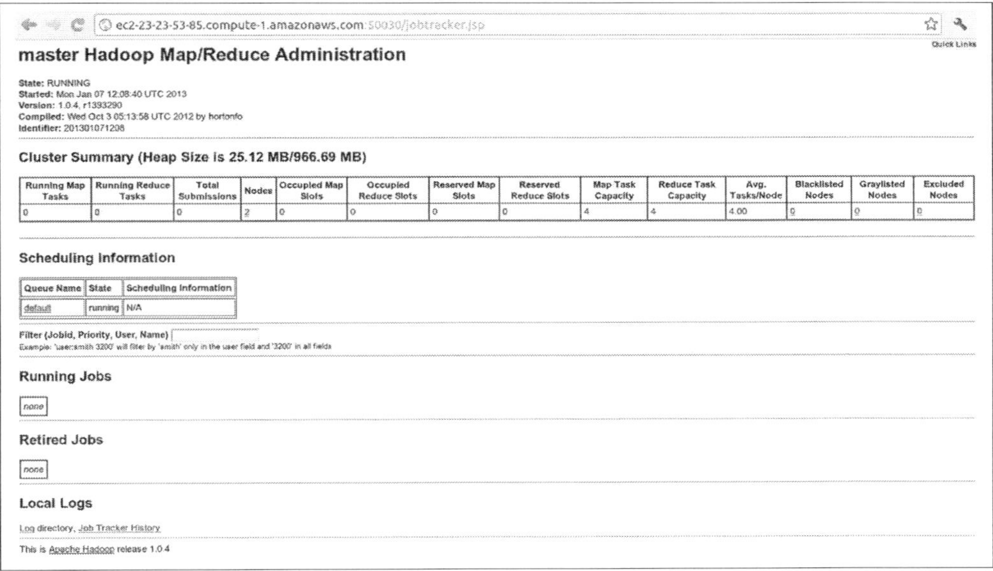

Figure 4.11: Hadoop MapReduce administration page

NameNode - http://<NameNodeHostName>:50070/
JobTracker - http://<JobTrackerHostName>:50030/
Figure 4.10 shows the Hadoop NameNode status page which provides information about NameNode uptime, the number of live, dead, and decommissioned nodes, host and port information, safe mode status, heap information, audit logs, garbage collection metrics, total load, file operations, and CPU usage.

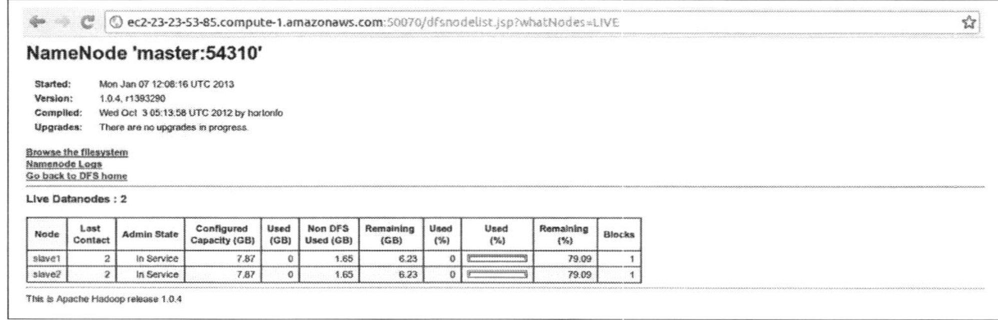

Figure 4.12: Hadoop HDFS status page showing live data nodes

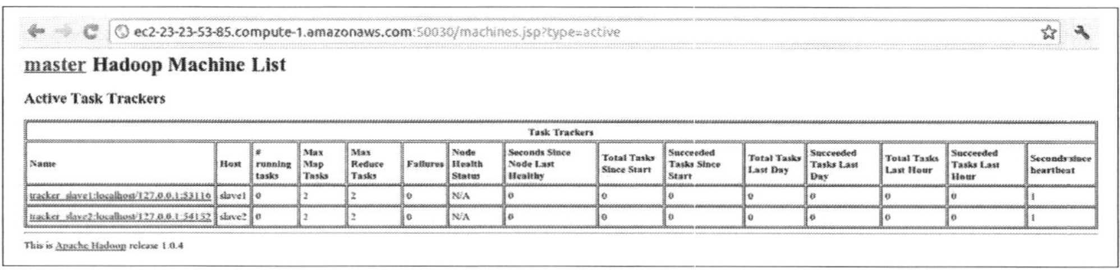

Figure 4.13: Hadoop MapReduce status page showing active TaskTrackers

Figure 4.11 shows the MapReduce administration page which provides host and port information, start time, tracker counts, heap information, scheduling information, current running jobs, retired jobs, job history log, service daemon logs, thread stacks, and a cluster utilization summary.

Figure 4.12 shows the status page of the live data nodes of the Hadoop cluster. The status page shows two live data nodes – slave1 and slave2.

Figure 4.13 shows the status page of the active TaskTrackers of the Hadoop cluster. The status page shows two active TaskTrackers that run on the slave1 and slave2 nodes of the cluster.

Summary

In this chapter you learned about the Apache Hadoop framework and the MapReduce parallel programming model. Hadoop is an open source framework for distributed batch processing of massive scale data. Hadoop ecosystem consist of a number of projects such as Hadoop Common, HDFS, Hadoop MapReduce, YARN, HBase, Zookeeper, Pig, Hive, Chukwa, Mahout, Cassandra, Avro, Oozie, Flume, Sqoop, etc. HDFS is a distributed file system that runs on large clusters and provides high throughput access to data. The Hadoop MapReduce provides a data processing model and an execution environment for MapReduce jobs for large scale data processing. YARN is framework for job scheduling and cluster resource management. HBase is a scalable, non-relational, distributed, column-oriented database. Zookeeper is a high performance distributed coordination service. Pig is a data flow language and an execution environment for analyzing large datasets. Hive is a distributed data warehouse infrastructure for Hadoop. Chukwa is a data collection system for monitoring large distributed systems. Mahout is a scalable machine learning library for Hadoop. Cassandra is scalable multi-master database with no single points of failure. Avro is a data serialization system. Oozie is a workflow scheduler system for managing Hadoop jobs. Flume is a distributed, service for collecting, analyzing and moving large amounts of data from applications to HDFS. Sqoop is a tool that allows transferring bulk data between Hadoop and structured datastores. Key processes of Hadoop include NameNode, Secondary NameNode, JobTracker, TaskTracker and DataNode. NameNode keeps the directory tree of all files in the file system, and tracks where across the cluster the file data is kept. Secondary NameNode creates checkpoints of the namespace. JobTracker distributes MapReduce tasks to specific nodes in the cluster. TaskTracker accepts Map, Reduce and Shuffle tasks from the JobTracker. DataNode stores data in an HDFS file system. Hadoop scheduler is a pluggable component that makes it open to support different scheduling algorithms. The default scheduler in Hadoop is FIFO (first in, first out). In addition to this, two advanced schedulers are also available - the Fair Scheduler and the Capacity Scheduler, developed at Yahoo. Fair Scheduler assigns resources to jobs such that each job gets an equal share of the available resources on average over time. In Capacity Scheduler, you define a number of named queues each with a configurable number of map and reduce slots and each queue is also assigned a guaranteed capacity.

Review Questions

1. What are the stages of a MapReduce job?
2. What are the functions of Hadoop NameNode and Secondary NameNode?
3. How does a Hadoop TaskTracker assign map and reduce slots?
4. What is the purpose of a TaskTracker heartbeat message?
5. What are the key components of YARN?
6. How does Fair Scheduler provide capacity guarantees?
7. What mechanism allows Capacity Scheduler queues to get their fair share?

Lab Exercises

1. In this exercise you will create a multi-node Hadoop cluster on a cloud. Follow the steps below:
   - Create and Amazon Web Services account.
   - From Amazon EC2 console launch two *m1.small* EC2 instances.
   - When the instances start running, note the public DNS addresses of the instances.
   - Connect to the instances using SSH.
   - Run the commands given in Box 4.1 to install Java on each instance.
   - Run the commands given in Box 4.1 to install Hadoop on each instance.
   - Configure Hadoop. Use the templates for core-site.xml, hdfs-site.xml, mapred-site.xml and master and slave files shown in Boxes 4.3 - 4.6.
   - Start the Hadoop cluster using the commands shown in Box 4.7.
   - In a browser open the Hadoop cluster status pages:
     public-DNS-of-hadoop-master:50070
     public-DNS-of-hadoop-master:50030

2. In this exercise you will run a MapReduce job on a Hadoop cluster. Follow the steps below:
   - Follow the steps in Exercise-1 to create a Hadoop cluster.
   - Copy some text files to the Hadoop master instance. Use scp or copy or wget to download files. Copy the text files in a single folder named 'data'.
   - Copy the files from the Hadoop master node local filesystem to HDFS:
     bin/hadoop dfs -copyFromLocal data/ input
   - Run a word count MapReduce job as follows:
     bin/hadoop jar hadoop-examples-*.jar wordcount -D mapred.reduce.tasks=16 input output
   - View the output as follows:
     bin/hadoop dfs -cat output/part-00000

3. In this exercise you will configure Fair Scheduler for Hadoop and run MapReduce jobs.
   - Follow the steps in Exercise-1 to create a Hadoop cluster.
   - On both the master and slave nodes of the Hadoop cluster, edit the mapred-site.xml and fair-scheduler.xml files. Use the templates given in Boxes 9.2 and 9.3.
   - Create three users on the Hadoop master as follows:
     sudo useradd user1
     sudo useradd user2
     sudo useradd user3
   - Generate some random data using the Hadoop RandomWriter program for each user as follows:
     sudo -u user1 bin/hadoop jar hadoop-examples-1.0.4.jar randomwriter
     -D test.randomwrite.bytes_per_map=1000000 random-data
   - Submit three different MapReduce jobs, one from each user as follows:
     sudo -u user2 bin/hadoop jar hadoop-examples-1.0.4.jar sort
     -D mapred.job.queue.name=queueA random-data sort-output2
     sudo -u user1 bin/hadoop jar hadoop-examples-1.0.4.jar wordcount
     -D mapred.job.queue.name=queueA -D mapred.reduce.tasks=16 random-data word-count-output2
     sudo -u user3 bin/hadoop jar invertedindex.jar pkg.InvertedIndex
     -D mapred.job.queue.name=queueA random-data inverted-index-output2
   - View the progress of jobs on the Hadoop MapReduce scheduler page:
     public-DNS-of-hadoop-master:50030/scheduler

4. In this exercise you will configure Capacity Scheduler for Hadoop and run MapReduce jobs.
   - Follow the steps in Exercise-1 to create a Hadoop cluster.
   - On both the master and slave nodes of the Hadoop cluster, edit the mapred-

site.xml and capacity-scheduler.xml files. Use the templates given in Boxes 9.4 and 9.5.

- Generate some random data using the Hadoop RandomWriter program for each user as follows:
  bin/hadoop jar hadoop-examples-1.0.4.jar randomwriter
  -D test.randomwrite.bytes_per_map=1000000 random-data

- Submit three different MapReduce jobs to the capacity scheduler queues as follows:
  bin/hadoop jar hadoop-examples-1.0.4.jar wordcount -D
  mapred.job.queue.name=queueA -D mapred.reduce.tasks=16 random-data wordcount-output
  bin/hadoop jar hadoop-examples-1.0.4.jar sort -D
  mapred.job.queue.name=queueB random-data sort-output
  bin/hadoop jar invertedindex.jar pkg.InvertedIndex -D
  mapred.job.queue.name=queueC random-data inverted-index-output

- View the progress of jobs on the Hadoop MapReduce scheduler page:
  public-DNS-of-hadoop-master:50030/scheduler

Part II

DEVELOPING FOR CLOUD

5 — Cloud Application Design

This Chapter Covers

- Cloud Application Design Considerations
- Cloud Application Reference Architectures
- Design Methodologies
- Data Storage
- Data Analytics
- Deployment & Management

5.1 Introduction

Web applications have evolved significantly in the past decade and are now quite dynamic in nature allowing users to interact and collaborate, include user generated content such as comments and discussions, integrate social networks and multimodal content such as text, images, audio, video, presentations, etc., in various formats. Due to this dynamic nature of modern web applications, the traffic patterns for such applications are becoming more and more unpredictable. Some applications experience seasonal variations in their workloads, e.g., e-Commerce websites see elevated user traffic in holiday seasons. Traditional approaches that were based on the 'one size fits all' paradigm no longer work for modern applications. In this chapter you will learn about the design considerations for cloud applications, the reference architectures for various types of applications and design methodologies such as SOA, CCM and MVC.

5.2 Design Considerations for Cloud Applications

In this section we will look at the important design considerations for developing applications that can leverage the benefits of cloud computing.

5.2.1 Scalability

Scalability is an important factor that drives the application designers to move to cloud computing environments. Building applications that can serve millions of users without taking a hit on their performance has always been challenging. With the growth of cloud computing application designers can provision adequate resources to meet their workload levels. However, simply provisioning more and more resources may not bring performance gains if the applications are not designed to scale well. There are several design considerations that the developers need to keep in mind. Traditional approaches were based on either over-provisioning of resources to handle the peak workload levels expected or provisioning based on average workload levels. Both approaches have their disadvantages. While the over-provisioning approach leads to underutilization of resources and increased costs, the approach based on average workload levels can lead to traffic overloads, slow response times, low throughputs and hence loss of opportunity to serve the customers. In order to leverage the benefits of cloud computing such as dynamic scaling, the following design considerations must be kept in mind:

- **Loose coupling of components:** Traditional application design methodologies with tightly coupled application components, limit the scalability. Tightly coupled components use procedure based tight coupling and hard-wired links which make it difficult to scale application components independently. By designing loosely coupled components, it is possible to scale each component independently.
- **Asynchronous communication:** In traditional application designs, it is a common practice to process a request and return immediately. This limits the scalability of the application. By allowing asynchronous communication between components, it is possible to add capacity by adding additional servers when the application load increases.
- **Stateless design:** Stateless designs that store state outside of the components in a separate database allow scaling the application components independently.

- **Database choice and design:** Choice of the database and the design of data storage schemes affect the application scalability. Decisions such as whether to choose a traditional relational database (SQL approach) with strict schemas or a schema-less database (No-SQL approach) should be made after careful analysis of the application's data storage and analysis requirements.

5.2.2 Reliability & Availability

Reliability of a system is defined as the probability that a system will perform the intended functions under stated conditions for a specified amount of time. Availability is the probability that a system will perform a specified function under given conditions at a prescribed time. The important considerations to be kept in mind while developing highly reliable and available applications are:

- **No single point of failure:** Traditional application design approaches which have single points of failure such as a single database server or a single application server have the risk of complete breakdowns in case the of failure of the critical resource. To high achieve reliability and availability, having a redundant resource or an automated fallback resource is important.
- **Trigger automated actions on failures:** Traditional application design approaches handled failures by giving exceptions. By using failures and triggers for automated actions it is possible to improve the application reliability and availability. For example, if an application server experiences high CPU usage and is a unable to server new requests, a new application server is automatically launched.
- **Graceful degradation:** Applications should be designed to gracefully degrade in the event of outages of some parts or components of the application. Graceful degradation means that if some component of the application becomes unavailable the application as a whole would still be available and continue to serve the users, though, with limited functionality. For example, in an e-Commerce application, if a component that manages a certain category of products becomes unavailable, the users should still be able to view products from other categories.
- **Logging:** Logging all events in all the application components can help in detecting bottlenecks and failures so that necessary design/deployment changes can be made to improve application reliability and availability.
- **Replication:** All application data should be replicated. Replication is used to create and maintain multiple copies of the data in the cloud. In the event of data loss at the primary location, organizations can continue to operate their applications from secondary data sources. In Chapter 2 we discussed replication approaches such as array-based replication, network-based replication, host-based replication.

5.2.3 Security

Security is an important design consideration for cloud applications given the outsourced nature of cloud computing environments. In domains such as healthcare there are several government laws that require the applications to ensure security of health information of patients. The security aspects for cloud applications are described in detail in Chapter 12. Key security considerations for cloud computing environments include:

- Securing data at rest
- Securing data in motion
- Authentication
- Authorization
- Identity and access management
- Key management
- Data integrity
- Auditing

5.2.4 Maintenance & Upgradation

To achieve a rapid time-to-market, businesses typically launch their applications with a core set of features ready and then incrementally add new features as and when they are complete. Businesses may need to adapt their applications based on the feedback from the users. In such scenarios, it is important to design applications with low maintenance and upgradation costs. Design decisions such as loosely coupled components help in reducing the application maintenance and upgradation time. In applications with loosely coupled components, changes can be made to a component without affecting other components. Moreover, components can be tested individually. Other decisions such as logging and triggering automated actions also help in lowering the maintenance costs.

5.2.5 Performance

Applications should be designed while keeping the performance requirements in mind. Performance requirements depend on the type of the application. For example applications which experience high database read-intensive workloads, can benefit from read-replication or caching approaches. There are various metrics that are used to evaluate the application performance, such as response time, throughput, etc. In Chapter 11, the performance evaluation metrics and approaches are described in detail. For a good user experience a response time less than 4 seconds is generally acceptable. However certain applications may have even more strict requirements.

5.3 Reference Architectures for Cloud Applications

Multi-tier cloud applications can have various deployment architecture alternatives. Choosing the right deployment architecture is important to ensure that the application meets the specified performance requirements. In this chapter you will learn about the reference architectures for different classes of multi- tier cloud applications.

Figure 5.1 shows a typical deployment architecture for e-Commerce, Business-to-Business, Banking and Financial applications. The various tiers in this deployment include:

- **Load Balancing Tier:** The first tier is the load balancing tier. Load balancing tier consists of one or more load balancers. It is recommended to have at least two load balancer instances to avoid the single point of failure. Whenever possible, it is also recommended to provision the load balancer instances in separate availability zones of the cloud service provider to improve reliability

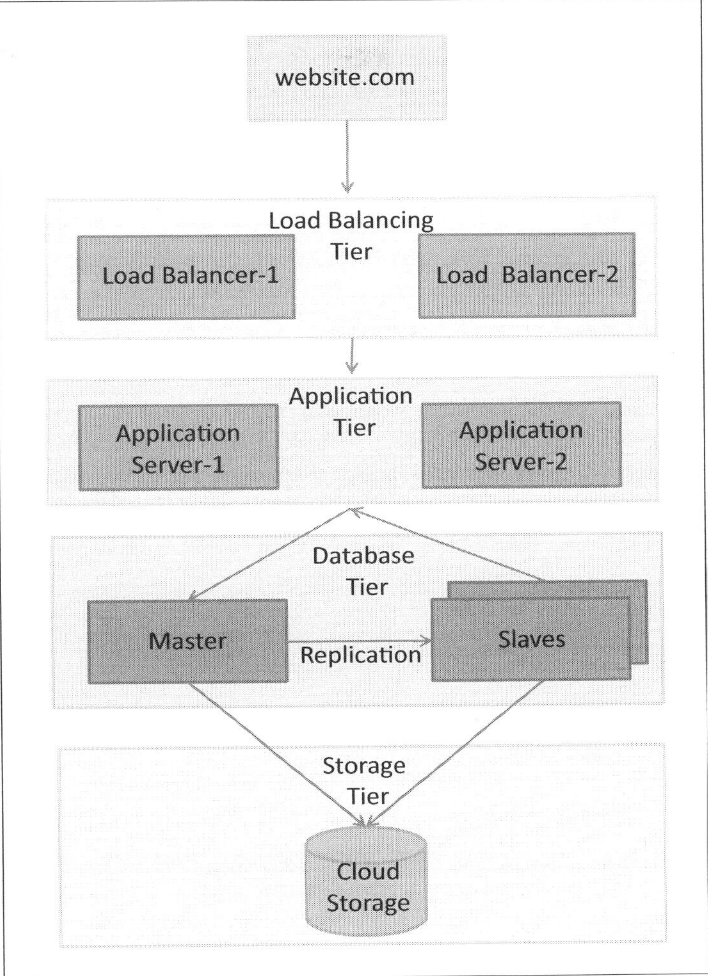

Figure 5.1: Typical deployment architecture for e-Commerce, Business-to-Business, Banking and Financial applications.

and availability.

- **Application Tier:** The second tier is the application tier that consists of one or more application servers. For this tier, it is recommended to configure auto scaling. Auto scaling can be triggered when the recorded values for any of the specified metrics such as CPU usage, memory usage, etc. goes above defined thresholds. The minimum and maximum size of the application server auto scaling groups can be configured. It is recommended to have at least two application servers running at all times to avoid a single point of failure. When an auto scaling event occurs, a new instance is launched. It may take a few minutes for the instance to get fully operational. Within this time period if the workload increases rapidly, the existing application server instances may fail to serve all requests. Therefore, it is recommended to set the threshold values for the auto scaling metrics conservatively to take care of the time lag involved in the new instances becoming operational. In the auto scaling options, the threshold for scaling down are also specified.

- **Database Tier:** The third tier is the database tier which includes a master database instance and multiple slave instances. The master node serves all the write requests and the read requests are served from the slave nodes. This improves the throughput for the database tier since most applications have a higher number of read requests than write requests. Multiple slave nodes also serve as a backup for the master node. In the event of failure of the master node, one of the slave nodes can be automatically configured to become the master. For both master and slave nodes, it is highly recommended to use a disk subsystem for storage and not the instance-attached store. This is important to ensure reliability and availability because in the event of failures if the instance-attached storage is used for the database, all data will be lost. Whereas, in the case of separate disk volumes, it is possible to restore the database. Regular snapshots of the database are recommended. The frequency of snapshots may be configured to be daily or hourly. It is recommended to store snapshots in distributed persistent cloud storage solutions (such as Amazon S3).

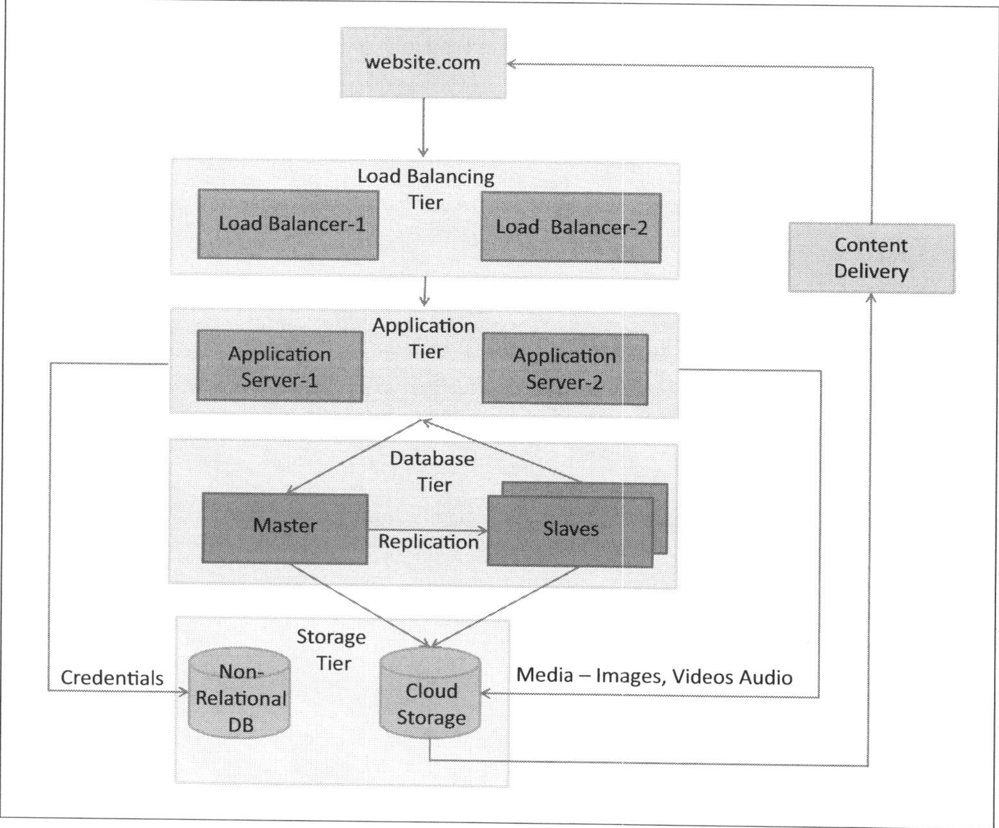

Figure 5.2: Typical deployment architecture for content delivery applications such as online photo albums, video webcasting, etc.

Figure 5.2 shows a typical deployment architecture for content delivery applications such as online photo albums, video webcasting, etc. Both relational and non-relational data stores are shown in this deployment. A content delivery network (CDN) which consists of a global network of edge locations is used for media delivery. CDN is used to speed up the delivery of static content such as images and videos.

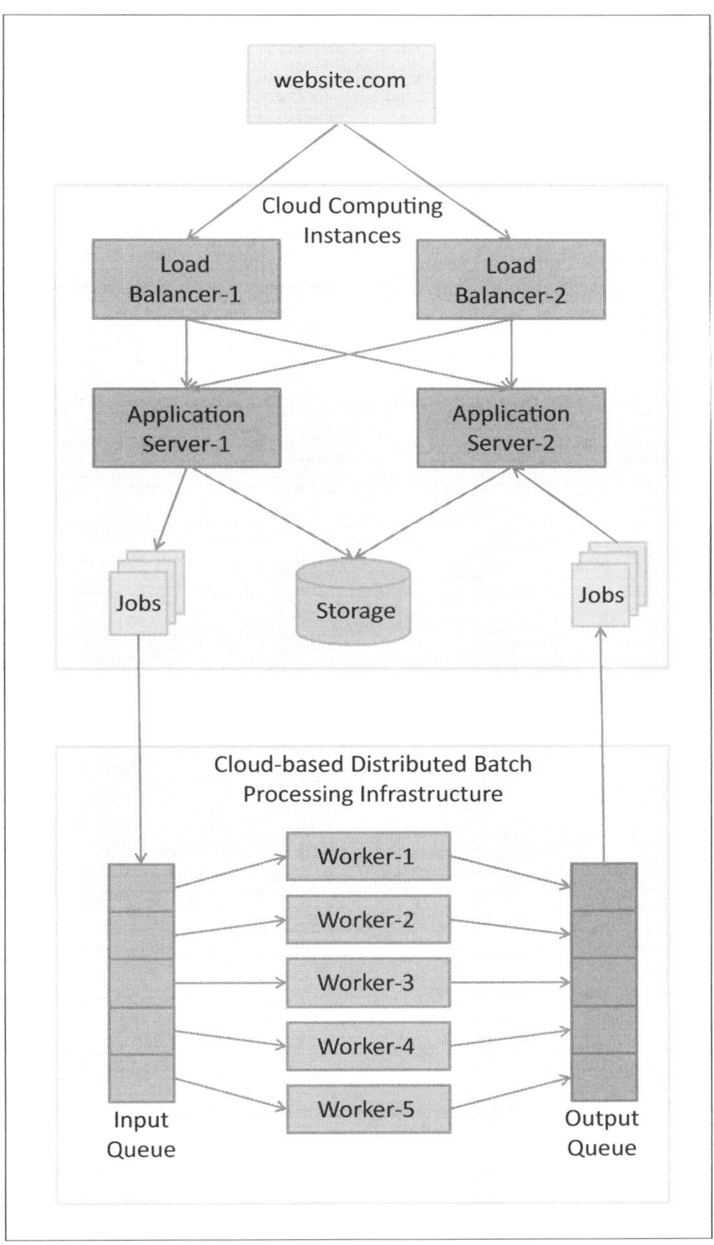

Figure 5.3: Typical deployment architecture for compute intensive applications such as Data Analytics, Media Transcoding, etc.

Figure 5.3 shows a typical deployment architecture for compute intensive applications such as Data Analytics, Media Transcoding, etc. The figure shows web, application, storage, computing/analytics and database tiers. The analytics tier consists of cloud-based distributed batch processing frameworks such as Hadoop which are suitable for analyzing big data. Data analysis jobs (such as MapReduce) jobs are submitted to the analytics tier from the application servers. The jobs are queued for execution and upon completion the analyzed data is presented from the application servers.

Java	PHP	.NET	Python
Apache Tomcat	Zend Server	Internet Information Services (IIS) web server	Django
Oracle WebLogic	Quercus	Windows Server AppFabric	Gunicorn
GlassFish			mod_python
IBM WebSphere			mod_wsgi
JBoss			Paste
ColdFusion			Tornado
Apache Geronimo			Zope
Orion			

Table 5.1: Examples of popular cloud deployment management tools

5.4 Cloud Application Design Methodologies

In this section you will learn about the design methodologies for cloud applications.

5.4.1 Service Oriented Architecture

Service Oriented Architecture (SOA) is a well established architectural approach for designing and developing applications in the form services that can be shared and reused. SOA is a collection of discrete software modules or services that form a part of an application and collectively provide the functionality of an application. SOA services are developed as loosely coupled modules with no hard-wired calls embedded in the services. The services communicate with each other by passing messages. Services are described using the Web Services Description Language (WSDL). WSDL is an XML-based web services description language that is used to create service descriptions containing information on the functions performed by a service and the inputs and outputs of the service.

Figure 5.4 shows the concepts of WSDL 2.0. A WSDL 2.0 description contains:

- **Service:** Service describes a discrete system function that is exposed as a web service.
- **Endpoint:** Endpoint is the address of the web service.
- **Binding:** Binding specifies the interface and transport protocol.

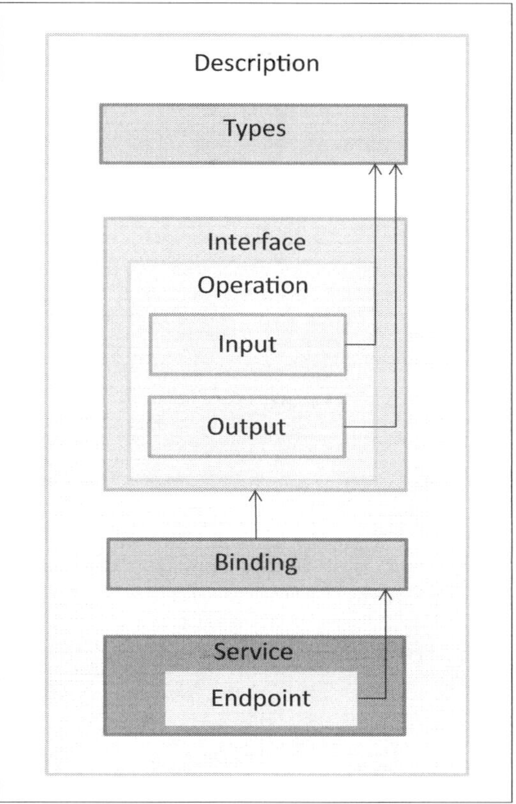

Figure 5.4: WSDL concepts for representation of web services.

- **Interface:** Interface defines a web service and the operations that can be performed by the service and the input and outputs.
- **Operation:** Operation defines how the message is decoded and the actions that can be performed.
- **Types:** Types describe the data.

SOA services communicate using the Simple Object Oriented Protocol (SOAP). SOAP is a protocol that allows exchange of structured information between web services. WSDL in combination with SOAP is used to provide web services over the internet.
SOA allows reuse of services for multiple applications. Since each service is designed to perform a small function (such as display the balance in a bank account, show a list of recent transactions, etc.) developers can orchestrate existing SOA services in an ad-hoc fashion to create new application without the need for re-implementing the services.
Figure 5.5 shows the layers of SOA including:

- **Business Systems:** This layer consists of custom built applications and legacy systems such as Enterprise Resource Planning (ERP), Customer Relationship Management (CRM), Supply Chain Management (SCM), etc.
- **Service Components:** The service components allow the layers above to interact with the business systems. The service components are responsible for

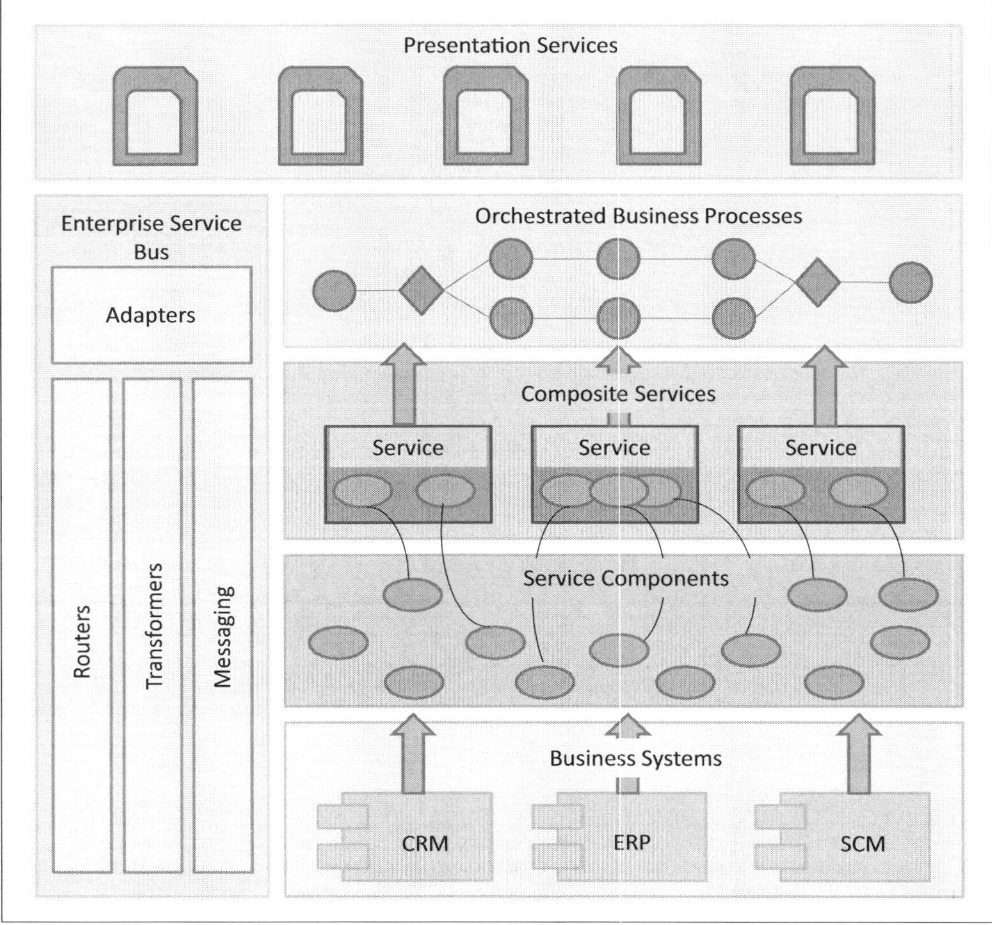

Figure 5.5: Layers of service oriented architecture

realizing the functionality of the services exposed.

- **Composite Services:** These are coarse-grained services which are composed of two or more service components. Composite services can be used to create enterprise scale components or business-unit specific components.
- **Orchestrated Business Processes:** Composite services can be orchestrated to create higher level business processes. In this layers the compositions and orchestrations of the composite services are defined to create business processes.
- **Presentation Services:** This is the topmost layer that includes user interfaces that exposes the services and the orchestrated business processes to the users.
- **Enterprise Service Bus:** This layer integrates the services through adapters, routing, transformation and messaging mechanisms.

IBM SOA Foundation [77] is based on an SOA reference architecture that defines the comprehensive IT services required to support SOA at the model, assemble, deploy, manage and governance stages of the SOA life cycle. Microsoft's Windows Communication Foundation (WCF) [78] is a runtime and a set of APIs for building connected, service-oriented applications. Oracle SOA Suite [79] is a comprehensive, pluggable software suite to build, deploy and manage service-oriented architectures. Software-based SOA requires deploying and maintaining software and infrastructure. Salesforce SOA [80] delivers SOA as a service, run on Salesforce.com's on-demand platform, and allows developers to reuse software components. Limitation of traditional SOA is that it uses a messaging layer above HTTP by using SOAP which imposes prohibitive constraints for web application developers and requires greater implementation effort.

5.4.2 Cloud Component Model

Cloud Component Model [75] is an application design methodology that provides a flexible way of creating cloud applications in a rapid, convenient and platform independent manner, unlike existing approaches that use architecture-specific and domain-specific templates. CCM is an architectural approach for cloud applications that is not tied to any specific programming language or cloud platform. Cloud applications designed with CCM approach can have innovative hybrid deployments in which different components of an application can be deployed on cloud infrastructure and platforms of different cloud vendors. Applications designed using CCM have better portability and interoperability. CCM based applications have better scalability by decoupling application components and providing asynchronous communication mechanisms. CCM makes maintainability of cloud applications easier as the functionality of individual components of the application can be improved or upgraded independent of other components. CCM approach provides cost benefits for cloud applications as components can be carefully mapped to cloud resources. Cost benefits come by scaling cloud resources up (or scaling out) only for those components which require additional computing capacity.
Figure 5.6 shows the steps involved in CCM approach for application design including:

Component Design

In the first step, a Cloud Component Model is created for the application based on comprehensive analysis of the application's functions and building blocks. Cloud component model allows identifying the building blocks of a cloud application which are classified based on the functions performed and type of cloud resources required. Each building block performs a set of actions to produce the desired outputs for other components. Figure 5.6 (b) shows the architecture of a CCM component. Each component takes specific inputs, performs a pre-defined set of actions and produces the desired outputs. Components offer their functions as services through a functional interface which can be used by other components. Components report their performance to a performance database through a performance interface. Components have number of resources such as web pages, images, documents, database tables, etc. Auto-scaling performance constraints and conditions can be specified for each component. Component-based approach is applicable to both web-based applications and mobile applications. Figure 5.7 shows a CCM component map for an e-Commerce application.

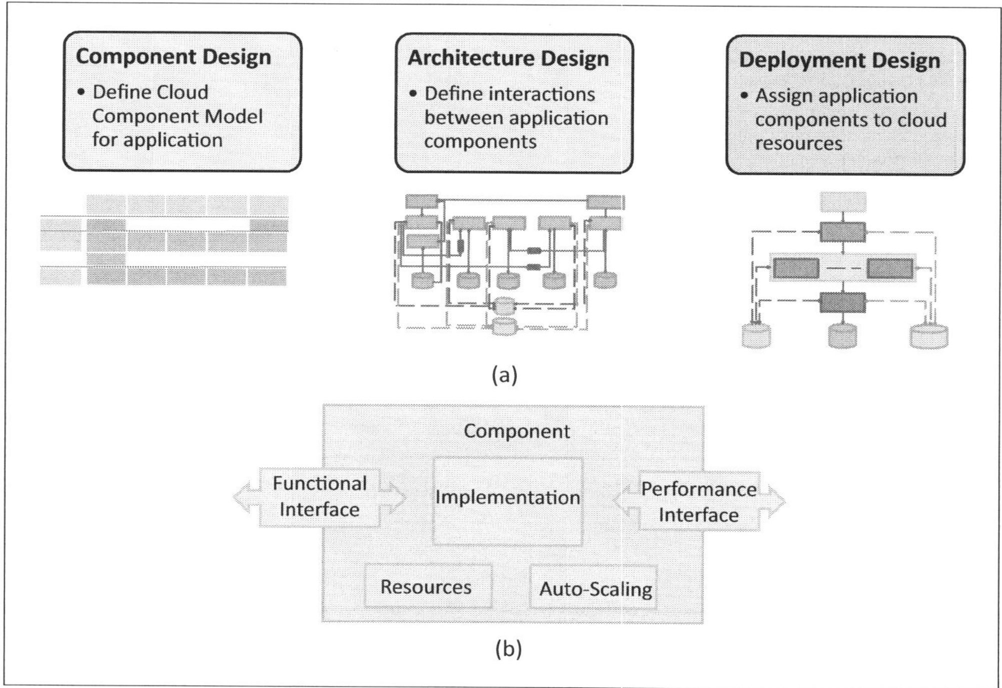

Figure 5.6: (a) Steps involved in application design using Cloud component model methodology, (b) Architecture of a CCM component.

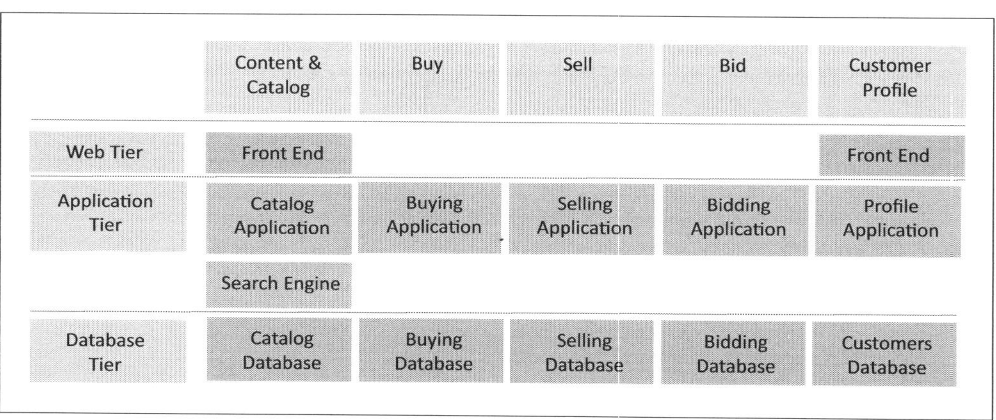

Figure 5.7: Component design step. The figure shows CCM map for an e-Commerce application.

Architecture Design

The second step in the CCM design methodology is architecture design. In this step, interactions between the application components are defined as shown in Figure 5.8. CCM components have the following characteristics:

- **Loose Coupling:** Components in the Cloud Component Model are loosely coupled. Instead of hard-wiring the links, the components interface through clearly defined functional and service boundaries. Links between the components are established and broken as they respond to service requests. Loose coupling of components relies on the use of REST communication protocol that allows components developed in different programming languages to communicate with each other.

- **Asynchronous Communication:** Tightly coupled components use procedure based tight coupling. Whereas, loosely coupled components communicate asynchronously through message based communication. Loose coupling isolates various components of the application so that each component interacts asynchronously with the others, treating other components as black boxes. In traditional application designs, it is a common practice to process a request and return immediately. This limits the scalability of the application. By allowing asynchronous communication between components, it is possible to add capacity by adding additional servers when the application load increases. Asynchronous communication is made possible by using messaging queues. The benefit of messaging queues is that the overall application can continue to perform even though individual components may go offline temporarily. If a component becomes temporarily unavailable, the messages are buffered and processed when the component becomes available again.
- **Stateless Design:** Components in the Cloud Component Model are stateless. By storing session state outside of the component (e.g. in a database), stateless component design enables distribution and horizontal scaling. In distributed computing (with horizontal scaling of components), successive requests to a component may be serviced by different servers. Therefore the state is maintained outside the components in a database.

Deployment Design

The third step in CCM design methodology is deployment design. In this step, application components are mapped to specific cloud resources such as web servers, application servers, database servers, etc. Since the application components are designed to be loosely coupled and stateless with asynchronous communication, components can be deployed independently of each other. Moreover, multiple clouds can be used for application deployment. This approach makes it easy to migrate application components from one cloud to the other. With this flexibility in application design and deployment, the application developers can ensure that the applications meet the performance and cost requirements with changing contexts. Figure 5.9 shows the deployment design for an e-Commerce application.

CCM and SOA share guiding principles such as reuse, loose coupling, statelessness, etc. Figure 5.10 lists the similarities and differences between SOA and CCM. CCM uses REST over HTTP for messaging which is native to all programming languages and it is better suited for cloud-based applications that are accessed from browsers.

5.4.3 IaaS, PaaS and SaaS services for cloud applications

Cloud service providers such as Amazon [81], Google [82], Microsoft [83], etc. provide diverse infrastructure (IaaS), platform (PaaS) and software (SaaS) services that the developers

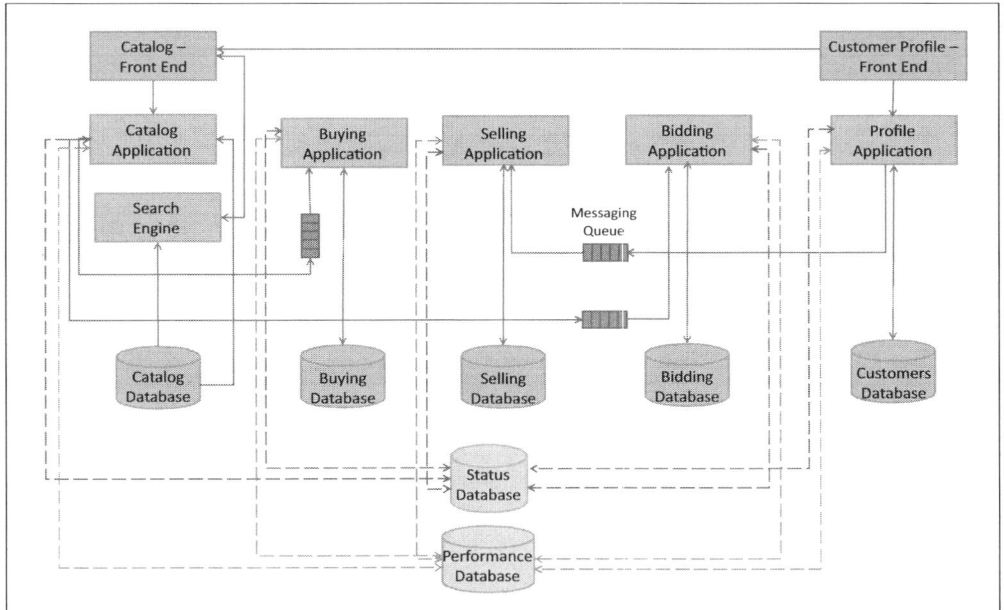

Figure 5.8: Architecture design step. The figure shows web interaction diagram for an e-Commerce application.

can use for developing and deploying applications in cloud computing environments. Cloud service providers make cloud resources available to the users with cloud APIs via a web-based interface. There are numerous cloud service providers with their own cloud APIs. For example, Salesforce PaaS (Force.com) allows developers to create applications using Apex (a proprietary programming language) and Visualforce (an XML-like syntax for building user interfaces). Similarly, applications designed for Google App Engine (GAE) [82] platform must implement GAE specific interfaces and have a GAE specific deployment descriptor. Amazon CloudFormation [84] allows developers to create, provision and manage cloud deployments using Amazon specific resources such as Amazon EC2, Amazon EBS, etc. Red Hat's open source PaaS, OpenShift [85], provides built-in support for a variety of programming languages (Ruby, Python, PHP, Java, etc.) and frameworks (Ruby on Rails, Django, etc.). CloudFoundry [86] is another open PaaS offering that supports a variety of clouds (Amazon Web Services, Rackspace, etc.), frameworks (Spring for Java, Scala, etc.) and application services (MySQL, MongoDB, etc.). Open PaaS offerings provide greater flexibility than vendor-specific PaaS offerings (such as GAE, Force.com, etc.) as they support more programming languages and frameworks and provide a greater choice of clouds for deployment, thus ending the vendor lock-in.

5.4.4 Model View Controller

Model View Controller (MVC) is a popular software design pattern for web applications.

The MVC pattern consists of three parts:

- **Model:** Model manages the data and the behavior of the applications. Model processes events sent by the controller. Model has no information about the views and

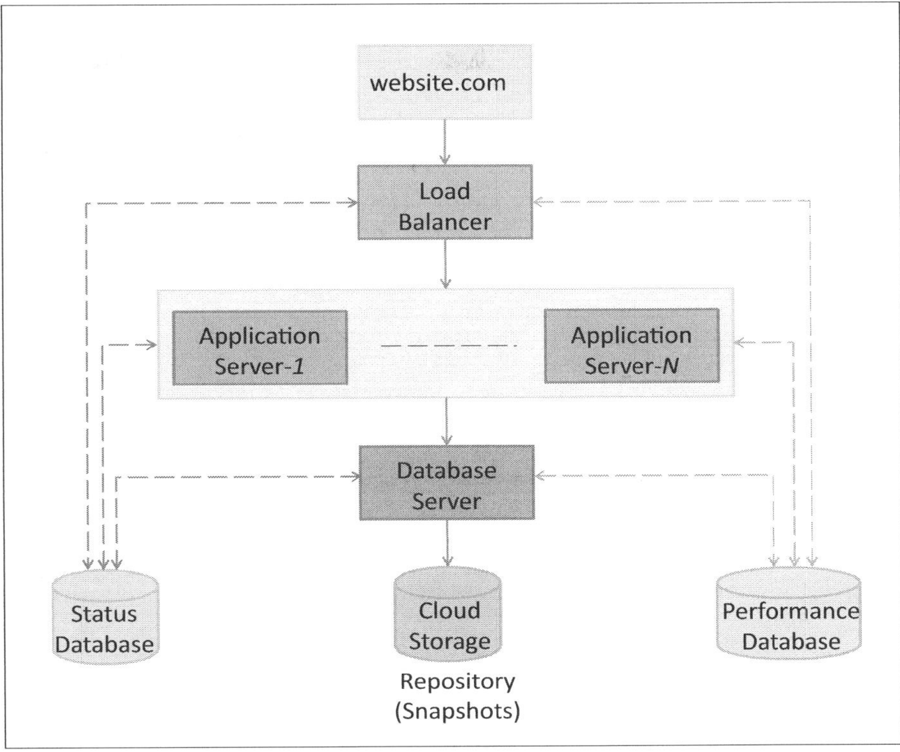

Figure 5.9: Deployment design step. The figure shows multi-tier cloud deployment for an e-Commerce application.

controllers. Model responds to the requests for information about its state (from the view) and responds to the instructions to change state (from controller).

- **View:** View prepares the interface which is shown to the user. Users interact with the application through views. Views present the information that the model or controller tell the view to present to the user and also handle user requests and sends them to the controller.
- **Controller:** Controller glues the model to the view. Controller processes user requests and updates the model when the user manipulates the view. Controller also updates the view when the model changes.

MVC separates the application logic, the data, and the user interface. The benefit of using MVC is that improves the maintainability of the application and allows reuse of code. The applications built with MVC architecture can be updated easily due to the separation of the model from the view. In MVC, both the view and controller depend on the model, however, the model does not depend on either. This allows the model to be developed and tested independently. Similarly the separation between the view and the controller is also well defined for web applications.

In traditional applications the view is generally tightly coupled with the model. Since views are likely to change more frequently than the model, this tight coupling requires re-wiring the links. With MVC, the views can be changed without affecting the model.

Similarities

	SOA	CCM
Standardization & Re-use	SOA advocates principles of reuse and well defined relationship between service provider and service consumer.	CCM is based on reusable components which can be used by multiple cloud applications.
Loose coupling	SOA is based on loosely coupled services that minimize dependencies.	CCM is based on loosely coupled components that communicate asynchronously
Statelessness	SOA services minimize resource consumption by deferring the management of state information.	CCM components are stateless. State is stored outside of the components.

Differences

	SOA	CCM
End points	SOA services have small and well-defined set of endpoints through which many types of data can pass.	CCM components have very large number of endpoints. There is an endpoint for each resource in a component, identified by a URI.
Messaging	SOA uses a messaging layer above HTTP by using SOAP which provide prohibitive constraints to developers.	CCM components use HTTP and REST for messaging.
Security	Uses WS-Security , SAML and other standards for security	CCM components use HTTPS for security.
Interfacing	SOA uses XML for interfacing.	CCM allows resources in components represent different formats for interfacing (HTML, XML, JSON, etc.).
Consumption	Consuming traditional SOA services in a browser is cumbersome.	CCM components and the underlying component resources are exposed as XML, JSON (and other formats) over HTTP or REST, thus easy to consume in the browser.

Figure 5.10: (a) Similarities between SOA and CCM, (b) Differences between SOA and CCM.

5.4.5 RESTful Web Services

Representational State Transfer (REST) [32] is a set of architectural principles by which you can design web services and web APIs that focus on a system's resources and how

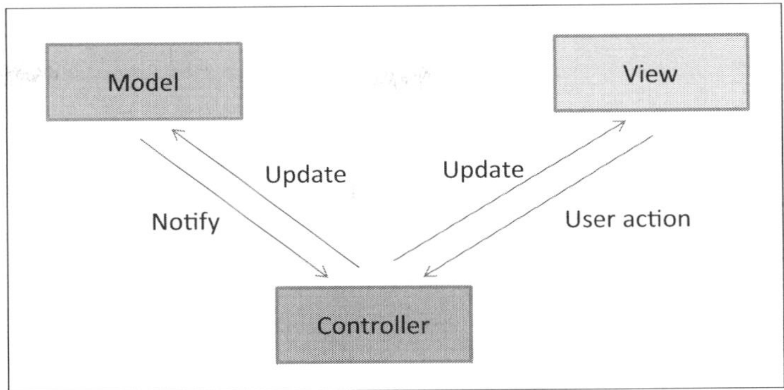

Figure 5.11: Model View Controller

resource states are addressed and transferred. The REST architectural constraints apply to the components, connectors, and data elements, within a distributed hypermedia system. The REST architectural constraints are as follows:

- **Client-Server**: The principle behind the client-server constraint is the separation of concerns. For example, clients should not be concerned with the storage of data which is a concern of the server. Similarly, the server should not be concerned about the user interface, which is a concern of the client. Separation allows client and server to be independently developed and updated.
- **Stateless**: Each request from client to server must contain all of the information necessary to understand the request, and cannot take advantage of any stored context on the server. The session state is kept entirely on the client.
- **Cacheable**: Cache constraint requires that the data within a response to a request be implicitly or explicitly labeled as cacheable or non-cacheable. If a response is cacheable, then a client cache is given the right to reuse that response data for later, equivalent requests. Caching can partially or completely eliminate some interactions and improve efficiency and scalability.
- **Layered System**: Layered system constraint constrains the behavior of components such that each component cannot see beyond the immediate layer with which they are interacting. For example, a client cannot tell whether it is connected directly to the end server, or to an intermediary along the way. System scalability can be improved by allowing intermediaries to respond to requests instead of the end server, without the client having to do anything different.
- **Uniform Interface**: Uniform Interface constraint requires that the method of communication between a client and a server must be uniform. Resources are identified in the requests (by URIs in web based systems) and are themselves separate from the representations of the resources that are returned to the client. When a client holds a representation of a resource it has all the information required to update or delete the resource (provided the client has required permissions). Each message includes enough information to describe how to process the message.
- **Code on demand**: Servers can provide executable code or scripts for clients to execute in their context. This constraint is the only one that is optional.

A RESTful web service is a web API implemented using HTTP and REST principles. RESTful web service is a collection of resources which are represented by URIs. RESTful web API has a base URI (e.g. http://example.com/api/tasks/). The clients send requests to these URIs using the methods defined by the HTTP protocol (e.g., GET, PUT, POST, or DELETE). A RESTful web service can support various Internet media types (JSON being the most popular media type for RESTful web services).

HTTP Method	Resource Type	Action	Example
GET	Collection URI	List all the resources in a collection	http://example.com/api/tasks/ (list all tasks)
GET	Element URI	Get information about a resource	http://example.com/api/tasks/1/ (get information on task-1)
POST	Collection URI	Create a new resource	http://example.com/api/tasks/ (create a new task from data provided in the request)
POST	Element URI	Generally not used	
PUT	Collection URI	Replace the entire collection with another collection	http://example.com/api/tasks/ (replace entire collection with data provided in the request)
PUT	Element URI	Update a resource	http://example.com/api/tasks/1/ (update task-1 with data provided in the request)
DELETE	Collection URI	Delete the entire collection	http://example.com/api/tasks/ (delete all tasks)
DELETE	Element URI	Delete a resource	http://example.com/api/tasks/1/ (delete task-1)

Table 5.2: HTTP request methods and actions

5.5 Data Storage Approaches

In this section you will learn about two broad categories of approaches for databases and their pros and cons.

5.5.1 Relational (SQL) Approach

A relational database is database that conforms to the relational model that was popularized by Edgar Codd in 1970 [76]. Table 5.3 summarizes the 12 rules that Codd introduced for relational databases. A relational database has a collection of relations (or tables). A relation is a set of tuples (or rows). Each relation has a fixed schema that defines the set of attributes (or columns in a table) and the constraints on the attributes. Each tuple in a relation has the

Rule	Description
Information rule	All information in a relational database is represented explicitly at the logical level and in exactly one way - by values in tables.
Guaranteed access rule	All data must be accessible. Every individual scalar value in a relational database is guaranteed to be logically accessible by specifying the table name, primary key value, and column name.
Systematic treatment of null values	DBMS must allow null values for all fields. Null values are supported in fully relational DBMS for representing missing information and inapplicable information in a systematic way.
Dynamic online catalog based on relational model	The system must support an online, relational catalog to authorized users using the same relational language.
Comprehensive sub-language rule	A relational system must support at least one language whose statements are expressible, by a well-defined syntax, as character strings, that is comprehensive in supporting all of the following items: Data Definition, View Definition, Data manipulation, Integrity Constraints, Authorization, Transaction boundaries.
View updating rule	All views that are theoretically updatable are also updatable by the system.
High level insert, update, delete	The system must support set-at-a-time insert, update, and delete operators. This means that the capability of handling a base relation or a derived relation as a single operand applies not only to the retrieval of data but also to the insertion, update, and deletion of data.
Physical data independence	Any changes made in either storage representations or access methods, should not require the application to be changed.
Logical data independence	Changes to the logical level (tables, columns, rows, and so on) must not require a change to an application based on the structure.
Integrity independence	Integrity constraints specific to a particular relational database must be definable in the relational data sub-language and storable in the catalog, not in the application programs.
Distribution independence	A relational DBMS has distribution dependence. That is, existing applications should continue to operate successfully, when a distributed version of the DBMS is first introduced and when existing distributed data are redistributed around the system.
Non-subversion rule	If a relational system has a low-level (single record at a time) language, that low level cannot be used to subvert or bypass the integrity rules and constraints expressed in the higher-level relational language (multiple records at a time).

Table 5.3: Codd's rules for Relational Databases [76]

same attributes (columns). The tuples in a relation can have any order and the relation is not sensitive to the ordering of the tuples. Each attribute has a domain, which is the set of possible values for the attribute. Relations can be modified using insert, update and delete operations. Every relation has a primary key that uniquely identifies each tuple in the relation. An attribute can be made a primary key if it does not have repeated values in different tuples. That is, no two tuples can have the same value for the primary key attribute.

Pros	Cons
Well defined consistent model. An application that runs on one relational database (such as MySQL) can be easily changed to run on other relational databases (eg. Microsoft SQL server). The underlying model remains unchanged.	Performance is the major constraint for relational databases. The performance depends on the number of relations and the size of the relations. Scaling out relational database deployments is difficult.
Provide ACID guarantees.	Limited support for complex data structures. Eg. If the data is naturally organized in a hierarchical manner and stored as such, the hierarchical approach can allow quick analysis of data.
Relational integrity maintained through entity and referential integrity constraints.	A complete knowledge of the database structure is required to create ad hoc queries.
Well suited for Online Transaction Processing (OLTP) applications.	Most relation database systems are expensive.
Sound theoretical foundation (based on relational model) which has been tried and tested for several years. Stable and standardized databases available.	Some relational databases have limits on the size of the fields.
The database design and normalization steps are well defined and the underlying structure is well understood.	Integrating data from multiple relational database systems can be cumbersome.

Table 5.4: Pros and Cons of relational databases

A relational database has various constraints described as follows:

- **Domain Constraint:** Domain constraints restrict the domain of each attribute or the set of possible values for the attribute. Domain constraints specify that each in tuple, the value of each attribute must be a value from the domain of the attribute.
- **Entity Integrity Constraint:** Entity integrity constraint states that no primary key value can be null. Since primary key is used to uniquely identify each tuple in a relation, having null value for a primary key value will make it impossible to identify tuples in the relation.
- **Referential Integrity Constraint:** Referential integrity constraints are required to maintain consistency among the tuples in two relations. Referential integrity requires

Relational Database
Oracle database
Microsoft SQL Server
DB2
SAP Sybase Adaptive Server Enterprise
SAP Sybase IQ
MySQL
PostgreSQL
Teradata
Informix
Ingres
Aster Data
Netezza
OpenLink Virtuoso
SQLite
Vertica

Table 5.5: Examples of popular relational databases

every value of one attribute of a relation to exist as a value of another attribute in another relation. In other words, tuples in a relation that refers to another relation must refer to tuples that exists in the other relation.

- **Foreign Key:** For cross-referencing between multiple relations foreign keys are used. Foreign key is a key in a relation that matches the primary key of another relation.

Relational databases support at least one comprehensive sub-language, the most popular being the Structured Query Language (SQL). Relational databases provide ACID guarantees that are a set of properties that guarantee that database transactions are processed reliably, described as follows:

- **Atomicity:** Atomicity property ensures that each transaction is either "all or nothing". In other words, an atomic transaction ensures that all parts of the transaction complete or the database state is left unchanged. Partially completed transactions in the event of system outages can lead to an invalid state. Atomicity ensures that the transaction is indivisible and is either committed or aborted.
- **Consistency:** Consistency property ensures that each transaction brings the database from one valid state to another. In other words, the data in a database always conforms to the defined schema and constraints.
- **Isolation:** Isolation property ensures that the database state obtained after a set of concurrent transactions is the same as would have been if the transactions were executed serially. This provides concurrency control, i.e. the results of incomplete transactions are not visible to other transactions. The transactions are isolated from each other until they finish.

- **Durability:** Durability property ensures that once a transaction is committed, the data remains as it is, i.e. it is not affected by system outages such as power loss. Durability guarantees that the database can keep track of changes and can recover from abnormal terminations.

Table 5.4 lists some pros and cons of relational databases and Table 5.5 lists some popular relational databases.

5.5.2 Non-Relational (No-SQL) Approach

Non-relational databases (or popularly called No-SQL databases) are becoming popular with the growth of cloud computing. Non-relational databases have better horizontal scaling capability and improved performance for big data at the cost of less rigorous consistency models. Unlike relational databases, non-relational databases do not provide ACID guarantees. Most non-relational databases offer "eventual" consistency, which means that given a sufficiently long period of time over which no updates are made, all updates can be expected to propagate eventually through the system and the replicas will be consistent. Some authors have referred to the term BASE (Basically Available, Soft state, Eventual consistency) guarantees for non-relational databases as opposed to ACID guarantees provided by relational databases. The driving force behind the non-relational databases is the need for databases that can achieve high scalability, fault tolerance and availability. These databases can be distributed on a large cluster of machines. Fault tolerance is provided by storing multiple replicas of data on different machines. For, example with a replication factor set equal to N for a non-relational database, each record has N replicas on different machines.

Non-relational databases are popular for applications in which the scale of data involved is massive, the data may not be structured and real-time performance is important as opposed to consistency. These systems are optimized for fast retrieval and appending operations on records. Unlike relational databases, the non-relational databases do not have a strict schema. The records can be in the form of key-value pairs or documents. Most non-relational databases are classified in terms of the data storage model or type of records that can be stored. The commonly used categories include:

- **Key-value store:** Key-value store databases are suited for applications that require storing unstructured data without a fixed schema. Most key-value stores have support for native programming language data types.
- **Document store:** Document store databases store semi-structured data in the form of documents which are encoded in different standards such as JSON, XML, BSON, YAML, etc. Semi-structured data means that the documents in a document store are similar to each other (similar fields, keys or attributes) but there are no strict requirements for a schema. Documents are organized in different ways in different solutions such as collections, buckets, tags, etc.
- **Graph store:** Graph stores are designed for storing data that has graph structure (nodes and edges). These solutions are suitable for applications that involve graph data such as social networks, transportation systems, etc.
- **Object store:** Object store solutions are designed for storing data in the form of objects defined in an object-oriented programming language.

Table 5.6 lists some pros and cons of non-relational databases and Table 5.7 lists some popular non-relational databases.

Pros	Cons
Easy to scale-out. Higher performance for massive scale data as compared to relational databases. Allows sharing of data across multiple servers.	Do not provide ACID guarantees, therefore less suitable for applications such as transaction processing that require strong consistency.
Most solutions are either open-source or cheaper as compared to relational databases.	No fixed schema. There is no common data storage model. Different solutions have different data storage models.
High availability and fault tolerance provided by data replication.	Limited support for aggregation (SUM, AVG, COUNT, GROUP BY) as compared to relational databases.
Support complex data structures and native programming objects.	Performance for complex joins is poor as compared to relational databases.
No fixed schema. Support unstructured data.	No well defined approach for database design, since different solutions have different data storage models.
Very fast retrieval of data. Suitable for real-time applications.	Lack of a consistent model can lead to solution lock-in, i.e., migrating from one solution to other may require significant remodeling of the application.
Most solutions provide support for MapReduce programming model for processing massive scale data.	

Table 5.6: Pros and Cons of non-relational databases

Summary

In this chapter you learned design considerations for cloud applications and cloud application design methodologies. Scalability is an important factor that drives the application designers to move to cloud computing environments. In order to leverage the benefits of cloud computing such as dynamic scaling, design considerations such as loose coupling of components, asynchronous communication, stateless design and database choice and design must be kept in mind. Reliability is another another design consideration for cloud applications. Reliability of a system is defined as the probability that a system will perform the intended functions under stated conditions for a specified amount of time. To make an application reliable, it should not have any single point of failure and should support automated triggering of actions on failures, graceful degradation, logging and replication. Security considerations for cloud applications include data security, authentication, authorization, identity & access management, key management, data integrity and auditing. Cloud applications must be designed with low maintenance and upgrade costs. Design decisions such as loosely coupled components help in reducing the application maintenance and upgradation time. Applications should be designed while keeping the performance requirements in mind. You learned about reference architecture for e-Commerce, Business-to-Business, Banking and Financial

Key-value	Document	Graph	Object
Apache Cassandra	BaseX	AllegroGraph	db4o
Amazon DynamoDB	ArangoDB	ArangoDB	GemStone/S
Google App Engine Datastore	Cassandra	Bigdata	JADE
BigTable	Clusterpoint	Bitsy	NeoDatis ODB
Project Voldemort	Couchbase	BrightstarDB	ObjectDB
OpenLink Virtuoso	CouchDB	DEX	Objectivity/DB
Berkeley DB	eXist	Filament	ObjectStore
Velocity	FleetDB	GraphBase	OpenLink Virtuoso
Freebase	Jackrabbit	Graphd	Versant Object Database
	Lotus Notes	Horton	Wakanda
	MarkLogic	HyperGraphDB	ZODB
	MongoDB	InfiniteGraph	
	OrientDB	InfoGrid	
	Redis	jCoreDB Graph	
		Neo4j	
		Oracle Spatial and Graph	
		OrientDB	
		OQGRAPH	
		VertexDB	

Table 5.7: List of popular non-relational databases

applications that comprises of load balancing, application, database and storage tiers. The reference architecture for content delivery applications such as online photo albums, video webcasting, etc., comprises of load balancing, application, database, storage and content delivery tiers. The reference architecture for compute intensive applications such as Data Analytics, Media Transcoding, etc. comprises of load balancing, application, storage and analytics tiers. You learned about design methodologies for cloud applications such as SOA, CCM and MVC. SOA is a collection of discrete software modules or services that form a part of an application and collectively provide the functionality of an application. Cloud Component Model is an application design methodology that provides a flexible way of creating cloud applications in a rapid, convenient and platform independent manner. MVC is a popular software design pattern for web applications that includes a Model, a View and a Controller. You also learned about the characteristics of relational and non-relational databases.

Review Questions

1. How can a cloud application be made scalable?
2. What are the design considerations to make a cloud applicable reliable?
3. What are the various layers of SOA?
4. What is the benefit of loose coupling in the CCM model?
5. What are the functions of model, view and controller in MVC model?
6. What is the difference between entity integrity and referential integrity constraint?
7. What are the benefits and limitations of non-relational databases over relational databases?
8. What is ACID guarantee?

Lab Exercises

1. In this exercise you will create a cloud-based photo gallery application. Use the architecture shown in Figure 8.2 as the baseline. Follow the steps below:
    - Create a Django application that uses the Django authentication system.
    - Create pages for viewing uploaded photos and uploading new photos.
    - Store the uploaded photos on a cloud storage.
    - In the upload new photo form, add an option to make the photo public.
    - Serve the public photos through a CDN (such as Amazon CloudFront).

2. In this exercise you will create a cloud-based employee records application. Use the architecture shown in Figure 8.1 as the baseline. Follow the steps below:
    - Create a Django application that uses the Django authentication system. Use a relational database such as MySQL as the backend.
    - Define Django models for Employee (with fields such as employee ID, first name, last name, gender, age, salary and department number) and Department (with fields such as department ID and department name).
    - Use the Django admin site to add new records and delete existing records.
    - Create Django views for viewing all employees and searching employees by employee ID.

3. Repeat Exercise-2 with a No-SQL database backend instead of a relational database.

4. Re-design the Social Media Analytics application described in section 7.4 using the Cloud Component Model (CCM) methodology. Follow the component design, architecture design and deployment design steps of CCM methodology.

6 — Python Basics

This Chapter covers

- Introduction to Python
- Installing Python
- Python Data Types & Data Structures
- Control Flow
- Functions
- Modules
- Packages
- File Input/Output
- Date/Time Operations
- Classes

6.1 Introduction

Python is a general-purpose high level programming language and suitable for providing a solid foundation to the reader in the area of cloud computing. Python 2.0 was released in the year 2000 and Python 3.0 was released in the year 2008. The 3.0 version is not backward compatible with earlier releases. The most recent release of Python is version 3.3. Currently, there is limited library support for the 3.x versions with operating systems such as Linux and Mac still using Python 2.x as default language. The exercises and examples in this book have been developed with Python version 2.7. The main characteristics of Python are:

Multi-paradigm programming language

Python supports more than one programming paradigms including object-oriented programming and structured programming

Interpreted Language

Python is an interpreted language and does not require an explicit compilation step. The Python interpreter executes the program source code directly, statement by statement, as a processor or scripting engine does.

Interactive Language

Python provides an interactive mode in which the user can submit commands at the Python prompt and interact with the interpreter directly.

The key benefits of Python are:

Easy-to-learn, read and maintain

Python is a minimalistic language with relatively few keywords, uses English keywords and has fewer syntactical constructions as compared to other languages. Reading Python programs feels like English with pseudo-code like constructs. Python is easy to learn yet an extremely powerful language for a wide range of applications. Due to its simplicity, programs written in Python are easy to maintain.

Object and Procedure Oriented

Python supports both procedure-oriented programming and object-oriented programming. Procedure oriented paradigm allows programs to be written around procedures or functions that allow reuse of code. Procedure oriented paradigm allows programs to be written around objects that include both data and functionality.

Extendable

Python is an extendable language and allows integration of low-level modules written in languages such as C/C++. This is useful when you want to speed up a critical portion of a program.

Scalable

Due to the minimalistic nature of Python, it provides a manageable structure for large programs.

Portable

Since Python is an interpreted language, programmers do not have to worry about compilation, linking and loading of programs. Python programs can be directly executed from source code and copied from one machine to other without worrying about portability. The Python interpreter converts the source code to an intermediate form called byte codes and then translates this into the native language of your specific system and then runs it.

Broad Library Support

Python has a broad library support and works on various platforms such as Windows, Linux, Mac, etc. There are a large number of Python packages available for various applications such as machine learning, image processing, network programming, cryptography, etc.

6.2 Installing Python

Python is a highly portable language that works on various platforms such as Windows, Linux, Mac, etc. This section describes the Python installation steps for Windows and Linux:

Windows

Python binaries for Windows can be downloaded from http://www.python.org/getit . For the examples and exercise in this book, you would require Python 2.7 which can be directly downloaded from: http://www.python.org/ftp/python/2.7.5/python-2.7.5.msi Once the python binary is installed you can run the python shell at the command prompt using
> python

Linux

Box 6.1 provides the commands for installing Python on Ubuntu.

■ Box 6.1: Installing Python on Ubuntu Linux

```
#Install Dependencies
sudo apt-get install build-essential
sudo apt-get install libreadline-gplv2-dev libncursesw5-dev libssl-dev libsqlite3-dev tk-dev
libgdbm-dev libc6-dev libbz2-dev

#Download Python
wget http://python.org/ftp/python/2.7.5/Python-2.7.5.tgz
tar -xvf Python-2.7.5.tgz
cd Python-2.7.5

#Install Python
./configure
make
sudo make install
```

6.3 Python Data Types & Data Structures

6.3.1 Numbers

Number data type is used to store numeric values. Numbers are immutable data types, therefore changing the value of a number data type results in a newly allocated object. Box 6.2 shows some examples of working with numbers.

■ Box 6.2: Working with Numbers in Python

```
#Integer
>>>a=5
>>>type(a)
<type 'int'>

#Floating Point
>>>b=2.5
>>>type(b)
<type 'float'>

#Long
>>>x=9898878787676L
>>>type(x)
<type 'long'>

#Complex
>>>y=2+5j
>>>y
(2+5j)
>>>type(y)
<type 'complex'>
>>>y.real
2
>>>y.imag
5

#Addition
>>>c=a+b
>>>c
7.5
>>>type(c)
<type 'float'>

#Subtraction
>>>d=a-b
>>>d
2.5
>>>type(d)
<type 'float'>

#Multiplication
>>>e=a*b
>>>e
12.5
>>>type(e)
<type 'float'>

#Division
>>>f=b/a
>>>f
0.5
```

```
>>>type(f)
<type 'float'>

#Power
>>>g=a**2
>>>g
25
```

6.3.2 Strings

A string is simply a list of characters in order. There are no limits to the number of characters you can have in a string. A string which has 0 characters is called an empty string. Box 6.3 shows examples of working with strings.

■ Box 6.3: Working with Strings in Python

```
#Create string
>>>s="Hello World!"
>>>type(s)
<type 'str'>

#String concatenation
>>>t="This is sample program."
>>>r = s+t
>>>r
'Hello World!This is sample program.'

#Get length of string
>>>len(s)
12

#Convert string to integer
>>>x="100"
>>>type(s)
<type 'str'>
>>>y=int(x)
>>>y
100

#Print string
>>>print s
Hello World!

#Formatting output
>>>print "The string (The string (Hello World!) has 12 characters

#Convert to upper/lower case
>>>s.upper()
'HELLO WORLD!'
>>>s.lower()
'hello world!'

#Accessing sub-strings
```

```
>>>s(0)
'H'
>>>s(6:)
'World!'
>>>s(6:-1)
'World'

#strip: Returns a copy of the string with the leading and trailing characters removed.
>>>s.strip("!")
'Hello World'
```

6.3.3 Lists

List a compound data type used to group together other values. List items need not all have the same type. A list contains items separated by commas and enclosed within square brackets. Box 6.4 shows examples of working with lists.

■ Box 6.4: Working with Lists in Python

```
>>>fruits=['apple','orange','banana','mango']
>>>type(fruits)
<type 'list'>
>>>len(fruits)
4

>>>fruits[1]
'orange'
>>>fruits[1:3]
['orange', 'banana']
>>>fruits[1:]
['orange', 'banana', 'mango']

#Appending an item to a list
>>>fruits.append('pear')
>>>fruits
['apple', 'orange', 'banana', 'mango', 'pear']

#Removing an item from a list
>>>fruits.remove('mango')
>>>fruits
['apple', 'orange', 'banana', 'pear']

#Inserting an item to a list
>>>fruits.insert(1,'mango')
>>>fruits
['apple', 'mango', 'orange', 'banana', 'pear']

#Combining lists
>>>vegetables=['potato','carrot','onion','beans','radish']
>>>vegetables
['potato', 'carrot', 'onion', 'beans', 'radish']
>>>eatables=fruits+vegetables
>>>eatables
```

```
['apple', 'mango', 'orange', 'banana', 'pear', 'potato', 'carrot', 'onion', 'bea
ns', 'radish']

#Mixed data types in a list
>>>mixed=['data',5,100.1,8287398L]
>>>type(mixed)
<type 'list'>
>>>type(mixed[0])
<type 'str'>
>>>type(mixed[1])
<type 'int'>
>>>type(mixed[2])
<type 'float'>
>>>type(mixed[3])
<type 'long'>

#It is possible to change individual elements of a list
>>>mixed[0]=mixed[0]+" items"
>>>mixed[1]=mixed[1]+1
>>>mixed[2]=mixed[2]+0.05
>>>mixed
['data items', 6, 100.14999999999999, 8287398L]

#Lists can be nested
>>>nested=[fruits,vegetables]
>>>nested
[['apple', 'mango', 'orange', 'banana', 'pear'], ['potato', 'carrot', 'onion', '
beans', 'radish']]
```

6.3.4 Tuples

A tuple is a sequence data type that is similar to the list. A tuple consists of a number of values separated by commas and enclosed within parentheses. Unlike lists, the elements of tuples cannot be changed, so tuples can be thought of as read-only lists. Box 6.5 shows examples of working with tuples.

■ Box 6.5: Working with Tuples in Python

```
>>>fruits=("apple","mango","banana","pineapple")
>>>fruits
('apple', 'mango', 'banana', 'pineapple')
>>>type(fruits)
<type 'tuple'>

#Get length of tuple
>>>len(fruits)
4

#Get an element from a tuple
>>>fruits[0]
'apple'
>>>fruits[:2]
('apple', 'mango')
```

```
#Combining tuples
>>>vegetables=('potato','carrot','onion','radish')
>>>eatables=fruits+vegetables
>>>eatables
('apple', 'mango', 'banana', 'pineapple', 'potato', 'carrot', 'onion', 'radish')
```

6.3.5 Dictionaries

Dictionary is a mapping data type or a kind of hash table that maps keys to values. Keys in a dictionary can be of any data type, though numbers and strings are commonly used for keys. Values in a dictionary can be any data type or object. Box 6.6 shows examples on working with dictionaries.

■ Box 6.6: Working with Dictionaries in Python

```
>>>student={'name':'Mary','id':'8776','major':'CS'}
>>>student
{'major': 'CS', 'name': 'Mary', 'id': '8776'}
>>>type(student)
<type 'dict'>

#Get length of a dictionary
>>>len(student)
3

#Get the value of a key in dictionary
>>>student['name']
'Mary'

#Get all items in a dictionary
>>>student.items()
[('gender', 'female'), ('major', 'CS'), ('name', 'Mary'), ('id', '8776')]

#Get all keys in a dictionary
>>>student.keys()
['gender', 'major', 'name', 'id']

#Get all values in a dictionary
>>>student.values()
['female', 'CS', 'Mary', '8776']

#Add new key-value pair
>>>student['gender']='female'
>>>student
{'gender': 'female', 'major': 'CS', 'name': 'Mary', 'id': '8776'}

#A value in a dictionary can be another dictionary
>>>student1={'name':'David','id':'9876','major':'ECE'}
>>>students={'1': student,'2':student1}
>>>students
{'1': {'gender': 'female', 'major': 'CS', 'name': 'Mary', 'id': '8776'}, '2': {'
major': 'ECE', 'name': 'David', 'id': '9876'}}
```

```
#Check if dictionary has a key
>>>student.has_key('name')
True
>>>student.has_key('grade')
False
```

6.3.6 Type Conversions

Box 6.7 shows examples of type conversions.

■ Box 6.7: Type conversion examples

```
#Convert to string
>>>a=10000
>>>str(a)
'10000'

#Convert to int
>>>b="2013"
>>>int(b)
2013

#Convert to float
>>>float(b)
2013.0

#Convert to long
>>>long(b)
2013L

#Convert to list
>>>s="aeiou"
>>>list(s)
['a', 'e', 'i', 'o', 'u']

#Convert to set
>>>x=['mango','apple','banana','mango','banana']
>>>set(x)
set(['mango', 'apple', 'banana'])
```

6.4 Control Flow

Lets us look at the control flow statements in Python.

6.4.1 if

The *if* statement in Python is similar to the *if* statement in other languages. Box 6.8 shows some examples of the *if* statement.

■ Box 6.8: if statement examples

```
>>>a = 25**5
>>>if a>10000:
    print "More"
else:
    print "Less"

More

>>>if a>10000:
    if a<1000000:
        print "Between 10k and 100k"
    else:
        print "More than 100k"
elif a==10000:
    print "Equal to 10k"
else:
    print "Less than 10k"

More than 100k

>>>s="Hello World"
>>>if "World" in s:
    s=s+"!"
    print s

Hello World!

>>>student={'name':'Mary','id':'8776'}
>>>if not student.has_key('major'):
student('major')='CS'
>>>student
{'major': 'CS', 'name': 'Mary', 'id': '8776'}
```

6.4.2 for

The *for* statement in Python iterates over items of any sequence (list, string, etc.) in the order in which they appear in the sequence. This behavior is different from the *for* statement in other languages such as C in which an initialization, incrementing and stopping criteria are provided. Box 6.9 shows examples of the *for* statement.

■ **Box 6.9: for statement examples**

```
helloString = "Hello World"
fruits=['apple','orange','banana','mango']
student = 'name': 'Mary', 'id': '8776','gender': 'female', 'major': 'CS'

#Looping over characters in a string
for c in helloString:
    print c


#Looping over items in a list
i=0
```

```
for item in fruits:
    print "Fruit-%d: %s" % (i,item)
    i=i+1

#Looping over keys in a dictionary
for key in student:
    print "%s: %s" % (key,student(key))
```

6.4.3 while

The *while* statement in Python executes the statements within the *while* loop as long as the *while* condition is true. Box 6.10 shows a *while* statement example.

■ Box 6.10: while statement examples

```
#Prints even numbers upto 100
>>> i = 0
>>> while i<=100:
if i%2 == 0:
print i
i = i+1
```

6.4.4 range

The *range* statement in Python generates a list of numbers in arithmetic progression. Examples of *range* statement are shown in Box 6.11.

■ Box 6.11: range examples

```
#Generate a list of numbers from 0 - 9
>>>range (10)
[0, 1, 2, 3, 4, 5, 6, 7, 8, 9]

#Generate a list of numbers from 10 - 100 with increments of 10
>>>range(10,110,10)
[10, 20, 30, 40, 50, 60, 70, 80, 90,100]
```

6.4.5 break/continue

The *break* and *continue* statements in Python are similar to the statements in C. The *break* statement breaks out of the for/while loop whereas the *continue* statement continues with the next iteration. Box 6.12 shows examples of *break* and *continue* usage.

■ Box 6.12: break/continue examples

```
#Break statement example
>>>y=1
>>>for x in range(4,256,4):
        y = y * x
        if y > 512:
            break
        print y
```

```
4
32
384

#Continue statement example
>>>fruits=('apple','orange','banana','mango')
>>>for item in fruits:
    if item == "banana":
        continue
    else:
        print item

apple
orange
mango
```

6.4.6 pass

The *pass* statement in Python is a null operation. The *pass* statement is used when a statement is required syntactically but you do not want any command or code to execute. Box 6.13 shows an example of *pass* statement.

■ **Box 6.13: pass statement example**

```
fruits=['apple','orange','banana','mango']
for item in fruits:
    if item == "banana":
        pass
    else:
        print item

apple
orange
mango
```

6.5 Functions

A function is a block of code that takes information in (in the form of parameters), does some computation, and returns a new piece of information based on the parameter information. A function in Python is a block of code that begins with the keyword *def* followed by the function name and parentheses. The function parameters are enclosed within the parenthesis. The code block within a function begins after a colon that comes after the parenthesis enclosing the parameters. The first statement of the function body can optionally be a documentation string or docstring. Box 6.14 shows an example of a function that computes the average grade given a dictionary containing student records.

■ **Box 6.14: Example of a function in Python**

```
students = { '1': {'name': 'Bob', 'grade': 2.5},
```

```
    '2': {'name': 'Mary', 'grade': 3.5},
    '3': {'name': 'David', 'grade': 4.2},
    '4': {'name': 'John', 'grade': 4.1},
    '5': {'name': 'Alex', 'grade': 3.8}}


def averageGrade(students):
    "This function computes the average grade"
    sum = 0.0
    for key in students:
        sum = sum + students(key)('grade')
        average = sum/len(students)
        return average

avg = averageGrade(students)
print "The average garde is: %0.2f" % (avg)
```

Functions can have default values of the parameters. If a function with default values is called with fewer parameters or without any parameter, the default values of the parameters are used as shown in the example in Box 6.15.

■ Box 6.15: Example of function with default arguments

```
>>>def displayFruits(fruits=['apple','orange']):
    print "There are %d fruits in the list" % (len(fruits))
    for item in fruits:
        print item

#Using default arguments
>>>displayFruits()
apple
orange

>>>fruits = ['banana', 'pear', 'mango']
>>>displayFruits(fruits)
banana
pear
mango
```

All parameters in the Python functions are passed by reference. Therefore, if a parameter is changed within a function the change also reflected back in the calling function. Box 6.16 shows an example of parameter passing by reference.

■ Box 6.16: Example of passing by reference

```
>>>def displayFruits(fruits):
    print "There are %d fruits in the list" % (len(fruits))
    for item in fruits:
        print item
    print "Adding one more fruit"
    fruits.append('mango')
```

```
>>>fruits = ['banana', 'pear', 'apple']
>>>displayFruits(fruits)
There are 3 fruits in the list
banana
pear
apple
Adding one more fruit

>>>print "There are %d fruits in the list" % (len(fruits))
There are 4 fruits in the list
```

Functions can also be called using keyword arguments that identifies the arguments by the parameter name when the function is called. Box 6.17 shows examples of keyword arguments.

■ Box 6.17: Examples of keyword arguments

```
>>>def printStudentRecords(name,age=20,major='CS'):
    print "Name: " + name
    print "Age: " + str(age)
    print "Major: " + major

#This will give error as name is required argument
>>>printStudentRecords()
Traceback (most recent call last):
File "<stdin>", line 1, in <module>
TypeError: printStudentRecords() takes at least 1 argument (0 given)

>>>printStudentRecords(name='Alex')
Name: Alex
Age: 20
Major: CS

>>>printStudentRecords(name='Bob',age=22,major='ECE')
Name: Bob
Age: 22
Major: ECE

>>>printStudentRecords(name='Alan',major='ECE')
Name: Alan
Age: 20
Major: ECE

#name is a formal argument.
#**kwargs is a keyword argument that receives all arguments except the formal argument
as a dictionary.
>>>def student(name, **kwargs):
    print "Student Name: " + name
    for key in kwargs:
        print key + ': ' + kwargs(key)
```

```
>>>student(name='Bob', age='20', major = 'CS')
Student Name: Bob
age: 20
major: CS
```

Python functions can have variable length arguments. The variable length arguments are passed to as a tuple to the function with an argument prefixed with asterix (*) as shown in Box 6.18.

■ Box 6.18: Example of variable length arguments

```
def student(name, *varargs):
    print "Student Name: " + name
    for item in varargs:
        print item

>>>student('Nav')
Student Name: Nav

>>>student('Amy', 'Age: 24')
Student Name: Amy
Age: 24

>>>student('Bob', 'Age: 20', 'Major: CS')
Student Name: Bob
Age: 20
Major: CS
```

6.6 Modules

Python allows organizing the program code into different modules which improves the code readability and management. A module is a Python file that defines some functionality in the form of functions or classes. Modules can be imported using the import keyword. Modules to be imported must be present in the search path. Box 6.19 shows the example of a student module that contains two functions and Box 6.20 shows an example of importing the student module and using it.

■ Box 6.19: Module student

```
def averageGrade(students):
    sum = 0.0
    for key in students:
        sum = sum + students[key]['grade']
    average = sum/len(students)
    return average

def printRecords(students):
    print "There are %d students" %(len(students))
    i=1
    for key in students:
```

```
        print "Student-%d: " % (i)
        print "Name: " + students[key]['name']
        print "Grade: " + str(students[key]['grade'])
        i = i+1
```

■ **Box 6.20: Using module student**

```
>>>import student

>>>students = '1': 'name': 'Bob', 'grade': 2.5,
        '2': 'name': 'Mary', 'grade': 3.5,
        '3': 'name': 'David', 'grade': 4.2,
        '4': 'name': 'John', 'grade': 4.1,
        '5': 'name': 'Alex', 'grade': 3.8

>>>student.printRecords(students)
There are 5 students
Student-1:
Name: Bob
Grade: 2.5

Student-2:
Name: David
Grade: 4.2

Student-3:
Name: Mary
Grade: 3.5

Student-4:
Name: Alex
Grade: 3.8

Student-5:
Name: John
Grade: 4.1

>>>avg = student. averageGrade(students)
>>>print "The average garde is: %0.2f" % (avg)
3.62
```

The import keyword followed by the module name imports all the functions in the module. If you want to use only a specific function it is recommended to import only that function using the keyword *from* as shown in the example in Box 6.21.

■ **Box 6.21: Importing a specific function from a module**

```
»>from student import averageGrade

>>>students = '1': 'name': 'Bob', 'grade': 2.5,
        '2': 'name': 'Mary', 'grade': 3.5,
```

```
        '3': 'name': 'David', 'grade': 4.2,
        '4': 'name': 'John', 'grade': 4.1,
        '5': 'name': 'Alex', 'grade': 3.8

>>>avg = averageGrade(students)
>>>print "The average garde is: %0.2f" % (avg)
3.62
```

Python comes with a number of standard modules such as system related modules (sys), OS related module (os), mathematical modules (math, fractions, etc.), internet related modules (email, json. etc), etc. The complete list of standard modules is available in the Python documentation [31]. Box 6.22 shows an example of listing all names defined in a module using the built-in dir function.

■ Box 6.22: Listing all names defines in a module

```
>>>import email

>>>dir (email)
['Charset', 'Encoders', 'Errors', 'FeedParser', 'Generator', 'Header', 'Iterator
s', 'LazyImporter', 'MIMEAudio', 'MIMEBase', 'MIMEImage', 'MIMEMessage', 'MIMEMu
ltipart', 'MIMENonMultipart', 'MIMEText', 'Message', 'Parser', 'Utils', '_LOWERN
AMES', '_MIMENAMES', '__all__', '__builtins__', '__doc__', '__file__', '__name__
', '__package__', '__path__', '__version__', '_name', 'base64MIME', 'email', 'im
porter', 'message_from_file', 'message_from_string', 'mime', 'quopriMIME', 'sys'
]
```

6.7 Packages

Python package is hierarchical file structure that consists of modules and subpackages. Packages allow better organization of modules related to a single application environment. For example, Box 6.23 shows the listing of the skimage package that provides image processing algorithms. The package is organized into a root directory (skimage) with sub-directories (color, draw, etc) which are sub-packages within the skimage package. Each directory contains a special file named __init__.py which tells Python to treat directories as packages. This file can either be an empty file or contain some initialization code for the package.

■ Box 6.23: skimage package listing

```
skimage/                          Top level package
    __init__.py                   Treat directory as a package
    color/                        color subpackage
        __init__.py
        colorconv.py
        colorlabel.py
        rgb_colors.py
    draw/                         draw subpackage
        __init__.py
```

```
        draw.py
        setup.py
    exposure/                           exposure subpackage
        __init__.py
        _adapthist.py
        exposure.py
    feature/                            feature subpackage
        __init__.py
        _brief.py
        _daisy.py
        ...
    ...
```

6.8 File Handling

Python allows reading and writing to files using the file object. The open(filename, mode) function is used to get a file object. The mode can be read (r), write (w), append (a), read and write (r+ or w+), read-binary (rb), write-binary (wb), etc. Box 6.24 shows an example of reading an entire file with read function. After the file contents have been read the close function is called which closes the file object.

■ Box 6.24: Example of reading an entire file

```
>>>fp = open('file.txt','r')
>>>content = fp.read()
>>>print content
Python supports more than one programming paradigms including object-oriented pro-
gramming and structured programming
Python is an interpreted language and does not require an explicit compilation
step.
The Python interpreter executes the program source code directly, statement by statement,
as a processor or scripting engine does.
Python provides an interactive mode in which the user can submit commands at the
Python prompt and interact directly with programs.
>>>fp.close()
```

Box 6.25 shows an example of reading line by line from a file using the readline function.

■ Box 6.25: Example of reading line by line

```
>>>fp.close()
>>>fp = open('file.txt','r')
>>>print "Line-1: " + fp.readline()
Line-1: Python supports more than one programming paradigms including object-oriented
programming and structured programming

>>>print "Line-2: " + fp.readline()
Line-2: Python is an interpreted language and does not require an explicit
compilation step.

>>>fp.close()
```

Box 6.26 shows an example of reading lines of a file in a loop using the readlines function.

■ Box 6.26: Example of reading lines in a loop

```
>>>fp = open('file.txt','r')
>>>lines = fp.readlines()
>>>for line in lines:
    print line

Python supports more than one programming paradigms including object-oriented
programming and structured programming

Python is an interpreted language and does not require an explicit compilation
step.

The Python interpreter executes the program source code directly, statement by
statement, as a processor or scripting engine does.

Python provides an interactive mode in which the user can submit commands at the
Python prompt and interact with the interpreter directly to programs.
```

Box 6.27 shows an example of reading a certain number of bytes from a file using the read(size) function.

■ Box 6.27: Example of reading a certain number of bytes

```
>>>fp = open('file.txt','r')
>>>fp.read(10)
'Python sup'
>>>fp.close()
```

Box 6.28 shows an example of getting the current position of read using the tell function.

■ Box 6.28: Example of getting the current position of read

```
>>>fp = open('file.txt','r')
>>>fp.read(10)
'Python sup'
>>>currentpos = fp.tell
>>>print currentpos
<built-in method tell of file object at 0x0000000002391390>
>>>fp.close()
```

Box 6.29 shows an example of seeking to a certain position in a file using the seek function.

■ Box 6.29: Example of seeking to a certain position

```
>>>fp = open('file.txt','r')
>>>fp.seek(10,0)
>>>content = fp.read(10)
>>>print content
```

```
ports more
>>>fp.close()
```

Box 6.30 shows an example of writing a file using the write function.

■ **Box 6.30: Example of writing to a file**

```
>>>fo = open('file1.txt','w')
>>>content='This is an example of writing to a file in Python.'
>>>fo.write(content)
>>>fo.close()
```

6.9 Date/Time Operations

Python provides several functions for date and time access and conversions. The datetime module allows manipulating date and time in several ways. Box 6.31 shows examples of manipulating with date.

■ **Box 6.31: Examples of manipulating with date**

```
>>>from datetime import date
>>>now = date.today()
>>>print "Date: " + now.strftime("%m-%d-%y")
Date: 07-24-13
>>>print "Day of Week: " + now.strftime("%A")
Day of Week: Wednesday
>>>print "Month: " + now.strftime("%B")
Month: July
>>>
>>>then = date(2013, 6, 7)
>>>timediff = now - then
>>>timediff.days
47
```

The time module in Python provides various time-related functions. Box 6.32 shows examples of manipulating with time.

■ **Box 6.32: Examples of manipulating with time**

```
>>>import time
>>>nowtime = time.time()
>>>time.localtime(nowtime)
time.struct_time(tm_year=2013, tm_mon=7, tm_mday=24, tm_
ec=51, tm_wday=2, tm_yday=205, tm_isdst=0)
>>>time.asctime(time.localtime(nowtime))
'Wed Jul 24 16:14:51 2013'

>>>time.strftime("The date is %d-%m-%y. Today is a %A. It is %H hours, %M minutes and %S
seconds now.")
```

'The date is 24-07-13. Today is a Wednesday. It is 16 hours, 15 minutes and 14 seconds now.'

6.10 Classes

Python is an Object-Oriented Programming (OOP) language. Python provides all the standard features of Object Oriented Programming such as classes, class variables, class methods, inheritance, function overloading, and operator overloading. Let us briefly look at these OOP concepts:

Class

A class is simply a representation of a type of object and user-defined prototype for an object that is composed of three things: a name, attributes, and operations/methods.

Instance/Object

Object is an instance of the data structure defined by a class.

Inheritance

Inheritance is the process of forming a new class from an existing class or base class.

Function overloading

Function overloading is a form of polymorphism that allows a function to have different meanings, depending on its context.

Operator overloading

Operator overloading is a form of polymorphism that allows assignment of more than one function to a particular operator.

Function overriding

Function overriding allows a child class to provide a specific implementation of a function that is already provided by the base class. Child class implementation of the overridden function has the same name, parameters and return type as the function in the base class.

Box 6.33 shows an example of a Class. The variable *studentCount* is a class variable that is shared by all instances of the class *Student* and is accessed by *Student.studentCount*. The variables *name*, *id* and *grades* are instance variables which are specific to each instance of the class. There is a special method by the name *__init__*() which is the class constructor. The class constructor initializes a new instance when it is created. The function *__del__*() is the class destructor.

■ Box 6.33: Examples of a class

```
>>>class Student:
    studentCount = 0
    def __init__(self, name, id):
        print "Constructor called"
        self.name = name
        self.id = id
        Student.studentCount = Student.studentCount + 1
        self.grades=
```

```
    def __del__(self):
        print "Destructor called"

    def getStudentCount(self):
        return Student.studentCount

    def addGrade(self,key,value):
        self.grades[key]=value

    def getGrade(self,key):
        return self.grades[key]

    def printGrades(self):
        for key in self.grades:
            print key + ": " + self.grades[key]

>>>s = Student('Steve','98928')
Constructor called
>>>s.addGrade('Math','90')
>>>s.addGrade('Physics','85')
>>>s.printGrades()
Physics: 85
Math: 90
>>>mathgrade = s.getGrade('Math')
>>>print mathgrade
90
>>>count = s.getStudentCount()
>>>print count
1
>>>del s
Destructor called
```

Box 6.34 shows an example of class inheritance. In this example *Shape* is the base class and *Circle* is the derived class. The class *Circle* inherits the attributes of the *Shape* class. The child class *Circle* overrides the methods and attributes of the base class (eg. *draw*() function defined in the base class *Shape* is overridden in child class *Circle*). It is possible to hide some class attributes by naming them with a *double underscore* prefix. For example, *__label* attribute is hidden and cannot be directly accessed using the object (*circ.__label* gives an error). To hide the attributes with double underscore prefix, Python changes their names internally and prefixes the class name (e.g. *__label* is changed to *_Circle__label*).

■ Box 6.34: Examples of class inheritance

```
>>>class Shape:
    def __init__(self):
        print "Base class constructor"
        self.color = 'Green'
        self.lineWeight = 10.0
    def draw(self):
        print "Draw - to be implemented"
```

```
    def setColor(self, c):
        self.color = c
    def getColor(self):
        return self.color
    def setLineWeight(self,lwt):
        self.lineWeight = lwt
    def getLineWeight(self):
        return self.lineWeight

>>>class Circle(Shape):
    def __init__(self, c,r):
        print "Child class constructor"
        self.center = c
        self.radius = r
        self.color = 'Green'
        self.lineWeight = 10.0
        self.__label = 'Hidden circle label'
    def setCenter(self,c):
        self.center = c
    def getCenter(self):
        return self.center
    def setRadius(self,r):
        self.radius = r
    def getRadius(self):
        return self.radius
    def draw(self):
        print "Draw Circle (overridden function)"

>>>class Point:
    def __init__(self, x, y):
        self.xCoordinate = x
        self.yCoordinate = y

    def setXCoordinate(self,x):
        self.xCoordinate = x
    def getXCoordinate(self):
        return self.xCoordinate
    def setYCoordinate(self,y):
        self.yCoordinate = y
    def getYCoordinate(self):
        return self.yCoordinate

>>>p = Point(2,4)
>>>circ = Circle(p,7)
Child class constructor
>>>circ.getColor()
'Green'
>>>circ.setColor('Red')
>>>circ.getColor()
'Red'

>>>circ.getLineWeight()
10.0
>>>circ.getCenter().getXCoordinate()
2
```

```
>>>circ.getCenter().getYCoordinate()
4

>>>circ.draw()
Draw Circle (overridden function)

>>>circ.radius
7
>>>circ.__label
Traceback (most recent call last):
File "<stdin>", line 1, in <module>
AttributeError: Circle instance has no attribute '__label'

>>>circ._Circle__label
'Hidden circle label'
```

Summary

In this chapter you learned about the basics of Python programming language. Python is a general-purpose, high level programming language that supports more than one programming paradigms including object-oriented programming and structured programming. Python is an interpreted language and does not require an explicit compilation step. Python provides an interactive mode in which the user can submit commands at the Python prompt and interact with the interpreter directly. Python supports both procedure-oriented programming and object-oriented programming. Python programs can be directly executed from source code and copied from one machine to another without worrying about portability. Python Data Types & Data Structures include Numbers, Strings, Lists, Tuples and Dictionaries. Control flow statements in Python include *if*, *for*, *while*, *break*, *continue*, *range* and *pass*. A function in Python is a block of code that begins with the keyword *def* followed by the function name and parentheses. Python allows organizing the program code into different modules which improves the code readability and makes it easy to manage. Python packages allow better organization of modules related to a single application environment. Python provides all the standard features of Object Oriented Programming such as classes, class variables, class methods, inheritance, function overloading, and operator overloading.

Review Questions

1. What is the difference between procedure-oriented programming and object-oriented programming?
2. What is an interpreted language?
3. Describe a use case of Python dictionary?
4. What is a keyword argument in Python?
5. What are variable length arguments?
6. What is the difference between a Python module and a package?
7. How is function overriding implemented in Python?

Lab Exercises

1. In this exercise you will create a Python program to compute document statistics. Follow the steps below:
   - Create a text file with some random text.
   - Create a Python program with functions for reading the file, computing word count and top 10 words. Use the template below:

     ```
     def readFile(filename):
     #Implement this

     def wordCount(contents):
     #Implement this

     def topTenWords(wordCountDict):
     #Implement this

     def main():
         filename = sys.argv[1]
         contents = readFile(filename)
         wordCountDict=wordCount(contents)
         topTenWords(wordCountDict)

     if __name__ == '__main__':
         main()
     ```

   - Run the Python program as follows:
     python documentstats.py filename.txt

2. Extend Exercise-1 to compute top 10 keywords in a file. To ignore stop-words (commonly occurring words such as 'an', 'the', 'how', etc) create a list of stop-words. Ignore stop-words when computing top 10 keywords.

3. In this exercise you will create a sentiment extractor program that finds the sentiment of the given input.
   - Sentiment can be positive, negative or neutral. For sentiment analysis use a sentiment lexicon such as AFINN [103] (which is a list of English words rated for valence with an integer between minus five (negative sentiment) and plus five (positive sentiment)). Alternatively, create your own sentiment lexicon with a few words as follows:
     confusing -2
     congrats 2
     happy 5
     sad -5
     :
   - To compute the sentiment, parse each word in the input and add the sentiment

scores of the words obtained from the sentiment lexicon.

- Test the program as follows:
  python sentimentExtractor.py "I am very happy today"

7 — Python for Cloud

This Chapter covers

- Python for Amazon Web Services
- Python for Google Cloud
- Python for Windows Azure
- Python for MapReduce
- Python Packages of Interest
- Python Web Application Framework - Django
- Development with Django
- Django Case Study

In the previous chapter you learned about the basics of Python. In this chapter you will learn how to use Python for provisioning and managing cloud resources and developing applications for the cloud.

7.1 Python for Amazon Web Services

In this section you will learn how to use Python for Amazon Web Services. Boto is a Python package that provides interfaces to Amazon Web Services (AWS) [87]. Currently Boto supports the following AWS services:

- Compute
  - Amazon Elastic Compute Cloud (EC2)
  - Amazon Elastic MapReduce (EMR)
  - AutoScaling
  - Content Delivery
  - Amazon CloudFront
- Database
  - Amazon Relational Data Service (RDS)
  - Amazon DynamoDB
  - Amazon SimpleDB
  - Amazon ElastiCache
  - Amazon Redshift
- Deployment and Management
  - AWS Elastic Beanstalk
  - AWS CloudFormation
  - AWS Data Pipeline
- Identity & Access
  - AWS Identity and Access Management (IAM)
- Application Services
  - Amazon CloudSearch
  - Amazon Simple Workflow Service (SWF)
  - Amazon Simple Queue Service (SQS)
  - Amazon Simple Notification Server (SNS)
  - Amazon Simple Email Service (SES)
- Monitoring
  - Amazon CloudWatch
- Networking
  - Amazon Route53
  - Amazon Virtual Private Cloud (VPC)
  - Elastic Load Balancing (ELB)
  - Payments and Billing
  - Amazon Flexible Payment Service (FPS)
- Storage
  - Amazon Simple Storage Service (S3)
  - Amazon Glacier
  - Amazon Elastic Block Store (EBS)

- Google Cloud Storage

7.1.1 Amazon EC2

Amazon EC2, an Infrastructure as a Service (IaaS), is provided by Amazon. EC2 delivers scalable, pay-as-you-go compute capacity in the cloud. EC2 is a web service that provides computing capacity in the form of virtual machines that are launched in Amazon's cloud computing environment.

Box 7.1 shows the Python code for launching an EC2 instance. In this example, a connection to EC2 service is first established by calling *boto.ec2.connect_to_region*. The EC2 region, AWS access key and AWS secret key are passed to this function. After connecting to EC2 , a new instance is launched using the *conn.run_instances* function. The AMI-ID, instance type, EC2 key handle and security group are passed to this function. This function returns a reservation. The instances associated with the reservation are obtained using *reservation.instances*. Finally the status of an instance associated with a reservation is obtained using the *instance.update* function. In the example shown in Box 7.1, the program waits till the status of the newly launched instance becomes *running* and then prints the instance details such as public DNS, instance IP, and launch time.

■ Box 7.1: Python program for launching an EC2 instance

```
import boto.ec2
from time import sleep

ACCESS_KEY="<enter access key>"
SECRET_KEY="<enter secret key>"

REGION="us-east-1"
AMI_ID = "ami-d0f89fb9"
EC2_KEY_HANDLE = "<enter key handle>"
INSTANCE_TYPE="t1.micro"
SECGROUP_HANDLE="default"

print "Connecting to EC2"

conn = boto.ec2.connect_to_region(REGION,
    aws_access_key_id=ACCESS_KEY,
    aws_secret_access_key=SECRET_KEY)

print "Launching instance with AMI-ID %s, with keypair %s, instance type %s, security
group %s"%(AMI_ID,EC2_KEY_HANDLE,INSTANCE_TYPE,SECGROUP_HANDLE)

reservation = conn.run_instances(image_id=AMI_ID,
            key_name=EC2_KEY_HANDLE,
            instance_type=INSTANCE_TYPE,
            security_groups = [ SECGROUP_HANDLE, ] )

instance = reservation.instances[0]

print "Waiting for instance to be up and running"
```

```
status = instance.update()
while status == 'pending':
    sleep(10)
    status = instance.update()

if status == 'running':
    print " \n Instance is now running. Instance details are:"
    print "Intance Size: " + str(instance.instance_type)
    print "Intance State: " + str(instance.state)
    print "Intance Launch Time: " + str(instance.launch_time)
    print "Intance Public DNS: " + str(instance.public_dns_name)
    print "Intance Private DNS: " + str(instance.private_dns_name)
    print "Intance IP: " + str(instance.ip_address)
    print "Intance Private IP: " + str(instance.private_ip_address)
```

Box 7.2 shows the Python code for viewing all running instances. In this example the *conn.get_all_instances* function is used to get information on all running instances.

■ Box 7.2: Python program for viewing details of running instances

```
import boto.ec2
from time import sleep

ACCESS_KEY="<enter access key>"
SECRET_KEY="<enter secret key>"

REGION="us-east-1"

print "Connecting to EC2"

conn = boto.ec2.connect_to_region(REGION,
    aws_access_key_id=ACCESS_KEY,
    aws_secret_access_key=SECRET_KEY)

print "Getting all running instances"

reservations = conn.get_all_instances()
print reservations

for item in reservations:
    instances = item.instances
    for instance in instances:
        print "—— \n"
        print "Intance Size: " + str(instance.instance_type)
        print "Intance State: " + str(instance.state)
        print "Intance Launch Time: " + str(instance.launch_time)
        print "Intance Public DNS: " + str(instance.public_dns_name)
        print "Intance Private DNS: " + str(instance.private_dns_name)
        print "Intance IP: " + str(instance.ip_address)
        print "Intance Private IP: " + str(instance.private_ip_address)
```

Box 7.3 shows the Python code for stopping an EC2 instance. In this example the *conn.get_all_instances* function is called to get information on all running instances. This function returns reservations. Next, the IDs of instances associated with each reservation are obtained. The instances are stopped by calling *conn.stop_instances* function to which the IDs of the instances to stop are passed.

■ Box 7.3: Python program for stopping an EC2 instance

```
import boto.ec2
from time import sleep


ACCESS_KEY="<enter access key>"
SECRET_KEY="<enter secret key>"

REGION="us-east-1"

print "Connecting to EC2"

conn = boto.ec2.connect_to_region(REGION,
    aws_access_key_id=ACCESS_KEY,
    aws_secret_access_key=SECRET_KEY)

print "Getting all running instances"
reservations = conn.get_all_instances()
print reservations

instance_rs = reservations[0].instances
instance = instance_rs[0]
instanceid=instance_rs[0].id
print "Stopping instance with ID: " + str(instanceid)

conn.stop_instances(instance_ids=[instanceid])

status = instance.update()
while not status == 'stopped':
    sleep(10)
    status = instance.update()

print "Stopped instance with ID: " + str(instanceid)
```

7.1.2 Amazon AutoScaling

Amazon AutoScaling allows automatically scaling of Amazon EC2 capacity up or down according to user defined conditions. Therefore, with AutoScaling users can increase the number of EC2 instances running their applications seamlessly during spikes in the application workloads to meet the application performance requirements and scale down capacity when the workload is low to save costs.

Box 7.4 shows the Python code for creating an AutoScaling group. In this example, a connection to AutoScaling service is first established by calling *boto.ec2.autoscale.connect_to_region* function. The EC2 region, AWS access key and AWS secret key are passed to this function. After connecting to AutoScaling service, a new launch configuration is created by calling *conn.create_launch_configuration*. Launch configuration contains instructions on how to launch new instances including the AMI-ID, instance type, security groups, etc. After creating a launch configuration, it is then associated with a new AutoScaling group. AutoScaling group is created by calling *conn.create_auto_scaling_group*. The settings for AutoScaling group such as the maximum and minimum number of instances in the group, the launch configuration, availability zones, optional load balancer to use with the group, etc. After creating an AutoScaling group, the policies for scaling up and scaling down are defined. In this example, a scale up policy with adjustment type *ChangeInCapacity* and *scaling_adjustment* = 1 is defined. Similarly a scale down policy with adjustment type *ChangeInCapacity* and *scaling_adjustment* = −1 is defined. With the scaling policies defined, the next step is to create Amazon CloudWatch alarms that trigger these policies. In this example, alarms for scaling up and scaling down are created. The scale up alarm is defined using the *CPUUtilization* metric with the *Average* statistic and threshold greater 70% for a period of 60 sec. The scale up policy created previously is associated with this alarm. This alarm is triggered when the average CPU utilization of the instances in the group becomes greater than 70% for more than 60 seconds. The scale down alarm is defined in a similar manner with a threshold less than 50%.

■ Box 7.4: Python program for creating an AutoScaling group

```
import boto.ec2.autoscale
from boto.ec2.autoscale import LaunchConfiguration
from boto.ec2.autoscale import AutoScalingGroup
from boto.ec2.cloudwatch import MetricAlarm
from boto.ec2.autoscale import ScalingPolicy
import boto.ec2.cloudwatch

ACCESS_KEY="<enter access key>"
SECRET_KEY="<enter secret key>"

REGION="us-east-1"
AMI_ID = "ami-d0f89fb9"
EC2_KEY_HANDLE = "<enter key handle>"
INSTANCE_TYPE="t1.micro"
SECGROUP_HANDLE="default"

print "Connecting to Autoscaling Service"

conn = boto.ec2.autoscale.connect_to_region(REGION,
        aws_access_key_id=ACCESS_KEY,
        aws_secret_access_key=SECRET_KEY)


print "Creating launch configuration"


lc = LaunchConfiguration(name='My-Launch-Config-2',
            image_id=AMI_ID,
            key_name=EC2_KEY_HANDLE,
            instance_type=INSTANCE_TYPE,
            security_groups = [ SECGROUP_HANDLE, ])
```

```
conn.create_launch_configuration(lc)

print "Creating auto-scaling group"

ag = AutoScalingGroup(group_name='My-Group',
          availability_zones=['us-east-1b'],
          launch_config=lc, min_size=1, max_size=2,
          connection=conn)

conn.create_auto_scaling_group(ag)

print "Creating auto-scaling policies"

scale_up_policy = ScalingPolicy(name='scale_up',
              adjustment_type='ChangeInCapacity',
              as_name='My-Group',
              scaling_adjustment=1,
              cooldown=180)

scale_down_policy = ScalingPolicy(name='scale_down',
              adjustment_type='ChangeInCapacity',
              as_name='My-Group',
              scaling_adjustment=-1,
              cooldown=180)


conn.create_scaling_policy(scale_up_policy)
conn.create_scaling_policy(scale_down_policy)


scale_up_policy = conn.get_all_policies( as_group='My-Group',
policy_names=['scale_up'])[0]
scale_down_policy = conn.get_all_policies( as_group='My-Group',
policy_names=['scale_down'])[0]

print "Connecting to CloudWatch"

cloudwatch = boto.ec2.cloudwatch.connect_to_region(REGION,
          aws_access_key_id=ACCESS_KEY,
          aws_secret_access_key=SECRET_KEY)

alarm_dimensions = "AutoScalingGroupName": 'My-Group'

print "Creating scale-up alarm"

scale_up_alarm = MetricAlarm(
       name='scale_up_on_cpu', namespace='AWS/EC2',
       metric='CPUUtilization', statistic='Average',
       comparison='>', threshold='70',
       period='60', evaluation_periods=2,
       alarm_actions=[scale_up_policy.policy_arn] ,
       dimensions=alarm_dimensions)
```

```
cloudwatch.create_alarm(scale_up_alarm)

print "Creating scale-down alarm"

scale_down_alarm = MetricAlarm(
        name='scale_down_on_cpu', namespace='AWS/EC2',
        metric='CPUUtilization', statistic='Average',
        comparison='<', threshold='50',
        period='60', evaluation_periods=2,
        alarm_actions=[scale_down_policy.policy_arn],
        dimensions=alarm_dimensions)

cloudwatch.create_alarm(scale_down_alarm)
print "Done!"
```

Box 7.5 shows the Python code for deleting an AutoScaling group. Before deleting a group all the instances in the group must be terminated by calling *group.shutdown_instances*.

■ Box 7.5: Python program for deleting an Autoscaling group

```
import boto.ec2.autoscale
from boto.ec2.autoscale import LaunchConfiguration
from boto.ec2.autoscale import AutoScalingGroup
from boto.ec2.cloudwatch import MetricAlarm
from boto.ec2.autoscale import ScalingPolicy
import boto.ec2.cloudwatch

ACCESS_KEY="<enter access key>"
SECRET_KEY="<enter secret key>"
REGION="us-east-1"

print "Connecting to Autoscaling Service"

conn = boto.ec2.autoscale.connect_to_region(REGION,
    aws_access_key_id=ACCESS_KEY,
    aws_secret_access_key=SECRET_KEY)

print "Get all groups"

groups = conn.get_all_groups()

print groups

group_to_delete = groups[0]

print "Shutting down all instances from group: " + str(group_to_delete)

group_to_delete.shutdown_instances()

print "Deleting group"

group_to_delete.delete()

print "Done!"
```

7.1.3 Amazon S3

Amazon S3 is an online cloud-based data storage infrastructure for storing and retrieving any amount of data. S3 provides highly reliable, scalable, fast, fully redundant and affordable storage infrastructure.

Box 7.6 shows the Python code for uploading a file to Amazon S3 cloud storage. In this example, a connection to S3 service is first established by calling *boto.connect_s3* function. The AWS access key and AWS secret key are passed to this function. This example defines two functions *upload_to_s3_bucket_path* and *upload_to_s3_bucket_root*.

The *upload_to_s3_bucket_path* function uploads the file to the S3 bucket specified at the specified path. The *upload_to_s3_bucket_root* function uploads the file to the S3 bucket root.

■ Box 7.6: Python program for uploading a file to an S3 bucket

```
import boto.s3

ACCESS_KEY="<enter access key>"
SECRET_KEY="<enter secret key>"

conn = boto.connect_s3(aws_access_key_id=ACCESS_KEY,
    aws_secret_access_key=SECRET_KEY)

def percent_cb(complete, total):
    print ('.')

def upload_to_s3_bucket_path(bucketname, path, filename):
    mybucket = conn.get_bucket(bucketname)
    fullkeyname=os.path.join(path,filename)
    key = mybucket.new_key(fullkeyname)
    key.set_contents_from_filename(filename, cb=percent_cb, num_cb=10)

def upload_to_s3_bucket_root(bucketname, filename):
    mybucket = conn.get_bucket(bucketname)
    key = mybucket.new_key(filename)
    key.set_contents_from_filename(filename, cb=percent_cb, num_cb=10)

upload_to_s3_bucket_path('mybucket2013', 'data', 'file.txt')
```

7.1.4 Amazon RDS

Amazon RDS is a web service that allows you to create instances of MySQL, Oracle or Microsoft SQL Server in the cloud. With RDS, developers can easily set up, operate, and scale a relational database in the cloud.

Box 7.7 shows the Python code for launching an Amazon RDS instance. In this example, a connection to RDS service is first established by calling *boto.rds.connect_to_region* function. The RDS region, AWS access key and AWS secret key are passed to this function. After connecting to RDS service, the *conn.create_dbinstance* function is called to launch a new RDS instance. The input parameters to this function include the instance ID, database size, instance type, database username, database password, database port, database engine (e.g. MySQL5.1), database name, security groups, etc. The program shown in Box 7.7 waits till the status of the RDS instance becomes *available* and then prints the instance details such as instance ID, create time, instance end point, etc.

■ Box 7.7: Python program for launching an RDS instance

```
import boto.rds
from time import sleep

ACCESS_KEY="<enter access key>"
SECRET_KEY="<enter secret key>"

REGION="us-east-1"
INSTANCE_TYPE="db.t1.micro"
ID = "MySQL-db-instance"
USERNAME = 'root'
PASSWORD = 'password'
DB_PORT = 3306
DB_SIZE = 5
DB_ENGINE = 'MySQL5.1'
DB_NAME = 'mytestdb'
SECGROUP_HANDLE="default"

print "Connecting to RDS"

conn = boto.rds.connect_to_region(REGION,
    aws_access_key_id=ACCESS_KEY,
    aws_secret_access_key=SECRET_KEY)

print "Creating an RDS instance"

db = conn.create_dbinstance(ID, DB_SIZE, INSTANCE_TYPE, USERNAME, PASSWORD,
port=DB_PORT, engine=DB_ENGINE, db_name=DB_NAME,
security_groups = [ SECGROUP_HANDLE, ] )
print db

print "Waiting for instance to be up and running"

status = db.status
while not status == 'available':
    sleep(10)
    status = db.status

if status == 'available':
    print " \n RDS Instance is now running. Instance details are:"
    print "Intance ID: " + str(db.id)
    print "Intance State: " + str(db.status)
    print "Intance Create Time: " + str(db.create_time)
    print "Engine: " + str(db.engine)
    print "Allocated Storage: " + str(db.allocated_storage)
    print "Endpoint: " + str(db.endpoint)
```

Box 7.8 shows the Python code for viewing the running RDS instances.

■ Box 7.8: Python program for viewing all RDS instances

```
import boto.rds

ACCESS_KEY="<enter access key>"
SECRET_KEY="<enter secret key>"

REGION="us-east-1"
ID = "MySQL-db-instance"
DB_NAME = 'mytestdb'


print "Connecting to RDS"

conn = boto.rds.connect_to_region(REGION,
    aws_access_key_id=ACCESS_KEY,
    aws_secret_access_key=SECRET_KEY)

print "Getting all instances"

instances = conn.get_all_dbinstances(ID)

print instances

for db in instances:
    print "—— \n"
    print "Intance ID: " + str(db.id)
    print "Intance State: " + str(db.status)
    print "Intance Create Time: " + str(db.create_time)
    print "Engine: " + str(db.engine)
    print "Allocated Storage: " + str(db.allocated_storage)
    print "Endpoint: " + str(db.endpoint)
```

Box 7.9 shows the Python code for creating a MySQL table, writing and reading from the table. This example uses the MySQLdb Python package. To connect to the MySQL RDS instance, the *MySQLdb.connect* function is called and the end point of the RDS instance, database username, password and port are passed to this function. After the connection to the RDS instance is established, a cursor to the database is obtained by calling *conn.cursor*. Next, a new database table named *Student* is created with *Id* as primary key and other columns. After creating the table some values are inserted. To execute the SQL commands for database manipulation, the commands are passed to the *cursor.execute* function.

■ Box 7.9: Python program for creating a MySQL table, writing and reading from the table

```
import MySQLdb

USERNAME = 'root'
PASSWORD = 'password'
DB_NAME = 'mytestdb'
```

```
print "Connecting to RDS instance"

conn = MySQLdb.connect (host =
"mysql-db-instance-3.c35qdifuf9ko.us-east-1.rds.amazonaws.com",
user = USERNAME,
passwd = PASSWORD,
db = DB_NAME,
port = 3306)

print "Connected to RDS instance"

cursor = conn.cursor ()
cursor.execute ("SELECT VERSION()")
row = cursor.fetchone ()
print "server version:", row[0]

cursor.execute ("CREATE TABLE Student(Id INT PRIMARY KEY, Name TEXT, Major TEXT,
Grade FLOAT) ")
cursor.execute ("INSERT INTO Student VALUES(100, 'John', 'CS', 3)")
cursor.execute ("INSERT INTO Student VALUES(101, 'David', 'ECE', 3.5)")
cursor.execute ("INSERT INTO Student VALUES(102, 'Bob', 'CS', 3.9)")
cursor.execute ("INSERT INTO Student VALUES(103, 'Alex', 'CS', 3.6)")
cursor.execute ("INSERT INTO Student VALUES(104, 'Martin', 'ECE', 3.1)")

cursor.execute("SELECT * FROM Student")
rows = cursor.fetchall()

for row in rows:
    print row

cursor.close ()
conn.close ()
```

7.1.5 Amazon DynamoDB

Amazon DynamoDB is a fully-managed, scalable, high performance No-SQL database service.

Box 7.10 shows the Python code for creating a DynamoDB table. In this example, a connection to DynamoDB service is first established by calling *boto.dynamodb.connect_to_region*. The DynamoDB region, AWS access key and AWS secret key are passed to this function. After connecting to DynamoDB service, a schema for the new table is created by calling *conn.create_schema*. The schema includes the hash key and range key names and types. A DynamoDB table is then created by calling *conn.create_table* function with the table schema, read units and write units as input parameters.

■ Box 7.10: Python program for creating a DynamoDB table

```
import boto.dynamodb
import time
from datetime import date

ACCESS_KEY="<enter access key>"
```

```
SECRET_KEY="<enter secret key>"
REGION="us-east-1"

print "Connecting to DynamoDB"

conn = boto.dynamodb.connect_to_region(REGION,
    aws_access_key_id=ACCESS_KEY,
    aws_secret_access_key=SECRET_KEY)

table_schema = conn.create_schema(
    hash_key_name='msgid',
    hash_key_proto_value=str,
    range_key_name='date',
    range_key_proto_value=str
    )

print "Creating table with schema:"
print table_schema


table = conn.create_table(
    name='my-test-table',
    schema=table_schema,
    read_units=1,
    write_units=1
    )

print "Creating table:"
print table

print "Done!"
```

Box 7.11 shows the Python code for writing and reading from a DynamoDB table. After establishing a connection with DynamoDB service, the *conn.get_table* is called to retrieve an existing table. The data written in this example consists of a JSON message with keys - *Body*, *CreatedBy* and *Time*. After creating the JSON message, a new DynamoDB table item is created by calling *table.new_item* and the hash key and range key is specified. The data item is finally committed to DynamoDB by calling *item.put*. To read data from DynamoDB, the *table.get_item* function is used with the hash key and range key as input parameters.

■ Box 7.11: Python program for writing and reading from a DynamoDB table

```
import boto.dynamodb
import time
from datetime import date

ACCESS_KEY="<enter access key>"
SECRET_KEY="<enter secret key>"
REGION="us-east-1"

print "Connecting to DynamoDB"
```

```
conn = boto.dynamodb.connect_to_region(REGION,
    aws_access_key_id=ACCESS_KEY,
    aws_secret_access_key=SECRET_KEY)

print "Listing available tables"
tables_list = conn.list_tables()
print tables_list

print "my-test-table description"
desc = conn.describe_table('my-test-table')
print desc

msg_datetime = time.asctime(time.localtime(time.time()))

print "Writing data"

table = conn.get_table("my-test-table")

hash_attribute = "Entry/" + str(date.today())

item_data =
    'Body': 'Test message',
    'CreatedBy': 'Bob',
    'Time': msg_datetime,


item = table.new_item(
    hash_key=hash_attribute,
    range_key=str(date.today()),
    attrs=item_data
)
item.put()

print "Reading data"

table = conn.get_table('my-test-table')

read_data = table.get_item(
        hash_key=hash_attribute,
        range_key=str(date.today())
        )

print read_data
print "Done!"
```

7.1.6 Amazon SQS

Amazon SQS offers a highly scalable and reliable hosted queue for storing messages as they travel between distinct components of applications.

Box 7.12 shows the Python code for creating an SQS queue. In this example, a connection to SQS service is first established by calling *boto.sqs.connect_to_region*. The AWS region, access key and secret key are passed to this function. After connecting to SQS service, *conn.create_queue* is called to create a new queue with queue name as input parameter. The function *conn.get_all_queues* is used to retrieve all SQS queues.

■ Box 7.12: Python program for creating an SQS queue

```
import boto.sqs

ACCESS_KEY="<enter access key>"
SECRET_KEY="<enter secret key>"
REGION="us-east-1"

print "Connecting to SQS"

conn = boto.sqs.connect_to_region(
        REGION,
        aws_access_key_id=ACCESS_KEY,
        aws_secret_access_key=SECRET_KEY)

queue_name = 'mytestqueue'

print "Creating queue with name: " + queue_name
q = conn.create_queue(queue_name)

print "Created queue with name: " + queue_name

print " \n Getting all queues"

rs = conn.get_all_queues()

for item in rs:
    print item
```

Box 7.13 shows the Python code for writing an SQS queue. After connecting to an SQS queue, the *queue.write* is called with the message as input parameter.

■ Box 7.13: Python program for writing to an SQS queue

```
import boto.sqs
from boto.sqs.message import Message
import time

ACCESS_KEY="<enter access key>"
SECRET_KEY="<enter secret key>"

REGION="us-east-1"

print "Connecting to SQS"

conn = boto.sqs.connect_to_region(
        REGION,
        aws_access_key_id=ACCESS_KEY,
        aws_secret_access_key=SECRET_KEY)

queue_name = 'mytestqueue'

print "Connecting to queue: " + queue_name
```

```
q = conn.get_all_queues(prefix=queue_name)

msg_datetime = time.asctime(time.localtime(time.time()))

msg = "Test message generated on: " + msg_datetime
print "Writing to queue: " + msg

m = Message()
m.set_body(msg)
status = q[0].write(m)

print "Message written to queue"

count = q[0].count()

print "Total messages in queue: " + str(count)
```

Box 7.14 shows the Python code for reading from an SQS queue. After connecting to an SQS queue, the *queue.read* is called to read a message from a queue.

■ Box 7.14: Python program for reading from an SQS queue

```
import boto.sqs
from boto.sqs.message import Message

ACCESS_KEY="<enter access key>"
SECRET_KEY="<enter secret key>"

REGION="us-east-1"

print "Connecting to SQS"

conn = boto.sqs.connect_to_region(
        REGION,
        aws_access_key_id=ACCESS_KEY,
        aws_secret_access_key=SECRET_KEY)

queue_name = 'mytestqueue'

print "Connecting to queue: " + queue_name
q = conn.get_all_queues(prefix=queue_name)

count = q[0].count()

print "Total messages in queue: " + str(count)

print "Reading message from queue"

for i in range(count):
    m = q[0].read()
    print "Message %d: %s" % (i+1,str(m.get_body()))
    q[0].delete_message(m)

print "Read %d messages from queue" % (count)
```

7.1.7 Amazon EMR

Amazon EMR is a web service that utilizes Hadoop framework running on Amazon EC2 and Amazon S3. EMR is suitable for massive scale data processing for applications such as data mining, data warehousing, scientific simulations, etc.

Box 7.15 shows the Python code for launching an Elastic MapReduce job. In this example, a connection to EMR service is first established by calling *boto.emr.connect_to_region*. The AWS region, access key and secret key are passed to this function. After connecting to EMR service, a jobflow step is created. There are two types of steps - streaming and custom jar. To create a streaming job an object of the *StreamingStep* class is created by specifying the job name, locations of the mapper, reducer, input and output. The job flow is then started using the *conn.run_jobflow* function with streaming step object as input. When the MapReduce job completes, the output can be obtained from the output location on the S3 bucket specified while creating the streaming step.

■ Box 7.15: Python program for launching an EMR job

```
import boto.emr
from boto.emr.step import StreamingStep
from time import sleep

ACCESS_KEY="<enter access key>"
SECRET_KEY="<enter secret key>"
REGION="us-east-1"

print "Connecting to EMR"

conn = boto.emr.connect_to_region(REGION,
        aws_access_key_id=ACCESS_KEY,
        aws_secret_access_key=SECRET_KEY)

print "Creating streaming step"

step = StreamingStep(name='Word Count',
        mapper='s3n://mybucket/wordCountMapper.py',
        reducer='s3n://mybucket/wordCountReducer.py',
        input='s3n://mybucket/data/',
        output='s3n://mybucket/wordcountoutput/')


print "Creating job flow"

jobid = conn.run_jobflow(name='Word Count Jobflow',
        log_uri='s3n://mybucket/wordcount_logs',
        steps=[step])

print "Submitted job flow"

print "Waiting for job flow to complete"

status = conn.describe_jobflow(jobid)
print status.state
```

```
while status.state != 'COMPLETED' or status.state != 'FAILED':
    sleep(10)
    status = conn.describe_jobflow(jobid)

print "Job status: " + str(status.state)

print "Done!"
```

Box 7.16 shows the word count mapper program in Python. The mapper reads the data from standard input (stdin) and splits the data into words. For each word in input, the mapper emits a key-value pair where key is the word and value is equal to 1.

■ Box 7.16: Word count Mapper in Python

```
#!/usr/bin/env python
import sys

for line in sys.stdin:
    line = line.strip()
    words = line.split()
    for word in words:
        print '%s%s' % (word, 1)
```

Box 7.17 shows the word count reducer program in Python. The key-value pairs emitted by the map phase are shuffled to the reducers and grouped by the key. The reducer reads the key-value pairs grouped by the same key from the standard input (stdin) and sums up the occurrences to compute the count for each word.

■ Box 7.17: Word count Reducer in Python

```
#!/usr/bin/env python
from operator import itemgetter
import sys

current_word = None
current_count = 0
word = None

for line in sys.stdin:
    line = line.strip()
    word, count = line.split('', 1)

    try:
        count = int(count)
    except ValueError:
        continue

    if current_word == word:
        current_count += count
else:
```

```
    if current_word:
        print '%s%s' % (current_word, current_count)
    current_count = count
    current_word = word

if current_word == word:
    print '%s%s' % (current_word, current_count)
```

7.2 Python for Google Cloud Platform

In this section you will learn how to use Python for Google Cloud Platform. The examples in this section use the Google-APIs Python Client library for accessing Google APIs.

7.2.1 Google Compute Engine

Google Compute Engine provides scalable and flexible virtual machine computing capabilities in the cloud [4].

Box 7.18 shows the credentials file that is used for all the Google Cloud examples in this section. The client ID and client secret can be obtained from the Google APIs console.

■ Box 7.18: Credentials file for Google Cloud examples - client_secrets.json

```
{
    "installed": {
        "client_id": "<enter client id>",
        "client_secret":"<enter client secret>",
        "redirect_uris": ["http://localhost:8080/", "urn:ietf:wg:oauth:2.0:oob"],
        "auth_uri": "https://accounts.google.com/o/oauth2/auth",
        "token_uri": "https://accounts.google.com/o/oauth2/token"
    }
```

Box 7.19 shows the Python program for launching Google Compute Engine instance. This example uses the OAuth 2.0 scope (https://www.googleapis.com/auth/compute) and credentials in the credentials file to request a refresh and access token, which is then stored in the oauth2.dat file. The access token saved in the oauth2.dat eliminates the need for further authorizations. After completing the OAuth authorization, an instance of the Google Compute Engine service is obtained. To launch a new instance the *instances().insert* method of the Google Compute Engine API is used. The request body to this method contains the properties such as instance name, machine type, zone, network interfaces, etc., specified in JSON format.

■ Box 7.19: Python program for launching GCE instance

```
import httplib2
from oauth2client.client import flow_from_clientsecrets
from oauth2client.file import Storage
from apiclient.errors import HttpError
from oauth2client.client import AccessTokenRefreshError
```

```
from oauth2client.tools import run
from apiclient.discovery import build
from httplib2 import HttpLib2Error


API_VERSION = 'v1beta15'
GCE_SCOPE = 'https://www.googleapis.com/auth/compute'
GCE_URL = 'https://www.googleapis.com/compute/%s/projects/' % (API_VERSION)
DEFAULT_ZONE = 'us-central1-b'
CLIENT_SECRETS = 'client_secrets.json'
OAUTH2_STORAGE = 'oauth2.dat'
PROJECT_ID = 'mycloudproject'
NEW_INSTANCE_NAME='myinstance'

def main():
    #OAuth 2.0 authorization.
    flow = flow_from_clientsecrets(CLIENT_SECRETS, scope=GCE_SCOPE)
    storage = Storage(OAUTH2_STORAGE)
    credentials = storage.get()

    if credentials is None or credentials.invalid:
        credentials = run(flow, storage)

    http = httplib2.Http()
    auth_http = credentials.authorize(http)

    gce_service = build('compute', API_VERSION)

    # Construct the request body
    instance = {
        "kind": "compute#instance",
        "disks": [],
        "networkInterfaces": [
        {
        "kind": "compute#instanceNetworkInterface",
        "network":"https://www.googleapis.com/
         compute/v1beta15/projects/mycloudproject/global/netw orks/default",
        "accessConfigs": [
        {
         "name": "External NAT",
         "type": "ONE_TO_ONE_NAT"
        }
        ]
        }
        ],
        "serviceAccounts": [
        {
        "kind": "compute#serviceAccount",
        "email": "default",
        "scopes": [
        "https://www.googleapis.com/auth/userinfo.email",
        "https://www.googleapis.com/auth/compute",
         "https://www.googleapis.com/auth/devstorage.full_control"
        ]
```

```
        }
        ],
        "zone":
"https://www.googleapis.com/
compute/v1beta15/projects/mycloudproject/zones/us-c entral1-b",
        "metadata": {
        "items": []
        },
        "machineType": "https://www.googleapis.com/
compute/v1beta15/projects/mycloudproject/zones/us-ce ntral1-b/machineTypes/n1-standard-
1",
        "image":
"https://www.googleapis.com/
compute/v1beta15/projects/debian-cloud/global/images /debian-7-wheezy-v20130723",
        "name": "myinstance"
    }

    # Create the instance
    request = gce_service.instances().insert(
            project=PROJECT_ID, body=instance, zone=DEFAULT_ZONE)
    response = request.execute(auth_http)

    print response

if __name__ == '__main__':
main()
```

Box 7.20 shows the Python program for launching Google Compute Engine instance. To list instances the *instances().list* method of the Google Compute Engine API is used.

■ Box 7.20: Python program for listing GCE instances

```
import httplib2
from oauth2client.client import flow_from_clientsecrets
from oauth2client.file import Storage
from apiclient.errors import HttpError
from oauth2client.client import AccessTokenRefreshError
from oauth2client.tools import run
from apiclient.discovery import build
from httplib2 import HttpLib2Error


API_VERSION = 'v1beta15'
GCE_SCOPE = 'https://www.googleapis.com/auth/compute'
GCE_URL = 'https://www.googleapis.com/compute/%s/projects/' % (API_VERSION)
DEFAULT_ZONE = 'us-central1-b'
CLIENT_SECRETS = 'client_secrets.json'
OAUTH2_STORAGE = 'oauth2.dat'
PROJECT_ID = 'mycloudproject'
NEW_INSTANCE_NAME='myinstance'

def main():
    #OAuth 2.0 authorization.
    flow = flow_from_clientsecrets(CLIENT_SECRETS, scope=GCE_SCOPE)
```

```
    storage = Storage(OAUTH2_STORAGE)
    credentials = storage.get()

    if credentials is None or credentials.invalid:
        credentials = run(flow, storage)
    http = httplib2.Http()
    auth_http = credentials.authorize(http)

    gce_service = build('compute', API_VERSION)

    #List instances
    request = gce_service.instances().list(project=PROJECT_ID, zone=DEFAULT_ZONE, fil-
ter=None)
    response = request.execute(auth_http)
    if response and 'items' in response:
        instances = response['items']
        for instance in instances:
        print instance['name']
    else:
    print 'No instances found'


if __name__ == '__main__':
main()
```

7.2.2 Google Cloud Storage

Google Cloud Storage is a cloud service for storing data in the Google's cloud [106]. Data stored on Google Cloud Storage is organized into buckets. Box 7.21 shows the Python program for uploading a file to a Google Cloud Storage bucket. This example uses the OAuth 2.0 scope (https://www.googleapis.com/auth/devstorage.full_control) and credentials in the credentials file to request a refresh and access token, which is then stored in the oauth2.dat file. After completing the OAuth authorization, an instance of the Google Cloud Storage service is obtained. To upload a file the *objects().insert* method of the Google Cloud Storage API is used. The request to this method contains the bucket name, file name and media body containing the *MediaIoBaseUpload* object created from the file contents.

■ Box 7.21: Python program for uploading a file to Google Cloud Storage

```
import httplib2
from oauth2client.client import flow_from_clientsecrets
from oauth2client.file import Storage
from apiclient.errors import HttpError
from oauth2client.client import AccessTokenRefreshError
from oauth2client.tools import run
from apiclient.discovery import build
from httplib2 import HttpLib2Error
from apiclient.http import MediaIoBaseUpload

import io

API_VERSION = 'v1beta2'
```

```
GS_SCOPE = 'https://www.googleapis.com/auth/devstorage.full_control'
CLIENT_SECRETS = 'client_secrets.json'
OAUTH2_STORAGE = 'oauth2.dat'
BUCKET='mybucket'
FILENAME = 'file.txt'
FILE_TYPE = 'text/plain'

def main():
    #OAuth 2.0 authorization.
    flow = flow_from_clientsecrets(CLIENT_SECRETS, scope=GS_SCOPE)
    storage = Storage(OAUTH2_STORAGE)
    credentials = storage.get()

    if credentials is None or credentials.invalid:
        credentials = run(flow, storage)
    http = httplib2.Http()
    auth_http = credentials.authorize(http)

    gs_service = build('storage', API_VERSION, http=auth_http)

    # Upload file
    fp= open(FILENAME,'r')
    fh = io.BytesIO(fp.read())
    media = MediaIoBaseUpload(fh, FILE_TYPE)
    request = gs_service.objects().insert(bucket=BUCKET, name=FILENAME, media_body=media)
    response = request.execute()
    print response

if __name__ == '__main__':
main()
```

Box 7.22 shows the Python program for downloading a file from a Google Cloud Storage bucket. For downloading a file the *objects().get_media* method of the Google Cloud Storage API is used. The request to this method contains the bucket name and file name.

■ Box 7.22: Python program for downloading a file from Google Cloud Storage

```
import httplib2
from oauth2client.client import flow_from_clientsecrets
from oauth2client.file import Storage
from apiclient.errors import HttpError
from oauth2client.client import AccessTokenRefreshError
from oauth2client.tools import run
from apiclient.discovery import build
from httplib2 import HttpLib2Error
from apiclient.http import MediaIoBaseDownload

import io

API_VERSION = 'v1beta2'
GS_SCOPE = 'https://www.googleapis.com/auth/devstorage.full_control'
CLIENT_SECRETS = 'client_secrets.json'
OAUTH2_STORAGE = 'oauth2.dat'
```

```
PROJECT_ID = 'mycloudproject'
BUCKET='mybucket'
FIELDS = 'bucket,name,metadata(my-key)'

FILENAME = 'file.txt'

def main():
    #OAuth 2.0 authorization.
    flow = flow_from_clientsecrets(CLIENT_SECRETS, scope=GS_SCOPE)
    storage = Storage(OAUTH2_STORAGE)
    credentials = storage.get()

    if credentials is None or credentials.invalid:
        credentials = run(flow, storage)
    http = httplib2.Http()
    auth_http = credentials.authorize(http)

    gs_service = build('storage', API_VERSION, http=auth_http)

    # Get Metadata
    request = gs_service.objects().get(bucket=BUCKET, object=FILENAME, fields=FIELDS)
    response = request.execute()
    print response


    # Get Payload Data
    req = gs_service.objects().get_media(bucket=BUCKET, object=FILENAME)
    fh = io.BytesIO()
    downloader = MediaIoBaseDownload(fh, req, chunksize=1024*1024)
    done = False
    while not done:
        status, done = downloader.next_chunk()
        if status:
            print 'Download %d%%.' % int(status.progress() * 100)
        print 'Download Complete!'

    fp=open(FILENAME,'w')
    fp.write(fh.getvalue())
    fp.close()

if __name__ == '__main__':
main()
```

Box 7.23 shows the Python program for listing files in a GCS bucket. For listing files the *objects().list* method of the Google Cloud Storage API is used.

■ **Box 7.23: Python program for listing files in a GCS bucket**

```
import httplib2
from oauth2client.client import flow_from_clientsecrets
from oauth2client.file import Storage
from apiclient.errors import HttpError
from oauth2client.client import AccessTokenRefreshError
from oauth2client.tools import run
```

```
from apiclient.discovery import build
from httplib2 import HttpLib2Error


API_VERSION = 'v1beta2'
GS_SCOPE = 'https://www.googleapis.com/auth/devstorage.full_control'
CLIENT_SECRETS = 'client_secrets.json'
OAUTH2_STORAGE = 'oauth2.dat'
PROJECT_ID = 'mycloudproject'
BUCKET='mybucket'
FIELDS = 'items(bucket,name,metadata(my-key))'

def main():
    #OAuth 2.0 authorization.
    flow = flow_from_clientsecrets(CLIENT_SECRETS, scope=GS_SCOPE)
    storage = Storage(OAUTH2_STORAGE)
    credentials = storage.get()

    if credentials is None or credentials.invalid:
        credentials = run(flow, storage)
    http = httplib2.Http()
    auth_http = credentials.authorize(http)

    gs_service = build('storage', API_VERSION)

    #List objects
    request = gs_service.objects().list(bucket=BUCKET, fields=FIELDS)
    response = request.execute(auth_http)
    print response

if __name__ == '__main__':
main()
```

7.2.3 Google Cloud SQL

Google Cloud SQL is a MySQL database in the Google's cloud [109]. Box 7.24 shows the Python program for launching a Google Cloud SQL instance. This example uses the OAuth 2.0 scope (https://www.googleapis.com/auth/sqlservice.admin) and credentials in the credentials file to request a refresh and access token, which is then stored in the oauth2.dat file. After completing the OAuth authorization, an instance of the Google Cloud SQL service is obtained. To launch a new instance the *instances().insert* method of the Google Cloud SQL API is used. The request body of this method contains properties such as instance, project, tier, pricingPlan and replicationType.

■ Box 7.24: Python program for launching a Google Cloud SQL instance

```
import httplib2
from oauth2client.client import flow_from_clientsecrets
from oauth2client.file import Storage
from apiclient.errors import HttpError
from oauth2client.client import AccessTokenRefreshError
from oauth2client.tools import run
```

```
from apiclient.discovery import build
from httplib2 import HttpLib2Error

import io

API_VERSION = 'v1beta1'
GS_SCOPE = 'https://www.googleapis.com/auth/sqlservice.admin'
CLIENT_SECRETS = 'client_secrets.json'
OAUTH2_STORAGE = 'oauth2.dat'
PROJECT_ID = 'mycloudproject'

def main():
    #OAuth 2.0 authorization.
    flow = flow_from_clientsecrets(CLIENT_SECRETS, scope=GS_SCOPE)
    storage = Storage(OAUTH2_STORAGE)
    credentials = storage.get()

    if credentials is None or credentials.invalid:
        credentials = run(flow, storage)

    http = httplib2.Http()
    auth_http = credentials.authorize(http)

    gcs_service = build('sqladmin', API_VERSION, http=auth_http)

    instance={
            "instance": "mydb",
            "project": "mycloudproject",
            "settings":
        {
            "tier": "D0",
            "pricingPlan": "PER_USE",
            "replicationType": "SYNCHRONOUS"
        }
    }

    # Create the instance
    request = gcs_service.instances().insert(project=PROJECT_ID, body=instance)
    response = request.execute()

    print response

if __name__ == '__main__':
main()
```

Box 7.25 shows the Python program for listing Google Cloud SQL instances. For listing instances the *instances().list* method of the Google Cloud SQL API is used.

■ Box 7.25: Python program for listing Google Cloud SQL instances

```
import httplib2
from oauth2client.client import flow_from_clientsecrets
from oauth2client.file import Storage
from apiclient.errors import HttpError
```

```
from oauth2client.client import AccessTokenRefreshError
from oauth2client.tools import run
from apiclient.discovery import build
from httplib2 import HttpLib2Error

import io

API_VERSION = 'v1beta1'
GS_SCOPE = 'https://www.googleapis.com/auth/sqlservice.admin'
CLIENT_SECRETS = 'client_secrets.json'
OAUTH2_STORAGE = 'oauth2.dat'
PROJECT_ID = 'mycloudproject'

def main():
    #OAuth 2.0 authorization.
    flow = flow_from_clientsecrets(CLIENT_SECRETS, scope=GS_SCOPE)
    storage = Storage(OAUTH2_STORAGE)
    credentials = storage.get()

    if credentials is None or credentials.invalid:
        credentials = run(flow, storage)

    http = httplib2.Http()
    auth_http = credentials.authorize(http)

    gcs_service = build('sqladmin', API_VERSION, http=auth_http)

    # List instances
    request = gcs_service.instances().list(project=PROJECT_ID)
    response = request.execute()

    print response

if __name__ == '__main__':
main()
```

Box 7.26 shows the Python program for creating a native MySQL connection with a Google Cloud SQL instance. This example uses the MySQLdb Python package. To connect to the MySQL RDS instance, the *MySQLdb.connect* function is called. After the connection to the RDS instance is established, a cursor to the database is obtained by calling *conn.cursor*. Next, a new database table named *Student* is created with *Id* as primary key and other columns. After creating the table some values are inserted. To execute the SQL commands for database manipulation, the commands are passed to the *cursor.execute* function.

■ Box 7.26: MySQL example using a Google Cloud SQL instance

```
import MySQLdb

USERNAME = 'root'
DB_NAME = 'mydb'
```

```
conn = MySQLdb.connect(unix_socket='/cloudsql/mycloudproject:mydb', user=USERNAME)

cursor = conn.cursor ()

cursor.execute ("CREATE TABLE Student(Id INT PRIMARY KEY, Name TEXT, Major TEXT, Grade
FLOAT) ")
cursor.execute ("INSERT INTO Student VALUES(100, 'John', 'CS', 3)")
cursor.execute ("INSERT INTO Student VALUES(101, 'David', 'ECE', 3.5)")
cursor.execute ("INSERT INTO Student VALUES(102, 'Bob', 'CS', 3.9)")
cursor.execute ("INSERT INTO Student VALUES(103, 'Alex', 'CS', 3.6)")
cursor.execute ("INSERT INTO Student VALUES(104, 'Martin', 'ECE', 3.1)")

rows = cursor.fetchall()
cursor.close ()
conn.close ()
```

7.2.4 Google BigQuery

Google BigQuery allows querying massive scale datasets with SQL-like queries [107]. The BigQuery queries are run against append-only tables and use the processing power of Google's infrastructure for speeding up queries.

Box 7.27 shows the Python program for creating a BigQuery dataset. This example uses the OAuth 2.0 scope (https://www.googleapis.com/auth/bigquery) and credentials in the credentials file to request a refresh and access token, which is then stored in the oauth2.dat file. After completing the OAuth authorization, an instance of the Google BigQuery service is obtained. The *jobs().insert* method of the Google BigQuery API is used for inserting a new dataset. The request body of this method contains properties such as configuration, load, and schema. In this example, the data is loaded from a CSV file. The schema property specifies the schema of the CSV file. The *jobs().insert* method returns immediately, therefore the *jobs.get* is called to get the job status.

■ Box 7.27: Python program for creating a BigQuery dataset

```
import httplib2
from oauth2client.client import flow_from_clientsecrets
from oauth2client.file import Storage
from apiclient.errors import HttpError
from oauth2client.client import AccessTokenRefreshError
from oauth2client.tools import run
from apiclient.discovery import build
from httplib2 import HttpLib2Error
import io
import time

API_VERSION = 'v2'
GS_SCOPE = 'https://www.googleapis.com/auth/bigquery'
CLIENT_SECRETS = 'client_secrets.json'
OAUTH2_STORAGE = 'oauth2.dat'
PROJECT_ID = 'mycloudproject'
DATASET_ID='mydataset'
```

```
def main():
    #OAuth 2.0 authorization.
    flow = flow_from_clientsecrets(CLIENT_SECRETS, scope=GS_SCOPE)
    storage = Storage(OAUTH2_STORAGE)
    credentials = storage.get()

    if credentials is None or credentials.invalid:
        credentials = run(flow, storage)

    http = httplib2.Http()
    auth_http = credentials.authorize(http)

    bigquery_service = build('bigquery', API_VERSION, http=auth_http)

    jobCollection = bigquery_service.jobs()

    jobData = {
    'projectId': PROJECT_ID,
    'configuration': {
    'load': {
    'sourceUris': ['gs://mybucket/yob2012.txt'],
    'schema': {
    'fields': [
        {
        'name': 'name',
        'type': 'STRING'
        },
        {
        'name': 'gender',
        'type': 'STRING'
        },
        {
        'name': 'count',
        'type': 'INTEGER'
        }
    ]
    },
    'destinationTable': {
    'projectId': PROJECT_ID,
    'datasetId': DATASET_ID,
    'tableId': 'namesdata'
    },
    }
    }
    }

    insertResponse = jobCollection.insert(projectId=PROJECT_ID,body=jobData).execute()

    while True:
        job = jobCollection.get(projectId=PROJECT_ID,
        jobId=insertResponse['jobReference']['jobId']).execute()
        if 'DONE' == job['status']['state']:
            print 'Done!'
            break
```

```
        print 'Loading data...'
        time.sleep(10)


if __name__ == '__main__':
    main()
```

Box 7.28 shows the Python program for querying a dataset with BigQuery. The *jobs().query* method of the Google BigQuery API is used for querying the dataset. This method runs a BigQuery SQL query synchronously and returns query results.

■ Box 7.28: Python program for querying a dataset with BigQuery

```
import httplib2
from oauth2client.client import flow_from_clientsecrets
from oauth2client.file import Storage
from apiclient.errors import HttpError
from oauth2client.client import AccessTokenRefreshError
from oauth2client.tools import run
from apiclient.discovery import build
from httplib2 import HttpLib2Error

import io

API_VERSION = 'v2'
GS_SCOPE = 'https://www.googleapis.com/auth/bigquery'
CLIENT_SECRETS = 'client_secrets.json'
OAUTH2_STORAGE = 'oauth2.dat'
PROJECT_ID = 'mycloudproject'

def main():
    #OAuth 2.0 authorization.
    flow = flow_from_clientsecrets(CLIENT_SECRETS, scope=GS_SCOPE)
    storage = Storage(OAUTH2_STORAGE)
    credentials = storage.get()

    if credentials is None or credentials.invalid:
    credentials = run(flow, storage)
    http = httplib2.Http()
    auth_http = credentials.authorize(http)

    bigquery_service = build('bigquery', API_VERSION, http=auth_http)

    # Query
    query_request = bigquery_service.jobs()
    query_data = {'query':'SELECT name,count FROM mydataset.names WHERE gender =
ḾÓRDER BY count DESC LIMIT 5;'}

    query_response = query_request.query(projectId=PROJECT_ID,
body=query_data).execute()

    print query_response
```

```
    print 'Query Results:'
    for row in query_response['rows']:
        result_row = []
        for field in row['f']:
            result_row.append(field['v'])
        print ('').join(result_row)


if __name__ == '__main__':
main()
```

7.2.5 Google Cloud Datastore

Google Cloud Datastore is a No-SQL (i.e., schema-less) object datastore that provides robust and scalable storage [108]. Data objects in the Datastore are known as entities. An entity has one or more named properties, each of which can have one or more values. Entities of the same kind need not have the same properties, and an entity's values for a given property need not all be of the same data type. Box 7.29 shows the Python program for creating a Google Cloud Datastore entity. This example uses the OAuth 2.0 scopes (https://www.googleapis.com/auth/datastore and https://www.googleapis.com/auth/userinfo.email) and credentials in the credentials file to request a refresh and access token, which is then stored in the oauth2.dat file. After completing the OAuth authorization, an instance of the Google Cloud Datastore service is obtained. The *datasets().blindWrite* method of the Google Cloud Datastore API is used for creating a new entity.

■ Box 7.29: Python program for creating a Google Cloud Datastore entity

```
import httplib2
from oauth2client.client import flow_from_clientsecrets
from oauth2client.file import Storage
from apiclient.errors import HttpError
from oauth2client.client import AccessTokenRefreshError
from oauth2client.tools import run
from apiclient.discovery import build
from httplib2 import HttpLib2Error

import io

API_VERSION = 'v1beta1'
GS_SCOPE = ['https://www.googleapis.com/auth/userinfo.email',
'https://www.googleapis.com/auth/datastore']
CLIENT_SECRETS = 'client_secrets.json'
OAUTH2_STORAGE = 'oauth2.dat'
PROJECT_ID='mycloudproject'

def main():
    #OAuth 2.0 authorization.
    flow = flow_from_clientsecrets(CLIENT_SECRETS, scope=GS_SCOPE)
    storage = Storage(OAUTH2_STORAGE)
```

```
credentials = storage.get()

if credentials is None or credentials.invalid:
credentials = run(flow, storage)
http = httplib2.Http()
auth_http = credentials.authorize(http)

gds_service = build('datastore', API_VERSION, http=auth_http)


query={
    "mutation":
    {
        "insert":
        [
            {
            "key":
            {
            "path":
            [
            {
            "kind": "Person",
            "id": "989871871"
            }
            ]
            },
            "properties":
            {
            "City":
            {
            "values":
            [
            {
            "stringValue": "Atlanta"
            }
            ]
            },
            "Age":
            {
            "values":
            [
            {
            "integerValue": "20"
            }
            ]
            },
            "Name":
            {
            "values":
            [
            {
            "stringValue": "Mary"
            }
            ]
```

```
                }
              }
            }
          ]
        }
    }

    # Create Entity
    request = gds_service.datasets().blindWrite(datasetId=PROJECT_ID, body=query)
    response = request.execute()
    print response

if __name__ == '__main__':
main()
```

Box 7.30 shows the Python program for querying Google Cloud Datastore entities. The *datasets().runQuery* method of the Google Cloud Datastore API is used for querying entities.

■ Box 7.30: Python program for querying Google Cloud Datastore entities

```
import httplib2
from oauth2client.client import flow_from_clientsecrets
from oauth2client.file import Storage
from apiclient.errors import HttpError
from oauth2client.client import AccessTokenRefreshError
from oauth2client.tools import run
from apiclient.discovery import build
from httplib2 import HttpLib2Error

import io

API_VERSION = 'v1beta1'
GS_SCOPE = ['https://www.googleapis.com/auth/userinfo.email',
'https://www.googleapis.com/auth/datastore']
CLIENT_SECRETS = 'client_secrets.json'
OAUTH2_STORAGE = 'oauth2.dat'
PROJECT_ID='mycloudproject'

def main():
    #OAuth 2.0 authorization.
    flow = flow_from_clientsecrets(CLIENT_SECRETS, scope=GS_SCOPE)
    storage = Storage(OAUTH2_STORAGE)
    credentials = storage.get()

    if credentials is None or credentials.invalid:
    credentials = run(flow, storage)
    http = httplib2.Http()
    auth_http = credentials.authorize(http)

    gds_service = build('datastore', API_VERSION, http=auth_http)

    query={
        "query":
```

```
        {
            "kinds":
            [
                {
                    "name": "Person"
                }
            ]
        }
    }

    # Querying entities
    request = gds_service.datasets().runQuery(datasetId=PROJECT_ID, body=query)
    response = request.execute()
    print response

if __name__ == '__main__':
main()
```

7.2.6 Google App Engine

Google App Engine is a web application hosting service [105]. Applications hosted in Google App Engine are are easy to build, maintain, and scale. Applications run in a secure sandbox environment that provides limited access to the underlying operating system. The sandbox isolates an application in its own secure, reliable environment that is independent of the hardware, operating system and physical location of the web server. The benefit of the sandbox is that it allows Google App Engine to distribute web requests for the application across multiple servers, and start and stop servers to meet application workloads.

Google App Engine includes a simple web application framework called webapp2. App Engine also supports any framework written in pure Python that speaks WSGI, including Django, CherryPy, Pylons, web.py, and web2py.

Box 7.31 shows the Python code for a simple Google App Engine application for student records. This application uses the App Engine Users service for signing into the application using Google accounts. For storing data, the App Engine Datastore is used. The application contains two request handlers, one for the main page (*MainPage*) and the other for saving records (*SaveRecord*).

■ Box 7.31: Python code for a Google App Engine application - student.py

```
import cgi
import urllib
from google.appengine.api import users
from google.appengine.ext import db
import webapp2
import datetime

MAIN_PAGE_TEMPLATE = """
<h1>New Student Record</h1>
<form method="post" action="/save">
Name: <input name="name"><br>
Major: <input name="major"><br>
```

```
Email: <input name="email"><br><br>
<input type="submit" value="Save">
</form>

<a href="%s">%s</a>

</body>
</html>
"""

class Student(db.Model):
    name = db.StringProperty(required=True)
    major = db.StringProperty()
    email = db.StringProperty()


class MainPage(webapp2.RequestHandler):

def get(self):

    if not users.get_current_user():
        url = users.create_login_url(self.request.uri)
        self.redirect(url)
    else:
        self.response.write('<html><body>')
        self.response.write('<h1>Student Records</h1><br><br>')

        students = db.GqlQuery("SELECT * FROM Student")

        self.response.write('<table border="1" cellpadding="0" cellspacing="0">
                <tr><td width="180"><h4>Name</h4></td>
                <td width="180"><h4>Major</h4></td>
                <td width="180"><h4>Email</h4></td>
                </tr>')

        for student in students:
         self.response.write('<tr><td>%s</td>' % student.name)
         self.response.write('<td>%s</td>' % student.major)
         self.response.write('<td>%s</td></tr>' % student.email)

        self.response.write('</table>')

        if users.get_current_user():
         url = users.create_logout_url(self.request.uri)
         url_linktext = 'Logout'

        self.response.write(MAIN_PAGE_TEMPLATE % (url, url_linktext))

class SaveRecord(webapp2.RequestHandler):

def post(self):
student_name = self.request.get('name')
student_major = self.request.get('major')
student_email = self.request.get('email')
```

```
    s = Student(name=student_name,major=student_major,email=student_email)
    s.put()

self.redirect('/' )

application = webapp2.WSGIApplication([
('/', MainPage),
('/save', SaveRecord),
], debug=True)
```

Every App Engine application requires a configuration file (app.yaml). Box 7.32 shows the configuration file for the student records application. This file describes which handler scripts should be used for which URLs.

App Engine SDK comes with a development web server that allows you to test the application locally. To test the application, the development server is launched by the following command:
$dev_appserver.py app-name

where app-name is the name of the folder containing the application files. After testing the application locally, it can be deployed on App Engine by the following command:
$appcfg.py update app-name

Figure 7.1 shows a screenshot of the login page of the student records application and Figure 7.2 shows a screenshot of the main page.

■ Box 7.32: Google App Engine application configuration file - app.yaml

```
application: studentrecordsapp
version: 1
runtime: python27
api_version: 1
threadsafe: true

handlers:
- url: /.*
script: student.application

libraries:
- name: webapp2
version: latest
```

7.3 Python for Windows Azure

Windows Azure provides three compute models that you can use to host web applications - Web Sites, Cloud Services, and Virtual Machines [83]. In this section you will learn how to use Python for Windows Azure.

7.3.1 Azure Cloud Service

An application that is run in Windows Azure is called a Windows Azure cloud service that includes the application code and configuration. To deploy an application in Windows Azure

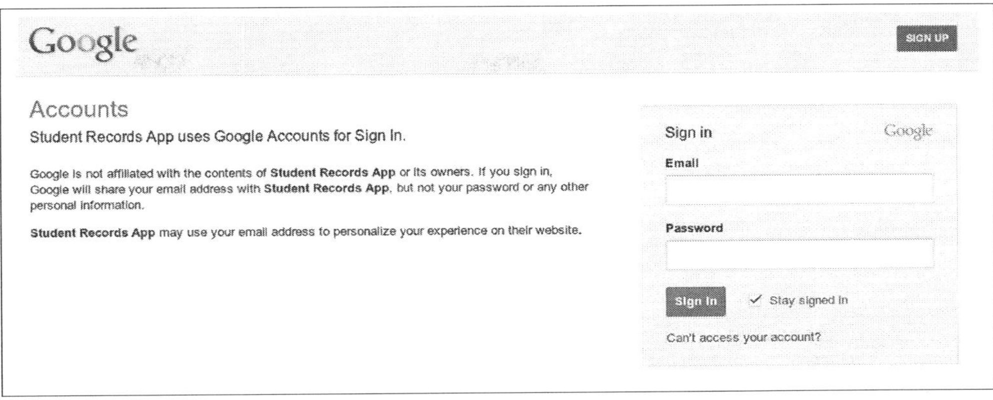

Figure 7.1: Student Records App - screenshot of login page

Student Records

Name	Major	Email
Joe	ECE	joe@mysite.com
Nav	CS	nav@mysite.com
Bob	ME	bob@mysite.com

New Student Record

Name:

Major:

Email:

Save

Logout

Figure 7.2: Student Records App - screenshot of home page

as a cloud service, three components are needed - service definition file, service configuration file and service package.

Box 7.33 shows an example of creating a cloud service using the Azure service management API. Cloud service is created using the *create_hosted_service* method.

■ **Box 7.33: Python example of creating an Azure cloud service**

```
from azure import *
from azure.servicemanagement import *

subscription_id='<enter subscription ID>'
certificate_path='<enter PEM file path>'

sms = ServiceManagementService(subscription_id, certificate_path)

name = 'mycloudservice'
label = 'mycloudservice'
desc = 'my hosted service'
location = 'West US'

# You can either set the location or an affinity_group
sms.create_hosted_service(name, label, desc, location)
```

7.3.2 Azure Virtual Machines

Windows Azure Virtual Machines allows you to provision on-demand, scalable compute infrastructure. Box 7.34 shows an example of creating a new Azure virtual machine. To create a virtual machine, a cloud service is first created. Virtual machine is created using the *create_virtual_machine_deployment* method of the Azure service management API.

■ Box 7.34: Python example of creating an Azure virtual machine

```
from azure import *
from azure.servicemanagement import *

subscription_id='<enter subscription ID>'
certificate_path='<enter PEM file path>'

sms = ServiceManagementService(subscription_id, certificate_path)

name = 'mycloudservice'
location = 'West US'

# You can either set the location or an affinity_group
sms.create_hosted_service(service_name=name,
    label=name,
    location=location)

# Name of an os image as returned by list_os_images
image_name = 'b39f27a8b8c64d52b05eac6a62ebad85__Ubuntu-12_04_2-LTS-amd64-
server-20130225-en-us-30GB'

# Destination storage account container/blob where the VM disk will be created
media_link = 'http://mystorage.blob.core.windows.net/mycontainer/ubuntu.vhd'
# Linux VM configuration
linux_config = LinuxConfigurationSet('mystorage', 'myusername', 'mypassword', True)

os_hd = OSVirtualHardDisk(image_name, media_link)

sms.create_virtual_machine_deployment(service_name=name,
```

```
deployment_name=name,
deployment_slot='production',
label=name,
role_name=name,
system_config=linux_config,
os_virtual_hard_disk=os_hd,
role_size='Small')
```

7.3.3 Azure Storage

Windows Azure Storage services allow you to store and access various forms of data (Blobs, Tables and Queues). Blobs are used to store unstructured binary and text data. Tables are used to store non-relational structured data. Queues are used to store messages that a client can access. A storage service must be created before storing data in blobs, tables or queues. Box 7.35 shows an example of creating a new Azure storage service using the *create_storage_account* method of the service management API. Box 7.36 shows an example of listing Azure storage services.

■ Box 7.35: Python example of creating an Azure storage service

```
from azure import *
from azure.servicemanagement import *

subscription_id='<enter subscription ID>'
certificate_path='<enter PEM file path>'

sms = ServiceManagementService(subscription_id, certificate_path)

name = 'mystorage'
label = 'mystorage'
location = 'West US'
desc = 'My storage account.'

result = sms.create_storage_account(name, desc, label, location=location)

operation_result = sms.get_operation_status(result.request_id)

print('Operation status: ' + operation_result.status)
```

■ Box 7.36: Python example of listing Azure storage services

```
from azure import *
from azure.servicemanagement import *

subscription_id='<enter subscription ID>'
certificate_path='<enter PEM file path>'

sms = ServiceManagementService(subscription_id, certificate_path)

result = sms.list_storage_accounts()
for account in result:
```

```
    print('Service name: ' + account.service_name)
    print('Affinity group: ' + account.storage_service_properties.affinity_group)
    print('Location: ' + account.storage_service_properties.location)
    print('')
```

Azure Blob Service

Azure Blobs service allows you to store large amounts of unstructured text or binary data such as video, audio and images. Box 7.37 shows an example of using the Blob service for storing a file. Blobs are organized in containers. The *create_container* method is used to create a new container. After creating a container the blob is uploaded using the *put_blob* method. Blobs can be listed using the *list_blobs* method. To download a blob, the *get_blob* method is used.

■ Box 7.37: Python example of using Azure Blob Service

```
from azure.storage import *

key="<enter key>"

blob_service = BlobService(account_name='myaccountname', account_key=key)

#Create Container
blob_service.create_container('mycontainer')

#Upload Blob
filename='images.txt'
myblob = open(filename, 'r').read()
blob_service.put_blob('mycontainer', filename, myblob, x_ms_blob_type='BlockBlob')

#List Blobs
blobs = blob_service.list_blobs('mycontainer')
for blob in blobs:
    print(blob.name)
    print(blob.url)

#Download Blob
output_filename='output.txt'
blob = blob_service.get_blob('mycontainer', 'myblob')
with open(output_filename, 'w') as f:
    f.write(blob)
```

Azure Table Service

Azure Table service provides No-SQL capabilities for applications that require storage of large amounts of unstructured data. Box 7.38 shows an example of using the Table service. The *create_table* method is used to create a new table. A table is a collection of entities. Tables don't have a fixed schema. Therefore entities in a table can have different sets of properties. Entity is a set of properties. To insert an entity into a table, the *insert_entity* method is used. Entities stored in a table can be queried using the *query_entities* method.

■ Box 7.38: Python example of using Azure Table Service

```
from azure.storage import *

key="<enter key>"

table_service = TableService(account_name='myaccountname', account_key=key)

#Create Table
table_service.create_table('gtstudents')

#Insert Entity
item = {'PartitionKey': 'CS-Students', 'RowKey': '1', 'Name' : 'Preet', 'Major': 'CS', 'Grade':
'3.8'}
table_service.insert_entity('gtstudents', item)

#Query Entities
items = table_service.query_entities('gtstudents', "PartitionKey eq 'CS-Students'")
for item in items:
    print(item.Name)
    print(item.Major)
    print(item.Grade)
```

Azure Queue Service

Windows Azure Queues store large numbers of messages. Box 7.39 shows an example of using the Queue service. To create a new queue the *create_queue* method is used. Messages are inserted into the queue using the *put_message* method and retrieved using the *get_messages* method.

■ Box 7.39: Python example of using Azure Queue Service

```
from azure.storage import *
import time

key="<enter key>"

queue_service = QueueService(account_name='myaccountname', account_key=key)
#Create Queue
queue_service.create_queue('myqueue')

# Insert Message into Queue
msg_datetime = time.asctime(time.localtime(time.time()))
msg = "Test message generated on: " + msg_datetime

queue_service.put_message('myqueue', msg)

#Get Queue Length
queue_metadata = queue_service.get_queue_metadata('myqueue')
count = queue_metadata['x-ms-approximate-messages-count']
print "Queue Length:" + count

#Retrieve Messages from Queue
```

```
messages = queue_service.get_messages('myqueue')
for message in messages:
    print(message.message_text)
    queue_service.delete_message('myqueue',
message.message_id, message.pop_receipt)
```

7.4 Python for MapReduce

In this section you will learn how to create a MapReduce job in Python and run it on a Hadoop cluster. Let us create a MapReduce job for computing an inverted index from a set of text files. An inverted index consists of a number of rows where each row holds a unique term and list document identifiers in which the term occurs.

Box 7.40 shows the inverted index mapper program. The map function reads the data from the standard input (stdin) and splits the tab-limited data into document-ID and contents of the document. The map function emits key-value pairs where key is each word in the document and value is the document-ID.

Box 7.41 shows the inverted index reducer program. The key-value pairs emitted by the map phase are shuffled to the reducers and grouped by the key. The reducer reads the key-value pairs grouped by the same key from the standard input (stdin) and creates a list of document-IDs in which the word occurs. The output of reducer contains key value pairs where key is a unique word and value is the list of document-IDs in which the word occurs.

Box 7.42 shows the commands to run the inverted index MapReduce program. First, we copy the directory containing the input to Hadoop filesystem. The input contains an aggregated file in which each line contains a document-ID and the contents of the document separated by a tab. A Hadoop streaming job is then created by specifying the input mapper and reducer programs and the locations of the input and output. When the streaming job completes, the output directory will have a file containing the inverted index.

■ **Box 7.40: Inverted Index Mapper in Python**

```
#!/usr/bin/env python
import sys

for line in sys.stdin:
    doc_id, content = line.split('')

    words = content.split()
    for word in words:
        print '%s%s' % (word, doc_id)
```

■ **Box 7.41: Inverted Index Reducer in Python**

```
#!/usr/bin/env python
import sys

current_word = None
```

```
current_docids = []
word = None

for line in sys.stdin:
    # remove leading and trailing whitespace
    line = line.strip()

    # parse the input we got from mapper.py
    word, doc_id = line.split('')

    if current_word == word:
        current_docids.append(doc_id)
    else:
        if current_word:
            print '%s%s' % (current_word, current_docids)
        current_docids = []
        current_docids.append(doc_id)
        current_word = word
```

■ Box 7.42: Running Inverted Index MapReduce on Hadoop Cluster

```
$HADOOP_HOME/bin/hadoop fs -copyFromLocal  /documents input

$ HADOOP_HOME/bin/hadoop jar contrib/streaming/hadoop-*streaming*.jar
-mapper mapper.py -reducer reducer.py
-file mapper.py
-file reducer.py
-input input/* -output output
```

7.5 Python Packages of Interest

7.5.1 JSON

JavaScript Object Notation (JSON) is an easy to read and write data-interchange format. JSON is used as an alternative to XML and is is easy for machines to parse and generate. JSON is built on two structures - a collection of name-value pairs (e.g. a Python dictionary) and ordered lists of values (e.g.. a Python list).

JSON format is often used for serializing and transmitting structured data over a network connection, for example, transmitting data between a server and web application. Box 7.43 shows an example of a Twitter tweet object encoded as JSON.

■ Box 7.43: JSON Example - A Twitter tweet object

```
{
    "created_at":
    "Sat Jun 01 11:39:43 +0000 2013",
    "id":340794787059875841,
    "text":"What a bright and sunny day today!",
    "truncated":false,
```

```
    "in_reply_to_status_id":null,
    "user":{
        "id":383825039,
        "name":"Harry",
        "followers_count":316,
        "friends_count":298,
        "listed_count":0,
        "created_at":"Sun Oct 02 15:51:16 +0000 2011",
        "favorites_count":251,
        "statuses_count":1707,
        :
        "notifications":null
        },
    "geo":{
        "type":"Point",
        "coordinates":[26.92782727,75.78908449]
        },
    "coordinates":{
        "type":"Point",
        "coordinates":[75.78908449,26.92782727]
        },
    "place":null,
    "contributors":null,
    "retweet_count":0,
    "favorite_count":0,
    "entities":{
        "hashtags":[],
        "symbols":[],
        "urls":[],
        "user_mentions":[]
        },
    "favorited":false,
    "retweeted":false,
    "filter_level":"medium",
    "lang":"nl"
}
```


Exchange of information encoded as JSON involves encoding and decoding steps. The Python JSON package [88] provides functions for encoding and decoding JSON.

Box 7.44 shows an example of JSON encoding and decoding.

■ Box 7.44: Encoding & Decoding JSON in Python

```
>>>import json

>>>message = {
    "created": "Wed Jun 31 2013",
    "id":"001",
    "text":"This is a test message.",
}

>>>json.dumps(message)
'{"text": "This is a test message.", "id": "001", "created": "Wed Jun 31 2013"}'
```

```
>>>decodedMsg = json.loads( '{"text": "This is a test message.", "id": "001", "created":
"Wed Jun 31 2013"}')

>>>decodedMsg['created']
u'Wed Jun 31 2013'
>>>decodedMsg['text']
u'This is a test message.'
```

7.5.2 XML

XML (Extensible Markup Language) is a data format for structured document interchange. Box 7.45 shows an example of an XML file. In this section you will learn how to parse, read and write XML with Python. The Python *minidom* library provides a minimal implementation of the Document Object Model interface and has an API similar to that in other languages. Box 7.46 shows a Python program for parsing an XML file. Box 7.47 shows a Python program for creating an XML file.

▪ Box 7.45: XML example

```
<?xml version="1.0"?>
<catalog>
< plant id='1' >
<common>Bloodroot</common>
<botanical>Sanguinaria canadensis</botanical>
<zone>4</zone>
<light>Mostly Shady</light>
<price> 2.44 </price>
<availability>031599</availability>
</plant>
<plant id='2' >
<common>Columbine</common>
<botanical>Aquilegia canadensis</botanical>
<zone>3</zone>
<light>Mostly Shady</light>
<price> 9.37</price >
<availability>030699</availability>
</plant>
<plant id='3' >
<common>Marsh Marigold</common>
<botanical>Caltha palustris</botanical>
<zone>4</zone>
<light>Mostly Sunny</light>
<price> 6.81</price>
<availability>051799</availability>
</plant>
</catalog>
```

■ Box 7.46: Parsing an XML file in Python

```
from xml.dom.minidom import parse
dom = parse("test.xml")
for node in dom.getElementsByTagName('plant'):
    id=node.getAttribute('id')
    print "Plant ID:", id
    common=node.getElementsByTagName('common')(0).childNodes(0) .nodeValue
    print "Common:", common
    botanical=node.getElementsByTagName('botanical')(0).childNodes(0) .nodeValue
    print "Botanical:", botanical
    zone=node.getElementsByTagName('zone')(0).childNodes(0) .nodeValue
    print "Zone:", zone
```

■ Box 7.47: Creating an XML file with Python

```
#Python example to create the following XML:
#' <?xml version="1.0" ?> <Class> <Student>
#<Name>Alex</Name> <Major>ECE</Major> </Student > </Class>

from xml.dom.minidom import Document
doc = Document()

# create base element
base = doc.createElement('Class')
doc.appendChild(base)

# create an entry element
entry = doc.createElement('Student')
base.appendChild(entry)

# create an element and append to entry element
name = doc.createElement('Name')
nameContent = doc.createTextNode('Alex')
name.appendChild(nameContent)
entry.appendChild(name)

# create an element and append to entry element
major = doc.createElement('Major')
majorContent = doc.createTextNode('ECE')
major.appendChild(majorContent)
entry.appendChild(major)

fp = open('foo.xml','w')
doc.writexml()
fp.close()
```

7.5.3 HTTPLib & URLLib

HTTPLib2 and URLLib2 are Python libraries used in network/internet programming [91, 92]. HTTPLib2 is an HTTP client library and URLLib2 is a library for fetching URLs.

Box 7.48 shows an example of an HTTP GET request using the HTTPLib. The variable *resp* contains the response headers and *content* contains the content retrieved from the URL.

■ Box 7.48: HTTP GET request example using HTTPLib

```
>>> import httplib2
>>> h = httplib2.Http()
>>> resp, content = h.request("http://example.com", "GET")
>>> resp
{'status': '200', 'content-length': '1270', 'content-location':
'http://example.com', 'x-cache': 'HIT', 'accept-ranges': 'bytes', 'server': 'ECS
(cpm/F858)', 'last-modified': 'Thu, 25 Apr 2013 16:13:23 GMT', 'etag':
'"780602-4f6-4db31b2978ec0"', 'date': 'Wed, 31 Jul 2013 12:36:05 GMT',
'content-type': 'text/html; charset=UTF-8'}

>>> content
'<!doctype html>\n<html>\n<head>\n
<title>Example Domain</title>\n\n
<meta charset="utf-8" />\n
:
```

Box 7.49 shows an HTTP request example using URLLib2. A request object is created by calling *urllib2.Request* with the URL to fetch as input parameter. Then *urllib2.urlopen* is called with the request object which returns the response object for the requested URL. The response object is read by calling *read* function.

■ Box 7.49: HTTP request example using URLLib2

```
>>> import urllib2
>>>
>>> req = urllib2.Request('http://example.com')
>>> response = urllib2.urlopen(req)
>>> response_page = response.read()
>>> response_page
'<!doctype html>\n<html>\n<head>\n
<title>Example Domain</title>\n\n
<meta charset="utf-8" />\n
```

Box 7.50 shows an example of an HTTP POST request. The data in the POST body is encoded using the *urlencode* function from urllib.

■ Box 7.50: HTTP POST example using HTTPLib2

```
>>> import httplib2
>>> import urllib
>>> h = httplib2.Http()
>>> data = {'title': 'Cloud computing'}
>>> resp, content = h.request("http://www.htmlcodetutorial.com/cgi-bin/mycgi.pl", "POST",
urllib.urlencode(data))
```

```
>>> resp
{'status': '200', 'transfer-encoding': 'chunked', 'server': 'Apache/2.0.64
(Unix) mod_ssl/2.0.64 OpenSSL/0.9.7a mod_auth_passthrough/2.1
mod_bwlimited/1.4 FrontPage/5.0.2.2635 PHP/5.3.10', 'connection': 'close',
'date': 'Wed, 31 Jul 2013 12:41:20 GMT', 'content-type': 'text/html;
charset=ISO-8859-1'}

>>> content
'<HTML>\n<HEAD>\n<TITLE>Idocs Guide to
HTML: My CGI</TITLE>\n</HEAD>
:
```

Box 7.51 shows an example of sending data to a URL using URLLib2 (e.g. an HTML form submission). This example is similar to the HTTP POST example in Box 7.50 and uses URLLib2 request object instead of HTTPLib2.

■ Box 7.51: Example of sending data to a URL

```
>>> import urllib
>>> import urllib2
>>>
>>> url = 'http://www.htmlcodetutorial.com/cgi-bin/mycgi.pl'
>>> values = {'title' : 'Cloud Computing',
... 'language' : 'Python' }
>>>
>>> data = urllib.urlencode(values)
>>> req = urllib2.Request(url, data)
>>> response = urllib2.urlopen(req)
>>> the_page = response.read()
>>> the_page
'<HTML>\n<HEAD>\n<TITLE>Idocs Guide to
HTML: My CGI</TITLE>\n</HEAD>
:
```

7.5.4 SMTPLib

Simple Mail Transfer Protocol (SMTP) is a protocol which handles sending email and routing e-mail between mail servers. The Python smtplib module provides an SMTP client session object that can be used to send email [93].

Box 7.52 shows a Python example of sending email from a Gmail account. The string *message* contains the email message to be sent. To send email from a Gmail account the Gmail SMTP server is specified in the *server* string.

To send an email, first a connection is established with the SMTP server by calling *smtplib.SMTP* with the SMTP server name and port. The user name and password provided are then used to login into the server. The email is then sent by calling *server.sendmail* function with the from address, to address list and message as input parameters.

■ Box 7.52: Python example of sending email

```
import smtplib

from_email = '<enter-gmail-address>'
recipients_list = ['<enter-sender-email>']
cc_list = [ ]
subject = 'Hello'
message = 'This is a test message.'
username = '<enter-gmail-username>'
password = '<enter-gmail-password>'
server = 'smtp.gmail.com:587'

def sendemail(from_addr, to_addr_list, cc_addr_list,
subject, message,
login, password,
smtpserver):

header = 'From: %s\n' % from_addr
header += 'To: %s\n' % ','.join(to_addr_list)
header += 'Cc: %s\n' % ','.join(cc_addr_list)
header += 'Subject: %s\n\n' % subject
message = header + message

server = smtplib.SMTP(smtpserver)
server.starttls()
server.login(login,password)
problems = server.sendmail(from_addr, to_addr_list, message)
server.quit()

#Send email
sendemail(from_email, recipients_list, cc_list, subject, message, username, password,
server)
```

Box 7.53 shows a Python example of sending an HTML email from a Gmail account.

■ Box 7.53: Python example of sending HTML email

```
import smtplib

from_email = '<enter-gmail-address>'
recipients_list = ['<enter-sender-email>']
cc_list = []
subject = 'Hello'
username = '<enter-gmail-username>'
password = '<enter-gmail-password>'
server = 'smtp.gmail.com:587'

#HTML Message to send
htmlmessage = "<h1>HTML Message Example</h1><p>This is a test message.</p>"

def sendemail(from_addr, to_addr_list, cc_addr_list,
        subject, message,
        login, password,
        smtpserver):
```

```
    header = 'From: %s\n' % from_addr
    header += 'To: %s\n' % ','.join(to_addr_list)
    header += 'Cc: %s\n' % ','.join(cc_addr_list)
    header += 'MIME-Version: 1.0\n'
    header += 'Content-type: text/html\n'
    header += 'Subject: %s\n\n' % subject
    message = header + message

    server = smtplib.SMTP(smtpserver)
    server.starttls()
    server.login(login,password)
    problems = server.sendmail(from_addr, to_addr_list, message)
    server.quit()

#Send email
sendemail(from_email, recipients_list, cc_list, subject, htmlmessage, username, password,
server)
```

Box 7.54 shows a Python example of sending an email attachment from a Gmail account. In this example the file to be sent is read and encoded with base64 encoding. The Content-type header is set to multipart/mixed in the message and Content-Transfer-Encoding is set to base64.

■ Box 7.54: Python example of sending email attachment

```
import smtplib
import base64

from_email = '<enter-gmail-address>'
receipients_list = ['<enter-sender-email>']
cc_list = []
subject = 'Hello'
username = '<enter-gmail-username>'
password = '<enter-gmail-password>'
server = 'smtp.gmail.com:587'

def sendemail(from_addr, to_addr_list, cc_addr_list,
    subject, message,
    login, password,
    smtpserver):

    header = 'From: %s\n' % from_addr
    header += 'To: %s\n' % ','.join(to_addr_list)
    header += 'Cc: %s\n' % ','.join(cc_addr_list)
    header += 'MIME-Version: 1.0\n'
    header += 'Content-Type: multipart/mixed; name=%s\n' % (filename)
    header += 'Content-Transfer-Encoding:base64\n'
    header += 'Content-Disposition: attachment; filename=%s\n' % (filename)
    header += 'Subject: %s\n\n' % subject
    message = header + message

    server = smtplib.SMTP(smtpserver)
    server.starttls()
```

```
    server.login(login,password)
    problems = server.sendmail(from_addr, to_addr_list, message)
    server.quit()


#read file
filename = "test.txt"
fo = open(filename, "rb")
filecontent = fo.read()
fo.close()

#encode to base64
encodedcontent = base64.b64encode(filecontent)

#send attachement
sendemail(from_email, receipients_list, cc_list, subject, encodedcontent, username, pass-
word, server)
```

7.5.5 NumPy

NumPy is a package for scientific computing in Python [94]. NumPy provides support for large multi-dimensional arrays and matrices

NumPy capabilities include:

- Creation and manipulation of arrays
- Matrix support
- Binary and string operations
- Linear algebra
- Discrete Fourier Transform
- Statistics
- Random sampling
- Sorting, searching and counting
- Financial functions
- Polynomials
- Logic functions

Box 7.55 shows examples of creating, indexing and manipulating NumPy arrays.

■ Box 7.55: NumPy array examples

```
#Creating arrays
from numpy import *
a = np.zeros((3,4))

>>>a = zeros((3,4))
>>>a
array([[ 0., 0., 0., 0.],
    [ 0., 0., 0., 0.],
    [ 0., 0., 0., 0.]])
>>>a.shape
(3, 4)
>>>a.ndim
2
```

```
>>>a.itemsize
8
>>>a.size
12
>>>type(a)
<type 'numpy.ndarray'>

#Reshaping arrays
>>>b = array([5,4,2,8,9,3,1,5,8,8,3,4,9,5,2])
>>>b
array([5, 4, 2, 8, 9, 3, 1, 5, 8, 8, 3, 4, 9, 5, 2])
>>>b.shape
(15,)
>>>c =b.reshape(3,5)
>>>c
array([[5, 4, 2, 8, 9],
    [3, 1, 5, 8, 8],
    [3, 4, 9, 5, 2]])
>>>c.shape
(3, 5)

#Accessing array elements
>>>c[2,3]
5
>>>c[2,3::]
array([5, 2])
>>>c[::,3]
array([8, 8, 5])

#Indexing with Boolean Arrays
>>>e = arange(30).reshape(5,6)
>>>e
array([[ 0, 1, 2, 3, 4, 5],
    [ 6, 7, 8, 9, 10, 11],
    [12, 13, 14, 15, 16, 17],
    [18, 19, 20, 21, 22, 23],
    [24, 25, 26, 27, 28, 29]])
>>>ee = e>>>ee
array([[ True, False, True, False, True, False],
    [ True, False, True, False, True, False],
    [ True, False, True, False, True, False],
    [ True, False, True, False, True, False],
    [ True, False, True, False, True, False]], dtype=bool)
>>>e[ee]
array([ 0, 2, 4, 6, 8, 10, 12, 14, 16, 18, 20, 22, 24, 26, 28])

#Indexing with Arrays of Indices
>>>e[[1,2],[3,4]]
array([ 9, 16])


#Array operations
>>>f = arange(30,60).reshape(5,6)
>>>f
```

```
array([[30, 31, 32, 33, 34, 35],
    [36, 37, 38, 39, 40, 41],
    [42, 43, 44, 45, 46, 47],
    [48, 49, 50, 51, 52, 53],
    [54, 55, 56, 57, 58, 59]])
>>>g = e+f
>>>g
array([[30, 32, 34, 36, 38, 40],
    [42, 44, 46, 48, 50, 52],
    [54, 56, 58, 60, 62, 64],
    [66, 68, 70, 72, 74, 76],
    [78, 80, 82, 84, 86, 88]])
>>>gef =e*f
>>>gef
array([[ 0, 31, 64, 99, 136, 175],
    [ 216, 259, 304, 351, 400, 451],
    [ 504, 559, 616, 675, 736, 799],
    [ 864, 931, 1000, 1071, 1144, 1219],
    [1296, 1375, 1456, 1539, 1624, 1711]])

>>>e.sum()
435
>>>e.mean()
14.5
>>>e.min()
0
>>>e.max()
29
```

Box 7.56 shows examples of creating and manipulating matrices with NumPy.

▪ Box 7.56: NumPy matrix examples

```
#Creating a matrix
>>>A = matrix('5,6,8;2,3,6;1,6,9')
>>>A
matrix([[5, 6, 8],
    [2, 3, 6],
    [1, 6, 9]])
>>>B = matrix('2,4,6;7,3,1;7,8,2')
>>>B
matrix([[2, 4, 6],
    [7, 3, 1],
    [7, 8, 2]])
>>>B = matrix('2,4;7,1;7,2')
>>>B
matrix([[2, 4],
    [7, 1],
    [7, 2]])

#Matrix transpose
>>>C=B.transpose()
>>>C
matrix([[2, 7, 7],
```

```
    [4, 1, 2]])

#Matrix multiplication
>>>D = A*B
>>>D
matrix([[108, 42],
    [ 67, 23],
    [107, 28]])
#Matrix inverse
>>>A.I
matrix([[ 0.2 , 0.13333333, -0.26666667],
    [ 0.26666667, -0.82222222, 0.31111111],
    [-0.2 , 0.53333333, -0.06666667]])
```

7.5.6 Scikit-learn

Scikit-learn is an open source machine learning library for Python that provides implementations of various machine learning algorithms for classification, clustering, regression and dimension reduction problems.

Scikit-learn is a very useful package for big data analytics applications. In Chapter 9 you will learn how to use scikit-learn for clustering and classification of big data. Scikit-learn capabilities include [95]:

- Supervised learning
  - Generalized Linear Models
  - Support Vector Machines
  - Stochastic Gradient Descent
  - Nearest Neighbors
  - Gaussian Processes
  - Partial Least Squares
  - Naive Bayes
  - Decision Trees
  - Ensemble methods
  - Multiclass and multilabel algorithms
  - Feature selection
  - Semi-Supervised
  - Linear and Quadratic Discriminant Analysis
  - Isotonic regression
- Unsupervised learning
  - Gaussian mixture models
  - Manifold learning
  - Clustering
  - Decomposing signals in components
  - Covariance estimation
  - Novelty and Outlier Detection
  - Hidden Markov Models
- Model selection and evaluation
  - Cross-Validation: evaluating estimator performance
  - Grid Search: setting estimator parameters

  - Pipeline: chaining estimators
  - FeatureUnion: Combining feature extractors
  - Model evaluation
- Dataset transformations
  - Preprocessing data
  - Feature extraction
  - Kernel Approximation
  - Random Projection
  - Pairwise metrics, Affinities and Kernels
- Dataset loading utilities
  - General dataset API
  - Sample images
  - Sample generators

7.6 Python Web Application Framework - Django

Django is an open source web application framework for developing web applications in Python [96]. A web application framework in general is a collection of solutions, packages and best practices that allows development of web applications and dynamic websites. Django is based on the Model-Template-View architecture and provides a separation of the data model from the business rules and the user interface. Django provides a unified API to a database backend. Thus web applications built with Django can work with different databases without requiring any code changes. With this flexibility in web application design combined with the powerful capabilities of the Python language and the Python ecosystem, Django is best suited for cloud applications. Django consists of an object-relational mapper, a web templating system and a regular-expression-based URL dispatcher.

7.6.1 Django Architecture

Django is Model-Template-View (MTV) framework. The roles of model, template and view are:

Model

The model acts as a definition of some stored data and handles the interactions with the database. In a web application, the data can be stored in a relational database, non-relational database, an XML file, etc. A Django model is a Python class that outlines the variables and methods for a particular type of data.

Template

In a typical Django web application, the template is simply an HTML page with a few extra placeholders. Django's template language can be used to create various forms of text files (XML, email, CSS, Javascript, CSV, etc.)

View

The view ties the model to the template. The view is where you write the code that actually generates the web pages. View determines what data is to be displayed, retrieves the data from the database and passes the data to the template.

7.6.2 Starting Development with Django

Appendix B provides the instructions for setting up Django. In this section you will learn how to start developing web applications with Django.

Creating a Django Project and App

Box 7.57 provides the commands for creating a Django project and an application within a project.

When you create a new django project a number of files are created:

- __init__.py: This file tells Python that this folder is a Python package
- manage.py: This file contains an array of functions for managing the site.
- settings.py: This file contains the website's settings
- urls.py: This file contains the URL patterns that map URLs to pages.

A Django project can have multiple applications. Apps are where you write the code that makes your website function. Each project can have multiple apps and each app can be part of multiple projects.

When a new application is created a new directory for the application is created which has a number of files including:

- model.py: This file contains the description of the models for the application.
- views.py: This file contains the application views.

■ Box 7.57: Creating a new Django project and an app in the project

```
#Create a new project
django-admin.py startproject blogproject

#Create an application within the project
python mangage.py startapp myapp

#Starting development server
python manage.py runserver

#Django uses port 8000 by default
#The project can be viewed at the URL:
#http://localhost:8000
```

Django comes with a built-in, lightweight Web server that can be used for development purposes. When the Django development server is started the default project can be viewed at the URL: http://localhost:8000. Figure 7.3 shows a screenshot of the default project.

Configuring a Database

Till now you have learned how to create a new Django project and an app within the project. Most web applications are database backend. Developers have a wide choice of databases that can be used for web applications including both relational and non-relational databases. Django provides a unified API for database backends thus giving the freedom to

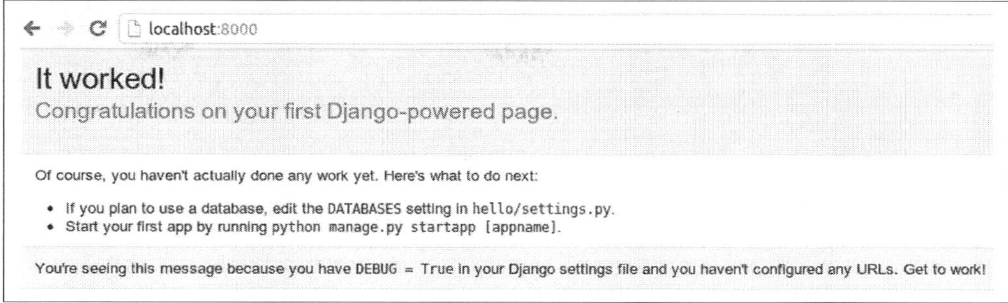

Figure 7.3: Django default project

choose the database. Django supports various relational database engines including MySQL, PostgreSQL, Oracle and SQLite3. Support for non-relational databases such as MongoDB can be added by installing additional engines (e.g. Django-MongoDB engine for MongoDB).

Let us look at examples of setting up a relational and a non-relational database with a Django project. The first step in setting up a database is to install and configure a database server. After installing the database, the next step is to specify the database settings in the setting.py file in the Django project.

Box 7.58 shows the commands to setup MySQL. Box 7.59 shows the database setting to use MySQL with a Django project.

■ Box 7.58: Setting up MySQL database

```
#Install MySQL
sudo apt-get install mysql-server mysql-client
sudo mysqladmin -u root -h localhost password 'mypassword'
```

■ Box 7.59: Configuring MySQL with Django - settings.py

```
DATABASES = {
    'default': {
        'ENGINE': 'django.db.backends.mysql',
        'NAME': '<database-name>'
        'USER': 'root'
        'PASSWORD': 'mypassword'
        'HOST': '<hostname>', # set to empty for localhost
        'PORT': '<port>', #set to empty for default port
}
}
```

Box 7.60 shows the commands to setup MongoDB and the Django-MongoDB engine. Box 7.61 shows the database setting to use MongoDB with a Django project.

■ Box 7.60: Setting up MongoDB and Django-MongoDB engine

```
#Install MongoDB
sudo apt-key adv –keyserver keserver.ubuntu.com –recv 7F0CEB10
echo 'deb http://downloads-distro.mongodb.org/repo/ubuntu-upstart dist 10gen' | sudo
tee /etc/apt/sources.list.d/10gen.list

sudo apt-get update
sudo apt-get install mongodb-10gen

#Setup Django MongoDB Engine
sudo pip install https://bitbucket.org/wkornewald/django-nonrel/get/tip.tar.gz
sudo pip install https://bitbucket.org/wkornewald/djangotoolbox/get/tip.tar.gz
sudo pip install https://github.com/django-nonrel/mongodb-engine/tarball/master
```

■ Box 7.61: Configuring MongoDB with Django - settings.py

```
DATABASES = {
    'default': {
        'ENGINE': 'django_mongodb_engine',
        'NAME': '<database-name>'
        'HOST': '<mongodb-hostname>', # set to empty for localhost
        'PORT': '<mongodb-port>', #set to empty for default port
}
}
```

Defining a Model

Model acts as a definition of the data in the database. Box 7.62 shows an example of a Django model for *Student*, *Course* and *Instructor* tables in a database. The *Student*, *Course* and *Instructor* tables in the database are defined as Classes in the Django model.

Each class that represents a database table is a subclass of *django.db.models.Model* which contains all the functionality that allows the models to interact with the database. The *Student* class has *first_name* and *last_name* as *CharField*, *email* as an *EmailField* and courses as a *ManyToManyField* field with a many-to-many relationship with the *Course* class (because a student can take many courses and a course can be taken by many students). The *Course* class has a name (*CharField*) and an instructor (one-many field defined with a foreign key to the Instructor table).

To sync the models with the database simply run the following command:
>python manage.py syncdb

When the *syncdb* command is run the first time, it creates all the tables defined in the Django model in the configured database. For more information about the Django models refer to the Django documentation [97].

■ Box 7.62: Example of a Django model

```
from django.db import models
```

```
class Instructor(models.Model):
    first_name = models.CharField(max_length=30)
    last_name = models.CharField(max_length=40)
    email = models.EmailField()
    def __unicode__(self):
        return self.first_name

class Course(models.Model):
    name = models.CharField(max_length=30)
    semester_year = models.CharField(max_length=30)
    instructor = models.ForeignKey(Instructor)
    def __unicode__(self):
        return self.name

class Student(models.Model):
    first_name = models.CharField(max_length=30)
    last_name = models.CharField(max_length=40)
    email = models.EmailField()
    courses = models.ManyToManyField(Course)
    def __unicode__(self):
        return self.first_name
```

Django Admin Site

Django provides an administration system that allows you to manage the website without writing additional code. The admin system reads the Django model and provides an interface that can be used to add content to the site. The Django admin site is enabled by adding *django.contrib.admin* and *django.contrib.admindocs* to the INSTALLED_APPS section in the settings.py file. The admin site also requires URL pattern definitions in the urls.py file described later in the URLs sections.

To define which of your application models should be editable in the admin interface, a new file named admin.py is created in the application folder as shown in Box 7.63.

■ Box 7.63: Enabling admin for Django models

```
from django.contrib import admin
from myapp.models import Instructor
from myapp.models import Course
from myapp.models import Student

admin.site.register(Instructor)
admin.site.register(Course)
admin.site.register(Student)
```

Figure 7.4 shows a screenshot of the default admin interface. You can see all the tables corresponding to the Django models in this screenshot. Figures 7.5, 7.6 and 7.7 show how to add new items in the Instructor, Course and Student tables using the admin site.

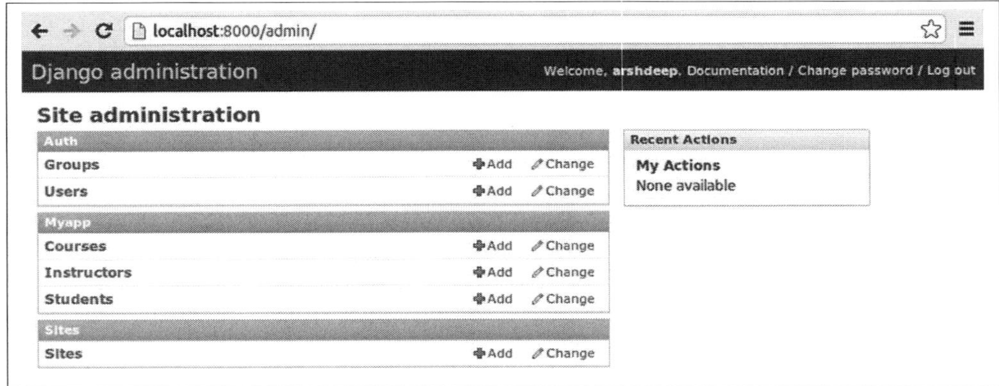

Figure 7.4: Screenshot of Django admin site

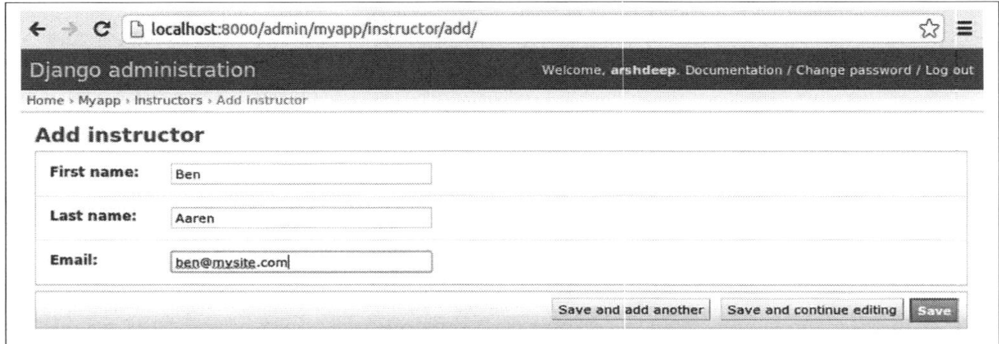

Figure 7.5: Django admin site - adding new items to Instructor table

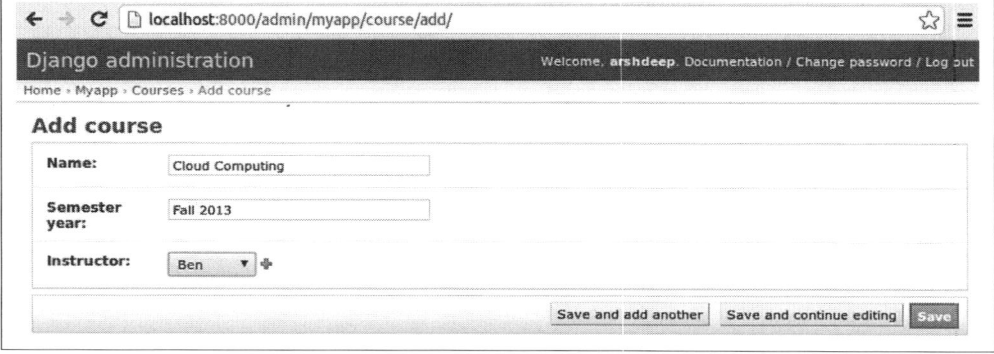

Figure 7.6: Django admin site - adding new items to Course table

Defining a View

View contains the logic that glues the model to the template. The view determines the data to be displayed in the template, retrieves the data from the database and passes it to the template. Conversely, the view also extracts the data posted in a form in the template and inserts it in the database. Typically, each page in the website has a separate view, which is

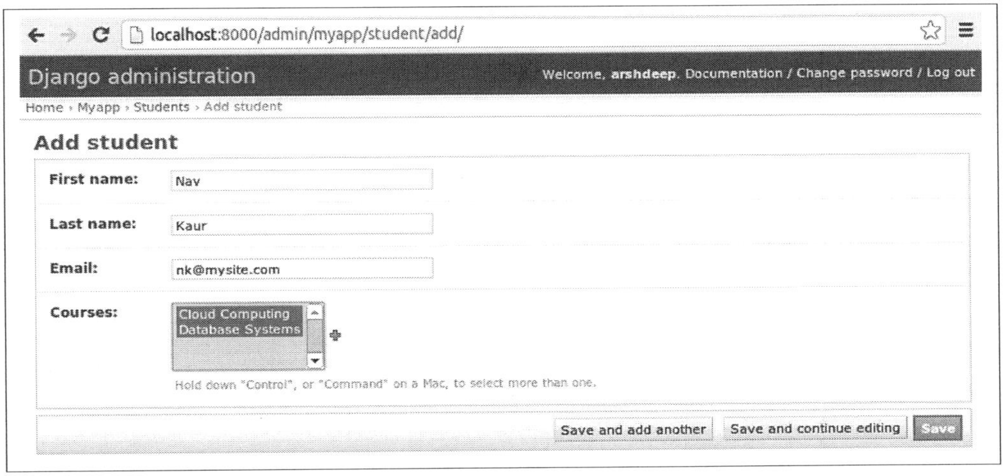

Figure 7.7: Django admin site - adding new items to Student table

basically a Python function in the views.py file. Views can also perform additional tasks such as authentication, sending emails, etc.

Box 7.64 shows an example of a Django view for the Student Records app. This view corresponds to the webpage that displays all the entries in the Instructor, Course and Student tables. In this view the Django's built in object-relational mapping API is used to retrieve the data from the Instructor, Course and Student tables. The object-relational mapping API allows the developers to write generic code for interacting with the database without worrying about the underlying database engine. So the same code for database interactions works with different database backends. You can optionally choose to use a Python library specific to the database backend used (e.g. MySQLdb for MYSQL, PyMongo for MongoDB, etc.) to write database backed specific code. For more information about the Django views refer to the Django documentation [98].

In the view shown in Box 7.64, the $table.objects.all$ query returns a QuerySet with all the entries in a table. To retrieve specific entries, you can use $table.objects.filter(**kwargs)$ to filter out queries that match the specified condition. For example, the query $Course.objects.filter(semester\_year='Fall\ 2013')$ return all courses of Fall 2013.

To render the retrieved entries in the template, the $render\_to\_response$ function is used. This function renders a given template with a given context dictionary and returns an $HttpResponse$ object with that rendered text.

■ Box 7.64: Example of a Django view

```
from django.shortcuts import render_to_response
from myapp.models import *

def home(request):
    student_entries = Student.objects.all()
    course_entries = Course.objects.all()
    instructor_entries = Instructor.objects.all()
```

```
return render_to_response('index.html',
    {'student_entries':student_entries, 'course_entries':course_entries,
    'instructor_entries': instructor_entries})
```

Defining a Template

A Django template is typically an HTML file (though it can be any sort of text file such as XML, email, CSS, Javascript, CSV, etc.). Django templates allow separation of the presentation of data from the actual data by using placeholders and associated logic (using template tags). A template receives a context from the view and presents the data in context variables in the placeholders. Box 7.65 shows an example of a template for the Student Records demo app. In the previous section you learned how the data is retrieved from the database in the view and passed to the template in the form of a context dictionary. In the example shown in Box 7.65, the variables containing the retrieved Instructor, Course and Student records are passed to the template. The *for* tags in the template loop over each item in a sequence and the items are inserted with the placeholder tags (variable name surrounded by braces, e.g. {{entry.email}}). Template tag is any text that is surrounded by curly braces and percent signs (e.g. {% for entry in student_entries %}). Django's template language offers basic tags such as *for*, *if*, etc. and a number of built-in filters for modifying the output of variables. Filters are attached to variables using a pipe character (|). For example the filter *join* in {{entry.courses.all|join:", "}} joins a list with a string. For more information about the Django templates refer to the Django documentation [99].

■ Box 7.65: Example of a Django template

```
<html>
<head>
<meta http-equiv="Content-Type" content="text/html; charset=UTF-8">
<title>Student Records</title>
<link href="/static/styles/demo_style.css" rel="stylesheet" type="text/css">
<link href="/static/styles/bootstrap.css" rel="stylesheet" type="text/css">
</head> <body>

<div class="demoHead">
<div>
<div style="float:left;">
<h1>Student Records</h1>
<h2>Django demo app</h2>
</div>

<div style="clear:both;"> </div>
</div> </div>
<br>
<center>
<h2>Students</h2>
</center>
<hr/>
<table align="center" border="0" cellpadding="0" cellspacing="0">
<tr>
<td width="200"> <h4>First Name</h4> </td>
```

```
<td width="200"> <h4>Last Name</h4> </td>
<td width="200"> <h4>Email</h4> </td>
<td width="250"> <h4>Courses</h4> </td>
</tr>
    {% for entry in student_entries %}
    <tr>
    <td >{{ entry.first_name }} </td>
    <td >{{ entry.last_name }}</td>
    <td >{{entry.email}}</td>
    <td >{{entry.courses.all | join:", "}}</td>
    </tr>
    {% endfor %}
</table>
<center>
<h2>Courses</h2>
</center>
<table align="center" border="0" cellpadding="0" cellspacing="0">
<tr>
<td width="200"> <h4>Name</h4> </td>
<td width="200"> <h4>Instructor</h4> </td>
<td width="200"> <h4>Semester-Year</h4> </td>
</tr>
    {% for entry in course_entries %}
    <tr>
    <td>{{ entry.name }} </td>
    <td>{{ entry.instructor}}</td>
    <td>{{entry.semester_year}}</td>
    </tr>
    {% endfor %}
</table>
<center>
<h2>Instructors</h2>
</center>
<table align="center" border="0" cellpadding="0" cellspacing="0">
<tr>
<td width="200"> <h4>First Name</h4> </td>
<td width="200"> <h4>Last Name</h4> </td>
<td width="300"> <h4>Email</h4> </td>
</tr>
    {% for entry in instructor_entries %}
    <tr>
    <td>{{ entry.first_name }} </td>
    <td>{{ entry.last_name}}</td>
    <td>{{entry.email}}</td>
    </tr>
    {% endfor %}
</table>
</body>
</html>
```

Figure 7.8 shows the home page for the Student Records app. The home page is rendered from the template shown in Box 7.65.

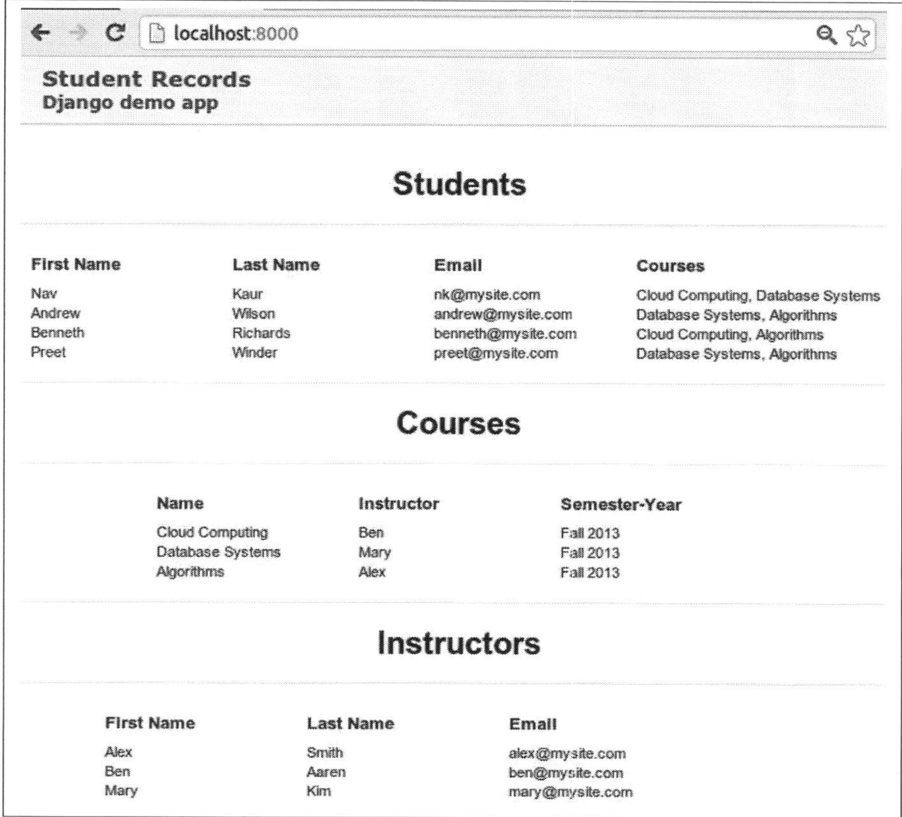

Figure 7.8: Screenshot of home page of Student Records app rendered from template in Box 7.65

Defining the URL Patterns

URL Patterns are a way of mapping the URLs to the views that should handle the URL requests. The URLs requested by the user are matched with the URL patterns and the view corresponding to the pattern that matrices the URL is used to handle the request. Box 7.66 shows an example of the URL patterns for the Student Records project. As seen in this example, the URL patterns are constructed using regular expressions. The simplest regular expression (r' ^ $') corresponds to the root of the website or the home page. More complex URLs allow capturing values. For example the pattern:
url(r'^ records/(?P<studentname>\w+)', 'myapp.views.studentrecord')

would capture the student name from the URL (such as http://myside.com/records/bob) to the variable *studentname* that is passed to the *studentrecord* view. For more information about the Django URL patterns refer to the Django documentation [100].

■ Box 7.66: Example of a URL configuration

```
from django.conf.urls.defaults import *
```

```
from django.contrib import admin
admin.autodiscover()

urlpatterns = patterns('',
    url(r'^$', 'myapp.views.home', name='home'),
    url(r'^admin/doc/', include('django.contrib.admindocs.urls')),
    url(r'^admin/', include(admin.site.urls)),
)
```

7.6.3 Django Case Study - Blogging App

This section provides a case study on building a multi-tier blogging application with Python, Django and MongoDB. Figure 7.9 shows the cloud deployment architecture for the blogging application. The deployment consists of a load balancer (HAProxy), application servers (Django) and database server (MongoDB).

MongoDB is a popular open-source No-SQL database. MongoDB stores data in JSON-like documents with dynamic schemas. An element of data in MongoDB is called a document, and documents are stored in collections. A collection may have any number of documents.

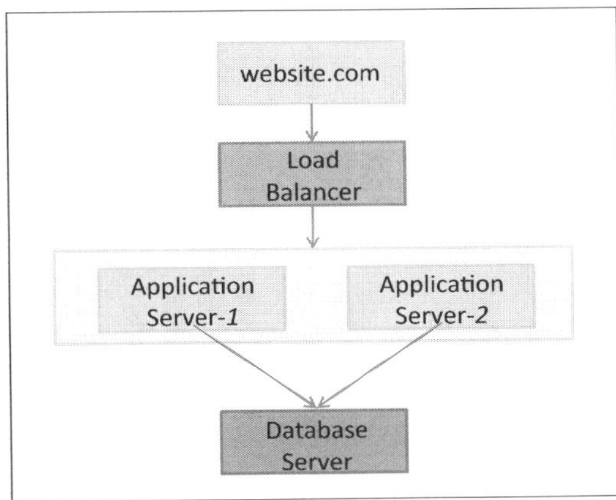

Figure 7.9: Multi-tier deployment architecture for blogging app

Launch 3 Ubuntu instances on a cloud platform (such as Amazon EC2) and setup Django on two instances and MongoDB on one instance.

■ Box 7.67: Django Model - models.py

```
from django.db import models
from djangotoolbox.fields import ListField, EmbeddedModelField

class Post(models.Model):
    created_at = models.DateTimeField(auto_now_add=True, db_index=True)
    title = models.CharField(max_length=255)
    body = models.TextField()

    def __unicode__(self):
        return self.title
```

```
    class Meta:
        ordering = ["-created_at"]
```

■ **Box 7.68: URL patterns - urls.py**

```
from django.conf.urls.defaults import patterns, include, url

from django.views.generic import ListView
from myapp.models import Post

urlpatterns = patterns('',
url(r'^$', ListView.as_view(
    queryset=Post.objects.all(),
    context_object_name="posts"),
    name="home"
),
)
```

■ **Box 7.69: Base template: /myapp/template/base.html**

```
<!DOCTYPE html>
<html lang="en">
<head>
    <meta charset="utf-8">
    <title>My Blog Application</title>
    <link href="http://twitter.github.com/bootstrap/1.4.0/bootstrap.css" rel="stylesheet">
    <style>.content padding-top: 80px;</style>
</head>
<body>

    <div class="topbar">
    <div class="fill">
    <div class="container">
     <h1><a href="/" class="brand">My Blog</a>!
    <small>Powerd by Django and MongoDB</small></h1>
    </div>
    </div>
    </div>

    <div class="container">
    <div class="content">
    % block page_header %% endblock %
    % block content %% endblock %
    </div>
    </div>

</body>
</html>
```

■ Box 7.70: Posts template - /myapp/template/myapp/posts.html

```
% extends "base.html" %

% block content %
    % for post in posts_list %
        <h2> post.title </h2>
        <p> post.body | truncatewords:20 </p>
        <p>
         post.created_at
        % endwith %
        </p>
    % endfor %
% endblock %
```

■ Box 7.71: Django project settings - settings.py

```
DATABASES =
    'default':
        'ENGINE': 'django_mongodb_engine',
        'NAME': 'myapp'
        'HOST': '<mongodb-hostname>',
        'PORT': '<mongodb-port>',



TEMPLATE_DIRS = (
    "/home/ubuntu/django/blogproject/myapp/templates",
)
```

■ Box 7.72: Setting up HAProxy load balancer

```
#Install HAProxy
wget http://haproxy.1wt.eu/download/1.4/src/haproxy-1.4.18.tar.gz
tar -zxf haproxy-1.4.18.tar.gz
cd haproxy-1.4.18
make TARGET=linux26
make install

#Edit config
vim /etc/haproxy.cfg

#To Check Config:
haproxy -f /etc/haproxy.cfg -c

#To Start:
haproxy -f /etc/haproxy.cfg

#Sample config file:
```

```
listen mycluster
    bind *:8080
    mode http
    stats enable
    stats auth admin:123456
    balance roundrobin
    option httpclose
    option forwardfor
    option httpchk
    server sv1 <server-1 IP>:8000 check inter 3000 rise 2 fall 3 maxconn 255
    server sv2 <server-2 IP>:8000 check inter 3000 rise 2 fall 3 maxconn 255
```

■ Box 7.73: Inserting new data and running Django server

```
# Insert new data using the shell interface provided by manage.py
python manage.py shell
from myapp.models import *
post = Post(title="Wecome!",
slug="welcome",
body = "Welcome to my new Blog! "
)
post.save()


#Running Django server
python manage.py runserver 0.0.0.0:8000
```

Box 7.67 shows the source code for the model of the blog application. Box 7.68 contains the source code for the urls.py file of the Django project. This file contains the URL patterns that tells Django how to serve the URL requests. Since django-mongodb engine tightly integrates Django with MongoDB you can use generic views such as the ListView to display the posts page as specified in the urls.py file. Since generic views are used, there is no need for a separate views.py file. Having created the model and configured the URL patterns the next step is to create templates. Box 7.69 shows the source code for the base template and Box 7.70 shows the source code for the posts page. The next step is to provide the database settings in the settings.py file of the Django project and also the path to the templates as shown in Box 7.71.

So far we have launched two Ubuntu instances and setup Django and the blog project on them. We also launched another instance for the database and setup MongoDB on it. The next step is to setup the Load Balancer instance. Box 7.72 shows the commands to setup the HAProxy load balancer on an Ubuntu instance. The IP addresses of the instances running the application servers are specified in the configuration file of HAProxy.

Finally, we insert some data and launch the application servers as shown in Box 7.73. Figure 7.10 shows the screenshot of the Blog application we created in this section. This application runs on a multi-tier deployment on cloud with one load balancer, two application servers and one database server.

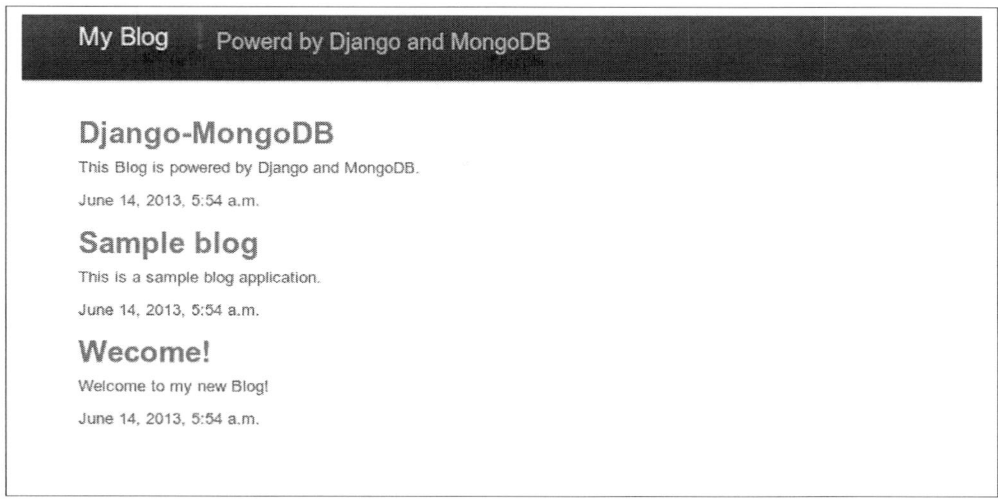

Figure 7.10: Screenshot of the Blog application

7.7 Designing a RESTful Web API

In Chapter 5 you learned about the characteristics of Representational State Transfer (REST) systems and RESTful web APIs. In this section you will learn how to develop a RESTful web API. The example in this section uses the Django REST framework [33] for building a REST API. With the Django framework already installed, the Django REST framework can be installed as follows:

```
pip install djangorestframework
pip install markdown
pip install django-filter
```

After installing the Django REST framework, create a new Django project named *restfulapi*, and then start a new app called *myapp*, as follows:

```
django-admin.py startproject restfulapi
cd restfulapi
python manage.py startapp myapp
```

The REST API described in this section allows you to create, view, update and delete a collection of resources where each resource represents a Book object. Box 7.74 shows the Django model for a Book. The Book model contains four fields - book name, ISBN number, publication date and publisher name. Box 7.75 shows the Django views for the REST API. ViewSets are used for the views that allow you to combine the logic for a set of related views in a single class.

Box 7.76 shows the serializers for the REST API. Serializers allow complex data (such as querysets and model instances) to be converted to native Python datatypes that can then be easily rendered into JSON, XML or other content types. Serializers also provide deserialization, allowing parsed data to be converted back into complex types, after first validating the incoming data.

Box 7.77 shows the URL patterns for the REST API. Since ViewSets are used instead of views, we can automatically generate the URL conf for our API, by simply registering the viewsets with a router class. Routers automatically determining how the URLs for an application should be mapped to the logic that deals with handling incoming requests. Box 7.78 shows the settings for the REST API Django project.

■ Box 7.74: Django model for Book - models.py

```
from django.db import models

class Book(models.Model):
    name = models.CharField(max_length=50)
    isbn = models.CharField(max_length=50)
    pub_date = models.DateField()
    pub_name = models.CharField(max_length=50)
```

■ Box 7.75: Django views for Book REST API - views.py

```
from myapp.models import Book
from rest_framework import viewsets
from myapp.serializers import BookSerializer


class BookViewSet(viewsets.ModelViewSet):
    queryset = Book.objects.all()
    serializer_class = BookSerializer
```

■ Box 7.76: Serializers for Book REST API- serializers.py

```
from myapp.models import Book
from rest_framework import serializers

class BookSerializer(serializers.HyperlinkedModelSerializer):
    class Meta:
        model = Book
        fields = ('url', 'name', 'isbn', 'pub_date', 'pub_name')
```

■ Box 7.77: Django URL patterns for Book REST API - urls.py

```
from django.conf.urls import patterns, include, url
from django.contrib import admin
admin.autodiscover()
from rest_framework import routers
from myapp import views
```

```
router = routers.DefaultRouter()
router.register(r'books', views.BookViewSet)

# Wire up our API using automatic URL routing.
# Additionally, we include login URLs for the browseable API.
urlpatterns = patterns('',
    url(r'^', include(router.urls)),
    url(r'^api-auth/', include('rest_framework.urls', namespace='rest_framework')),
    url(r'^admin/', include(admin.site.urls)),
)
```

■ Box 7.78: Django project settings for Book REST API project - settings.py

```
DATABASES =
    'default':
        'ENGINE': 'django.db.backends.sqlite3',
        'NAME': os.path.join(BASE_DIR, 'db.sqlite3'),


REST_FRAMEWORK =
    'DEFAULT_PERMISSION_CLASSES': ('rest_framework.permissions.IsAdminUser',),
    'PAGINATE_BY': 10


INSTALLED_APPS = (
    'django.contrib.admin',
    'django.contrib.auth',
    'django.contrib.contenttypes',
    'django.contrib.sessions',
    'django.contrib.messages',
    'django.contrib.staticfiles',
    'myapp',
    'rest_framework',
)
```

After creating the Books REST API source files, the next step is to setup the database and then run the Django development web server as follows:
python manage.py syncdb
python manage.py runserver

■ Box 7.79: Using the Book REST API - CURL examples

```
#——POST Example———

$curl -i -H "Content-Type: application/json" -H "Accept: application/json; indent=4"
-X POST -d '"name":"Cloud Computing","isbn":"989-1-9881818","pub_date":"2013-12-04",
"pub_name":"XYZ Publishers"' -u arshdeep http://127.0.0.1:8000/books/
```

```
HTTP/1.0 201 CREATED
Server: WSGIServer/0.1 Python/2.7.3
Vary: Accept, Cookie
X-Frame-Options: SAMEORIGIN
Content-Type: application/json; indent=4
Location: http://127.0.0.1:8000/books/1/
Allow: GET, POST, HEAD, OPTIONS

    "url": "http://127.0.0.1:8000/books/1/",
    "name": "Cloud Computing",
    "isbn": "989-1-9881818",
    "pub_date": "2013-12-04",
    "pub_name": "XYZ Publishers"


#——GET Examples————

$curl -i -H "Accept: application/json; indent=4" -u arshdeep http://127.0.0.1:8000/books/

HTTP/1.0 200 OK
Server: WSGIServer/0.1 Python/2.7.3
Vary: Accept, Cookie
X-Frame-Options: SAMEORIGIN
Content-Type: application/json; indent=4
Allow: GET, POST, HEAD, OPTIONS

    "count": 2,
    "next": null,
    "previous": null,
    "results": [

            "url": "http://127.0.0.1:8000/books/1/",
            "name": "Cloud Computing",
            "isbn": "989-1-9881818",
            "pub_date": "2013-12-04",
            "pub_name": "XYZ Publishers"
        ,

            "url": "http://127.0.0.1:8000/books/2/",
            "name": "Database Systems",
            "isbn": "981-3-8128989",
            "pub_date": "2013-02-14",
            "pub_name": "ABC Publishers"

    ]

$curl -i -H "Accept: application/json; indent=4" -u arshdeep http://127.0.0.1:8000/books/1/

HTTP/1.0 200 OK
Server: WSGIServer/0.1 Python/2.7.3
```

```
Vary: Accept, Cookie
X-Frame-Options: SAMEORIGIN
Content-Type: application/json; indent=4
Allow: GET, PUT, PATCH, DELETE, HEAD, OPTIONS

    "url": "http://127.0.0.1:8000/books/1/",
    "name": "Cloud Computing",
    "isbn": "989-1-9881818",
    "pub_date": "2013-12-04",
    "pub_name": "XYZ Publishers"

#——PUT Example———

$curl -i -H "Content-Type: application/json" -H "Accep: application/json; indent=4"
-X PUT -d '"name":"Cloud Computing: Concepts & Technologies", "isbn":"989-1-9881818",
"pub_date":"2013-12-04","pub_name":"XYZ Publishers"'
-u arshdeep http://127.0.0.1:8000/books/1/

HTTP/1.0 200 OK
Server: WSGIServer/0.1 Python/2.7.3
Vary: Accept, Cookie
X-Frame-Options: SAMEORIGIN
Content-Type: application/json; indent=4
Allow: GET, PUT, PATCH, DELETE, HEAD, OPTIONS

    "url": "http://127.0.0.1:8000/books/1/",
    "name": "Cloud Computing: Concepts & Technologies",
    "isbn": "989-1-9881818",
    "pub_date": "2013-12-04",
    "pub_name": "XYZ Publishers"

#——DELETE Example———

$curl -i -X DELETE -H "Accept: application/json; indent=4"
-u arshdeep http://127.0.0.1:8000/books/2/

HTTP/1.0 204 NO CONTENT
Server: WSGIServer/0.1 Python/2.7.3
Vary: Accept, Cookie
X-Frame-Options: SAMEORIGIN
Content-Type: application/json; indent=4
Content-Length: 0
Allow: GET, PUT, PATCH, DELETE, HEAD, OPTIONS
```

Box 7.79 shows examples of interacting with the Books REST API using CURL. The HTTP POST method is used to create a new resource, GET method is used to obtain information about a resource, PUT method is used to update a resource and DELETE method is used to delete a resource. Figures 7.11 and 7.12 show the screenshots from the web browsable Books REST API.

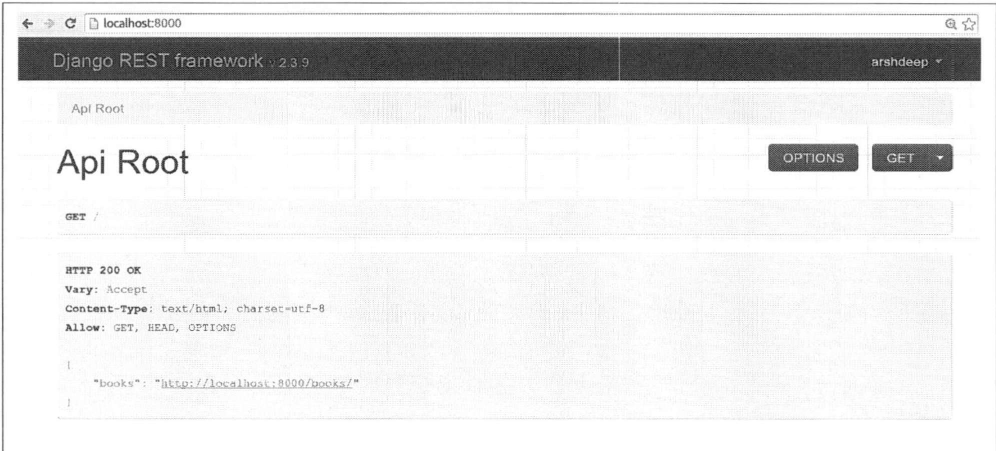

Figure 7.11: Screenshot from the web browsable Books REST API - API root

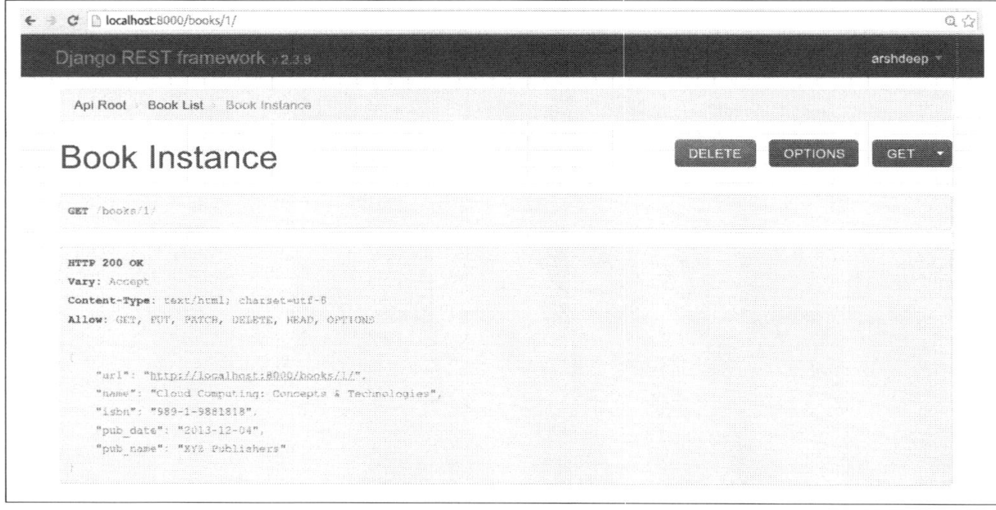

Figure 7.12: Screenshot from the web browsable Books REST API - viewing a particular book

Summary

In this chapter you learned how to use Python for Amazon Web Services, Google Cloud Platform and Windows Azure Platform. Boto is a Python package that provides interfaces to Amazon Web Services (AWS). Amazon EC2 is a computing service from Amazon. You learned how to programmatically launch an Amazon EC2 instance, view instance details and stop running instances. Amazon AutoScaling allows automatically scaling Amazon EC2 capacity up or down according to user defined conditions. You learned how to programmatically create an AutoScaling group, define AutoScaling policies and CloudWatch alarms for triggering the AutoScaling policies. Amazon S3 is an online cloud-based data storage from Amazon. You learned how to programmatically upload a file to an S3 bucket. Amazon RDS is a cloud-based relational database service. You learned how to programmatically launch an RDS instance, view running instances, connect to an instance, create a MySQL table, write and read from the table on the RDS instance. Amazon DynamoDB is a No-SQL database service. You learned how to programmatically create a DynamoDB table, write and read from a DynamoDB table. Amazon SQS is a scalable queuing service from Amazon. You learned how to programmatically create an SQS queue, write messages to a queue and read messages from a queue. Amazon EMR is a MapReduce web service. You learned how to programmatically create an EMR job. Google Compute Engine is a computing service from Google. You also learned how to programmatically launch GCE instances and view running instances. Google Cloud Storage is a cloud service for storing data in the Google's cloud. You learned how to programmatically upload and download files from Google Cloud Storage. Google Cloud SQL is a relational database service from Google. You learned how to programmatically launch a Google Cloud SQL instance, list running instances and create MySQL table on a Cloud SQL instance. Google BigQuery allows querying massive scale datasets with SQL-like queries. You also learned how to programmatically create a BigQuery dataset and query the dataset. Google Cloud Datastore is a No-SQL datastore. You learned how to programmatically create a Datastore entity and query existing entities. Google App Engine is a PaaS from Google. You also learned how to create and deploy an App Engine application. Windows Azure Virtual Machines is a compute service from Microsoft. You learned how to programmatically create an Azure virtual machine. Windows Azure Storage is a cloud storage service that allows you to store and access various forms of data (Blobs, Tables and Queues). You learned how to programmatically create blobs, tables and queues. MapReduce is a parallel programming model. You learned how to create MapReduce programs. You also learned about Python packages such as JSON, HTTPLib, URLLib, SMTPLib, NumPy and Scikit-learn. Django is an open source web application framework for developing web applications in Python. Django is based on the Model-Template-View architecture. You also learned how to develop a Django application made up of model, view and templates. Finally, you learned how to develop a RESTful web API.

Review Questions

1. What is the purpose of an Amazon AutoScaling group? Describe the steps involved in creating an AutoScaling group.
2. What is Amazon DynamoDB? Describe an application that can benefit from Amazon DynamoDB.
3. What are the uses of messaging queues? What are the message formats supported by Amazon SQS, Google Task Queue and Windows Azure Queue service?
4. What does a MapReduce job comprise of?
5. Describe the steps involved in Google Compute Engine authorization.
6. Describe an application of Google BigQuery.
7. Describe a use of the Windows Azure Table service.
8. Describe the architecture of a Django application.
9. What is the function of URL patterns in Django?
10. Describe scaling options for a database tier.

Lab Exercises

1. In this exercise you will programmatically create a web tier of a cloud application. Follow the steps below:
   - Create a static website with one or two HTML pages and copy the pages and dependent files in an Amazon S3 bucket.
   - Create a startup script to install Apache server and copy the website files from S3 to the instance.
   - Create a Python program using boto to launch an *m1.small* Ubuntu instance. Supply the startup script you created in previous step while launching a new instance from the program. Use a security group with port 80 open.
   - Your program should check the status of the newly launched instance and return the public DNS address of the instance when the status changes to 'running'.
   - Open the public DNS of the newly launched instance in a browser and verify if the static website works.

2. In this exercise you will programmatically create an auto-scaling configuration for the web tier of a cloud application. Follow the steps below:
   - Create a static website with one or two HTML pages and copy the pages and dependent files in an Amazon S3 bucket.
   - Create a startup script to install Apache server and copy the website files from S3 to the instance.
   - Create a Python program using boto that creates an Amazon AutoScaling group. Define scale up and scale down policies and the corresponding CloudWatch alarms. Supply the startup script you created in previous step while launching a new instance from the program. Use a security group with port 80 open.
   - Open the public DNS of the newly launched instance in a browser and verify if the static website works.

3. In this exercise you will extend the Exercise-2 to define a time-based auto-scaling schedule. Follow the steps below:
   - Create a Python program using boto that creates an Amazon AutoScaling group. Define a scheduled group action to the auto-scaling group that scales up the group by adding one more instance during day-time from 9:00am to 6:00pm everyday and then scales down the group.
   - Open the public DNS of the newly launched instance in a browser and verify if the static website works. Verify if the scheduled group action works.

4. Repeat Exercise-1 using Google Compute Engine and Google Cloud Storage.

5. Repeat Exercise-1 using Windows Azure Virtual Machines and Windows Azure Storage.

6. Extend the Student Records app described in section 6.2.6 and create separate pages for viewing student records, adding new records and deleting existing records.

7. In this exercise you will develop a MapReduce application which has multiple independent components. The job submission component accepts MapReduce jobs and enqueues them into a queue. The job execution component retrieves jobs from the queue and creates Amazon EMR jobs. Follow the steps below:
   - Using the programs in Box 6.13 and 6.15 as the baseline, develop a Python program that accepts MapReduce jobs from the user. The user specifies the location of the Mapper, Reducer and input data from command line. The MapReduce job configuration (as a JSON) is submitted to an Amazon SQS queue.
   - Write a Python program to read MapReduce job requests from the SQS queue and create EMR jobs. Use programs 6.14 and 6.15 as baseline.

8. Extend the Student Records Django application described in section 6.6 to include separate pages for students, courses and instructors. Each page should have links to create a new record and delete existing records. Develop your own interface for creating and deleting records (similar to the Django admin interface).

9. Extend the Blog application described in section 6.6 to allow adding new blog entities from the web interface, instead of using Django shell.

10. Deploy the Blog application developed in Exercise-9 on a multi-tier deployment comprising of an Amazon Elastic Load Balancer, Amazon AutoScaling group for the web tier and an AutoScaling group for the database tier.

8 — Cloud Application Development in Python

This Chapter Covers

Cloud application case studies including

- Image Processing App
- Document Storage App
- MapReduce App
- Social Media Analytics App

This chapter provides case studies on cloud applications developed in Python. For each application, the reference architecture, source code and screenshots are provided.

8.1 Design Approaches

In this section you will learn about application design approaches that leverage the Infrastructure-as-a-Service (IaaS) and Platform-as-a-Service (PaaS) cloud service models.

8.1.1 Design methodology for IaaS service model

Traditional application design approaches such as service-oriented architecture (SOA) use component-based designs. However the components in these approaches can span multiple tiers (such as web, application and database tiers), which makes it difficult to map them to multi-tier cloud architectures. In Chapter 5, you learned about the Cloud Component Model (CCM) approach for designing cloud applications, which is a more recent approach that classifies the components based on the types of functions performed and types of cloud resources used. The CCM design approach is suited for applications that use the Infrastructure-as-a-Service (IaaS) cloud service model. With the IaaS model the developers get the flexibility to map the CCM architectures to cloud deployments. Virtual machines for various tiers (such as web, application and database tiers) can be provisioned and auto scaling options for each tier can be defined.

Figure 8.1 shows the steps involved in a CCM based application design approach. In the first step, the building blocks of an application are identified. These building blocks are then grouped based on the functions performed and type of cloud resources required and the application components are identified based on these groupings. In the second step, the interactions between the application components are defined. CCM approach is based on loosely coupled and stateless designs. Messaging queues are used for asynchronous communication. CCM components expose functional interfaces (such as REST APIs for loose coupling) and performance interfaces (for reporting the performance of components). An external status database is used for storing the state. In the third step, the application components are mapped to specific cloud resources (such as web servers, application servers, database servers, etc.)

The benefits of CCM approach are as follows:

- **Improved Application Performance**: CCM uses loosely coupled components that communicate asynchronously. Designing an application with loosely components makes it possible to scale up (or scale out) the application components that limit the performance.
- **Savings in Design, Testing & Maintenance Time**: The CCM methodology achieves savings in application design, testing and maintenance time. Savings in design time come from use of standard components. Savings in testing time come from the use of loosely coupled components which can be tested independently.
- **Reduced Application Cost**: Applications designed with CCM can leverage both vertical and horizontal scaling options for improving the application performance. Both types of scaling options involve additional costs for provisioning servers with higher computing capacity or launching additional servers. Costs for cloud resources can be reduced by identifying the application components which limit the performance

and scaling up (or scaling out) cloud resources for only those components. This is not possible for applications which have tightly coupled and hard wired systems.

- **Reduced Complexity**: A simplified deployment architecture can be more easier to design and manage. Therefore, depending on application performance and cost requirements, it may be more beneficial to scale vertically instead of horizontally. For example, if equivalent amount of performance can be obtained at a more cost-effective rate, then deployment architectures can be simplified using small number of large server instances (vertical scaling) rather than using a large number of small server instances (horizontal scaling). CCM provides the flexibility to use both vertical and horizontal scaling for application components.

Component Design

- Indentify the building blocks of the application and the functions to be performed by each block
- Group the building blocks based on the functions performed and type of cloud resources required and identify the application components based on the groupings
- Identify the inputs and outputs of each component
- List the interfaces that each component will expose
- Evaluate the implementation alternatives for each component (design patters such as MVC, etc.)

Architecture Design

- Define the interactions between the application components
- Guidelines for loosely coupled and stateless designs - use messaging queues (for asynchronous communication), functional interfaces (such as REST APIs for loose coupling) and external status database (for stateless design)

Deployment Design

- Map the application components to specific cloud resources (such as web servers, application servers, database servers, etc.)

Figure 8.1: Design methodology for IaaS service model (component-based approach)

8.1.2 Design methodology for PaaS service model

For applications that use the Platform-as-a-service (PaaS) cloud service model, the architecture and deployment design steps shown in Figure 8.1 are not required since the platform takes care of the architecture and deployment. In the component design step, the developers have to take into consideration the platform specific features. For example, applications designed with Google App Engine (GAE) can leverage the GAE Image Manipulation service for image processing tasks. Different PaaS offerings such as Google App Engine, Windows Azure Web Sites, etc., provide platform specific software development kits (SDKs) for developing cloud applications. Applications designed for specific PaaS offerings run in sandbox environments and are allowed to perform only those actions that do not interfere with the performance of other applications. The deployment and scaling is handled by the platform while the developers focus on the application development using the platform-specific SDKs. Portability is a major constraint for PaaS based applications as it is difficult to move the application from one cloud vendor to the other due to the use of vendor-specific APIs and PaaS SDKs.

8.2 Image Processing App

In this section you will learn how to develop a cloud-based Image Processing application. This application provides online image filtering capability. Users can upload image files and choose the filters to apply. The selected filters are applied to the image and the processed image can then be downloaded.

Figure 8.2 shows the component design step for the image processing app. In this step we identify the application components and group them based on the type of functions performed and type of resources required. The web tier for the image processing app has front ends for image submission and displaying processed images. The application tier has components for processing the image submission requests, processing the submitted image and processing requests for displaying the results. The storage tier comprises of the storage for processed images.

Figure 8.3 shows the architecture design step which defines the interactions between the application components. This application uses the Django framework, therefore, the web tier components map to the Django templates and the application tier components map to the Django views. A cloud storage is used for the storage tier. For each component, the corresponding code box numbers are mentioned.

Figure 8.4 shows the deployment design for the image processing app. This is a multi-tier architecture comprising of load balancer, application servers and a cloud storage for processed images. For each resource in the deployment the corresponding Amazon Web Services (AWS) cloud service is mentioned.

Figure 8.5 shows a screenshot of the first step of the image submission wizard in the Image Processing app. In the first step, the user selects the image to filter. Figure 8.6 shows a screenshot of the second step in which the user selects a filter to apply to the image. Figure 8.7 shows a screenshot of the final step in which the user submits the image for filtering. Figure 8.8 shows a screenshot of the processed image in the Image Processing app to which the selected filter has been applied.

Box 8.1 shows the source code for the Django template for the image submission page. Box 8.2 shows the source code for the Django template for the processed image page. Box 8.3 shows the source code for Django form that is displayed in the image submission page.

■ Box 8.1: Image submission front end - Django template

```
<html xmlns="http://www.w3.org/1999/xhtml">
<head>
<meta http-equiv="Content-Type" content="text/html; charset=UTF-8">
<title>Image Processing App</title>
<link href="/static/styles/demo_style.css" rel="stylesheet" type="text/css">
<link href="/static/styles/smart_wizard.css" rel="stylesheet" type="text/css">
<link href="/static/styles/bootstrap.css" rel="stylesheet" type="text/css">
<script type="text/javascript" src="/static/js/jquery-1.4.2.min.js"></script>
<script type="text/javascript" src="/static/js/jquery.smartWizard.js"></script>
```

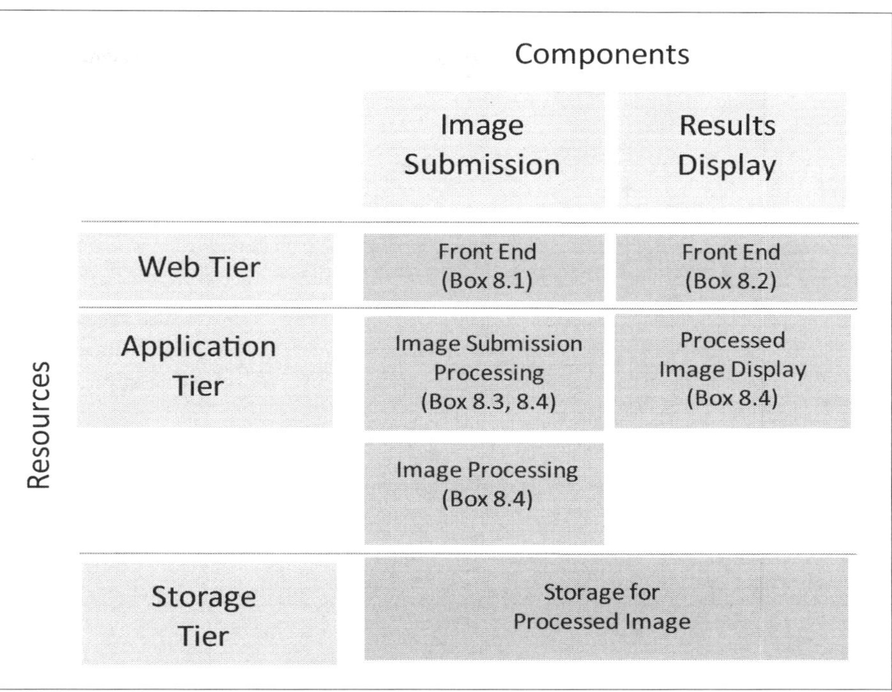

Figure 8.2: Component design for Image Processing App

```
<script type="text/javascript">
$(document).ready(function(){
$('#wizard').smartWizard({transitionEffect:'fade',onFinish:onFinishCallback} );
function onFinishCallback(){
$('form').submit();
}
});
</script>
</head>
<body>
<div class="demoHead">
<div>
<div style="float:left;">
<h1>Image Processing App</h1>
<h2>a cloud-based app for Image Processing</h2>
</div>

<div style="clear:both;"></div>
</div>
</div>

<form action="/" method="post" enctype="multipart/form-data">
{% csrf_token %}
<br>
<table align="center" border="0" cellpadding="0" cellspacing="0">
<tr><td>
<!- Smart Wizard ->
```

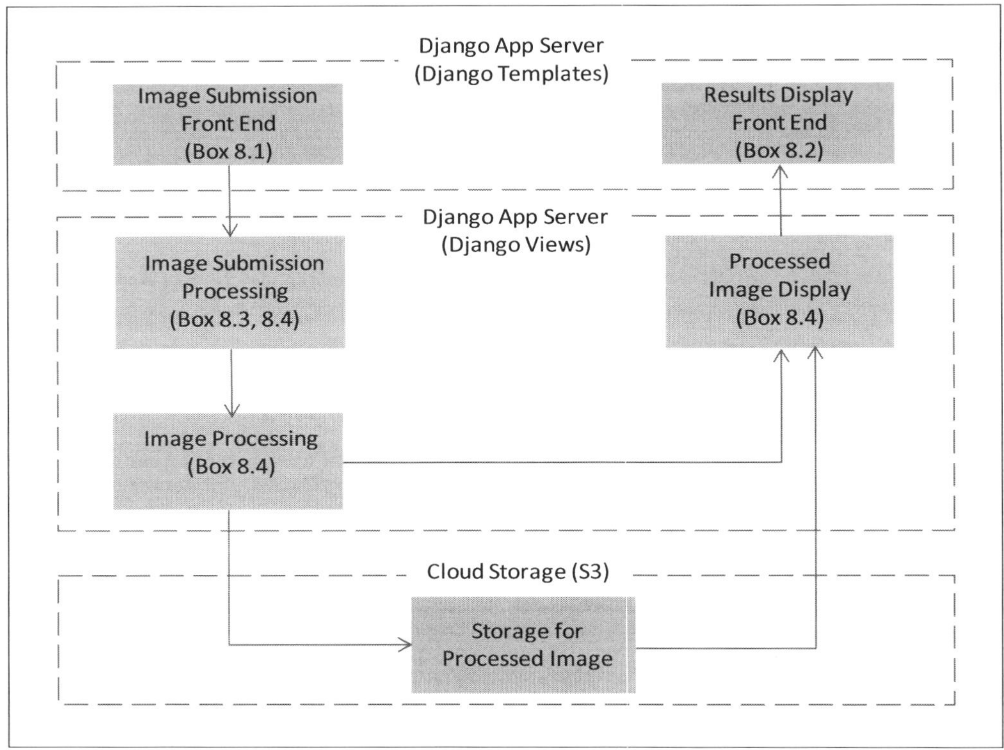

Figure 8.3: Architecture design for Image Processing App

```
<h2>Upload image file </h2>
<div id="wizard" class="swMain">
<ul>
<li><a href="#step-1">
<label class="stepNumber">1</label>
<span class="stepDesc">
Step 1<br />
<small>Select image file</small>
</span>
</a></li>
<li><a href="#step-2">
<label class="stepNumber">2</label>
<span class="stepDesc">
Step 2<br />
<small>Select image filter</small>
</span>
</a></li>
<li><a href="#step-3">
<label class="stepNumber">3</label>
<span class="stepDesc">
Step 3<br />
<small>Apply filter</small>
</span>
</a></li>
```

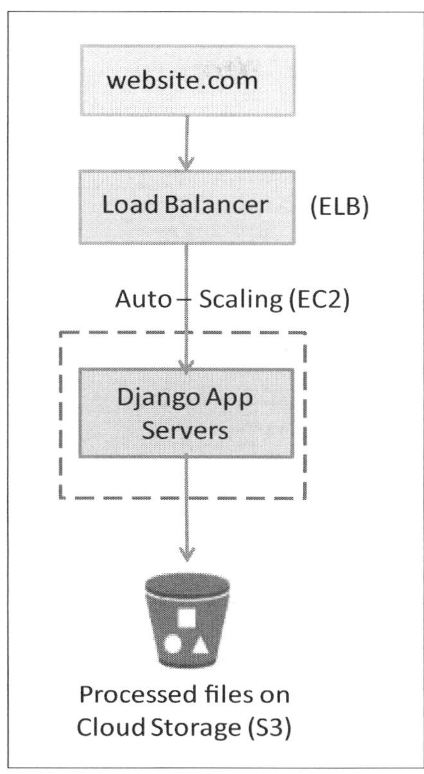

Figure 8.4: Deployment design for Image Processing App

```
</ul>
<div id="step-1">
<h2 class="StepTitle">Select image file</h2>

<h4>Choose the image file:</h4>

<p>{{ form.non_field_errors }}</p>
<p>
{{ form.myfilefield.errors }}
{{ form.myfilefield }}
</p>
</div>
<div id="step-2">
<h2 class="StepTitle">Select Image Filter</h2> <br>
<h4>Choose Filter:</h4>
<h4>
<table border = '0' width = 90% align="center">
<tr>
<td><input type="radio" name="preset" value="gray"> Gray</td>
<td><input type="radio" name="preset" value="sepia"> Sepia</td>
<td><input type="radio" name="preset" value="poster"> Poster</td>
</tr>
<tr>
<td><img src = '/static/images/gray.jpg' width='120px' ></td>
```

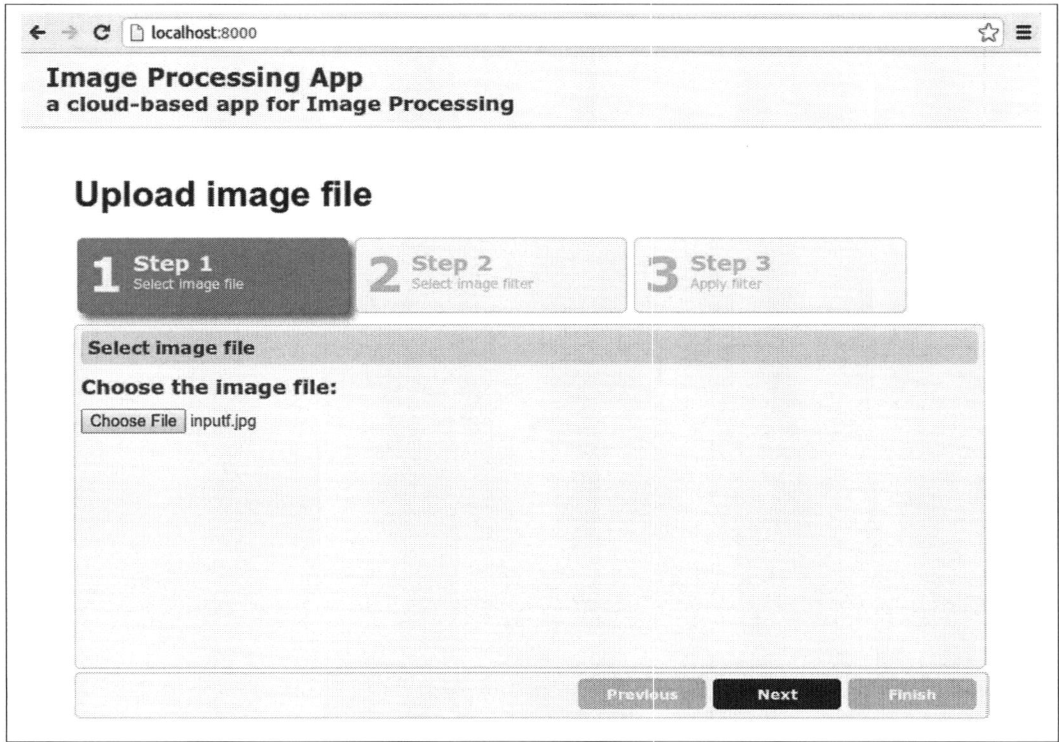

Figure 8.5: Screenshot of Image Processing App - choosing image

```
<td><img src = '/static/images/sepia.jpg' width='120px' ></td>
<td><img src = '/static/images/poster.jpg' width='120px' ></td>
</tr>
<tr>
<td><input type="radio" name="preset" value="blur"> Blur</td>
<td><input type="radio" name="preset" value="edge"> Edge</td>
<td><input type="radio" name="preset" value="solar"> Solar</td>
</tr>
<td><img src = '/static/images/blur.jpg' width='120px' ></td>
<td><img src = '/static/images/edge.jpg' width='120px' ></td>
<td><img src = '/static/images/solar.jpg' width='120px' ></td>
</tr>
</h4>
</table>
</div>
<div id="step-3">
<h2 class="StepTitle">Apply Filter</h2>
<br>
<h4>Click finish to apply filter to image.</h4><br>
</div>
</div>
</td></tr>
</table>
</form>
```

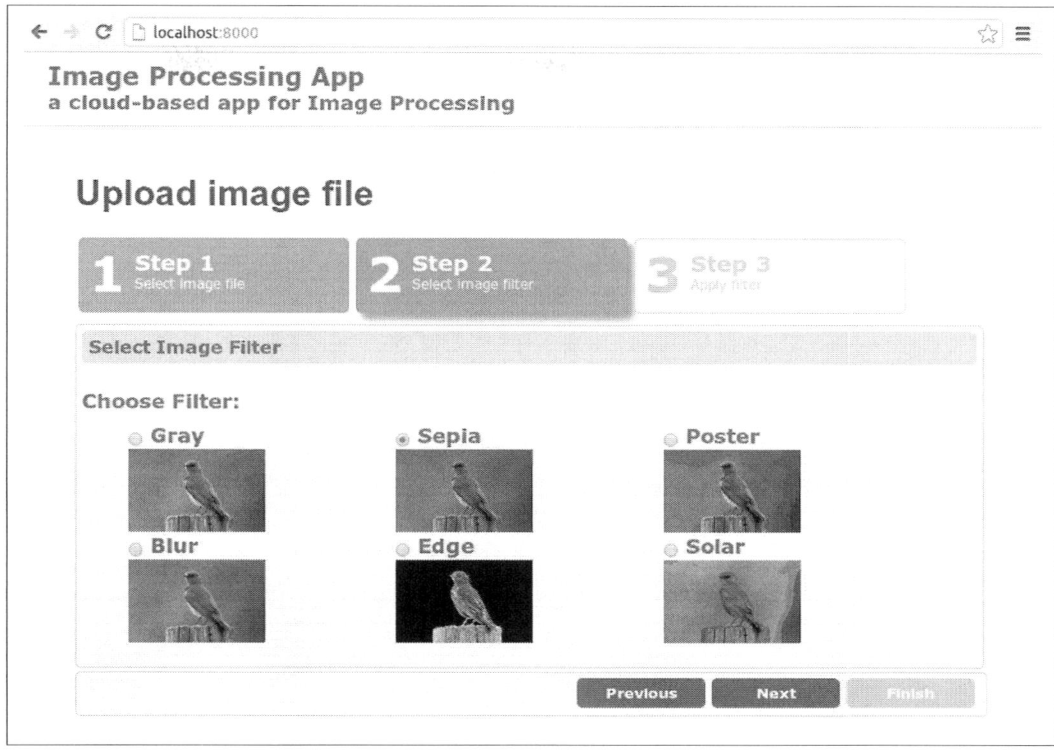

Figure 8.6: Screenshot of Image Processing App - selecting filter

```
</body>
</html>
```

■ **Box 8.2: Results display front end - Django template**

```
<html xmlns="http://www.w3.org/1999/xhtml">
<head>
<meta http-equiv="Content-Type" content="text/html; charset=UTF-8">
<title>Image Processing App</title>
<link href="/static/styles/demo_style.css" rel="stylesheet" type="text/css">
<link href="/static/styles/smart_wizard.css" rel="stylesheet" type="text/css">
<link href="/static/styles/bootstrap.css" rel="stylesheet" type="text/css">
<script type="text/javascript" src="/static/js/jquery-1.4.2.min.js"></script>
<script type="text/javascript" src="/static/js/jquery.smartWizard.js"></script>
</head>
<body>
<div class="demoHead">
<div>
<div style="float:left;">
<h1>Image Processing App</h1>
<h2>a cloud-based app for Image Processing</h2>
</div>
<div style="clear:both;"></div>
```

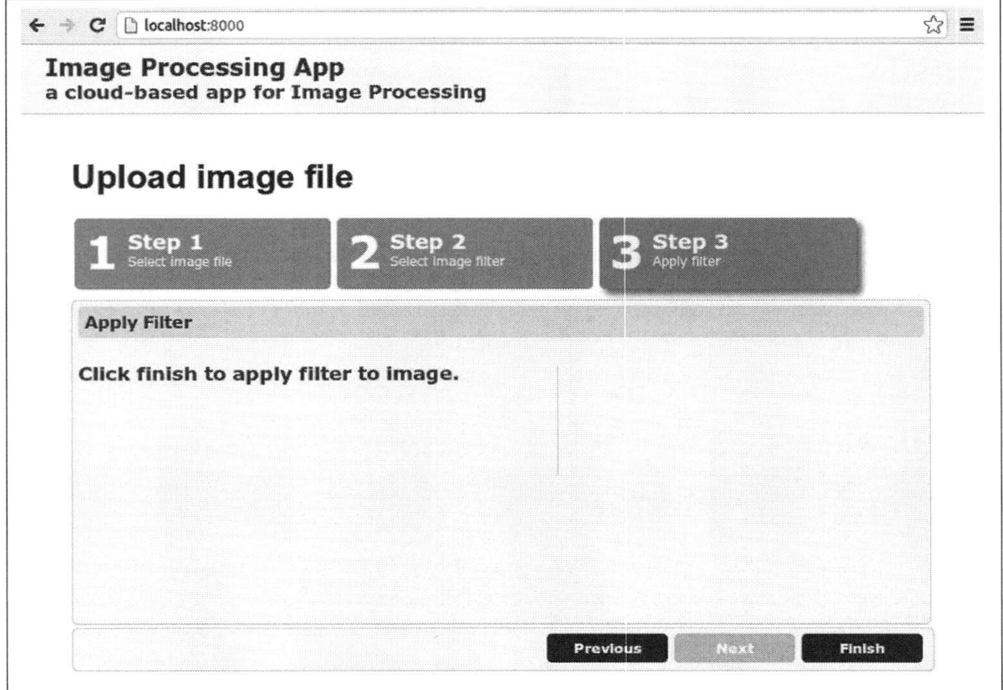

Figure 8.7: Screenshot of Image Processing App - submitting image

```
</div>
</div>
<table align="center" border="0" cellpadding="0" cellspacing="0">
<tr><td>
<center>
<h4>Image filter has been successfully applied. </h4>
</center>
<br>
<img src = '/static/output/{{outputfilename}}' width='800px' >
</td></tr>
</table>
</body>
</html>
```

■ **Box 8.3: Django form - image processing app**

```
from django import forms

class UploadFileForm(forms.Form):
    myfilefield = forms.FileField()
```

Box 8.4 shows the source code of the Django View of the Image Processing app. The function *home*() in the view renders the image submission page. This function checks if the request method is POST or not. If the request method is not POST then the file upload form is rendered in the template. Whereas, if the request is POST, the file selected by the user

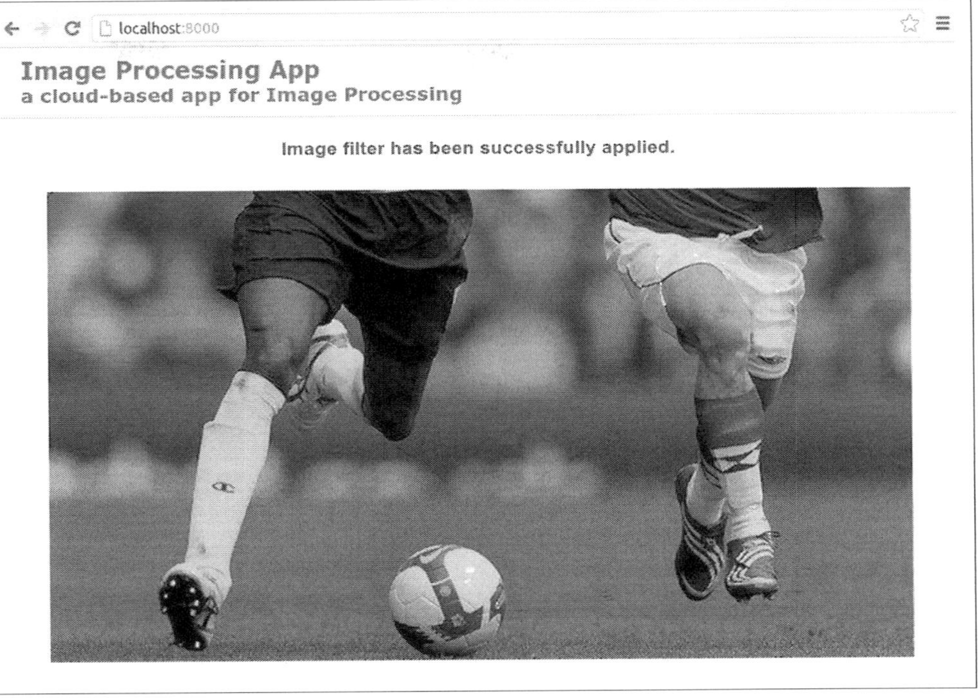

Figure 8.8: Screenshot of Image Processing App - processed image

is uploaded to the *media* directory (specified in the Django project settings). The selected filter is then applied on the uploaded file in the *applyfilter*() function. This example uses the Python Imaging Library (PIL) for image filtering operations.

■ Box 8.4: Django View - image processing app

```
from django.shortcuts import render_to_response
from django.template import RequestContext
from myapp.forms import UploadFileForm
from PIL import Image, ImageOps,ImageFilter

def applyfilter(filename, preset):
    inputfile = '/home/arshdeep/django/imagepro/media/' + filename

    f=filename.split('.')
    outputfilename = f[0] + '-out.jpg'

    outputfile = '/home/arshdeep/django/imagepro/myapp/templates/static/output/'
+
        outputfilename

    im = Image.open(inputfile)
    if preset=='gray':
        im = ImageOps.grayscale(im)
```

```
    if preset=='edge':
        im = ImageOps.grayscale(im)
        im = im.filter(ImageFilter.FIND_EDGES)

    if preset=='poster':
        im = ImageOps.posterize(im,3)

    if preset=='solar':
        im = ImageOps.solarize(im, threshold=80)

    if preset=='blur':
        im = im.filter(ImageFilter.BLUR)

    if preset=='sepia':
        sepia = []
        r, g, b = (239, 224, 185)
        for i in range(255):
            sepia.extend((r*i/255, g*i/255, b*i/255))
        im = im.convert("L")
        im.putpalette(sepia)
        im = im.convert("RGB")

    im.save(outputfile)
    return outputfilename

def handle_uploaded_file(f,preset):
    uploadfilename='media/' + f.name
    with open(uploadfilename, 'wb+') as destination:
        for chunk in f.chunks():
            destination.write(chunk)

    outputfilename=applyfilter(f.name, preset)
    return outputfilename

def home(request):
    if request.method == 'POST':
        form = UploadFileForm(request.POST,request.FILES)
        if form.is_valid():
         preset=request.POST['preset']
            outputfilename = handle_uploaded_file(request.FILES['myfilefield'],preset)
            return render_to_response('process.html',{'outputfilename': outputfilename},
             context_instance=RequestContext(request))
    else:
        form = UploadFileForm()
    return render_to_response('index.html',{'form': form},
        context_instance=RequestContext(request))
```

Box 8.5 shows the URL patterns for the Image Processing application.

■ Box 8.5: URL patterns for image processing app

```
from django.conf.urls.defaults import *
urlpatterns = patterns('',
    url(r'^$', 'myapp.views.home'),    )
```

8.3 Document Storage App

In this section you will learn how to develop a cloud-based document storage (Cloud Drive) application. This application allows users to store documents on a cloud-based storage.

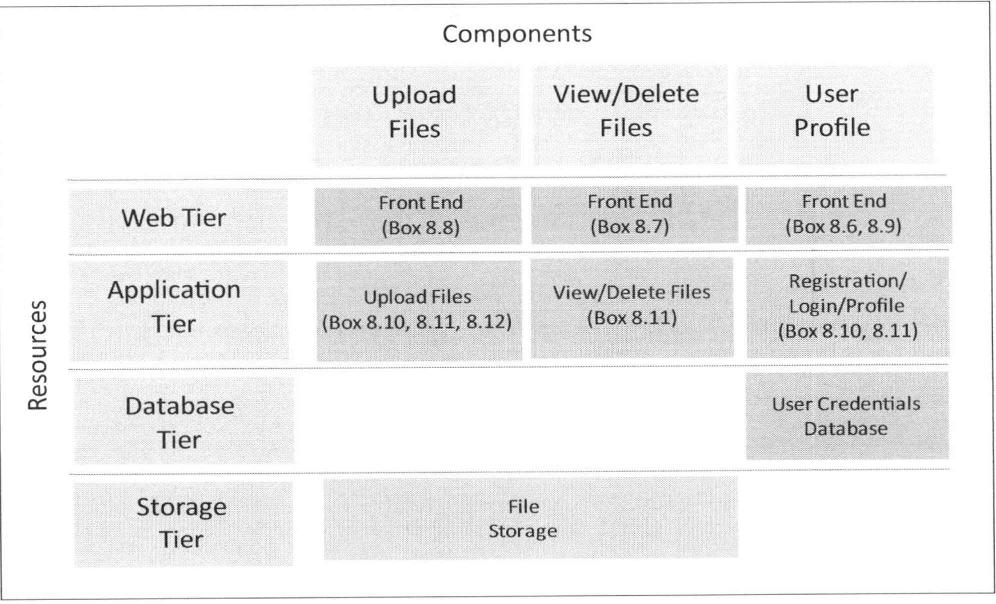

Figure 8.9: Component design for Cloud Drive App

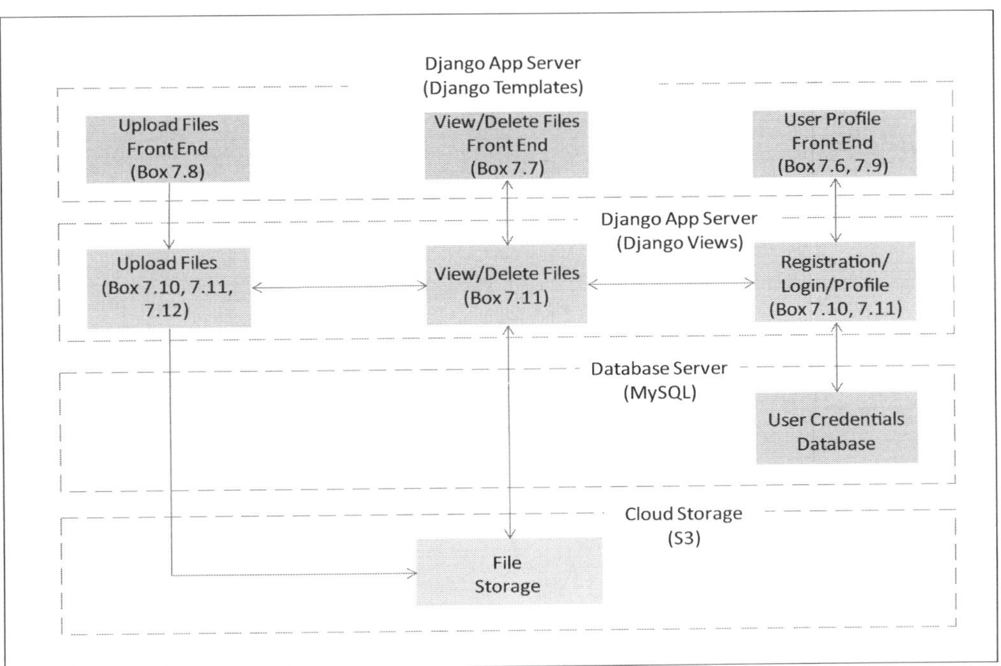

Figure 8.10: Architecture design for Cloud Drive App

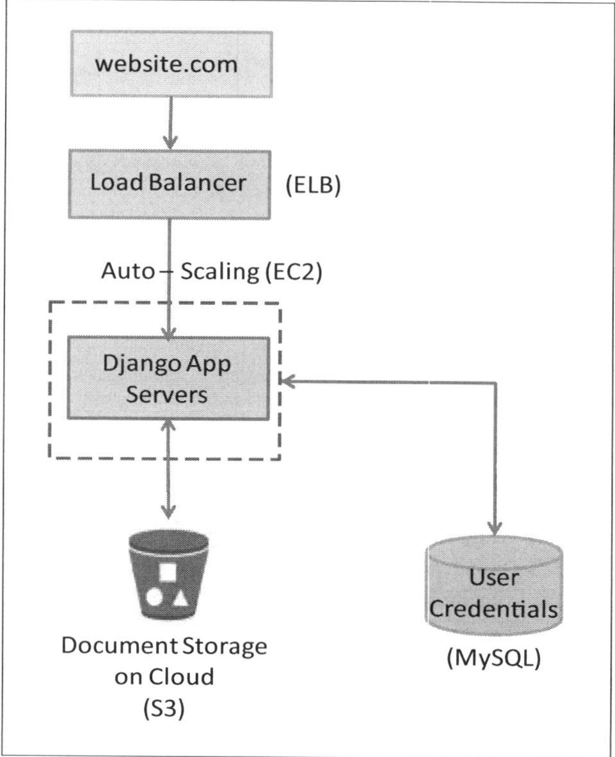

Figure 8.11: Deployment design for Cloud Drive App

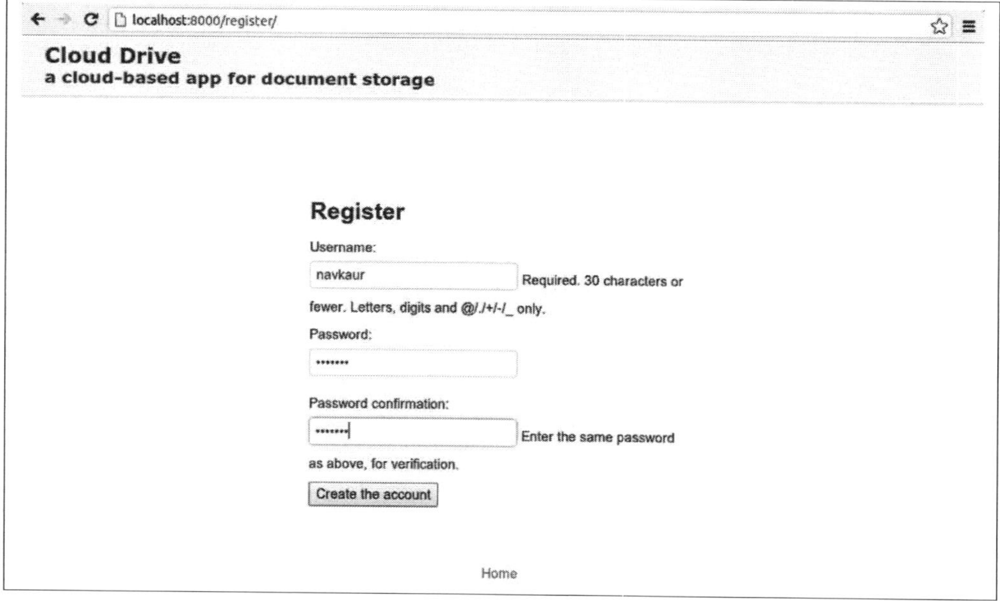

Figure 8.12: Screenshot of Cloud Drive App - registration page

Figure 8.9 shows the component design step for the Cloud Drive app. In this step we

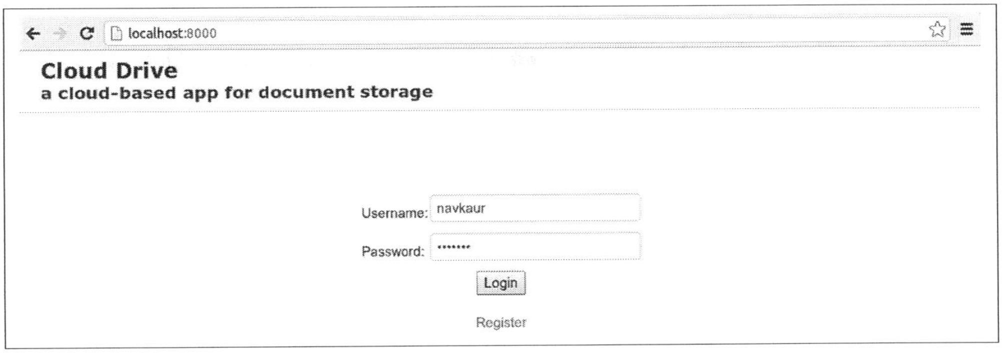

Figure 8.13: Screenshot of Cloud Drive App - login page

identify the application components and group them based on the type of functions performed and type of resources required. The web tier for the Cloud Drive app has front ends for uploading files, viewing/deleting files and user profile. The application tier has components for processing requests for uploading files, processing requests for viewing/deleting files and the component that handles the registration, profile and login functions. The database tier comprises of a user credentials database. The storage tier comprises of the storage for files.

Figure 8.10 shows the architecture design step which defines the interactions between the application components. This application uses the Django framework, therefore, the web tier components map to the Django templates and the application tier components map to the Django views. A MySQL database is used for the database tier and a cloud storage is used for the storage tier. For each component, the corresponding code box numbers are mentioned.

Figure 8.11 shows the deployment design for the Cloud Drive app. This is a multi-tier deployment comprising of load balancer, application servers, cloud storage for storing documents and a database server for storing user credentials. For each resource in the reference architecture the corresponding Amazon Web Services (AWS) cloud service is mentioned.

Figure 8.12 shows a screenshot of the user registration page and Figure 8.13 shows a screenshot of the login page. The Cloud Drive app uses the Django's in-built user authentication system. Box 8.6 shows the source code for the Django template for the registration page.

■ Box 8.6: Django template - registration page

```
<html xmlns="http://www.w3.org/1999/xhtml">
<head>
<meta http-equiv="Content-Type" content="text/html; charset=UTF-8">
<title>Cloud Drive</title>
<link href="/static/styles/demo_style.css" rel="stylesheet" type="text/css">
<link href="/static/styles/bootstrap.css" rel="stylesheet" type="text/css">
</head>
<body>
<div class="demoHead">
```

```
<div>
<div style="float:left;">
<h1>Cloud Drive</h1>
<h2>a cloud-based app for document storage</h2>
</div>
<div style="clear:both;"></div>
</div>
</div>
<br><br><br><br>
<center>
<table width="40%" align="center" border="0">
<tr>
<td>
<h3>Register</h3>
</center>
<form action="" method="post">{% csrf_token %}
{{ form.as_p }}
<input type="submit" value="Create the account">
</form>
</td>
</tr>
</table>
<br><br>
<center>
<a href='/'>Home</a>
</center>
</body>
</html>
```

Figure 8.14 shows a screenshot of the home page of Cloud Drive that shows the files uploaded by a user. Box 8.7 shows the source code for the Django template for the home page.

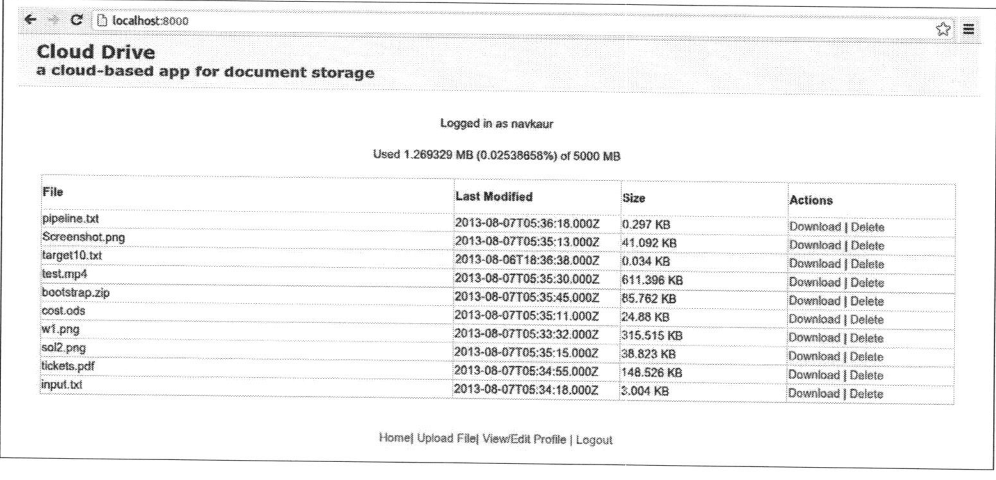

Figure 8.14: Screenshot of Cloud Drive App - uploaded files

■ Box 8.7: Django template - view files page

```
<html xmlns="http://www.w3.org/1999/xhtml">
<head>
<meta http-equiv="Content-Type" content="text/html; charset=UTF-8">
<title>Cloud Drive</title>
<link href="/static/styles/demo_style.css" rel="stylesheet" type="text/css">
<link href="/static/styles/bootstrap.css" rel="stylesheet" type="text/css">
</head><body>
<div class="demoHead">
<div>
<div style="float:left;">
<h1>Cloud Drive</h1>
<h2>a cloud-based app for document storage</h2>
</div>
<div style="clear:both;"></div>
</div>
</div>
<center>
<br>
Logged in as {{username}}
<br><br>
Used {{totalsize}} MB ({{percentused}}%) of {{limit}} MB
<br><br>
<table border='1' bordercolor='#cccccc'>
<tr>
<td width="500"><h5>File</h5></td>
<td width="200"><h5>Last Modified</h5></td>
<td width="100"><h5>Size</h5></td>
<td width="200"><h5>Actions</h5></td>
</tr>
{% for key,val in userfiles.items %}
<tr>
<td width="500">{{key}}</td>
<td width="200">{{val.0}}</td>
<td width="200">{{val.1}} KB</td>
<td width="200"><a href="#">Download</a> | <a href="/delete/{{key}}">Delete</a></td>
</tr>
{% endfor %}
</table>
<br><br>
<a href='/'>Home</a> |
<a href='/upload'>Upload File</a> |
<a href='/profile'>View/Edit Profile</a> |
<a href='/logout'>Logout</a>
</center>
</body>
</html>
```

Figure 8.15 shows a screenshot of the page for uploading files. Box 8.8 shows the source code for the Django template for the upload files page.

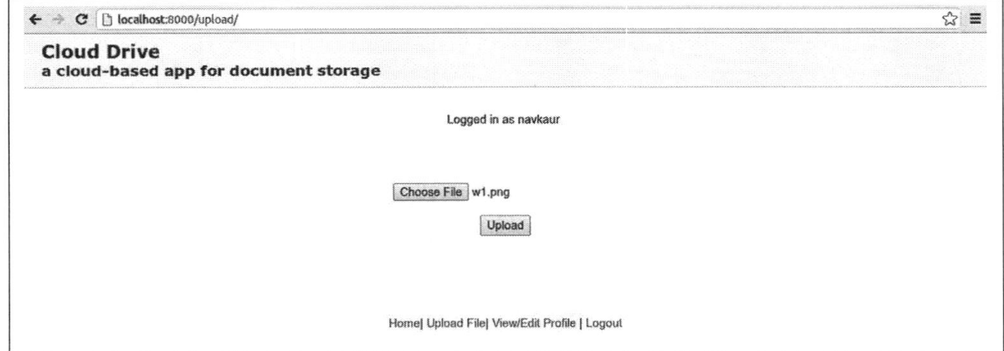

Figure 8.15: Screenshot of Cloud Drive App - file upload page

■ Box 8.8: Django template - upload file page

```
<html xmlns="http://www.w3.org/1999/xhtml">
<head>
<meta http-equiv="Content-Type" content="text/html; charset=UTF-8">
<title>Cloud Drive</title>
<link href="/static/styles/demo_style.css" rel="stylesheet" type="text/css">
<link href="/static/styles/bootstrap.css" rel="stylesheet" type="text/css">
</head><body>
<div class="demoHead">
<div>
<div style="float:left;">
<h1>Cloud Drive</h1>
<h2>a cloud-based app for document storage</h2>
</div>

<div style="clear:both;"></div>
</div>
</div>
<center>
<br>
Logged in as {{username}}
<br><br><br><br>

<form action="/upload/" method="post" enctype="multipart/form-data">
{% csrf_token %}

<p>{{ form.non_field_errors }}</p>
<p>
{{ form.myfilefield.errors }}
{{ form.myfilefield }}
</p>

<input type="submit" value="Upload" />
</form>
<br><br><br><br>
<a href='/'>Home</a> |
```

```
<a href='/upload'>Upload File</a> |
<a href='/profile'>View/Edit Profile</a> |
<a href='/logout'>Logout</a>
</center>
</body>
</html>
```

Figure 8.16 shows a screenshot of the user profile page. Box 8.9 shows the source code for the Django template for the profile page.

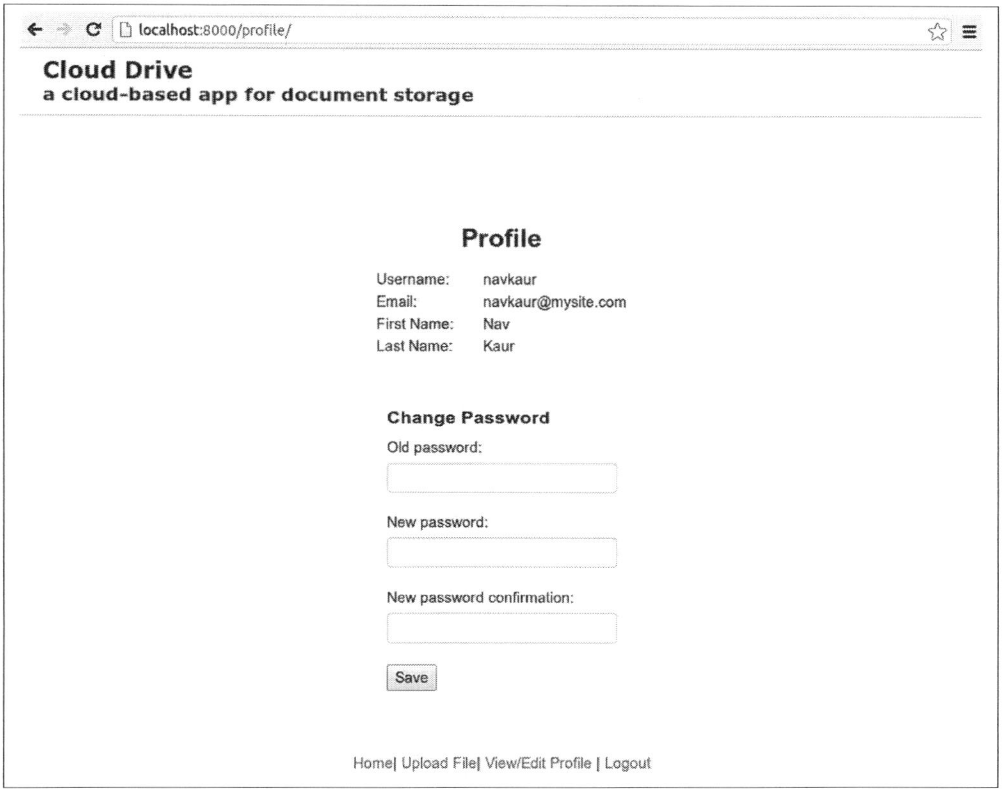

Figure 8.16: Screenshot of Cloud Drive App - profile page

■ Box 8.9: Django template - profile page

```
<html xmlns="http://www.w3.org/1999/xhtml">
<head>
<meta http-equiv="Content-Type" content="text/html; charset=UTF-8">
<title>Cloud Drive</title>
<link href="/static/styles/demo_style.css" rel="stylesheet" type="text/css">
<link href="/static/styles/bootstrap.css" rel="stylesheet" type="text/css">
</head><body>

<div class="demoHead">
<div>
```

```
<div style="float:left;">
<h1>Cloud Drive</h1>
<h2>a cloud-based app for document storage</h2>
</div>
<div style="clear:both;"></div>
</div>
</div>
<br><br><br><br>
<center>
<h3>Profile</h3>

<table>
<tr>
<td width = "100">Username:</td>
<td>{{username}}</td>
</tr>
<tr>
<td width = "100">Email:</td>
<td>{{email}}</td>
</tr>
<tr>
<td width = "100">First Name:</td>
<td>{{fname}}</td>
</tr>
<tr>
<td width = "100">Last Name:</td>
<td>{{lname}}</td>
</tr>
</table>

<br><br>
</center>
<table width="10%" align="center" border="0">
<tr>
<td>
<h4>Change Password</h4>
</center>
<form action="" method="post">{% csrf_token %}
{{ form.as_p }}
<input type="submit" value="Save">
</form>
</td>
</tr>
</table>
<br><br>
<center>
<a href='/'>Home</a> |
<a href='/upload'>Upload File</a> |
<a href='/profile'>View/Edit Profile</a> |
<a href='/logout'>Logout</a>
</center>

</body>
</html>
```

Box 8.10 shows the source code for the Django forms for login and file upload.

■ Box 8.10: Django form - cloud drive app

```
from django import forms

class LoginForm(forms.Form):
    username = forms.CharField()
    password = forms.CharField(widget=forms.PasswordInput())

class UploadFileForm(forms.Form):
    myfilefield = forms.FileField()
```

Box 8.11 shows the source code for the Django View. The *home*() function handles the request for the home page. This function renders the login page by default. If the request method is POST (generated when the user submits the login information in the login page) the username and password are obtained from the login form data and the user is authenticated by calling the *authenticate*() function. If the password is valid for the given username, the *authenticate*() function returns a *User* object. The authenticated user is then attached to the current session by calling the *login*() function. The *login* function takes an *HttpRequest* object and a *User* object and saves the user ID in the session, using Django's session framework. After attaching the authenticated user to the current session, the user files are retrieved by calling the *getuserfiles* function to which the Amazon S3 bucket name and username are passed. The *getuserfiles*() function returns a dictionary of the user files and their attributes, which is then rendered in the template.

The function *upload_view*() handles the requests for uploading a file submitted from the upload file page. The *handle_uploaded_file*() function uploads the selected file to an Amazon S3 bucket. Files from different users are stored in the same S3 bucket, but in separate directories named as the usernames.

The function *register_view*() handles the requests for registering a new user. The function *delete_view*() handles the requests for deleting a file. The *delete_from_s3*() function deletes the file specified.

■ Box 8.11: Django views - cloud drive app

```
from django.shortcuts import render_to_response
from django.shortcuts import render
from django.shortcuts import redirect
from django.template import RequestContext
from django.contrib.auth import authenticate, login
from forms import LoginForm, UploadFileForm
from django.contrib.auth.forms import UserCreationForm
from django.contrib.auth.forms import PasswordChangeForm
from django.contrib.auth import logout
from django.contrib.auth.decorators import login_required
from s3upload import *


def logout_view(request):
    logout(request)
    return redirect('/')
```

```
@login_required
def profile_view(request):
    if request.method == 'POST':
        form = PasswordChangeForm(request.user, data=request.POST)
        if form.is_valid():
            form.save()
            return redirect('/')

    username = request.user.username
    email = request.user.email
    fname = request.user.first_name
    lname = request.user.last_name
    form = PasswordChangeForm(request.POST)
    return render_to_response('profile.html',{'form': form, 'username': username,
            'email': email, 'fname':fname, 'lname': lname},
            context_instance=RequestContext(request))


def register_view(request):
if request.method == 'POST':
form = UserCreationForm(request.POST)
if form.is_valid():
new_user = form.save()
return redirect('/')
else:
form = UserCreationForm()
return render_to_response('register.html',{'form': form},
            context_instance=RequestContext(request))


def handle_uploaded_file(f,username):
    uploadfilename='media/' + f.name
    with open(uploadfilename, 'wb+') as destination:
        for chunk in f.chunks():
            destination.write(chunk)

    upload_to_s3_bucket_path('mybucket', username, uploadfilename)
    return uploadfilename


@login_required
def delete_view(request,filename):
    username = request.user.username
    delete_from_s3('mybucket', username,filename)
    userfiles,totalsize = getuserfiles('mybucket', username)
    limit=5000
    percentused = totalsize*100/limit
    return render_to_response('index.html',{'username':username,'userfiles': userfiles,
                'totalsize':totalsize,'limit':limit,'percentused':percentused},
                context_instance=RequestContext(request))
```

```
@login_required
def upload_view(request):
    if request.method == 'POST':
        form = UploadFileForm(request.POST, request.FILES)
        if form.is_valid():
            username = request.user.username
            outputfilename = handle_uploaded_file(request.FILES['myfilefield'],username)
            userfiles,totalsize = getuserfiles('mybucket', username)
            limit=5000
            percentused = totalsize*100/limit
            return render_to_response('index.html',{'username':username,'userfiles': user-
files,
                    'totalsize':totalsize,'limit':limit,'percentused':percentused},
                    context_instance=RequestContext(request))
    else:
        form = UploadFileForm()
        username = request.user.username
    return render_to_response('upload.html',{'form': form,'username':username},
              context_instance=RequestContext(request))


def home(request):
    if request.method == 'POST':
        username = request.POST['username']
        password = request.POST['password']
        user = authenticate(username=username, password=password)
        if user is not None:
            if user.is_active:
                login(request, user)
                username = request.user.username
                userfiles,totalsize = getuserfiles('mybucket', username)
                limit=5000
                percentused = totalsize*100/limit
                return render_to_response('index.html',{'username':username,'userfiles': user-
files,
                    'totalsize':totalsize,'limit':limit,'percentused':percentused},
                    context_instance=RequestContext(request))
    else:
        if request.user.is_authenticated():
            username = request.user.username
            userfiles,totalsize = getuserfiles('mybucket', username)
            limit=5000
            percentused = totalsize*100/limit
            return render_to_response('index.html',{'username':username,'userfiles': user-
files,
                    'totalsize':totalsize,'limit':limit,'percentused':percentused},
                    context_instance=RequestContext(request))

    form = LoginForm()
    return render_to_response('login.html',{'form': form},
        context_instance=RequestContext(request))
```

Box 8.12 shows the source code of the functions for interacting with the Amazon S3 service. These functions are used in the Django View.

■ Box 8.12: S3 functions - cloud drive app

```
import os
import boto.s3

conn = boto.connect_s3(aws_access_key_id='<enter key>',
    ws_secret_access_key='<enter key>')

def percent_cb(complete, total):
    print ('.')

def upload_to_s3_bucket_path(bucketname, path, filename):
    mybucket = conn.get_bucket(bucketname)
    fullkeyname=os.path.join(path,filename)
    key = mybucket.new_key(fullkeyname)
    key.set_contents_from_filename(filename, cb=percent_cb, num_cb=10)
    #key.make_public(recursive=False)

def getuserfiles(bucketname,username):
    mybucket = conn.get_bucket(bucketname)
    keys = mybucket.list(username)
    totalsize=0.0
    userfiles = {}
    for key in keys:
        value=[]
        #value.append(key.name)
        filename = key.name
        filename=filename.replace(username+'/media/','')
        value.append(key.last_modified)
        keysize = float(key.size)/1000.0
        value.append(str(keysize))
        userfiles[filename]=value
        totalsize = totalsize + float(key.size)
    totalsize = totalsize/1000000.0
    return userfiles,totalsize

def delete_from_s3(bucketname, username,filename):
    mybucket = conn.get_bucket(bucketname)
    mybucket.delete_key(username+'/media/'+filename)
```

Box 8.13 shows the URL patterns for the Cloud Drive app.

■ Box 8.13: URL patterns for cloud drive app

```
from django.conf.urls.defaults import *
from django.contrib import admin
from django.contrib.auth import views as auth_views

admin.autodiscover()

urlpatterns = patterns('',
url(r'^$', 'myapp.views.home'),
url(r'^logout/$', 'myapp.views.logout_view'),
```

```
url(r'^register/$', 'myapp.views.register_view'),
url(r'^profile/$', 'myapp.views.profile_view'),
url(r'^upload/$', 'myapp.views.upload_view'),
url(r'^delete/(?P<filename> [\w\. ]+)$', 'myapp.views.delete_view'),
url(r'^process/$', 'myapp.views.process'),
url(r'^admin/doc/', include('django.contrib.admindocs.urls')),
url(r'^admin/', include(admin.site.urls)),
url(r'^password/change/$', auth_views.password_change,
name='auth_password_change'),
url(r'^password/change/done/$', auth_views.password_change_done,
name='auth_password_change_done'),)
```

The Cloud Drive app uses a MySQL database for storing the user credentials which is configured in the Django settings. The user credentials can be managed from the Django admin site. Figure 8.17 shows a screenshot of the Django admin site for the Cloud Drive app.

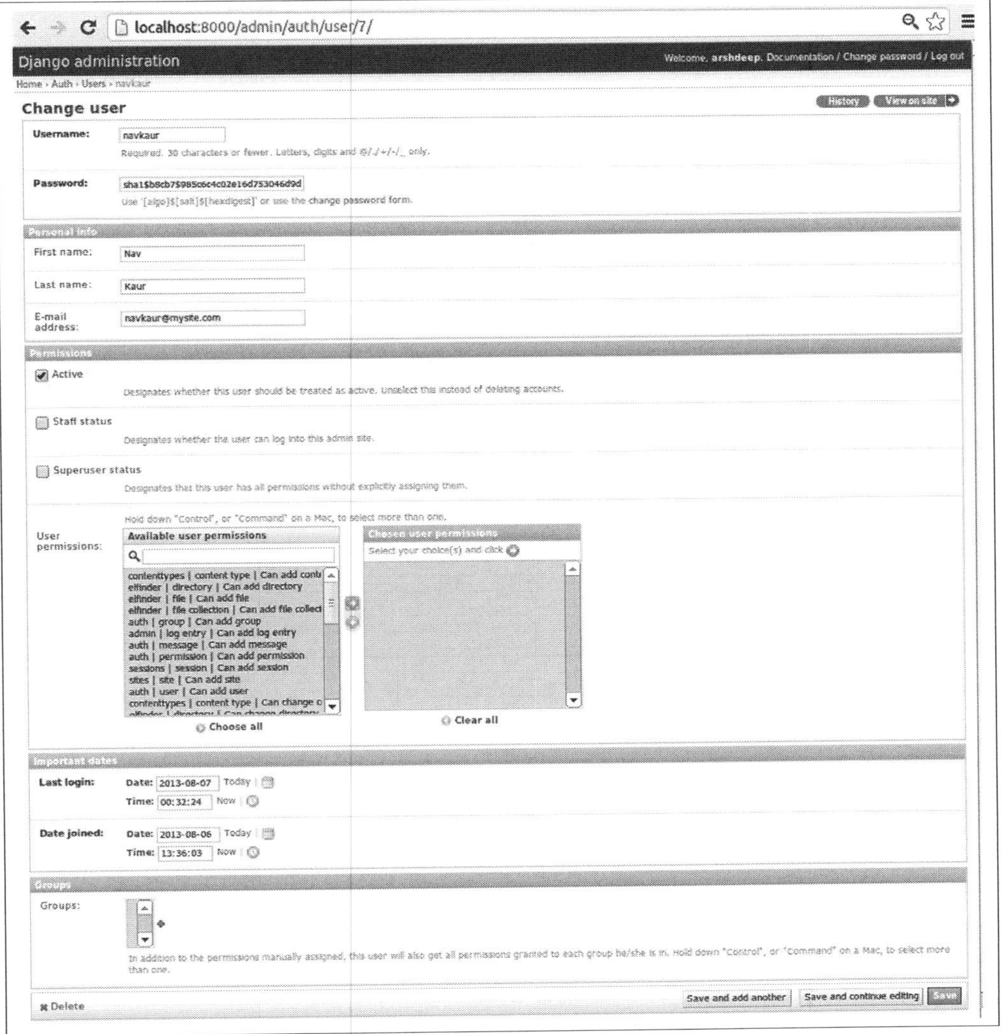

Figure 8.17: Cloud Drive App - Django admin site

8.4 MapReduce App

In this section you will learn how to develop a MapReduce application. This application allows users to submit MapReduce jobs for data analysis. This application is based on the Amazon Elastic MapReduce (EMR) service. Users can upload data files to analyze and choose/upload the Map and Reduce programs. The selected Map and Reduce programs along with the input data are submitted to a queue for processing.

Figure 8.18 shows the component design step for the MapReduce app. In this step we identify the application components and group them based on the type of functions performed and type of resources required. The web tier for the MapReduce app has a front end for MapReduce job submission. The application tier has components for processing requests for uploading files, creating MapReduce jobs and enqueuing jobs, MapReduce consumer and the component that sends email notifications. The Hadoop framework is used for the analytics tier and a cloud storage is used for the storage tier.

Figure 8.19 shows the architecture design step which defines the interactions between the application components. This application uses the Django framework, therefore, the web tier components map to the Django templates and the application tier components map to the Django views. For each component, the corresponding code box numbers are mentioned. To make the application scalable the job submission and job processing components are separated. The MapReduce job requests are submitted to a queue. A consumer component that runs on a separate instance retrieves the MapReduce job requests from the queue and creates the MapReduce jobs and submits them to the Amazon EMR service. The user receives an email notification with the download link for the results when the job is complete.

Figure 8.20 shows the deployment design for the MapReduce app. This is a multi-tier architecture comprising of load balancer, application servers and a cloud storage for storing MapReduce programs, input data and MapReduce output. For each resource in the deployment the corresponding Amazon Web Services (AWS) cloud service is mentioned.

Figure 8.21 shows a screenshot of the first step of the MapReduce job submission wizard in the MapReduce app. In the first step, the user selects the data to analyze. Figure 8.22 shows a screenshot of the second step in which the user selects Map and Reduce programs. The user can either choose from the list of predefined programs or upload custom Map and Reduce programs. Figure 8.23 shows a screenshot of the final step in which the user submits the MapReduce job. Figure 8.24 shows a screenshot of the MapReduce job submission confirmation page.

Box 8.14 shows the source code for the Django template for the MapReduce job submission page. Box 8.15 shows the source code for the Django template for the job confirmation page. Box 8.16 shows the source code for Django form that is displayed in the job submission page.

■ Box 8.14: Django template - job submission page

```
<html xmlns="http://www.w3.org/1999/xhtml">
<head>
<meta http-equiv="Content-Type" content="text/html; charset=UTF-8">
<title>MapReduce App</title>
<link href="/static/styles/demo_style.css" rel="stylesheet" type="text/css">
```

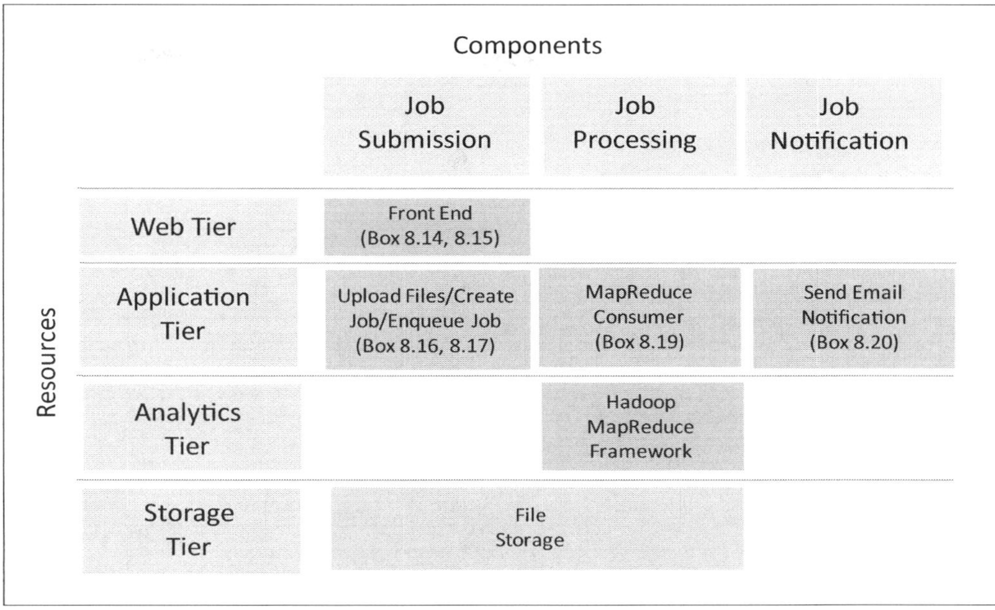

Figure 8.18: Component design for MapReduce App

```
<link href="/static/styles/smart_wizard.css" rel="stylesheet" type="text/css">
<link href="/static/styles/bootstrap.css" rel="stylesheet" type="text/css">
<script type="text/javascript" src="/static/js/jquery-1.4.2.min.js"></script>
<script type="text/javascript" src="/static/js/jquery.smartWizard.js"></script>
<script type="text/javascript">
$(document).ready(function(){

    $('#wizard').smartWizard({transitionEffect:'fade',onFinish:onFinishCallback} );
function onFinishCallback(){
$('form').submit();
}
});
</script>
</head>
<body>
<div class="demoHead">
<div>
<div style="float:left;">
<h1>MapReduce App</h1>
<h2>a cloud-based app for MapReduce</h2>
</div>

<div style="clear:both;"></div>
</div>
</div>

<form action="/" method="post" enctype="multipart/form-data">
{% csrf_token %}
<br>
```

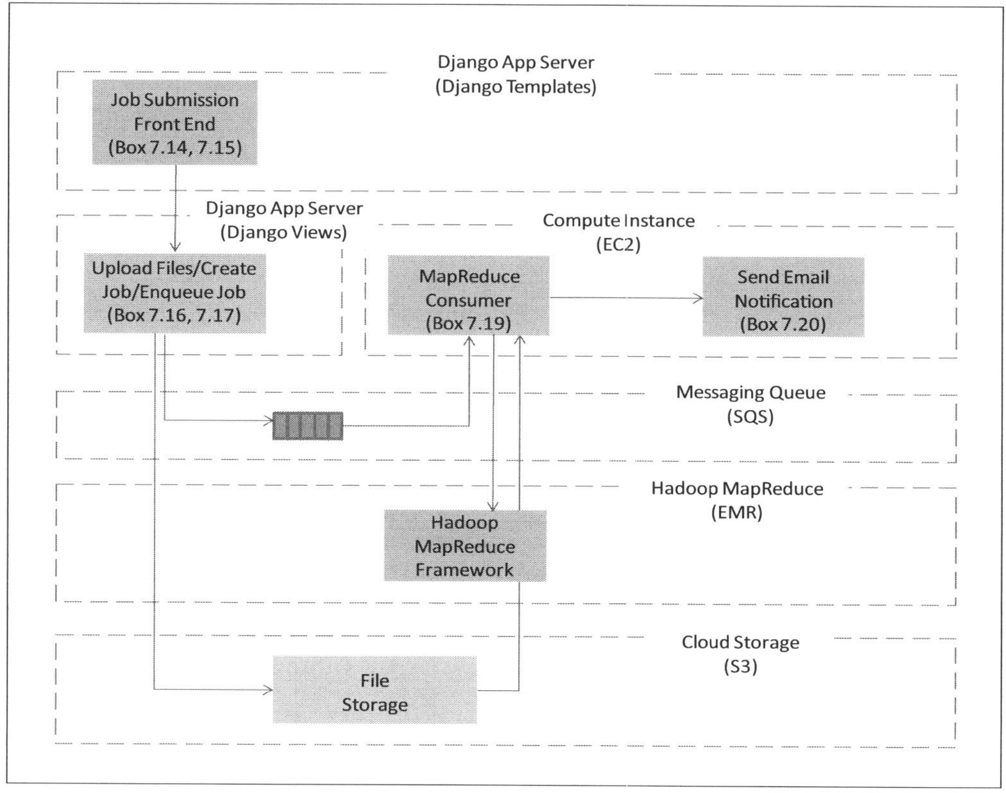

Figure 8.19: Architecture design for MapReduce App

```
<table align="center" border="0" cellpadding="0" cellspacing="0">
<tr><td>
<!- Smart Wizard ->
<h2>Submit MapReduce Job</h2>
<div id="wizard" class="swMain">
<ul>
<li><a href="#step-1">
<label class="stepNumber">1</label>
<span class="stepDesc">
Step 1<br />
<small>Select data to analyze</small>
</span>
</a></li>
<li><a href="#step-2">
<label class="stepNumber">2</label>
<span class="stepDesc">
Step 2<br />
<small>Select MapReduce programs</small>
</span>
</a></li>
<li><a href="#step-3">
<label class="stepNumber">3</label>
<span class="stepDesc">
```

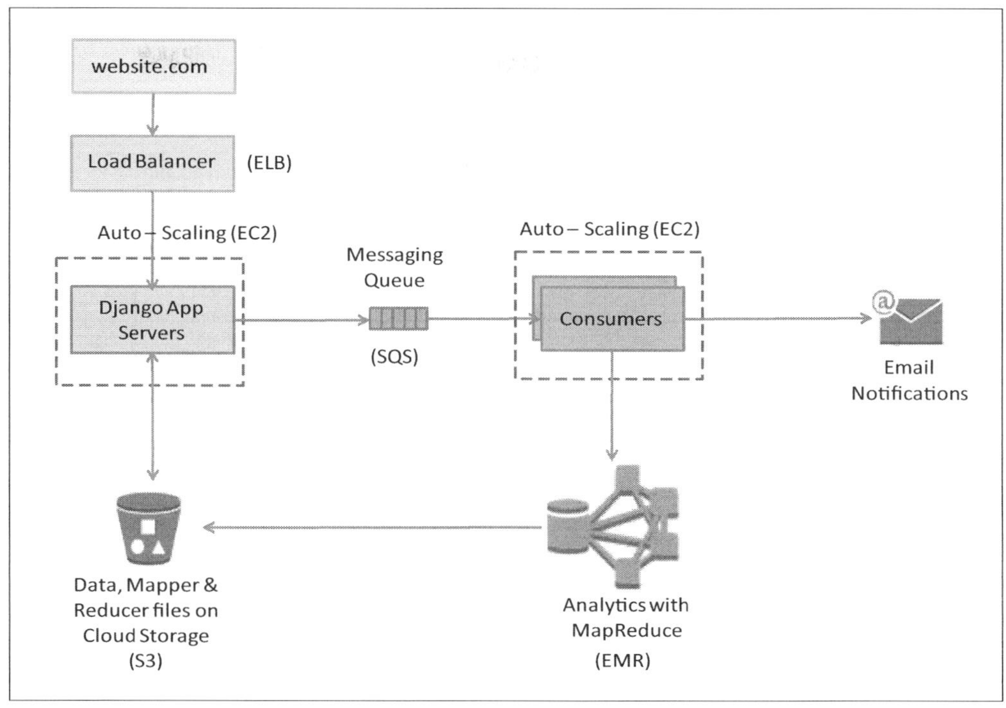

Figure 8.20: Deployment design for MapReduce App

```
Step 3<br />
<small>Submit job</small>
</span>
</a></li>
</ul>
<div id="step-1">
<h2 class="StepTitle">Select data to analyze</h2>

<h4>Choose the data file:</h4>

<p>{{ form.non_field_errors }}</p>
<p>
{{ form.myfilefield.errors }}
{{ form.myfilefield }}
</p>

</div>
<div id="step-2">
<h2 class="StepTitle">Select Map and Reduce programs</h2> <br>
<h5>Choose Predefined Map and Reduce:</h5>
<select name="mapreduceprogram">
<option value="none">Select map-reduce programs...</option>
<option value="wordcount">Word Count</option>
<option value="invertedindex">Inverted Index</option>
</select>
<h4>OR</h4>
```

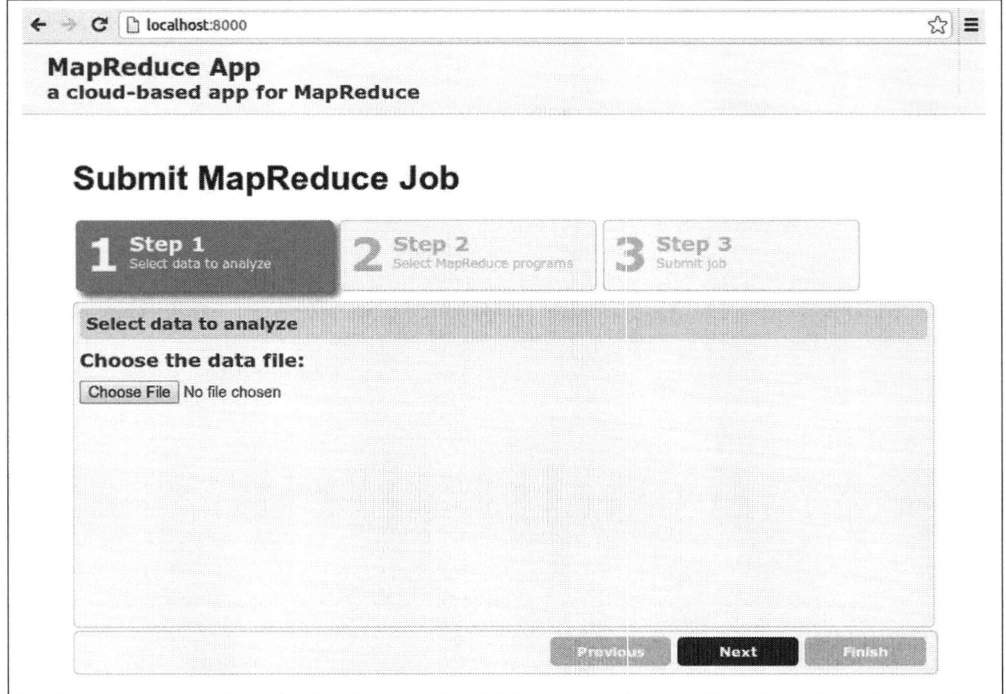

Figure 8.21: Screenshot of MapReduce App - choosing data file

```
<h5>Choose Custom Mapper:</h5>
<p>{{ mapform.non_field_errors }}</p>
<p>
{{ mapform.mymapfield.errors }}
{{ mapform.mymapfield }}
</p>
<h5>Choose Custom Reducer:</h5>
<p>{{ reduceform.non_field_errors }}</p>
<p>
{{ reduceform.myreducefield.errors }}
{{ reduceform.myreducefield }}
</p>
</div>
<div id="step-3">
<h2 class="StepTitle">Submit job</h2>
<br>
<h4>Enter email to get job completion notification.</h4><br>
<input type="text" name="email">
</div>
</div>
</td></tr>
</table>
</form>
</body>
</html>
```

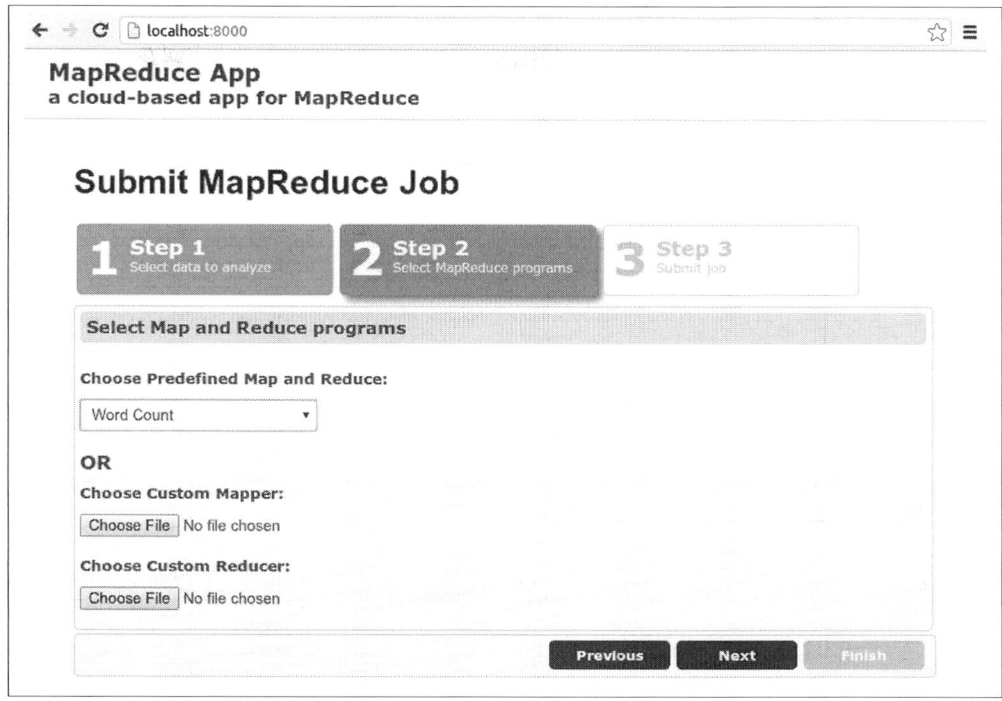

Figure 8.22: Screenshot of MapReduce App - selecting mapper and reducer

■ **Box 8.15: Django template - job submission confirmation page**

```
<html xmlns="http://www.w3.org/1999/xhtml"><head>
<meta http-equiv="Content-Type" content="text/html; charset=UTF-8">
<title>MapReduce App</title>
<link href="/static/styles/demo_style.css" rel="stylesheet" type="text/css">
<link href="/static/styles/smart_wizard.css" rel="stylesheet" type="text/css">
<link href="/static/styles/bootstrap.css" rel="stylesheet" type="text/css">
<script type="text/javascript" src="/static/js/jquery-1.4.2.min.js"></script>
<script type="text/javascript" src="/static/js/jquery.smartWizard.js"></script>
</head>
<body>
<div class="demoHead">
<div>
<div style="float:left;">
<h1>MapReduce App</h1>
<h2>a cloud-based app for MapReduce</h2>
</div>
<div style="clear:both;"></div>
</div>
</div>
<table align="center" border="0" cellpadding="0" cellspacing="0">
<tr><td>
<center>
<h4>MapReduce job has been successfully submitted.</h4>
```

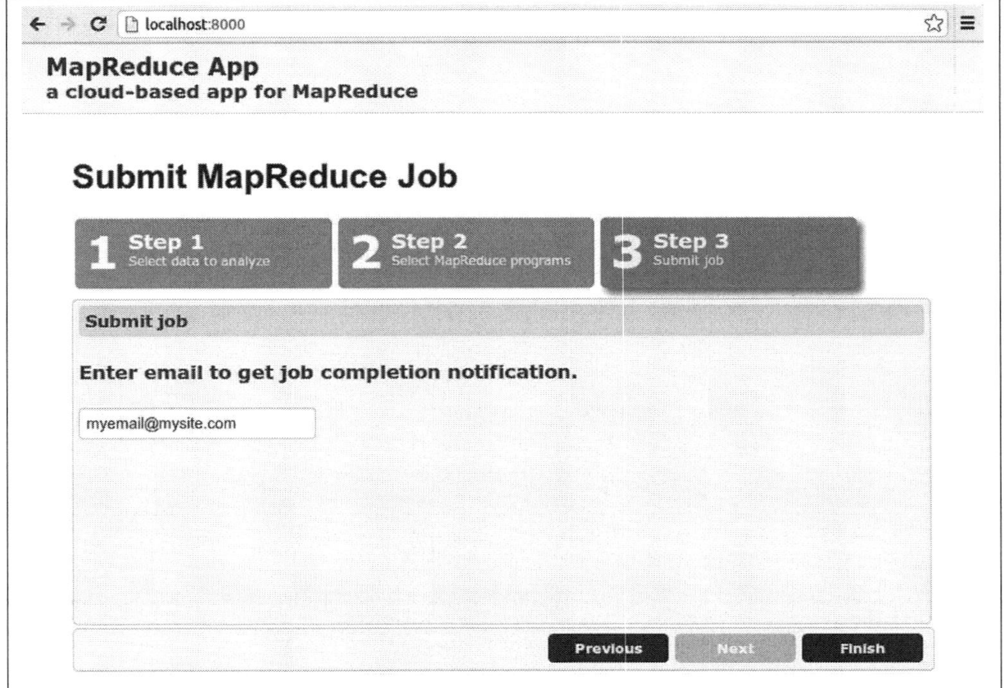

Figure 8.23: Screenshot of MapReduce App - submitting job

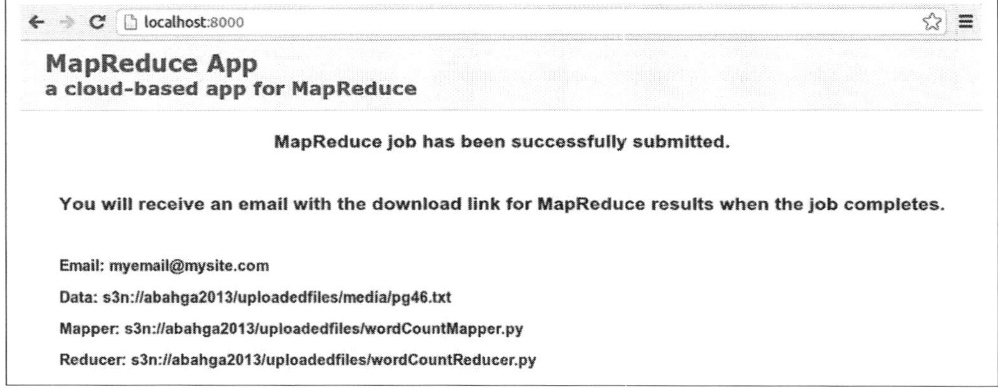

Figure 8.24: Screenshot of MapReduce App - job confirmation

```
<br>
<h4>You will receive an email with the download link for MapReduce results when the job
completes.</h4>
</center>
<br>
<h5>Email: {{emailaddress}}</h5>
<h5>Data: {{datafile}}<h5>
<h5>Mapper: {{mapper}}</h5>
<h5>Reducer: {{reducer}}</h5>
```

```
</td></tr>
</table>
</body>
</html>
```

■ Box 8.16: Django form - MapReduce app

```
from django import forms

class UploadFileForm(forms.Form):
    myfilefield = forms.FileField()

class UploadMapForm(forms.Form):
    mymapfield = forms.FileField()

class UploadReduceForm(forms.Form):
    myreducefield = forms.FileField()
```

Box 8.17 shows the source code for the Django View for the MapReduce app. The *home*() function handles the request for the job submission page. The function checks if the request method is POST or not. If the request method is POST, the form submitted by the user is processed and the data file, Map and Reduce programs are uploaded to the *media* directory (which is specified in the Django project settings). The *createjob*() function is then called which creates a MapReduce job definition which has information on the input data, Mapper, Reducer and user email address for job completion notification. The files submitted by the user are uploaded to an S3 bucket. The *enqueuejob*() function is then called which enqueues a MapReduce job request to an Amazon SQS queue.

■ Box 8.17: Django views - MapReduce app

```
from django.shortcuts import render_to_response
from django.template import RequestContext
from myapp.forms import UploadFileForm
from myapp.forms import UploadMapForm
from myapp.forms import UploadReduceForm
from s3upload import upload_to_s3_bucket_path
import cPickle
import boto.sqs
from boto.sqs.message import Message

ACCESS_KEY="<enter access key>"
SECRET_KEY="<enter secret key>"
REGION="us-east-1"

def handle_uploaded_file(f):
    uploadfilename='media/' + f.name
    with open(uploadfilename, 'wb+') as destination:
        for chunk in f.chunks():
            destination.write(chunk)
    return uploadfilename
```

```
def enqueuejob(datafile,mapper,reducer,emailaddress):
    conn = boto.sqs.connect_to_region(
        REGION,
        aws_access_key_id=ACCESS_KEY,
        aws_secret_access_key=SECRET_KEY)

    queue_name = 'arsh-queue'

    q = conn.get_all_queues(prefix=queue_name)

    msgdict={'datafile': datafile,'mapper': mapper,
        'reducer':reducer, 'emailaddress': emailaddress}

    msg = cPickle.dumps(msgdict)

    m = Message()
    m.set_body(msg)
    status = q[0].write(m)

def createjob(datafilename, mapfilename, reducefilename,
        mapreduceprogram, emailaddress):
    upload_to_s3_bucket_path('mybucket', 'uploadedfiles', datafilename)
    datafile = 's3n://mybucket/uploadedfiles/' + datafilename
    if mapreduceprogram == 'wordcount':
        mapper = 's3n://mybucket/uploadedfiles/wordCountMapper.py'
        reducer = 's3n://mybucket/uploadedfiles/wordCountReducer.py'
    elif mapreduceprogram == 'invertedindex':
        mapper = 's3n://mybucket/uploadedfiles/invertedindexMapper.py'
        reducer = 's3n://mybucket/uploadedfiles/invertedindexReducer.py'
    else:
        upload_to_s3_bucket_path('mybucket', 'uploadedfiles', mapfilename)
        upload_to_s3_bucket_path('mybucket', 'uploadedfiles', reducefilename)
        mapper = 's3n://mybucket/uploadedfiles/' + mapfilename
        reducer = 's3n://mybucket/uploadedfiles/'    + reducefilename

    enqueuejob(datafile,mapper,reducer,emailaddress)
    return datafile,mapper,reducer,emailaddress

def home(request):
    if request.method == 'POST':
        datafilename = ''
        mapfilename = ''
        reducefilename = ''
        mapreduceprogram = ''
        form = UploadFileForm(request.POST, request.FILES)
        if form.is_valid():
            datafilename = handle_uploaded_file(request.FILES['myfilefield'])

        mapform = UploadMapForm(request.POST, request.FILES)
        if mapform.is_valid():
            mapfilename = handle_uploaded_file(request.FILES['mymapfield'])

        reduceform = UploadReduceForm(request.POST, request.FILES)
```

```
        if reduceform.is_valid():
            reducefilename = handle_uploaded_file(request.FILES('myreducefield'))

        mapreduceprogram=request.POST('mapreduceprogram')
        emailaddress=request.POST('email')

        datafile,mapper,reducer,emailaddress =
            createjob(datafilename, mapfilename, reducefilename,
                        mapreduceprogram, emailaddress)
        return render_to_response('process.html',{'datafile': datafile,
        'mapper': mapper, 'reducer': reducer,
        'emailaddress': emailaddress}, context_instance=RequestContext(request))
    else:
        form = UploadFileForm()
        mapform = UploadMapForm()
        reduceform = UploadReduceForm()
    return render_to_response('index.html',{'form': form,
        'mapform': mapform, 'reduceform': reduceform},
        context_instance=RequestContext(request))
```

Box 8.18 shows the URL patterns for the MapReduce app.

■ Box 8.18: URL patterns for MapReduce app

```
from django.conf.urls.defaults import *

urlpatterns = patterns('',
    url(r'^$', 'myapp.views.home'),
)
```

Box 8.19 shows the source code for the consumer program that retrieves the MapReduce job request from the SQS queue and creates a MapReduce job that is submitted to the Amazon EMR service for execution. The consumer program processes the MapReduce job requests in a First-In, First-Out (FIFO) manner from the queue. The consumer program waits till the execution of a MapReduce job completes and then calls the *sendnotification*() function which sends an email notification to the user.

■ Box 8.19: MapReduce app - consumer program

```
import boto.sqs
from boto.sqs.message import Message
import cPickle
import boto.emr
from boto.emr.step import StreamingStep
import time
from sendemailnotification import sendemail

ACCESS_KEY="<enter access key>"
SECRET_KEY="<enter secret key>"
REGION="us-east-1"

def sendnotification(msg, status, downloadlink):
```

```
    receipients_list = (msg('emailaddress'))
    subject = 'MapReduce Job Notification'

    if status == 'COMPLETED':
        message = "Your MapReduce job is complete. Download results from: " + download-
link

    sendemail(receipients_list, subject, message)

def createemrjob(msg):
    print "Connecting to EMR"

    conn = boto.emr.connect_to_region(REGION,
     aws_access_key_id=ACCESS_KEY,
     aws_secret_access_key=SECRET_KEY)

    print "Creating streaming step"

    t=time.localtime(time.time())
    job_datetime = str(t.tm_year) + str(t.tm_mon) + str(t.tm_mday) +
            str(t.tm_hour) + str(t.tm_min) + str(t.tm_sec)

    outputlocation = 's3n://mybucket/uploadedfiles/' + job_datetime
    step = StreamingStep(name=job_datetime,
            mapper=msg('mapper'),
            reducer=msg('reducer'),
            input=msg('datafile'),
            output=outputlocation)

    print "Creating job flow"

    jobid = conn.run_jobflow(name=job_datetime,
            log_uri='s3n://mybucket/uploadedfiles/mapred_logs',
            steps=(step))

    print "Submitted job flow"

    print "Waiting for job flow to complete"

    status = conn.describe_jobflow(jobid)
    print status.state

    while status.state == 'STARTING' or status.state == 'RUNNING' or
        status.state == 'WAITING' or status.state == 'SHUTTING_DOWN':
        time.sleep(10)
        status = conn.describe_jobflow(jobid)

    print "Job status: " + str(status.state)

    print "Completed Job: " + job_datetime

    downloadlink = 'http://mybucket.s3.amazonaws.com/uploadedfiles/' +
            job_datetime + '/part-00000'
    sendnotification(msg, status.state, downloadlink)
```

```
print "Connecting to SQS"

conn = boto.sqs.connect_to_region(
REGION,
aws_access_key_id=ACCESS_KEY,
aws_secret_access_key=SECRET_KEY)

queue_name = 'arsh-queue'

print "Connecting to queue: " + queue_name
q = conn.get_all_queues(prefix=queue_name)

count = q[0].count()

print "Total messages in queue: " + str(count)

print "Reading message from queue"

for i in range(count):
    m = q[0].read()
    msg=cPickle.loads(m.get_body())
    print "Message %d: %s" % (i+1, msg)
    q[0].delete_message(m)
    createemrjob(msg)

print "Read %d messages from queue" % (count)
```

Box 8.20 shows the source code for the email notification program. This program uses a Gmail account for sending notification emails. Alternatively, the Amazon Simple Notification Service (SNS) can be used.

■ Box 8.20: MapReduce app - email notification program

```
import smtplib

from_addr = '<enter email here>'
cc_addr_list = []
username = '<username>'
password = '<password>'
smtpserver = 'smtp.gmail.com:587'

def sendemail(to_addr_list, subject, message):
    header = 'From: %s\n' % from_addr
    header += 'To: %s\n' % ','.join(to_addr_list)
    header += 'Cc: %s\n' % ','.join(cc_addr_list)
    header += 'Subject: %s\n \n' % subject
    message = header + message
    server = smtplib.SMTP(smtpserver)
    server.starttls()
    server.login(username,password)
    problems = server.sendmail(from_addr, to_addr_list, message)
    server.quit()
```

Figure 8.25 shows a screenshot of an email notification about a MapReduce job completion. The email also contains the download link for the results.

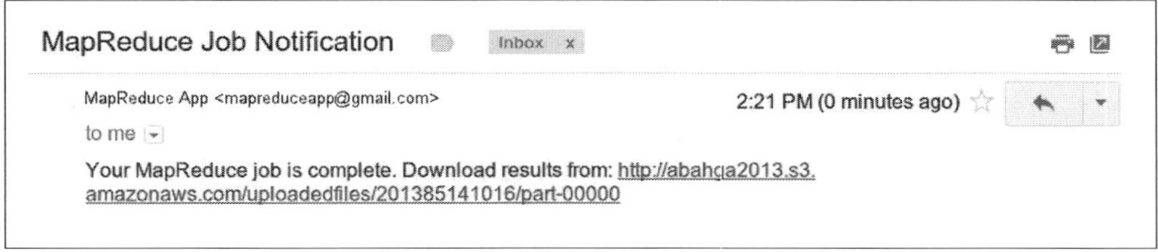

Figure 8.25: MapReduce job completion notification email

8.5 Social Media Analytics App

In this section you will learn how to develop a Social Media Analytics application. This application collects the social media feeds (Twitter tweets) on a specified keyword in real time and analyzes the sentiments of the tweets and provides aggregate results.

Figure 8.26 shows the component design step for the Social Media Analytics app. In this step we identify the application components and group them based on the type of functions performed and type of resources required. The web tier has a front end for displaying results. The application tier has a listener component that collects social media feeds, a consumer component that analyzes tweets and a component for rendering the results in the dashboard. A MongoDB database is used for the database tier and a cloud storage is used for the storage tier.

Figure 8.27 shows the architecture design step which defines the interactions between the application components. For each component, the corresponding code box numbers are mentioned. To make the application scalable the feeds collection component (Listener) and feeds processing component (Consumer) are separated. The Listener component uses the Twitter API to get feeds on a specific keyword (or a list of keywords) and enqueues the feeds to a queue. The Consumer component (that runs on a separate instance) retrieves the feeds from the queue and analyzes the feeds and stores the aggregated results in a separate database. The aggregate results are displayed to the users from a Django application.

Figure 8.28 shows the deployment design for the Social Media Analytics app. This is a multi-tier architecture comprising of load balancer, application servers, listener and consumer instances, a cloud storage for storing raw data and a database server for storing aggregated results. For each resource in the deployment the corresponding Amazon Web Services (AWS) cloud service is mentioned.

Figure 8.29 shows a screenshot of the Social Media Analytics app. This app shows the total number of tweets collected, the number of positive, negative and neutral tweets, hourly activity, top tweets and top hashtags.

Box 8.21 shows the source code for the Listener component. The lister uses the tweepy Python package [104] for obtaining twitter feeds in real-time. The list of keywords can be configured in the listener. In the listener, the *on_data*() method is called whenever a new tweet related to the list of keywords is received. The tweets data (which is in the form of a JSON object) is then serialized and written to an SQS queue.

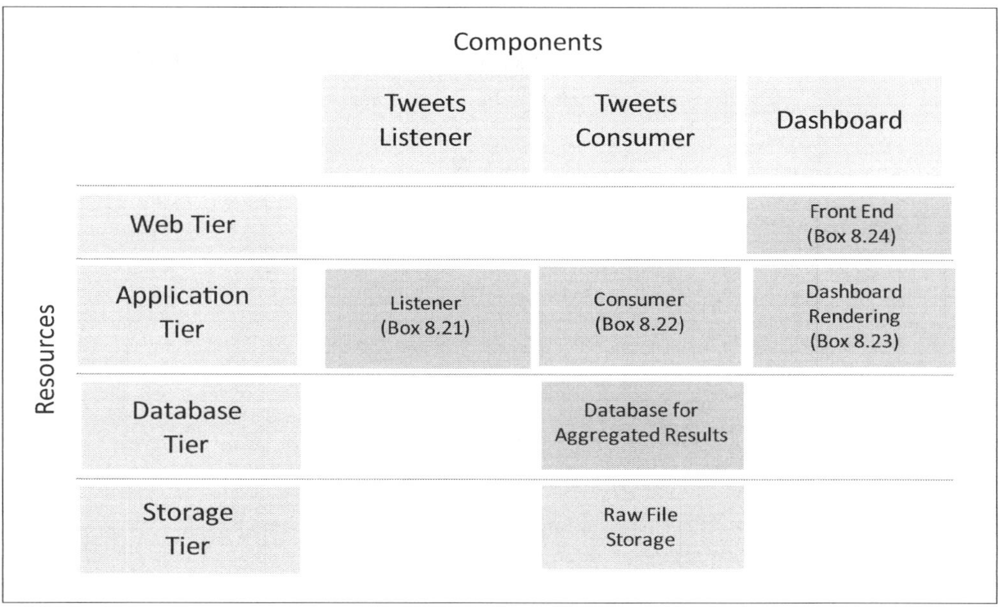

Figure 8.26: Component design for Social Media Analytics App

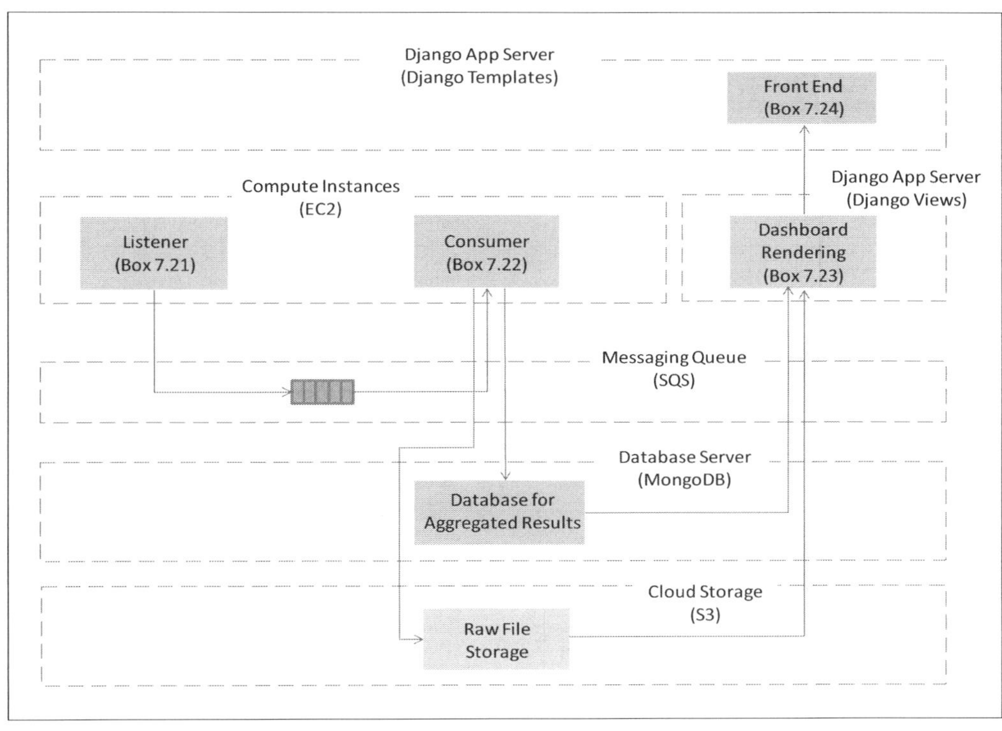

Figure 8.27: Architecture design for Social Media Analytics App

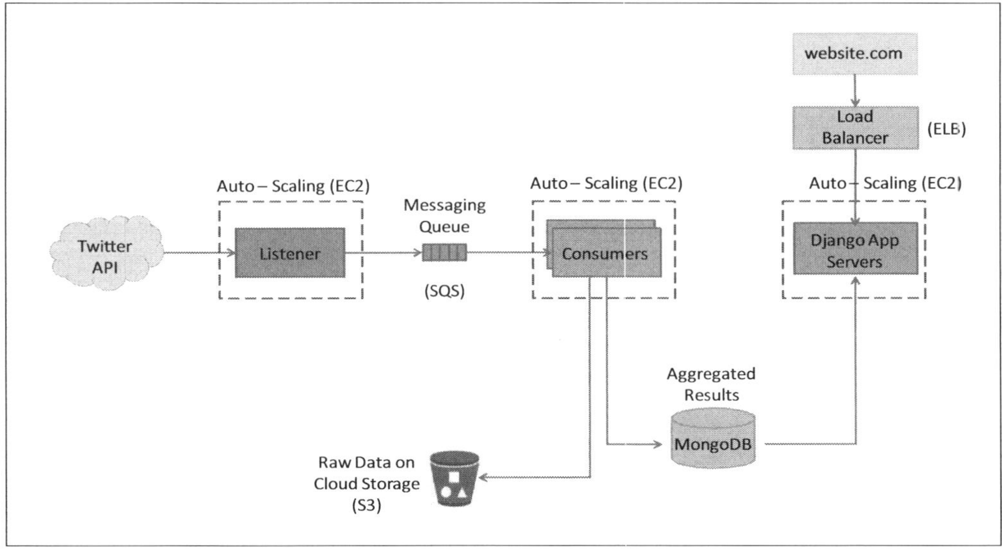

Figure 8.28: Deployment design for Social Media Analytics App

■ **Box 8.21: Tweets Listener**

```
from tweepy.streaming import StreamListener
from tweepy import OAuthHandler
from tweepy import Stream
from boto.sqs.message import Message
import cPickle


consumer_key="<enter key>"
consumer_secret="<enter secret>"
access_token = "<enter access token>"
access_token_secret = "<enter access secret>"


import boto.sqs
conn = boto.sqs.connect_to_region(
    "us-east-1",
    aws_access_key_id='<enter key>',
     aws_secret_access_key='<enter secret>')

q = conn.get_all_queues(prefix='arsh-queue')

class StdOutListener(StreamListener):
    def on_data(self, data):
        #print data
        msg=cPickle.dumps(data)
        m = Message()
        m.set_body(msg)
        status = q[0].write(m)
        return True
```

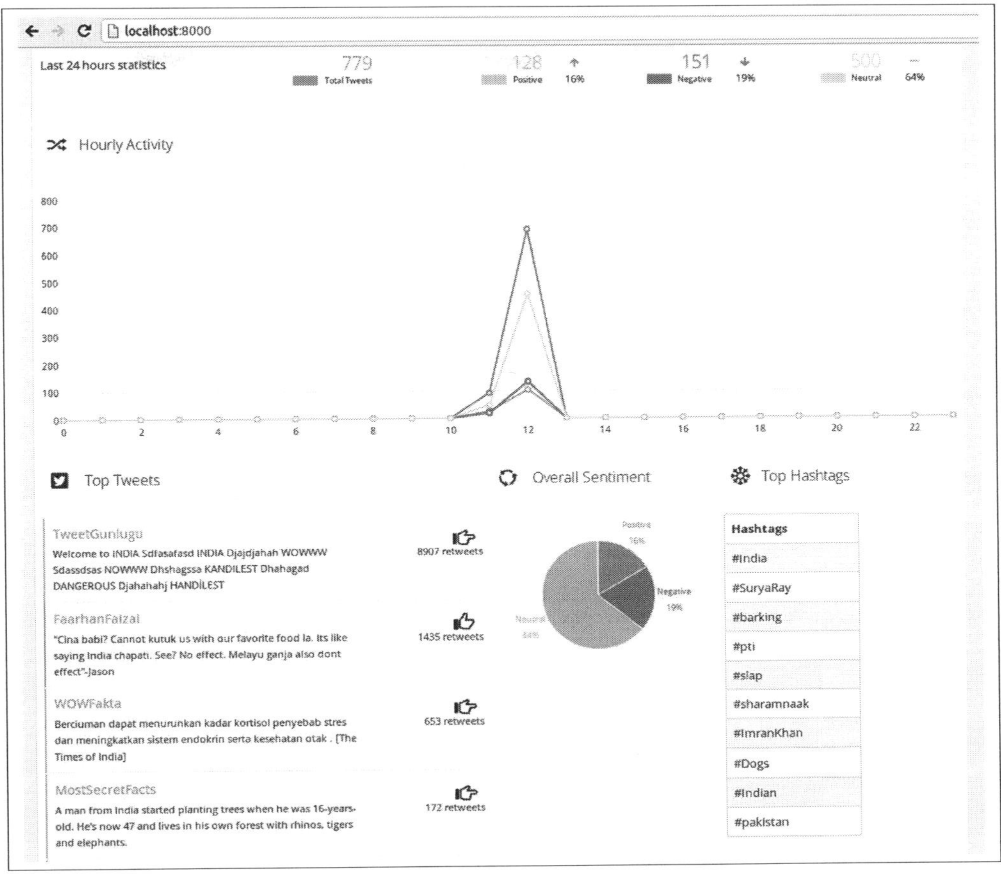

Figure 8.29: Screenshot of Social Media Analytics App

```
    def on_error(self, status):
        print status


if __name__ == '__main__':
    keywords=['india']
    l = StdOutListener()
    auth = OAuthHandler(consumer_key, consumer_secret)
    auth.set_access_token(access_token, access_token_secret)
    stream = Stream(auth, l)
    stream.filter(track=keywords)
```

Box 8.22 shows the source code for the Consumer component. The consumer component runs on a separate instance than the listener. The consumer retrieves the tweets from the SQS queue and analyzes them one by one. The *parseTweet*() function parses the fields in the tweet object (which is a JSON object). The *findsentiment*() computes the sentiment of the parsed tweet. For sentiment analysis, a sentiment lexicon is used which has a list of English words each with a sentiment score. The sentiment lexicon used in this example is AFINN [103] which contains about 2500 words each marked with a sentiment score between

-5 and 5. The *analyzeTweet*() function analyzes and aggregates the results. The aggregated results are stored in a MongoDB database.

■ Box 8.22: Tweets Consumer

```
from pymongo import MongoClient
import datetime
import boto.sqs
from boto.sqs.message import Message
import cPickle
from datetime import date
import json
from topia.termextract import extract
from collections import OrderedDict
import re
import ast
import random
import sys

parseddic={}
aggregatedic={}
TERMS={}
global conn
global q
global client
global db
global keyword

###########Setup Consumer function###############
def setupConsumer():
    global conn
    global q
    global client
    global db
    global keyword

    #——Initialize keyword list———
    keyword='india'

    #——Load Sentiments Dict—————
    sent_file = open('AFINN-111.txt')
    sent_lines = sent_file.readlines()
    for line in sent_lines:
        s = line.split("")
        TERMS[s[0]] = s[1]
    sent_file.close()

    #——Connect to SQS Queue—————
    conn = boto.sqs.connect_to_region(
        "us-east-1",
        aws_access_key_id='<enter access key>',
        aws_secret_access_key='<enter secret key>')
```

```
    q = conn.get_queue('arsh-queue')
    queuecount=q.count()
    print "Queue count= "+str(queuecount)

    #——-Connect to MongoDB——————
    client = MongoClient()
    client = MongoClient('localhost', 27017)
    db = client['myapp']

################ Find Sentiment function ################
def findsentiment(tweet):
    splitTweet=tweet.split()
    sentiment=0.0
    for word in splitTweet:
        if TERMS.has_key(word):
            sentiment = sentiment+ float(TERMS[word])
    return sentiment

################ Parse Tweet function ########################
def parseTweet(tweet):
    if tweet.has_key('created_at'):
        createdat = tweet['created_at']
        hourint=int(createdat[11:13])
        parseddic['hour'] = str(hourint)

#—————————-Retweets———
    parseddic['toptweets']={}
    if tweet.has_key('retweeted_status'):
        retweetcount= tweet['retweeted_status']['retweet_count']
        retweetscreenname= tweet['retweeted_status']['user']['screen_name'].encode('utf-
8',errors='ignore')
        retweetname= tweet['retweeted_status']['user']['name'].encode('utf-8',
errors='ignore')
        retweettext=tweet['retweeted_status']['text'].encode('utf-8',errors='ignore')
        retweetdic={}
        retweetdic['retweetcount']=retweetcount
        retweetdic['retweetscreenname']=retweetscreenname
        retweetdic['retweetname']=retweetname
        retweetdic['retweettext']=retweettext

            retweetdic['retweetsentiment']=findsentiment(retweettext)
        parseddic['toptweets']=retweetdic


#————-Text, Sentiment————
    if tweet.has_key('text'):
        text = tweet['text'].encode('utf-8',errors='ignore')
        parseddic['text']=text
        sentiment=findsentiment(text)
        parseddic['sentimentscore']=sentiment
        parseddic['positivesentiment']=0
        parseddic['negativesentiment']=0
        parseddic['neutralsentiment']=0

        if sentiment>0:
```

```
            parseddic['positivesentiment']=1
        elif sentiment<0:
            parseddic['negativesentiment']=1
        elif sentiment==0:
            parseddic['neutralsentiment']=1

    #————————Hashtags——————
    if tweet.has_key('entities'):
        res1 = tweet['entities']
        taglist = res1["hashtags"]
        hashtaglist=[]
        for tagitem in taglist:
            hashtaglist.append(tagitem["text"])
        parseddic['hashtags']=hashtaglist

#### Analyze Tweet function###########
def analyzeTweet(tweetdic):
    text =tweetdic['text']
    text =text.lower()

    if not aggregatedic.has_key(keyword):
        valuedic={'totaltweets':0,
'positivesentiment':0,'negativesentiment':0,'neutralsentiment': 0, 'hashtags':
{}, 'toptweets': {}, 'totalretweets':0, 'hourlyaggregate':{'0': {'totaltweets':0, 'positivesenti-
ment':0,'negativesentiment':0,'neutralsentiment': 0},'1':
{'totaltweets':0, 'positivesentiment':0,'negativesentiment':0,'neutralsentiment': 0},'2':
{'totaltweets':0, 'positivesentiment':0,'negativesentiment':0,'neutralsentiment': 0},'3':
{'totaltweets':0, 'positivesentiment':0,'negativesentiment':0,'neutralsentiment': 0},'4':
{'totaltweets':0, 'positivesentiment':0,'negativesentiment':0,'neutralsentiment': 0},'5':
{'totaltweets':0, 'positivesentiment':0,'negativesentiment':0,'neutralsentiment': 0},'6':
{'totaltweets':0, 'positivesentiment':0,'negativesentiment':0,'neutralsentiment': 0},'7':
{'totaltweets':0, 'positivesentiment':0,'negativesentiment':0,'neutralsentiment': 0},'8':
{'totaltweets':0, 'positivesentiment':0,'negativesentiment':0,'neutralsentiment': 0},'9':
{'totaltweets':0, 'positivesentiment':0,'negativesentiment':0,'neutralsentiment': 0},'10':
{'totaltweets':0, 'positivesentiment':0,'negativesentiment':0,'neutralsentiment': 0},'11':
{'totaltweets':0, 'positivesentiment':0,'negativesentiment':0,'neutralsentiment': 0},'12':
{'totaltweets':0, 'positivesentiment':0,'negativesentiment':0,'neutralsentiment': 0},'13':
{'totaltweets':0, 'positivesentiment':0,'negativesentiment':0,'neutralsentiment': 0},'14':
{'totaltweets':0, 'positivesentiment':0,'negativesentiment':0,'neutralsentiment': 0},'15':
{'totaltweets':0, 'positivesentiment':0,'negativesentiment':0,'neutralsentiment': 0},'16':
{'totaltweets':0, 'positivesentiment':0,'negativesentiment':0,'neutralsentiment': 0},'17':
{'totaltweets':0, 'positivesentiment':0,'negativesentiment':0,'neutralsentiment': 0},'18':
{'totaltweets':0, 'positivesentiment':0,'negativesentiment':0,'neutralsentiment': 0},'19':
{'totaltweets':0, 'positivesentiment':0,'negativesentiment':0,'neutralsentiment': 0},'20':
{'totaltweets':0, 'positivesentiment':0,'negativesentiment':0,'neutralsentiment': 0}, '21':
{'totaltweets':0, 'positivesentiment':0,'negativesentiment':0,'neutralsentiment': 0}, '22':
{'totaltweets':0, 'positivesentiment':0,'negativesentiment':0,'neutralsentiment': 0},'23':
{'totaltweets':0, 'positivesentiment':0,'negativesentiment':0,'neutralsentiment': 0}} }

        aggregatedic[keyword]=valuedic

#————————Counts——————
    valuedic=aggregatedic[keyword]
    valuedic['totaltweets']+=1
```

```
    valuedic['positivesentiment']+=tweetdic['positivesentiment']
    valuedic['negativesentiment']+=tweetdic['negativesentiment']
    valuedic['neutralsentiment']+=tweetdic['neutralsentiment']
#--------Hourly Aggregate----------
    hour=tweetdic['hour']
    valuedic['hourlyaggregate'][hour]['positivesentiment']+=tweetdic['positivesentiment']
    valuedic['hourlyaggregate'][hour]['negativesentiment']+=tweetdic['negativesentiment']
    valuedic['hourlyaggregate'][hour]['neutralsentiment']+=tweetdic['neutralsentiment']
    valuedic['hourlyaggregate'][hour]['totaltweets']+=1
#-------------Top Hashtags---------
    tagsdic=valuedic['hashtags']
    for tag in tweetdic['hashtags']:
        if tagsdic.has_key(tag):
            tagsdic[tag]+=1
        else:
            tagsdic[tag]=1

#-------------Top Tweets----------
    if tweetdic.has_key('toptweets'):
        if tweetdic['toptweets'].has_key('retweetscreenname'):
            toptweetsdic=valuedic['toptweets']
            retweetkey= tweetdic['toptweets']['retweetscreenname']

            if toptweetsdic.has_key(retweetkey):
                toptweetsdic[retweetkey]['retweetcount']=
            tweetdic['toptweets']['retweetcount']
            else:
                toptweetsdic[retweetkey]=tweetdic['toptweets']


#-------------Aggregate-----------
    aggregatedic[keyword]=valuedic

################ Post Processing function #######################
def postProcessing():
    print aggregatedic
    valuedic= aggregatedic[keyword]


#--------Top 10 Hashtags----------
    keysdic=valuedic['hashtags']
    sortedkeysdic = OrderedDict(sorted(keysdic.items(),key = lambda x:x[1],reverse=True))
    tophashtagsdic={}
    i=0
    for item in sortedkeysdic:
        if i>9:
            break
        i = i+1
        tophashtagsdic[item]= keysdic[item]

    valuedic['hashtags']=tophashtagsdic

#-----Total Retweets & Top 10 Tweets---------
```

```
        toptweetsdic=valuedic['toptweets']
    for key in toptweetsdic:
        valuedic['totalretweets']+=toptweetsdic[key]['retweetcount']

    sortednames=sorted(toptweetsdic,key =
     lambda x:toptweetsdic[x]['retweetcount'],reverse=True)
    sortedtoptweetsdic = OrderedDict()
    i=0
    for k in sortednames:
        if i>99:
            break
        i = i+1
        sortedtoptweetsdic[k]=toptweetsdic[k]

    valuedic['toptweets'] = sortedtoptweetsdic
    #print valuedic['toptweets']

#------------Create Key for MongoDB document------------------
    valuedic['_id'] = str(date.today())+"/"+keyword
    valuedic['metadata'] = {'date': str(date.today()), 'key': keyword}


#------------Insert into MongoDB---------------------------
    print valuedic
    print "Inserting data into MongoDB"
    postid=db.myapp_micollection.insert(valuedic)

#################### Main Function: Configure consumeCount ###############
def main():
    print "Setting up consumer..."
    setupConsumer()
    print "Completed consumer setup..."

    #---enter no. of tweets to consume---------
    consumeCount=800

    print "Consuming "+ str(consumeCount) +" feeds..."

    consumeCount=consumeCount/10 #get 10 in each batch
    for i in range(consumeCount):
        rs = q.get_messages(10) #gets max 10 msgs at a time.
        if len(rs) > 0:
         for m in rs:
            post=m.get_body()
             deserializedpost=cPickle.loads(post)
             postdic=json.loads(deserializedpost)

            parseTweet(postdic)
            analyzeTweet(parseddic)
        conn.delete_message_batch(q,rs)

    queuecount=q.count()
    print "Remaining Queue count= "+str(queuecount)
    print "Completed consuming..."
```

```
    print "Starting post processing..."
    postProcessing()
    print "Completed post processing..."
    print "Done!"

###########Entry Point####################
if __name__ == '__main__':
main()
```

Box 8.23 shows the source code for the Django View for the Social Media Analytics app. The *home*() function processes the request for the home page. This function retrieves the aggregated results from the MongoDB database and renders the results in the Django template. Box 8.24 shows the source code of the Django template of the Social Media Analytics app.

■ **Box 8.23: Django View - social media analytics app**

```
from django.shortcuts import render_to_response
import json
from pymongo import MongoClient
from collections import OrderedDict
from datetime import date, timedelta

today = str(date.today())

client = MongoClient()
client = MongoClient('localhost', 27017)
db = client['myapp']

def home(request):
    results=db.myapp_micollection.find({'metadata.key':'india', 'metadata.date':today})
    #results=db.myapp_micollection.find({'metadata.key':query, 'metadata.date':'2013-
06-30'})

    for postdic in results:
        totaltweets=postdic['totaltweets']
        positivesentiment=postdic['positivesentiment']
        negativesentiment=postdic['negativesentiment']
        neutralsentiment=postdic['neutralsentiment']

        pospercent=positivesentiment*100/totaltweets
        negpercent=negativesentiment*100/totaltweets
        neupercent=neutralsentiment*100/totaltweets

        hashtags=postdic['hashtags']
        hashtags = OrderedDict(sorted(hashtags.items(),key = lambda x:x[1],reverse=True))

        toptweetsdic=postdic['toptweets']
        sortednames=sorted(toptweetsdic,key =
        lambda x:toptweetsdic[x]['retweetcount'],reverse=True)
        sortedtoptweetsdic = OrderedDict()

        i=0
```

```
        for k in sortednames:
            if i>4:
                break
            i = i+1
            sortedtoptweetsdic[k]=toptweetsdic[k]

        toptweets=OrderedDict()
        for key in sortedtoptweetsdic:
            t=[]
            t.append(sortedtoptweetsdic[key]['retweetscreenname'])
            t.append(sortedtoptweetsdic[key]['retweetname'])
            t.append(sortedtoptweetsdic[key]['retweettext'])
            t.append(sortedtoptweetsdic[key]['retweetcount'])
            t.append(sortedtoptweetsdic[key]['retweetsentiment'])
            t.append(sortedtoptweetsdic[key]['retweetimage'])
            toptweets[key]=t

        hourlyaggregate=postdic['hourlyaggregate']

            total={}
        positive={}
        negative={}
        neutral={}
        hi={}
        for key in hourlyaggregate:
            hi[int(key)]=hourlyaggregate[key]

        hourlyaggregate = OrderedDict(sorted(hi.items()))

        for entry in hourlyaggregate:
            total[entry]=hourlyaggregate[entry]['totaltweets']
            positive[entry]=hourlyaggregate[entry]['positivesentiment']
            negative[entry]=hourlyaggregate[entry]['negativesentiment']
            neutral[entry]=hourlyaggregate[entry]['neutralsentiment']

    return render_to_response('index.html', {'totaltweets': totaltweets, 'positivesentiment':
positivesentiment, 'negativesentiment': negativesentiment, 'neutralsentiment': neutralsen-
timent, 'pospercent': pospercent, 'negpercent': negpercent, 'neupercent': neupercent,
'hashtags': hashtags, 'hourlyaggregate': hourlyaggregate, 'total': total, 'positive': positive,
'negative': negative, 'neutral': neutral, 'toptweets': toptweets })
```

■ **Box 8.24: Django template - social media analytics app**

```
<!DOCTYPE html>
<html lang="en">
<head>
<meta charset="utf-8" />
<title>Mood-India</title>
<link id="bootstrap-style" href="/static/css/bootstrap.css" rel="stylesheet" />
<link id="base-style" href="/static/css/style.css" rel="stylesheet" />
<script src="/static/js/jquery-1.7.2.min.js"></script>
<script src="/static/js/jquery-ui-1.8.21.custom.min.js"></script>
<script src="/static/js/jquery.flot.js"></script>
```

```
<script src="/static/js/jquery.flot.pie.js"></script>
<script>
function showplots() {
/* ——— Pie chart start——— */
var data = [
{ label: "Positive", data: {{positivesentiment}}},
{ label: "Negative", data: {{negativesentiment}}},
{ label: "Neutral ", data: {{neutralsentiment}}}
];
if($("#mipiechart").length)
{
$.plot($("#mipiechart"), data,
{
series: {
pie: {
show: true
}
},
grid: {
hoverable: true,
clickable: true
},
legend: {
show: false
},
colors: ["#78CD51", "#FA5833", "#FABB3D","#2FABE9"]
});

function pieHover(event, pos, obj)
{
if (!obj)
return;
percent = parseFloat(obj.series.percent).toFixed(2);
$("#hover").html('<span style="font-weight: bold; color:
'+obj.series.color+'">'+obj.series.label+' ('+percent+'%)</span>');
}
$("#mipiechart").bind("plothover", pieHover);
}
/* ——— Pie chart end ——— */
/* ——— hourlychart start ——— */
if($("#mihourlychart").length)
{
var totaldata = [
{% for key,val in total.items %}
[{{key}},{{val}}],
{% endfor %}
];
var positivedata = [
{% for key,val in positive.items %}
[{{key}},{{val}}],
{% endfor %}
];
var negativedata = [
{% for key,val in negative.items %}
```

```
[{{key}},{{val}}],
{% endfor %}
];
var neutraldata = [
{% for key,val in neutral.items %}
[{{key}},{{val}}],
{% endfor %}
];

var plot = $.plot($("#mihourlychart"),
[ { data: totaldata, label: "Total Tweets"},
{ data: positivedata, label: "Positive Tweets"},
{ data: negativedata, label: "Negative Tweets" },
{ data: neutraldata, label: "Neutral Tweets"} ], {
series: {
lines: { show: true,
lineWidth: 2
},
points: { show: true,
lineWidth: 2
},
shadowSize: 0
},
grid: { hoverable: true,
clickable: true,
tickColor: "#f9f9f9",
borderWidth: 0
},
legend: {
show: false
},
colors: ["#2FABE9", "#74DF00", "#FF0000", "#eae874" ],
xaxis: {ticks:15, tickDecimals: 0},
yaxis: {ticks:5, tickDecimals: 0},
});

}
}
</script>
</head>
<body onload="showplots()">
<div class="container-fluid">

<div class="row-fluid">
<div id="content" class="span11">
<div class="row-fluid">
<div class="stats-date span3">
<div>Last 24 hours statistics</div>
</div>
<div class="stats span9">
<div class="stat">
<div class="left">
<div class="number blue">{{totaltweets}}</div>
<div class="title"><span class="color blue"></span> Total Tweets</div>
```

```
</div></div>
<div class="stat">
<div class="left">
<div class="number green">{{positivesentiment}}</div>
<div class="title"><span class="color green"></span> Positive</div>
</div>
<div class="right">
<div class="arrow">
<i class="fa-icon-arrow-up green"></i>
</div>
<div class="percent">{{pospercent}}%</div>
</div></div>
<div class="stat">
<div class="left">
<div class="number red">{{negativesentiment}}</div>
<div class="title"><span class="color red"></span> Negative</div>
</div>
<div class="right">
<div class="arrow">
<i class="fa-icon-arrow-down red"></i>
</div>
<div class="percent">{{negpercent}}%</div>
</div></div>
<div class="stat">
<div class="left">
<div class="number yellow">{{neutralsentiment}}</div>
<div class="title"><span class="color yellow"></span> Neutral</div>
</div>
<div class="right">
<div class="arrow">
<i class="fa-icon-minus yellow"></i>
</div>
<div class="percent">{{neupercent}}%</div>
</div></div></div></div>

<div class="row-fluid">
<div class="widget span12">
<h2><span class="glyphicons random"><i></i></span>Hourly Activity</h2>
<hr />
</div>

<div class="row-fluid">
<div id="mihourlychart" class="span12" style="height:300px"></div>
</div>

<div class="row-fluid">
<div class="widget span6">
<h2><span class="glyphicons twitter"><i></i></span> Top Tweets</h2>
<hr />
{% for key,val in toptweets.items %}
{% if val.4 < 0 %}
<div class="task high">
{% else %}
{% if val.4 > 0 %}
```

```
<div class="task low">
{% else %}
<div class="task medium">
{% endif %}{% endif %}
<div class="desc">
<a href="http://twitter.com/{{key}}" target="_blank">
<div class="title blue">{{key}}</div>
<div> {{val.2}} </div>
</div>
<div class="time">
<div class="date">
{% if val.4 < 0 %}
<span class="glyphicons thumbs_down"><i></i></span>
{% else %}
{% if val.4 > 0 %}
<span class="glyphicons thumbs_up"><i></i></span>
{% else %}
<span class="glyphicons hand_right"><i></i></span>
{% endif %}{% endif %}
</div>
<div> {{val.3}} retweets</div>
</div>
</div>
{% endfor %}
<div class="clearfix"></div>
</div>
<div class="widget span3">
<h2><span class="glyphicons roundabout"><i></i></span>
Overall Sentiment</h2><hr/>
<div id="mipiechart" style="height:200px"></div>
</div>
<div class="widget span2" >
<h2><span class="glyphicons snowflake"><i></i></span>Top Hashtags</h2>
<hr>
<table class="table table-striped table-bordered">
<thead>
<tr>
<th>Hashtags</th>
</tr>
</thead>
<tbody>
{% for key,val in hashtags.items %}
<tr><td>#{{key}}</td></tr>
{% endfor %}
</tbody>
</table>
</div></div></div></div>
</body>
</html>
```

Box 8.25 shows the URL patterns for the Social Media Analytics app.

■ Box 8.25: URL patterns for social media analytics app

```
from django.conf.urls.defaults import *

urlpatterns = patterns('',
    url(r'^$', 'myapp.views.home'),
)
```

Summary

In this chapter you learned how to develop cloud applications using Python and Django. This chapter provided case studies on Image Processing App, Document Storage App, MapReduce App and Social Media Analytics App. The Image Processing App demonstrated how to develop a multi-tier application comprising of load balancer, application servers and a cloud storage. The Document Storage App demonstrated how to integrate authentication with a Django application and interface with a cloud storage service. The MapReduce app demonstrated how to develop an application with loosely coupled components that communicate via a messaging queue. Decoupling the application component makes the application scalable since the application components can be scaled independently of each other. The Social Media Analytics app demonstrated how to develop an application that collects real-time social media feeds and analyzes them. The application had multiple components that communicated via a messaging queue. The analyzed results were stored in a non-relational database. An application front end was developed for visualization of results using Django.

Review Questions

1. What is the benefit of decoupling application components?
2. What is the use of messaging queues?
3. How can application components be scaled independently?
4. What are the benefit of a non-relational database over relational databases?

Lab Exercises

1. Extend the Image Processing app described in section 7.1 to match the reference architecture shown in Figure 7.1. Create an Amazon AutoScaling group for the application tier and the Amazon Elastic Load Balancer for load balancing. On successful completion of an image processing task, generate an Amazon SNS notification and send an email along with a link to the processed image.

2. Extend the Cloud Drive app described in section 7.2 to match the reference architecture shown in Figure 7.2. Create an Amazon AutoScaling group for the application tier and the Amazon Elastic Load Balancer for load balancing.

3. Extend the MapReduce app described in section 7.3 to accept Pig scripts.

4. Extend the Social Media Analytics app described in section 7.4 to display top keywords and top users (users who tweet the most in a day).

Part III

ADVANCED TOPICS

9 — Big Data Analytics

This Chapter Covers

- Big Data analytics approaches
- Approaches for clustering big data
- Approaches for classification of big data
- Recommendation Systems

9.1 Introduction

Big data is defined as collections of data sets whose volume, velocity in terms of time variation, or variety is so large that it is difficult to store, manage, process and analyze the data using traditional databases and data processing tools. In the recent years there has been an exponential growth in the both structured and unstructured data generated by information technology, industrial, healthcare, and other systems. Some examples of big data are described as follows:

- Data generated by social networks including text, images, audio and video data.
- Click-stream data generated by web applications such as e-Commerce to analyze user behavior.
- Machine sensor data collected from sensors embedded in industrial and energy systems for monitoring their health and detecting failures.
- Healthcare data collected in electronic health record (EHR) systems.
- Logs generated by web applications
- Stock markets data

The underlying characteristics of big data include:

- **Volume:** Though there is no fixed threshold for the volume of data to be considered as big data, however, typically, the term big data is used for massive scale data that is difficult to store, manage and process using traditional databases and data processing architectures. The volumes of data generated by modern IT, industrial, healthcare and systems is growing exponentially driven by the lowering costs of data storage and processing architectures and the need to extract valuable insights from the data to improve business processes, efficiency and service to consumers.
- **Velocity:** Velocity is another important characteristic of big data and the primary reason for exponential growth of data. Velocity of data refers to how fast the data is generated. Modern IT, industrial and other systems are generating data at increasingly higher speeds generating big data.
- **Variety:** Variety refers to the forms of the data. Big data comes in different forms such as structured or unstructured data, including text data, image, audio, video and sensor data.

Big data analytics involves several steps starting from data cleansing, data munging (or wrangling), data processing and visualization. Big data analytics is enabled by several technologies such as cloud computing, distributed parallel processing frameworks, in-memory databases, etc. In this chapter you will learn how to implement big data analytics including approaches for clustering and classification of big data.

9.2 Clustering Big Data

Clustering is the process of grouping similar data items together such that data items that are more similar to each other (with respect to some similarity criteria) than other data items are put in one cluster. Clustering big data is of much interest, and happens in applications such as:

- Clustering social network data to find a group of similar users
- Clustering electronic health record (EHR) data to find similar patients.
- Clustering sensor data to group similar or related faults in a machine

- Clustering market research data to group similar customers
- Clustering clickstream data to group similar users

Clustering is achieved by clustering algorithms that belong to a broad category algorithms called unsupervised machine learning. Unsupervised machine learning algorithms find the patterns and hidden structure in data for which no training data is available. Let us now look at some popular clustering algorithms and their applications to big data.

9.2.1 k-means clustering

K-means is a clustering algorithm that groups data items into k clusters, where k is user defined. Each cluster is defined by a centroid point. All points in a cluster are closer (with respect to some distance measure) to their centroid as compared to the centroids of neighboring clusters. K-means clustering begins with a set of k centroid points which are either randomly chosen from the dataset or chosen using some initialization algorithm such as canopy clustering. The algorithm proceeds by finding the distance between each data point in the data set and the centroid points. Based on the distance measure, each data point is assigned to a cluster belonging to the closest centroid. In the next step the centroids are recomputed by taking the mean value of all the data points in a cluster. This process is repeated till the centroids no longer move more than a specified threshold. The k-means clustering algorithms is shown in Box 9.1.

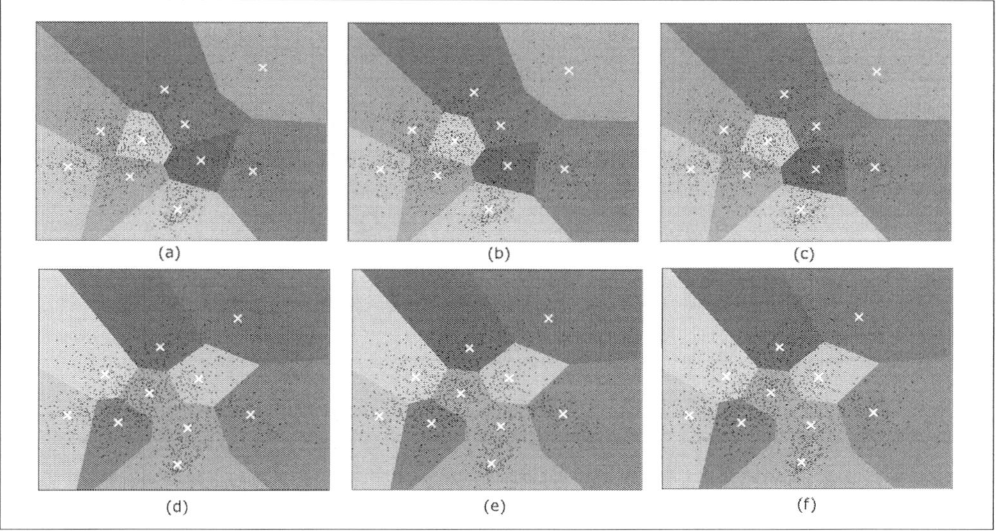

Figure 9.1: Example of clustering 300 points with k-means: (a) iteration 1, (b) iteration 2, (c) iteration 3, (d) iteration 5, (e) iteration 10, (f) iteration 100.

■ Box 9.1: k-means clustering algorithm

Start with k centroid points

while the centroids no longer move beyond a threshold or maximum number of itera-

```
tions reached:
    for each point in the dataset:
        for each centroid:
            find the distance between the point and the centroid
            assign the point to the cluster belonging to the nearest centroid
    for each cluster:
        recompute the centroid point by taking mean value of all points in the cluster
```

Figure 9.1 shows an example of clustering 300 data points. The centroid points are recomputed after each iteration and as seen in this figure there is little movement of centroids after 10 iterations.

There are various distance measures that can be used for clustering algorithms including:

- **Euclidean distance measure:** This is the simplest of all distance measures. The Euclidean distance between points p and q in N-dimensional space is given as:

$$d(p,q) = \sqrt{\sum_{i=1}^{N}(p_i - q_i)^2} \tag{9.1}$$

- **Cosine distance measure:** Cosine distance measure finds the cosine of angle between two vectors (vectors drawn from origin to the points).

$$d = cos(\theta) = \frac{A.B}{||A||||B||} \tag{9.2}$$

- **Manhattan distance measure:** Manhattan distance measure is the sum of the absolute differences of the coordinates of two points given as:

$$d(p,q) = \left|\sum_{i=1}^{N}(p_i - q_i)\right| \tag{9.3}$$

■ Box 9.2: k-means clustering in Python

```
import numpy as np
from sklearn.cluster import KMeans
from sklearn.datasets.samples_generator import make_blobs
import pylab as pl

# Generate sample data
centers = [[1, 1], [-1, 1], [-1, -1], [1, -1]]
X, labels_true = make_blobs(n_samples=750, centers=centers, cluster_std=0.4)

kmeans = KMeans(init='k-means++', n_clusters=4, n_init=10)
kmeans.fit(X)

centroids = kmeans.cluster_centers_
labels = kmeans.labels_

# Number of clusters in labels, ignoring noise if present.
```

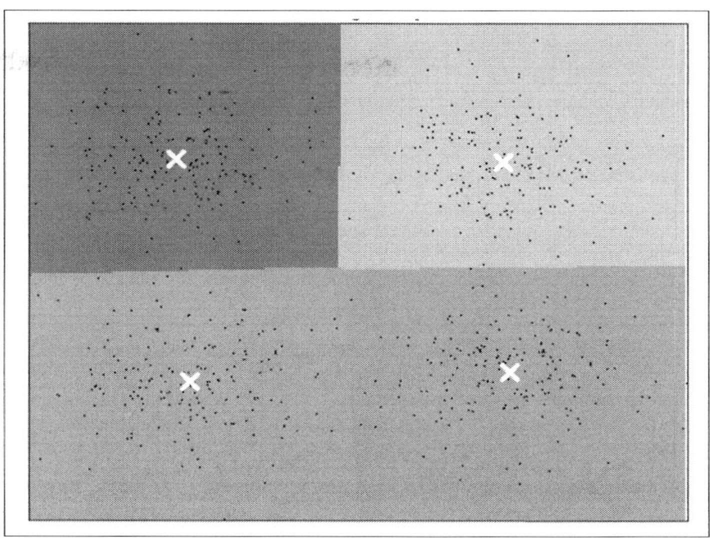

Figure 9.2: Clusters generated using k-means clustering

```
n_clusters_ = len(set(labels)) - (1 if -1 in labels else 0)

# Plot result

# Step size of the mesh.
h = .02

# Plot the decision boundary. For that, we will asign a color to each
x_min, x_max = X[:, 0].min(), X[:, 0].max()
y_min, y_max = X[:, 1].min(), X[:, 1].max()
xx, yy = np.meshgrid(np.arange(x_min, x_max, h), np.arange(y_min, y_max, h))

# Obtain labels for each point in mesh. Use last trained model.
Z = kmeans.predict(np.c_[xx.ravel(), yy.ravel()])

# Put the result into a color plot
Z = Z.reshape(xx.shape)
pl.figure(1)
pl.clf()
pl.imshow(Z, interpolation='nearest',
    extent=(xx.min(), xx.max(), yy.min(), yy.max()),
    cmap=pl.cm.Paired,
    aspect='auto', origin='lower')

pl.plot(X[:, 0], X[:, 1], 'k.', markersize=2)
# Plot the centroids as a white X
centroids = kmeans.cluster_centers_
pl.scatter(centroids[:, 0], centroids[:, 1],
    marker='x', s=169, linewidths=3,
    color='w', zorder=10)
pl.xlim(x_min, x_max)
pl.ylim(y_min, y_max)
```

```
pl.xticks(())
pl.yticks(())
pl.show()
```

Let us look at a k-means clustering example using Python. The scikit-learn Python package provides implementations of popular machine learning algorithms such as clustering and classification. Box 9.2 shows a Python program for clustering synthetic data generated using *make_blobs* synthetic data generator. In this program we generate 750 data points and then cluster them using k-means. Figure 9.2 shows the clusters that are generated. The centroid points for these clusters are very close to the centers used for generating the synthetic data.

■ Box 9.3: Document clustering with k-means

```
from sklearn.feature_extraction.text import TfidfVectorizer
from sklearn.feature_extraction.text import TfidfTransformer
from sklearn.cluster import KMeans
import os
import fnmatch

#Get data from all .txt files in the directory specified in input_data_path
input_data_path='data'
data=[]
for dirpath, dirs, files in os.walk(input_data_path):
    for filename in fnmatch.filter(files, '*.txt'):
        fp= open(os.path.join(dirpath, filename))
        lines=fp.readlines()
        content=''
        for line in lines:
            content+= line[:-1]
        fp.close()
        data.append(content)

vectorizer = TfidfVectorizer(max_df=1.0, max_features=100,
stop_words='english', use_idf=True)

X = vectorizer.fit_transform(data)

km = KMeans(n_clusters=2, init='k-means++', max_iter=100, n_init=1, verbose=1)

print "Clustering data with %s" % km

res=km.fit(X)

print "Labels: %s" % km.labels_

print "Cluster Centers: %s" % km.cluster_centers_.squeeze()
```

Lets us now look at another example that clusters documents by topics. Document clustering is the most commonly used application of k-means clustering algorithm. Document clustering problem occurs in many big data applications such as finding similar news articles, finding similar patients using electronic health records, etc. Before applying k-means algorithm for document clustering, the documents need to be vectorized. Since documents contain textual information, the process of vectorization is required for clustering documents. The process of generating document vectors involves several steps. In the first step, a dictionary of all words used in the tokenized records is generated. Each word in the dictionary has a dimension number assigned to it which is used to represent the dimension the word occupies in the document vector. In the second step, the number of occurrences or term frequency (TF) of each word is computed. In the third step, the Inverse Document Frequency (IDF) for each word is computed. Document Frequency (DF) for a word is the number of documents (or records) in which the word occurs. IDF_i for a word-i is calculated as follows:

$$IDF_i = \frac{N}{DF_i} \tag{9.4}$$

where N is the number of documents. In the fourth step, the weight for each word is computed as follows:

$$W_i = TF_i log \frac{N}{DF_i} \tag{9.5}$$

The term weight W_i is used in the document vector as the value for the dimension-i. Similarity between documents is computed using a distance measure such as Euclidean distance measure. Box 9.3 shows a Python implementation of document clustering. This program loads the document data from all text files in an input directory and then converts the documents into vectors using TfidfVectorizer. TfidfVectorizer maps the most frequent words to features indices and computes a word occurrence frequency (sparse) matrix. The word frequencies are then re-weighted using the IDF vector collected feature-wise over the corpus.

9.2.2 DBSCAN clustering

DBSCAN (density-based spatial clustering of applications with noise) is another algorithm of interest; See Ester *et. al.* [67]. DBSCAN is a density clustering algorithm that works on the notions of density reachability and density connectivity. Density reachability is defined on the basis of Eps-neighborhood, where Eps-neighborhood means that for every point p in a cluster C there is a point q in C so that p is inside of the Eps-neighborhood of q and there are at least a minimum number ($MinPts$) of points in an Eps-neighborhood of that point. A point p is called directly density-reachable from a point q if it is not farther away than a given distance (Eps) and if it is surrounded by at least a minimum number ($MinPts$) of points that may be considered to be part of a cluster. A point p is density-reachable from a point q if there is a chain of points $p_1, ..., p_n, p_1 = q, p_n = p$ such that $p_i + 1$ is directly density-reachable from p_i . A point p is density connected to a point q if there is a point o such that both, p and q are density-reachable from o wrt. Eps and $MinPts$.

A cluster, is then defined based on the following two properties:

- **Maximality:** For all point p, q if p belongs to cluster C and q is density-reachable from p (wrt. Eps and $MinPts$), then q also belongs to the cluster C.

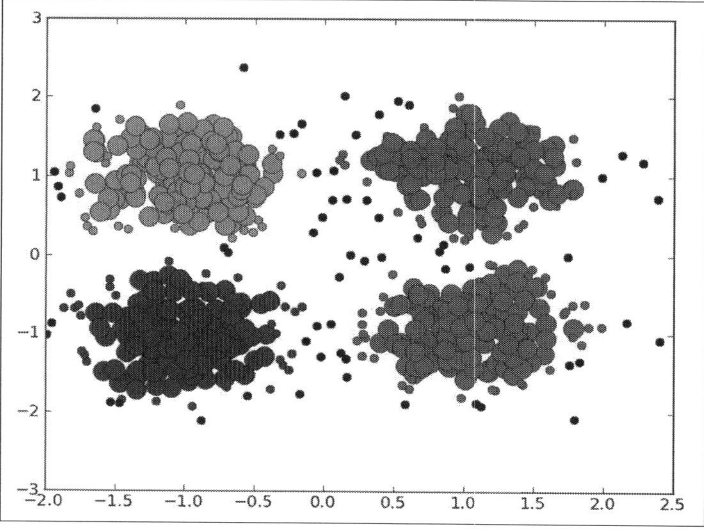

Figure 9.3: Clusters generated using DBSCAN clustering

- **Connectivity:** For all point p, q in cluster C, p is density-connected to q (wrt. Eps and $MinPts$).

■ Box 9.4: DBSCAN clustering algorithm

```
DBSCAN (Dataset, Eps, MinPts)
ClusterId = 0;
for each Point in Dataset
    P.Visited= TRUE
    NeighborPoints = regionQuery(Point, Eps)
    if sizeof(NeighborPoints) < MinPts
        P.ClusterId=0 // p is noise
    else
        C = nextID(ClusterId) //next cluster
        expandCluster(Point, NeighborPoints, C, Eps, MinPts)

regionQuery(Point, eps)
    return all points within Eps-neighborhood of Point

expandCluster(Point, NeighborPoints, C, Eps, MinPts)
    P.ClusterId = C
    for each point Q in NeighborPoints
        if Q.Visited ==FALSE
            Q.Visited= TRUE
            NeighborPointsQ = regionQuery(Q, Eps)
        if sizeof(NeighborPointsQ) >= MinPts
            NeighborPoints = NeighborPoints.append(NeighborPointsQ)
        if Q.ClusterId ==NULL
            Q.ClusterId = C
```

■ **Box 9.5: DBSCAN clustering example in Python**

```
import numpy as np
from scipy.spatial import distance
from sklearn.cluster import DBSCAN
from sklearn import metrics
from sklearn.datasets.samples_generator import make_blobs
import pylab as pl
from itertools import cycle

# Generate sample data
centers = [[1, 1], [-1, 1], [-1, -1], [1, -1]]
X, labels_true = make_blobs(n_samples=750, centers=centers, cluster_std=0.4)

# Compute similarities
D = distance.squareform(distance.pdist(X))
S = 1 - (D / np.max(D))

# Compute DBSCAN
db = DBSCAN(eps=0.95, min_samples=10).fit(S)
core_samples = db.core_sample_indices_
labels = db.labels_

# Number of clusters in labels, ignoring noise if present.
n_clusters_ = len(set(labels)) - (1 if -1 in labels else 0)

# Plot result

pl.figure(1)
pl.clf()

# Black removed and is used for noise instead.
colors = cycle('bgrcmybgrcmybgrcmybgrcmy')
for k, col in zip(set(labels), colors):
    if k == -1:
        # Black used for noise.
        col = 'k'
        markersize = 6
    class_members = [index[0] for index in np.argwhere(labels == k)]
    cluster_core_samples = [index for index in core_samples
    if labels[index] == k]
        for index in class_members:
        x = X[index]
        if index in core_samples and k != -1:
            markersize = 14
        else:
            markersize = 6
            pl.plot(x[0], x[1], 'o', markerfacecolor=col,
            markeredgecolor='k', markersize=markersize)

pl.show()
```

Let us now rework the example shown in Box 9.2 using DBSCAN. Box 9.5 shows the

DBSCAN clustering example using Python. In this program we generate 750 data points and then cluster them using DBSCAN. Figure 9.3 shows the clusters generated. As seen in this figure, DBSCAN clusters densely clustered points and the far off points are considered noise. DBSCAN requires two inputs, the distance measure Eps and $MinPts$. The advantage of DBSCAN over k-means clustering algorithm is that it does not require the number of clusters as an input. Moreover, DBSCAN considers far off points (not density-connected) as noise.

■ Box 9.6: Document clustering with DBSCAN

```
from sklearn.feature_extraction.text import TfidfVectorizer
from sklearn.feature_extraction.text import TfidfTransformer
from sklearn.cluster import KMeans
import os
import fnmatch

#Get data from all .txt files in the directory specified in input_data_path
input_data_path='data'
data=[]
for dirpath, dirs, files in os.walk(input_data_path):
    for filename in fnmatch.filter(files, '*.txt'):
        fp= open(os.path.join(dirpath, filename))
        lines=fp.readlines()
        content=''
        for line in lines:
            content+= line[:-1]
        fp.close()
        data.append(content)

vectorizer = TfidfVectorizer(max_df=1.0, max_features=100,
stop_words='english', use_idf=True)

X = vectorizer.fit_transform(data)

# Compute similarities
D = distance.squareform(distance.pdist(X))
S = 1 - (D / np.max(D))

# Compute DBSCAN
db = DBSCAN(eps=0.95, min_samples=10)

print "Clustering data with %s" % db
db.fit(S)

print "Labels: %s" % db.labels_
print "Core Samples: %s" % db.core_sample_indices_
```

Figure 9.4 shows a comparison of k-means and DBSCAN clustering. As seen in this figure DBSCAN gives the correct results whereas k-means incorrectly clusters two of the clusters. DBSCAN can find irregular shaped clusters as seen from this example and can even find a cluster completely surrounded by a different cluster. Also as seen in the DBSCAN example in Figure 9.4, some of the points are considered noise and not assigned to any

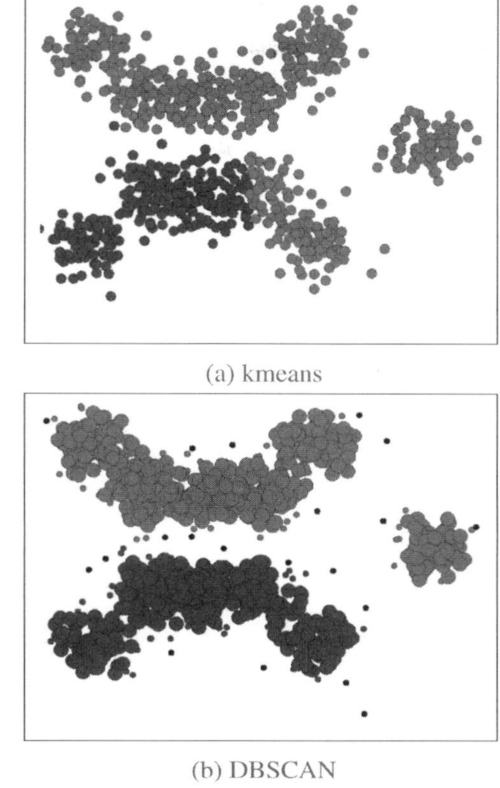

(a) kmeans

(b) DBSCAN

Figure 9.4: Comparison of k-means and DBSCAN clustering

cluster.

Lets us now rework the document clustering example using DBSCAN. Box 9.6 shows the Python code for document clustering using DBCSAN. The benefit of using DBSCAN for document clustering is that it is not required to specify the number of clusters in the input. Since in real world problems, the number of clusters may not be known in advance, DBSCAN is useful and efficient clustering algorithm for such problems.

9.2.3 Parallelizing Clustering Algorithms using MapReduce

The clustering implementations described so far are serial implementations that are performed in-memory. However, when the data to be clustered is so big that it cannot fit into the memory of a single machine, in-memory clustering is not possible. MapReduce programming model can be used for parallelizing clustering algorithms. Figure 9.5 shows a parallel implementation of k-means clustering with MapReduce. The data to be clustered is distributed on a distributed file system such as HDFS and split into blocks which are replicated across different nodes in the cluster. Clustering begins with an initial set of centroids. The client program controls the clustering process. In the Map phase, the distances between the data samples and centroids are calculated and each sample is assigned to the nearest centroid. In the Reduce phase, the centroids are recomputed using the mean of all the points in each cluster. The new centroids are then fed back to the client which checks whether convergence is reached or maximum number of iterations are completed. Convergence criteria used in k-means is the difference between the coordinates of the new centroids and the centroids in the old centroids. If the movement of centroids is below a specified threshold, convergence is achieved.

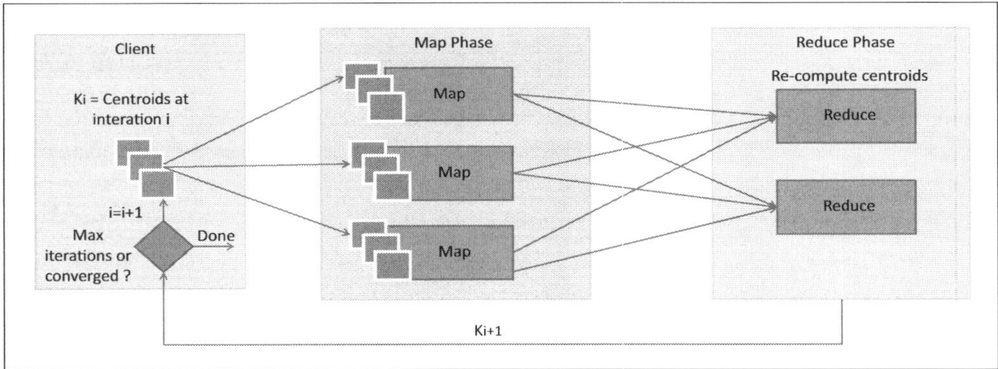

Figure 9.5: Parallel implementation of k-means clustering with MapReduce

■ **Box 9.7: Installing Mahout**

```
sudo apt-get install maven2

HADOOP_HOME=/root/hadoop
export HADOOP_HOME
HADOOP_CONF_DIR=/root/hadoop/conf
export HADOOP_CONF_DIR
JAVA_HOME=/usr/lib/jvm/java-6-sun-1.6.0.26
export JAVA_HOME

wget http://apache.techartifact.com/mirror/mahout/0.7/mahout-distribution-0.7-src.tar
.gz
tar xzf mahout-distribution-0.7-src.tar.gz
cd mahout-distribution-0.7
mvn compile
mvn clean install -DskipTests=true
```

■ **Box 9.8: Parallel document clustering with k-means using Mahout**

```
#Requires Hadoop installation.

#Run Hadoop
bin/hadoop namenode -format
bin/start-dfs.sh
bin/start-mapred.sh
jps

cd /root/hadoop
```

```
#Copy input documents to HDFS
bin/hadoop fs -put /root/input input

cd /root/mahout-distribution-0.7
#Convert input to SequenceFiles
bin/mahout seqdirectory -c UTF-8 -i input -o input-seqfiles

#Generate document vectors from SequenceFiles
bin/mahout seq2sparse -i input-seqfiles/ -o input-vectors -ow -a
org.apache.lucene.analysis.WhitespaceAnalyzer -chunk 200 -wt tfidf -s 5 -md 3 -x
90 -ng 2 -ml 50 -seq -n 2

#Run k-means clustering with random seeds
bin/mahout kmeans -i input-vectors/tfidf-vectors/ -c input-initial-clusters -o
input-kmeans-random-clusters -dm
org.apache.mahout.common.distance.SquaredEuclideanDistanceMeasure -cd 1.0 -k 4
-x 20 -cl –ow

#Dump clusters
bin/mahout clusterdump -i input-kmeans-random-clusters/clusters-*-final -o
/root/dumps/kmeans_random_clusterdump -d input-vectors/dictionary.file-0 -dt
sequencefile -b 20 -n 20 -sp 0
```

Apache Mahout provides distributed and scalable machine learning algorithms on top of the Hadoop platform. Mahout provides a collection of algorithms for clustering, classification and prediction problems. Scalability is achieved using MapReduce implementations of the machine learning algorithms. Mahout contains various implementations of clustering including k-means, Fuzzy k-means, meanshift, Dirichlet, etc. In this section you will learn how to use Mahout for clustering documents using a parallel implementation k-means algorithm. Box 9.7 provides the commands for installing Mahout.

Box 9.8 shows an example of document clustering on a Hadoop cluster using Mahout. In this example the input data (collection of text documents) is first copied from the local directory to HDFS. The input documents are then converted to Hadoop SequenceFiles. The seq2sparse command is used to read the data from SequenceFiles and write the vectors generated by the dictionary-based vectorizer to the output directory. The options used with seq2sparse include:

- -a: The class name of the analyzer to use. In this example the Lucene WhitespaceAnalyzer is used.
- -ow: Overwrite flag. If set, the ouput folder is overwritten.
- -ng: N-gram size. This flag specifies the maximum number of N-grams to use.
- -x: The maximum number of documents a term should occur in to be considered for the dictionary. This is useful for filtering stop words (common words which occur in most documents).
- -s: The minimum frequency of the term in the document collection to be considered a part of the dictionary.
- -ml: Maximum log-likelihood ratio (valid only when N-gram size is greater than 1).
- -seq: Create sequential access sparse vectors.
- -n: The normalization value to use.

- -wt: Weighting scheme to use. In this example, the tfidf scheme is used.
- -chunk: Chunk size in MB. Documents larger than the chunk size are split during vectorization.
- -i: Input path
- -o: Output path

With the document vectors generated, finally, k-means clustering is performed. The options used with Mahout kmeans launcher include:

- -i: Path to the directory containing the input vectors
- -o: Output path
- -d: Distance measure to use with kmeans. In this example, the Squared Euclidean distance measure is used.
- -c: Path to the directory containing initial clusters.
- -cd: Convergence threshold.
- -ow: Overwrite flag.
- -k: Number of clusters. In this example, the RandomSeedGenerator is used to seed the initial centroids.
- -x: Maximum number of iterations.

When kmeans clustering is launched with Mahout, multiple MapReduce jobs are created that cluster the data in parallel.

9.3 Classification of Big Data

Classification is the process of categorizing objects into predefined categories. Classification is achieved by classification algorithms that belong to a broad category of algorithms called supervised machine learning. Supervised learning involves inferring a model from a set of input data and known responses to the data (training data) and then using the inferred model to predict responses to new data. There are various types of classification approaches for big data analytics including:

- **Binary classification:** Binary classification involves categorizing the data into two categories. For example, classifying the sentiment of a news article into positive or negative, classifying the state of a machine into good or faulty, classifying the heath test into positive or negative, etc.
- **Multi-class classification:** Multi-class classification involves more than two classes into which the data is categorized. For example, gene expression classification problem involves multiple classes.
- **Document classification:** Document classification is a type of multi-class classification approach in which the data to the classified is in the form of text document. For classifying news articles into different categories such as politics, sports, etc.

The performance of classification algorithms can be evaluated using the following metrics:

- **Precision:** Precision is the fraction of objects that are classified correctly. Precision is defined as,

$$Precision = \frac{TruePositive}{(TruePositive + FalsePositive)} \tag{9.6}$$

- **Recall:** Recall is the fraction of objects belonging to a category that are classified correctly.

$$Recall = \frac{TruePositive}{(TruePositive + FalseNegative)} \tag{9.7}$$

- **Accuracy:** Accuracy is defined as,

$$Accuracy = \frac{(TruePositive + TrueNegative)}{(TruePositive + TrueNegative + FalsePositive + FalseNegative)} \tag{9.8}$$

- **F1-score:** F1-score is a measure of accuracy that considers both precision and recall. F1-score is the harmonic means of precision and recall given as,

$$F1 - Score = \frac{2(Precision)(Recall)}{(Precision + Recall)} \tag{9.9}$$

9.3.1 Naive Bayes

Naive Bayes is a probabilistic classification algorithm based on the Bayes theorem with a naive assumption about the independence of feature attributes. Given a class variable C and feature variables $F_1, ..., F_n$, the conditional probability (posterior) according to Bayes theorem is given as,

$$P(C|F_1, ..., F_n) = \frac{P(F_1, ..., F_n|C)P(C)}{P(F_1, ..., F_n)} \tag{9.10}$$

where, $P(C|F_1, ..., F_n)$ is the posterior probability, $P(F_1, ..., F_n|C)$ is the likelihood and $P(C)$ is the prior probability and $P(F_1, ..., F_n)$ is the evidence. Naive Bayes makes a naive assumption about the independence every pair of features given as,

$$P(F_1, ..., F_n|C) = \prod_{i=1}^{n} P(F_i|C) \tag{9.11}$$

In practice, since the evidence $P(F_1, ..., F_n)$ is constant for a given input and does not depend on the class variable C, only the numerator of the posterior probability is important for classification. Therefore we get,

$$P(C|F_1, ..., F_n) \propto P(C) \prod_{i=1}^{n} P(F_i|C) \tag{9.12}$$

With this simplification, classification can then be done as follows,

$$C = argmax_C P(C) \prod_{i=1}^{n} P(F_i|C) \tag{9.13}$$

There are different versions of Naive Bayes which differ in the naive assumption made. Some of them include:

- **Gaussian Naive Bayes:** Gaussian Naive Bayes assumes the likelihood $P(F_1,...,F_n|C)$ as,

$$P(F_1,...,F_n|C) = \prod_{i=1}^{n} P(F_i|C) \tag{9.14}$$

where,

$$P(F_i|C) = \frac{1}{\sqrt{2\pi\sigma_C^2}} exp\Big(\frac{-(F_i - \mu_C)^2}{2\pi\sigma_C^2}\Big) \tag{9.15}$$

where μ is the mean and σ_C is the standard deviation for values in F_i in class C. Gaussian Naive Bayes is suitable for problems in which the feature variables have continuous values which are assumed to have a Gaussian distribution.

- **Multinomial Naive Bayes:** Multinomial Naive Bayes uses multinomial distribution for each of the feature variables. This is suitable for problems which have discrete features such as document classification.
- **Bernoulli Naive Bayes:** Bernoulli Naive Bayes is also suitable for problems which have discrete features. The likelihood in Bernoulli Naive Bayes is as follows,

$$P(F_i|C) = P(i|CF_i(1 - P(i|C))(1 - F_i) \tag{9.16}$$

where each feature is assumed to be binary valued.

Let us now look at some examples of Naive Bayes. Box 9.9 shows an example of binary classification using Gaussian Naive Bayes. In this example, three data sets are generated using the *make_classification* method in scikit-learn, which generates by default 100 samples. The total number of features specified for all three datasets is 2. In the first dataset, the number of informative features is 1 and the number of clusters per features is also 1. In the second dataset, the number of informative features is 2 and the number of clusters per feature is 1. In the third dataset, the number of informative features is 2 and the number of clusters per feature is 2.

■ Box 9.9: Naive Bayes classification in Python

```
import numpy as np
import pylab as pl
from matplotlib.colors import ListedColormap
from sklearn.cross_validation import train_test_split
from sklearn.preprocessing import StandardScaler
from sklearn.datasets import make_classification
from sklearn.naive_bayes import GaussianNB

name="Naive Bayes"
clf= GaussianNB()
h = .02 # step size in the mesh

datasetname=['One informative feature, one cluster','Two informative features, one clus-
```

```
ter','Two informative features, two clusters']
X1, Y1 = make_classification(n_features=2, n_redundant=0, n_informative=1,
n_clusters_per_class=1)
ds1 = (X1, Y1)

X2, Y2 = make_classification(n_features=2, n_redundant=0, n_informative=2,
n_clusters_per_class=1)
ds2 = (X2, Y2)

X3, Y3 = make_classification(n_features=2, n_redundant=0, n_informative=2)
ds3 = (X3, Y3)

datasets = [ds1,ds2,ds3]

figure = pl.figure(figsize=(12, 12))
i = 1
j=0

for ds in datasets:
    # Split into training and test part
    X, y = ds
    X = StandardScaler().fit_transform(X)
    X_train, X_test, y_train, y_test = train_test_split(X, y, test_size=.4)

    x_min, x_max = X[:, 0].min() - .5, X[:, 0].max() + .5
    y_min, y_max = X[:, 1].min() - .5, X[:, 1].max() + .5
    xx, yy = np.meshgrid(np.arange(x_min, x_max, h),
        np.arange(y_min, y_max, h))

    # Plot dataset
    cm = pl.cm.PiYG
    cm_bright = ListedColormap(['red', 'green'])
    ax = pl.subplot(3, 2, i)

    # Plot the training points
    ax.scatter(X_train[:, 0], X_train[:, 1], c=y_train, cmap=cm_bright)

    # Plot testing points
    ax.scatter(X_test[:, 0], X_test[:, 1], c=y_test, cmap=cm_bright, alpha=0.6)
    ax.set_xlim(xx.min(), xx.max())
    ax.set_ylim(yy.min(), yy.max())
    ax.set_xticks(())
    ax.set_yticks(())
 ax.set_title(datasetname[j])
    i += 1
    j+=1

    ax = pl.subplot(3, 2, i)
    clf.fit(X_train, y_train)
    score = clf.score(X_test, y_test)

    # Plot the decision boundary.
    if hasattr(clf, "decision_function"):
        Z = clf.decision_function(np.c_[xx.ravel(), yy.ravel()])
    else:
```

```
        Z = clf.predict_proba(np.c_[xx.ravel(), yy.ravel()])[:, 1]

    # Put the result into a color plot
    Z = Z.reshape(xx.shape)
    ax.contourf(xx, yy, Z, cmap=cm, alpha=.8)

    # Plot the training points
    ax.scatter(X_train[:, 0], X_train[:, 1], c=y_train, cmap=cm_bright)
    # Plot the testing points
    ax.scatter(X_test[:, 0], X_test[:, 1], c=y_test, cmap=cm_bright,
            alpha=0.6)

    ax.set_xlim(xx.min(), xx.max())
    ax.set_ylim(yy.min(), yy.max())
    ax.set_xticks(())
    ax.set_yticks(())
    ax.set_title(name)
    ax.text(xx.max() - .2, yy.max() - .5, ('Accuracy= %.2f' % score),
        size=15, horizontalalignment='right')
    i += 1

pl.show()
```

Figure 9.6 shows the classification results using Naive Bayes and the classifier seems to work very well for first two datasets.

Let us look at a document classification example using Multinomial Naive Bayes. Box 9.10 shows the Python implementation for document classification using the *MultinomialNB* classifier of scikit-learn package. The dataset used in this example is the 4 Universities dataset [69] which contains web-pages collected from computer science departments of various universities in January 1997 by the webkb project of the CMU text learning group. This dataset contains 8,282 pages manually classified into the following categories: student (1641), faculty (1124), staff (137), department (182), course (930), project (504), other (3764). In this example, first the training set is loaded and features are extracted from the training set using a TF-IDF vectorizer. The classifier is then trained with the training data and used for predicting classes of the test data. Finally, the performance metrics are printed using the *classification_report* method. Box 9.11 shows the performance results of document classification example.

■ Box 9.10: Document classification with Naive Bayes

```
import sys
import os
from sklearn.datasets import load_mlcomp
from sklearn.feature_extraction.text import TfidfVectorizer
from sklearn.metrics import classification_report
from sklearn.naive_bayes import MultinomialNB

if 'MLCOMP_DATASETS_HOME' not in os.environ:
    print "Set MLCOMP_DATASETS_HOME as:"
    print "export MLCOMP_DATASETS_HOME=<path_to_dataset_directory>"
    sys.exit(0)
```

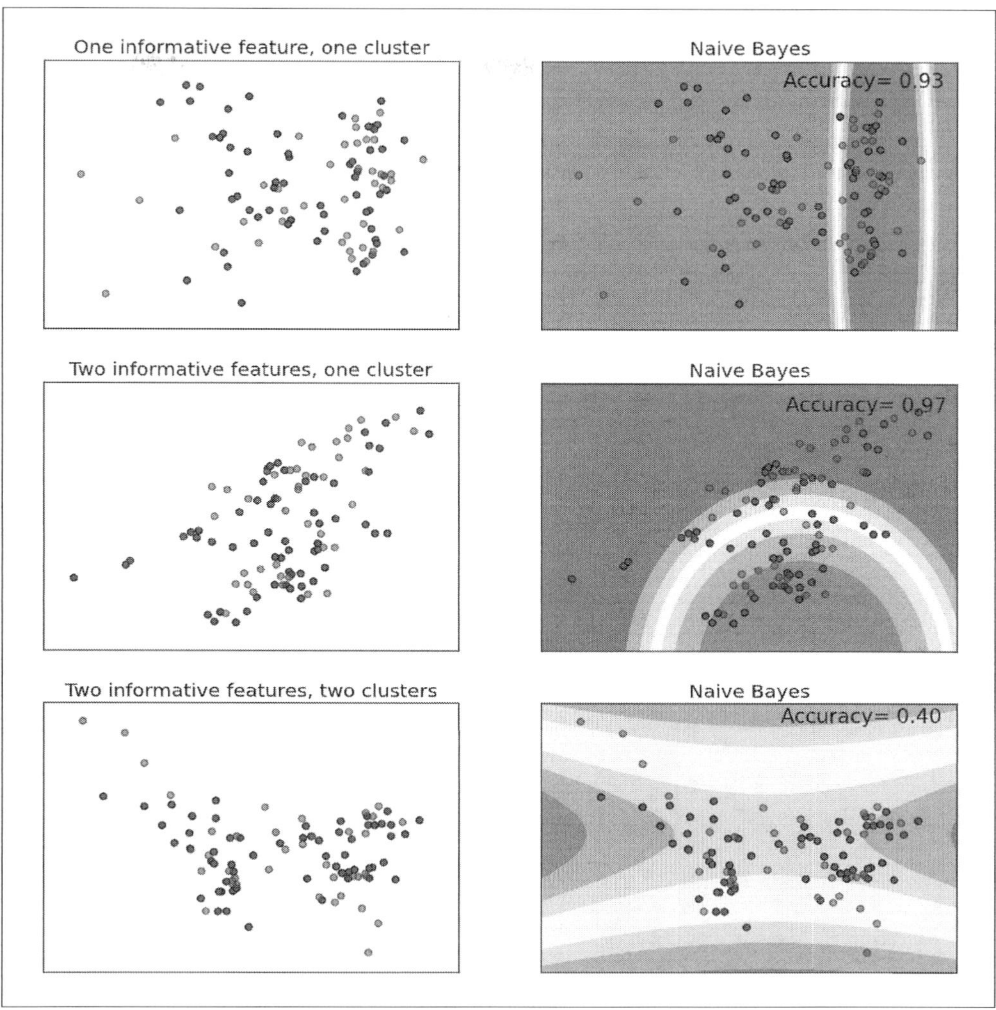

Figure 9.6: Binary classification with Naive Bayes

```
# Load the training set
data_train = load_mlcomp('webkb-4-universities-wisconsin-test', 'train')

#Extracting features from the dataset using a sparse vectorizer"
vectorizer = TfidfVectorizer(charset='latin1')
X_train = vectorizer.fit_transform((open(f).read() for f in data_train.filenames))
y_train = data_train.target

#—Load test set... "
data_test = load_mlcomp('webkb-4-universities-wisconsin-test', 'test')

#Extracting features from the dataset using the same vectorizer
X_test = vectorizer.transform((open(f).read() for f in data_test.filenames))
y_test = data_test.target
```

```
#——Train Classifier——————
clf= MultinomialNB()
clf = clf.fit(X_train, y_train)

#—Predict———————
pred = clf.predict(X_test)

#—Print classification report—
print classification_report(y_test, pred, target_names=data_test.target_names)
```

■ Box 9.11: Classification report for document classification with Naive Bayes

	precision	recall	f1-score	support
course	0.67	0.07	0.13	85
department	0.00	0.00	0.00	1
faculty	0.00	0.00	0.00	42
other	0.77	0.98	0.86	942
project	0.00	0.00	0.00	25
staff	0.00	0.00	0.00	12
student	0.69	0.22	0.34	156
avg/total	0.70	0.76	0.69	1263

The Naive Bayes implementations described so far in this section are serial implementations. Let us now look at parallel implementation of Naive Bayes based on MapReduce. Apache Mahout provides MapReduce implementations of several machine learning classifiers including Naive Bayes. Box 9.12 shows an example of document clustering with Naive Bayes classifier using the Apache Mahout framework. The dataset used for this example is the 20 newsgroup data set [70]. The 20 newsgroups dataset is a collection of approximately 20,000 newsgroup documents, partitioned (nearly) evenly across 20 different newsgroups. The 20 newsgroups dataset is one of the most popular datasets for machine learning experiments such as document clustering and document classification. The output of this example is shown in Box 9.13.

■ Box 9.12: Parallel document classification with Naive Bayes using Mahout

```
#Requires Hadoop installation.

#Run Hadoop
bin/hadoop namenode -format
bin/start-dfs.sh
bin/start-mapred.sh
jps

cd /root/hadoop

#Get the 20 newsgroup dataset
wget http://people.csail.mit.edu/jrennie/20Newsgroups/20news-bydate.tar.gz
```

```
tar xzf 20news-bydate.tar.gz

#Copy traning and test datasets to HDFS
bin/hadoop fs -put /home/ubuntu/20news-bydate-train/ 20news-bydate-train
bin/hadoop fs -put /home/ubuntu/20news-bydate-test/ 20news-bydate-test

#Convert traning and test datasets to SequenceFiles
cd /root/mahout-distribution-0.7
/bin/mahout seqdirectory -i 20news-bydate-train -o 20news-bydate-train-seq
/bin/mahout seqdirectory -i 20news-bydate-test -o 20news-bydate-test-seq

#Generate document vectors from SequenceFiles
/bin/mahout seq2sparse -i 20news-bydate-train-seq -o 20news-bydate-train-vectors -lnorm
-nv -wt tfidf
/bin/mahout seq2sparse -i 20news-bydate-test-seq -o 20news-bydate-test-vectors -lnorm
-nv -wt tfidf
#Train Naive Bayes classifier
/bin/mahout trainnb -i 20news-bydate-train-vectors -el -o model -li labelindex -ow naive-
bayes

#Test Naive Bayes classifier
/bin/mahout testnb -i 20news-bydate-test-vectors -m model -l labelindex -ow -o 20news-
testing naivebayes
```

■ Box 9.13: Output of document classification with Naive Bayes using Mahout

```
INFO driver.MahoutDriver: Program took 24713 ms (Minutes: 0.41188333333333333)

Summary
-------------------------------------------------------
Correctly Classified Instances : 6800      90.3054%
Incorrectly Classified Instances : 730     9.6946%
Total Classified Instances : 7530
```

9.3.2 Decision Trees

Decision Trees are a supervised learning method that use a tree created from simple decision rules learned from the training data as a predictive model. The predictive model is in the form of a tree that can be used to predict the value of a target variable based on a several attribute variables. Each node in the tree corresponds to one attribute in the dataset on which the "split" is performed. Each leaf in a decision tree represents a value of the target variable. The learning process involves recursively splitting on the attributes until all the samples in the child node have the same value of the target variable or splitting further results in no further information gain. To select the best attribute for splitting at each stage, different metrics can be used. The two most popular metrics used to determine the best attribute for splitting are:

- **Information Gain:** Information content of a discrete random variable X with probability mass function (PMF), $P(X)$, is defined as,

$$I(X) = -\log_2 P(X) \tag{9.17}$$

Information gain is defined based on the entropy of the random variable which is defined as,

$$H(X) = E[I(X)] = E[-\log_2 P(X)] = -\sum_i \log_2 P(x_i) \tag{9.18}$$

Entropy is a measure of uncertainty in a random variable and choosing the attribute with the highest information gain results in a split that reduces the uncertainty the most at that stage.

- **Gini Coefficient:** Gini coefficient measures the inequality, i.e. how often a randomly chosen sample that is labeled based on the distribution of labels, would be labeled incorrectly. Gini coefficient is defined as,

$$G(X) = 1 - \sum_i P(x_i)^2 \tag{9.19}$$

There are different algorithms for building decisions trees, popular ones being ID3 and C4.5. Let us look at the steps involved in the ID3 algorithm:

- Attributes are discrete. If not, discretize the continuous attributes.
- Calculate the entropy of every attribute using the dataset.
- Choose the attribute with the highest information gain.
- Create branches for each value of the selected attribute.
- Repeat with the remaining attributes.

■ Box 9.14: Binary classification with Decision Trees

```
from sklearn.tree import DecisionTreeClassifier

name="Decision Tree"
clf= DecisionTreeClassifier(max_depth=5)

#Using same datasets as in Box 9.9
datasets = [ds1,ds2,ds3]

#Use same logic as in Box 9.9 to
#1. Split into training and test part
#2. Plot dataset
#3. Plot the training points
#4. Plot testing points
#5. Plot the decision boundary
#6. Put the result into a color plot
```

■ Box 9.15: Classification with Decision Tree

```
#This example uses the UCI Parkinsons dataset. The data is in ASCII CSV format. The
rows of the CSV file contain an instance #corresponding to one voice recording. There are
around six recordings per patient. This example uses a modified CSV file #where the first
column is "status".

import numpy as np
```

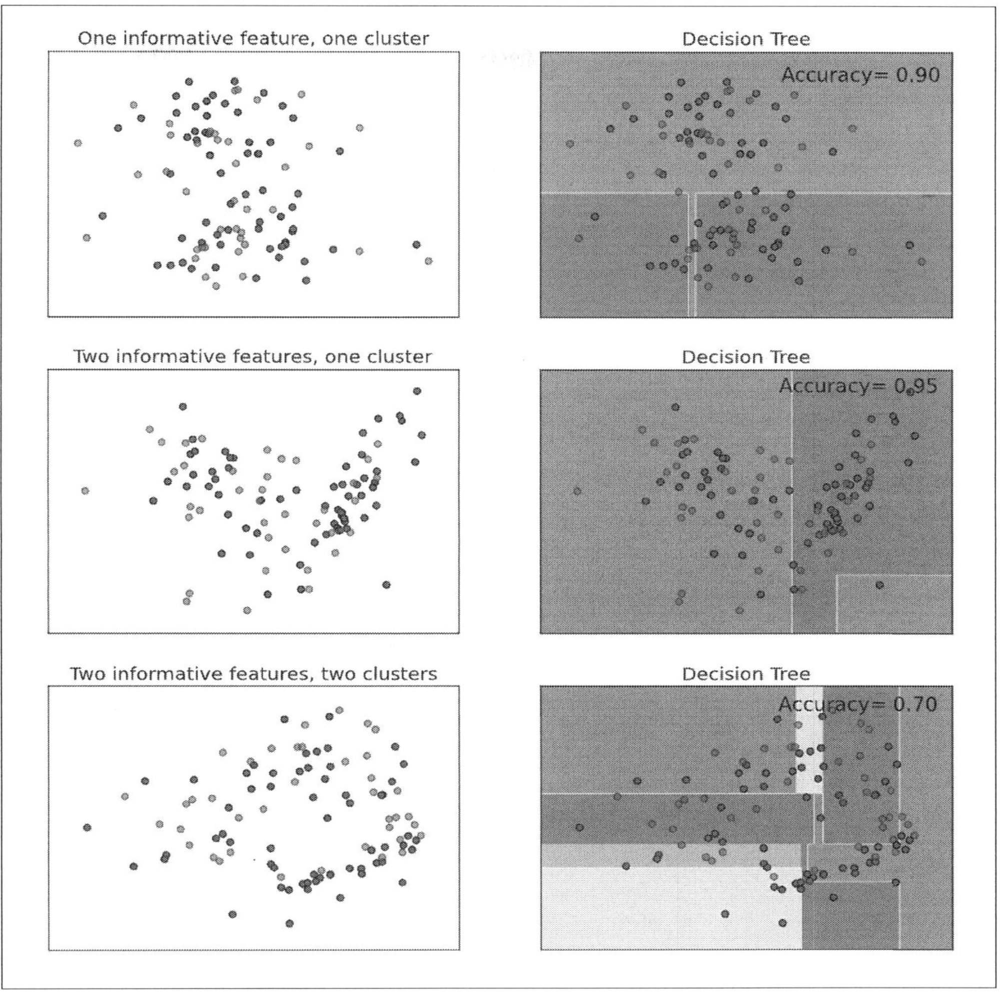

Figure 9.7: Binary classification with Decision Trees

```
from sklearn.tree import DecisionTreeClassifier
import csv as csv

csv_file_object = csv.reader(open('train.csv', 'rb')) #Load in the training csv file
train_data=[] #Creat a variable called 'train_data'
for row in csv_file_object: #Skip through each row in the csv file
    train_data.append(row) #adding each row to the data variable

train_data = np.array(train_data) #Then convert from a list to an array
X_train = train_data[0::,1::]

#"status" column which is set to 0 for healthy and 1 for Parkinson's disease.
y_train = train_data[0::,0]

csv_file_object = csv.reader(open('test.csv', 'rb')) #Load in the training csv file
```

```
test_data=[]
for row in csv_file_object:
    test_data.append(row)

test_data = np.array(test_data)

X_test = test_data[0::,1::]
y_test = test_data[0::,0]

clf= DecisionTreeClassifier(max_depth=None, min_samples_split=1,random_state=0)

#train Decision Tree classifier
clf = clf.fit(X_train, y_train)

#Score
score = clf.score(X_test, y_test)
print score
```

The ID3 algorithm can be result in over-fitting to the training data and can be expensive to train especially for continuous attributes. The C4.5 algorithm is an extension of the ID3 algorithm. C4.5 supports both discrete and continuous attributes. To support continuous attributes, C4.5 finds thresholds for the continuous attributes and then splits based on the threshold values. C4.5 prevents over-fitting by pruning trees after they have been created. Pruning involves removing or aggregating those branches which provide little discriminatory power. Box 9.14 shows an example of binary classification using Decision Trees. Figure 9.7 shows the classification results using Decision Trees and the classifier seems to work very well for first two datasets with accuracy above 90%.

Box 9.15 shows another classification example using Decision Trees. The dataset used in this example is the UCI Parkinsons dataset [71] that is composed of a range of biomedical voice measurements from 31 people, 23 with Parkinsons disease. Each column in the table is a particular voice measure, and each row corresponds to one of the 195 voice recordings from these individuals. The main aim of the data is to discriminate healthy people from those with Parkinsons disease, according to "status" column which is set to 0 for healthy and 1 for Parkinson's disease.

Figure 9.8 shows the decision tree generated for the Parkinsons dataset classification example. The tree shows the attributes on which splitting is done at each step and the split values. Also shows are the error, total number of samples at each node and the number of samples in each class (in the value array). For example, the first split is done on the 19th column (attribute X[18]) and the total number of samples in the training set is 137. On the first split there are 30 samples in first class and 107 samples in the second class.

9.3.3 Random Forest

Random Forest is an ensemble learning method that is based on randomized decision trees [72]. Random Forest trains a number decision trees and then takes the majority vote by using the mode of the class predicted by the individual trees. The Random Forest algorithm (Breiman's algorithm) is shown in Box 9.16.

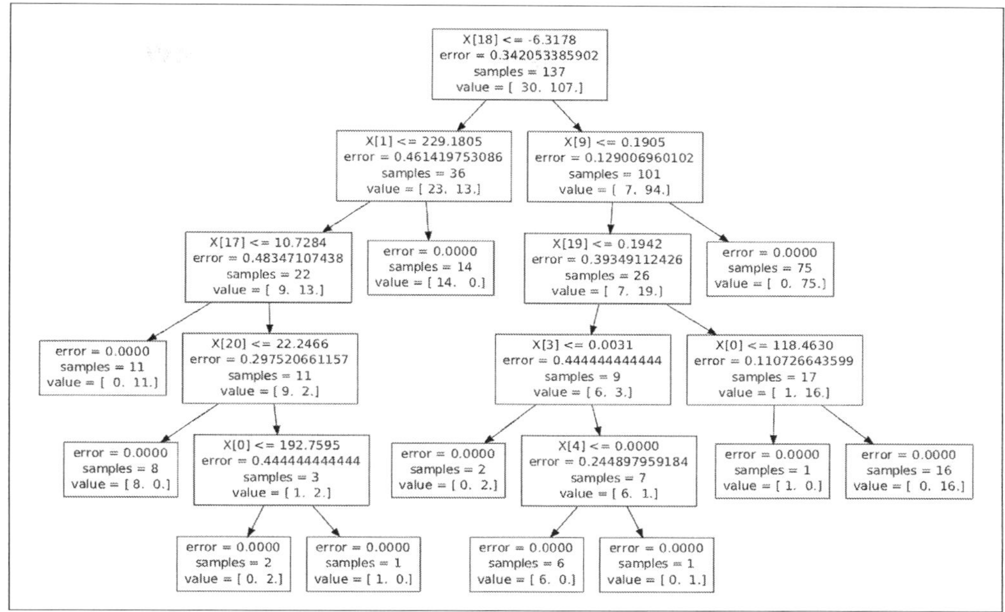

Figure 9.8: Example of a generated decision tree

■ Box 9.16: Random Forest algorithm

1. Draw a bootstrap sample (n times with replacement from the N samples in the training set) from the dataset
2. Train a decision tree
    - Until the tree is fully grown (maximum size)
        – Choose next leaf node
        – Select m attributes (m is much less than the total number of attributes M) at random.
        – Choose the best attribute and split as usual
3. Measure out-of-bag error
    - Use the rest of the samples (not selected in the bootstrap) to estimate the error of the tree, by predicting their classes.
4. Repeat steps 1-3 k times to generate k trees.
5. Make a prediction by majority vote among the k trees

■ Box 9.17: Binary classification with Random Forest

```
from sklearn.ensemble import RandomForestClassifier

name="Random Forest"
clf= RandomForestClassifier(max_depth=5, n_estimators=10, max_features=1)

#Using same datasets as in Box 9.9
datasets = [ds1,ds2,ds3]
```

```
#Use same logic as in Box 9.9 to
#1. Split into training and test part
#2. Plot dataset
#3. Plot the training points
#4. Plot testing points
#5. Plot the decision boundary
#6. Put the result into a color plot
```

Randomness is injected in each tree in a Random Forest by two ways:

- A bootstrap sample (selecting n times with replacement from N samples in the training set) is used for building a tree.
- When a tree leaf is split, only a random subsets of attributes are considered for splitting.

■ Box 9.18: Classification with Random Forest

```
import numpy as np
from sklearn.ensemble import RandomForestClassifier
import csv as csv

csv_file_object = csv.reader(open('train.csv', 'rb')) #Load in the training csv file
train_data=[] #Creat a variable called 'train_data'
for row in csv_file_object: #Skip through each row in the csv file
train_data.append(row) #adding each row to the data variable

train_data = np.array(train_data) #Then convert from a list to an array
X_train = train_data[0::,1::]

#"status" column which is set to 0 for healthy and 1 for Parkinson's disease.
y_train = train_data[0::,0]

csv_file_object = csv.reader(open('test.csv', 'rb')) #Load in the training csv file
test_data=[]
for row in csv_file_object:
    test_data.append(row)

test_data = np.array(test_data)

X_test = test_data[0::,1::]
y_test = test_data[0::,0]

clf= RandomForestClassifier(n_estimators=100, max_depth=None, min_samples_split=1,
random_state=0,
max_features='auto')

#train Decision Tree classifier
clf = clf.fit(X_train, y_train)

#Score
score = clf.score(X_test, y_test)
print score
```

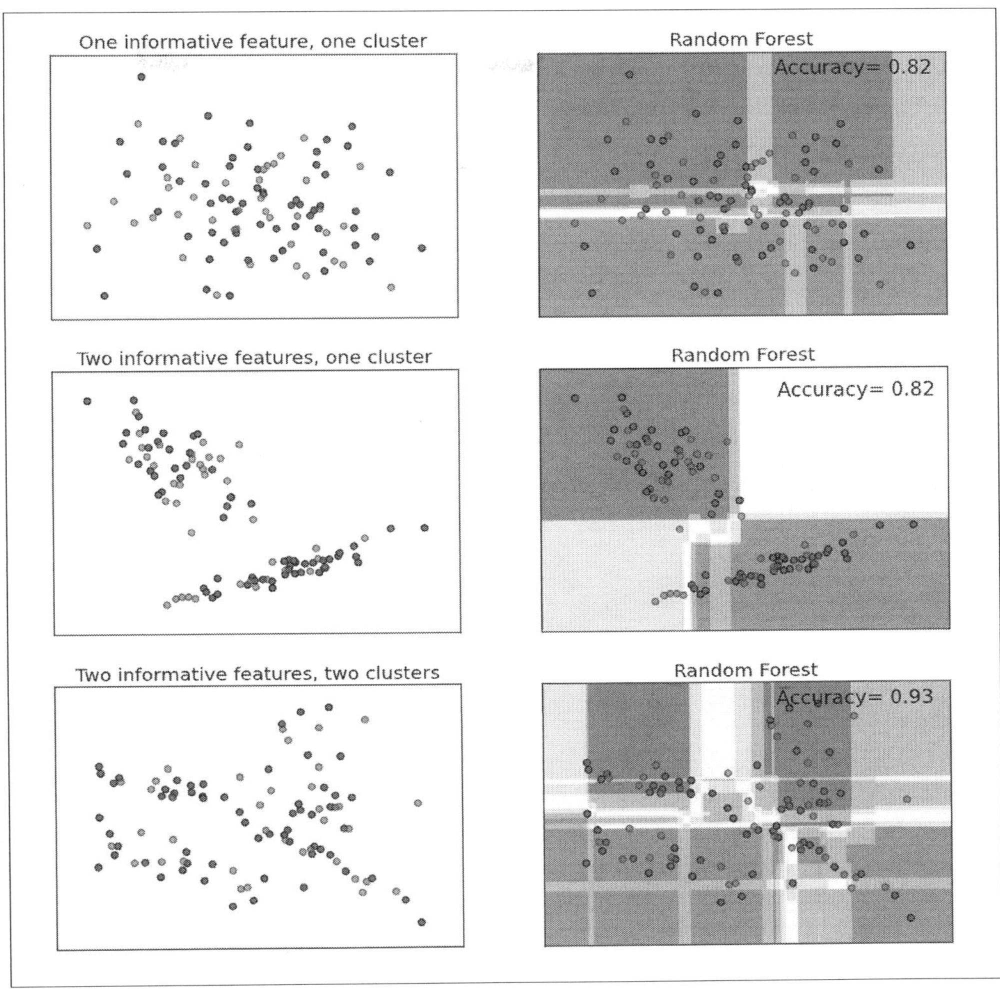

Figure 9.9: Binary classification with Random Forest

Box 9.17 shows an example of binary classification using Random Forest. Figure 9.9 shows the classification results using Random Forest and the classifier seems to work very well for the third data set and gives reasonably well results for first two datasets.

Box 9.18 shows a classification example using Random Forest for the Parkinsons disease dataset. Box 9.19 shows an example of Random Forest using the Apache Mahout framework that provides a parallel implementation of Random Forest. In this example the UCI breast cancer dataset [73] is used, that consists of 699 instances with 10 attributes each describing the features computed from a digitized image of a fine needle aspirate (FNA) of a breast mass. The class variable has two values (2 for benign, 4 for malignant). This example runs for 10 iterations and builds 100 trees in each iteration. In each iteration, 10% of the data is kept for testing and two random forests are created one with random inputs and another with a single input. The forest that gives the lowest out-of-bag error is chosen to compute the test set error. Box 9.20 shows the output of the random forest example. The results show that even with a single input random forest, results are comparable to random forest with more than one input.

■ **Box 9.19: Brieman Random Forest example in Mahout**

```
#Requires Hadoop installation.

#Run Hadoop
bin/hadoop namenode -format
bin/start-dfs.sh
bin/start-mapred.sh
jps

cd /root/hadoop

#Get the breast cancer dataset
wget http://archive.ics.uci.edu/ml/machine-learning-databases/breast-cancer-wisconsin
/breast-cancer-wisconsin.data

#Copy traning and test datasets to HDFS
bin/hadoop fs -put /home/ubuntu/breast-cancer-wisconsin.data
breast-cancer.data

#Generate a file descriptor for the dataset
bin/hadoop jar /home/ubuntu/mahout-distribution-0.7/core/target/mahout-core-0.7-job.jar
org.apache.mahout.classifier.df.tools.Describe -p breast-cancer.data -f
breast-cancer.info -d I 9 N L

#Run the example
bin/hadoop jar /home/ubuntu/mahout-distribution-0.7/examples/target/mahout-examples-
0.7-job.jar
org.apache.mahout.classifier.df.BreimanExample -d breast-cancer.data -ds
breast-cancer.info -i 10 -t 100
```

■ **Box 9.20: Output of Brieman Randon Forest example in Mahout**

```
INFO df.BreimanExample: Iteration 0
:
INFO df.BreimanExample: Splitting the data
:
INFO df.BreimanExample: Growing a forest with m=4
:
INFO df.BreimanExample: Growing a forest with m=1
:
INFO df.BreimanExample: Iteration 1
:
INFO df.BreimanExample: Splitting the data
:
INFO df.BreimanExample: Growing a forest with m=4
:
:
INFO df.BreimanExample: Random Input Test Error : 0.04852941176470589
```

```
INFO df.BreimanExample: Single Input Test Error : 0.062093942054433714
INFO df.BreimanExample: Mean Random Input Time : 0h 0m 0s 460
INFO df.BreimanExample: Mean Single Input Time : 0h 0m 0s 158
INFO df.BreimanExample: Mean Random Input Num Nodes : 4406
INFO df.BreimanExample: Mean Single Input Num Nodes : 8259
```

9.3.4 Support Vector Machine

Support Vector Machine (SVM) is a supervised machine learning approach used for classification and regression. The basic form is SVM is a binary classifier that classifies the data points into one of the two classes [74]. SVM training involves determining the maximum margin hyperplane that separates the two classes. The maximum margin hyperplane is one which has the largest separation from the nearest training data point. Figure 9.10 shows the margins for an SVM. Given a training data set (x_i, y_i) where x_i is an n dimensional vector and $y_i = 1$ if x_i is in class 1 and $y_i = -1$ if x_i is in class 2. A standard SVM finds a hyperplane $\mathbf{w}.\mathbf{x} - b = 0$, which correctly separates the training data points and has a maximum margin which is the distance between the two hyperplanes $\mathbf{w}.\mathbf{x} - b = 1$ and $\mathbf{w}.\mathbf{x} - b = -1$, as shown in Figure 9.11.

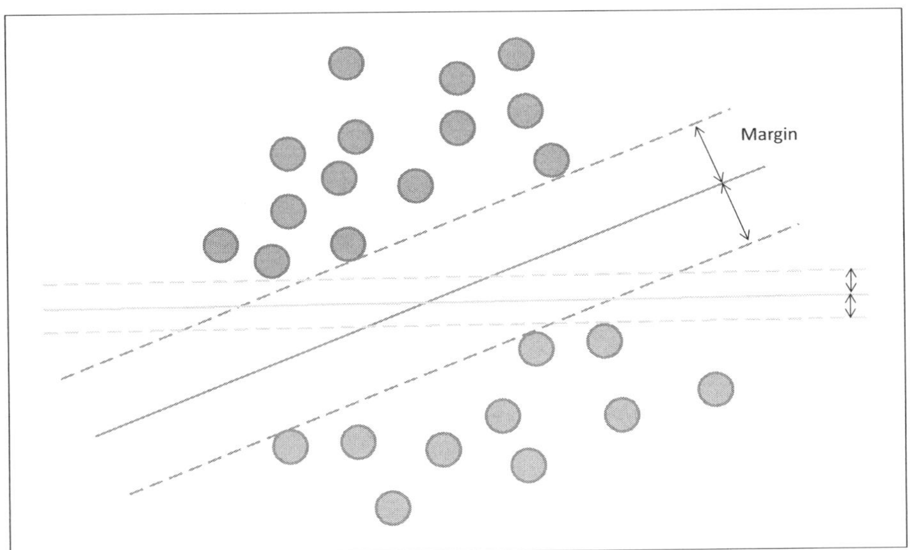

Figure 9.10: Margins for an SVM

The optimal hyperplane with maximum margin can be obtained by solving the following quadratic programming problem,

$$min_{\{w,b\}} \frac{1}{2} ||w||^2 + C \sum_{i=1}^{l} \xi_i \tag{9.20}$$

subject to $y_i(w.x_i - b) \geq 1 - \xi_i$, $\xi_i > 0$, $1 < i < l$ where C is the soft margin parameter and ξ is a slack variable for the non-separable case. The optimal hyperplane is given as,

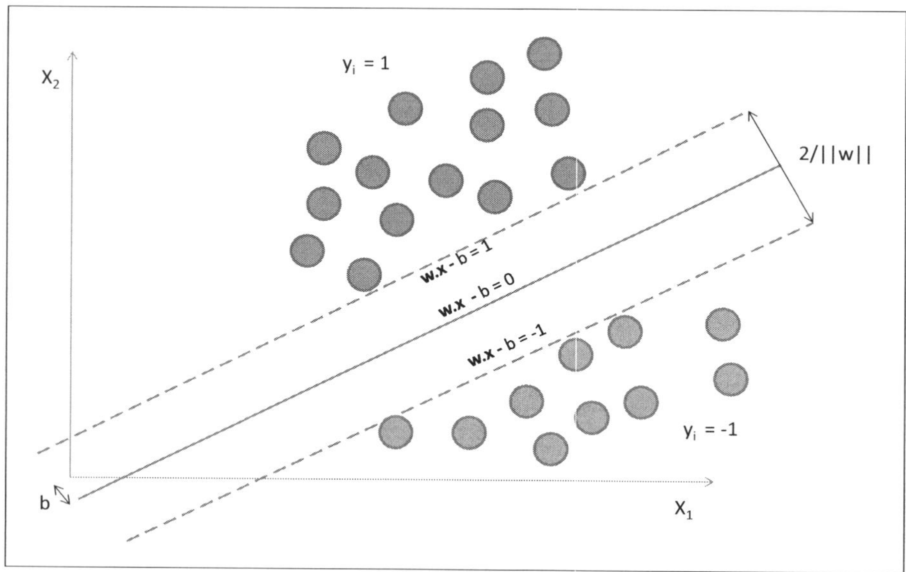

Figure 9.11: Maximum margin hyperplane

$$f(x) = sign\Big(C\sum_{i=1}^{l} \alpha_i y_i K(x_i, x) - b\Big) \tag{9.21}$$

where α_i is the Lagrange multiplier and $K(x_i, x)$ is the kernel function. A standard SVM is a two-class classier where the outcome is 1 or -1. When sets are not linearly separable, the data points in the original finite-dimensional space are mapped to a higher dimensional space where they can be separated easily. The performance of an SVM classifier depends on the selection of kernel, the kernel's parameters, and soft margin parameter C. The commonly used kernels include:

- Linear: $k(x_i, x_j) =< x_i, x_j >$
- Polynomial: $k(x_i, x_j) = (\gamma < x_i, x_j > +r)^d$
- Radial Basis Function (RBF): $k(x_i, x_j) = exp(-\gamma||x_i - x_j||^2)$
- Sigmoid: $k(x_i, x_j) = (tanh < x_i, x_j > +r)$

■ Box 9.21: Binary classification with SVM

```
from sklearn.svm import SVC

#For Linear SVM
name="RBF SVM"
clf= SVC(kernel="linear")

#For RBF-SVM
#name="RBF SVM"
#clf= SVC(kernel="rbf")
```

```
#Using same datasets as in Box 9.9
datasets = [ds1,ds2,ds3]

#Use same logic as in Box 9.9 to
#1. Split into training and test part
#2. Plot dataset
#3. Plot the training points
#4. Plot testing points
#5. Plot the decision boundary
#6. Put the result into a color plot
```

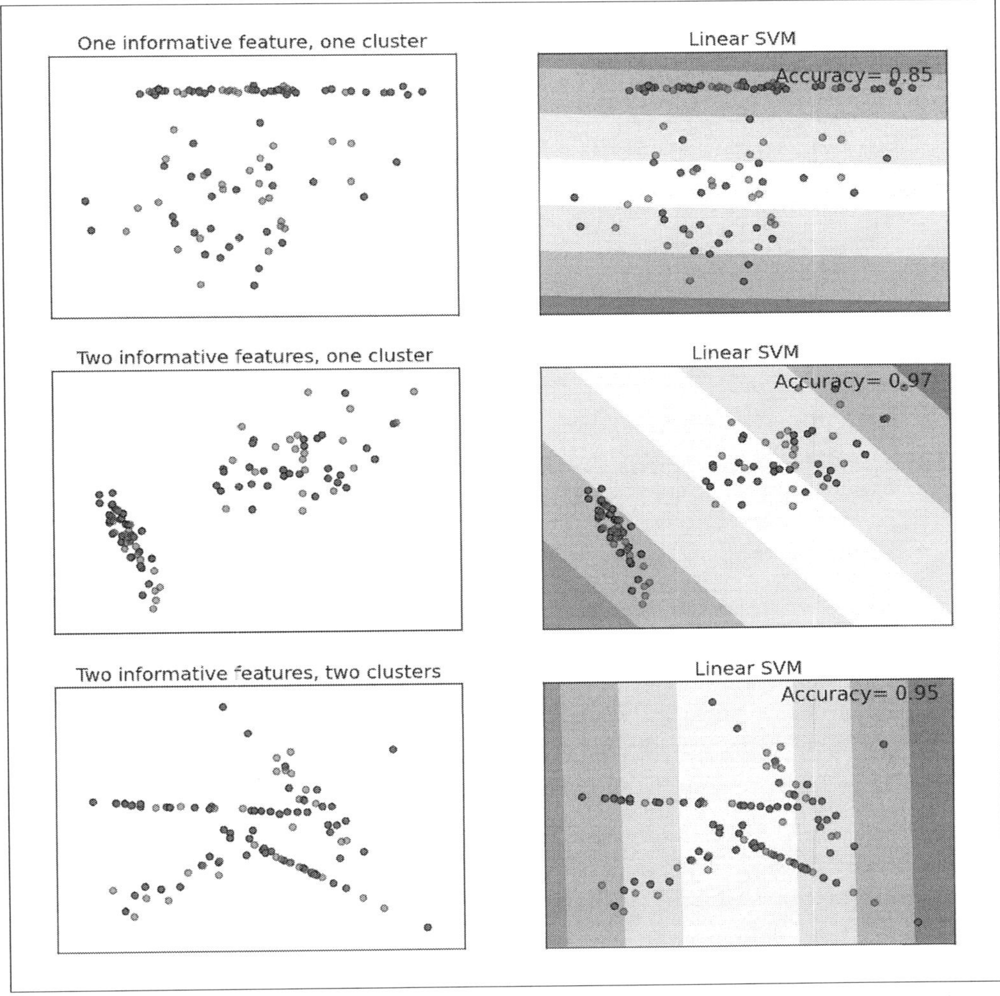

Figure 9.12: Binary classification with Linear SVM

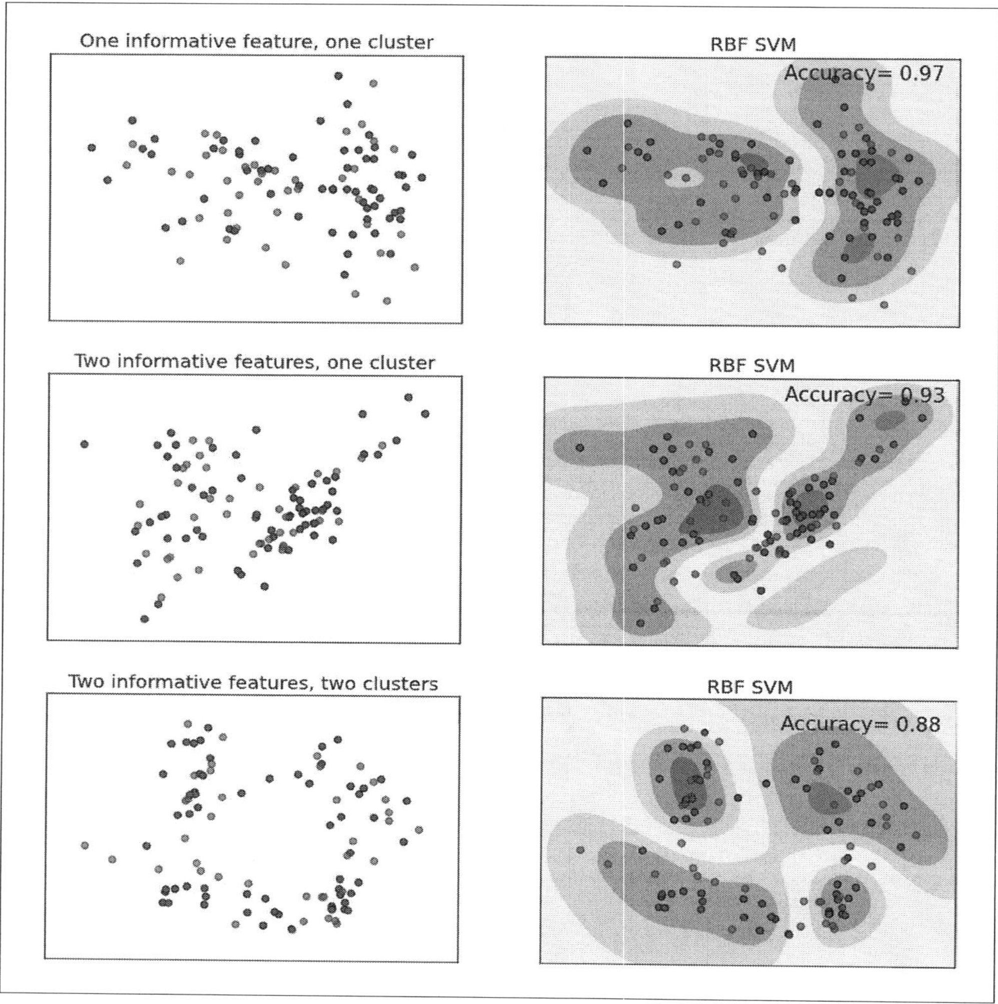

Figure 9.13: Binary classification with RBF SVM

■ **Box 9.22: Classification with SVM**

```
import numpy as np
from sklearn.ensemble import RandomForestClassifier
import csv as csv
from sklearn.svm import SVC

csv_file_object = csv.reader(open('train.csv', 'rb')) #Load in the training csv file
train_data=[] #Creat a variable called 'train_data'
for row in csv_file_object: #Skip through each row in the csv file
    train_data.append(row) #adding each row to the data variable

train_data = np.array(train_data) #Then convert from a list to an array
X_train = train_data[0::,1::]
```

```
#"status" column which is set to 0 for healthy and 1 for Parkinson's disease.
y_train = train_data[0::,0]

csv_file_object = csv.reader(open('test.csv', 'rb')) #Load in the training csv file
test_data=[]
for row in csv_file_object:
    test_data.append(row)

test_data = np.array(test_data)

X_test = test_data[0::,1::]
y_test = test_data[0::,0]

clf= SVC(kernel='linear')

#train Decision Tree classifier
clf = clf.fit(X_train, y_train)

#Score
score = clf.score(X_test, y_test)
print score
```

Box 9.21 shows an example of binary classification using SVM. Figures 9.12 and 9.13 show the classification results using Linear SVM and RBF SVM respectively. Both SVM classifiers work well for the three datasets. Box 9.22 shows an example of classification with SVM for the Parkinsons dataset.

9.4 Recommendation Systems

Recommendation systems are an important part of modern cloud applications such as e-Commerce, social networks, content delivery networks, etc. A recommendation system provides recommendations to users (for items such as books, movies, songs,or restaurants) for unrated items based on the characteristics of the item or the ratings given by the user and other users to similar items. The former approach is called item-based or content-based recommendation, and the latter is called collaborative filtering.

In this section you will learn how to build a simple recommendation system in Python. The input to any recommendation system is the data about user ratings for different items. Figure 9.14 shows an example of user ratings matrix where each row belongs to a user and the columns are the ratings given to items.

Box 9.23 shows a python implementation of a simple recommendation engine. Box 9.24 shows an improved implementation of a recommendation engine using SVD.

■ Box 9.23: Simple recommendation system in Python

```
import numpy as np
import csv as csv

def getdata(data_file):
    csv_file_object = csv.reader(open(data_file, 'rb')) #Load in the training csv file
```

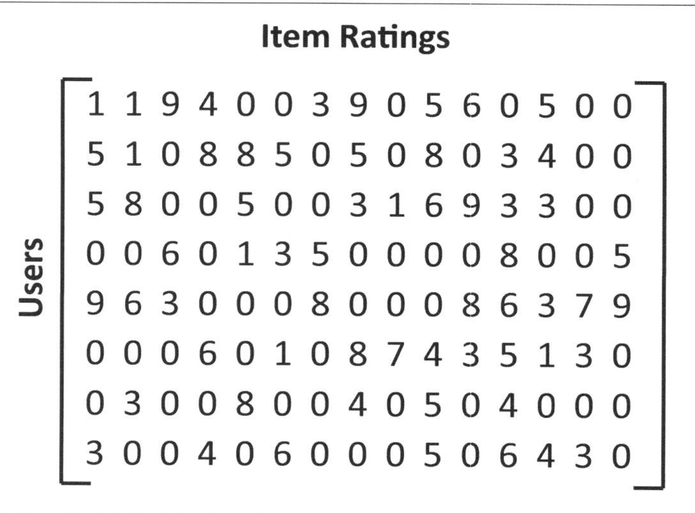

Figure 9.14: Example of user item ratings on a scale of 10

```
    user_ratings=[]
    for row in csv_file_object: #Skip through each row in the csv file
        user_ratings.append(row) #adding each row to the data variable

    user_ratings = np.array(user_ratings) #Then convert from a list to an array
    return user_ratings.astype(np.int)

def getRating(user_ratings,user,item):
    numItems= np.shape(user_ratings)[1]
    total=0
    simialrityRating=0
    for i in range(numItems):
        if user_ratings[user,i]!=0:
            similarity=0.5+0.5*np.corrcoef(user_ratings[::,item],user_ratings[::,i])[0][1]
            total += similarity
            simialrityRating += similarity*user_ratings[user,i]
    return simialrityRating/total

def main():
    data_file=' data.csv'
    user_ratings=getdata(data_file)
    numUsers= np.shape(user_ratings)[0]
    for user in range(numUsers):
        not_rated=np.nonzero(user_ratings[user,:]==0)[0]
        itemRatings={}
        for item in not_rated:
         rating=getRating(user_ratings,user,item)
            itemRatings[item]=rating

        topItemRatings=sorted(itemRatings.items(),key = lambda x:x[1],reverse=True)[:3]

        print "Top 3 items recommended for user-%d: "%(user)
```

```
        for key in topItemRatings:
            print key[0]

if __name__ == '__main__':
    main()
```

■ **Box 9.24: Improved recommendation system using SVD**

```
import numpy as np
import csv as csv

def getdata(data_file):
    csv_file_object = csv.reader(open(data_file, 'rb')) #Load in the training csv file
    user_ratings=[]
    for row in csv_file_object: #Skip through each row in the csv file
        user_ratings.append(row) #adding each row to the data variable

    user_ratings = np.array(user_ratings) #Then convert from a list to an array
    return user_ratings.astype(np.int)

def getRatingSVD(user_ratings,user_ratings_ld,user,item):
    numItems= np.shape(user_ratings)[1]
    total=0
    simialrityRating=0
    for i in range(numItems):
        if user_ratings[user,i]!=0:
            similarity=0.5+0.5*np.corrcoef(user_ratings_ld[item,::],user_ratings_ld[i,::])[0][1]
            total += similarity
            simialrityRating += similarity*user_ratings[user,i]
    return simialrityRating/total

def main():
    data_file='data.csv'
    user_ratings=getdata(data_file)

    numUsers= np.shape(user_ratings)[0]
    U,S,V=np.linalg.svd(user_ratings)
    Sigma=np.mat(np.eye(4)*S[:4])

    #Transform to lower dimensional space
    usigma = U[:,:4]*Sigma.I
    user_ratings_ld = user_ratings.T * usigma

    for user in range(numUsers):
        not_rated=np.nonzero(user_ratings[user,:]==0)[0]
        itemRatings={}
        for item in not_rated:
            rating=getRatingSVD(user_ratings, user_ratings_ld,user,item)
            itemRatings[item]=rating

        topItemRatings=sorted(itemRatings.items(),key = lambda x:x[1],reverse=True)[:3]
```

```
        print "Top 3 items recommended for user-%d: "%(user)
        for key in topItemRatings:
            print key[0]

if __name__ == '__main__':
    main()
```

Summary

In this chapter you learned big data analytics approaches including approaches for clustering big data, classification of big data and recommendation systems. Big data is defined as collections of datasets whose volume, velocity or variety is so large that it is difficult to store, manage, process and analyze the data using traditional databases and data processing tools. The underlying characteristics of big data include volume, velocity and variety. You learned about clustering algorithms such as k-means and DBSCAN. k-means is a clustering algorithm that groups data items into k clusters, where k is user defined. DBSCAN is a density clustering algorithm that works on the notions of density reachability and density connectivity. You learned how to cluster documents with k-means and DBSCAN. Clustering algorithms can be parallelized using MapReduce. You learned how to use Apache Mahout that provides distributed and scalable machine learning algorithms on top of the Hadoop platform. Classification is the process of categorizing objects into predefined categories. You learned classification algorithms such as Naive Bayes, Decision Trees, Random Forest and Support Vector Machine. Naive Bayes is a probabilistic classification algorithm based on the Bayes theorem with a naive assumption about the independence of feature attributes. Decision Trees are a supervised learning method that use a tree created from simple decision rules learned from the training data as a predictive model. Random Forest is an ensemble learning method that is based on randomized decision trees. SVM is a supervised machine learning approach used for classification and regression. This chapter provided examples of binary classification and document classification with various classification algorithms. Finally, you learned about recommendation systems that provide recommendations to users for unrated items based on the characteristics of the items or the ratings given by the user and other users to similar items.

Review Questions

1. What are the characteristics of big data?
2. What is the stopping criteria used in k-means clustering?
3. What is the difference between density reachability and density connectivity?
4. What is the difference between precision and accuracy?
5. What is the naive assumption made by Naive Bayes algorithm?
6. What is information gain?
7. What is an ensemble learning method?
8. What is a maximum margin hyperplane in SVM?
9. What is the difference between content-based recommendation and collaborative filtering?

Lab Exercises

1. Develop a Django application for document clustering. The application should include a wizard for uploading a set of documents as a single compressed file (gzip) and selecting a clustering algorithm (implement k-means and DBSCAN). Display the clustered results on a separate web page.

2. Develop a Django application for document classification. The application should include a wizard for uploading a set of documents as a single compressed file (gzip) and selecting the classification algorithm (implement Naive Bayes). Display the results on a separate web page.

3. Extend the Social Media Analytics application described in Chapter 8 and to find sentiment of social media feeds using a Naive Bayes classifier.

4. Extend the Social Media Analytics application described in Chapter 8 and to categorize social media feeds into categories such as sports, entertainment, politics, etc. Compare Naive Bayes and Decision Tree classifiers for feed classification.

5. Develop a recommendation system based on collaborative filtering and test it with the Jester Collaborative Filtering Dataset (http://goldberg.berkeley.edu/jester-data/). This dataset contains data from 24,983 users who have rated 36 or more jokes, a matrix with dimensions 24983 x 101. Use the example in described in section 11.4 as the baseline.

6. Repeat Exercise-5 using the collaborative filtering algorithm provided in Apache Mahout framework.

10 — Multimedia Cloud

This Chapter Covers

- Reference architecture for Multimedia Cloud
- Case study of a live video streaming cloud application
- Case study of a video transcoding cloud application

10.1 Introduction

With the development of web 2.0 and higher and through the increasing reach of high speed internet to wireless applications, multimedia rich web applications have become widely popular in recent years. There are various types of multimedia web applications including multimedia storage, processing, transcoding and streaming applications. Due the higher resource requirements for multimedia applications, cloud computing is proving to be an efficient and cost effective solution. With the increasing demand for multimedia rich web applications on wireless platforms, a new paradigm of multimedia cloud is emerging that provides multimedia storage, processing and streaming services to millions of mobile users around the world.

Figure 10.1 shows a reference architecture for a multimedia cloud. In this architecture, the first layer is the infrastructure services layer that includes computing and storage resources. On top of the infrastructure services layer is the platform services layer that includes frameworks and services for streaming and associated tasks such as transcoding and analytics that can be leveraged for rapid development of multimedia applications. The topmost layer is the applications such as live video streaming, video transcoding, video-on-demand, multimedia processing etc. Cloud-based multimedia applications alleviates the burden of installing and maintaining multimedia applications locally on the multimedia consumption devices (desktops, tablets, smartphone, etc) and provide access to rich multimedia content. A multimedia cloud can have various service models such as IaaS, PaaS and SaaS that offer infrastructure, platform or application services as shown in Figure 10.1.

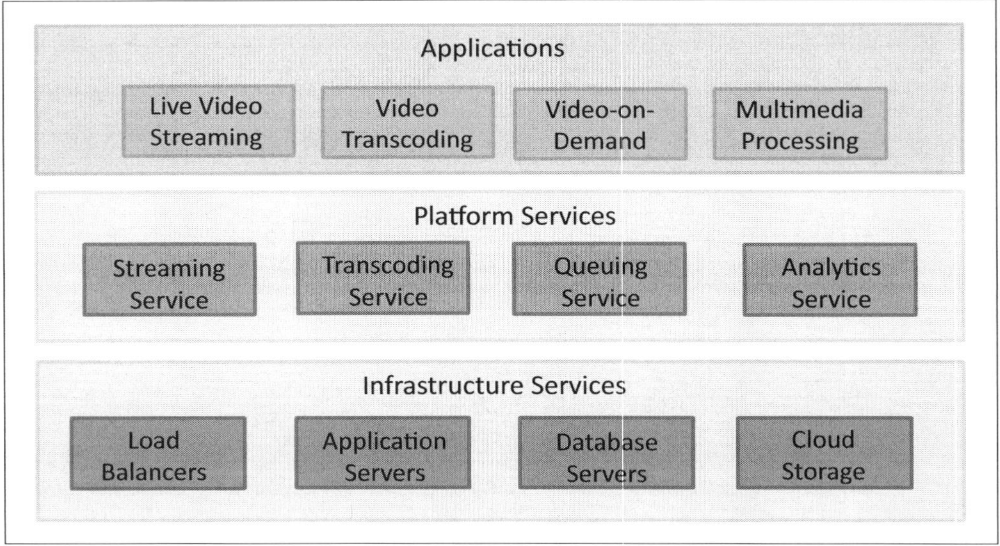

Figure 10.1: Multimedia Cloud reference architecture

10.2 Case Study: Live Video Streaming App

This chapter provides case studies of cloud-based multimedia applications. You will learn how to develop and deploy multimedia applications on the cloud. Let us begin with a cloud-based live video streaming application. Video streaming applications have become very popular in the recent years with more and more users watching events broadcast live on the internet. Live streamed events can be viewed by audiences around the world on different types of devices connected to the internet such as laptops, desktops, tablets, smartphones, internet-TVs, etc. This capability to reach a much wider audience across a much larger geographic area is one of the most unique and exciting applications of streaming technology. Figure 10.2 shows a workflow of a live video streaming application that uses multimedia cloud. In this workflow the video and audio feeds generated by a number cameras and microphones are mixed/multiplexed with video/audio mixers and then encoded by a client application which then sends the encoded feeds to the multimedia cloud. On the cloud, streaming instances are created on-demand and the streams are then broadcast over the internet. The streaming instances also record the event streams which are later moved to the cloud storage for video archiving.

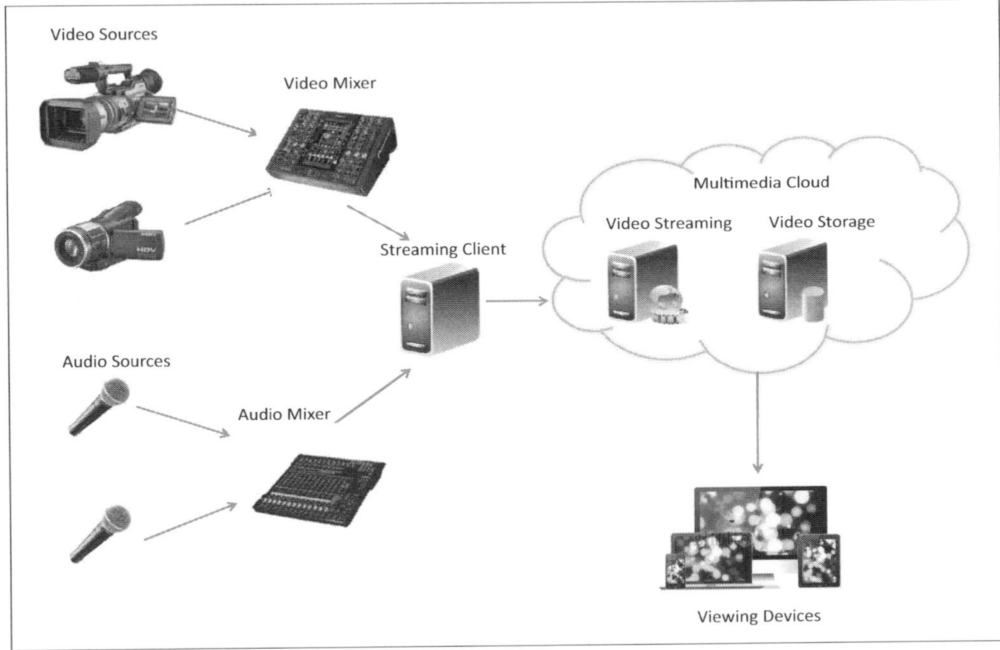

Figure 10.2: Workflow for live video streaming using multimedia cloud

Figure 10.3 shows a screenshot of a live video streaming demo application that is described in this section. This application allows on-demand creation of video streaming instances in the cloud. Figure 10.3 shows the first step in the stream instance creation workflow in which the details of the stream are specified. Figures 10.4 and 10.5 show the second and third steps in which an instance size is selected and then the instance is launched.

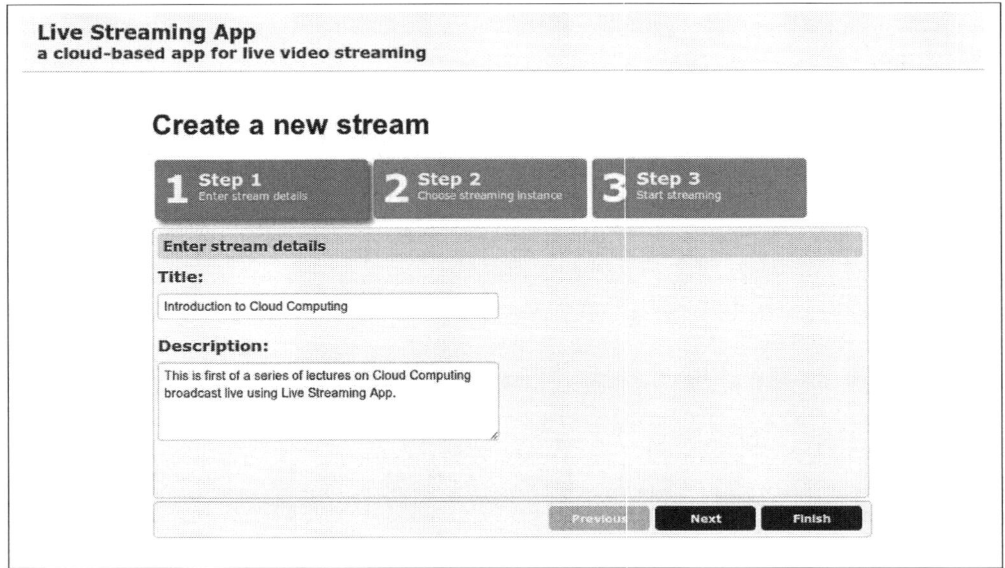

Figure 10.3: Screenshot of live video streaming application showing step-1 (entering stream details)

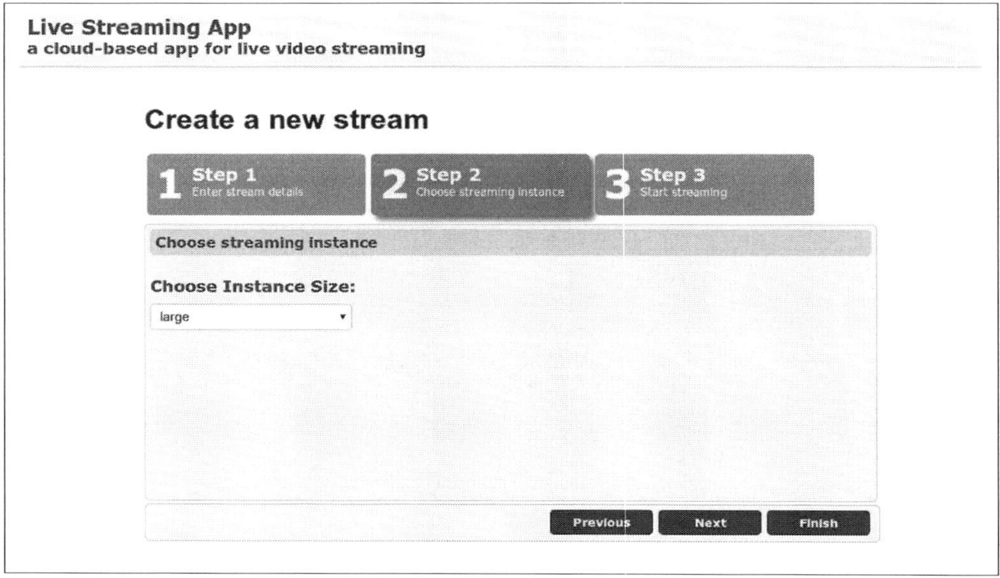

Figure 10.4: Screenshot of live video streaming application showing step-2 (choosing stream instance)

The live streaming application is created using the Django framework and uses Amazon EC2 cloud instances. For video stream encoding and publishing, the Adobe Flash Media Live Encoder and Flash Media Server are used [41]. Box 10.1 shows the source code for the Django template for start stream page shown in Figures 10.3, 10.4 and 10.5. This template uses the jQuery smart wizard to get user inputs for the streaming instance. The form inputs

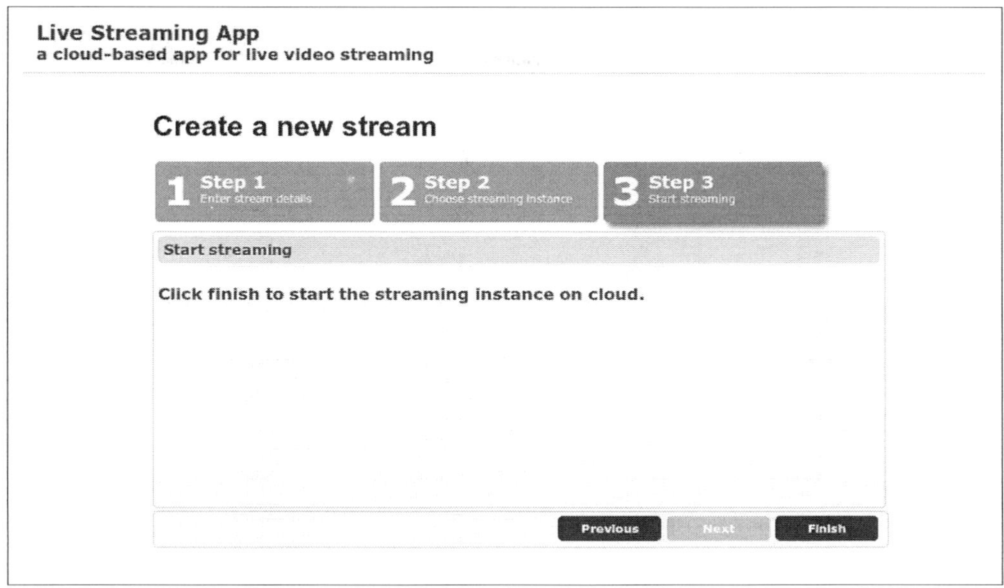

Figure 10.5: Screenshot of live video streaming application showing step-3 (starting streaming instance)

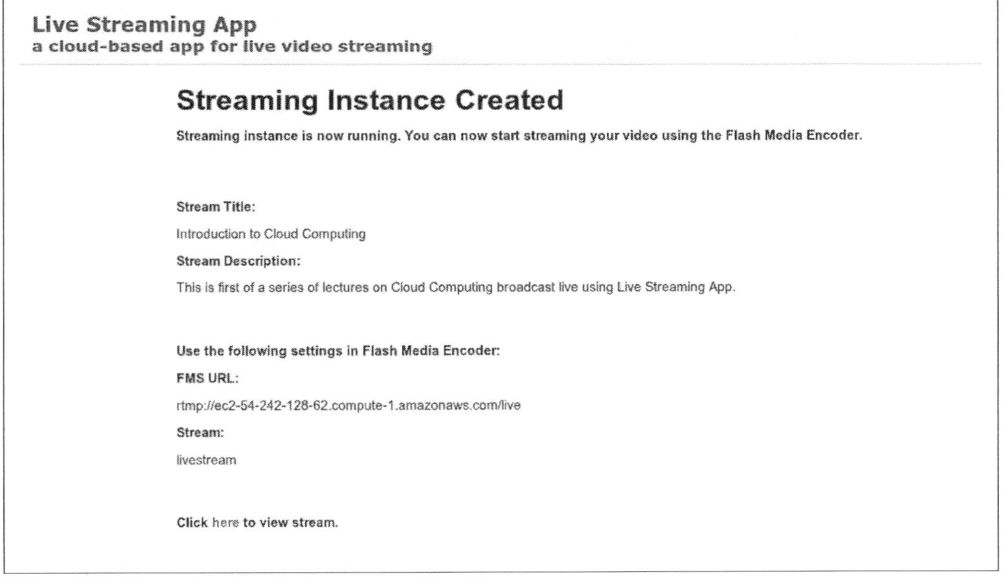

Figure 10.6: Screenshot of live video streaming application showing details of streaming instance

are processed in a Django view described later in this section.

After the user completes the stream instance creation wizard, an instance of Flash Media Server is created in the Amazon cloud. Figure 10.6 shows the screenshot of the stream details page which provides the settings to use with the Flash Media Encoder application on the client. This page also provides a link to the page in which the live stream can be viewed. Box 10.2 shows the Django template for the stream details page.

■ Box 10.1: Django Template for Live Streaming App - Start Stream Page

```
<html><head>
<meta http-equiv="Content-Type" content="text/html; charset=UTF-8">
<title>Live Streaming App</title>
<link href="/static/styles/demo_style.css" rel="stylesheet" type="text/css">
<link href="/static/styles/smart_wizard.css" rel="stylesheet" type="text/css">
<link href="/static/styles/bootstrap.css" rel="stylesheet" type="text/css">
<script type="text/javascript" src="/static/js/jquery-1.4.2.min.js"></script>
<script type="text/javascript" src="/static/js/jquery.smartWizard.js"></script>

<script type="text/javascript">
$(document).ready(function(){
$('#wizard').smartWizard({transitionEffect:'fade',onFinish:onFinishCallback} );

function onFinishCallback(){
$('form').submit();
}
});
</script>
</head><body>

<div class="demoHead">
<div>
<div style="float:left;">
<h1>Live Streaming App</h1>
<h2>a cloud-based app for live video streaming</h2>
</div>

<div style="clear:both;"></div>
</div>

</div>

<form action="/startinstance/" method="get"><br>
<table align="center" border="0" cellpadding="0" cellspacing="0">
<tr><td>
<!- Smart Wizard ->
<h2>Create a new stream</h2>
<div id="wizard" class="swMain">
<ul>
<li>
<a href="#step-1">
<label class="stepNumber">1</label>
<span class="stepDesc">
Step 1<br />
<small>Enter stream details</small>
</span>
</a>
</li>
<li>
```

```
<a href="#step-2">
<label class="stepNumber">2</label>
<span class="stepDesc">
Step 2<br />
<small>Choose streaming instance</small>
</span>
</a>
</li>
<li>
<a href="#step-3">
<label class="stepNumber">3</label>
<span class="stepDesc">
Step 3<br />
<small>Start streaming</small>
</span>
</a>
</li>
</ul>

<div id="step-1">
<h2 class="StepTitle">Enter stream details</h2>
<h4>Title: </h4><input type="text" name="title" class="span5" ><br>
<h4>Description: </h4> <textarea rows="4" class="span5" name="description"></textarea>
</div>

<div id="step-2">
<h2 class="StepTitle">Choose streaming instance</h2> <br>
<h4>Choose Instance Size:</h4>
<select name="size">
<option value="t1.micro">micro</option>
<option value="m1.small">small</option>
<option value="m1.medium">medium</option>
<option value="m1.large">large</option>
<option value="m1.xlarge">extra-large</option>
</select>
</div>

<div id="step-3">
<h2 class="StepTitle">Start streaming</h2>
<br>
<h4>Click finish to start the streaming instance on cloud. </h4><br>
</div>

</div>

</td></tr>
</table>
</form>

</body>
</html>
```

■ **Box 10.2: Django Template for Live Streaming App - Stream Details Page**

```
<html>
<head>
<meta http-equiv="Content-Type" content="text/html; charset=UTF-8">
<title>Live Streaming App</title>
<link href="/static/styles/bootstrap.css" rel="stylesheet" type="text/css">
</head>
<body>

<div class="demoHead">
<div>
<div style="float:left;">
<h1>Live Streaming App</h1>
<h2>a cloud-based app for live video streaming</h2>
</div>

<div style="clear:both"> </div>
</div>

</div>

< table align="center" border="0" cellpadding="0" cellspacing="0" >
<tr> <td>
<!– Smart Wizard –>
<h2>Streaming Instance Created</h2>
<div id="streampage">
<h5>Streaming instance is now running. You can now start streaming your video using the
Flash Media Encoder. </h5> <br> <br>
<h5>Stream Title: </h5> {{title}}
<h5>Stream Description: </h5> {{description}}<br> <br> <br>

<h5>Use the following settings in Flash Media Encoder:</h5>
<h5>FMS URL:</h5> rtmp://{{publicdns}}/live
<h5>Stream: </h5> livestream
<br> <br> <br>

<h5>Click <a href="/viewstream/?title={{titleescaped}}
&description={{descriptionescaped}} &dns={{publicdns}}/">here</a> to view stream.</h5>
</div>
</td> </tr>
</table>
</body>
</html>
```

The FMS URL and Stream details provided in the stream details page are then entered in the Flash Media Encoder (FME) application that runs on the client machine. Figure 10.7 shows a screenshot of FME application. The client gets the video and audio feed from a camera and microphone or gets a multiplexed feed from video/audio mixers. The video and audio formats and bit rates can be specified in FME. After all the settings are complete, streaming can be started by clicking on the start button. In this example, RTMP protocol is used for streaming which is described later in this chapter.

Figure 10.7: Screenshot of Adobe Flash Media Live Encoder used for video streaming

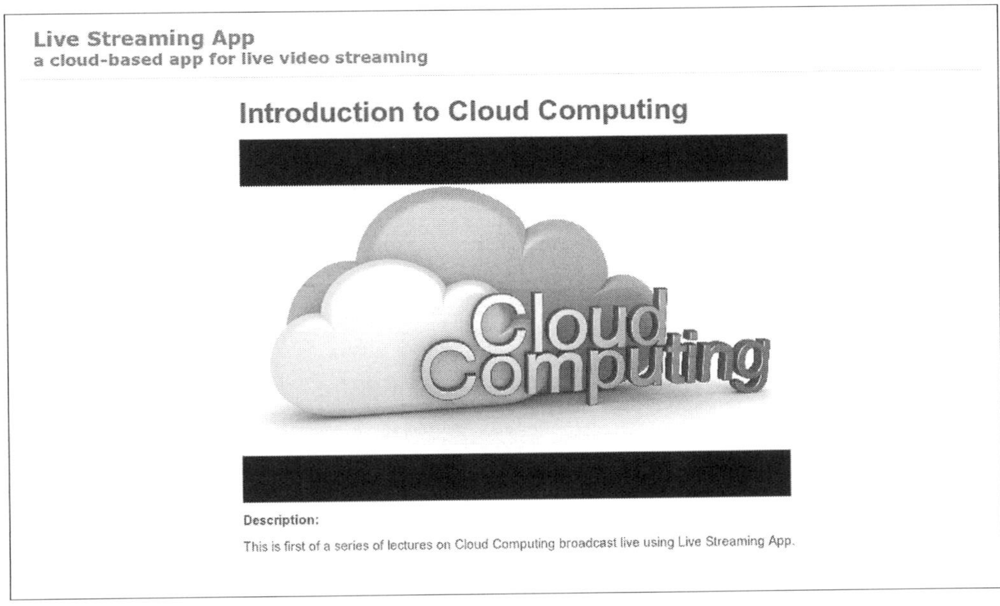

Figure 10.8: Screenshot of live video streaming application showing video streaming page

■ Box 10.3: Django Template for Live Streaming App - View Stream Page

```
<html>
<meta http-equiv="Content-Type" content="text/html; charset=UTF-8">
<title>Live Streaming App</title>
<link href="/static/styles/bootstrap.css" rel="stylesheet" type="text/css">
</head>
<body>

<div class="demoHead">
<div>
<div style="float:left;">
<h1>Live Streaming App</h1>
<h2>a cloud-based app for live video streaming</h2>
</div>

<div style="clear:both;"> </div>
</div>

</div>

<table align="center" border="0" cellpadding="0" cellspacing="0">
<tr> <td>
<!- Smart Wizard ->
<h2>{{title}}</h2>

<object width="600" height="409"> <param name="movie"
value="http://fpdownload.adobe.com/strobe/FlashMediaPlayback.swf">
</param>
<param name="flashvars" value="src=rtmp://{{publicdns}}
/live/livestream/&poster=/static/cloud.jpg"> </param>
<param name="allowFullScreen" value="true"> </param>

<param name="allowscriptaccess" value="always"> </param>
<embed src="http://fpdownload.adobe.com/strobe/FlashMediaPlayback.swf"
type="application/x-shockwave-flash"
allowscriptaccess="always" allowfullscreen="true" width="600" height="409"
flashvars="src=rtmp://{{publicdns}}
/live/livestream/&poster=/static/cloud.jpg"> </embed>
</object>
<h5>Description: </h5> {{description}}

</td> </tr>
</table>

</body>
</html>
```

Figure 10.8 shows a screenshot of the page in which the live video stream broadcast by the streaming client is viewed. Box 10.3 provides the source code of the Django template for this page.

■ Box 10.4: Django URL patterns for Live Streaming App

```
rom django.conf.urls.defaults import *

urlpatterns = patterns('',
    url(r'^$', 'myapp.views.home'),
    url(r'^startinstance/$', 'myapp.views.startinstance'),
    url(r'^viewstream/$', 'myapp.views.viewstream'),
)
```

So far you have seen the application screenshots and source code of the Django templates. Now lets us look at the back-end processing and settings part. Box 10.4 shows the URL patterns for the live streaming application. This application uses three URL patterns which map to different views.

■ Box 10.5: Django View for Live Streaming App

```
from django.http import HttpResponseRedirect
from django.shortcuts import render
from django.shortcuts import render_to_response

import boto.ec2
from time import sleep

ACCESS_KEY="<enter access key here>"
SECRET_KEY="<enter secret key here>"

REGION="us-east-1"
AMI_ID = "<enter ami-id of FMS>"
EC2_KEY_HANDLE = "<enter key name>"
SECGROUP_HANDLE="default"

def viewstream(request):
    title=request.GET['title']
    description=request.GET['description']
    publicdns=request.GET['dns']
    return render_to_response('viewstream.html', {'title':title,
        'description': description, 'publicdns':publicdns})

def home(request):
    return render_to_response('index.html')

def startinstance(request):
    title=request.GET['title']
    description=request.GET['description']
    size=request.GET['size']
    titleescaped = title.replace(' ','+')
    descriptionescaped=description.replace(' ','+')

    publicdns=startFMSinstance(size)
    return render_to_response('stream.html', {'title':title,
    'description': description,'titleescaped':titleescaped, 'descriptionescaped':
```

```
    descriptionescaped, 'publicdns':publicdns})

def startFMSinstance(size):
    conn = boto.ec2.connect_to_region(REGION,
        aws_access_key_id=ACCESS_KEY,
        aws_secret_access_key=SECRET_KEY)

    reservation = conn.run_instances(image_id=AMI_ID,
            key_name=EC2_KEY_HANDLE,
            instance_type=size,
            security_groups = [ SECGROUP_HANDLE, ] )

    instance = reservation.instances[0]

    status = instance.update()
    while status == 'pending':
        sleep(5)
        status = instance.update()

    publicdns="none"
    if status == 'running':
        publicdns=instance.public_dns_name

    return publicdns
```

Box 10.5 shows the source code for the Django views for live streaming application. The access and secret keys for the Amazon account to be used for this application are specified in this view. The specifications for the Flash Media Server EC2 instance are also provided in the view including the AMI-ID, region, security key handle and security group. The *startinstance* function processes the form submitted by the user in the start stream page. This function parses the form input and then calls the *startFMSinstance* function. In the *startFMSinstance* function an instance of the Flash Media Server is created on Amazon EC2 and the public DNS of the created instance is returned. The stream details specified by the user and the public DNS of the created instance are then rendered in the stream details page.

The live streaming application described in this section demonstrates a simple use case of multimedia cloud. This application can be extended further to provide scale up and scale out options to serve a larger number of viewers. The choice of number of instances to launch and size of the instances can be made based on the number of expected viewers.

10.3 Streaming Protocols

The live streaming application described in the previous section uses RTMP streaming protocol. There are a number of streaming methods used by stream servers such as Flash Media Server including [41]:

- **RTMP Dynamic Streaming (Unicast)**: High-quality, low-latency media streaming with support for live and on-demand and full adaptive bitrate.
- **RTMPE (encrypted RTMP)**: Real-time encryption of RTMP.
- **RTMFP (multicast)**: IP multicast encrypted with support for both ASM or SSM multicast for multicast-enabled network.

- **RTMFP (P2P)**: P2P live video delivery between Flash Player clients.
- **RTMFP (multicast fusion)**: IP and P2P working together to support higher QoS within enterprise networks.
- **HTTP Dynamic Streaming (HDS)**: Enabling on-demand and live adaptive bitrate video streaming of standards-based MP4 media over regular HTTP connections.
- **Protected HTTP Dynamic Streaming (PHDS)**: Real-time encryption of HDS.
- **HTTP Live Streaming (HLS)**: HTTP streaming to iOS devices or devices that support the HLS format; optional encryption with AES128 encryption standard.

The streaming methods listed above are based on the RTMP and HTTP streaming protocols.

10.3.1 RTMP Streaming

Real Time Messaging Protocol (RTMP) [42] is a protocol for streaming audio, video and data over the Internet, between Adobe Flash Platform technologies, including Adobe Flash Player and Adobe AIR. RTMP is available as an open specification to create products and technology that enable delivery of video, audio, and data in the open AMF, SWF, FLV, and F4V formats compatible with Adobe Flash Player. RTMP protocol has several variations. The plain version of RTMP protocol works on top of TCP. RTMPS is a secure variation of RTMP that works over TLS/SSL.

RTMP provides a bidirectional message multiplex service over a reliable stream transport, such as TCP. RTMP maintains persistent TCP connections that allow low-latency communication. RTMP is intended to carry parallel streams of video, audio, and data messages, with associated timing information, between a pair of communicating peers. Streams are split into fragments so that delivery of the streams smoothly. The size of the stream fragments is either fixed or negotiated dynamically between the client and server. Default fragment sizes used are 64-bytes for audio data, and 128 bytes for video data. RTMP implementations typically assign different priorities to different classes of messages, which can affect the order in which messages are enqueued to the underlying stream transport when transport capacity is constrained. In practice, the interleaving and multiplexing is done at the packet level, with RTMP packets across several different active channels being interleaved in such a way as to ensure that each channel meets its bandwidth, latency, and other quality-of-service requirements.

10.3.2 HTTP Live Streaming

HTTP Live Streaming (HLS) was proposed by Apple and is a part of the Apple iOS [43]. HLS can dynamically adjust playback quality to match the available speed of wired or wireless networks. HLS supports multiple alternate streams at different bit rates, and the client software can switch streams intelligently as network bandwidth changes. HLS also provides for media encryption and user authentication over HTTPS, allowing publishers to protect their work. The protocol works by splitting the stream into small chunks which are specified in a playlist file. Playlist file is an ordered list of media URIs and informational tags. The URIs and their associated tags specify a series of media segments. To play the stream, the client first obtains the playlist file and then obtains and plays each media segment in the playlist.

10.3.3 HTTP Dynamic Streaming

HTTP Dynamic Streaming (HDS) protocol is supported by Adobe [44]. HDS enables on-demand and live adaptive bitrate video delivery of standards-based MP4 media (H.264 or VPC) over regular HTTP connections. HDS combines HTTP (progressive download) and RTMP (streaming download) to provide the ability to deliver video content in a steaming manner over HTTP. HDS supports adaptive bitrate which allows HDS to detect the client's bandwidth and computer resources and serve content fragments encoded at the most appropriate bitrate for the best viewing experience. HDS supports high-definition video up to 1080p, with bitrates from 700 kbps up to and beyond 6 Mbps, using either H.264 or VP6 video codecs, or AAC and MP3 audio codecs. HDS allows leveraging existing caching infrastructures, content delivery networks (CDNs) and standard HTTP server hardware to deliver on-demand and live content.

10.4 Case Study: Video Transcoding App

Let us now look to develop a video transcoding application based on multimedia cloud. The demo application shown in this section is built upon the Amazon Elastic Transcoder [45]. Elastic Transcoder is highly scalable, relatively easy to use service from Amazon that allows converting video files from their source format into versions that will playback on mobile devices like smartphones, tablets and PCs. In this section we will describe the steps involved in building a video transcoding application using Python and Django. The transcoding application allows users to upload video files and choose the conversion presets. Figure 10.9, 10.10 and 10.11 show screenshots of the video file submission wizard.

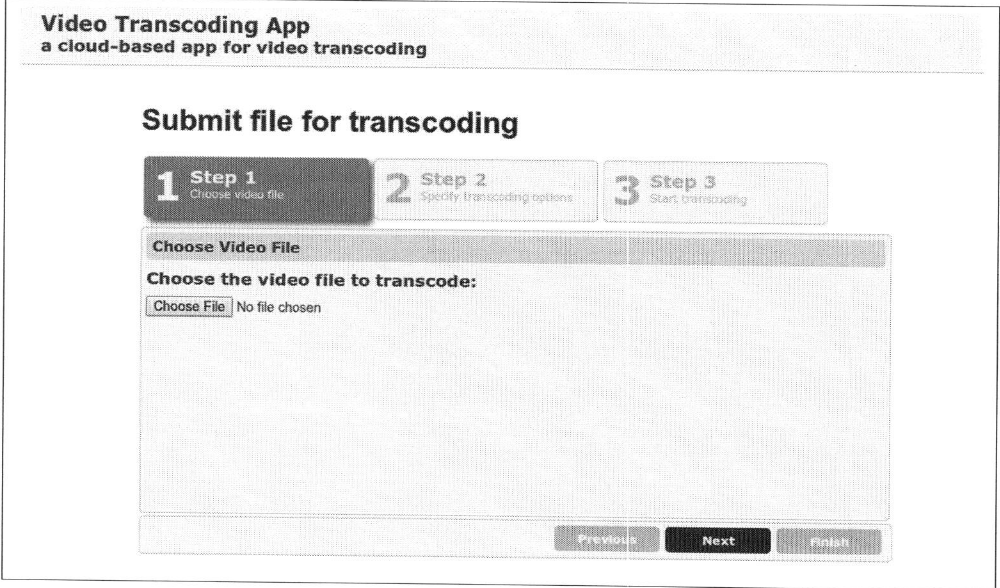

Figure 10.9: Screenshot of video transcoding app showing video uploading form

The source code for the Django template for the home page is provided in Box 10.6. This template uses the jQuery smart wizard to get user inputs. The form inputs are processed in a

Video Transcoding App
a cloud-based app for video transcoding

Submit file for transcoding

1 Step 1 Choose video file
2 Step 2 Specify transcoding options
3 Step 3 Start transcoding

Specify Transcoding Options

Choose Preset:

Generic 1080p

Previous Next Finish

Figure 10.10: Screenshot of video transcoding app showing preset options

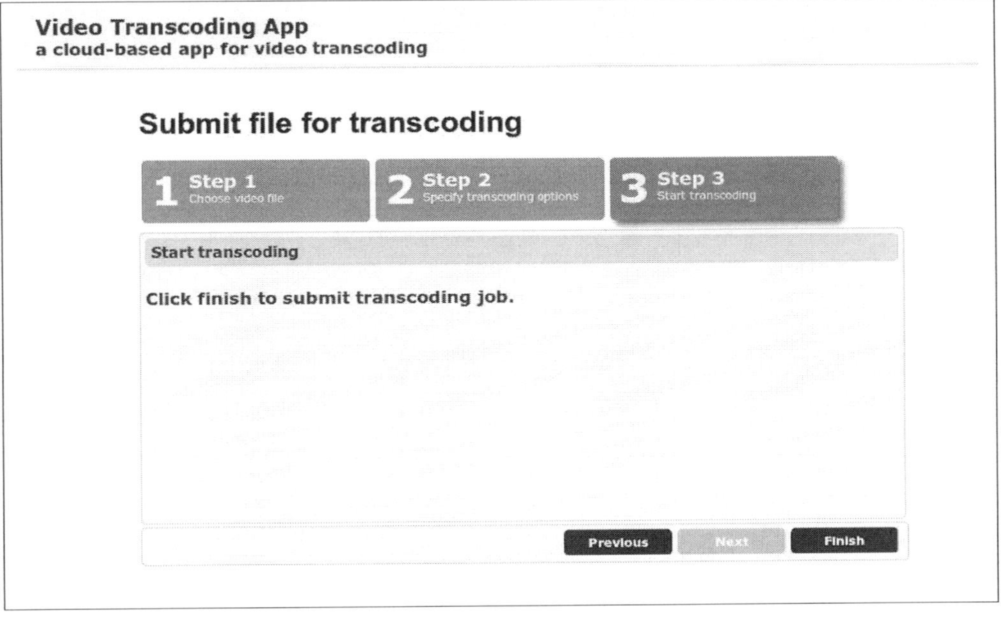

Figure 10.11: Screenshot of video transcoding app showing job submission form

Django view described later in this section.

■ Box 10.6: Django Template for Video Transcoding App - Home Page

```
<html xmlns="http://www.w3.org/1999/xhtml"><head>
<meta http-equiv="Content-Type" content="text/html; charset=UTF-8">
<title>Video Transcoding App</title>
<link href="/static/styles/demo_style.css" rel="stylesheet" type="text/css">
<link href="/static/styles/smart_wizard.css" rel="stylesheet" type="text/css">
<link href="/static/styles/bootstrap.css" rel="stylesheet" type="text/css">
<script type="text/javascript" src="/static/js/jquery-1.4.2.min.js"></script>
<script type="text/javascript" src="/static/js/jquery.smartWizard.js"></script>
<script type="text/javascript">
$(document).ready(function(){

    $('#wizard').smartWizard({transitionEffect:'fade',onFinish:onFinishCallback} );

function onFinishCallback(){
$('form').submit();
}
});
</script>
</head>

<body>
<div class="demoHead">
<div>
<div style="float:left;">
<h1>Video Transcoding App</h1>
<h2>a cloud-based app for video transcoding</h2>
</div>

<div style="clear:both;"></div>
</div>
</div>

<form action="/" method="post" enctype="multipart/form-data">
{% csrf_token %}
<br>
<table align="center" border="0" cellpadding="0" cellspacing="0">
<tr><td>
<h2>Submit file for transcoding</h2>
<div id="wizard" class="swMain">
<ul>
<li><a href="#step-1">
<label class="stepNumber">1</label>
<span class="stepDesc">
Step 1<br />
<small>Choose video file</small>
</span>
</a></li>
<li><a href="#step-2">
<label class="stepNumber">2</label>
<span class="stepDesc">
Step 2<br />
<small>Specify transcoding options</small>
</span>
</a></li>
```

```
<li><a href="#step-3">
<label class="stepNumber">3</label>
<span class="stepDesc">
Step 3<br />
<small>Start transcoding</small>
</span>
</a></li>

</ul>
<div id="step-1">
<h2 class="StepTitle">Choose Video File</h2>

<h4>Choose the video file to transcode:</h4>

<p>{{ form.non_field_errors }}</p>
<p>
{{ form.myfilefield.errors }}
{{ form.myfilefield }}
</p>

</div>
<div id="step-2">
<h2 class="StepTitle">Specify Transcoding Options</h2> <br>
<h4>Choose Preset:</h4>
<select name="preset">
<option value="1351620000001-000001">Generic 1080p</option>
<option value="1351620000001-000010">Generic 720p</option>
<option value="1351620000001-000020">Generic 480p 16:9</option>
<option value="1351620000001-000030">Generic 480p 4:3</option>
<option value="1351620000001-000040">Generic 360p 16:9</option>
<option value="1351620000001-000050">Generic 360p 4:3</option>
<option value="1351620000001-000060">Generic 320x240</option>
<option value="1351620000001-100070">Web</option>
</select>
</div>
<div id="step-3">
<h2 class="StepTitle">Start transcoding</h2>
<br>
<h4>Click finish to submit transcoding job.</h4><br>
</div>
</div>
</td></tr>
</table>
</form>

</body>
</html>
```

Figure 10.12 shows a screenshot of the video transcoding app after the video file is submitted by the user. The video files submitted for transcoding are uploaded to an Amazon S3 bucket and a new transcoding job is then created. The source for the Django template for video file submission confirmation page is provided in Box 10.7.

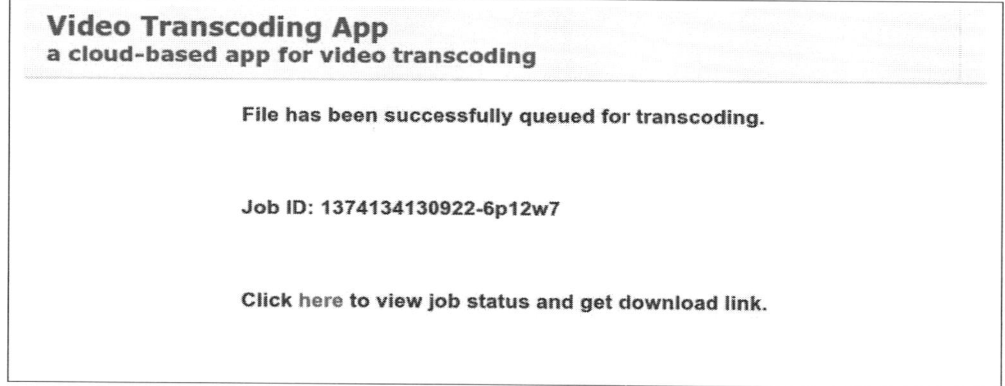

Figure 10.12: Screenshot of video transcoding app showing submitted job

■ Box 10.7: Django Template for Video Transcoding App - File Submitted Page

```
<html xmlns="http://www.w3.org/1999/xhtml"><head>
<meta http-equiv="Content-Type" content="text/html; charset=UTF-8">
<title>Video Transcoding App</title>
<link href="/static/styles/bootstrap.css" rel="stylesheet" type="text/css">
</head>
<body>

<div class="demoHead">
<div>
<div style="float:left;">
<h1>Video Transcoding App</h1>
<h2>a cloud-based app for video transcoding</h2>
</div>

<div style="clear:both;"></div>
</div>
</div>

<table align="center" border="0" cellpadding="0" cellspacing="0">
<tr><td>

<h4>File has been successfully queued for transcoding.</h4>
<br>
<br>
<h4>Job ID: {{jobid}}</h4>
<br>
<br>
<h4>Click <a href="jobstatus/{{jobid}}">here</a>

to view job status and get download link.</h4>

</td></tr>
</table>
</body>
```

```
</html>
```

After the video file is uploaded and a new transcoding job is created, the user can view the job status and obtain the download link for the transcoded video from the job status page. Figure 10.13 shows a screenshot the job status page. The source code for the Django template for the job status page is provided in Box 10.8.

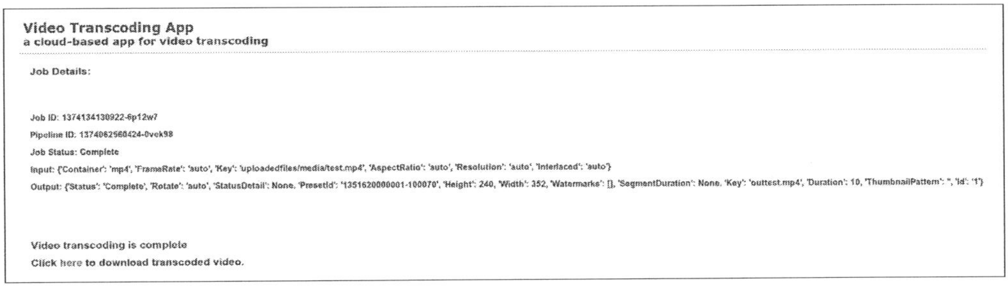

Figure 10.13: Screenshot of video transcoding app showing job status and download link

■ Box 10.8: Django Template for Video Transcoding App - Job Status Page

```
<html xmlns="http://www.w3.org/1999/xhtml">
<head>
<meta http-equiv="Content-Type" content="text/html; charset=UTF-8">
<title>Video Transcoding App</title>
<link href="/static/styles/bootstrap.css" rel="stylesheet" type="text/css">
</head>

<body>
<div class="demoHead">
<div>
<div style="float:left;">
<h1>Video Transcoding App</h1>
<h2>a cloud-based app for video transcoding</h2>
</div>

<div style="clear:both;"></div>
</div>
</div>

<table align="center" border="0" cellpadding="0" cellspacing="0">
<tr><td>
<h4>Job Details:</h4>
<br><br><h5>Job ID: {{jobid}}</h5>
<h5>Pipeline ID: {{pipelineid}}</h5>
<h5>Job Status: {{status}}</h5>
<h5>Input: {{jobinput}}</h5>
<h5>Output: {{jobputput}}</h5>
<br><br><br>
{% if status == 'Complete' %}
<h4>Video transcoding is complete</h4>
```

```
<h4>Click <a href="http://mybucketname.s3.amazonaws.com/{{outputfilename}} ">
here</a> to download transcoded video.</h4>
{% endif %}

</td></tr>
</table>
</body>
</html>
```

Box 10.9 provides the URL patterns for the Django application for video transcoding.

■ Box 10.9: Django URL Patterns for Video Transcoding App

```
from django.conf.urls.defaults import *

urlpatterns = patterns('',
    url(r'$', 'myapp.views.home'),
    url(r'process/$', 'myapp.views.process'),
    url(r'jobstatus/(?P<jobid>($w$ -)+)$', 'myapp.views.jobstatus'),
)
```

Box 10.10 provides the source code for the Django form for uploading the video file. In this form a FileField is defined. The form is processed in the View.

■ Box 10.10: Django Form for Video Transcoding App

```
from django import forms

class UploadFileForm(forms.Form):
    myfilefield = forms.FileField()
```

■ Box 10.11: Django View for Video Transcoding App

```
    from django.shortcuts import render_to_response
from django.template import RequestContext
from django.http import HttpResponseRedirect
from myapp.forms import UploadFileForm
from s3upload import upload_to_s3_bucket_path
import boto.elastictranscoder

ACCESS_KEY="<enter access key>"
SECRET_KEY="<enter sectret key>"
REGION="us-east-1"
PIPELINEID="<enter pipeline id>"

def transcode(filenamepath, filename,preset):
    conn = boto.elastictranscoder.connect_to_region(REGION,
     aws_access_key_id=ACCESS_KEY,
```

```
    aws_secret_access_key=SECRET_KEY)

    outfilename = "out"+filename

    jobinput={
     "Key":filenamepath,
     "FrameRate":"auto",
     "Resolution":"auto",
     "AspectRatio":"auto",
     "Interlaced":"auto",
     "Container":"mp4"
     }

    joboutputs=(
     {
         "Key":outfilename,
         "ThumbnailPattern":"",
         "Rotate":"auto",
         "PresetId":preset,
         "Watermarks":()
     }
     )

    result = conn.create_job(pipeline_id=PIPELINEID, input_name=jobinput,
    output=None, outputs=joboutputs, output_key_prefix=None, playlists=None)
    jobid=result('Job')('Id')
    status=result('Job')('Status')
    return jobid,status


def handle_uploaded_file(f,preset):
    uploadfilename='media/' + f.name
    with open(uploadfilename, 'wb+') as destination:
        for chunk in f.chunks():
            destination.write(chunk)

    upload_to_s3_bucket_path('mybucketname', 'uploadedfiles', uploadfilename)
    jobid,status=transcode('uploadedfiles/'+uploadfilename, f.name,preset)
    return jobid,status

def home(request):
    if request.method == 'POST':
        form = UploadFileForm(request.POST, request.FILES)
        if form.is_valid():
         preset=request.POST('preset')
         jobid,status=handle_uploaded_file(request.FILES('myfilefield'),preset)
        return          render_to_response('process.html',{'jobid':          jobid, 'status': sta-
tus},
context_instance=RequestContext(request))
    else:
        form = UploadFileForm()
    return render_to_response('index.html',{'form': form},
        context_instance=RequestContext(request))
```

```
def process(request):
    return render_to_response('process.html', {})


def jobstatus(request,jobid):
    conn = boto.elastictranscoder.connect_to_region(REGION,
     aws_access_key_id=ACCESS_KEY,
     aws_secret_access_key=SECRET_KEY)

    result = conn.read_job(id=jobid)

    jobinput=result['Job']['Input']
    jobputput=result['Job']['Outputs'][0]
    pipelineid=result['Job']['PipelineId']
    outputfilename=jobputput['Key']

    status=result['Job']['Status']

    return render_to_response('jobstatus.html', {'jobid':jobid,
        'jobinput': jobinput,          'jobputput': jobputput, 'pipelineid': pipelineid,
        'outputfilename':outputfilename, 'status': status})
```

■ **Box 10.12: Source code for uploading file to S3 bucket**

```
import os
import boto.s3

ACCESS_KEY="<enter access key>"
SECRET_KEY="<enter sectret key>"

conn = boto.connect_s3(aws_access_key_id=ACCESS_KEY,
    aws_secret_access_key=SECRET_KEY)

def percent_cb(complete, total):
    print ('.')

def upload_to_s3_bucket_path(bucketname, path, filename):
    mybucket = conn.get_bucket(bucketname)
    fullkeyname=os.path.join(path,filename)
    key = mybucket.new_key(fullkeyname)
    key.set_contents_from_filename(filename, cb=percent_cb, num_cb=10)
```

Box 10.11 provides the source code for the Django View for the video transcoding app. The *home* function processes the home page request and renders the home page with the file submission wizard. This function checks if a request has been submitted and then processed the request and handles the file upload using *handle_uploaded_file* function. The video file submitted by the user is uploaded to the media directory in the Django application (defined as MEDIA_ROOT and MEDIA_URL in the Django project settings). After the file is uploaded to the media directory, the *upload_to_s3_bucket_path* function is called which uploads the file to an S3 bucket. This step is required because the Amazon Elastic Transcoder accepts video files for transcoding from S3 buckets only. After the file is uploaded to S3 bucket, the transcode function is called. In this function a new transcoding job is created and job-ID and job status are returned. The *jobstatus* function processes the request for the job status page. In this function the status of the transcoding job is retrieved and rendered in the Django template. When the job is complete the download link for the transcoded video file is rendered in the job status template.

Box 10.12 provides the source code of the *upload_to_s3_bucket_path* function which is called in the Django View. This function uploads a file to an S3 bucket.

Summary

In this chapter you learned about a reference architecture for multimedia cloud consisting of infrastructure services, platform services and applications. This chapter describes actual application development for live video streaming and video transcoding applications. RTMP and HTTP Live Streaming and HTTP Dynamic Streaming are popular streaming protocols. RTMP is a protocol for streaming audio, video and data over the Internet, between Adobe Flash Platform technologies, including Adobe Flash Player and Adobe AIR. HTTP Live Streaming supports multiple alternate segment-based streams at different bit rates, and the mobile client software can switch streams intelligently as network bandwidth changes. HTTP Dynamic Streaming combines HTTP (progressive download) and RTMP (streaming download) and provides the ability to deliver video content in a streaming manner over HTTP using standard Web servers.

Review Questions

1. What is the difference between HTTP Live Streaming and HTTP Dynamic Streaming?
2. What are the benefits of HTTP Live Streaming and HTTP Dynamic Streaming over RTMP?
3. What is the function of a pipeline in Amazon Elastic Transcoder?

Lab Exercises

1. Extend the live video streaming app described in section 12.2 to support archiving of live streamed videos. Use a cloud storage such as Amazon S3 for archiving videos.

2. In this exercise you will develop a video gallery application. Follow the steps below:
   - Create a Django application that allows you to browse and videos stored on a cloud storage and upload new videos.
   - When a new video is uploaded it is transcoded to MP4 format. Use Amazon Elastic Transcoder for video transcoding.

11 — Cloud Application Benchmarking & Tuning

This Chapter Covers

- Cloud application workload characteristics
- Performance metrics for cloud applications
- Cloud application testing
- Performance testing tools
- Load test and bottleneck detection case study

11.1 Introduction

Multi-tier applications deployed in cloud computing environments can experience rapid changes in their workloads, which is also the reason why cloud computing has been preferred over traditional in-house resources. To ensure market readiness of such applications, adequate resources need to be provisioned so that the applications can meet the demands of specified workload levels and at the same time ensure that service level agreements are met.

Provisioning and capacity planning is a challenging task for complex multi-tier applications such as e-Commerce, Business-to-Business, Health care, Banking and Financial, Retail and Social Networking applications deployed in cloud computing environments. Each class of applications has different deployment configurations with web servers, application servers and database servers. Over-provisioning in advance for such systems is not economically feasible. Cloud computing provides a promising approach of dynamically scaling up or scaling down the capacity based on the application workload. For resource management and capacity planning decisions, it is important to understand the workload characteristics of such systems, measure the sensitivity of the application performance to the workload attributes and detect bottlenecks in the systems. Performance testing of cloud-based applications prior to deployment can reveal bottlenecks in the system and support provisioning and capacity planning decisions. With performance testing it is possible to predict application performance under heavy workloads and identify bottlenecks in the system so that failures can be prevented. Bottlenecks, once detected, can be resolved by provisioning additional computing resources, by either scaling up systems (instances with more computing capacity) or scaling out systems (more instances of the same kind).

Multi-tier cloud applications can have complex deployment configurations with load balancers, web servers, application servers and database servers relating to both data and business backends. Complex dependencies may exist between servers in various tiers. To support provisioning and capacity planning decisions, performance testing approaches with synthetic workloads are used. Accuracy of a performance testing approach is determined by how closely the generated synthetic workloads mimic the realistic workloads. In this chapter you will learn about the need for benchmarking cloud applications, workload characteristics and workload modeling approaches.

Benchmarking of cloud applications is important or the following reasons:

- Provisioning and capacity planning: The process of provisioning and capacity planning for cloud applications involves determining the amount of computing, memory and network resources to provision for the application. Though from the standpoint of a user, the cloud computing resources should look limit-less, however due to complex dependencies that exist between servers in various tiers, applications can experience performance bottlenecks. Benchmarking can help in comparing alternative deployment architectures and choosing the best and most cost effective deployment architecture that can meet the application performance requirements. Since multi-tier applications can experience seasonal variations in workloads, benchmarking may need to be done on a regular basis to ensure the market readiness of such applications at all times.
- Ensure proper utilization of resources: Benchmarking can help in determining the utilization of computing, memory and network resources for applications and identify resources which are either under-utilized or over-provisioned and hence save

deployments costs.

- Market readiness of applications: Performance of an application depends on the characteristics of the workloads it experiences. Different types of workloads can dead to different performance for the same application. To ensure the market readiness of an application it is important to model all types of workloads the application can experience and benchmark the application with such workloads.

The steps involved in benchmarking of cloud applications are described below:

11.1.1 Trace Collection/Generation

The first step in benchmarking cloud applications is to collect/generate traces of real application workloads. For generating a trace of workload, the application is instrumented to log information such as the requests submitted by the users, the time-stamps of the requests, etc.

11.1.2 Workload Modeling

Workload modeling involves creation of mathematical models that can be used for generation of synthetic workloads. Workloads of applications are often recorded as traces of workload related events such as arrival of requests along with the time-stamps, details about the users requesting the services, etc. Analysis of such traces can provide insights into the workload characteristics which can be used for formulating mathematical models for the workloads.

11.1.3 Workload Specification

Since the workload models of each class of cloud computing applications can have different workload attributes, a Workload Specification Language (WSL) is often used for specification of application workloads. WSL can provide a structured way for specifying the workload attributes that are critical to the performance of the applications. WSL can be used by synthetic workload generators for generating workloads with slightly varying the characteristics. This can be used to perform sensitivity analysis of the application performance to the workload attributes by generating synthetic workloads.

11.1.4 Synthetic Workload Generation

Synthetic workloads are used for benchmarking cloud applications. An important requirement for a synthetic workload generator is that the generated workloads should be representative of the real workloads and should preserve the important characteristics of real workloads such as inter-session and intra-session intervals, etc. There are two approaches to synthetic workload generation:

- Empirical approach: In this approach traces of applications are sampled and replayed to generate the synthetic workloads.
- Analytical approach: This approach uses mathematical models to define the workload characteristics that are used by a synthetic workload generator.

The empirical approach lacks flexibility as the real traces obtained from a particular system are used for workload generation which may not well represent the workloads on other systems with different configurations and load conditions. On the other hand, the analytical approach is flexible and allows generation of workloads with different characteristics by varying the workload model attributes. With the analytical approach it is possible to modify the workload model parameters one at a time and investigate the effect on application performance to measure the application sensitivity to different parameters.

11.1.5 User Emulation vs Aggregate Workloads

The commonly used techniques for workload generation are user emulation and aggregate workload generation. In user emulation, each user is emulated by a separate thread that mimics the actions of a user by alternating between making requests and lying idle. The attributes for workload generation in the user emulation method include think time, request types, inter-request dependencies, for instance. User emulation allows fine grained control over modeling the behavioral aspects of the users interacting with the system under test, however, it does not allow controlling the exact time instants at which the requests arrive the system. This is because in user emulation, a new request is issued only after the response to the previous request has been received. Thus, due to network delays, heavy loads on system under test, for instance, the intervals between successive requests increase.

Aggregate workload generation is another approach that allows specifying the exact time instants at which the requests should arrive the system under test. However, there is no notion of an individual user in aggregate workload generation, therefore, it is not possible to use this approach when dependencies between requests need to be satisfied. Dependencies can be of two types inter-request and data dependencies. An inter-request dependency exists when the current request depends on the previous request, whereas a data dependency exists when the current requests requires input data which is obtained from the response of the previous request.

11.2 Workload Characteristics

Each class of multi-tier applications can have their own characteristic workloads. A successful performance evaluation methodology should be able to accurately model the application workloads. Workload modeling involves creation of mathematical models that can be used for generation of synthetic workloads. Characteristics of application workloads include:

- **Session:** A set of successive requests submitted by a user constitute a session.
- **Inter-Session Interval:** Inter-session interval is the time interval between successive sessions.
- **Think Time:** In a session, a user submits a series of requests in succession. The time interval between two successive requests is called think time. Think time is the inactive period between subsequent requests in a session. It is the time taken by the user to review the response of a request and decide what the next request should be.
- **Session Length:** The number of requests submitted by a user in a session is called the session length.
- **Workload Mix:** Workload mix defines the transitions between different pages of an application and the proportion in which the pages are visited. Multi-tier cloud applications can experience rapid changes in their workloads. Workload characteristics of an application may also vary widely based on the kind of user interactions with an application. An e-Commerce application, for example, can experience database write-intensive workloads during the times of a year when a large number of users are purchasing products online. Whereas, the same application can have a read-intensive

workload mix when users are only browsing for products.

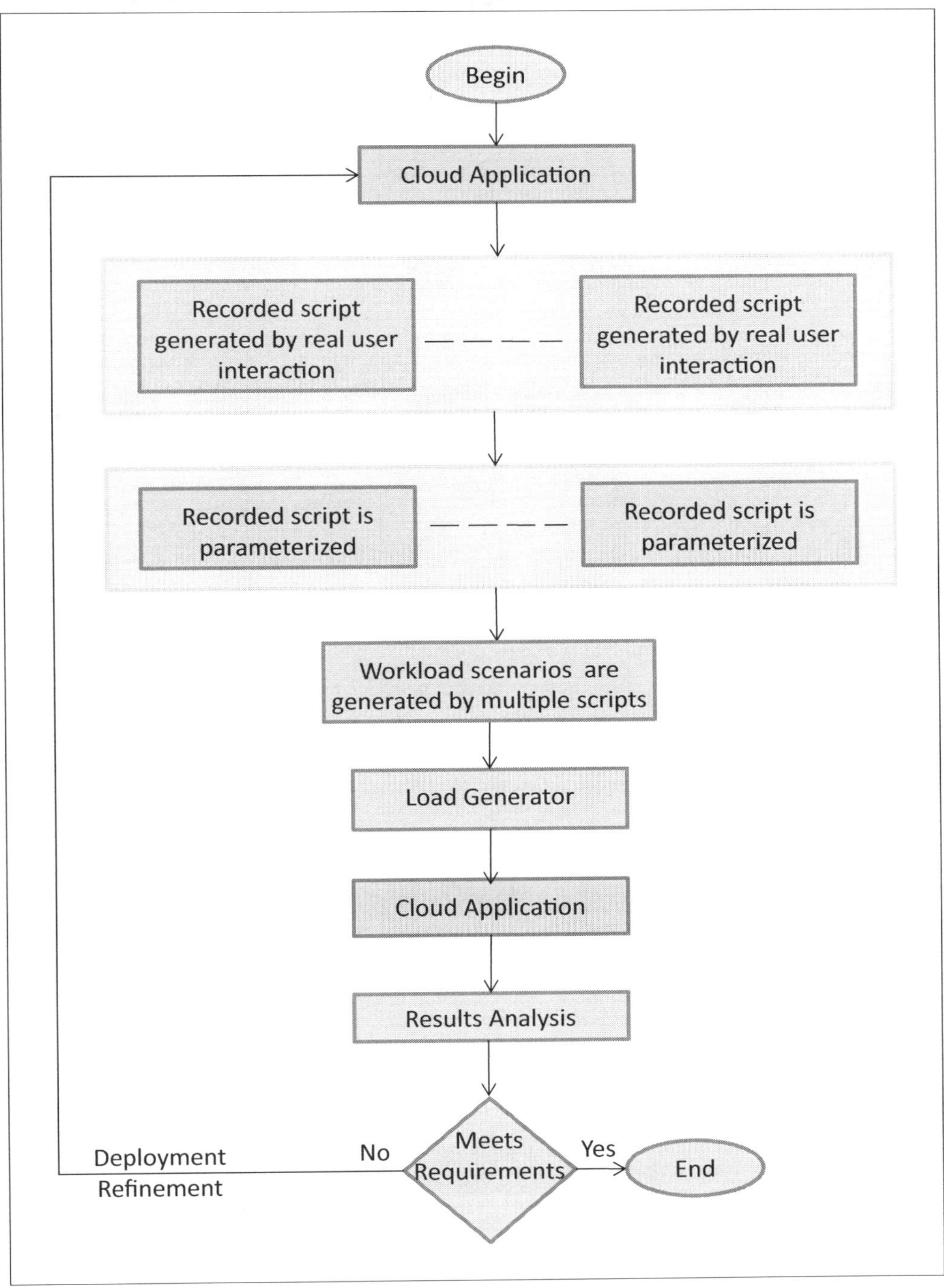

Figure 11.1: Traditional performance evaluation workflow based on a semi- automated approach. A real user has to first manually interact with the application to record scripts and then parameterize recorded scripts to generate scripts for creating virtual users.

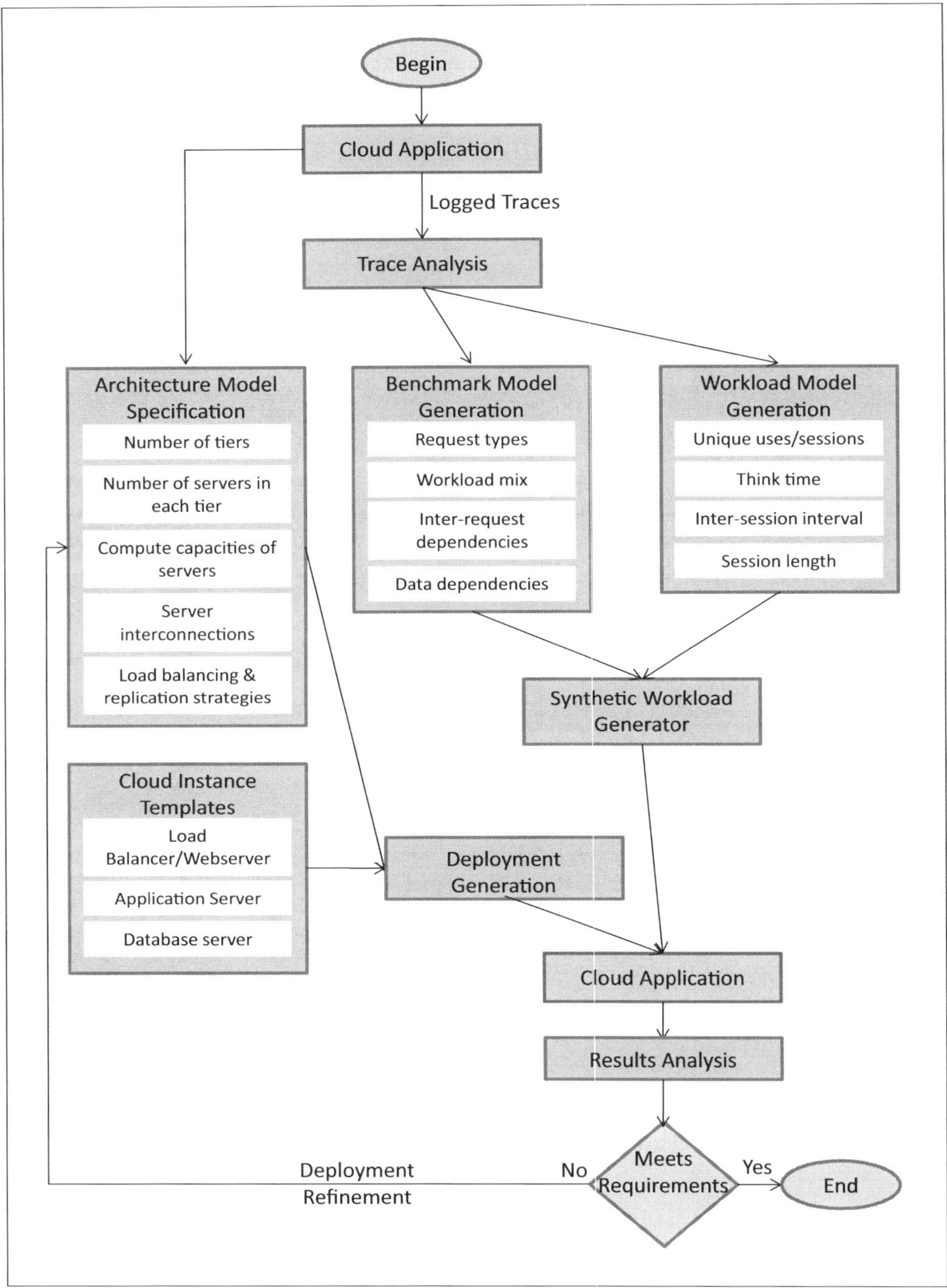

Figure 11.2: Automated performance evaluation workflow used by recent tools such as GT-CAT.

Tool	Application & Approach	Input/Output & Model
httperf [52]	Application: A tool that generates various HTTP workloads for measuring server performance. Approach: Has a core HTTP engine, a workload generation module and a statistics collection module.	Input: Request URLs, specifications of the request rates, number of connections, for instance. Output: Requests generated at the specified rate. Models: No models used.
SURGE [53]	Application: Request generation for testing network and server performance Approach: Uses an offline trace generation engine to create traces of requests. Web characteristics such as file sizes, request sizes, popularity, temporal locality, etc are statistically modeled.	Input: Pre-computed datasets consisting of the sequence of requests to be made. Output: Synthetic workload that agrees with six distributional models. Model: Six distributional models make up the SURGE model.
SWAT [54]	Application: Stress testing session-based web applications. Approach: Uses a trace generation engine that takes sessionlets (a sequence of request types from a real system user) as input and produces an output trace of sessions for stress test. SWAT uses httperf for request generation.	Input: Trace of sessionlets obtained from access logs of a live system under test, specifications of think time, session length, session inter-arrival time, for instance. Output: Trace of sessions for stress test. Model: Workload model used that consists of attributes such as session inter-arrival time, session length, think time, request inter-arrival time and workload mix.
HP Load-Runner [55]	Application: Performance testing of web applications. Approach: Based on empirical modeling approach. A browser based Virtual User Generator is used for interactive recording and scripting. Scripts are generated by recording activities of a real user interaction with the application.	Input: Load generators take the virtual user scripts as input. Output: Synthetic workloads. Model: Empirical modeling approach used. Recorded scripts are parameterized to account for randomness in application and workload parameters.
GT-CAT [56]	Application: Performance testing of multi-tier cloud applications. Approach: Based on analytical modeling approach. Benchmark and workload models are generated by analysis of real traces of the application. Synthetic workload generator generates synthetic workloads.	Input: Logged traces of real application. Output: Synthetic workload that has the same workload characteristics as real workloads. Model: Benchmark, Workload & Architecture models used.

Table 11.1: Performance evaluation tools for cloud applications

11.3 Application Performance Metrics

The most commonly used performance metrics for cloud applications are as follows:

Response Time

Response time is the time interval between the moment when the user submits a request to the application and the moment when the user receives a response. Response time includes various components as given in the following equation,

$$R = \frac{D}{B} + T_{RTT} + T_S + T_C \tag{11.1}$$

where D is the amount of data transfer required to serve the user request, B is the minimum bandwidth across all links in the network from the user to the application deployment, T_{RTT} is the round trip time for user-application interactions that are needed to generate the response, T_S is the total processing time required by all the tiers of the application deployment and T_C is the total processing time required by the user's device.

Throughput

Throughput is the number of requests that can be serviced per second. If an application receives N requests per second and only $(N-M)$ can be serviced in a second, then M requests will wait in a queue.

Performance requirements are typically specified as a series of service level objectives (SLOs) that define response time or throughput requirements for each request in the application.

11.4 Design Considerations for a Benchmarking Methodology

Let us look at the important design considerations for a benchmarking methodology:

- **Accuracy:** The effectiveness of any benchmarking methodology is defined by how accurately it is able to model the performance of the application. Accuracy of a benchmarking methodology is determined by how closely the generated synthetic workloads mimic the realistic workloads. Aggregate workload generation techniques can run into difficulties when inter-request or data dependencies exist. In such cases the user emulation approach is preferred where the workload characterizations are in the form of the behavior of an individual user. Accurate modeling of application workload characteristics is required to generate workloads that are representative of the real workloads.
- **Ease of Use:** A good benchmarking methodology should be user friendly and should involve minimal hand coding effort for writing scripts for workload generation that take into account the dependencies between requests, workload attributes, for instance.
- **Flexibility:** A good benchmarking methodology should allow fine grained control over the workload attributes such as think time, inter-session interval, session length, workload mix, for instance. to perform sensitivity analysis. Sensitivity analysis is performed by varying one workload characteristic at a time while keeping the others constant.

- **Wide Application Coverage:** A good benchmarking methodology is one that works for a wide range of applications and not tied to the application architecture or workload types.

11.5 Benchmarking Tools

There are several workload generation tools developed to study web applications such as httperf [52], SURGE [53], SWAT [54], HP LoadRunner [55], and SPECweb99 [57]. Such workload generation tools repeatedly send requests from machines configured as clients to the intended systems under test. Table 11.1 provides a comparison of few workload generation tools. Several other tools generate synthetic workloads through transformation (eg. permutation) of empirical workload traces [58, 59, 60]. Several studies on analysis and modeling of web workloads have been done [61, 62]. Since obtaining real traces from complex multi-tier systems is difficult, a number of benchmarks have been developed to model the real systems [63, 64, 65]. Figure 11.1 shows a workflow used by traditional performance evaluation approaches, which require a real user to interact with the application to record scripts that are used by load generators. Figure 11.2 shows the performance evaluation workflow used by recent tools such as GT-CAT [56] developed by the authors.

Let us look at the differences between the approaches shows in Figures 11.1 and 11.2.

- **Capturing Workload Characteristics:** In traditional approach shown in Figure 11.1, to capture workload characteristics, a real user's interactions with a cloud application are first recorded as virtual user scripts. The recorded virtual user scripts then are parameterized to account for randomness in application and workload parameters. There is no underlying statistical model involved in such approaches as recorded scripts are used to drive the load generators. In the automated approach shown in Figure 11.2, real traces of a multi-tier application which are logged on web servers, application servers and database servers are analyzed to generate benchmark and workload models that capture the cloud application and workload characteristics. A statistical analysis of the user requests in the real traces is performed to identify the right distributions that can be used to model the workload model attributes.
- **Automated Performance Evaluation:** In the traditional approach, multiple scripts have to be recorded to create different workload scenarios. This approach involves a lot of manual effort. In order to add new specifications for workload mix and new requests, new scripts need to be recorded and parameterized. Writing additional scripts for new requests may be complex and time consuming as inter-request dependencies need to be taken care of. In the automated approach, real traces are analyzed to generate benchmark and workload models. Various workload scenarios can be created by changing the specifications of the workload model. New specifications for workload mix and new requests can be specified by making changes in the benchmark model. This approach is faster as compared to the traditional approach in which multiple virtual user scripts have to be recorded and parameterized to generate various workload scenarios. The benchmark and workload models drive the synthetic workload generator. The approach shown in Figure 11.2 automates the entire performance evaluation workflow right from capturing user behavior into workload and benchmark models to generating synthetic workloads which have the same characteristics as real workloads.

- **Realistic Workloads:** Traditional approaches which are based on manually generating virtual user scripts by interacting with a cloud application, are not able to generate synthetic workloads which have the same characteristics as real workloads. Although the traditional approaches allow creation of various workload scenarios using multiple recorded virtual user scripts, however, these workload scenarios are generally over simplifications of real-world scenarios in which a very large number of users may be simultaneously interacting with a cloud application. In the automated approach, since real traces from a cloud application are used to capture workload and application characteristics into workload and benchmark models, the generated synthetic workloads have the same characteristics as real workloads. By statistical analysis of the user requests in the real traces, the automated approach is able to identify the right distributions that can be used to model the workload model attributes such as think time, inter-session interval and session length.
- **Rapid Deployment Prototyping:** Traditional approaches do now allow rapidly comparing various deployment architectures. Based on the performance evaluation results, the deployments have to be refined manually and additional virtual user scripts have to be generated with new deployments. In the automated approach, an architecture model captures the deployment configurations of multi-tier applications. With this approach complex deployments can be created rapidly, and a comparative performance analysis on various deployment configurations can be accomplished.

11.5.1 Types of Tests

There are various types of tests that can be done using the benchmarking tools described in Table 11.1, including:

- **Baseline Tests:** Baseline tests are done to collect the performance metrics data of the entire application or a component of the application. The performance metrics data collected from baseline tests is used to compare various performance tuning changes which are subsequently made to the application or a component. Base line tests are usually done with a small number of users (eg. 1, 10 and 100) and the data on performance metrics such as response time, throughput, CPU, memory and network utilization of various servers, for instance. is collected. Whenever a change in the application is done, the baseline tests can be used to compare if the performance improves or degrades with the changes.
- **Load Tests:** Load tests evaluate the performance of the system with multiple users and workload levels that are encountered in the production phase. The number of users and workload mix are usually specified in the load test configuration.
- **Stress Tests:** Stress tests load the application to a point where it breaks down. The workload levels in stress tests are set beyond what are anticipated in the production phase. These tests are done to determine how the application fails, the conditions in which the application fails and the metrics to monitor which can warn about impending failures under elevated workload levels.
- **Soak Tests:** Soak tests involve subjecting the application to a fixed workload level for long periods of time. Soak tests help in determining the stability of the application under prolonged use and how the performance changes with time.

11.6 Deployment Prototyping

From the standpoint of a user, the cloud computing resources should look limit-less, however due to complex dependencies that exist between servers in various tiers, applications can experience performance bottlenecks. Deployment prototyping can help in making deployment architecture design choices. By comparing performance of alternative deployment architectures, deployment prototyping can help in choosing the best and most cost effective deployment architecture that can meet the application performance requirements. Since multi-tier applications can experience seasonal variations in workloads, deployment prototyping may need to be done on a regular basis to ensure the market readiness of such applications at all times.

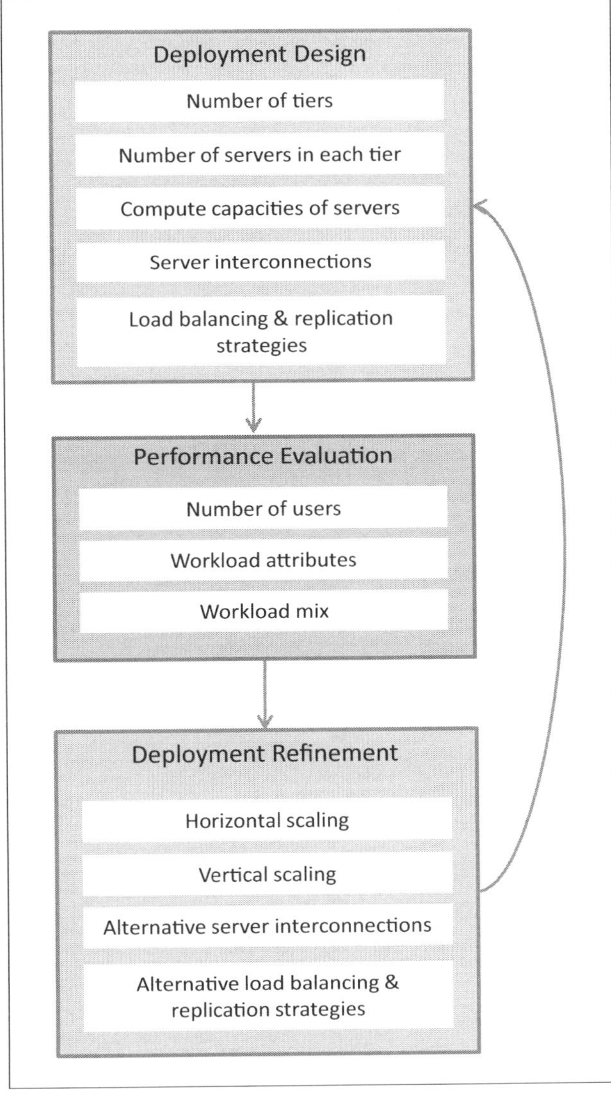

Figure 11.3: Steps involved in deployment prototyping for a cloud application

Figure 11.3 shows the steps involved in the deployment prototyping along with the variables involved in each step. Given the performance requirements for an application, the deployment design is an iterative process that involves the following steps:

- **Deployment Design:** Create the deployment with various tiers as specified in the deployment configuration and deploy the application.
- **Performance Evaluation:** Verify whether the application meets the performance requirements with the deployment.
- **Deployment Refinement:** Deployments are refined based on the performance evaluations. Various alternatives can exist in this step such as vertical scaling, horizontal scaling, for instance.

11.7 Load Testing & Bottleneck Detection Case Study

This section provides a case study of load testing and benchmarking an application with a multi-tier cloud deployment as shown in Figure 11.4. For this case study, the Rice University Bidding System [64] benchmark is used. RUBiS is an auction site prototype which has been loosely modeled after the internet auction website eBay. The RUBiS PHP application is deployed on the application servers and a MySQL database is setup on the database server. For measuring system statistics *collectd* utility is used. *collectd* is a daemon which collects system performance statistics periodically and provides mechanisms to store the values in a variety of ways, for example in RRD files, CSV files, for instance. collectd gathers statistics about the system it is running on and stores this information. The collected statistics can then be used to find performance bottlenecks and predict future system load. *collectd* comes with over 90 plugins including plugins for monitoring CPU, Disk, Memory, Network, for instance. Box 11.1 shows the commands for installing and configuring *collectd*.

■ Box 11.1: Configuring collectd for monitoring resources

```
#Install collectd
$sudo apt-get install collectd

#Configure collectd
$vim /etc/collectd.conf

#Add the following configuration settings
#to the collectd.conf file:
_______________________________
Hostname "master"
Interval 10
ReadThreads 5
LoadPlugin syslog
<Plugin syslog>
LogLevel info
</Plugin>
LoadPlugin csv
<Plugin csv>
DataDir "/var/lib/collectd/csv"
StoreRates true
```

```
</Plugin>
LoadPlugin cpu
LoadPlugin df
LoadPlugin disk
LoadPlugin load
LoadPlugin memory
LoadPlugin swap
LoadPlugin users
LoadPlugin interface
<Plugin interface>
Interface "eth0"
</Plugin>
Include "/etc/collectd.d/*.conf"
```

```
#Restart collectd
$/etc/init.d/collectd restart
```

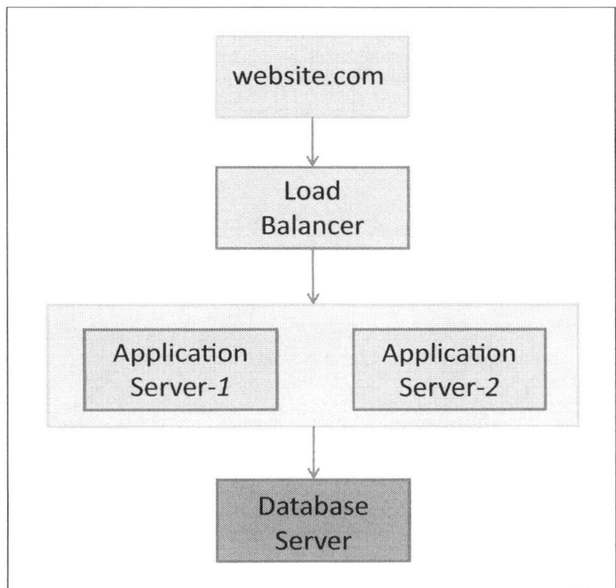

Figure 11.4: Multi-tier deployment architecture for sample application for case study

Box 11.2 shows a python program used for load testing the application. This program uses httperfpy package [66] which is a wrapper over httpef tool. The program in Box 11.2 shows how to perform multiple tests at different demanded request rates. In each step the demanded request rate is increased by 10 and various metrics are recorded such as the observed request rate, response time, for instance.

Figure 11.5 (a) shows the average throughput and response time. The observed throughput increases as demanded request rate increases. As more number of requests are served per second by the application, the response time also increases. The observed throughput saturates beyond a demanded request rate of 50 req/sec. Figure 11.5 (b) shows the CPU usage density of one of the application servers. This plot shows that the application server CPU is non-saturated resource. Figure 11.5 (c) shows the database server CPU usage density.

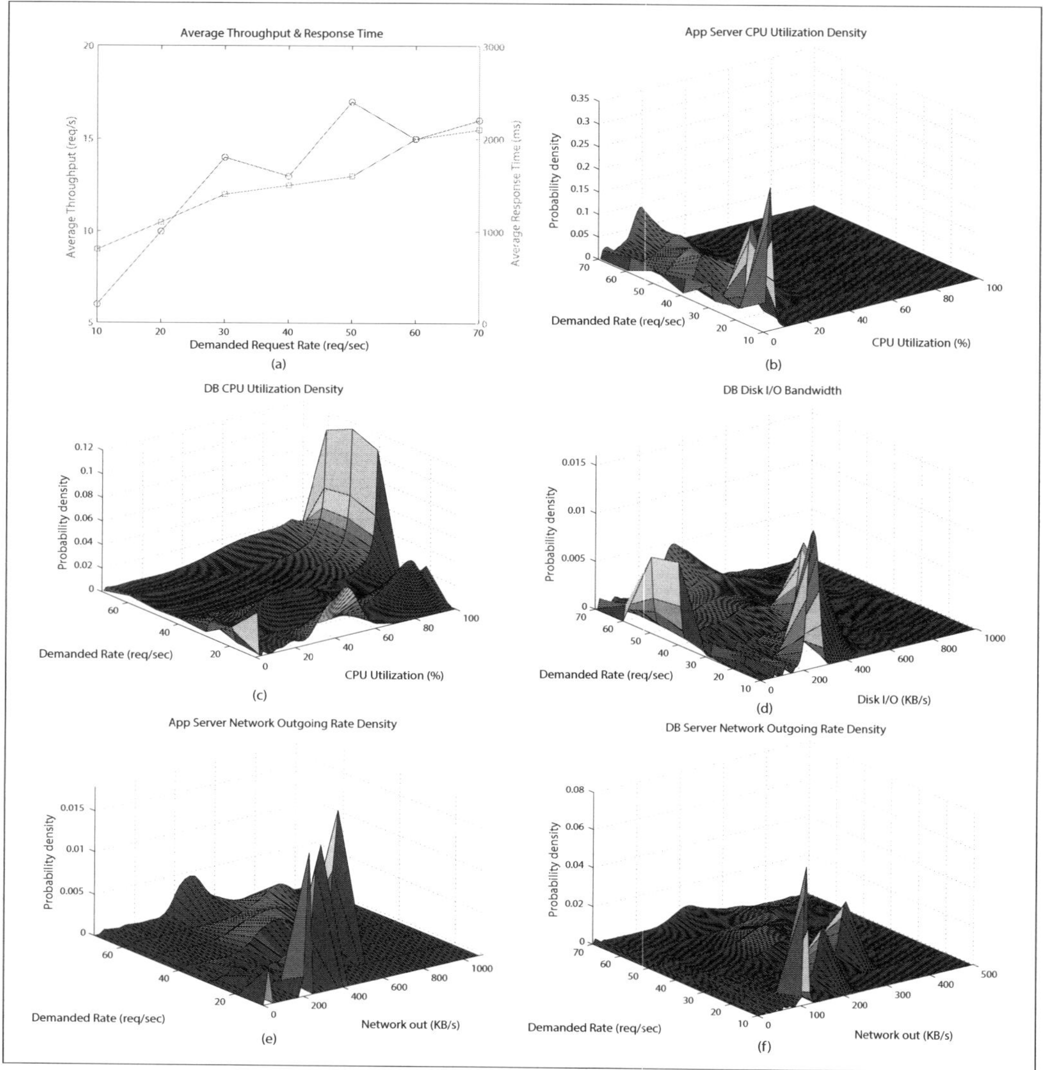

Figure 11.5: (a) Plot of average throughput and response time results obtained from load testing with httperf, (b) Application server-1 CPU utilization density, (c) Database server CPU utilization density, (d) Database server disk I/O bandwidth, (e) Application server-1 network outgoing rate density, (f) Database server network outgoing rate density.

From this density plot we observe that the database CPU spends a large percentage of time at high utilization levels for demanded request rate more than 40 req/sec. Figure 11.5 (d) shows the density plot of the database disk I/O bandwidth. Figure 11.5 (e) shows the network out rate for one of the application servers and Figure 11.5 (f) shows the density plot of the network out rate for the database server. From this plot we observe a continuous saturation of the network out rate around 200 KB/s.

■ Box 11.2: Python program for load testing a cloud application using httperf

```
#!/usr/bin/env python

from httperfpy import Httperf

#Run in 5 steps and increment request rate by 10 in each step
for i in range(10,60,10):
    print 'Rate='+str(i)
    perf = Httperf(server="www.mywebsite.com",
            port=80,rate=i,num_calls=50, num_conns=400,timeout=60,
        send_buffer=4096,recv_buffer=16384)

    perf.parser = True

    results = perf.run()

    print 'Request rate per sec, Connection rate per sec,
        Avg reply rate, Max reply rate, Response Time'
    print results("request_rate_per_sec") + ', '+ results("connection_rate_per_sec") + ', '+
            results("reply_rate_avg") + ',
        '+ results("reply_rate_max")+', '+ results("reply_time_response")
```

Analyzing the plots in Figure 11.5 we observe that throughput continuously increases as the demanded request rate increases from 10 to 40 req/sec. Beyond 40 req/sec demanded request rate, we observe that throughput saturates, which is due to the high CPU utilization density of the database server CPU. From the analysis of density plots of various system resources we observe that the database CPU is a system bottleneck.

This case study demonstrates that by running the load tests with httperf several times with monotonically increasing request rates, the observed throughput saturates. Further, by analyzing the CPU, disk I/O and network utilizations of the various servers in the application deployment, we were able to detect the bottleneck in the deployment. This bottleneck can be resolved by scaling up (vertical scaling) or scaling out (horizontal scaling) the database tier.

11.8 Hadoop Benchmarking Case Study

In Chapter 4 you have learned about the components of Hadoop, MapReduce job execution flow, Hadoop schedulers, and how to setup a Hadoop cluster. In this section you will learn how to configure different schedulers in Hadoop and benchmark the performance of a Hadoop cluster. For the experiments in this section, a Hadoop cluster comprising of two nodes (master and slave) is created. Fair Scheduler and Capacity Schedulers are configured for the experiments and their performance is benchmarked.

■ Box 11.3: Configuring Fair Scheduler - mapred-site.xml

```
<?xml version="1.0"?>
<?xml-stylesheet type="text/xsl" href="configuration.xsl"?>

<configuration>
```

```
<property>
<name>mapred.job.tracker</name>
<value>master:54311</value>
</property>

<property>
<name>mapred.jobtracker.taskScheduler</name>
</property>

</configuration>
```

■ Box 11.4: Configuring Fair Scheduler - fair-scheduler.xml

```
<?xml version="1.0"?>
<allocations>
<pool name="user1">
<minMaps>5</minMaps>
<minReduces>5</minReduces>
<maxMaps>25</maxMaps>
<maxReduces>25</maxReduces>
<minSharePreemptionTimeout>300</minSharePreemptionTimeout>
</pool>
<user name="user1">
<maxRunningJobs>6</maxRunningJobs>
</user>
<userMaxJobsDefault>3</userMaxJobsDefault>
<fairSharePreemptionTimeout>600</fairSharePreemptionTimeout>
:
<pool name="user3">
<minMaps>5</minMaps>
<minReduces>5</minReduces>
<maxMaps>25</maxMaps>
<maxReduces>25</maxReduces>
<minSharePreemptionTimeout>300</minSharePreemptionTimeout>
</pool>
<user name="user3">
<maxRunningJobs>6</maxRunningJobs>
</user>
</allocations>
```

Box 11.4 shows the fair-scheduler.xml file that is used to specify the allocations for each pool, as well as the per-pool and per-user limits on the number of running jobs. The allocations shown in Box 11.4 consist of three pools – user1, user2 and user3, each having a guarantee of 5 map slots and 5 reduce slots. The maximum number of map and reduce slots for each pool are fixed at 25. The maximum number of running jobs per user is fixed to 6 for all users.

The allocations for the pool and the user and pool running job limits can be modified at runtime by editing the allocation configuration file. This file is reloaded by the scheduler 10-15 seconds after the file is modified. With the Fair Scheduler configured, the Hadoop cluster is launched. The Fair Scheduler administration page can be viewed at the URL:

http://<JobTracker-URL>:50030/scheduler

The administration page of the Fair Scheduler shows the pools and their allocations. The status of the MapReduce jobs submitted to different pools can also be viewed on this page. For each pool, the minimum and maximum share for map and reduce slots, number of running map and reduce tasks, and the fair share for map and reduce tasks can be viewed. The fair share denotes the average number of task slots that a job should have at any given time according to fair sharing. Now let us move on to the Capacity Scheduler. Box 11.5 shows the mapred-site.xml configuration file used for configuring the Capacity Scheduler. Box 11.6 shows the capacity-scheduler.xml configuration file. In this file multiple queues are defined to which the users can submit jobs with the Capacity Scheduler. Properties for each queue are specified in this file. For example, to specify a property for a queue, the property name is used as - mapred.capacity-scheduler.queue.<queue-name>.<property-name>.

■ Box 11.5: Configuring Capacity Scheduler - mapred-site.xml

```
<?xml version="1.0"?>
<?xml-stylesheet type="text/xsl" href="configuration.xsl"?>

<configuration>
<property>
<name>mapred.job.tracker</name>
<value>master:54311</value>
</property>

<property>
<name>mapred.jobtracker.taskScheduler</name>
<value>org.apache.hadoop.mapred.CapacityTaskScheduler</value>
</property>

<property>
<name>mapred.queue.names</name>
<value>userA,userB,userC</value>
</property>

</configuration>
```

■ Box 11.6: Configuring Capacity Scheduler - capacity-scheduler.xml

```
<?xml version="1.0"?>
<configuration>

<property>
<name>mapred.capacity-scheduler.maximum-system-jobs</name>
<value>3000</value>
<description>Maximum number of jobs in the system which can be initialized,
concurrently, by the CapacityScheduler.
</description>
</property>
```

```
<property>
<name>mapred.capacity-scheduler.queue.default.capacity</name>
<value>10</value>
</property>
<property>

    <name>mapred.capacity-scheduler.queue.default.supports-priority</name>

    <value>false</value>
</property>
<property>

    <name>mapred.capacity-scheduler.queue.default.minimum-user-limit-percent
</name>
<value>10</value>
</property>
<property>

    <name>mapred.capacity-scheduler.queue.default.user-limit-factor</name>

    <value>10</value>
</property>
<property>

    <name>mapred.capacity-scheduler.queue.default.maximum-initialized-active-tas ks
</name>
<value>200000</value>
</property>
<property>

    <name>mapred.capacity-scheduler.queue.default.maximum-initialized-active-tas ks-
per-user</name>
<value>100000</value>
</property>
<property>

    <name>mapred.capacity-scheduler.queue.default.init-accept-jobs-factor
</nam e>
<value>100</value>
</property>

<property>
<name>mapred.capacity-scheduler.queue.userA.capacity </name>
<value>30</value>
</property>
<property>

    <name>mapred.capacity-scheduler.queue.userA.supports-priority </name>
<value>false</value>
</property>
<property>

    <name>mapred.capacity-scheduler.queue.userA.minimum-user-limit-percent
</na me>
```

```
<value>20</value>
</property>
<property>

    <name>mapred.capacity-scheduler.queue.userA.user-limit-factor </name>
<value>10</value>
</property>
<property>

    <name>mapred.capacity-scheduler.queue.userA.maximum-initialized-active-tasks
</name>
<value>200000 </value>
</property>
<property>

    <name>mapred.capacity-scheduler.queue.userA.maximum-initialized-active-tasks
-per-user</name>
<value>100000 </value>
</property>
<property>

    <name>mapred.capacity-scheduler.queue.userA.init-accept-jobs-factor
</name>
<value>100</value>
</property>

:
</configuration>
```

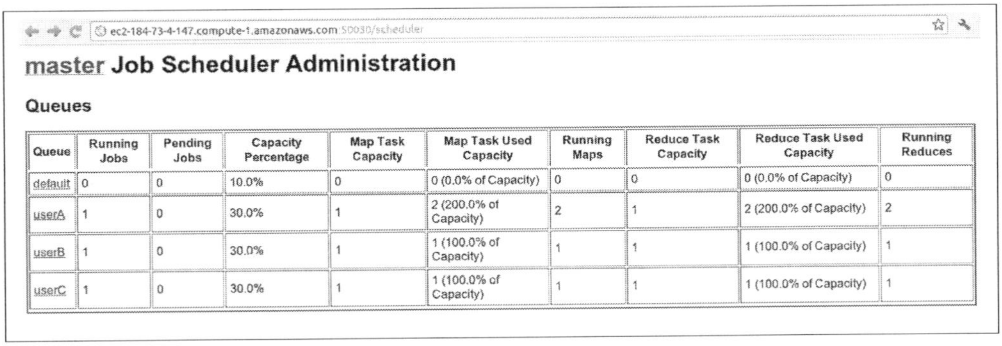

ec2-184-73-4-147.compute-1.amazonaws.com:50030/scheduler

master Job Scheduler Administration

Queues

Queue	Running Jobs	Pending Jobs	Capacity Percentage	Map Task Capacity	Map Task Used Capacity	Running Maps	Reduce Task Capacity	Reduce Task Used Capacity	Running Reduces
default	0	0	10.0%	0	0 (0.0% of Capacity)	0	0	0 (0.0% of Capacity)	0
userA	1	0	30.0%	1	2 (200.0% of Capacity)	2	1	2 (200.0% of Capacity)	2
userB	1	0	30.0%	1	1 (100.0% of Capacity)	1	1	1 (100.0% of Capacity)	1
userC	1	0	30.0%	1	1 (100.0% of Capacity)	1	1	1 (100.0% of Capacity)	1

Figure 11.6: Hadoop Capacity Scheduler administration page

With the Capacity Scheduler configured, the Hadoop cluster is launched. The Capacity Scheduler administration page can be viewed at the URL: http://<JobTracker-URL>:50030/scheduler, as shown in Figure 11.6. The administration page of the Capacity Scheduler shows the queues and their allocated capacities, map and reduce task capacities used and number of running map and reduce tasks.

For monitoring the performance of the nodes in the Hadoop cluster you can use performance monitoring tools such as *collectd*, *nmon*, for instance. For the experiments shown in this section, the *collectd* tool is used.

Benchmark	Description
TestDFSIO	TestDFSIO tests the I/O performance of HDFS. This benchmark is useful for stress testing HDFS. TestDFSIO uses a MapReduce job to read or write files in parallel. Each file is read or written in a separate map task, and the output of the map is used for collecting statistics relating to the file just processed. The reduce phase accumulates the statistics to produce a summary.
MRBench	MRBench runs a small job a number of times. MRBench is a complimentary benchmark to the Sort benchmark. MRBench checks whether small job runs are responsive and running efficiently on the cluster.
NNBench	NNBench is useful for load testing the NameNode hardware and configuration. This benchmark generates a lot of HDFS-related requests with normally very small payloads for the sole purpose of putting a high HDFS management stress on the NameNode. The benchmark can simulate requests for creating, reading, renaming and deleting files on HDFS.
Gridmix	GridMix is a suite of benchmarks that model that characteristics of realistic workloads for submitting a mix of synthetic jobs. GridMix requires a MapReduce job trace describing the job mix for a given cluster, and input data from which the synthetic jobs will read bytes.
Sort	The Sort MapReduce program is included in the hadoop-*-examples.jar file. This program does a partial sort of its input. The Sort program is useful for benchmarking the whole MapReduce system. This program can test both MapReduce runtime performance and HDFS I/O performance.

Table 11.2: Hadoop benchmarks

Hadoop comes with several benchmarks that are packaged in the JAR file - hadoop-*-test.jar. Table 11.2 shows a list of Hadoop benchmarks. For benchmarking the Hadoop cluster, the Sort MapReduce program is used in this section. The Sort program does a partial sort of its input. This is useful for benchmarking the whole MapReduce system. This program can test both MapReduce runtime performance and HDFS I/O performance.

Box 11.7 lists the commands used for running the sort benchmark. The first step in benchmarking with sort is to generate input data for the sort program. The RandomWriter MapReduce program is used for generating random data. This program runs a MapReduce job with 10 maps per node by default, and each map generates approximately 10 GB of random binary data, with key and values of various sizes. The number of maps per node and the bytes per map can be changed by setting the properties *test.randomwriter.maps_per_host* and *test.randomwrite.bytes_per_map*.

■ Box 11.7: Running Sort Benchmark

```
# Submitting job from a particular user with Fair Scheduler configured:

$sudo -u userA bin/hadoop jar hadoop-examples-1.0.4.jar randomwriter -D
test.randomwrite.bytes_per_map=1000000 random-data

$ sudo -u userA bin/hadoop jar hadoop-examples-1.0.4.jar sort random-data1
sorted-data

#Submitting job to a particular queue of Capacity Scheduler:

$bin/hadoop jar hadoop-examples-1.0.4.jar randomwriter -D
test.randomwrite.bytes_per_map=1000000 -D mapred.job.queue.name=userA
random-data

$bin/hadoop jar hadoop-examples-1.0.4.jar sort -D mapred.job.queue.name=userA
random-data sorted-data
```

After running the benchmark, the statistics of the Hadoop nodes collected by the *collectd* performance monitoring tool are analyzed. Figures 9.7 (a) and (b) show the idle CPU for the master and slave nodes for a benchmark run. From these plots it is observed that for both nodes, high CPU utilization is observed when the benchmark is run. Figures 9.7 (c) and (d) show the disk I/O for the master and slave nodes. Figure 9.8 (a) and (b) show the network I/O for the master and slave nodes. Figure 9.8 (c) and (d) show the memory used for the master and slave nodes.

Analysis of statistics collected after a benchmark run can help locate the bottlenecks. The performance can then be tuned by changing properties such as the allocations for pools in the case of the Fair Scheduler and capacities of the queues in case of the Capacity Scheduler. Table 11.3 lists the properties of Hadoop that can be configured for tuning the performance of a Hadoop cluster.

Summary

In this chapter you learned about cloud application benchmarking approaches. Benchmarking for cloud-based applications is important to ensure market readiness of applications. Adequate resources must be be provisioned so that the applications can meet the workload demands. Provisioning and capacity planning for cloud applications involves determining the amount of computing, memory and network resources to provision for the application. For resource management and capacity planning decisions, it is important to understand the workload characteristics of applications and measure the sensitivity of the application performance to the workload attributes and detect bottlenecks in the systems. Benchmarking is done with synthetic workloads. To generate synthetic workloads, workload models are used. Workload models are generated from the analysis of traces of application workloads. Synthetic workloads are generated using either an empirical approach or analytical approach. In empirical approach traces of applications are sampled and replayed to generate the synthetic workloads. Analytical approach uses mathematical models to define the workload

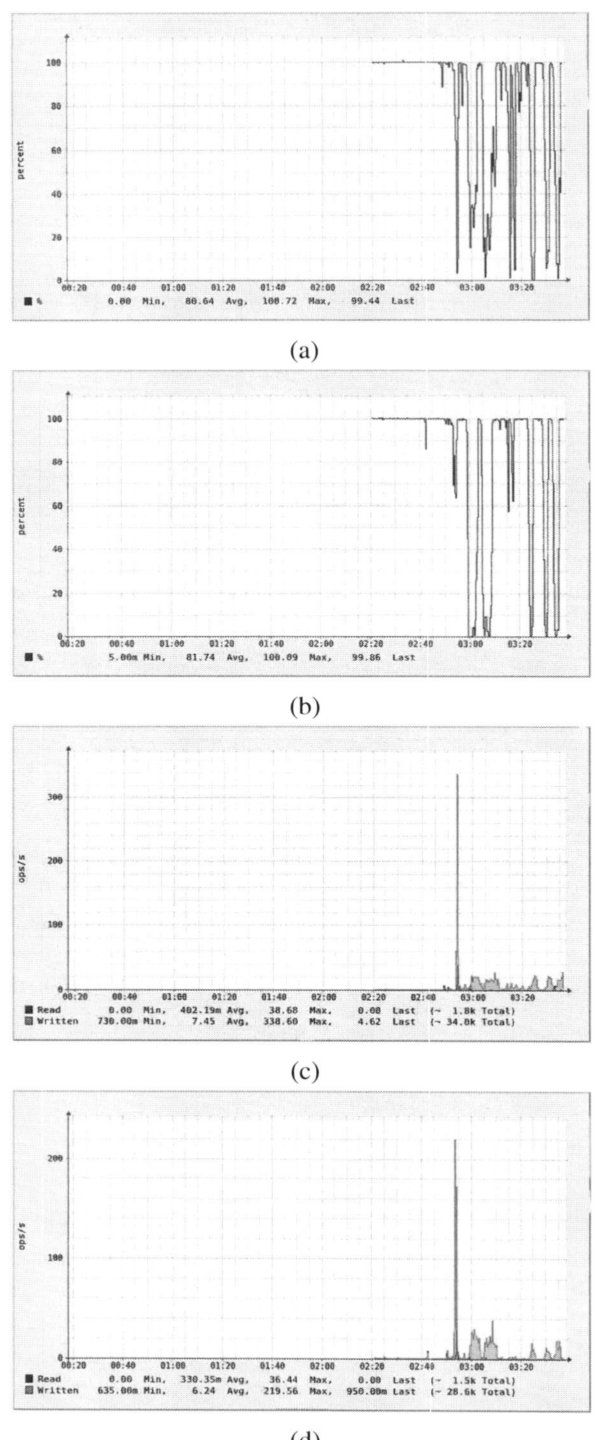

Figure 11.7: CPU-idle for: (a) master node, (b) slave node. Disk read/write for: (c) master node, (d) slave node

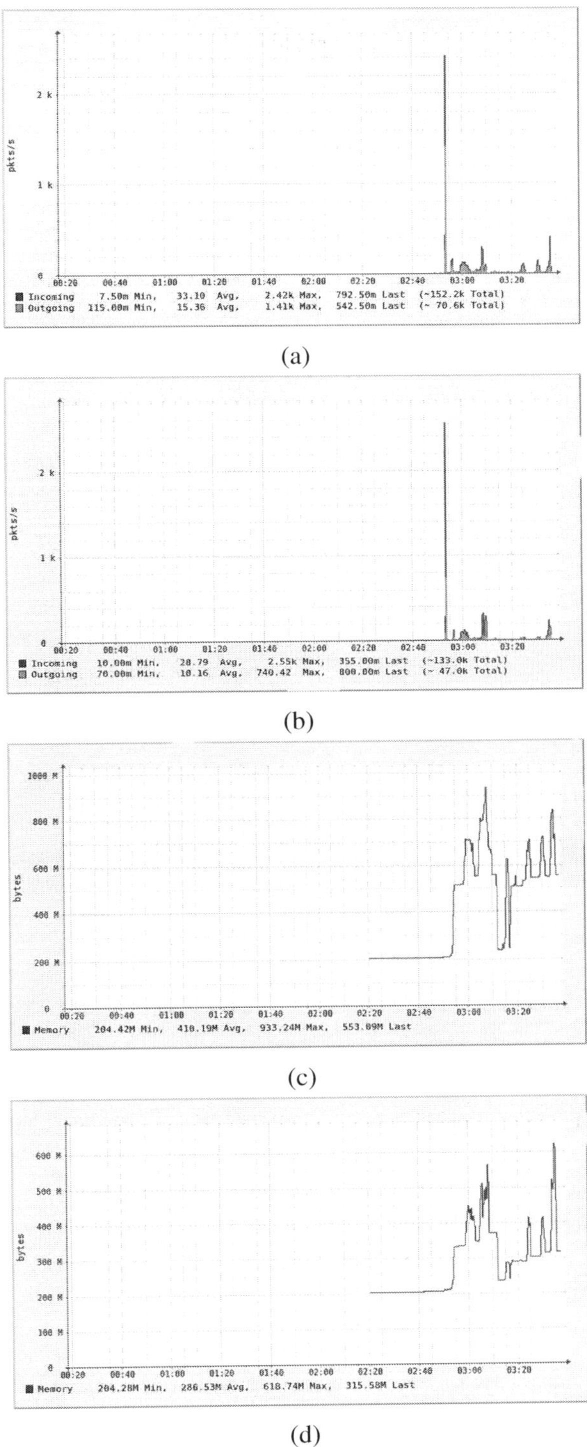

Figure 11.8: Network I/O for: (a) master node, (b) slave node. Memory used for: (c) master node, (d) slave node

File	Property	Description
mapred-default.xml	io.sort.mb	The number of streams to merge at once while sorting files. This determines the number of open file handles.
mapred-default.xml	io.sort.factor	The total amount of buffer memory to use while sorting files, in megabytes. By default, gives each merge stream 1MB, which should minimize seeks.
mapred-default.xml	mapred.map.tasks	The default number of map tasks per job.
mapred-default.xml	mapred.reduce.tasks	The default number of reduce tasks per job.
mapred-default.xml	mapred.reduce. parallel.copies	The default number of parallel transfers run by reduce during the copy (shuffle) phase.
mapred-default.xml	mapred.tasktracker. map.tasks.maximum	The maximum number of map tasks that will be run simultaneously by a task tracker.
mapred-default.xml	mapred.tasktracker. reduce.tasks.maximum	The maximum number of reduce tasks that will be run simultaneously by a task tracker.
mapred-default.xml	mapred.child.java.opts	Java opts for the task tracker child processes.
mapred-default.xml	mapred.child.ulimit	The maximum virtual memory, in KB, of a process launched by the Map-Reduce framework.
mapred-default.xml	mapred.job.reduce. input.buffer.percent	The percentage of memory- relative to the maximum heap size- to retain map outputs during the reduce.
mapred-default.xml	mapred.output.compress	Specify whether the job outputs be compressed.
mapred-default.xml	mapred.compress. map.output	Should the outputs of the maps be compressed before being sent across the network. Uses SequenceFile compression.
mapred-default.xml	mapred.map.output. compression.codec	Specify the codec to be used for compressing the map outputs.
mapred-site.xml	mapred.tasktracker. reduce.tasks.maximum	The maximum number of map tasks, which are run simultaneously on a given TaskTracker, individually.
mapred-site.xml	mapred.tasktracker. reduce.tasks.maximum	The maximum number of reduce tasks, which are run simultaneously on a given TaskTracker, individually.

Table 11.3: Properties for tuning Hadoop performance

characteristics that are used by a synthetic workload generator. Characteristics of application workloads include session length, workload mix, inter-session interval, think time, for instance. A good benchmarking methodology is one that is accurate, flexible and provides a wide application coverage. Accuracy of a benchmarking methodology is determined by how closely the generated synthetic workloads mimic the realistic workloads. The commonly used performance metrics for cloud applications are response time and throughput. There are various types of tests that can be done in benchmarking such as baseline test, load tests, stress tests, soak tests, for instance. Deployment prototyping can help in making deployment architecture design choices by comparing performance of alternative deployment architectures. This chapter provided case studies on benchmarking a multi-tier application and a Hadoop cluster.

Review Questions

1. What is workload modeling?
2. What is the difference between user emulation and aggregate workload generation?
3. What is the difference between empirical and analytical approach for workload generation?
4. What are the important design considerations for a benchmarking methodology?
5. What are the steps involved in generating synthetic workloads for benchmarking applications?
6. What is the difference between soak test and load test?
7. What are the various alternatives for deployment refinement?

Lab Exercises

1. In this exercise you will benchmark a cloud-based application. Follow the steps below:
    - Deploy the Blogging application described in Chapter-7 on Amazon EC2 instances (*t1.micro* instances for application and database tiers).
    - Perform load testing using httpef tool. Extend the example in Box 9.1 for load testing.

2. In this exercise you will extend the benchmarking Exercise-1. Follow the steps below:
    - Deploy the Blogging application described in Chapter-7 on Amazon EC2 instances (*t1.micro* instances for application and database tiers).
    - Use Amazon CloudWatch metrics for CPU usage and monitor each instance in the deployment.
    - Perform load testing using httpef tool. Increment the request rate in steps of 10, until the throughput no longer increases.
    - Identify the bottleneck tier.
    - Scale up the bottleneck tier (use a larger instance size) and run the load test again.
    - Note the performance gains by scaling up.

3. Repeat Exercise-2 by scaling-out (adding more instances of the same size) instead of scaling up.

12 — Cloud Security

This Chapter covers

- Cloud security challenges
- Authorization
- Authentication
- Identify & Access Management
- Data Security
- Data Integrity
- Encryption & Key Management

12.1 Introduction

More and more organizations are moving their applications and associated data to cloud to reduce costs and reduce the operational and maintenance overheads, and one of the important considerations is that of security of the data in the cloud. Most cloud service providers implement advanced security features similar to those that exist in in-house IT environments. However, due the out-sourced nature of the cloud, resource pooling and multi-tenanted architectures, security remains an important concern in adoption of cloud computing. In addition to the traditional vulnerabilities that exist for web applications, the cloud applications have additional vulnerabilities because of the shared usage of resources and virtualized resources. Key security challenges for cloud applications include:

Authentication

Authentication refers to digitally confirming the identity of the entity requesting access to some protected information. In a traditional in-house IT environment authentication polices are under the control of the organization and the process of confirming identity is usually restricted to the employees of the organization. Even in scenarios where users outside an organization need to be authenticated, the authentication policies are always under the organization's control and can be altered at their own convenience. However, in cloud computing environments, where applications and data are accessed over the internet, the complexity of digital authentication mechanisms increases rapidly. Alteration of authentication and authorization policies requires the involvement of the cloud service provider's systems and services.

Authorization

Authorization refers to digitally specifying the access rights to the protected resources using access policies. In a traditional in-house IT environment, the access policies are controlled by the organization and can be altered at their convenience. An organization, for example, can provide different access policies for different departments. Authorization in a cloud computing environment requires the use of the cloud service providers services for specifying the access policies.

Security of data at rest

Due to the multi-tenant environments used in the cloud, the application and database servers of different applications belonging to different organizations can be provisioned side-by-side increasing the complexity of securing the data. Appropriate separation mechanisms are required to ensure the isolation between applications and data from different organizations.

Security of data in motion

In traditional in-house IT environments all the data exchanged between the applications and users remains within the organization's control and geographical boundaries. Organizations believe that they have complete visibility of all the data exchanged and control the IT infrastructure. With the adoption of the cloud model, the applications and the data are moved out of the in-house IT infrastructure to the cloud provider. In such a scenario, organizations have to access their applications with the data moving in and out of the cloud over the internet. Therefore, appropriate security mechanisms are required to ensure the security of data in, and while in, motion.

Data Integrity

Data integrity ensures that the data is not altered in an unauthorized manner after it is created, transmitted or stored. Due to the outsourcing of data storage in cloud computing environments, ensuring integrity of data is important. Appropriate mechanisms are required for detecting accidental and/or intentional changes in the data.

Auditing

Auditing is very important for applications deployed in cloud computing environments. In traditional in-house IT environments, organizations have complete visibility of their applications and accesses to the protected information. For cloud applications appropriate auditing mechanisms are required to get visibility into the application, data accesses and actions performed by the application users, including mobile users and devices such as wireless laptops and smartphones.

12.2 CSA Cloud Security Architecture

The Cloud Security Alliance (CSA) provides a Trusted Cloud Initiative (TCI) Reference Architecture [46] which is a methodology and a set of tools that enable cloud application developers and security architects to assess where their internal IT and their cloud providers are in terms of security capabilities, and to plan a roadmap to meet the security needs of their business. The Security and Risk Management (SRM) domain within the TCI Reference Architecture provides the core components of an organization's information security program to safeguard assets and detect, assess, and monitor risks inherent in operating activities. Figure 12.1 shows the SRM domain within the TCI Reference Architecture of CSA. The sub-domains of SRM include:

Governance, Risk Management, and Compliance

This sub-domain deals with the identification and implementation of the appropriate organizational structures, processes, and controls to maintain effective information security governance, risk management and compliance.

Information Security Management

This sub-domain deals with the implementation of appropriate measurements (such as capability maturity models, capability mapping models, security architectures roadmaps and risk portfolios) in order to minimize or eliminate the impact that security related threats and vulnerabilities might have on an organization.

Privilege Management Infrastructure

The objective of this sub-domain is to ensure that users have access and privileges required to execute their duties and responsibilities with Identity and Access Management (IAM) functions such as identity management, authentication services, authorization services, and privilege usage management.

Threat and Vulnerability Management

This sub-domain deals with core security such as vulnerability management, threat management, compliance testing, and penetration testing.

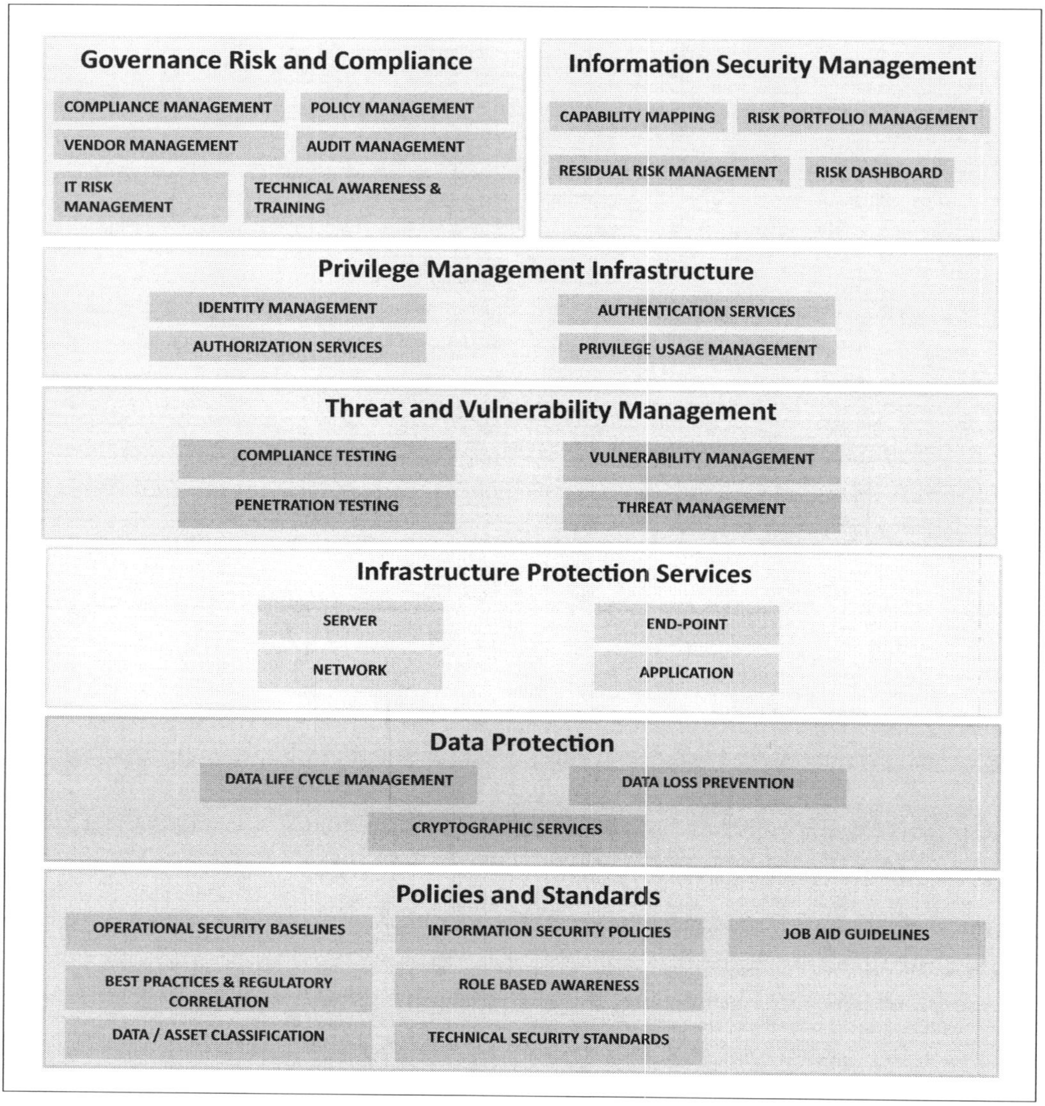

Governance Risk and Compliance
COMPLIANCE MANAGEMENT
POLICY MANAGEMENT
VENDOR MANAGEMENT
AUDIT MANAGEMENT
IT RISK MANAGEMENT
TECHNICAL AWARENESS & TRAINING

Information Security Management
CAPABILITY MAPPING
RISK PORTFOLIO MANAGEMENT
RESIDUAL RISK MANAGEMENT
RISK DASHBOARD

Privilege Management Infrastructure
IDENTITY MANAGEMENT
AUTHENTICATION SERVICES
AUTHORIZATION SERVICES
PRIVILEGE USAGE MANAGEMENT

Threat and Vulnerability Management
COMPLIANCE TESTING
VULNERABILITY MANAGEMENT
PENETRATION TESTING
THREAT MANAGEMENT

Infrastructure Protection Services
SERVER
END-POINT
NETWORK
APPLICATION

Data Protection
DATA LIFE CYCLE MANAGEMENT
DATA LOSS PREVENTION
CRYPTOGRAPHIC SERVICES

Policies and Standards
OPERATIONAL SECURITY BASELINES
INFORMATION SECURITY POLICIES
JOB AID GUIDELINES
BEST PRACTICES & REGULATORY CORRELATION
ROLE BASED AWARENESS
DATA / ASSET CLASSIFICATION
TECHNICAL SECURITY STANDARDS

Figure 12.1: Security and Risk Management (SRM) domain within the TCI Reference Architecture of CSA [46]

Infrastructure Protection Services

This objective of this sub-domain is to secure Server, End-Point, Network and Application layers.

Data Protection

This sub-domain deals with data lifecycle management, data leakage prevention, intellectual property protection with digital rights management, and cryptographic services such as key management and PKI/symmetric encryption.

Policies and Standards

Security policies and standards are derived from risk-based business requirements and exist at a number of different levels including Information Security policy, Physical Security Policy, Business Continuity Policy, Infrastructure Security Policies, Application Security Policies as well as the over-arching Business Operational Risk Management Policy.

12.3 Authentication

Authentication refers to confirming the digital identity of the entity requesting access to some protected information. The process of authentication involves, but is not limited to, validating the at least one factor of identification of the entity to be authenticated. A factor can be something the entity or the user knows (password or pin), something the user has (such as a smart card), or something that can uniquely identify the user (such as fingerprints). In multifactor authentication more than one of these factors are used for authentication. In this section you will learn about authentication mechanisms such as SSO, SAML-Token, OTP, etc.

12.3.1 Single Sign-on (SSO)

Single Sign-on (SSO) enables users to access multiple systems or applications after signing in only once, for the first time. When a user signs in, the user identity is recognized and there is no need to sign in again and again to access related systems or applications. Since different systems or applications may be internally using different authentication mechanisms, SSO upon receiving initial credential translates to different credentials for different systems or applications. The benefit of using SSO is that it reduces human error and saves time spent in authenticating with different systems or applications for the same identity. There are different implementation mechanisms for SSO described as follows:

SAML-Token

Security Assertion Markup Language (SAML) is an XML-based open standard data format for exchanging security information (authentication and authorization data) between an identity provider and a service provider. Figure 12.2 shows the authentication flow for a cloud application using SAML SSO. When a user tries to access the cloud application, a SAML request is generated and the user is redirected to the identity provider. The identity provider parses the SAML request and authenticates the user. A SAML token is returned to the user, who then accesses the cloud application with the token. SAML prevents man-in-the-middle and replay attacks by requiring the use of SSL encryption when transmitting assertions and messages. SAML also provides a digital signature mechanism that enables the assertion to have a validity time range to prevent replay attacks.

Kerberos

Kerberos is an open authentication protocol that was developed at MIT [47]. Kerberos uses tickets for authenticating client to a service that communicate over an un-secure network. Kerberos provides mutual authentication, i.e. both the client and the server authenticate with each other. Figure 12.3 shows the Kerberos authentication flow for a user who is using a client machine to connect to a remote service. The steps involved in authentication are as follows:

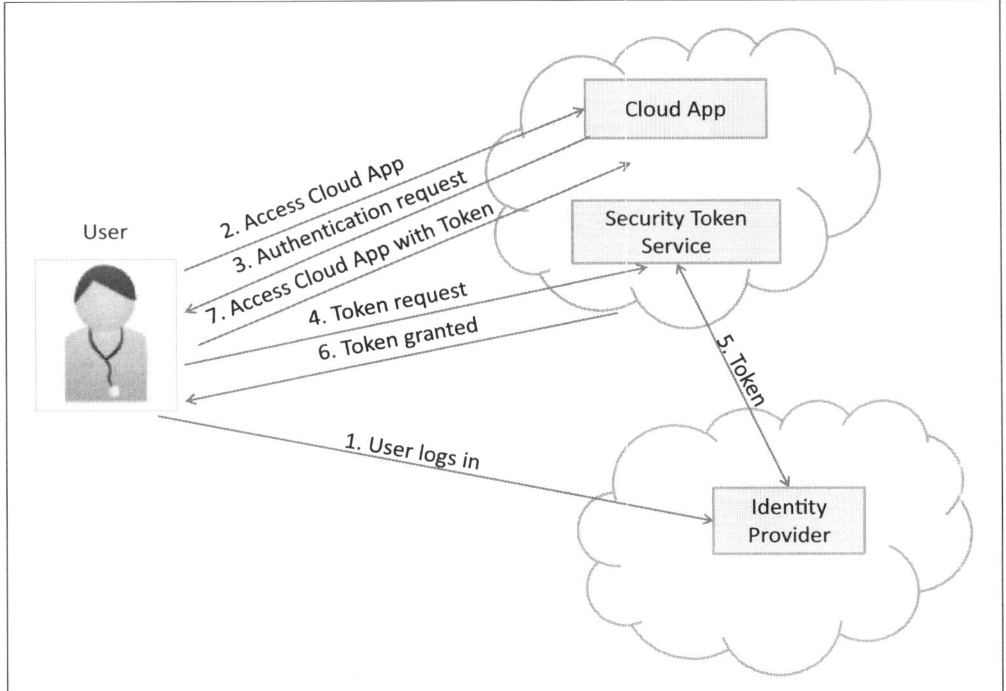

Figure 12.2: SAML-token based SSO authentication

- The client authenticates itself to the Authentication Server (AS) that resides on the Key Distribution Center (KDC). The client does not need to send the user password to the AS. Instead the client sends a clear-text message to the AS containing the user ID to the AS requesting to authenticate the user to the remote service.
- The AS checks if the client is in the database and generates a Client/TGS Session Key that will be used by the client and the remote service. The AS encrypts the session key with the user's password. The KDC also prepares the Ticket Granting Ticket (TGT) (which includes the client ID, client network address, ticket validity period, and the session key) and encrypts it using the secret key of the TGS. KDC then sends both the session key and TGT to the client. On receiving the session key and TGT, the client decrypts the Client/TGS Session Key using its password and extracts the session key. The client cannot decrypt the TGT as it does not know the secret key of the TGS.
- The client encrypts the client ID and current time using the session key to prepare an authenticator. The client then sends the authenticator and the TGT that it received from the KDC to the TGS.
- On receiving the authenticator and TGT from the client, the TGS decrypts the TGT using its own secret key and retrieves the session key. The TGS then uses the session key to decrypt the authenticator and extracts the client ID and time. The TGS then sends two pieces of data to the client. The first piece contains the client-server ticket (which includes the client ID, client network address, validity period and Client/Server Session Key) encrypted using the service's secret key. The second piece of data contains the Client/Server Session Key encrypted with the Client/TGS Session Key.

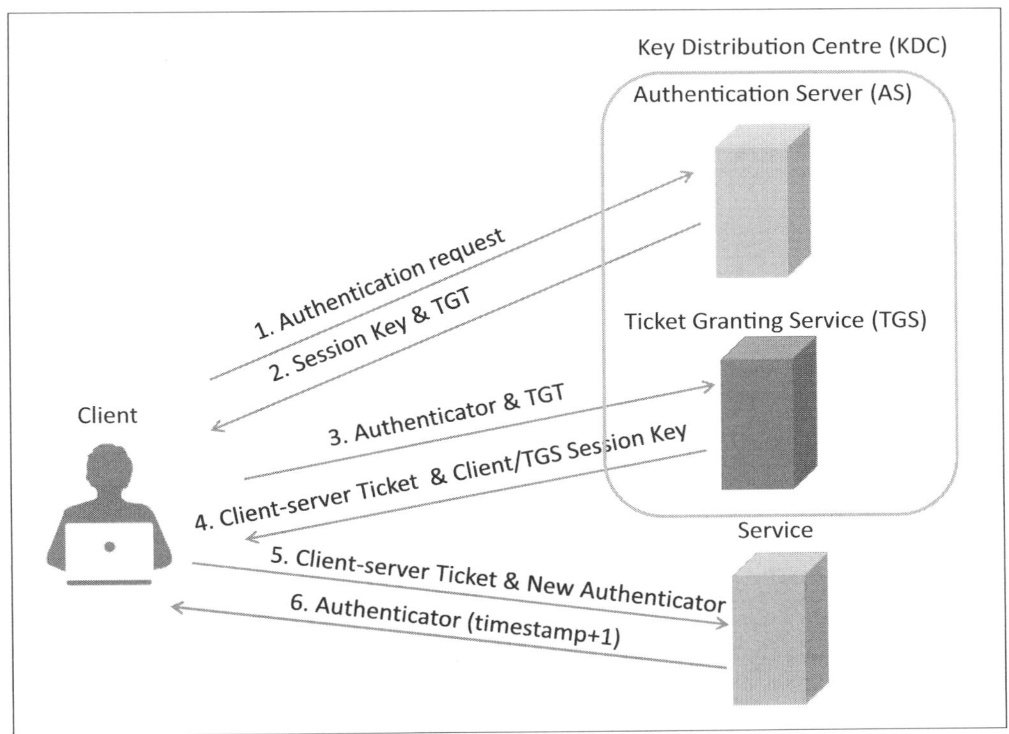

Figure 12.3: Kerberos authentication flow

- On receiving the client-server ticket and Client/TGS Session Key from the TGS, the client has enough information to authenticate itself to the remote service. The client then sends two pieces of data to the remote service. The first piece contains the client-server ticket which is encrypted using the service's secret key (that it received from the TGS). The second piece of data contains a new authenticator which includes the client ID, timestamp and is encrypted using Client/Server Session Key.
- On receiving the client-server ticket and new authenticator from the client, the remote service decrypts the client-server ticket using its own secret key and retrieves the Client/Server Session Key. Using the sessions key, remote service decrypts the authenticator. At this point the true identity of the client is confirmed to the remote service and it responds to the client with the timestamp found in client's authenticator plus 1, encrypted using the Client/Server Session Key.
- On receiving the new authenticator from the remote service, the client decrypts it using the Client/Server Session Key and checks the timestamp. If the timestamp is correctly updated, the client can trust the server and start issuing service requests to the server.

One Time Password (OTP)

One time password is another authentication mechanism that uses passwords which are valid for single use only for a single transaction or session. Authentication mechanism based on OTP tokens are more secure because they are not vulnerable to replay attacks. Text messaging (SMS) is the most common delivery mode for OTP tokens. The most common approach for generating OTP tokens is time synchronization. Time-based OTP algorithm (TOTP) is a popular time synchronization based algorithm for generating OTPs [48].

12.4 Authorization

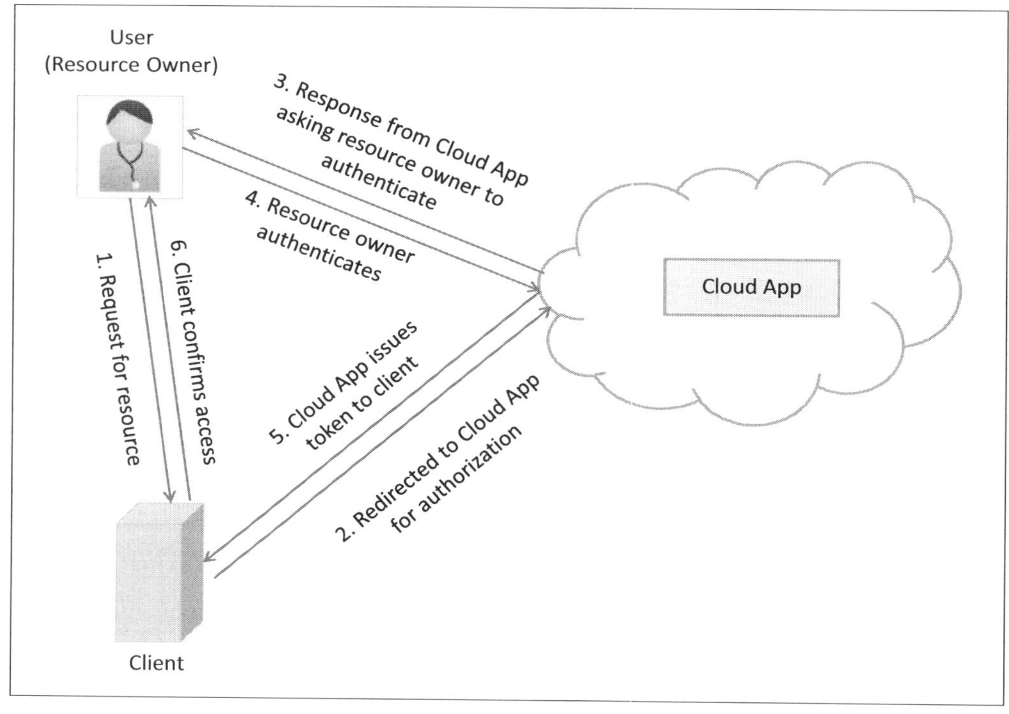

Figure 12.4: OAuth authorization flow

Authorization refers to specifying the access rights to the protected resources using access policies.

OAuth

OAuth is an open standard for authorization that allows resource owners to share their private resources stored on one site with another site without handing out the credentials [49, 50]. OAuth 1.0 protocol was published as an RFC in 2010 and the OAuth 2.0 framework was published in 2012. OAuth 2.0 is not backward compatible with OAuth 1.0. In the OAuth model, an application (which is not the resource owner) requests access to resources controlled by the resource owner (but hosted by the server). The resource owner grants permission to access the resources in the form of a token and matching shared-secret. Tokens make it unnecessary for the resource owner to share its credentials with the application. Tokens can be issued with a restricted scope and limited lifetime, and revoked independently. Figure 12.4 shows the OAuth authorization flow.

Let us look at the an example of an OAuth client. Box 12.1 shows the Python code for an OAuth client that provides methods for fetching request token, fetching access token, authorizing token and accessing resources [51].

■ Box 12.1: Example of an OAuth client in Python

```
import httplib
import time
import oauth.oauth as oauth

SERVER = 'hostname'
PORT = 8080

REQUEST_TOKEN_URL = 'request_token'
ACCESS_TOKEN_URL = 'access_token'
AUTHORIZATION_URL = 'authorize'
CALLBACK_URL = 'request_token_ready'
RESOURCE_URL = 'photos'

CONSUMER_KEY = 'key'
CONSUMER_SECRET = 'secret'

class MyOAuthClient(oauth.OauthClient):
    def __init__(self, server, port=httplib.HTTP_PORT,
    request_token_url=", access_token_url=", authorization_url="):
        self.server = server
        self.port = port
        self.request_token_url = request_token_url
        self.access_token_url = access_token_url
        self.authorization_url = authorization_url
        self.connection = httplib.HTTPConnection("%s:%d" % (self.server, self.port))

    def fetch_request_token(self, oauth_request):
        self.connection.request(oauth_request.http_method, self.request_token_url,
        headers=oauth_request.to_header())
        response = self.connection.getresponse()
        return oauth.OauthToken.from_string(response.read())

    def fetch_access_token(self, oauth_request):
        self.connection.request(oauth_request.http_method, self.access_token_url,
        headers=oauth_request.to_header())
        response = self.connection.getresponse()
        return oauth.OauthToken.from_string(response.read())

    def authorize_token(self, oauth_request):
        self.connection.request(oauth_request.http_method, oauth_request.to_url())
        response = self.connection.getresponse()
        return response.read()

    def access_resource(self, oauth_request):
        headers = 'Content-Type' :'application/x-www-form-urlencoded'
        self.connection.request('POST', RESOURCE_URL,
        body=oauth_request.to_postdata(), headers=headers)
        response = self.connection.getresponse()
        return response.read()
```

Box 12.2 shows the Python implementation of an OAuth authorization flow similar to the one shown in Figure 12.4. The authorization sequence begins with the requesting a token. The user is redirected to the authorization URL and provides consent (authorizes the access token). Upon user consent an OAuth token is returned to the application. The access token is then used to access some protected resources.

■ Box 12.2: Python implementation of an OAuth authorization flow

```
import httplib
import time
import oauth.oauth as oauth
import MyOAuthClient

def oauth_example():
    # setup
    client = MyOAuthClient(SERVER, PORT, REQUEST_TOKEN_URL,
    ACCESS_TOKEN_URL, AUTHORIZATION_URL)
    consumer = oauth.OAuthConsumer(CONSUMER_KEY, CONSUMER_SECRET)
    signature_method_plaintext = oauth.OAuthSignatureMethod_PLAINTEXT()
    signature_method_hmac_sha1 = oauth.OAuthSignatureMethod_HMAC_SHA1()

    # get request token
    print 'Obtain a request token ...'
    oauth_request =      oauth.OAuthRequest.from_consumer_and_token(consumer,
    callback=CALLBACK_URL,
    http_url=client.request_token_url)
    oauth_request.sign_request(signature_method_plaintext, consumer, None)
    print 'REQUEST (via headers)'
    print 'parameters: %s' % str(oauth_request.parameters)
    token = client.fetch_request_token(oauth_request)
    print 'GOT'
    print 'key: %s' % str(token.key)
    print 'secret: %s' % str(token.secret)
    print 'callback confirmed? %s' %     str(token.callback_confirmed)

    print 'Authorize the request token ...'
    oauth_request =
    oauth.OAuthRequest.from_token_and_callback(token=token,
    http_url=client.authorization_url)
    print 'REQUEST (via url query string)'
    print 'parameters: %s' % str(oauth_request.parameters)
    # this will actually occur only on some callback
    response = client.authorize_token(oauth_request)
    print 'GOT'
    print response
    # sad way to get the verifier
    import urlparse, cgi
    query = urlparse.urlparse(response)[4]
    params = cgi.parse_qs(query, keep_blank_values=False)
    verifier = params['oauth_verifier'][0]
    print 'verifier: %s' % verifier

    # get access token
    print 'Obtain an access token ...'
```

```
    oauth_request = oauth.OAuthRequest.from_consumer_and_token(consumer, token=token,
    verifier=verifier, http_url=client.access_token_url)
    oauth_request.sign_request(signature_method_plaintext, consumer, token)
    print 'REQUEST (via headers)'
    print 'parameters: %s' % str(oauth_request.parameters)
    token = client.fetch_access_token(oauth_request)
    print 'GOT'
    print 'key: %s' % str(token.key)
    print 'secret: %s' % str(token.secret)

    # access some protected resources
    print 'Access protected resources ...'
    parameters = 'file': 'file.pdf', 'size': 'original' # resource specific params
    oauth_request = oauth.OAuthRequest.from_consumer_and_token(consumer, token=token,
    http_method='POST', http_url=RESOURCE_URL, parameters=parameters)
    oauth_request.sign_request(signature_method_hmac_sha1, consumer, token)
    print 'REQUEST (via post body)'
    print 'parameters: %s' % str(oauth_request.parameters)
    params = client.access_resource(oauth_request)
    print 'GOT'
    print 'non-oauth parameters: %s' % params

if __name__ == '__main__':
    oauth_example()
```

12.5 Identity & Access Management

Identity management provides consistent methods for digitally identifying persons and maintaining associated identity attributes for the users across multiple organizations. Access management deals with user privileges. Identity and access management deal with user identities, their authentication, authorization and access policies. Authentication and authorization approaches were described in the previous section. Let us look at the Federated Identity Management approach. Federated identity management allows users of one domain to securely access data or systems of another domain seamlessly without the need for maintaining identity information separately for multiple domains. Federation is enabled through the use single sign-on mechanisms such as SAML token and Kerberos. With federated identify management the identity credentials stay with the identity provider at a trusted place and multiple applications from different organizations can use the identity credentials for user authentication.

Standardized access control policies ensure confidentially of data. Role-based access control approaches are used for restricting access to confidential information to authorized users. These access control policies allow defining different roles for different users. For example all users from a specific department within an organization can be put under one role and there can be different roles for different departments. Figure 12.5 shows an example of a the role based access control framework in the cloud. A user who wants to access the application data in the cloud is required to send his/her data to the system administrator who assigns permissions and access control policies which are stored in the User Roles and Data Access Policies databases respectively. The role based access control framework provides access to application data to the users based on the assigned roles and data access policies.

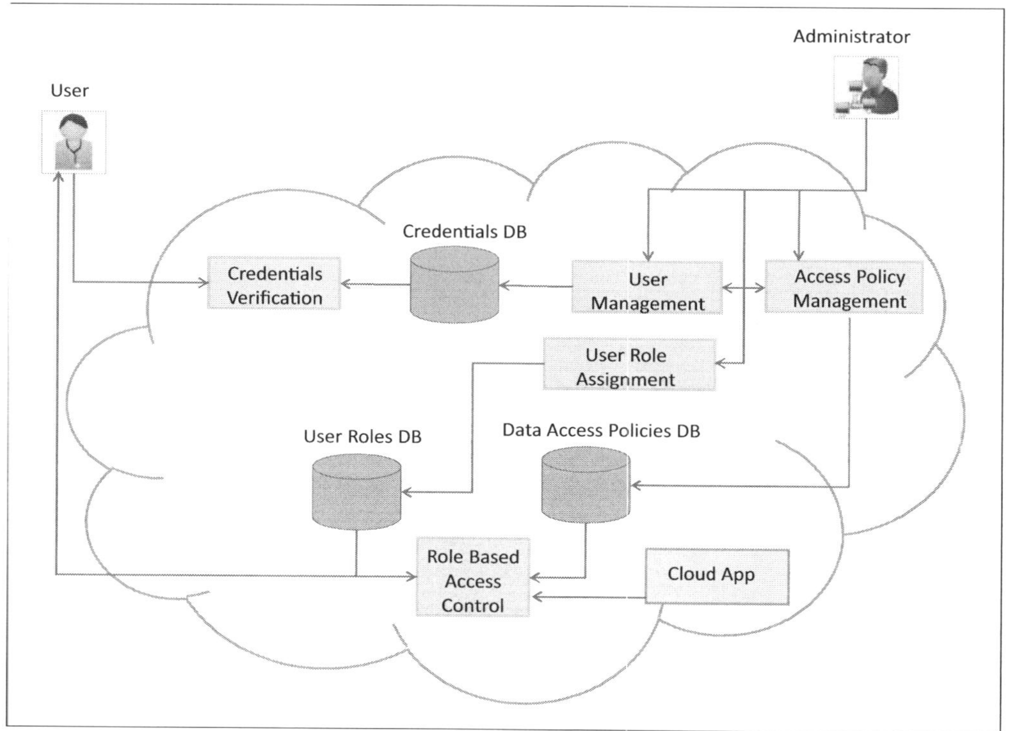

Figure 12.5: Role-based access control in the cloud

12.6 Data Security

Securing data in the cloud is critical for cloud applications as the data flows from applications to storage and vice versa. Cloud applications deal with both data at rest and data in motion. There are various types of threats that can exist for data in the cloud such as denial of service, replay attacks, man-in-the-middle attacks, unauthorized access/modification, etc.

12.6.1 Securing Data at Rest

Data at rest is the data that is stored in database in the form of tables/records, files on a file server or raw data on a distributed storage or storage area network (SAN). Data at rest is secured by encryption. Encryption is the process of converting data from its original form (i.e., plaintext) to a scrambled form (ciphertext) that is unintelligible. Decryption converts data from ciphertext to plaintext. Encryption can be of two types:

Symmetric Encryption (symmetric-key algorithms)

Symmetric encryption uses the same secret key for both encryption and decryption. The secret key is shared between the sender and the receiver. Symmetric encryption is best suited for securing data at rest since the data is accessed by known entities from known locations. Popular symmetric encryption algorithms include:

- **Advanced Encryption Standard (AES):** AES is the data encryption standard established by the U.S. National Institute of Standards and Technology (NIST) in 2001. AES uses Rijndael cipher (developed by Joan Daemen and Vincent Rijmen), and is the most widely-accepted encryption algorithm.

- **Twofish:** Twofish is a symmetric key block cipher with a block size of 128 bits and key sizes up to 256 bits. Twofish was one the top candidates for the AES contest.
- **Blowfish:** Blowfish has a 64-bit block size and a variable key length from 32 bits up to 448 bits.
- **Triple Data Encryption Standard (3DES):** This algorithm is a variation of Data Encryption Standard (DES) developed by IBM. 3DES uses a key-bundle comprising of three keys each of 56 bits. In the first step, DES is used to encrypt plaintext using the first key, then the data is decrypted using the second key and finally, the third key is used to encrypt the data using DES.
- **Serpent:** Serpent is a symmetric key block cipher that uses a block size of 128 bits and supports a key size of 128, 192 or 256 bits. Serpent was one of the top candidates for AES contest and came second.
- **RC6:** RC6 is a symmetric key block cipher designed by RSA Security and was a candidate for the AES contest. RC6 uses a block size of 128 bits and supports key sizes of 128, 192 and 256 bits.
- **MARS:** MARS is a block cipher that was designed by IBM as a candidate for the AES contest. It uses a 128-bit block size and a variable key size of between 128 and 448 bits.

Box 12.3 shows an example of symmetric encryption in Python.

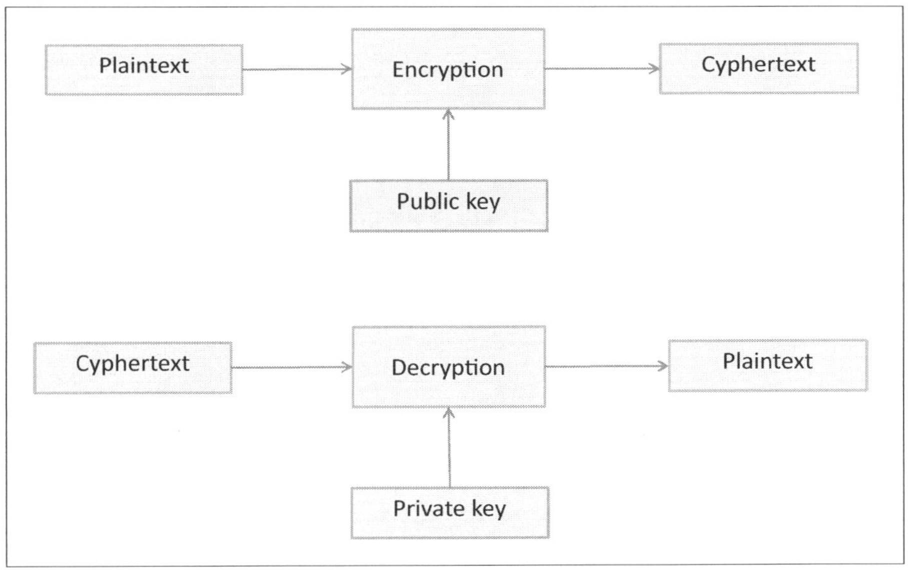

Figure 12.6: Asymmetric encryption using public/private keys

■ Box 12.3: Example of an AES Encryption/Decryption in Python

```
from Crypto.Cipher import AES
```

```
# create a cipher object using the random secret
aesObj = AES.new('This is a key123', AES.MODE_CBC, 'This is an IV456')
data = "Hello World!"

#Encrypt data
encrypted_data = obj.encrypt(data)
print encrypted_data

#Decrypt data
aesObj1 = AES.new('This is a key123', AES.MODE_CBC, 'This is an IV456')
decrypted_data= aesObj1.decrypt(encrypted_data)
print decrypted_data
```

Asymmetric Encryption (public-key algorithms)

Asymmetric encryption uses two keys, one for encryption (public key) and other for decryption (private key). The two keys are linked to each other such that one key encrypts plaintext to ciphertext and other decrypts ciphertext back to plaintext. Public key can be shared or published while the private key is known only to the user. Figure 12.6 shows the asymmetric encryption approach. Asymmetric encryption is best suited for securing data that is exchanged between two parties where symmetric encryption can be unsafe because the secret key has to be exchanged between the parties and anyone who manages to obtain the secret key can decrypt the data. In asymmetric encryption a separate key is used for decryption which is kept private. Box 12.4 shows an example of asymmetric encryption in Python.

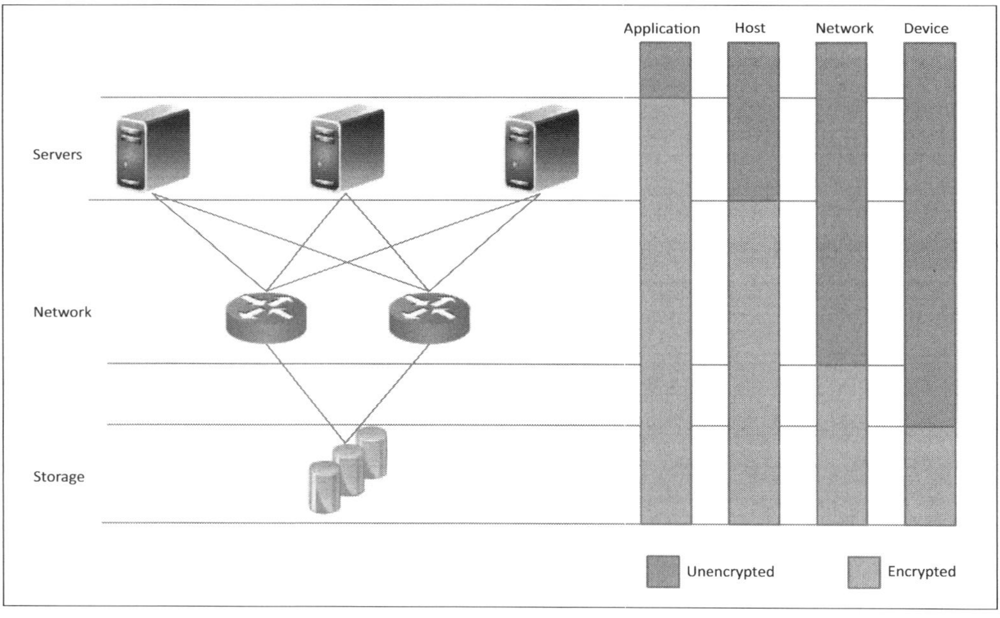

Figure 12.7: Encryption levels

■ **Box 12.4: Example of asymmetric encryption in Python**

```
from Crypto.PublicKey import RSA
from Crypto import Random
random_generator = Random.new().read


#Specify the size of the key in bits
key_size=1024

#Generate public/private key-pair
key = RSA.generate(key_size, random_generator)

#Get public key and to be published
public_key = key.publickey()
print public_key

data="Hello World!"

encrypted_data = public_key.encrypt(data, 32)

decrypted_data= key.decrypt(encrypted_data)
```

Encryption can be performed at various levels described as follows:

Application

Application level encryption involves encrypting application data right at the point where it originates i.e. within the application. Application level encryption provides security at the level of both the operating system and from other applications. Therefore one application cannot decrypt data of another application. An application encrypts all data generated in the application before it flows to the lower levels and presents decrypted data to the user. The advantage of application level encryption is that it provides security against operating system and network attacks and also data theft. However, key management is challenging task for application level encryption. Keys can be stored either in memory or a file or on a separate key server. The application performance is affected in case of key rotation, where the application reads and decrypts the data using an old key and then encrypts the data using the new key, while it is processing other requests.

Host

In host-level encryption, encryption is performed at the file-level for all applications running on the host. Host level encryption can be done in software in which case additional computational resource is required for encryption or it can be performed with specialized hardware such as a cryptographic accelerator card. The advantage of host-level encryption is that it is highly secure and suited well for active data files across all applications running on a host. However, like application-level encryption, key management can be challenging. Keys are stored in the host memory or a separate key server.

Network

Network-level encryption is best suited for cases where the threats to data are at the network or storage level and not at the application or host level. Network-level encryption is performed when moving the data form a creation point to its destination using a specialized hardware that encrypts all incoming data in real-time. The application and host levels remain unencrypted. Network-level encryption is operating system independent. The advantage of this network-level encryption is that it is simple to implement and requires no changes in the existing data infrastructure. Keys are managed in hardware. However, the disadvantage of this encryption level is that it is the least scalable of all the levels. As the data volume increases, a single encryption appliance can become a bottleneck.

Device

Device-level encryption is performed on a disk controller or a storage server. Device level encryption is easy to implement and is best suited for cases where the primary concern about data security is to protect data residing on storage media. Device level encryption is operating system, application, host and even transport independent. Encryption is performed in hardware in this method. Device-level encryption requires no changes in the existing data infrastructure. The disadvantage of this method is that all data that is transmitted to and from the storage media is unencrypted.

Figure 12.7 shows the various encryption levels.

12.6.2 Securing Data in Motion

Securing data in motion, i.e., when the data flows between a client and a server over a potentially insecure network, is important to ensure data confidentiality and integrity. Data confidentiality means limiting the access to data so that only authorized recipients can access it. Data integrity means that the data remains unchanged when moving from sender to receiver. Data integrity ensures that the data is not altered in an unauthorized manner after it is created, transmitted or stored. Transport Layer Security (TLS) and Secure Socket Layer (SSL) are the mechanisms used for securing data in motion. Though TLS and SSL are often used interchangeably, SSL is the predecessor of TLS. TLS 1.0 resembles closely to SSL 3.0. TLS and SSL are used to encrypt web traffic using Hypertext Transfer Protocol (HTTP). When HTTP is used with TLS/SSL, it is conventionally called HTTPS. TLS and SSL use asymmetric cryptography for authentication of key exchange, symmetric encryption for confidentiality and message authentication codes for message integrity. Figure 12.8 shows the TLS handshake protocol. The TLS handshake protocol is summarized as follows:

- **ClientHello:** The client sends a ClientHello message specifying the highest TLS protocol version it supports, a random number and the information on the private key encryption algorithms supported by the client.
- **ServerHello:** The server replies with the ServerHello message, containing the protocol version chosen, a random number and the settings of the private key encryption algorithms in use.
- **Server Certificate:** The server sends its Certificate to the client.
- **ServerHelloDone:** The server sends a ServerHelloDone message indicating to the client that it has completed handshake negotiation.
- **Client Certificate:** The client sends its Certificate to the server.
- **ClientKeyExchange:** The client creates a PreMaster secret (session key) encrypted with the server's public key (which is contained in the server's certificate) and it sends the encrypted session key to the server.

- **CertificateVerify:**The client sends a CertificateVerify message, which is a digital signature over the previous handshake messages using the client's certificate's private key. The digital signature can be verified by using the client's certificate's public key.
- **ChangeCipherSpec:** Client and server communicate to each other that the data that will be exchanged from now on will be encrypted with the session key previously exchanged.
- **Finished:** The client sends an encrypted message (containing a hash and MAC over the previous handshake messages) indicating the end of the handshake session, the server responds with its Finished message. At this point the handshake phase is complete and the client and the server use the session key to encrypt and decrypt the data that they mutually exchange to validate the integrity.

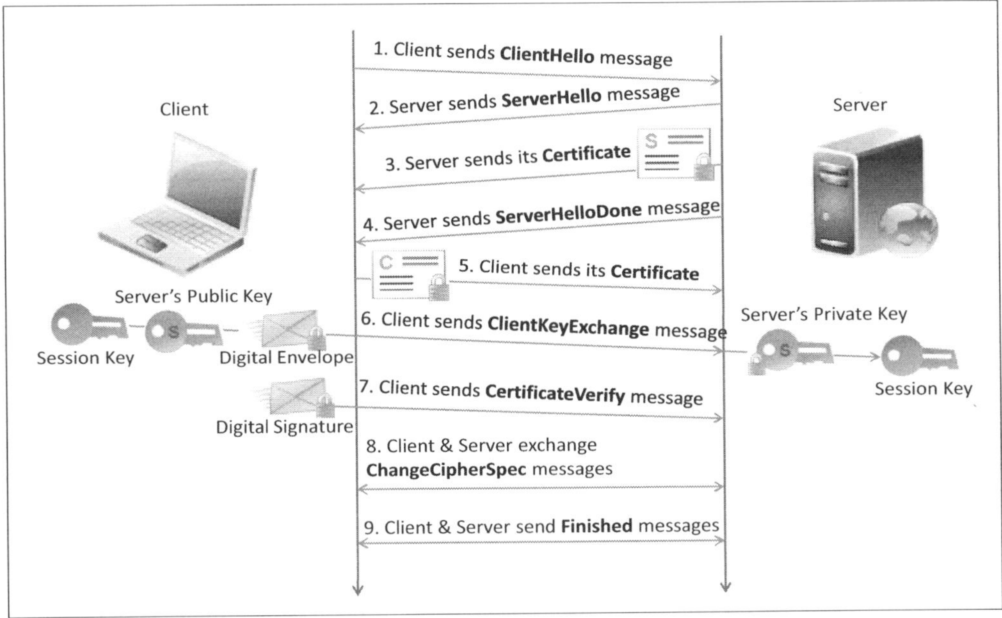

Figure 12.8: TLS Handshake

TLS/SSL use Message Authentication Codes (MAC) to detect both accidental or deliberate modifications in the data. MAC is a cryptographic checksum on the data that is used to provide an assurance that the data has not changed. Computation of MAC involves the use of (1) a secret key that is known only to the party that generates the MAC and the intended recipient, and (2) the data on which the MAC is computed.

12.7 Key Management

Management of encryption keys is critical to ensure security of encrypted data. The key management lifecycle involves different phases including:

- **Creation**: Creation of keys is the first step in the key management lifecycle. Keys must be created in a secure environment and must have adequate strength. It is recommended to encrypt the keys themselves with a separate master key.

- **Backup**: Backup of keys must be made before putting them into production because in the event of loss of keys, all encrypted data can become useless.
- **Deployment**: In this phase the new key is deployed for encrypting the data. Deployment of a new key involves re-keying existing data.
- **Monitoring**: After a key has been deployed, monitoring the performance of the encryption environment is done to ensure that the key has been deployed correctly.
- **Rotation**: Key rotation involves creating a new key and re-encrypting all data with the new key.
- **Expiration**: Key expiration phase begins after the key rotation is complete. It is recommended to complete the key rotation process before the expiry of the existing key.
- **Archival**: Archival is the phase before the key is finally destroyed. It is recommended to archive old keys for some period of time to account for scenarios where there is still some data in the system that is encrypted with the old key.
- **Destruction**: Expired keys are finally destroyed after ensuring that there is no data encrypted with the expired keys.

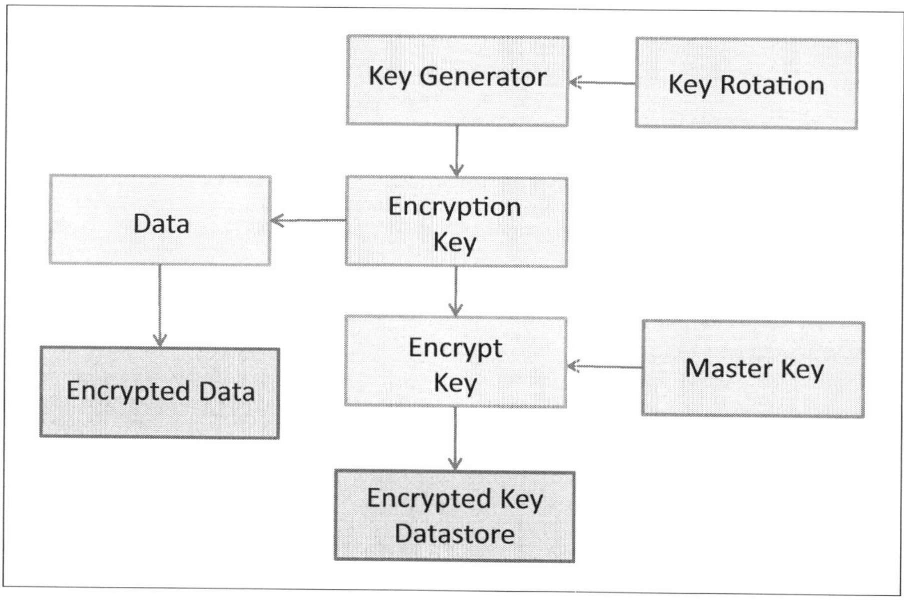

Figure 12.9: Example of a key management approach

Figure 12.9 shows an example of a key management approach. All keys for encryption must be stored in a data store which is separate and distinct from the actual data store. Additional security features such as key rotation and key encrypting keys can be used. Keys can be automatically or manually rotated. In the automated key change approach, the key is changed after a certain number of transactions. All keys can themselves be encrypted using a master key.

12.8 Auditing

Auditing is mandated by most data security regulations. Auditing requires that all read and write accesses to data be logged. Logs can include the user involved, type of access, timestamp, actions performed and records accessed. The main purpose of auditing is to find security breaches, so that necessary changes can be made in the application and deployment to prevent a further security breach. Auditing becomes even more important in cloud computing environments due to the outsourced resources and lack of direct control over the cloud infrastructure and platform which are managed by cloud service providers. The objectives of auditing include:

- Verify efficiency and compliance of identity and access management controls as per established access policies.
- Verifying that authorized users are granted access to data and services based on their roles.
- Verify whether access policies are updated in a timely manner upon change in the roles of the users.
- Verify whether the data protection policies are sufficient.
- Assessment of support activities such as problem management.

Summary

In this chapter you learned about common approaches to cloud security such as authorization, authentication, identify & access management, data security, data integrity, encryption & key management. Cloud Security Alliance provides a Trusted Cloud Initiative (TCI) Reference Architecture which is a methodology and a set of tools that enable cloud application developers and security architects to assess where their internal IT and their cloud providers are in terms of security capabilities and to plan a roadmap to meet the security needs of their business. Authentication refers to confirming the identity of the entity requesting access to some protected information. You learned about authentication mechanisms such as SSO, SAML-Token, OTP, etc. Two common SSO approaches are SAML-SSO and Kerberos. SAML-SSO uses SAML which is an XML-based open standard data format for exchanging security information (authentication and authorization data) between an identity provider and a service provider. Kerberos uses tickets for authenticating client to a service that communicate over an un-secure network. OTP uses passwords which are valid for single use only for a single transaction or session. Authorization refers to specifying the access rights to the protected resources using access policies. OAuth is an open standard for authorization that allows resource owners to share their private resources stored on one site with another site without handing out the credentials. Identity & access management deal with user identities, their authentication and authorization and access policies. Data at rest is secured by encryption which can be symmetric encryption or asymmetric encryption. Symmetric encryption uses the same secret key for both encryption and decryption. Asymmetric encryption uses two keys, one for encryption (public key) and the other for decryption (private key). Transport Layer Security (TLS) and Secure Socket Layer (SSL) are the mechanisms used for securing data in motion. The key management lifecycle involves creation, backup, deployment, monitoring, rotation, expiration, archival and destruction of keys. Auditing requires that all read and write accesses to data be logged and helps in find security breaches.

Review Questions

1. What is the difference between authentication and authorization?
2. How does SAML-SSO prevent man-in-the middle and replay attacks?
3. What are the steps involved in OAuth authorization?
4. What is the difference between symmetric-key and public-key algorithms?
5. What is the difference between host and device level encryption?
6. What are the steps involved in a TLS handshake?
7. What are the various stages in key management lifecycle?
8. What is the benefit of auditing?

Lab Exercises

1. Extend the example in Box 10.2 and integrate OAuth authorization in the Blogging app described in Chapter-7.

2. Implement a cloud-based component for key management using Figure 10.9 as the baseline. The component should have modules for key generation, key rotation (every month) and key-encrypting-key.

13 — Cloud for Industry, Healthcare & Education

This Chapter covers

Applications of cloud computing in:

- Healthcare
- Energy
- Industry
- Education

In this chapter you will learn about applications of cloud computing in healthcare, industry, energy systems and education.

13.1 Cloud Computing for Healthcare

The healthcare ecosystem consists of numerous entities including healthcare providers (primary care physicians, specialists, hospitals, for instance), payers (government, private health insurance companies, employers), pharmaceutical, device and medical service companies, IT solutions and services firms, and patients. The process of provisioning healthcare involves massive healthcare data that exists in different forms (structured or unstructured), can be coded but the skill and accuracy of that coding varies widely, is stored in disparate data sources (such as relational databases, file servers, for instance) and in many different formats. To promote more coordination of care across the multiple providers involved with patients, their clinical information is increasingly aggregated from diverse sources into Electronic Health Record (EHR) systems. Physicians diagnose patients based on information from many sources such as laboratory tests and medical devices (such as CT and MRI scanners,). In the diagnosis process, physicians retrieve and analyze the health information from the EHR. Chronic disease patients are typically seen by multiple physicians at different sites. Care is so distributed that the provider network around the average primary care physician includes some 200 other physicians. Information sharing among them is critical to high quality care. Physicians often seek expert advice from consulting specialists and this process depends on accurate and timely information sharing.

Figure 13.1 shows the application of cloud computing environments to the healthcare ecosystem. The cloud can provide several benefits to all the stakeholders in the healthcare ecosystem through systems such as Health Information Management System (HIMS), Laboratory Information System (LIS), Radiology Information System (RIS), Pharmacy Information System (PIS), for instance. Benefits of cloud computing to various stakeholder in healthcare include:

Providers & Hospitals

With public cloud based EHR systems hospitals don't need to spend a significant portion of their budgets on IT infrastructure. Public cloud service providers provide on-demand provisioning of hardware resources with pay-per-use pricing models. Thus hospitals using public cloud based EHR systems can save on upfront capital investments in hardware and data center infrastructure and pay only for the operating expenses of the cloud resources used. Hospitals can access patient data stored in the cloud and share the data with other hospitals.

Patients

Patients can provide access to their health history and information stored in the cloud (using SaaS applications) to hospitals so that the admissions, care and discharge processes can be streamlined. Physicians can upload diagnosis reports (such as pathology reports) to the cloud so that they can be accessed by doctors remotely for diagnosing the illness. Patients can manage their prescriptions and associated information such as dosage, amount and frequency, and provide this information to their healthcare provider.

Payers

Health payers can increase the effectiveness of their care management programs by providing value added services and giving access to health information to members.

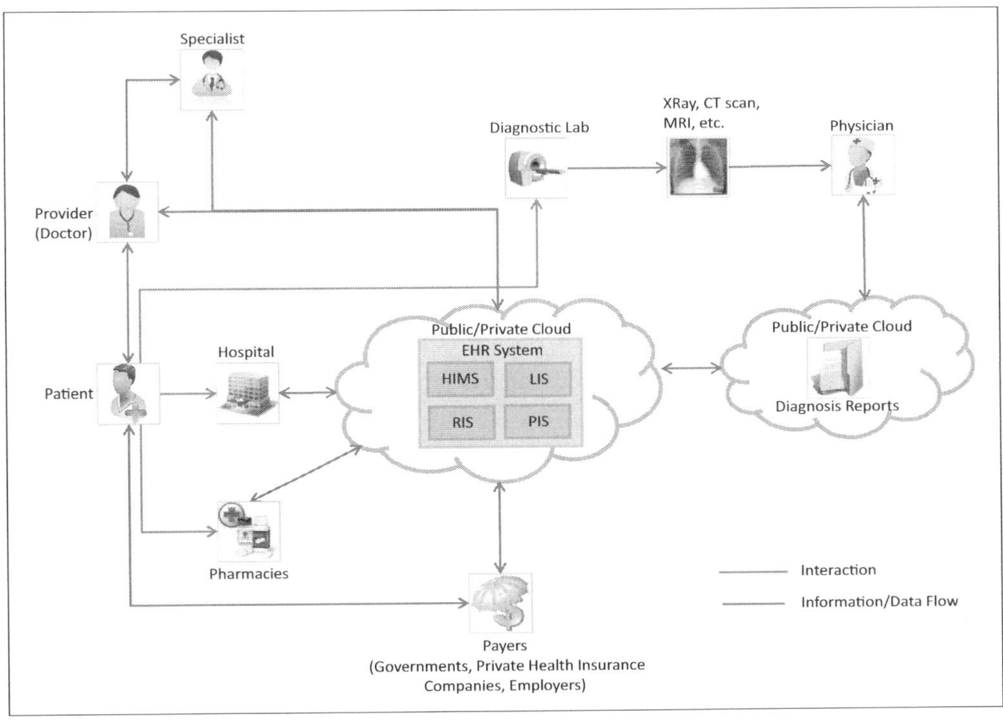

Figure 13.1: Cloud computing for healthcare

EHRs capture and store information on patient health and provider actions including individual-level laboratory results, diagnostic, treatment, and demographic data. Figure 13.2 shows a screenshot of a cloud-based EHR application. The figure shows a patient summary page of a Patient Health Record (PHR) application. The PHR application maintains information such as patient visits, allergies, immunizations, lab reports, prescribed medicines, vital signs, for instance. Though the primary use of EHRs is to maintain all medical data for an individual patient and to provide efficient access to the stored data at the point of care, EHRs can be the source for valuable aggregated information about overall patient populations. The EHR data can be used for advanced healthcare applications such as population-level health surveillance, disease detection, outbreak prediction, public health mapping, similarity-based clinical decision intelligence, medical prognosis, syndromic diagnosis, visual-analytics investigation, for instance. To exploit the potential to aggregate data for advanced healthcare applications there is a need for efficiently integrating information from distributed and heterogeneous healthcare IT systems and analyzing the integrated information. Figure 13.3 shows a screenshot of a HealthMapper application that uses a cloud-based analytics framework to query and analyze patient health records.

High Infrastructure Costs

Traditional client-server EHR systems with dedicated hosting require a team of IT experts to install, configure, test, run, secure and update hardware and software. With cloud-based EHR systems, organizations can save on the upfront capital investments for setting up the computing infrastructure as well as the costs of managing the infrastructure as all of that is done by the cloud provider.

Data Integration & Interoperability

Data integration and interoperability are the major challenges faced by traditional EHR systems. Traditional EHR systems use different and often conflicting technical and semantic standards which leads to data integration and interoperability problems. Traditional EHR systems are based on different EHR standards, different languages and different technology generations. The consequence is that EHR systems are fragmented and unable to exchange data. Acquiring medical data from different sources requires a high grade of data interoperability. Most medical information systems store clinical information about patients in proprietary formats. To address interoperability problems, several electronic health record (EHR) standards that enable structured clinical content for the purpose of exchange are currently under development. Interoperability of EHR systems will contribute to more effective and efficient patient care by facilitating the retrieval and processing of clinical information about a patient from different sites. Transferring patient information automatically between care sites will speed delivery and reduce duplicate testing and prescribing.

Scalability and Performance

Traditional EHR systems are built on a client-server model with dedicated hosting that involves a server which is installed within the organization's network and multiple clients that access the server. Data is stored on the server and can be accessed within the organization's network by authorized clients. Scaling up such systems requires additional hardware. Cloud computing is a hosting abstraction in which the underlying computing infrastructure is provisioned on demand and can be scaled up or down based on the workload. Public cloud-based applications run on cloud infrastructure which is managed by the cloud service provider. Scaling up cloud applications is easier as compared to client-server applications. For cloud-based applications, additional computing resources can be provisioned on-demand when the application workload increases. Cloud offers linear scalability without any changes in the application software.

So far we discussed the benefits of cloud computing for health IT systems. However, security of patient information is one of the biggest obstacles in the widespread adoption of cloud computing technology for EHR systems due to the outsourced nature of cloud computing. Government regulations require privacy protection and security of patient health information. For example, in the U.S., organizations called covered entities (CE), that create, maintain, transmit, use, and disclose an individual's protected health information (PHI) are required to meet Health Insurance Portability and Accountability Act (HIPAA) requirements. HIPAA requires covered entities (CE) to assure their customers that the integrity, confidentiality, and availability of PHI information they collect, maintain, use, or transmit is protected. HIPAA was expanded by the Health Information Technology for Economic and Clinical Health Act (HITECH), which addresses the privacy and security concerns associated with the electronic transmission of health information. Cloud-based

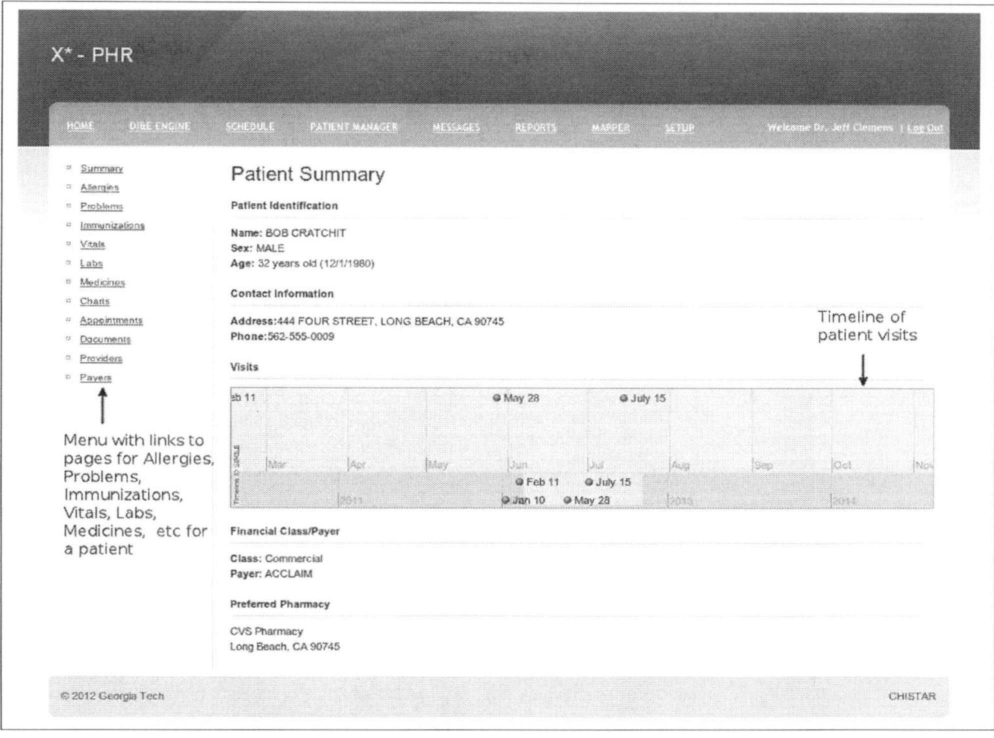

Figure 13.2: Screenshot of a cloud-based Patient Health Record application [10].

health IT systems require enhanced security features such as authorization services, identity management services and authentication services for providing secure access to healthcare data. You learned about these security aspects in Chapter 12.

Figure 13.4 shows the reference architecture for a cloud-based EHR system that can support both primary and secondary use of healthcare data with healthcare data storage and analytics in the cloud. In this architecture, tier-1 consists of web servers and load balancers, tier-2 consists of application servers and tier-3 consists of a cloud based distributed batch processing infrastructure such as Hadoop. HBase is used for the database layer. HBase is a distributed non-relational column oriented database that runs on top of HDFS. HBase provides a fault-tolerant way of storing large quantities of sparse data. HDFS is used for the storage layer for storing healthcare data in the form of flat files, images, for instance. Hive is used to provide a data warehousing infrastructure on top of Hadoop. Hive allows querying and analyzing data in HDFS/HBase using the SQL-like Hive Query Language (HQL). Zookeeper is used to provide a distributed coordination service for maintaining configuration information, naming, providing distributed synchronization, and providing group services.

13.2 Cloud Computing for Energy Systems

Complex clean energy systems (such as smart grids, power plants, wind turbine farms, for instance.) have a large number of critical components that must function correctly so that the

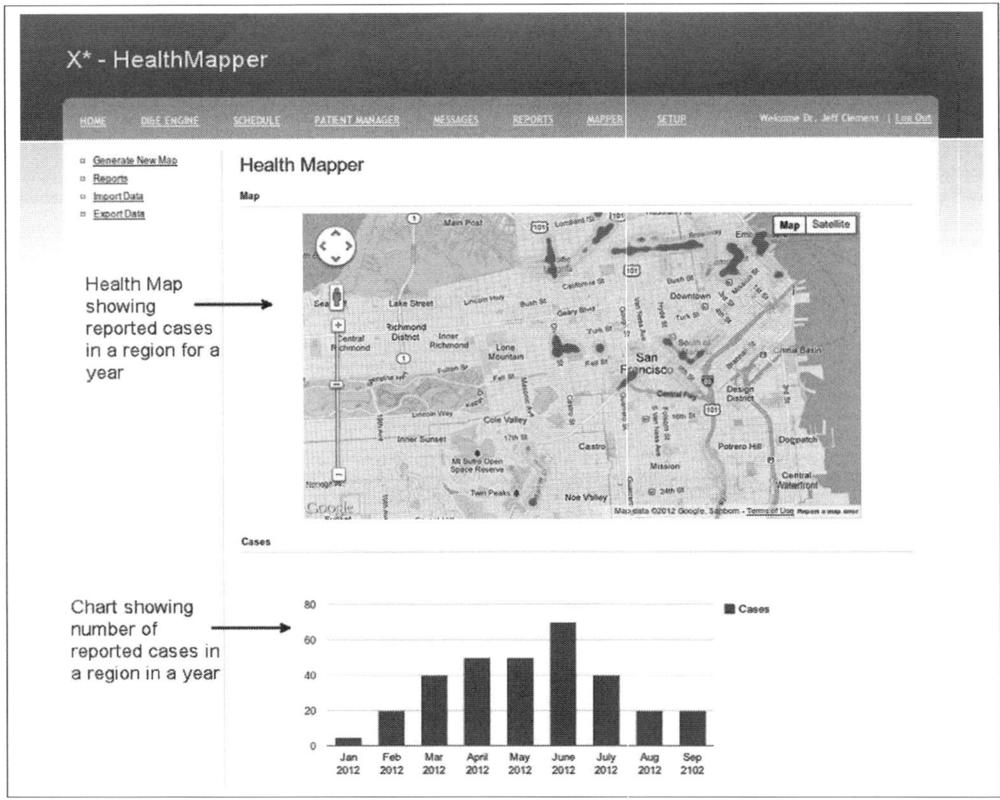

Figure 13.3: Screenshot of a cloud-based HealthMapper application that demonstrates the secondary use of healthcare data.

systems can perform their operations correctly. For example, a wind turbine has a number of critical components, e.g., bearings, turning gears, for instance. that must be monitored carefully as wear and tear in such critical components or sudden change in operating conditions of the machines can result in failures. In systems such as power grids, real-time information is collected using specialized electrical sensors called Phasor Measurement Units (PMU) at the substations. The information received from PMUs must be monitored in real-time for estimating the state of the system and for predicting failures. Energy systems have thousands of sensors that gather real-time maintenance data continuously for condition monitoring and failure prediction purposes. Maintenance and repair of such complex systems is not only expensive but also time consuming, therefore failures can cause huge losses for the operators, and supply outage for consumers.

Prognostic real-time health management involves predicting system performance by analyzing the extent of deviation of a system from its normal operating profiles. Analyzing massive amounts of maintenance data collected from sensors in energy systems and equipment can provide predictions for the impending failures (potentially in real-time) so that their reliability and availability can be improved. Reliability of a system is defined as the probability that a system will perform the intended functions under stated conditions for a specified amount of time. Availability is the probability that a system will perform a specified function

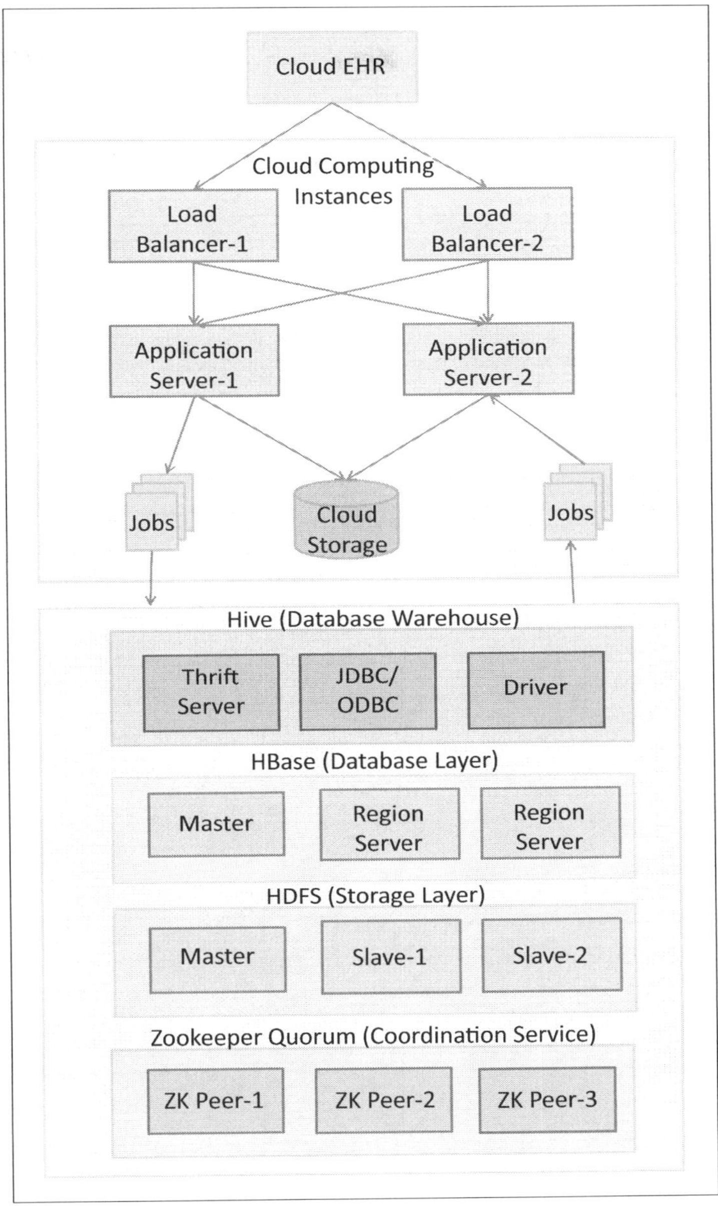

Figure 13.4: Reference architecture for a cloud-based EHR.

under given conditions at a prescribed time. Reliability of a system can be predicted using reliability models and the failure data of the various components of the system. The failure data can be available in the form of manual reports of the repairs of different components or provided in an automated manner by different sensors which monitor the health of the components. The failure data collected from machines is valuable as it can also be used to provide estimates of the reliability and availability that take into consideration the operating conditions and maintenance policies found in real world conditions and practice.

Prognostic health management systems have been developed for different energy systems.

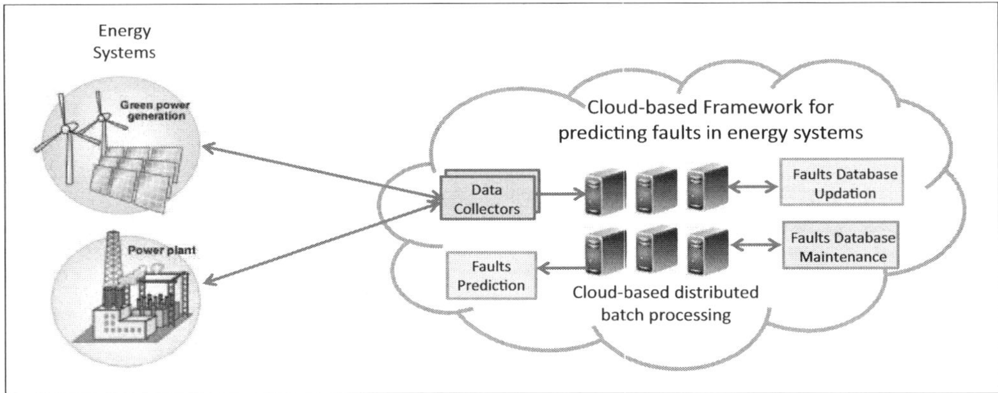

Figure 13.5: Cloud computing for energy systems

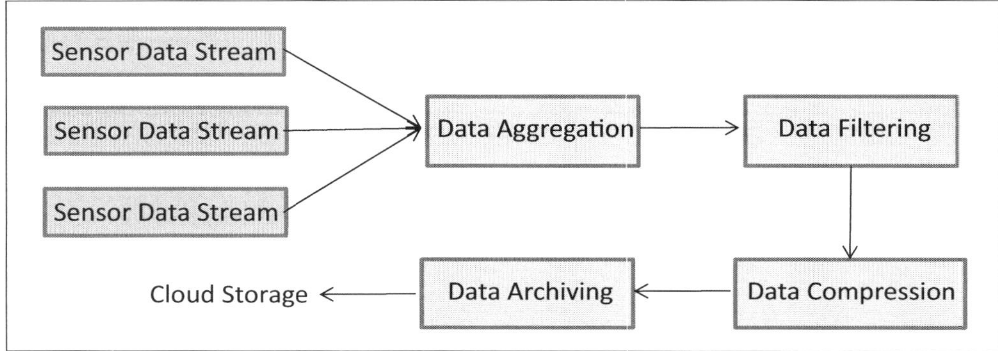

Figure 13.6: Workflow for collecting machine sensor data in a cloud.

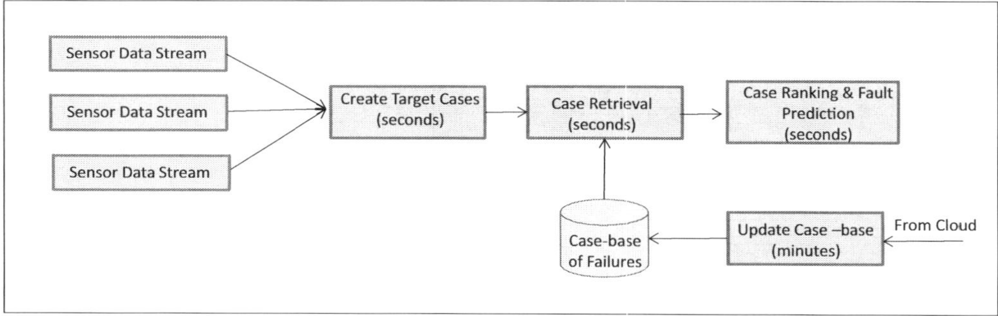

Figure 13.7: Approach for predicting failures in real-time using case-based reasoning demonstrated in [8].

GE has developed a system for gas turbine diagnostics [34]. SKF WindCon [35] is a condition monitoring solution for wind turbines developed by SKF. OpenPDC [36] is a set of applications for processing of streaming time-series data collected from Phasor Measurement Units (PMUs) in real-time. A generic framework for storage, processing and analysis of massive machine maintenance data, collected from a large number of sensors embedded in industrial machines, in a cloud computing environment was proposed in [8]. Figure 13.5 shows a generic use case of cloud for energy systems.

The scale of sensor data collected from energy systems is so large that it is not possible to fit the data on a single machine's disk. Cloud-based big sensor data storage and analytics systems are based on distributed storage systems (such as HDFS) and distributed batch processing frameworks (such as Hadoop). Cloud-based distributed batch processing infrastructures process large volumes of data using inexpensive commodity computers which are connected to work in parallel. Thus there is no need for expensive and reliable hardware for machine data processing. Such systems are designed to work on commodity hardware which has high probability of failure using techniques such as replication of file blocks on multiple machines in a cluster.

Figure 13.6 shows a workflow for aggregating sensor data in a cloud. The first step in this workflow is data aggregation. Each incoming data stream is mapped to a data aggregator. Since the raw sensor data comes from a large number of machines in the form of data streams, the data has to be preprocessed to make the data analysis using cloud-based parallel processing frameworks (such as Hadoop) more efficient. For example, the Hadoop MapReduce data processing model works more efficiently with a small number of large files rather than a large number of small files. The data aggregators buffer the streaming data into larger chunks. The next step is to filter data and remove bad records in which some sensor readings are missing. The filtered data then compressed and archived to a cloud storage.

With the sensor data collected in the cloud, the next step is to analyze the data to predict the state of the system and any impending faults. Faults in energy systems have unique signatures such as increase in temperature, increase in vibration levels, for instance. Various machine learning and analysis algorithms can be implemented over the distributed processing frameworks in the cloud for analyzing the machine sensor data. For example, by cluster analysis of big sensor data, sensor measurements can be assigned into clusters, so that measurements in the same cluster are more similar to each other than to the measurements in other clusters. Clustering algorithms can help in fault isolation. Case-based reasoning (CBR) is another popular method that has been used for fault prediction. CBR finds solutions to new problems based on past experience. CBR is an effective technique for problem solving in the fields in which it is hard to establish a quantitative mathematical model, such as prognostic health management. In CBR, the past experience is organized and represented as cases in a case-base. The steps involved in CBR are: (i) retrieving similar cases from case-base, (ii) reusing the information in the retrieved cases, (iii) revising the solution and (iv) retaining a new experience into the case-base. Figure 13.7 shows an approach based on CBR used for failure prediction in real-time as demonstrated in [8].

Lets us look the application of cloud computing for smart grids. Smart Grid is a data communications network integrated with the electrical grid that collects and analyzes data captured in near-real-time about power transmission, distribution, and consumption. Smart Grid technology provides predictive information and recommendations to utilities, their suppliers, and their customers on how best to manage power.

Figure 13.8 shows how smart grids can use cloud computing. Smart Grids collect data regarding electricity generation (centralized or distributed), consumption (instantaneous or predictive), storage (or conversion of energy into other forms), distribution and equipment health data. Smart grids use high-speed, fully integrated, two-way communication technolo-

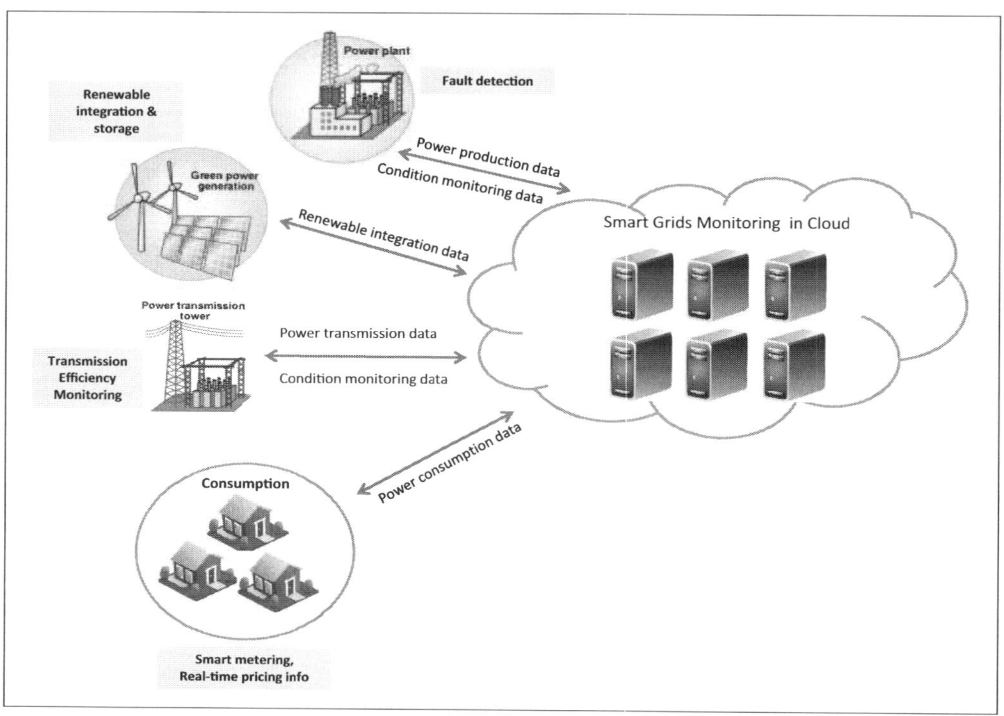

Figure 13.8: Cloud computing for smart grids

gies for real-time information and power exchange. Sensing and measurement technologies are used for evaluating the health of equipment and the integrity of the grid. Power thefts can be prevented using smart metering. By analyzing the data on power generation, transmission and consumption smart girds can improve efficiency throughout the electric system. Storage collection and analysis of smarts grids data in the cloud can help in dynamic optimization of system operations, maintenance, and planning. Cloud-based monitoring of smart grids data can improve energy usage levels via energy feedback to users coupled with real-time pricing information and from users with energy consumption status to reduce energy usage. Real-time demand response and management strategies can be used for lowering peak demand and overall load via appliance control and energy storage mechanisms. Condition monitoring data collected from power generation and transmission systems can help in detecting faults and predicting outages. Probabilistic risk assessments based on real-time measurements can help in identifying the equipment, power plants and transmission lines most likely to fail. Smarts grids data analytics can predict problems before they occur. This allows steps to be taken to minimize impacts and to respond more effectively.

13.3 Cloud Computing for Transportation Systems

Modern transportation systems are driven by data collected from multiple sources which is processed to provide new services to the stakeholders. By collecting large amount of data from various sources and processing the data into useful information, data-driven transportation systems can provide new services such as advanced route guidance [37,

38], dynamic vehicle routing [39], anticipating customer demands for pickup and delivery problem, for instance. Collection and organization of data from multiple sources in real-time and using the massive amounts data for providing intelligent decisions for operations and supply chains, is a major challenge, primarily because the size of the databases involved is very large, and real-time analysis tools have not been available. As a result large organizations are faced with a seemingly unsurmountable problem of analyzing terabytes of unorganized data stored on isolated and distinct geographical locations. However, recent advances in massive scale data processing systems, utilized for driving business operations of corporations provide a promising approach to massive intelligent transportation systems (ITS) data storage and analysis. Figure 13.9 shows a generic use case of cloud for transportation systems.

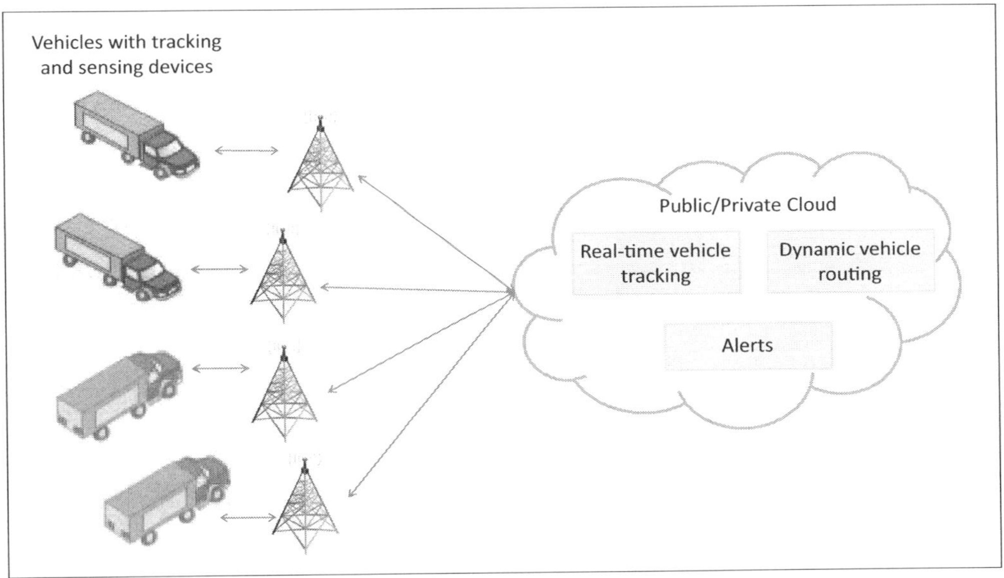

Figure 13.9: Cloud computing for transportation systems

Let us look at some of the applications of cloud computing for transportation systems:

Fleet Tracking

Vehicle fleet tracking systems use GPS technology to track the locations of the vehicles in real-time. Cloud-based fleet tracking systems can be scaled up on demand to handle large number of vehicles. Alerts can be generated in case of deviations in planned routes. The vehicle locations and routes data can be aggregated and analyzed for detecting bottlenecks in the supply chain such as traffic congestions on routes, assignments and generation of alternative routes, and supply chain optimization.

Route Generation & Scheduling

Route generation and scheduling systems can generate end-to-end routes using combination of route patterns and transportation modes and feasible schedules based on the availability of vehicles. As the transportation network grows in size and complexity, the number of possible route combinations increases exponentially. Route administrators find it is increasingly difficult to build and keep routes updated in a timely fashion. Cloud-based route generation and scheduling systems can provide fast response to the route generation queries and can be scaled up to serve a large transportation network.

Condition Monitoring

Condition monitoring solutions for transportation systems allow monitoring the conditions inside containers. For example, containers carrying fresh food produce can be monitored to prevent spoilage of food. Condition monitoring with sensors such as temperature, pressure, humidity, for instance. for a large fleet of vehicles can generate big data that can be difficult to analyze in real time. Cloud-based systems can be used for this purpose that not only detect food spoilage but also suggest alternative routes to prevent spoilage.

Planning, Operations & Services

Different transportation solutions (such as fleet tracking, condition monitoring, route generation, scheduling, cargo operations, fleet maintenance, customer service, order booking, billing & collection, for instance.) can be moved to the cloud to provide a seamless integration between order management, tactical planning & execution and customer facing processes & systems. Such integrated cloud-based systems for planning, operation and services for transportation systems enable the organizations to improve asset utilization, increase contribution, reduce network management costs (e.g. roll costs), and improve service levels.

Let us look at the example of fleet tracking and condition monitoring in more detail. Collecting and organizing location and sensor data from vehicles in transit and using the data for raising alerts about violation of certain conditions is a major challenge for the following reasons: 1) wide coverage is needed for collection of location and sensor data from vehicles carrying fresh food supply; 2) data needs to be collected from a large number of vehicles in real-time to raise timely alerts; 3) the collected data is massive scale, since the real-time data from a large number of vehicles is collected simultaneously; 4) the massive scale data needs to be organized and processed in real-time; 5) the infrastructure used for data collection should be low cost and easily deployable to ensure wide popularity. Cloud computing can be leveraged for such applications.

A cloud-based framework for real-time fresh food supply tracking and monitoring was proposed in [9]. Fresh food can be damaged during transit due to unrefrigerated conditions and changes in environmental conditions such as temperature and humidity, which can lead to microbial infections and biochemical reactions or mechanical damage due to rough handling. Spoilage of fruits and vegetables during transport and distribution not only results in losses to the distributors but also presents a hazard to the food safety. Therefore tracking and monitoring of fresh food supply is an important problem that needs to be addressed. Since fresh foods have short durability, tracking the supply of fresh foods and monitoring the transit conditions can help identification of potential food safety hazards. The analysis and interpretation of data on the environmental conditions in the container and food truck positioning can enable more effective routing decisions in real time. Therefore, it is possible to take remedial measures such as, (1) the food that has a limited time budget before it gets rotten can be re-routed to a closer destinations, (2) alerts can be raised to the driver and the distributor about the transit conditions, such as container temperature exceeding the allowed limit, humidity levels going out of the allowed limit, for instance., and corrective actions can be taken before the food gets damaged.

Monitoring and tracking supply chain transportation fleet involves a large amount of data. The scale of the location and sensor data involved for a fleet of vehicles is very large. For example, if the location and sensor readings are collected from 1000 vehicles every one minute then 1.44 million records will be created in one day on the server. Scalability is required both in terms of data storage and analysis. The advantage of using a cloud computing environment for data storage and analysis is that it is possible to organize and analyze real-time data from a large number of vehicles. Scalable algorithms for data analysis (such as generation of alerts and optimal routes) can be developed by leveraging the parallel computing capability of a computing cloud based on a large-scale distributed batch processing infrastructure. A cloud computing based approach also provides flexibility in data analysis jobs as the frequency of analysis jobs can be varied. Cloud computing resources can be provisioned on a just-in-time basis based on the demand. For example, if the number of vehicles registered with the tracking and monitoring service become large additional computing resources can be provisioned on-demand. The frequency of location and sensor data collection and data analysis in the cloud can also be increased or decreased depending on the requirements of the vehicles and type of food produce being transported.

13.4 Cloud Computing for Manufacturing Industry

Manufacturing industry researchers are exploring the potential of utilizing cloud computing for manufacturing that would enable collaborative design, distributed manufacturing and co-creation. There are two forms of cloud manufacturing, one that involves the use of cloud computing technologies for manufacturing and the other that involves service-oriented manufacturing that replicates the cloud computing environment using physical manufacturing resources (like computing resources in cloud computing). Cloud computing is well suited for manufacturing industry in which the computing needs vary significantly with the product lifecycle phase. Cloud computing can help in manufacturing by providing computational, storage and software services on demand. Cloud computing allows improved resource sharing, rapid prototyping, and reduces cost of manufacturing.

An application of cloud computing technologies for manufacturing is the Industrial Control Systems (ICS) data analytics. Industrial control systems such as supervisory control and data acquisition (SCADA) systems, distributed control systems (DCS), and other control system configurations such as Programmable Logic Controllers (PLC) found in the manufacturing industry continuously generate monitoring and control data. Real-time collection, management and analysis of data on production operations generated by ICS, in the cloud, can help in estimating the state of the systems, improve plant and personnel safety and thus take appropriate action in real-time to prevent catastrophic failures. Wu et. al. [40] have proposed to expand the paradigm of cloud computing to the field of computer-aided design and manufacturing and propose a new concept of cloud-based design and manufacturing (CBDM).

Figure 13.10 shows an example of services in cloud-based design and manufacturing including:

Software-as-a-Service (SaaS)

SaaS service model provides software applications such as customer relationship management (CRM), enterprise relationship management (ERP), computer aided design and manufacturing (CAD/CAM) hosted in a computing cloud, through thin clients such as web browsers. SaaS

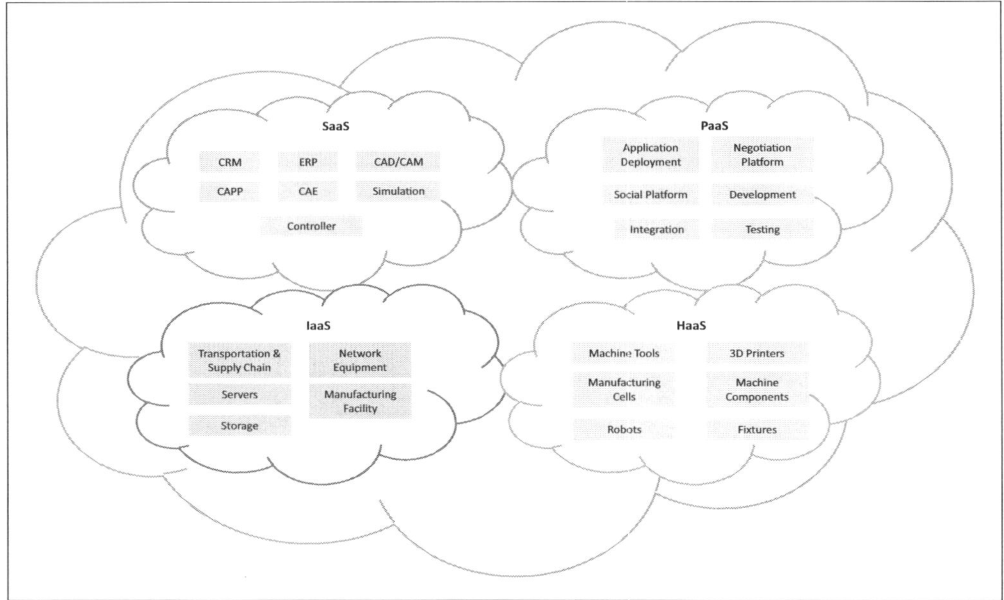

Figure 13.10: Cloud-based design and manufacturing

applications can be accessed by multiple teams spread across different locations working in a collaborative development environment.

Platform-as-a-Service (PaaS)

PaaS service model allows deployment of applications without the need for buying or managing the underlying infrastructure. PaaS provides services for developing, integrating and testing applications in an integrated development environment. Design teams can leverage PaaS for collaboration and enhance their productivity.

Infrastructure-as-a-Service (IaaS)

IaaS provides physical resources such as servers, storage that can be provisioned on demand.

Hardware-as-a-Service (HaaS)

HaaS provides access to machine tools, 3D printers, manufacturing cells, industrial robots, for instance. HaaS providers can rent hardware to consumers through the CBDM environment. For example, a HaaS service for 3D printing can be used by multiple organizations for printing 3D parts. Cloud connected 3D printers allow rapid tooling which makes rapid scalability possible for traditional manufacturing processes requiring tools.

13.5 Cloud Computing for Education

Cloud computing is bringing a transformative impact in the field of education by improving the reach of quality education to students through the use of online learning platforms and collaboration tools.

In the recent years the concept of Massively Online Open Courses (MOOCs) appears to be gaining popularity worldwide with large numbers students enrolling for online courses.

MOOCs are aimed for large audiences and use cloud technologies for providing audio/video content, readings, assignment and exams. Cloud-based auto-grading applications are used for grading exams and assignments. Cloud-based applications for peer grading of exams and assignments are also used in some MOOCs. MOOCs encourage discussions between students through online discussion boards. Cloud technologies make large-scale feedback and interactions possible by provisioning resources on demand and providing seamless scalability. Cloud computing thus has the potential of helping in bringing down the cost of education by increasing the student-teacher ratio through the use of online learning platforms and new evaluation approaches without sacrificing quality.

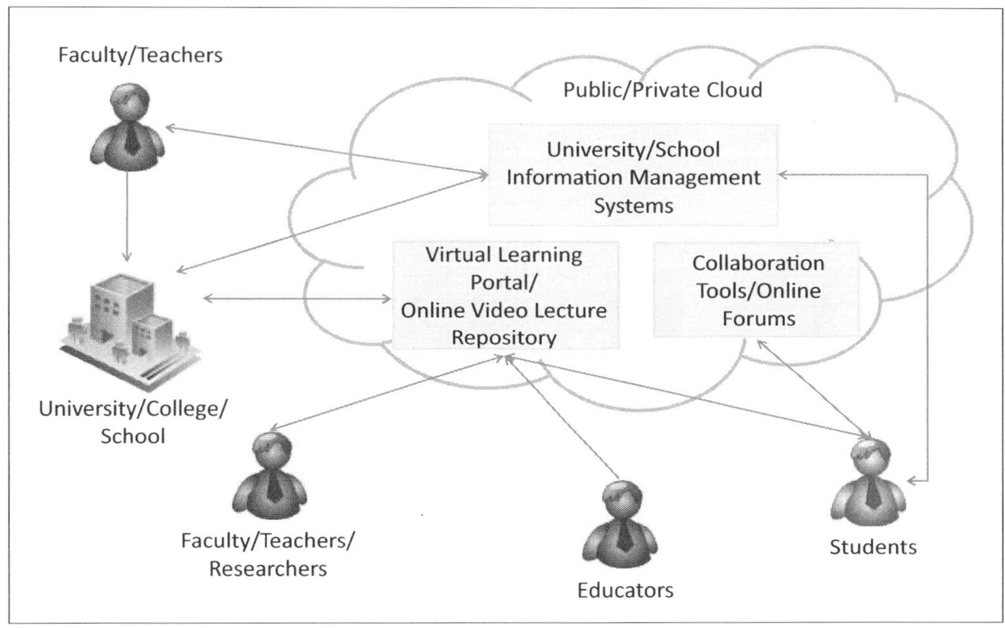

Figure 13.11: Cloud computing for education

Many universities across the world are using cloud platforms for providing online degree programs. Lectures are delivered through live/recorded video using cloud based content delivery networks to students across the world. Online proctoring for distance learning programs is also becoming popular through the use of cloud-based live video streaming technologies where online proctors observe test takers remotely through video. Access to virtual labs is provided to distance learning students through the cloud. Virtual labs provide remote access to the same software and applications that are used by students on campus. Cloud-based course management platforms are used to for sharing reading materials, providing assignments and releasing grades, for instance.

Cloud-based collaboration applications such as online forums, can help student discuss common problems and seek guidance from experts. Universities, colleges and schools can use cloud-based information management systems to improve administrative efficiency, offer online and distance education programs, online exams, track progress of students, collect feedback from students, for instance. Figure 13.11 shows a generic use case of cloud for education. Cloud-based systems can help universities, colleges and schools in cutting down the IT infrastructure costs and yet provide access to educational services to a large number of students.

Summary

In this chapter you learned about the applications of cloud computing in healthcare, industry, energy systems and education. The cloud can provide several benefits to all the stakeholders in the healthcare ecosystem (Providers & Hospitals, Patients and Payers) through systems such as Health Information Management System (HIMS), Laboratory Information System (LIS), Radiology Information System (RIS), Pharmacy Information System (PIS), for instance. You learned about a reference architecture for a cloud-based EHR. The benefit of moving healthcare applications to the cloud is that it improves scalability and performance, reduces infrastructure costs and enables data integration & interoperability. Cloud computing can be used for prognostic real-time health management applications that predict performance of energy systems (such as smart grids, power plants, wind turbine farms, for instance.) The scale of sensor data collected from energy systems is so large that it is not possible to fit the data on a single machine's disk. Cloud-based applications can analyze massive scale sensor data and predict the impending failures. Cloud computing has applications in transportation systems as well. Cloud-based applications for fleet tracking, route generation & scheduling, condition monitoring, for instance. can improve the efficiency and reduce wastage in transportation systems. Cloud enables various services for design and manufacturing such as Saas services (applications such CRM, ERP, CAD/CAM, for instance.), PaaS services (for development, integration and testing), IaaS services (for provisioning physical resources) and HaaS (provides access to machine tools, 3D printers, manufacturing cells, industrial robots, for instance.). In the education domain, cloud computing is helping to improve the reach of quality education to students through online learning platforms and collaboration tools.

Review Questions

1. What are the benefits of using cloud for EHR systems?
2. What aspects of cloud computing make it useful for prognostic health management applications for energy systems?
3. What are the steps involved in case-based reasoning?
4. What is cloud-based design and manufacturing?

Appendix-A - Setting up Ubuntu VM

Setting up Ubuntu Virtual Machine

The examples and exercises in this book have been developed and tested on Ubuntu Linux. This appendix provides the instructions for setting up an Ubuntu Linux virtual machine within other operating systems such as Windows. To set an Ubuntu virtual machine, the VirtualBox [110] software is used. VirtualBox is a virtualization software that allows you to run an entire operating system inside another operating system. VirtualBox runs on Windows, Linux, Macintosh, and Solaris hosts.

Download and install VirtualBox on your local machine. Also download the latest Ubuntu disk image (ISO file) from the Ubuntu website [111]. Launch VitualBox and then click on the New button to create a new virtual machine. Then enter a name for the virtual machine and choose the operating system as shown in Figure A1.1.

Then select the amount of memory to be allocated for the virtual machine.

Allocate a quarter of the RAM on your local machine for a good user experience as shown in Figure A1.2. For examples, if you have 4GB of RAM on your local machine, then allocate 1GB for the virtual machine.

Next, create a new virtual hard disk as shown in Figure A1.3. Select the virtual disk image (VDI) hard drive file type as shown in Figure A1.4. Then choose the fixed size storage for the hard disk as shown in Figure A1.5.

Next select the size of the virtual hard drive as shown in Figure A1.6. For Ubuntu, a virtual hard drive of atleast 4GB is required.

Create the virtual hard disk and then open the settings. In the storage section, click on the "Choose a virtual CD/DVD disk file“ and add the downloaded Ubuntu disk image (ISO file) as shown in Figure A1.7.

In the list of virtual machines, in the main window of VirtualBox, double-click your virtual machine to start it as shown in Figure A1.8. When the Ubuntu boots up you will see an option to install Ubuntu as shown in Figure A1.9.

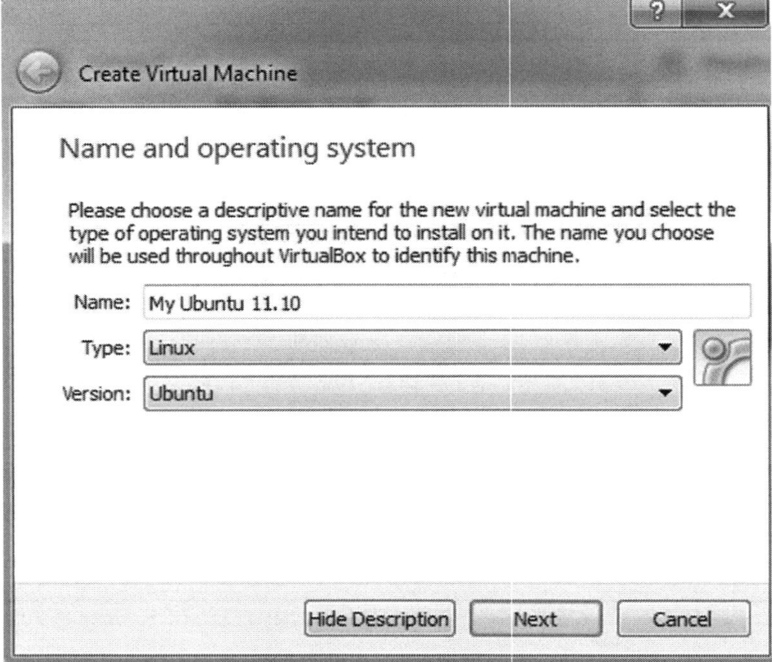

Figure A1.1: Creating a virtual machine with VitualBox

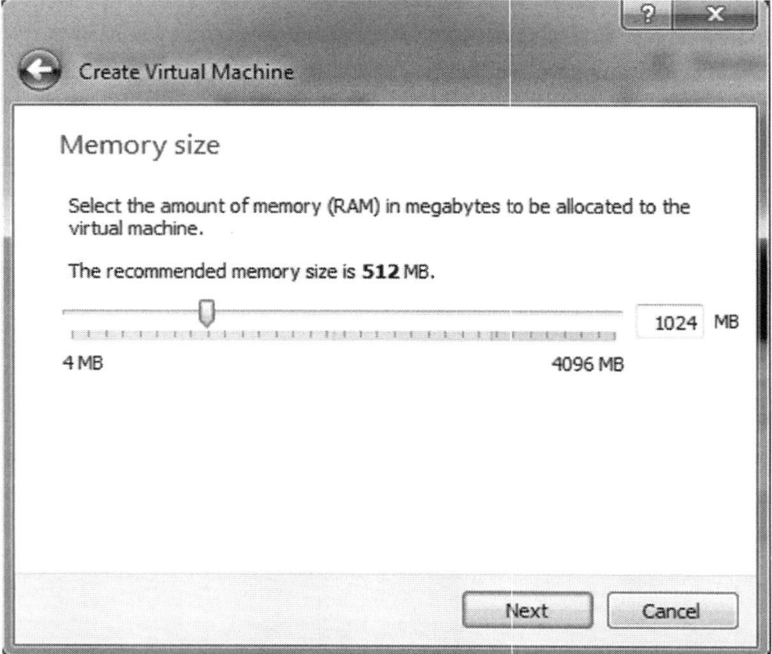

Figure A1.2: Selecting the memory size

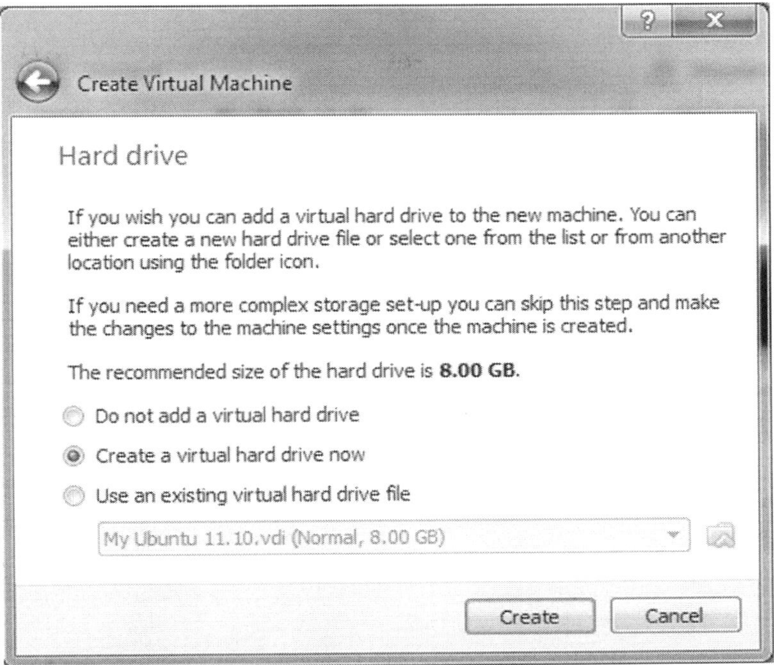

Figure A1.3: Creating a new virtual hard disk

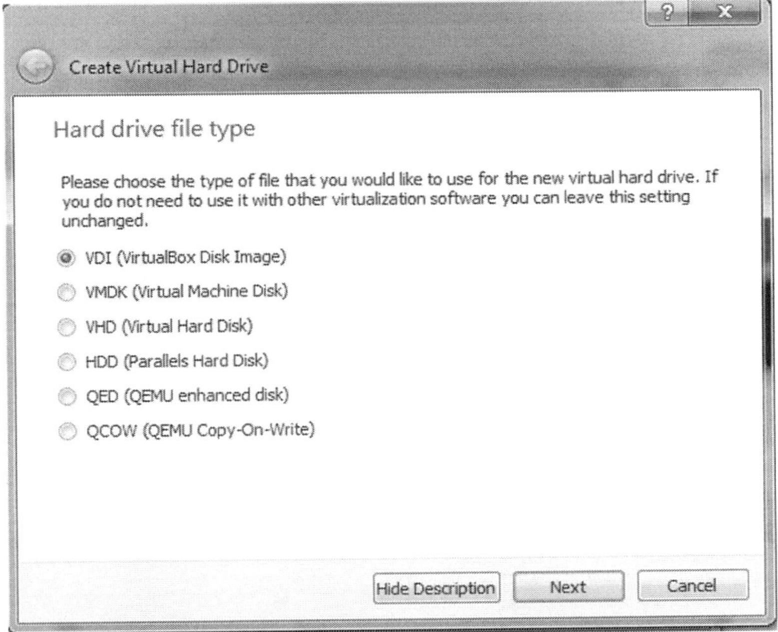

Figure A1.4: Selecting hard drive file type

Click on the Install Ubuntu button and select the installation type as shown in Figure A1.10. Choose the Erase disk option and start the installation as shown in Figures A1.11 and

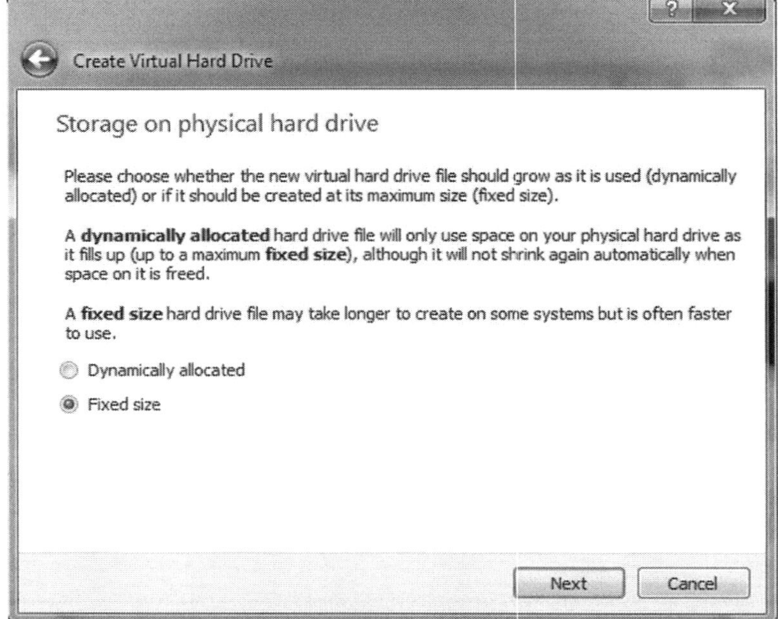

Figure A1.5: Choosing storage type

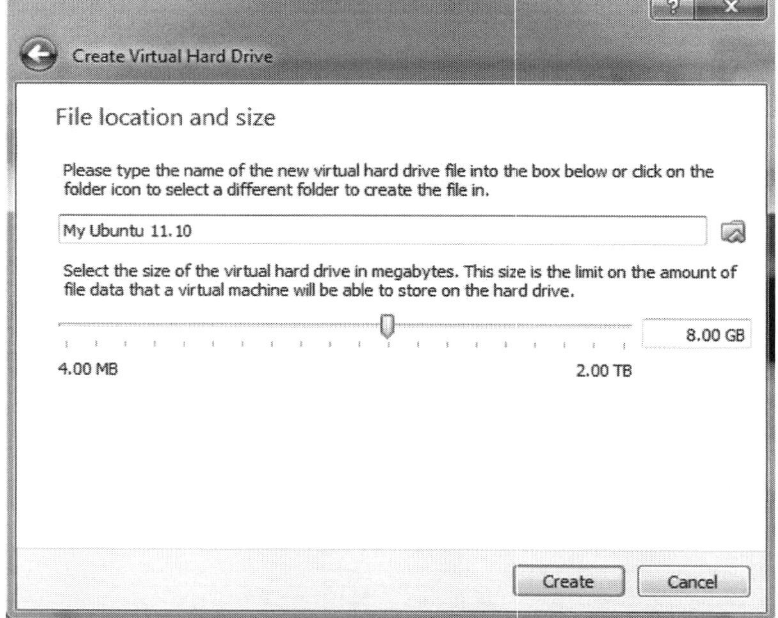

Figure A1.6: Choosing virtual hard drive size

A1.12.

When the installation completes, you will get a message to restart as shown in Figure A1.13. Restart the Ubuntu virtual machine. Ubuntu will boot and present the login screen as

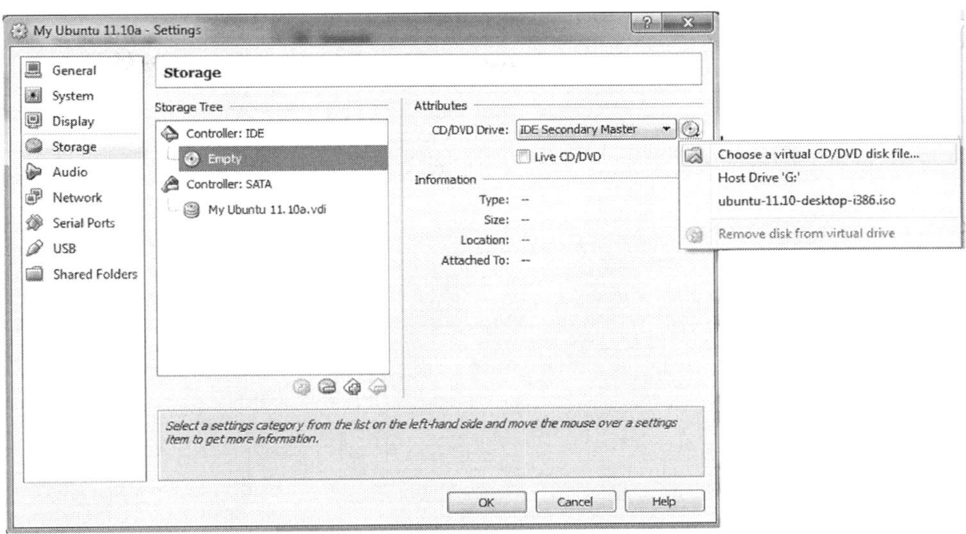

Figure A1.7: Adding Ubuntu disk image to virtual machine

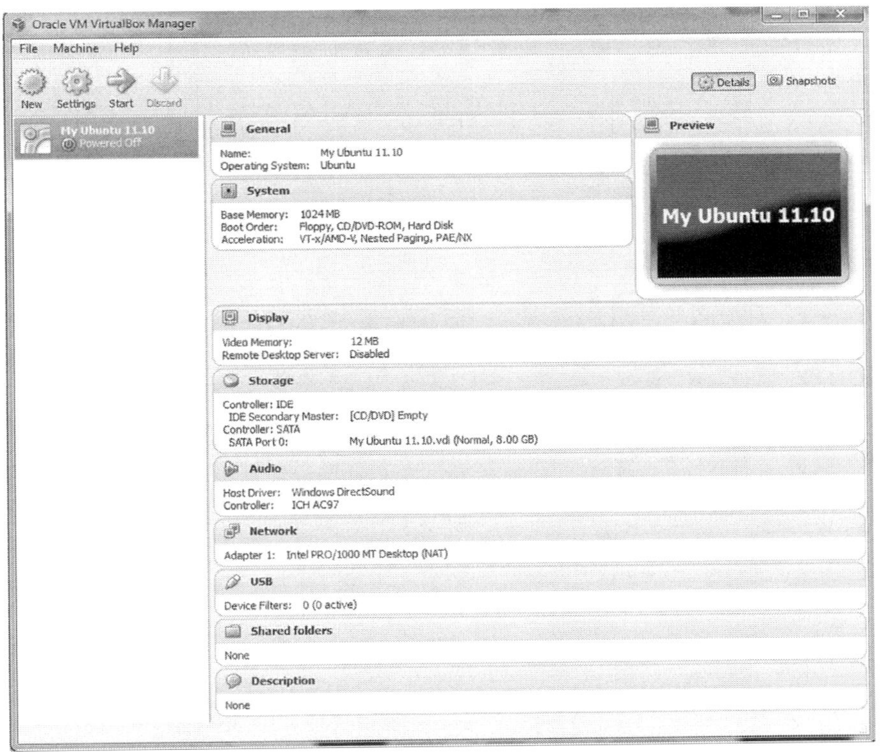

Figure A1.8: VirtualBox main window showing the Ubuntu virtual machine

shown in Figure A1.14. Enter the username and password you provided while installation to login.

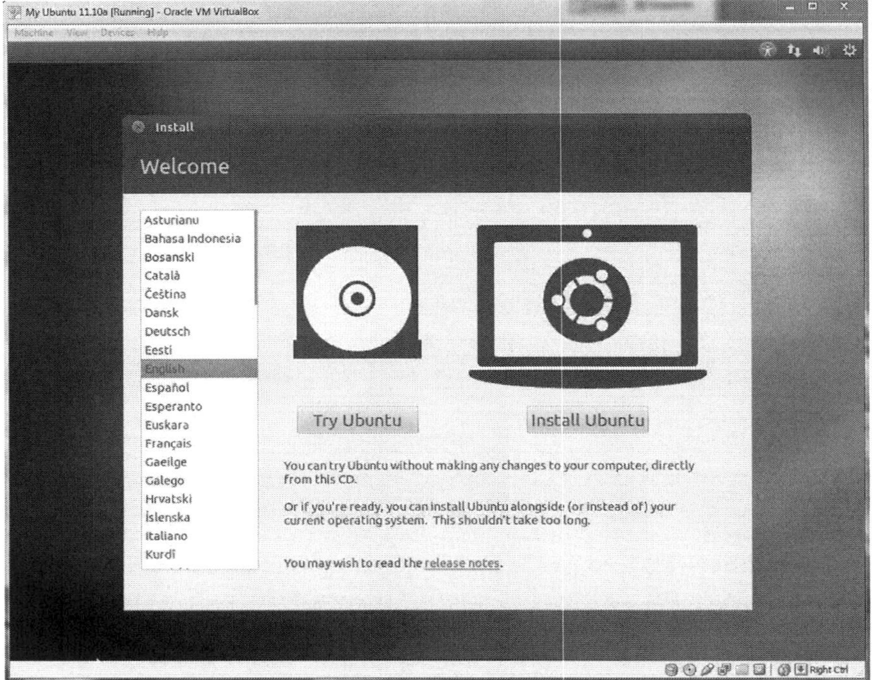

Figure A1.9: Ubuntu virtual machine running in VirtualBox

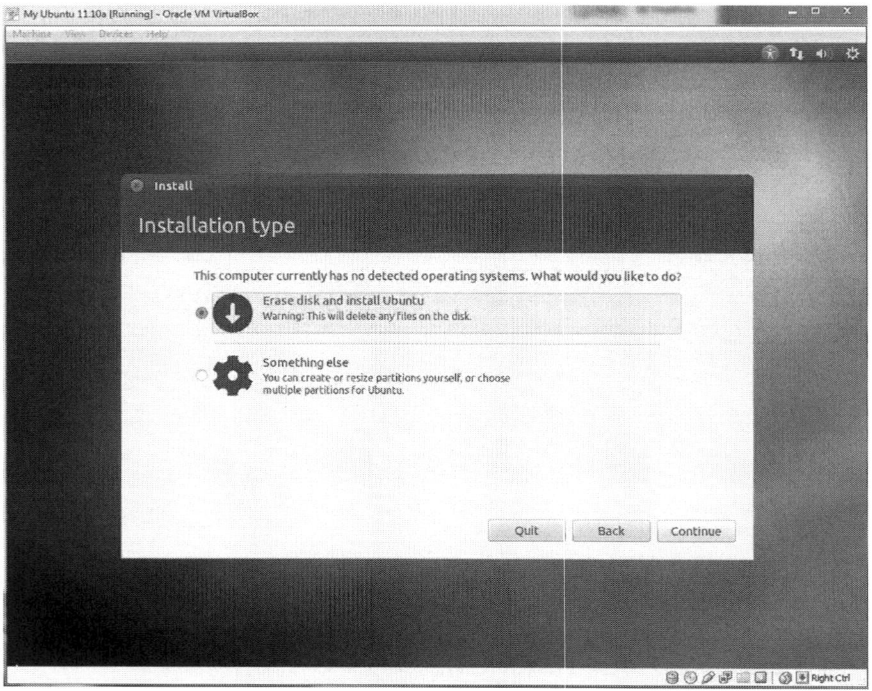

Figure A1.10: Selecting installation type.

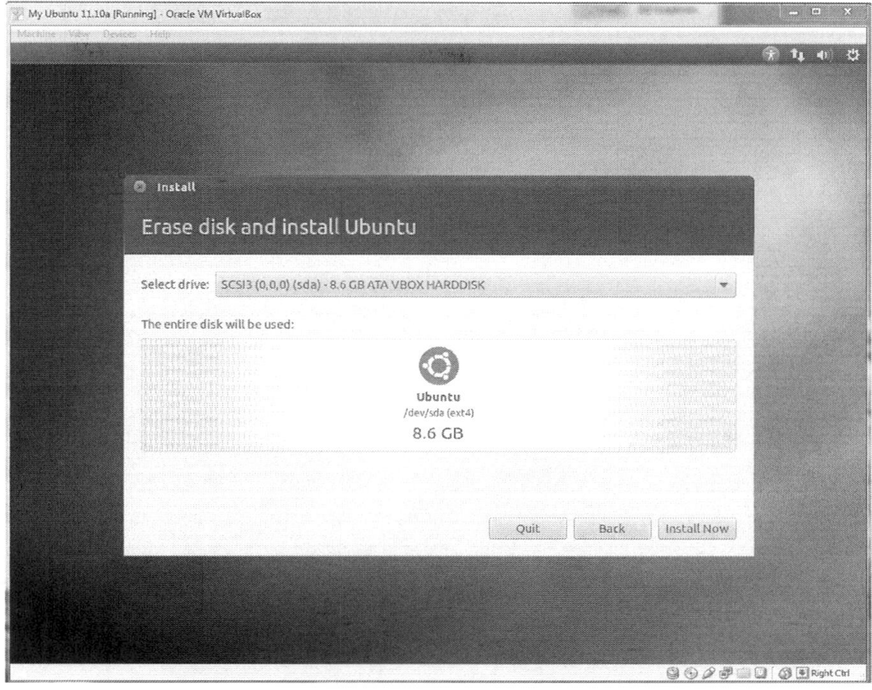

Figure A1.11: Starting installation

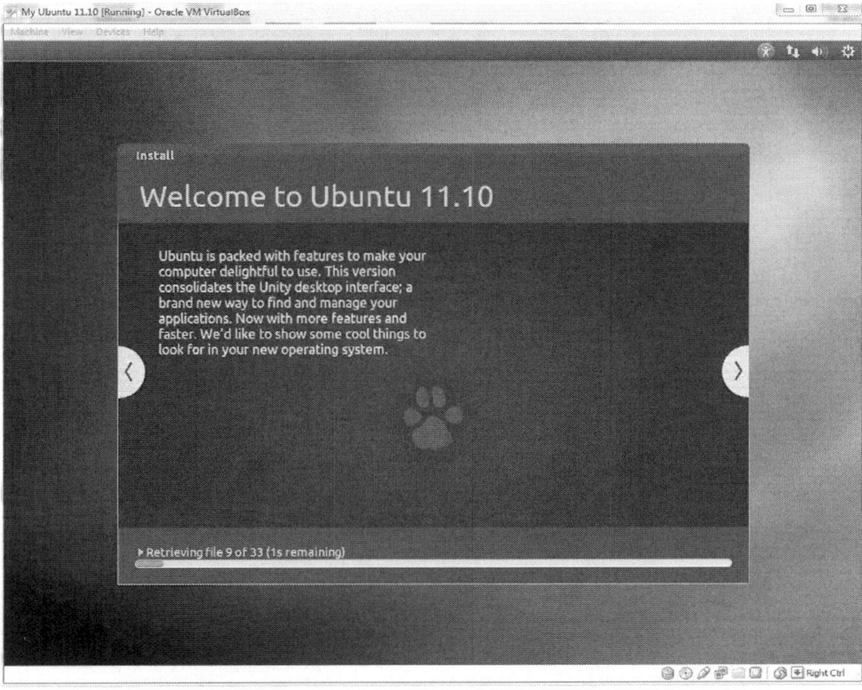

Figure A1.12: Installation in progress

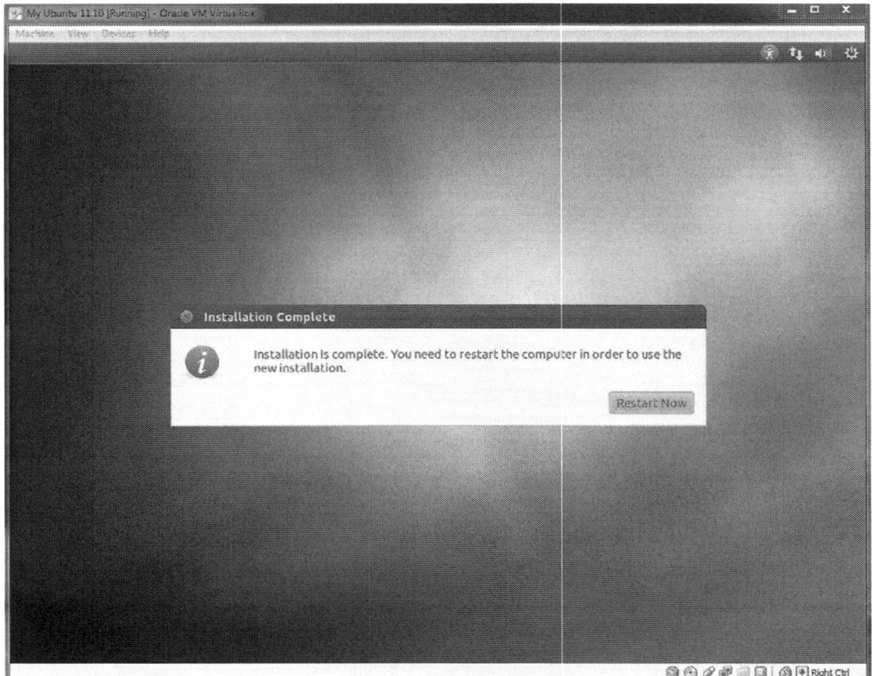

Figure A1.13: Installation complete message

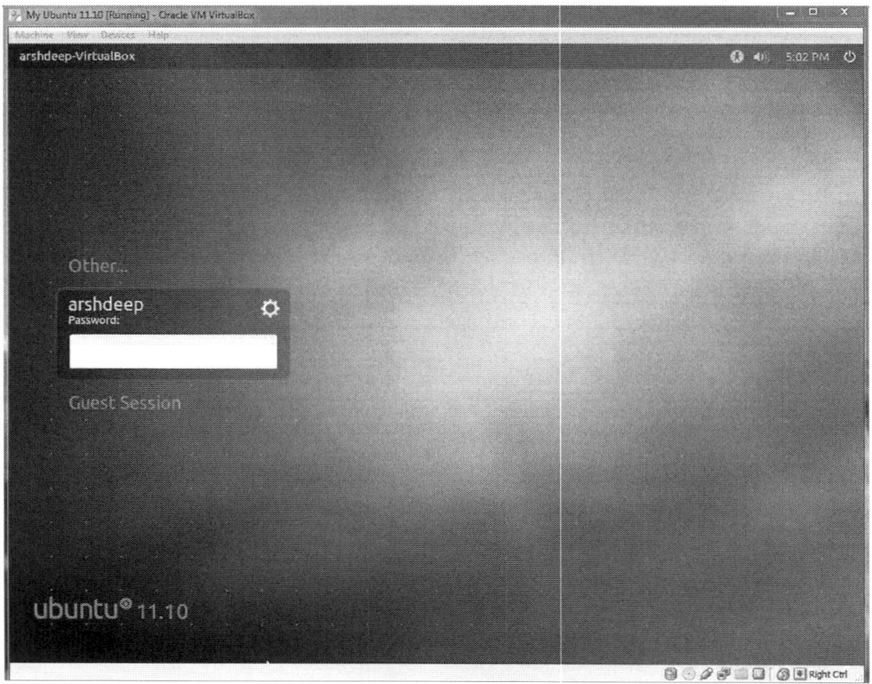

Figure A1.14: Ubuntu login screen

Appendix-B - Setting up Django

Setting up Django on Amazon EC2

This section provides instructions for setting up Django on an Amazon EC2 instance. To launch a new instance open the Amazon EC2 console and click on the launch instance button.

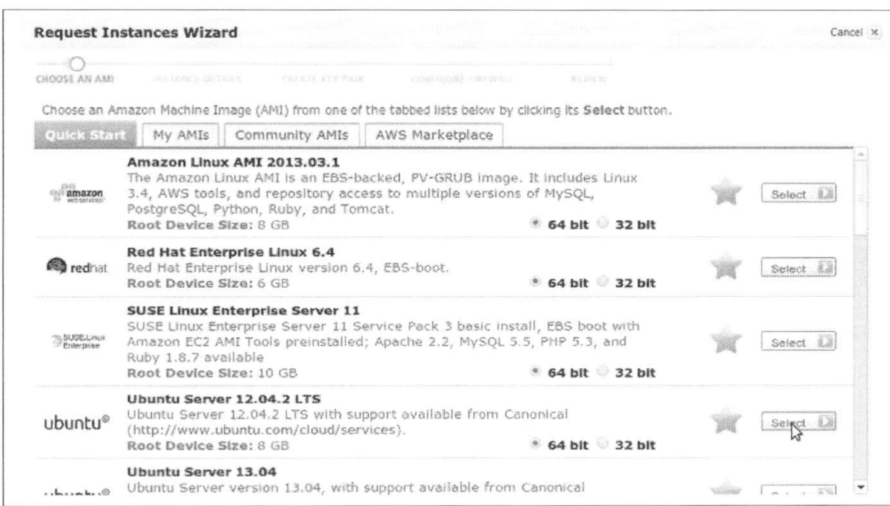

Figure A2.1: Amazon EC2 instance launch wizard showing AMIs

This will open a wizard where you can select the AMI with which you want to launch the instance as shown in Figure A2.1. Select an Ubuntu AMI. When you launch an instance you specify the instance type in the launch wizard as shown in Figure A2.2. In the instance details page you also specify the number of instances to launch based on the selected AMI and availability zones for the instances.

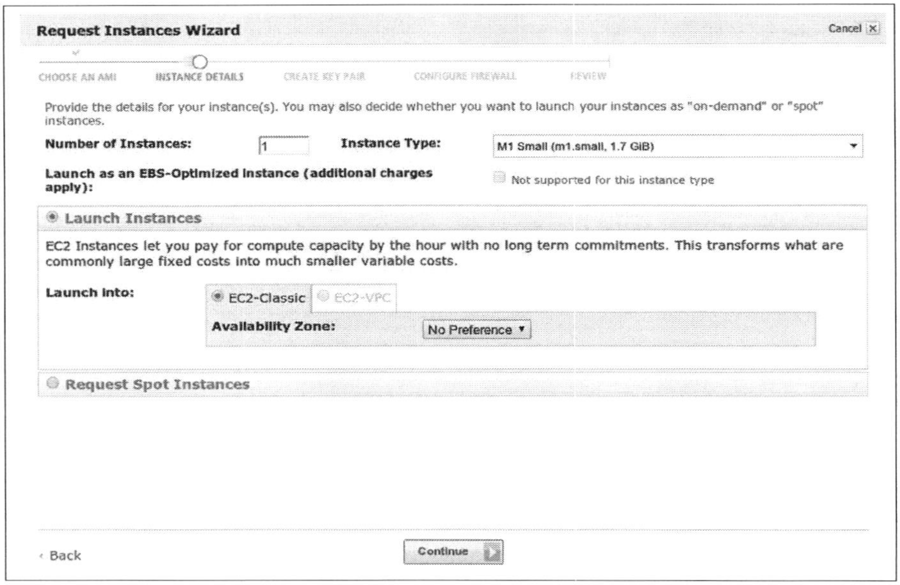

Figure A2.2: Amazon EC2 instance launch wizard showing instance details

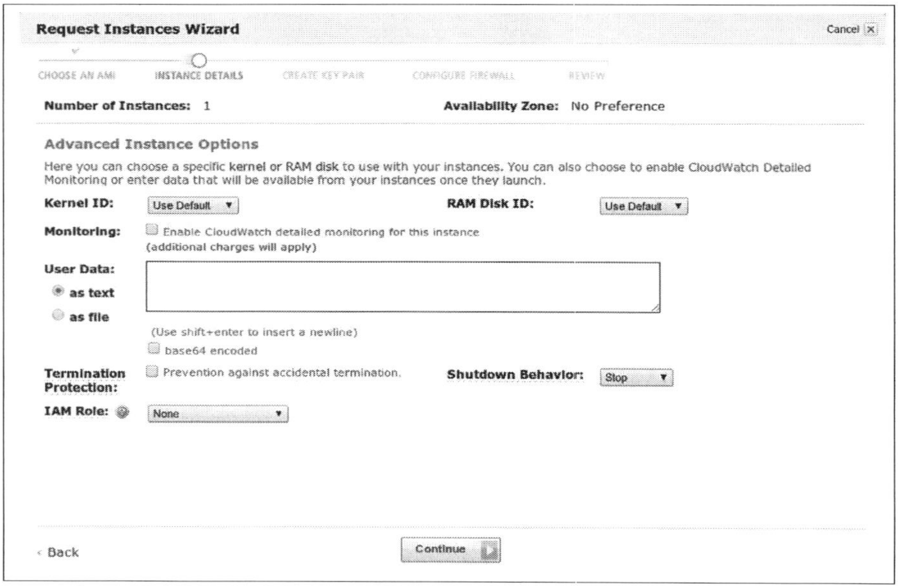

Figure A2.3: Amazon EC2 instance launch wizard showing advanced instance options

Next you specify the advanced instance options and storage device configuration shown in Figures A2.3 and A2.4. Proceed with the default options. In the next step you specify the meta-data tags for the instance as shown in Figure A2.5. These tags are used to simplify the administration of EC2 instances.

Figure A2.6 shows the keypair page of the instance launch wizard. This page allows you to choose an exisiting keypair or create a new keypair for the instance. Keypairs are used to

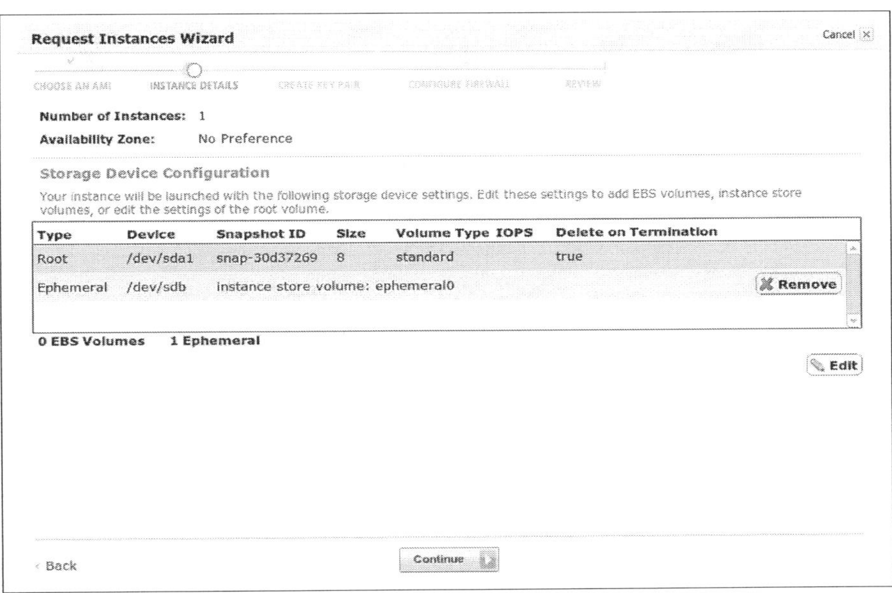

Figure A2.4: Amazon EC2 instance launch wizard showing storage device configuration

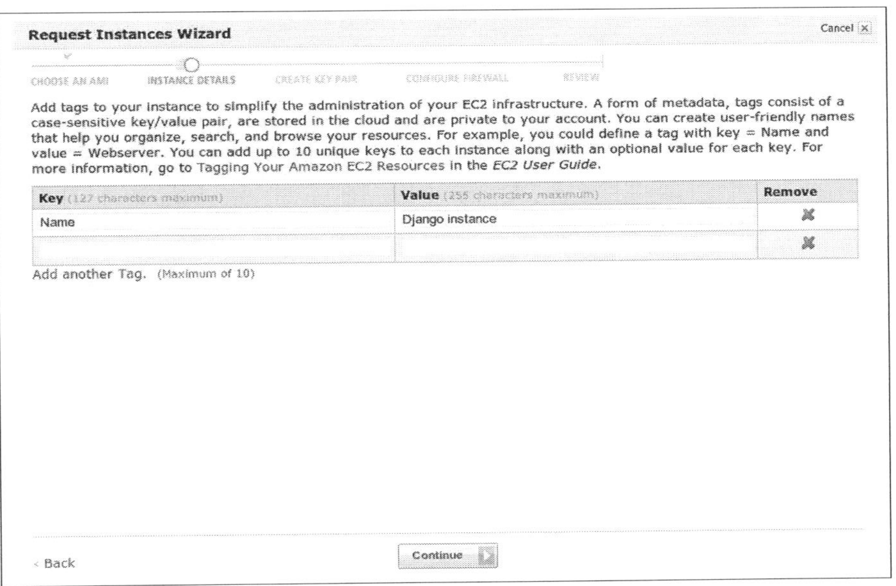

Figure A2.5: Amazon EC2 instance launch wizard showing instance tags

securely connect to an instance after it launches. Create a new pair and save it on your local machine. You will use this keypair later to connect to the instance.

Figure A2.7 shows the security groups page of the instance launch wizard. This page allows you to choose an existing security group or create a new security group. Security groups are used to open or block a specific network port for the launched instances. Create a new security group called and open ports 80 (HTTP), 8000 (Django server), 22 (SSH).

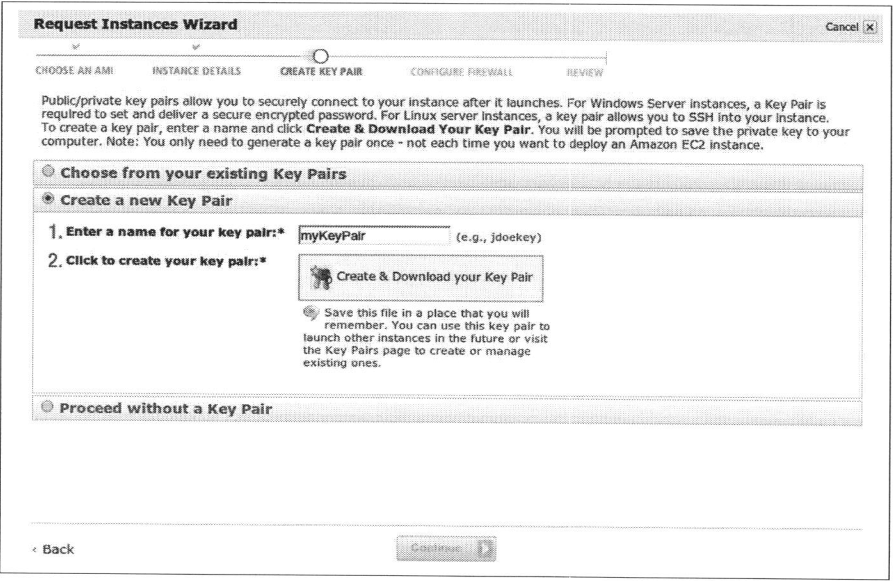

Figure A2.6: Amazon EC2 instance launch wizard showing keypairs

Figure A2.8 shows the summary of instance to be launched. Clicking on the launch button launches the instance.

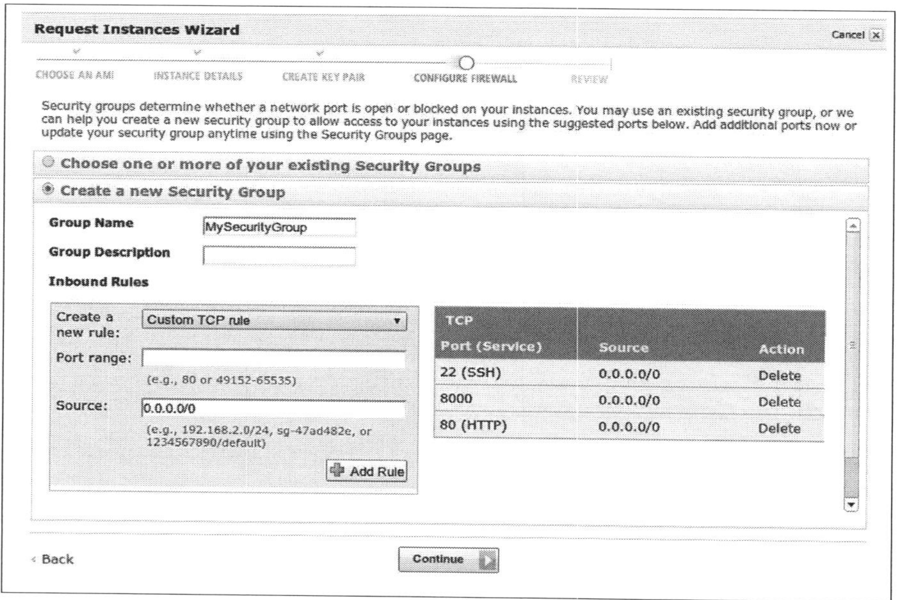

Figure A2.7: Amazon EC2 instance launch wizard showing security groups

The status of the launched instance can be viewed in the EC2 console as shown in Figure A2.9. When an instance is launched its state is pending. It takes a couple of minutes for the instance to come into the running state. When the instance comes into the running state, it is

Figure A2.8: Amazon EC2 instance launch wizard showing summary of instance to be launched

assigned a public DNS, private DNS, public IP and private IP. We will use the public DNS to securely connect to the instance using SSH.

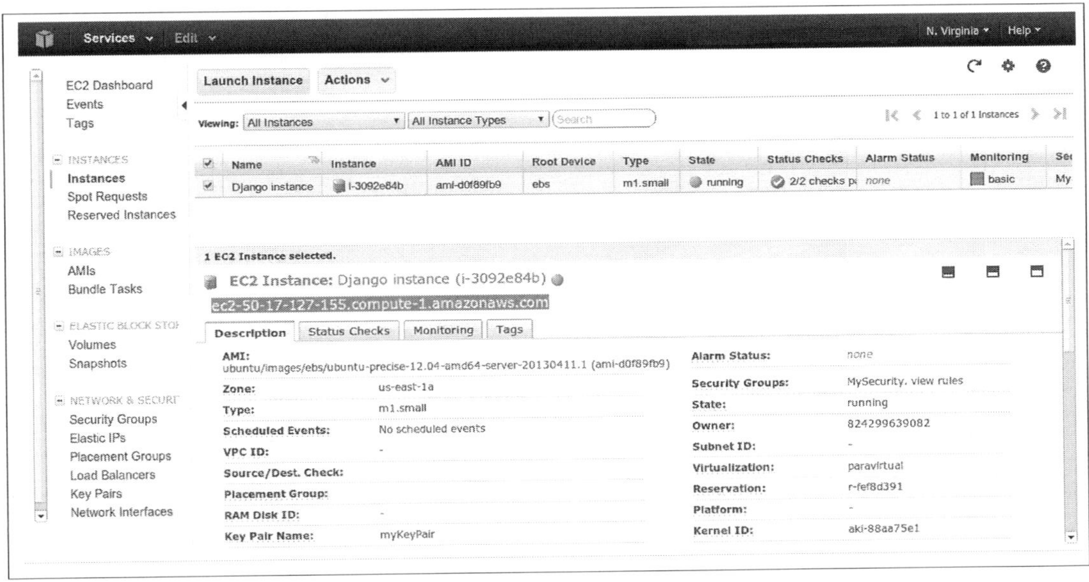

Figure A2.9: Amazon EC2 console showing the launched instance

Connect to the EC2 instance from your local machine using:

```
ssh -i myKeyPair.pem ubuntu@publicDNS
```

where publicDNS is the Public DNS of the instance you created.

Box A2.1 provides the commands for installing Django and verifying the Django installation.

■ Box A2.1: Installing Django

```
#On EC2 instance run following commands to install Django:
wget https://www.djangoproject.com/m/releases/1.5/Django-1.5.1.tar.gz
tar xzvf Django-1.5.1.tar.gz
cd Django-1.5.1
sudo python setup.py install

#Verifying Django installation
python
>>> import django
>>> django.VERSION
(1, 5, 1, 'final', 0)
```

Box A2.2 provides the commands for creating a blank Django project and running Django server. When you run the Django development server you can see the default Django project page as shown in Figure A2.10.

■ Box A2.2: Creating a Django project and running Django server

```
#Create a Django project
django-admin.py startproject myproject

#Starting development server
python manage.py runserver 0.0.0.0:8000

#Django uses port 8000 by default
#The project can be viewed at the URL:
#http://hostname:8000
```

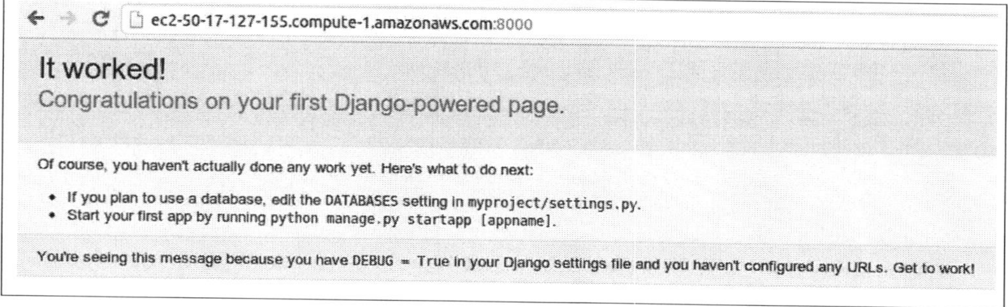

Figure A2.10: Django default project page

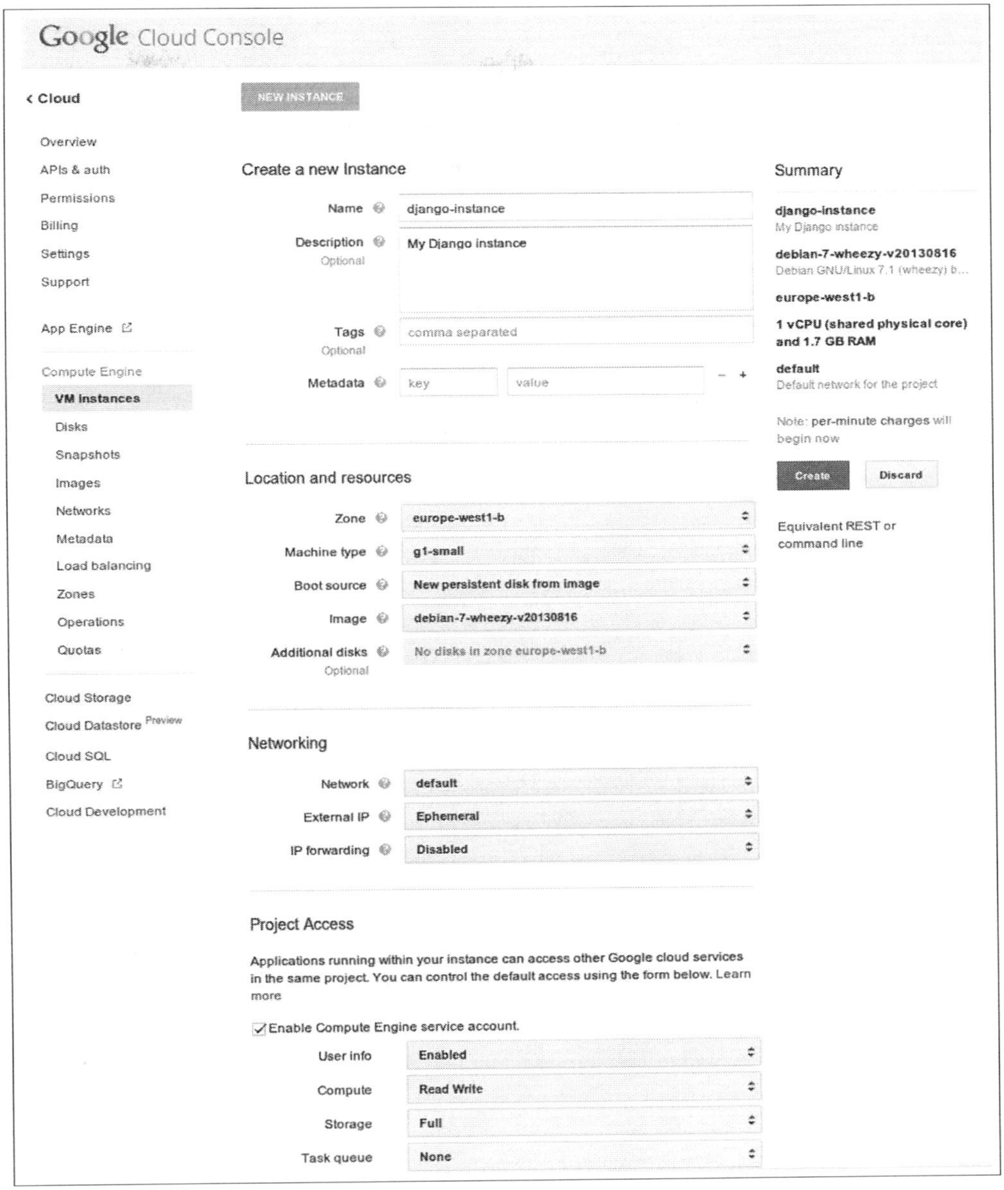

Figure A2.11: Launching a new instance from Google Compute Engine console

Setting up Django on Google Compute Engine

This section provides instructions on setting up Django on a Google Compute Engine instance. Figure A2.11 shows a screenshot of the new instance launch page of Google Compute Engine console. After launching the instance, connect to the instance from your local machine using:

```
gcutil getproject –project="myProject" –cache_flag_values
gcutil ssh django-instance
gcutil addfirewall django –description="Incoming HTTP" –allowed="tcp:8000"
```

Run the commands in Box A2.1 to install Django on the GCE instance. Open the instance IP address with port 8000 (http://<instance-IP>:8000) in a browser. You will be able to see the Django default project page.

Setting up Django on Windows Azure Virtual Machines

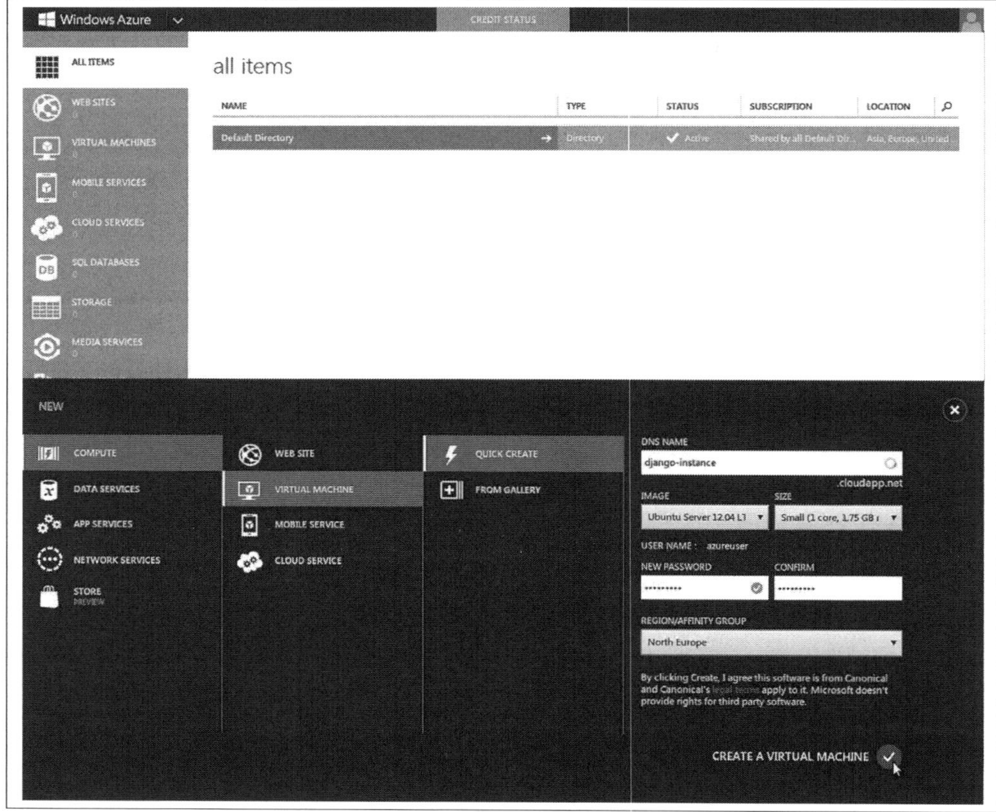

Figure A2.12: Launching a new instance from Windows Azure console

This section provides instructions for setting up Django on a Windows Azure Virtual Machines instance. Figure A2.12 shows a screenshot of the new instance launch wizard of Windows Azure Virtual Machines. After launching the instance, connect to the instance from your local machine using:
ssh <azure-instance-ip>

Enter the username and password you specified while creating the instance to connect to the instance. Run the commands in Box A2.1 to install Django on the Azure VM instance. Open the instance IP address with port 8000 (http://<instance-IP>:8000) in a browser. You will be able to see the Django default project page.

Taking Django to Production

Although Django comes with a built-in lightweight web-server, it is suited for development purposes only and not recommended for production environments.

The recommended method for taking Django to production is to deploy Django with Apache and mod_wsgi. mod_wsgi is an Apache module which can host any Python WSGI application, including Django [101]. mod_wsgi is suitable for use in hosting high performance production web sites. Box A2.3 shows the commands for installing Apache server with mod-wsgi on an Ubuntu machine.

■ Box A2.3: Installing Apache server with mod-wsgi

```
sudo aptitude install apache2 apache2.2-common apache2-mpm-prefork apache2-utils libexpat1 ssl-cert

sudo aptitude install libapache2-mod-wsgi

sudo service apache2 restart

sudo pip install django-storages boto
```

To provide mod_wsgi the access to a Django application, a wsgi configuration file inside the Django project directory is required. Box A2.4 shows a sample WSGI configuration for a Django project.

■ Box A2.4: Sample WSGI configuration - wsgi.py

```
import os
import sys
sys.path.append('/home/ubuntu/myproject/')
os.environ['DJANGO_SETTINGS_MODULE'] = 'myproject.settings'
import django.core.handlers.wsgi
application = django.core.handlers.wsgi.WSGIHandler()
```

Box A2.5 shows a sample WSGI configuration for Apache server. In this configuration the *WSGIScriptAlias* directive tells Apache that all requests below the base URL path specified (e.g. / is the root URL) should be handled by the WSGI application defined in that file.

■ Box A2.5: Sample Apache server configuration - httpd.conf

```
WSGIScriptAlias / /home/ubuntu/myproject/myproject/wsgi.py
WSGIPythonPath /home/ubuntu/myproject

<Directory /home/ubuntu/myproject>
<Files wsgi.py>
Order deny,allow
Allow from all
</Files>
</Directory>
```

After configuring the http.conf and wsgi.py files, Apache server must be restarted (/etc/init.d/apache2 restart). If all the configurations are in place, restarting the Apache server would deploy the Django application using mod_wsgi and ready for production.

Bibliography

[1] Peter Mell, Timothy Grance, *The NIST Definition of Cloud Computing*, NIST Special Publication 800-145, Sep 2011.

[2] VMware, *Understanding Full Virtualization, Paravirtualization, and Hardware Assist*, 2007.

[3] Amazon Elastic Compute Cloud, http://aws.amazom.com/ec2, 2012.

[4] Google Compute Engine, https://developers.google.com/compute/, Retrieved 2013.

[5] Windows Azure, http://www.windowsazure.com/, Retrieved 2013.

[6] Google App Engine, http://appengine.google.com, 2012.

[7] Salesforce, http://salesforce.com, 2012.

[8] A. Bahga, V. Madisetti, *Analyzing Massive Machine Maintenance Data in a Computing Cloud*, IEEE Transactions on Parallel & Distributed Systems, Vol. 23, Iss. 10, Oct 2012.

[9] A. Bahga, V. Madisetti, *On a Cloud-Based Information Technology Framework for Data Driven Intelligent Transportation Systems*, Journal of Transportation Technologies, Vol. 3, No. 2, April 2013.

[10] A. Bahga, V. Madisetti, *A Cloud-Based Approach to Interoperable Electronic Health Records (EHRs)*, IEEE Journal of Biomedical and Health Informatics, Vol. 17, Iss. 5, Sep 2013.

[11] Network Functions Virtualization, http://www.etsi.org/technologies-clusters/technologies/nfv, Retrieved 2013.

[12] OpenFlow Switch Specification, https://www.opennetworking.org, Retrieved 2013.

[13] S. Ghemawat, H. Gobioff, S. Leung, *The Google File System*, SOSP 2003.

[14] J. Dean, S. Ghemawat, *MapReduce: Simplified Data Processing on Large Clusters*, OSDI 2004.

[15] CloudStack, http://cloudstack.apache.org, Retrieved 2013.

[16] Eucalyptus, http://www.eucalyptus.com, Retrieved 2013.

[17] OpenStack, http://www.openstack.org, Retrieved 2013.

[18] Apache Hive, http://hive.apache.org, Retrieved 2013.

[19] Apache HBase, http://hbase.apache.org, Retrieved 2013.

[20] Apache Chukwa, http://chukwa.apache.org, Retrieved 2013.

[21] Apache Flume, http://flume.apache.org, Retrieved 2013.

[22] Apache Zookeeper, http://zookeeper.apache.org, Retrieved 2013.

[23] Apache Avro, http://avro.apache.org, Retrieved 2013.

[24] Apache Oozie, http://oozie.apache.org, Retrieved 2013.

[25] Apache Storm, http://storm-project.net, Retrieved 2013.

[26] Apache Tez, http://tez.incubator.apache.org, Retrieved 2013.

[27] Apache Cassandra, http://cassandra.apache.org, Retrieved 2013.

[28] Apache Mahout, http://mahout.apache.org, Retrieved 2013.

[29] Apache Pig, http://pig.apache.org, Retrieved 2013.

[30] Apache Sqoop, http://sqoop.apache.org, Retrieved 2013.

[31] The Python Standard Library, http://docs.python.org/2/library/, Retrieved 2013.

[32] Roy T. Fielding, Richard N. Taylor, *Principled Design of the Modern Web Architecture*, ACM Transactions on Internet Technology (TOIT), 2002.

[33] Django REST framework, http://django-rest-framework.org/, Retrieved 2013.

[34] Mark Devaney, Bill Cheetham, *Case-Based Reasoning for Gas Turbine Diagnostics*, 18th International FLAIRS Conference, 2005.

[35] Harry Timmerman, *SKF WindCon Condition Monitoring System for Wind Turbines*, New Zealand Wind Energy Conference, 2009.

[36] OpenPDC, http://openpdc.codeplex.com

[37] R. Claes, T. Holvoet and D. Weyns, *A Decentralized Approach for Anticipatory Vehicle Routing Using Delegate Multiagent Systems*, IEEE Transactions on Intelligent Transportation Systems, Vol. 12 No. 2, 2011.

[38] D. A. Steil, J. R. Pate, N. A. Kraft, R. K. Smith, B. Dixon, L. Ding and A. Parrish, *Patrol Routing Expression, Execution, Evaluation, and Engagement*, IEEE Transactions on Intelligent Transportation Systems, Vol. 12 No. 1, 2011.

[39] E. Schmitt and H. Jula, *Vehicle Route Guidance Systems: Classification and Comparison*, Proceedings of IEEE ITSC, Toronto, 2006.

[40] D. Wu, J.L. Thames, D.W. Rosen, & D. Schaefer, *Towards a Cloud-Based Design and Manufacturing Paradigm: Looking Backward, Looking Forward*, IDETC/CIE12, Chicago, U.S., 2012.

[41] Adobe Flash Media Family, http://www.adobe.com/in/products/adobe-media-server-family.html, Retrieved July 2013.

[42] Adobe's Real Time Messaging Protocol, http://www.adobe.com/devnet/rtmp.html, Retrieved July 2013.

[43] R. Pantos, *HTTP Live Streaming*, Internet Engineering Task Force, http://tools.ietf.org/html/draft-pantos-http-live-streaming-07, Retrieved July 2013.

[44] HTTP Dynamic Streaming, http://www.adobe.com/products/hds-dynamic-streaming.html, Retrieved July 2013.

[45] Amazon Elastic Transcoder, http://aws.amazon.com/elastictranscoder/, Retrieved July 2013.

[46] CSA Trusted Cloud Initiative, https://research.cloudsecurityalliance.org/tci/, 2013.

[47] Keberos, http://web.mit.edu/kerberos/, 2013.

[48] TOTP: Time-Based One-Time Password Algorithm http://tools.ietf.org/html/rfc6238, 2013.

[49] OAuth community site, http://oauth.net/, 2013.

[50] The OAuth 2.0 Authorization Framework, http://tools.ietf.org/html/rfc6749, 2013.

[51] Python OAuth2, https://github.com/simplegeo/python-oauth2, 2013.

[52] D. Mosberger, T. Jin, *httperf: A Tool for Measuring Web Server Performance*, ACM Performance Evaluation Review, Vol. 26, No. 3, pp. 31-37, 1998.

[53] P. Barford, M.E. Crovella, *Generating representative Web workloads for network and server performance evaluation*, In SIGMETRICS 98, pages 151-160, 1998.

[54] D. Krishnamurthy, J.A. Rolia, and S. Majumdar, *SWAT: A Tool for Stress Testing Session-based Web Applications*, in Proc. Int. CMG Conference, pp.639-649, 2003.

[55] HP LoadRunner, http://www8.hp.com/us/en/software/softwareproduct.html?compURI=tcm:245-935779, 2012.

[56] A. Bahga, V. Madisetti, *Performance Evaluation Approach for Multi-tier Cloud Applications*, Journal of Software Engineering and Applications, Vol. 6, No. 2, pp. 74-83, Mar 2013.

[57] SPECweb99, http://www.spec.org/osg/web99, 2012.

[58] A. Mahanti, C. Williamson, D. Eager, *Traffic Analysis of a Web Proxy Caching Hierarchy*, IEEE Network, vol. 14, no. 3, pp. 16-23, 2000.

[59] S. Manley, M. Seltzer, M. Courage, *A Self-Scaling and Self-Configuring Benchmark for Web Servers*, Proceedings of the ACM SIGMETRICS Conference, Madison, WI, 1998.

[60] Webjamma, http://www.cs.vt.edu/ chitra/webjamma.html, 2012.

[61] G. Abdulla, *Analysis and modeling of world wide web traffic*, PhD thesis, Chair-Edward A. Fox, 1998.

[62] M. Crovella, A. Bestavros, *Self-Similarity in World Wide Web Traffic: Evidence and Possible Causes*, IEEE/ACM Trans. Networking,vol. 5, no. 6, pp. 835-846, 1997.

[63] D. Garcia, J. Garcia, *TPC-W E-Commerce Benchmark Evaluation*, IEEE Computer, pages 4248, 2003.

[64] RUBiS, http://rubis.ow2.org, 2012. [15] TPC-W, http://jmob.ow2.org/tpcw.html, 2012.

[65] TPC-W, http://jmob.ow2.org/tpcw.html, 2012.

[66] httperfpy, https://github.com/jmervine/httperfpy, 2013.

[67] Martin Ester, Hans-Peter Kriegel, Jorg Sander, Xiaowei Xu, *A density-based algorithm for discovering clusters in large spatial databases with noise*, Proceedings of the Second International Conference on Knowledge Discovery and Data Mining (KDD-96), 1996.

[68] Apache Mahout, http://mahout.apache.org/, 2013.

[69] Webkb-4-universities-wisconsin-test Dataset, http://mlcomp.org/datasets/523, 2013.

[70] 20 Newsgroup dataset, http://people.csail.mit.edu/jrennie/20Newsgroups/20news-bydate.tar.gz, 2013.

[71] Parkinsons Data Set , http://archive.ics.uci.edu/ml/datasets/Parkinsons, 2013.

[72] Leo Breiman, "Random Forests", Machine Learning 45 (1): 5–32, 2001.

[73] UCI Breast Cancer dataset, http://archive.ics.uci.edu/ml/datasets/Breast+Cancer+Wisconsin+(Diagnostic), 2013.

[74] Corinna Cortes, Vladimir N. Vapnik, "Support-Vector Networks", Machine Learning, 20, 1995.

[75] A. Bahga, V. Madisetti, *Rapid Prototyping of Advanced Cloud-Based Systems*, IEEE Computer, vol. 46, iss. 11, Nov 2013.

[76] E.F. Codd, *A Relational Model of Data for Large Shared Data Banks*, Communications of the ACM 13 (6): 377–387, 1970.

[77] IBM SOA Foundation, http://www-01.ibm.com/software/solutions/soa/offerings.html, IBM, 2012.

[78] Windows Communication Foundation, http://msdn.microsoft.com/en-us/library/vstudio/ms735119%28v=vs.90.

[79] Oracle SOA Suite, http://www.oracle.com/us/products/middleware/soa/suite/overview/index.html, Retrieved 2012.

[80] Salesforce SOA, http://wiki.developerforce.com/page/ Salesforce SOA Demo, Retrieved 2013.

[81] Amazon Web Services, http://aws.amazon.com, Retrieved 2013.

[82] Google Cloud Platform, https://cloud.google.com, Retrieved 2013.

[83] Microsoft Windows Azure, http://www.windowsazure.com, Retrieved 2013.

[84] Amazon CloudFormation, http://aws.amazon.com/cloudformation, Retrieved 2013.

[85] OpenShift, http://openshift.com, Retrieved 2013.

[86] CloudFoundry, http://cloudfoundry.com, Retrieved 2013.

[87] boto, http://boto.readthedocs.org/en/latest/, Retrieved 2013.

[88] Python JSON package, http://docs.python.org/library/json.html, Retrieved 2013.

[89] Python socket package, http://docs.python.org/2/library/socket.html, Retrieved 2013.

[90] Python email package, http://docs.python.org/2/library/email, Retrieved 2013.

[91] Python HTTPLib, http://code.google.com/p/httplib2/, Retrieved 2013.

[92] Python URLLib, http://docs.python.org/2/howto/urllib2.html, Retrieved 2013.

[93] Python SMTPLib, http://docs.python.org/2/library/smtplib.html, Retrieved 2013.

[94] NumPy, http://www.numpy.org/, Retrieved 2013.

[95] Scikit-learn, http://scikit-learn.org/stable/, Retrieved 2013.

[96] Django, https://docs.djangoproject.com/en/1.5/, Retrieved 2013.

[97] Django Models, https://docs.djangoproject.com/en/1.5/topics/db/models/, Retrieved 2013.

[98] Django Views, https://docs.djangoproject.com/en/1.5/topics/http/views/, Retrieved 2013.

[99] Django Templates, https://docs.djangoproject.com/en/1.5/ref/templates/builtins/, Retrieved 2013.

[100] Django URL dispatcher, https://docs.djangoproject.com/en/1.5/topics/http/urls/, Retrieved 2013.

[101] http://code.google.com/p/modwsgi/, Retrieved 2013.

[102] Apache Hadoop, http://hadoop.apache.org/, Retrieved 2013.

[103] AFINN, http://www2.imm.dtu.dk/pubdb/views/publication_details.php?id=6010, Retrieved 2013.

[104] Tweepy Package, https://github.com/tweepy/tweepy, Retrieved 2013.

[105] Google App Engine, https://developers.google.com/appengine/, Retrieved 2013.

[106] Google Cloud Storage, https://developers.google.com/storage/, Retrieved 2013.

[107] Google BigQuery, https://developers.google.com/bigquery/, Retrieved 2013.

[108] Google Cloud Datastore, http://developers.google.com/datastore/, Retrieved 2013.

[109] Google Cloud SQL, https://developers.google.com/cloud-sql/, Retrieved 2013.

[110] VirtualBox, https://www.virtualbox.org/, Retrieved 2013.

[111] Ubuntu, https://www.ubuntu.com, Retrieved 2013.

Index

Printed in Great Britain
by Amazon.co.uk, Ltd.,
Marston Gate.